CW00642896

CAMBRIDGE LIBRARY COLLECTIO

Books of enduring scholarly value

British and Irish History, Seventeenth and Eighteenth Centuries

The books in this series focus on the British Isles in the early modern period, as interpreted by eighteenth- and nineteenth-century historians, and show the shift to 'scientific' historiography. Several of them are devoted exclusively to the history of Ireland, while others cover topics including economic history, foreign and colonial policy, agriculture and the industrial revolution. There are also works in political thought and social theory, which address subjects such as human rights, the role of women, and criminal justice.

A Description of the Country from Thirty to Forty Miles Round Manchester

The late eighteenth century saw Manchester and its surrounding areas undergo significant change as industrialisation fuelled urbanisation and population growth. In this classic 1795 account, the physician and prolific writer John Aikin (1747–1822) gathers together information on the settlements at the heart of manufacturing and trade in north-west England, covering the vital network of waterways as well as the surrounding countryside. Revealing the fundamental importance of the textile industry, this survey provides a detailed portrait of an evolving region and its human geography. It is complemented by a number of illustrations, including maps, plans, and engravings of notable landmarks. Referred to by Karl Marx in his writings, the book remains a historically valuable resource. Also reissued in this series is Aikin's *Biographical Memoirs of Medicine in Great Britain from the Revival of Literature to the Time of Harvey* (1780).

Cambridge University Press has long been a pioneer in the reissuing of out-of-print titles from its own backlist, producing digital reprints of books that are still sought after by scholars and students but could not be reprinted economically using traditional technology. The Cambridge Library Collection extends this activity to a wider range of books which are still of importance to researchers and professionals, either for the source material they contain, or as landmarks in the history of their academic discipline.

Drawing from the world-renowned collections in the Cambridge University Library and other partner libraries, and guided by the advice of experts in each subject area, Cambridge University Press is using state-of-the-art scanning machines in its own Printing House to capture the content of each book selected for inclusion. The files are processed to give a consistently clear, crisp image, and the books finished to the high quality standard for which the Press is recognised around the world. The latest print-on-demand technology ensures that the books will remain available indefinitely, and that orders for single or multiple copies can quickly be supplied.

The Cambridge Library Collection brings back to life books of enduring scholarly value (including out-of-copyright works originally issued by other publishers) across a wide range of disciplines in the humanities and social sciences and in science and technology.

A Description of the Country from Thirty to Forty Miles Round Manchester

JOHN AIKIN

CAMBRIDGE
UNIVERSITY PRESS

University Printing House, Cambridge, CB2 8BS, United Kingdom

Cambridge University Press is part of the University of Cambridge.

It furthers the University's mission by disseminating knowledge in the pursuit of
education, learning and research at the highest international levels of excellence.

www.cambridge.org
Information on this title: www.cambridge.org/9781108075848

© in this compilation Cambridge University Press 2014

This edition first published 1795
This digitally printed version 2014

ISBN 978-1-108-07584-8 Paperback

This book reproduces the text of the original edition. The content and language reflect
the beliefs, practices and terminology of their time, and have not been updated.

Cambridge University Press wishes to make clear that the book, unless originally published
by Cambridge, is not being republished by, in association or collaboration with,
or with the endorsement or approval of, the original publisher or its successors in title.

Stothard del.^t   Grignion sculp.^t

Publish'd June 4. 1795. by I. Stockdale. Piccadilly.

A
DESCRIPTION
of
THE COUNTRY
from thirty to forty Miles round.
MANCHESTER.

The Materials arranged, & the Work composed.

By J. AIKIN, M.D.

Stothard del.t   Audinet sculp.t

Embellished with seventy-three Plates.

LONDON.

Printed for John Stockdale, Piccadilly.

June 4. 1795.

A

DESCRIPTION

OF THE

COUNTRY

FROM

THIRTY TO FORTY MILES ROUND

MANCHESTER;

CONTAINING

ITS GEOGRAPHY, NATURAL AND CIVIL; PRINCIPAL PRODUCTIONS; RIVER
AND CANAL NAVIGATIONS; A PARTICULAR ACCOUNT OF ITS TOWNS
AND CHIEF VILLAGES; THEIR HISTORY, POPULATION, COM-
MERCE, AND MANUFACTURES; BUILDINGS,
GOVERNMENT, &c.

THE MATERIALS ARRANGED, AND THE WORK COMPOSED

BY J. AIKIN, M.D.

EMBELLISHED AND ILLUSTRATED WITH SEVENTY-THREE PLATES.

     The echoing hills repeat
The ſtroke of ax and hammer; ſcaffolds riſe,
And growing edifices; heaps of ſtone
Beneath the chiſſel beauteous ſhapes aſſume
Of frize and column. Some with even line
New ſtreets are marking in the neighb'ring fields,
And ſacred domes of worſhip.   *Dyer's Fleece.*

London:

PRINTED FOR JOHN STOCKDALE.

PREFATORY ADVERTISEMENT.

TO his laborious undertaking, now completed, the Publisher begs leave to prefix some explanations and acknowledgements, which concern himself and his subscribers, as well as the persons to whom he has been obliged for assistance.

His original idea was merely to give an account of the town of Mottram in Longdendale, and the singular country around it, with which he has much personal acquaintance, and where he enjoys a circle of valuable friends. At the urgent solicitation of some Lancashire gentlemen, he was induced to enlarge his plan, and to make Manchester the centre of a descriptive work, the circumference of which gradually extended itself further and further. With, perhaps, too little reflection, he suffered himself to be engaged in a design of a magnitude and importance that involved him in toil and expence, the idea of which,

had

had he forefeen their extent, would probably have deterred him from the profecution of it. And notwithftanding he was fo fortunate as to obtain the co-operation of a
gentleman of acknowledged abilities for fuch a work, and
with whofe exertions he doubts not that the public will be
as well fatisfied as he himfelf is, yet the difficulties and
difappointments he has met with in the progrefs of the
bufinefs, particularly in collecting the neceffary materials,
have frequently brought him to the verge of repenting
his temerity. But the tafk is now finifhed; and he flat-
ters himfelf he fhall not be miftaken in the expectations
he forms of its being thought worthy of the public fupport.

As he has received no fubfcriptions in advance, and as
original fubfcribers have been left perfectly at liberty to
withdraw their names if they fhould think proper, he conceives no blame can attach to him for having raifed the
price, in proportion as the value of the work itfelf rofe in
fair eftimation, from the additional decorations and advantages beftowed upon it. He is confident that its cheapnefs at the prefent price will be apparent to all who are
capable of forming a juft comparifon between it and other

works

works of a fimilar kind, and of eftimating the coft of the
paper, print, and plates.

In deference to the opinion of fome of his beft friends,
though confiderably againft his own inclination, he was
induced to throw out a propofal for gentlemen refiding
within the limits of the plan to contribute plates reprefent-
ing views of their own houfes, or fuch other objects as
they might fix upon—a circumftance by no means unufual in topographical works. Left it fhould be thought
that the Publifher lies under obligations which he has not
incurred, or that the numerous views he has given were
intended to be gratuitoufly prefented to the public, it is
incumbent upon him to fay, that all the acknowledgements he has to make on this head are for *two plates alone*,
a part of the expence of which has been handfomely repaid him, one by a peer, the other by a commoner.

An account of the principal ancient families within the
diftrict defcribed, was an original part of the defign ; but
it was foon found that the compafs of the work would not
admit fuch notices, however abbreviated, without exclu-
ding circumftances more univerfally interefting, relative

to

to the *prefent flate* of fo very commercial a tract; whence that part of the plan was neceffarily relinquifhed.

After the work was fully planned, a great number of papers were circulated, containing heads of inquiry, which it was hoped gentlemen in their feveral towns and parifhes would take the pains to anfwer. But though many expectations of this kind were given, in few inftances comparatively were they fulfilled; which the Publifher can only attribute to the more important engagements which the arduous circumftances of the times occafioned. He has, however, his warm thanks to return to many for their valuable communications; and fhould have to more, by name, had they not chofen to remain concealed.

Among thofe to whom he may venture publicly to mention his obligations, are

Jofeph Pickford, Efq. of Royton-hall, who has not only contributed much information from his own knowledge, but with great liberality permitted him to make ufe of the manufcript collections of the late Thomas Percival, Efq.

and

and prefented him with the plans of Bucton Caftle, Caftle Shaw, Caftle Croft, and Caftle Steads.

Thomas Pennant, Efq. of Downing, fo well known by his valuable writings, who befides allowing the moft copious tranfcriptions from his printed works, favoured the Publifher with a manufcript tour acrofs the county of Lancafter, from which much ufeful matter has been derived, particularly relative to the hundreds of Leyland and Blackburn.

Mr. Jofeph Booth of Manchefter, for his readinefs in anfwering various queries, and his many kind offices in promoting the fuccefs of the work.

Dr. Percival of the fame place, for the communication of various papers, as well as for many judicious hints and remarks towards the execution of the defign.

It is proper alfo to acknowledge, that a great part of the hiftory of the trade and manufactures of Manchefter has been taken from the printed account of the fame by *Mr. James Ogden,* improved by his written communications ; and that this intelligent perfon has been employed

3   by

by the Publifher in the colletion of materials refpeting feveral of the manufaturing towns in the north-eaftern part of Lancafhire.

Thomas Butterworth Bayley, Efq. of Hope; *John Legh, Efq.* of Bedford-fquare, London; *John Entwiftle, Efq.* of Foxholes; *Nicholas Afhton, Efq.* of Woolton-hall; *Thomas Walker, Efq.* of Manchefter; *Mr. Archdeacon Travis*; the *Rev. Mr. Lyon*, of Preftwich; have afforded various affiftance and encouragement to the work.

The account of Leeds has been principally drawn up from the communications of the *Rev. Mr. Wood*; and that of Sheffield from thofe of the *Rev. Mr. Naylor*.

Some other acknowledgements by name are made under the articles to which they belong. Among the favours which muft remain anonymous, the Publifher cannot but diftinguifh thofe of the writers concerning the tenures and charters of Liverpool, and the improvements of Chat and Trafford Moffes, and the Staffordfhire Potteries, as peculiarly entitled to his grateful remembrance.

On

On the whole, the Publifher is fatisfied that he may offer this work, whatever be its defects and inequalities, as containing a fund of new and authentic information, drawn either from perfonal obfervation or from the beft and moft refpectable fources, relative to fome of the moft interefting objects this kingdom affords; and thus, with thanks to his friends and fubfcribers, he difmiffes it with honeft hopes of the public approbation and encouragement.

JOHN STOCKDALE.

June 4, 1795.

Explanation of the Frontifpiece and Vignette.

THE group of females in the frontifpiece reprefents *Agriculture, Induftry, Plenty* and *Commerce,* allegorical perfonages peculiarly connected with the diftrict which forms the fubject of the work. The Ship in the back-ground alludes to the port of Liverpool. The Cupids fporting above, exprefs the joy and fatisfaction refulting from fuch an affociation.

The Vignette in the title page, exhibiting an arch thrown acrofs an arm of the fea, under which a fleet of merchant fhips is paffing in full fail, while a veffel nearly as large fails over the aqueduct above, is a kind of vifionary anticipation of the future wonders of canal-navigation, probably not a greater advance from its prefent ftate, than the aqueduct at Barton-bridge was, from that in which it was found by Brindley.

LIST

LIST of PLATES.

———

LIST of PLATES.

Plan

LIST of PLATES.

* The value and utility of this map, as well for the direction of the reader, as for gentlemen travelling that country, is felf-evident.

† The approbation which the plan of Manchefter and Salford by Mr. Laurent has met with, induced the publifher to purchafe the plates, for the benefit of thofe of his fubfcribers who are not already in poffeffion of that performance. It was very extraordinary that a foreigner, without knowledge of the language, or previous acquaintance with the country, fhould be able, *by his eye alone*, without the affiftance of any inftrument (as was verified by the public teftimony of the furveyors and architects of Manchefter) during the moft rigorous feafon of the year, to furvey, in lefs than two months, two towns of fome miles in circumference, with all their intricate communications.

CONTENTS.

3   *Hudders-*

PART II.—Accounts of Particular Places.

I.—LANCASHIRE.

II.—CHESHIRE.

Northwich

CONTENTS.

A D D I T I O N S.

C A N A L S.

M A N C H E S T E R.

L I V E R P O O L.

LIST

LIST of SUBSCRIBERS.

A.

ABBOT, Charles, Efq. Lincoln's Inn
Ackers, James, Efq. Lark Hill, Manchefter
Addifon, Mr. Thomas, Manchefter
Alfop, Mr. Richard, jun. Manchefter
Andrews, Mr. John, Quebec, Manchefter
Andrews, James Pettit, Efq. Brompton
Antrobus, Mr. John, Craven-ftreet
Antrobus, Edmund, No. 10, New Street, Spring Gardens
Antrobus, Rev. P. Nether Whitby, Chefhire
Arden, John, Efq. Harden Hall, Chefhire
Arden, the Right Hon. Sir Richard Pepper, Mafter of the Rolls, M. P.
Armftrong, Jofeph, Efq. Princefs Street, Manchefter
Armftrong, Mr. John, Newton
Armftrong, Mr. John, Everton, Liverpool
Arnold, George, Efq. Afhley Lodge, Northamptonfhire
Afhton, Nicholas, Efq. Woolton, Liverpool
Atherton, John, Efq. Prefcot
Atherton, John Jofeph, Efq. Walton Hall, Liverpool
Atkinfon, Rev. Myles, Leek

B.

Bagfhaw, John, Efq. Oakes, Sheffield
Baker, Wm. Efq.
Balme, Rev. Edward, M. A. and F. S. A. Finchinfield, Effex
Bamford, William, Efq. Bamford
Bankes, William, Efq. Winftanley
Barclay, Robert, Efq. Lombard Street

Barker, Richard, Efq. Golden Square
Barker, Francis, Efq. Hans Place
Barker, Mr. Thomas, Manchefter
Barkley, Mr. James, Buxton
Barnard, H. H. Efq. South Cave, Yorkfhire
Barnard, Thomas, Efq.
Barnes, the Rev. Dr. Manchefter
Baron, Peter, Efq. Manchefter
Barrow, Thomas, Efq. Bath, 5 copies
Barton, James, Efq.
Bath and Wells, Bifhop of
Baxter, Mr. Robert, Chefter
Baxter, Stafford Squire, Efq. No. 5, Gray's Inn Square
Bayley, Thomas, B. Efq. F. R. S. Hope
Beckwith, Mr. Thomas, jun. Liverpool
Beckwith, Mr. William, Liverpool
Bellas, Rev. Thomas, M. A. Rochdale
Bennett, Mr. Robert, Attorney at Law, Mottram, in Longdendale
Bennett, Mr. William
Berdmore, Rev. Scrope, D. D. Warden of Merton College, Oxford
Bertram, Alexander, M. D. Manchefter
Beft, Rev. Henry, M. A. Fellow of St. Mary Magdalen's College, Oxford
Bew, George, M. D. Manchefter
Bickerdike, Mr. Gideon, Manchefter
Birch, John Peploe, Efq. Curzon Street
Birch, Thomas, Efq. Gorton
Birch, Major General, Ardwick
Birkley, Mr. John, Hallifax
Blackburne, John, Efq. M. P.
Blackburne, William, Efq.
Blinkhorn, Mr. William, Raven Row, Spital Fields
Booth, Sir George, Bart. Afhton-under-Line
Booth,

c

Booth, Mr. Joseph, Manchester
Booth, Mr. William, Stockport
Booth, Mr. Samuel, Stockport
Bootle, Edward Wilbraham, Esq.
Borough, Richard, Esq. Dublin
Bottomley, Mr. James, Manchester
Bowden, Mr. Benjamin, Liverpool
Bower, Mr. John, for Staley Wood Club
Bowness, Rev. Mr. Stockport
Bracken, Rev. Thomas
Bradley, Mr. Job, Chesterfield
Bradshaw, Mr. William, Stockport
Bray, Mr. Champion, Middleton, near Manchester
Bray, Mr. Great Russell Street, Bloomsbury
Brereton, Owen Salusbury, Esq. Soho Square, M. P.
Brewin, Mr. New College, Hackney
Bright, Richard, Esq.
Brodie, Mr. Alexander, Carey Street
Brooks, Mr. Lincoln
Broster, Mr. J. Chester
Brown, Mr. James, Heaton Norris, Stockport
Brown, Mr. David, Macclesfield
Brown, James Esq. Stoke Newington
Brown, Mr. Nicholas, Surveyor, Saddleworth
Browne, Rev. William, Camfield Place, Hatfield
Bruckshaw, John, Esq.
Bruckshaw, Mr. Bredbury
Buckley, Rev. William, Dukinfield
Buckley, Mr. John, Tunstead, Saddleworth
Bury, Mr. John, Salford
Buxton, J. Esq. Northampton

C.

Calamy, Edmund, Esq.
Cardwell, Mr. Thomas, Mottram, in Longdendale
Cardwell, Henry, Esq. Old Hall, Mottram
Cafe, George, Esq. Liverpool
Catherall, Mr. Thomas, No. 7, Great Rider Street
Cavendish, Richard, Esq. Manchester
Chadwick, Lieutenant Colonel, Royal Lancashire Militia
Chadwick, Thomas, Esq. Hampton, Middlesex
Chamberlaine, George, Esq. Burwood, Cobham
Chamberlaine, Mr. John, Chester
Chamberlin, H. C. Esq. Leicester
Checkley, Rev. G. Ormskirk
Cheetham, Robert, Farren, Esq. Stockport
Chester, Bishop of

Chiswell, R. M. T. Esq. M. P.
Cholmondeley, Thomas, Esq. Vate Royal, Cheshire
Cholmondeley, Charles, Esq. No. 9, Lincoln's Inn Fields
Clarke, George Hyde, Esq. Hyde Hall, Cheshire
Clarke, George, Esq.
Clarke, Edward, Esq. Lambridge House, Bath
Clarke, Richard Brown, Esq. Adelphi
Claxton, John, Esq. Shirley, Surry
Clay, Mr. Thomas, Liverpool
Clayton, Sir Richard, Bart. Bath
Clayton, Thomas, Esq. Carr Hall, Coln, Lancashire
Clayton, Edward, Esq. Bamber Bridge, Preston
Clegg, James, Esq. Kirkdale, near Liverpool
Clegg, Mr. William, Merchant, Oldham
Clerke, Price, Esq. Sutton, Derbyshire
Clowes, Samuel, jun. Esq. Broughton
Clowes, Charles, Esq. Iver, Uxbridge
Collett, Richard, Esq. No. 62, Chancery Lane
Colwell, Mr.
Commerell, J. W. Esq.
Constable, Marmaduke, Esq. Wassand, Yorkshire
Cookson, John, Esq. Cavendish Square
Cooper, Rev. W. D. Gorton, Manchester
Cotton, H. C. Esq. Harley Street
Cotton, Lieut. Col. 25th Dragoons
Cox, Mr. Quality Court, Chancery Lane
Crompton, Mrs. Clapham
Crook, Rev. George, O. S. B. Ormskirk
Crofs, W. Esq. Collector of Excise, Manchester
Cubbin, Mr. Liverpool
Curzon, Lord.

D.

Dale, Mr. George Edward, Stockport
Danby, William, Esq. Farnley Hall, Leeds
Darby, W. T. Esq.
Darnley, Earl of
Dartmouth, Earl of
Davis, Mr. Jacob, Manchester
Davies, Rev. David, Macclesfield
Davies, Mr. Thomas, Stockport
Dent, John, Esq. M. P.
Dillon, John Talbot, Esq. M. R. I. A. Under Secretary of the Board of Agriculture, Hon. Member of the Literary and Philosophical Society of Manchester
Disney, John, D. D. F. S. A.
Dixon, Mr. Samuel, Wallworth

Drake,

Drake, Rev. Thomas, D. D. Vicar of Rochdale
Drake, Rev. James, A. B. John's College, Cambridge
Drinkwater, Peter, Efq. Manchefter
Dukinfield, Sir Nathaniel, Bart.

E.

Earle, Thomas, Efq. Liverpool
Eccleſton, Thomas, Efq. Scariſbrick
Edge, James, Efq. Middle Hilton
Edwards, Bryan, Efq. Southampton
Edwards, Thomas, Efq. Long Melford, Suffolk
Edwardſon, Mr. James and Richard, Golborn, near Manchefter
Egerton, William, Efq. Tatton Hall, M. P.
Englifh, William, Trevor, Efq. Dublin
Entwiſtle, John, Efq. Fox-holes, Rochdale
Eſtcourt, Thomas, Efq. M. P.
Evans, Rev. Dr. Archdeacon of Cheſter

F.

Falkener, Edward, Efq. Fairfield, near Liverpool
Farrall, Mr. William, Liverpool
Fauconberg, Earl of, Newburgh
Fenton, William, Efq. Spring Grove, Huddersfield
Ferguſon, Mr. John, Liverpool
Fielding, Mr. John, Withy Grove, Manchefter
Fildies, Thomas, Efq. Rochdale
Flint, John, Efq. Salop
Foley, Hon. Edward, Stoke, Herefordfhire
Ford, Mr. William, Ormſkirk
Ford, Mr. William, Manchefter
Forſhaw, Mr. James, Lathom
Fowles, John, Efq. Leek
Foxley, Rev. Mr. Radcliffe
Fynney, Fielding Beſt, Efq. Leek, Staffordfhire

G.

Garbers, Mr. J. C. H. Liverpool
Gardner, Mr. Edward, Stockport
Gartfide, John, Efq. Crumpſall, Manchefter
Gates, Mr. Thomas, Norbury, near Stockport
Gery, William, Efq. Buſhmead Priory, Bedfordſhire
Gibſon, Rev. E. Heaton, near Stockport
Gibſon, Mr. William, Liverpool

Gilbert, John, Efq. jun. Wortley
Gill, Mr. John, Huddersfield
Gill, Mr. James, Liverpool
Gladſtone, Mr. John, Liverpool
Golightly, Thomas, Efq. Liverpool
Goodier, Mr. Pudding Lane
Gordon, James, Efq. Saville Row, M. P. 2 copies
Gore, Mr. John, Liverpool
Goſling, Wm. Efq. Victualing Office
Goſnell, Mr. S. No. 8, Little Queen Street, Holborn, 2 copies
Gough, Richard, Efq.
Graham, Mr. No. 6, New Square, Lincoln's Inn
Greaves, Edward, Efq. Nettleworth, Notts
Green, Mr. Organ Builder, Iſleworth
Green, Mr. William, Drawing Maſter, Manchefter
Gregory, Mr. James, Ormſkirk
Gregſon, Mr. Matthew, Liverpool
Grey de Wilton, Lord
Grey, the Hon. John
Grimſhaw, Robert, Efq. Gorton Houſe
Grindrod, Rev. William, Manchefter
Grinfield, Rev. Thomas, Fulneck
Gunning, the Rev. Joſeph, Rector of Spex Hall, Suffolk

H.

Hall, Edward, Efq. Long Acre
Hall, Micah, Efq. Caſtleton
Hall, Rev. Samuel, A. M. Manchefter
Hallet, James, Efq. Higham Houſe, Kent
Hamer, John, Efq. the Wood, Rochdale
Hamilton, Mrs. King Street, Manchefter
Hamilton, the Rev. Frederic
Hamilton, the Rev. Dr.
Hammerton, James, Efq. Tompſon Houſe, Wigan
Hammond, Mr. Benjamin, Liverpool
Hardey, Mr. Edward, Old Club, Mofsley
Hardman, William, Efq. Manchefter
Hardy, Mr. John, Cheadle, Stockport
Harrach, Count Charles
Harris, Mr. Thomas, Manchefter
Harriſon, Jaſper, Efq. Wickham
Harriſon, James, Efq. Cheadle, Chefhire
Harriſon, Mr. William, Manchefter
Harriſon, Mr. John, Liverpool
Harrop, Mr. John, Saddleworth
Harrop, Mr. Printer, Manchefter
Harrop, Joſeph, Efq. Upton, Macclesfield
Harrowby, Lord, Sandon, Litchfield
Harveſt, Mrs. Longſight, Manchefter
Harvey, Mr. Surgeon, Manchefter

Hallows.

Hallows, Mr. James, Manchefter
Haffal, Rev. William, Rochdale
Hawke, Lord
Hawkefbury, Lord
Hawkins, Edward, Efq. Macclesfield
Hawkins, Sir Chriftopher, Bart. M. P.
Hay, Mrs. Dukinfield
Hay, William Robert, Efq. Dukinfield
Heathcote, Thomas, Efq.
Henderfon, Sir John, Bart.
Hefketh, Mr. Jofeph, Manchefter
Heywood, B. A. Efq. Manchefter
Hibbert, Thomas, Efq. Upper Grofvenor Street
Hibbert, Robert, Efq. Manchefter Square
Hibbert, George, Efq. New Broad Street
Hibbert, William, Efq. Manchefter
Hibbert, Mr. Titus, Manchefter
Hickinbottom, Mr. Red Pump Street, Hyde
Higginfon, Mr. Jonathan, Peover
Hilton, Mr. Marfden, Manchefter
Hincks, Mrs. Chefter
Hirft, Mr. Charles, Stockport
Hoare, Charles, Efq. Fleet Street
Hobfon, Edward, Efq. Manchefter
Hodfon, Mr. William, Manchefter
Heghton, Sir Henry, Bart. M. P.
Holland, James, Efq. Rochdale
Holland, Mr. P. Liverpool
Hollins, Mr. John, Knutsford, Chefhire
Holt, Mr. Richard, Attorney at Law, Rochdale
Holt, Mr. William, Manchefter
Holt, Mr. John, Walton, Liverpool
Homfray, Rev. John, A. B. Merton College, Oxford
Hopwood, Edward Gregge, Efq. Hopwood
Horne, Mrs. Weymouth Street, Portland Place
Horton, Sir Watts, Bart. Chadderton
Horton, William, Efq. Chadderton
Howe, Rev. Chriftopher, Gloffop
Hoyland, Mr. William, Halifax
Hoyle, Rev. E. Stockport
Hughs, Henry, Efq. Bedford Square
Hulme, Mr. Jonathan, Stretford
Hunt, Mr. Alexander, Stockport
Hyde, Nathan, Efq. Ardwick, Manchefter

I. J.

Jackfon, Rev. Cyril, D. D. Dean of Chrift Church, Oxford
Inglefield, Sir Henry, Bart.
Inchiquin, Earl of, Taplow Court
Joddrell, John Bower, Efq. Henbury
Johnfon, Mr. William, Congleton
Jones, Jofeph, Efq. Rickmanfworth
Jones, Daniel, Efq. No. 43, Lothbury
Jones, William, Efq. Manchefter
Jones, Mr. Liverpool
Jones, Samuel, Efq. Manchefter
Jones, Mr. Thomas, Mofely Street, Manchefter
Ifherwood, Mrs. Marple Hall

K.

Kearfley, John, Efq. Manchefter
Kellie, Earl of, Kellie Caftle
Kent, Sir Charles, Bart.
Kériaval, Mr. George, near Afhton-under-Line
Keymer, Mr. Robert, Manchefter
Kinder, Mr. Charles, Chefterfield
Kinder, Mr. John, Cheapfide
Kinder, Rev. Mr. Mottram, in Longdendale
King, Mr. Jofeph, Liverpool
Kinfton, Thomas, Efq. Clifton, Briftol
Knowles, Mr. J. No. 25, Soho Square
Kynafton, John, Efq. M. P.

L.

Lampriere, Rev. Mr. Abingdon
Landaff, Bifhop of
Langford, Samuel, Efq. Macclesfield
Langley, Mrs. A. York
Lawfon, Mr. Charles, Manchefter
Leaf, John, Efq. Manchefter
Lees, Mr. Samuel, Stockport
Lees, John, Efq. Fairfield
Lees, Mr. James, Quick, Saddleworth
Lees, Mr. John, Afhton-under-Lyne
Legh, John, Efq. Bedford Square
Legh, Peter, Efq. Booths, Chefhire
Legh, Willoughby, Efq.
Leicefter, Sir John Fleming, Bart. M. P.
Leigh, Mr. Ralph, Lawton, Warrington
Leroux, J. Efq. Sommers Town
Lever, Mr. John, Manchefter
Library, Circulating, Bolton
Library, New Subfcription, Leeds
Library, Public, Bolton
Library of Chefterfield
Library, Ormfkirk
Library, Kendal
Library, Subfcription, Macclesfield
Library, Leeds
Library, Subfcription, Hull
Library, The Circulating, Halifax
Library, Public, Norwich
Library of Manchefter
Library, Birmingham
Library, Rochdale

Library.

Library of Liverpool
Library, Circulating, Manchefter
Lightbody, Mr. John, jun. Liverpool
Lingard, John, Efq. Bank, Stockport
Literary and Philofophical Society, Newcaftle upon Tyne
Littlewood, Mr. John, Ardwick, Manchefter
Lloyd, George, Efq. Welcombe Lodge, Stratford-upon-Avon
Lloyd, George, Efq. Manchefter
Lloyd, Rev. J. R. Afton, Ellefmere
Lloyd, Gamaliel, Efq. Bury St. Edmund
Lloyd, Mafter William Horton, ditto
Lockhart, James, jun. Efq. Pallmall
London Library Society, No. 5, Ludgate Street
Lonfdale, Mr. John and Son, Haflingden
Lowe, Mr. John, Manchefter
Lowe, Mr. Solomon, White Gate Houfe, Mottram, in Longdendale
Lowndes, Robert, Efq.
Lowndes, Milnes, Efq.
Lowndes, Thomas, Efq.
Lyon, Rev. James, Rector of Pseftwich, Manchefter

M.

Maddocks, Rev. Mr. Chefter
Mainwaring, Sir Henry, Bart.
Malden, Lord, St. James's Place
Manefty, Mr. Liverpool
Markland, Bertie, Efq. Blackburn
Markland, Edward, Efq. Leeds
Markland, Robert, Efq. Manchefter
Marfland, Mr. Samuel, Longfight, Manchefter
Martin, Mr. George, Stockport
Matthews, Captain, R. N. Bedford Square
Matthias, George, Efq.
Meredith, Mr. James, jun. Manchefter
Miles, Mr.
Mills, Thomas, Efq. Leek
Milnes, R. S. Efq. M. P.
Milnes, James, Efq. Thornes Houfe, Wakefield, Yorkfhire
Molineux, Bryan William, Efq. Hawkley
Molyneux, Mr. Edmund, Liverpool
Morris, Mr. T. Engineer, Liverpool
Mullion, Mr. John, Manchefter
Mufgrave, Jofeph, Efq.
Myers, Mr. John, Liverpool
Mytton, Rev. Mr. Ecclefton

N.

Nafh, John, Efq. Caermarthen
4

Nafh, Mrs. Mofely Street, Manchefter
Nelfon, Rev. William, Chefter
Newfham, Mr. Thomas, Liverpool
Newton, Robert, Efq. Stockport
Newton, Mr. James Antrobus, Stockport
Norris, Mr. Robert, Liverpool
Norris, Mr. Richard, Jermyn Street
North, Mr. John, Halifax
North, Mr. Ford, Liverpool
Nugent, Colonel, M. P.

O.

Oakes, Mr. Thomas, Liverpool
Ogden, Thomas, Efq. Sarum
Oldham, Jofeph, Efq. Melton, Suffolk
Ollivant, Mr. Thomas, Manchefter
Ormerod, Henry, M. D. Rochdale
Ormfby, Owen, Efq. Porkington, Shropfhire
Owen, William Moftyn, Efq.

P.

Pain, Mr. William, Manchefter
Park, James Allen, Efq. Carey Street, Lincoln's Inn
Parker, Mr. Sedman, Liverpool
Partington, Mr. James, No. 29, Bafinghall Street
Peachey, John, Efq.
Pearfon, Mr. Thomas, Liverpool
Peel, Robert, Efq. Bury, M. P.
Peel, Lawrence, Efq. Ardwick
Pennant, Thomas, Efq. Dowing, 2 copies
Penrhyn, Lord, M. P.
Percival, Thomas, M. D. F. R. S. Manchefter
Percival, Mr. James, Liverpool
Percival, the Hon. Spratton, near Northampton
Petrie, William, Efq.
Philips, Mr. Robert, Manchefter
Phillips, Mrs. Barehill
Pickford, W. P. Efq. Royton
Pickford, Jofeph, Efq. Royton Hall
Pickford, Mr. Matthew, Poynton
Pickford, Mr. John, Stockport
Pierrepont, C. Efq. M. P. Portman Square
Pilkington, John, Efq. Bolton
Plumpton, John, Efq. Everton
Pole, William, Efq. Liverpool
Pope, Rev. J. Manchefter
Pownall, Rev. Mr. Warningham, Chefhire
Prefcot, Rev. Charles, Stockport
Price, Mr. Samuel, Cheapfide, Manchefter
Prieftnall, Mr. Matthew, Stockport
Prince, Mr. John, Ormfkirk
Putland, William, Efq. Stoke Hall, Ipfwich
Radcliffe,

R.

Radcliffe, Charles, Efq. Smithoufe, Yorkfhire, Weft Riding
Radcliffe, the Rev. John, A. M. Manchefter
Radcliffe, Mr. John, Stone Braikes, Saddleworth
Radcliffe, Mr. John, Liverpool
Radclyffe, Efq. Foxdenton
Radford, Lieutenant, R. L. Manchefter
Radnor, Earl of
Rawlinfon, William, Efq. Manchefter
Rearfley, John, Efq. Manchefter
Reafton, F. B. Efq. Temple
Reddifh, Mr. John, ditto
Reyner, Mr. Thomas, Borough High Street, Southwark
Ridgway, Mr. James, Mottram in Longdendale
Ridgway, Mr. Jonathan, Afhton-under-Line
Ridgway, Mr. John, Dukinfield Bridge
Rigby, William, Efq. Oldfield, Altringham, Chefhire
Roberts, William, Efq.
Robinfon, Mr. Robert, Manchefter
Rogers, Edward, Efq. Everton, Liverpool
Rofcoe, Mr. William, Liverpool
Rothwell, Mr. William, Manchefter
Royds, James, Efq. Falinge, Rochdale
Rufhton, Mr. Edward, Manchefter
Rufhworth, Mr. William, Bridge Street
Ruffell, Thomas, Efq. Prefton
Ryder, Right Hon. Dudley, M. P.

S.

Salifbury, Marquis of
Salifbury, E. W. V. Efq.
Sandbach, Mr. William, Burton, Chefhire
Sandbach, Samuel, Efq. No. 15, Brompton Row
Sandiford, Mr. Thomas, Manchefter
Scott, Sir William
Sedgwick, John, Efq. Manchefter
Sedgwick, James, Efq. Grappenhall, Chefhire
Shawe, Richard, Efq.
Shearfon, Mr. John, Land Surveyor
Shepherd, Mr. Tuffin, Oxton, Notts
Shepley, Mr. Gloffop
Sherwin, Mr. James, Manchefter
Shore, Samuel, Efq. Meerfbrook, Sheffield
Shorthofe, Mr. James, Manchefter
Sibthorp, Col. R. South Lincoln Militia
Simpfon, John, Efq. Hart Hill, Manchefter

Sinclair, Sir John, Bart. M. P.
Sitwell, Captain, 85th Regiment
Sitwell, E. S. Wilmot, Efq.
Slater, Mr. John, Fairfield
Slater, Mr. Thomas, Manchefter,
Smallpage, Rev. Mr.
Smith, Theophilus, Efq. Smith Field, Staffordfhire,
Smith, Mr. Jofhua, Princefs Street, Manchefter
Smith, Mr. John, Manchefter
Smith, Mr. Samuel, St. Ann's Square, Manchefter
Smith, Sir John, Bart.
Smith, Samuel, Efq. M. P. Wilford, Nottinghamfhire
Smyth, John, Efq. Heath, Yorkfhire, M. P.
Sotheron, William, Efq. M. P.
St. Afaph, the Dean of
Stamford, Earl of, 2 copies
Standifh, Edward, Efq. Standifh, Wigan
Staniforth, Thomas, Efq. Liverpool
Stanley, John Thomas, Efq. M. P.
Stanley, Colonel, M. P.
Stanton, Mr. John, Liverpool
Starkey, James, Efq. Heywood
Stephens, Francis, Efq. Victualling Office
Stockdale, Mr. Jeremiah, Mill-maker to his Majefty
Storrs, Mr. Jofeph, Chefterfield
Stronge, John, Efq. Richmond, Liverpool
Suffield, Lord, Albemarle Street
Sykes, Lady, Sledmere, Yorkfhire

T.

Tarleton, John, Efq. M. P. Finch Houfe
Tarleton, Thomas, Efq. Bolefworth Caftle
Tarleton, Clayton, Efq. Liverpool
Tatterfal, Mr. Thomas, Liverpool
Tatton, William, Efq. Tatton Park
Taylor, Mr. John, Greenacre's Moor
Taylor, Mr. Charles, Manchefter
Taylor, Mr. John, Manchefter
Thackeray, Jofeph, Efq. Manchefter
Thomas, John, Efq. Liverpool
Thompfon, Mr. Wm. York
Thorley, Mr. William, Attorney, Macclesfield
Tipping, Jofeph, Efq. Crumpfal, Manchefter
Tipping, Thomas, Efq. Ardwick, ditto
Tollemache, Hon. Wilbraham
Tomlinfon, Mr. George, Manchefter
Tonge, Mr. Afhton, Worfley
Tooke, Edward, Efq. Manchefter
Topping, James, Efq. Whatcroft Hall, Northwich, Chefhire

Touchet,

Touchet, Mr. James, Manchester
Townley, Richard, Esq. Ambleside, Kendal
Travers, Mr. Surgeon, East Bergholt, Suffolk
Travis, Rev. George Archdeacon of Chester,
Travis, Mr. John, Manchester
Trafford, John, Esq. Trafford House
Turner, Edmund, Esq. Panton, Lincolnshire
Turner, Rev. James, Mottram
Turner, Rev. W. Newcastle-upon-Tyne
Twemlow, Mr. Thomas, Liverpool

U.

Uxbridge, Earl of

V.

Vanburgh, Rev. George, L. L. B. Rector of Aughton
Vansittart, Nicholas, Esq.
Vaughan, William, Esq.
Vause, Rev. John, A. B. Manchester, Fellow of King's College, Cambridge

W.

Wainwright, Mr. Robert, Hatton Street
Walker, Thomas, Esq. Manchester
Walkers, Miss, Fairfield
Walker, Mr. William, York
Walker, Mr. James, Manchester
Walmsley, Mr. Stephen, Liquor Merchant, Ormskirk
Walmsley, George, Esq. Goose Lane
Walmsley, John, jun. Esq. Castle Moor, Rochdale
Ward, Rev. Peploe, Prebendary of Ely
Wardleworth, Mr. Mottram, in Longdendale
Waring, Mr. No. 20, Charlotte Street, Bedford Square
Warren, Hon. Sir George, K. B. Poynton, Cheshire, M. P.
Warren, Sir John Borlase, Bart.
Waterhouse, Mr. Nicholas, Liverpool
Watson, Wenman Langham, Esq. Stone, Worcester
Watson, Holland, Esq. Stockport
Way, Benjamin, Esq. Denham, Bucks
Wedgwood, Thomas, Esq.
Wentworth, Lord
Western, George, Esq. Derby
Wheeler, Mr. C. Printer, Manchester

Whitaker, the Rev. John
Whitaker, John, Esq.
Whitaker, Mrs. Kensington
White, Charles, Esq. F. R. S. Manchester
White, Mr. James, Manchester
White, Rev. Henry, Sacrist of Lichfield Cathedral
White, Rev. Mr.
Whitehouse, Mr. William, Liverpool
Whittaker, Mr. James, Bristol
Whitworth, Mr. James, Rochdale
Whitworth, Adam, Esq. Spath, Roachdale
Wiatt, Thomas, Esq. Everton
Wightwick, John, Esq. Sandgates, Chertsey
Wilbraham, Randle, Rhode Hall, Esq. Cheshire
Wilckens, Mr. Henry, Liverpool
Wilkinson, William, Esq. Bersham
Wilkinson, Mr. Anthony, jun. Gold Balance Maker, Ormskirk
Wilkinson, Mr. Thomas, Manchester
Wilkinson, John, M. D. F. R. S.
Willmott, Mr. John, Ashton Mills
Wilson, Mr. Richard
Wilson, Mr. John, Liverpool
Winter, Mr. Benjamin, L. Wine Merchant, Manchester
Winterbotham, Mr. Chadkirk, near Stockport
Wood, Mr. A. Attorney at Law, Ardwick Green
Wood, Mr. Charles, Manchester
Wood, Mr. William, Lever Street, Manchester
Worthington, Isaac, Esq.
Worthington, Mr. George, Attorney at Law, Altringham
Wray, Sir Cecil, Bart.
Wray, Mr. Leonard, Southampton
Wright, Mr. Ralph, Liverpool
Wright, Mr. Edward, Liverpool
Wright, Mr. Thomas, Printer
Wright, Mr. Nathaniel, Poynton, Stockport

Y.

Yarmouth, Monthly Book Club
Yates, Joseph, Esq. Ormond Street, Queen Square
Yates, Mr. Richard, Manchester
York, Book Society
Young, William, Esq. Harley Street

Z.

Zouch, Rev. Henry, Sandal, Wakefield

LIST of SUBSCRIBERS.

BOOKSELLERS.

Arch, Meſſ. John and Arthur, Lombard Street, 6 copies
Banks, S. Warrington
Bate, Mr. 6 copies
Bonds, Mr.
Brown, Mr. 3 copies
Browne, Thomas, Hull
Clark, J. and W. Mancheſter
Cocker, Mr. Richard, Ormſkirk, 12 copies
Cooke, Mr. Joſeph, Oxford, 2 copies
Crane and Jones, Meſſrs. Liverpool, 6 copies
Deighton, Mr. J. 6 copies
Dilly, Mr. C. 6 ditto
Drewry, Mr. John, Derby
Edwards, Mr. I. 6 copies
Edwards, Mr. R. 3 ditto
Faulder, Mr. Robert, 6 ditto
Goulding, Mr. G. James Street, Covent Garden, 6 ditto
Greenwood, Mr. Leeds
Greenwood, Mr. Edward, Leeds

Haſlingden, Mr. Mancheſter
Johnſon, Mr. J. 12 copies
Law, Mr. Charles, 12 ditto
Longman, Mr. T. N. 6 ditto
Minſhull, Mr. W. Cheſter
Payne, Mr.
Pennington, Mr. Kendal
Phillips, Mr. Robert, Liverpool
Reed, Mr. John, Briſtol
Richardſon, Mr. W. 12 copies,
Rivingtons, Meſſrs. 12 ditto
Robinſons, Meſſrs. 20 ditto
Sael, Mr. Strand, 3 ditto
Savage, J. and W. Howden, Yorkſhire
Simcoe, Mr. 2 copies
Teſſeyman, Mr. York
Thomſon, Mr. James, Mancheſter
Todd, Mr. John, York, 2 copies
Vernor and Hood, Meſſrs. 25 ditto
Walker, Mr. Preſton, Lancaſhire
White, Meſſrs. B. and J. 6 copies

INTRO-

INDEX MAP
to the
CANALS, RIVERS, ROADS &c.

British Miles

Published Nov.r 13 1794. by I. Stockdale. Piccadilly.   I. Mutlow 6. James St.

INTRODUCTION.

THE circle of country which it is the object of the present work to defcribe, forms a confiderable part of the north-weftern quarter of England. Juft approaching the Irifh fea to the weft, it ftretches on the eaft acrofs the ridge of hills which perpendicularly divides the north of England into two portions, and projects fome way into the plain beyond; and extending northwards to the edge of thofe hilly and barren parts which compofe a great fhare of the northern extremity of the kingdom, it encroaches fouthwards on the limits of the midland counties.

On taking our central ftation at Manchefter, a grand fcenery of ftrongly contrafted ranges of land prefents itfelf. Weftward, a long level plain, broken by a few

B　　　　　　　　fcattered

scattered eminences, partitioned, for the most part, into green and woody inclosures, yet sprinkled with large patches of bare and brown morass, affords to the eye an interminable profpect, expanding from side to side, and embracing almost the whole county of Chester, and the broadest and best cultivated portion of that of Lancaster. Northward, the view is soon bounded by a mountainous ridge of moderate elevation, beyond which lies another tract of vale, which is at length lost amidst hills and moors. Southward, a rich and varied country extends for many miles, bounded in the distant horizon by lofty hills in Staffordshire and Cheshire. The country to the east is composed of a vast tract of that chain of mountains which, descending from Scotland, runs like a back-bone through all the north of England, till it terminates in the Peak of Derbyshire and the moorlands of Staffordshire, both within the limits of our circle. This rugged region, stretching many miles from east to west, includes a confused assemblage of high barren moors, lofty eminences, and interjacent vales, each watered and fertilized by its winding stream. Its eastern edge declines suddenly in the beautiful and highly-cultured plain of Yorkshire and Derbyshire.

I   Such

Such is the general face and fituation of the extenfive tract over which we are about to travel ;—confiderably interefting merely as a portion of the furface of our ifland, and as poffeffing a great variety of natural and artificial products of the earth. But it is principally as a manufacturing diftrict that it merits the diftinction of being made the fubject of a particular furvey ; and in this refpect it may confidently challenge any other tract of equal extent within the limits of Great Britain (the vicinity of the metropolis, perhaps, excepted) to exhibit the fame number of objects of national importance.

The centre we have chofen is that of the *cotton manufacture*; a branch of commerce, the rapid and prodigious increafe of which is, perhaps, abfolutely unparalleled in the annals of trading nations. Manchefter is, as it were, the heart of this vaft fyftem, the circulating branches of which fpread all around it, though to different diftances. To the north-weftern and weftern points it is moft widely diffufed, having in thofe parts eftablifhed various head-quarters, which are each the centres to their leffer circles. Bolton, Blackburn, Wigan, and feveral other Lancafhire towns, are ftations of this kind ; and the whole inter-

vening

vening country takes it charaðer from its relation to them. Stockport to the fouth, and Afhton to the eaft, of Manchefter, are fimilar appendages to this trade ; and its influence is fpread, more or lefs, over the greateft part of Lancafhire, and the north-eaftern portion of Chefhire. Under the general head of the cotton manufaðure may be comprized a variety of fabrics not ftriðly belonging to it, but accompanying it, and in like manner centering in Manchefter and its vicinity.

To the north-eaft and eaft the cotton trade is foon entrenched upon by the *woollen manufaðure*, an objeð, likewife, of vaft importance, which extends through great part of the Weft Riding of Yorkfhire, and fills its moft bleak and fterile traðs with population and opulence. This has not any one common centre, but the towns of Leeds, Halifax, Bradford, Wakefield, Huddersfield, Saddleworth, and Rochdale, are each centres of particular branches and varieties of the woollen manufaðure. This trade, though of older ftanding and flower advance than the cotton trade, and likewife rivalled in other parts of the kingdom, has, neverthelefs, experienced a very rapid increafe in late years. It would feem as if a hilly coun-

try

try was peculiarly adapted to it, fince it almoft ceafes where Yorkfhire defcends into the plain.

Southward of the limits of the clothing trade, our circle comprehends the town of Sheffield, fo famous for its *cutlery* and *hardware*. Paffing into Derbyfhire it includes all the *mining* and *mineral* country of the Peak, and extends to the commercial town of Chefterfield. Staffordfhire, befides other branches of manufacture, affords a moft curious and valuable one, the *pottery*, which may be faid, as a national object, to be the creation of a few years paft, produced by a fortunate combination of chymical fkill with tafte in the fine arts. This county alfo participates with Chefhire in the *fpinning and winding of filk*, which is carried on to a moderate extent in feveral places. Chefhire poffeffes another article of great importance to the national revenues,—the *falt*, which is obtained in inexhauftible abundance from its rock-pits and fprings.

Though the cotton-trade peculiarly characterifes Lancafhire as a commercial county, yet it has other confiderable branches of manufacture; as that of *fail-cloth* and

coarfe

coarſe linens, of *nails*, of *watch tools and movements*, of *caſt-plate* and *common glaſs*. Its great port of Liverpool, the ſecond for extent of buſineſs in the kingdom, and that which has received the moſt rapid increaſe, is alſo within our limits ; as is, likewiſe, the ancient port of Cheſter.

This general ſurvey of our ground, will, it is preſumed, amply juſtify the choice of Mancheſter as a grand centre from whence to take a tour, moſt peculiarly intereſting to thoſe who wiſh for information reſpecting the commerce and manufactures of this iſland. It now remains to give ſome account of the method propoſed to be followed in arranging the materials of the enſuing work.

We begin with breaking this large ſpace into its geo- graphical diviſions. As the greater part of *Lancaſhire*, and a ſtill larger proportion of *Cheſhire*, are comprehended within our bounds, it has been thought proper to give an entire general deſcription of theſe two counties. Their limits, diviſions, face of country, ſoil, climate, courſe of rivers, agriculture, and productions, are treated of in a ſummary way, and every circumſtance of importance by which they are characteriſed is noted. Though a much
ſmaller

smaller portion of *Derbyshire* belongs to our plan, yet, as the whole county is not very extensive, and as the two hundreds with which we are concerned are by much the most remarkable for their appearance and products, we have also extended our general description through the whole of it. *Yorkshire* being geographically divided into Three Ridings, of which a part of the West alone comes within our circle, we have given a general account of that Riding alone. Of *Staffordshire* the northern extremity only is described in this general manner. These several territorial descriptions are terminated by a particular account of the whole system of canal and river navigation which extends through and mutually connects these districts, and which cannot be properly understood without tracing the several trunks and communicating branches from county to county, disregarding all artificial boundaries.

The main body of the work then succeeds, consisting of the description of *particular places*. Beginning with our centre, we proceed through all the principal towns and villages in the same order in which the counties have been treated of. Details are given, as accurate as our

mate-

materials could fupply, (in the collection of which neither pains nor expenfe have been fpared) of population, government, inftitutions public and private, trade, manufactures, and all that is important in the *prefent ftate* of a place, not, however, entirely difregarding narrations of paft times, when they appeared interefting. The very different degree in which our inquiries have produced the defired information at different places, has prevented fuch a proportional adjuftment of fpace to the accounts given of them, as their refpective importance would feem always to require ; but we truft it will be found, that few matters of real utility have been paffed over without fome adequate degree of notice. It is hoped that the number of maps and plans for illuftration, which, befides the numerous views for ornament, have been allotted to this work, will materially aid the information it is intended to convey.

DESCRIP-

LANCASHIRE.

British Statute Miles.

Published October 13, 1794, by J. Stockdale Piccadilly.

DESCRIPTION

OF THE

COUNTRY ROUND MANCHESTER.

I. *LANCASHIRE in general.*

LANCASHIRE is bounded on its whole fouthern fide by Chefhire, the river Merfey marking the divifion from the fea as far as Stockport, and the Tame, for the remainder. Its whole eaftern fide joins to Yorkfhire, by a very irregular boundary line, not naturally marked, but for the moft part following a mountainous chain. To the north it is bounded by Weftmoreland; and to the weft, by the Irifh fea, and by a fmall part of Cumberland, which touches its north-weftern extremity.

It is an extenfive tract of country, of very unequal dimenfions in its different parts. The fouthern part, as far the middle, and fomewhat beyond, forms a quadrangular portion, keeping a pretty uniform breadth from the confines of Yorkfhire to the fea. The county then narrows fuddenly, by the encroachment of Yorkfhire, fo that the remaining portion, as far as the limits of Weftmoreland, has an inconfiderable breadth. A third portion is quite detached from the reft by an arm of the fea, and is a roundifh tract, lying to the north-weft of the whole

main

main part of the county.   A line drawn from the northern extremity of this detached part, to the Merſey, would meaſure full 70 miles ; but the length of the county, excluſive of this part, is about 54.   The medium breadth of its ſouthern portion is 40 miles.   Mr. Yates, the author of the Lancaſhire map by ſurvey, gives the county the following dimenſions : greateſt length 74 miles, breadth 44½, circumference (croſſing the Ribble at its mouth) 342 miles; ſurface 1765 ſquare miles, or 1,129,600 ſtatute acres.

Face of the country.—The ſouthern part of Lancaſhire is a tract of nearly level land extending from the high country of Yorkſhire to the ſea.   Through the eaſtern part of this tract various rivers and ſtreams take their winding courſe, finally terminating in the Merſey.   A number of moſſes, or peat-bogs, are found in various parts, ſome of great extent.   Theſe become more numerous on approaching the ſea-coaſt, which throughout this county is univerſally low and flat.   On advancing a little northerly, a ridge of hills, connected with the great Yorkſhire chain, makes a deep inroad, extending from eaſt to weſt as far as the centre of the county, and appearing in detached eminences pretty far to the weſt.   Behind this firſt ridge is an interval of level country ; and then commences another hilly tract, running along the borders of Yorkſhire, and puſhing more or leſs into Lancaſhire, but every where leaving a ſpace of flat land between it and the ſea.   This ſpace is, however, more and more narrowed on proceeding northwards, till at the Weſtmoreland border it is reduced to a very ſmall breadth.   On the whole, if a line were drawn from Lancaſter to Preſton, and thence through Mancheſter, to Aſhton-under-line, it would leave the hilly country to the eaſt, and the level to the weſt.

As

As to the detached part or diſtrict of Furneſs, it is throughout an irregular and romantic mixture of hills, narrow vales, lakes, and ſtreams, the mountains being moſt wild and lofty on the Cumberland border. But its ſouthern extremity, which projects into the ſea, contains a conſiderable tract of level land, fronted by the ſingular bow-like iſle of Walney, which is of the ſame nature.

RIVERS.

The *Merſey* will be traced among the rivers of Cheſhire.

The *Irwell*.—This may be conſidered as the principal river of the ſouth-eaſtern part of the county, as it unites all the reſt, and is the only one navigable. The Irwell may be traced up to the moors near the Yorkſhire border about the parallel of Haſlingden. From an union of ſtreams in that quarter, a rivulet is formed, which runs through the manor of Tottington to Bury, a little below which, receiving the Roch, it turns weſtward; but ſoon, meeting with a ſtream coming from Bolton, it is bent in an acute angle ſouth-eaſtwards, and takes its courſe to Mancheſter. Here, after receiving the Irk and the Medlock, its direction is again changed weſterly, and proceeding through Barton, where it is croſſed by the Duke of Bridgewater's canal, it mixes at length with the Merſey below Flixton. It is made navigable from Mancheſter to its junction with the Merſey, and thence to the ſea.

The *Roch*, riſing out of the bordering ridge of hills called Blackſtone-edge, and uniting ſeveral ſtreams from both ſides as it flows, paſſes Rochdale, and joins the Irwell near Radcliff.

The

The ſtreams which compoſe the *Irk* come principally from Royton and Oldham. It takes a ſhort courſe to empty itſelf into the Irwell at Mancheſter.

The *Medlock* coming out of Yorkſhire has alſo a branch from Old-ham, and terminates in the ſame manner as the former.

The *Douglas*, taking its riſe from the neighbourhood of Rivington Pike, runs firſt ſouthwards to Wigan, where, receiving other ſtreams from the ſouth, it is forced to a north-weſterly direction; and after being augmented by the Eller-brook from Ormſkirk, and the united Yarrow and Loſtock rivulets from Chorley and Cuerden, it empties itſelf into the broad eſtuary of the Ribble at Much-hool. It is made navigable from Wigan.

The *Darwent*, ſpringing from among the hills about Over Darwen and Roſendale, runs a little to the ſouth of Blackburn, receiving a ſtream from that town, and then winds away to the weſt, and mixes with the Ribble at Walton-le-dale.

The *Ribble*, the principal river of the middle of Lancaſhire, and which makes the ſeparation between its broader and narrower portion, riſes in the Weſt Riding of Yorkſhire, and flowing ſouthwards between the noted mountains Ingleborough and Penigent, paſſes Settle and Bol-ton, and reaches the confines of Lancaſhire above Clitheroe, becoming for a ſhort ſpace the boundary line. Then, receiving from the north-weſt the Hodder, (a Yorkſhire ſtream, which alſo ſerves ſome way for a boundary) and the Calder, from the eaſt, it holds on a weſterly courſe, winding through a rich vale, by Ribcheſter, to Walton near Preſton,

where

where it is joined by the Darwent. Immediately below Penwortham it widens into a fhallow and broad eftuary, which makes a great gap in the fea-coaft line of the county, but is unfit for the navigation of veffels of any burthen. The Ribble, at fome periods a very inconfiderable ftream, in time of floods brings down vaft quantities of water, and with great impetuofity.

The *Calder* rifes from the moors on the borders near Colne, and running wefterly, joins the Ribble near Whalley.

The *Wyer* unites the ftreams of the country between the Ribble and Lune. It takes its rife from the wild country of Wyerfdale, on the Yorkfhire border, and running fouth-weft to Garftang, receives many ftreams from the eaft and fouth, which turn it due weft; when paffing near Poulton, it bends northerly, expanding into a fort of bafon called Wyer-water, and again contracting, enters the fea by a narrow channel, which has depth of water enough to afford entrance and fafe harbour to fhips of burthen.

The *Loyne* or *Lune*, fpringing from the fells of Weftmoreland, holds a direct fouthern courfe to Kirkby-Lonfdale, below which town it arrives at the Lancafhire border, and running fouth-wefterly, receives the Greta and the Wenning out of Yorkfhire, and flowing through a delightfully romantic dale, reaches Lancafter. Hence it becomes navigable for fhips, though veffels of confiderable burthen cannot without difficulty come nearer the town than two miles. It expands below Lancafter into a bafon, and enters the fea at Sunderland Point.

The

The diſtrict of Furneſs is too ſmall to afford rivers of any conſequence. The *Winſter*, which makes its ſeparation from Weſtmoreland on the eaſt, empties into the mouth of the Ken. The waters of the lake of Winder-meer are diſcharged by the *Leven*, which, meeting with thoſe from Coniſton-meer, diſcharged by the *Crake*, forms with it Leven-water, a ſmall eſtuary fordable at low water. The *Duddon*, which ſeparates Furneſs from Cumberland, widens, below Broughton, into a ſimilar eſtuary, called Duddon-water.

LAKES.

Winander-meer, or *Winder-meer*, in Furneſs, is the moſt extenſive piece of water in England, being about ten miles in length, though no where one in breadth; its direction running north and ſouth. Its general depth in the middle is 90 feet, but oppoſite to Ecclefrig crag it is 222 feet, the bottom ſmooth horizontal ſlate rocks. Before ſtorms it has a current in the oppoſite direction from whence the wind comes. The diviſion of the counties of Weſtmoreland and Lancaſter paſſes through the northern part of this lake, but the ſouthern is all in Lancaſhire. Its iſlands or holms, however, all belong to Weſtmoreland. Winder-meer is a capital object to thoſe who make the tour of the northern lakes, and affords many ſtriking points of proſpect.

Coniſton-water is about half the ſize of the former. It is ſituated in Furneſs, parallel to Winder-meer, and a few miles diſtant from it. Between the two lies another ſmall meer, called *Eaſthwaite-water*.

SOIL.

The ſoil of the county is very various, though the changes are not ſo rapid as in ſome other parts. The greateſt portion of the diſtrict be-

2   tween

tween the Ribble and Merſey has at the ſurface a ſandy loam, well fitted for the production of moſt cultivated vegetables. The ſubſtratum is generally red rock or clay marl. There is alſo a black ſandy loam, ſomewhat different from the above, the ſubſtratum of which is white ſand, under which is clay, and then marl. There are like-wiſe tracts of white ſand lands, and a few pebbly gravel lands. Some ſtiff land is met with, but no obdurate clay. The vales are generally fertile; but the ſoil becomes more barren on approaching the hills, which are moſtly compoſed of moor-land in a ſtate of nature, over-run with heath and wild plants.

Moſſes.—Lancaſhire abounds in thoſe bogs or moraſſes which bear the provincial name of *moſſes*. Some of theſe are large tracts of land, and by their brown and ſterile appearance greatly deform the face of the country. They conſiſt of a ſpungy ſoil, compoſed evidently of the roots of decayed vegetables intermixed with a rotten mould of the ſame origin. This matter is of a light colour and texture near the ſurface, but becomes darker and heavier on deſcending, and is converted into the ſubſtance called turf or peat, which is uſed as a fuel, and ſome-times contains ſo much bituminous matter as to flame at a candle. This kind of ſoil is ſeveral feet in depth, and contains in many parts large trees buried, and preſerved from putrefaction by excluſion of the air. They are of different colours and very inflammable, but often ſo found as to be capable of being worked into furniture. On penetrating quite through the moſs-earth, ſand or clay, the common ſoil of the country, is met with. Hence there can be little reaſon to doubt that theſe tracts were once foreſt-land, which being neglected, and ſuffered to be inundated, at length became bogs. The trees that grew on them were overthrown, and then covered by the rank vegetation. As plants died, others ſuc-ceeded,

ceeded, and thus an artificial foil was produced, which continually increafed. Some of thofe moffes now rife feveral feet above the level of the furrounding country. They are covered with a variety of plants proper to them ; as all the tribes of heath, bilberry, cranberry, crow-berry, Andromeda polifolia, Lancafhire afphodel, fun-dew, cotton grafs, and the fragrant Myrica Gale, or bog-myrtle. In dry weather, the upper cruft of turf will bear the foot, but for a large fpace round the ground fhakes with the tread, and horfes or cattle cannot venture upon it. In wet feafons the moffes are impaffable, and fo fwollen in their fubftance as fometimes to conceal objects from the oppofite fides which are vifible in dry feafons. Some of them are partially drained by deep ditches, which difcharge a water deeply tinctured with brown, and unfit for ufe. Were it not for fuch drains, they would probably fometimes fwell to burfting, as Solway-mofs in Cumberland fome years ago did, and as Chat-mofs, one of the largeft in Lancafhire, is record-ed to have done in the age preceding Camden, when it difgorged into the Merfey, and by its black contents killed the fifh for a large fpace. Good land is continually gained from the edges of the moffes, after the peat is cut away for fuel. By marling, the remaining boggy earth is made folid, and the land proves extremely fertile. It is fcarcely to be doubted that the whole of them may in time be reclaimed by means of effectual draining ; though at prefent the great depth of the loofe bog in their central parts offers a formidable obftacle.

The quantity of wafte lands in Lancafhire is great. Mr. Yates cal-culated that the mofs-lands amount to 26,500 acres, the moors, marfhes, and commons, to 482,000 ; making together 508,500 acres. Much of this is incapable of tillage, but might be improved by draining, planting, and various other modes.

I

MANURES.

MANURES.

The chief manure of the county is marl, which is found in moſt parts of it, and of various qualities, adapted to different ſoils. To the ſtiff clay lands, the blue or reddiſh ſlate marl, full of calcareous earth, is moſt effectual; but to the light ſand lands, the ſtrong clayey marl is beſt ſuited. By its means, ſome of the barren ſandy heaths have been rendered productive, but at a conſiderable expence, ſince it is neceſſary to lay on ſo much as to give a new ſtaple to the ſoil. Near the ſea, ſea-ſlutch is uſed for a manure, and in ſome places a ſand full of ſea-ſhells is found, which anſwers inſtead of marl. Lime is occaſionally uſed; and the neighbourhood of towns is ſupplied with various articles of manure from the refuſe of manufactures.

CLIMATE.

It is commonly obſerved that the whole weſtern ſide of the kingdom is more ſubject to rain than the eaſtern, the evident cauſe of which is, that it firſt receives the clouds from the Atlantic ocean, by which this iſland is principally watered. The ſituation of Lancaſhire in a peculiar manner expoſes it to the operation of this general cauſe, as the hills which form its line of ſeparation from Yorkſhire arreſt the clouds in their progreſs, and cauſe them to depoſite their contents: hence, the quantity of rain that falls is augmented in proportion to the nearneſs of the hills. Thus at Townley it was found by obſervation, that 42 inches of rain fell annually at a medium, whereas at Mancheſter only 33 fell. This wetneſs of the climate is unfortunate to the growth of corn and the ripening of fruit, but it is ſerviceable to paſturage, and produces an almoſt perpetual verdure in the fields. The froſts, too, are leſs ſevere and laſting than on the eaſtern ſide of the hills, and cat-

D

tle

tle in common years can be kept abroad all the winter. On the whole, the climate, though unpleafant, is not unfalubrious, or unfavourable to the wants of man, efpecially fince the culture of potatoes has fecured a quantity of food not much liable to injury from the weather. The: healthinefs of the county is fhewn in the appearance of the inhabitants, who are, in general, a tall, florid, and comely race. Scrofulous affec- tions, indeed, are common among thofe who inhabit the wetteft parts, and live poorly; and confumptions arifing from this caufe are very frequent.

PRODUCTIONS.

The grain principally cultivated is oats, which, when ground to meal, is the principal food of the labouring clafs, efpecially in the northern and eaftern parts of the county. A good deal of barley, and fome wheat, is grown in Low Furnefs, the Filde, and in the fouth- weftern parts of the county; but, on the whole, it is fuppofed that Lancafhire does not raife more than one quarter of the grain it con- fumes. The lands near the great towns are chiefly employed in pafturage; and at a greater diftance, a large portion of the ground is in pafturage and meadow. A great number of cows are kept near the towns for the pur- pofe of fupplying them with milk and butter. Confiderable quantities of cheefe are alfo made in fome parts, of which the moft in repute is that from the neighbourhood of Leigh and Newborough, which is mild and rich, and particularly valued for toafting. Buttermilk is a great article of food among the poor in this county, either mixed with oatmeal or potatoes, or drank at meals with water.

That ineftimable root, the potatoe, was long an article of common diet in Lancafhire and Chefhire, before it was known otherwife than

as

as a garden vegetable in moſt other parts of the kingdom; and theſe counties are ſtill peculiarly celebrated for the fineſt and moſt productive kinds. The beſt in this county are ſuppoſed to grow in the light ſandy ſoil of ſome of the ſea-coaſt pariſhes, eſpecially the Meales near Orm-ſkirk. It is imagined that they were originally introduced into theſe parts from Ireland, where Sir Walter Raleigh, who brought them from America, had cultivated them; but at preſent large quantities are ſent from the Lancaſhire ports to Dublin.

With reſpect to woods, it is with difficulty that trees of any kind can be reared near the ſea on account of the violence of the weſtern winds. In Furneſs many acres of coppice wood are cut down in rota-tion every 15 years, and burned into charcoal for the uſe of the ſmelt-ing furnaces. Towards the centre of the county are ſome thriving woods with good timber; a conſiderable quantity is alſo grown in hedge rows; but on the whole, the growth of timber trees is on the decline, except in plantations about gentlemens' ſeats. Of late years, the alder has become an article of conſequence, both on account of the peculiar fitneſs of its food for making ſmooth poles for hanging cotton yarn to dry, as for its bark which is uſed for dying, and ſells at nearly 1d. per pound. Alders are planted on the looſe grounds on the ſide of the Duke of Bridgewater's canal by way of ſecuring the banks, and have proved in other reſpects a valuable plantation. Oſiers are found to be a very valuable production on account of the demand for them in making hampers, &c.

Lancaſhire is poſſeſſed of a peculiar breed of horned cattle, which forms a variety of the Lincolnſhire, being of ſmaller ſize, with wide ſpreading horns and ſtraight backs. Their hair is finely curled, and

the

the elegance and regularity of their shape render this the most beautiful race of cattle this kingdom produces. The tract adjacent to Garstang is the principal seat of this breed.

But few sheep are kept in the southern part of the county, except those purchased by butchers, or fed by gentlemen on their grounds. In the northern parts, sheep are bred and kept upon the moors and mountains. There is also a breed called the Warton or Silver-dale sheep, which is much esteemed for the flavour of its flesh, fineness of wool, and tendency to fatten.

A greater number of horses has been bred of late years than formerly, owing to the increased demand; but much attention has not been paid to the breed. Strong horses are most in use for ordinary purposes. The stock of swine is generally purchased from herds brought out of the neighbouring counties, or from Wales and Ireland.

That beautiful fish, the Charr, (*Umbla*) which is a native of the lakes of the northern and mountainous parts of Europe, is found also in Winder-meer and Coniston-water. Mr. Pennant says, that the largest and most beautiful specimens of this fish which he ever saw were taken in Winder-meer, and sent him under the names of case charr, gelt charr, and red charr. On the closest examination he could not discover any specific differences between these, and therefore considers them as a variety of the same species. There is, however, a remarkable difference in their time of spawning. The case charr spawns about Michaelmas, and chiefly in the river Brathy, which, uniting with another called the Rowthay, falls into the northern end of the lake. The Brathy has a black rocky bottom; that of the Rowthay is bright sand,

and

and the charr are never obferved to enter it. Some of them, however, fpawn in the lake, but only in its ftony parts. They are fuppofed to be in perfection about May, and continue fo all the fummer, yet are rarely caught after April. The red charr fpawns from the beginning of January to the end of March. They are never known to afcend the rivers, but lie in thofe parts of the lake where the bottom is fmooth and fandy, and the water warmeft. They are taken in the greateft plenty from the end of September to the end of November, and are much more efteemed for eating than the former. The Conifton charr are reckoned very fine, and are fifhed later than thofe of Winder-meer, and continue longer in the fpring.

Salmon are found in all the Lancafhire rivers. Smelts, called here fparlings, come in great fhoals up the Merfey to fpawn in the fpring, but not as long as there is any fnow water in the river. They are remarkably large and fine there. The graining is a fifh fuppofed peculiar to the Merfey; it much refembles a dace, but is more flender, with a ftraighter back.

MINERALS.

The moft valuable mineral production of Lancafhire is coal, the great plenty of which has been a confiderable encouragement to the fettlement of manufactures in the county. They abound moft in the two fouthern hundreds of Weft Derby and Salford, and the adjacent eaftern one of Blackburn. The tracts containing them run from the northeaft to the fouth-weft. None are met with north of the Ribble; and all the fea-coaft parts northwards are fupplied by means of the river Douglas, which carries the coals from the neighbourhood of Wigan to the mouth of the Ribble. The kinds of coal are as various, as the

quantity

is abundant. The greater part are quick-burning, not caking or turning to cinders, but leaving a light white afh; there are, however, coals of a different quality, excellent for the fmith's ufe. One of the moft noted fpecies of coal is that termed cannel, or kennel, which looks almoft like pure bitumen, is highly inflammable, fplits with a fine polifhed furface not foiling the fingers, and is occafionally wrought into figures and toys. It burns rapidly when ftirred, yielding a bright flame, and crackling; but if left to itfelf, it folders together, and keeps in a fmothering fire for a long time. The Lancafhire coals are chiefly ufed in the county and the adjacent parts of Chefhire; but fome are exported from Liverpool, and this quantity is increafed fince the canal from that port to Wigan has afforded a more copious fupply.

There are quarries of ftone of different kinds in various parts of the county. Near Lancafter is an extenfive quarry of free-ftone which admits of a fine polifh. The town is built of it. Flags and grey flates are dug at Holland near Wigan. The beft fcythe ftones are got at Rainsford, and alfo fine pipe clay. Lime-ftone is found in abundance in the northern and north-eaftern diftricts; but no calcareous earth, except in marl, is met with towards the fouthern parts, a fmall quantity of lime-ftone pebbles upon the banks of the Merfey excepted. There are few other mineral productions, except in the detached diftrict of Furnefs. This is properly a mineral tract. Its lower parts yield quantities of iron ftone, which is partly fmelted upon the fpot, partly exported. In the hilly parts are mines of copper and lead; and there are quarries of fine blue flate, which is a confiderable article of exportation. At Anglezark, a little to the eaft of Chorley, is a lead mine at prefent worked, though to a fmall extent. It is the only mine in England known to yield that curious mineral the Acrated Barytes, of

which

which a particular account is given in a paper by Mr. James Watt, jun printed in the 3d vol. of the *Manchester Transactions*.

PROPERTY.

Since the introduction of manufactures, property has become more minutely divided. But there remain proprietors who hold very extensive possessions ; and the remark of Camden, of the number of ancient families which bear the names of the places where they reside, is still applicable to this county. The yeomanry, formerly numerous and respectable, have greatly diminished of late, many of them having entered into trade : but in their stead, a number of small proprietors have been introduced, whose chief subsistence depends upon manufactures, but who have purchased land round their houses, which they cultivate by way of convenience and variety.

In most townships there is one farm, still distinguished by the name of the Old Hall, or manor-house (the former residence of the great proprietor of the district), which is of larger extent than any of the neighbouring farms ; few of them, however, exceed 600 statute acres ; and many do not reach 200. The more general size of farms is from 50 down to 20 acres, or even as much only as will keep a horse or cow.

But few open or common fields are now remaining, the inconveniencies attending them having caused great exertions to effect a division of property, so that each individual might have his grounds contiguous, and cultivate them after his own method. The enclosures are in general very small, so as to occasion much loss of ground in hedges and fences, and in some measure to obstruct the free action of the sun and

air.

air.   In the lands of large proprietors, however, this fault is amending.
There can be no doubt that in this county, inclofure has increafed population.

CIVIL AND ECCLESIASTICAL DIVISIONS.

The people of Lancafhire were comprehended under the Roman denomination of *Brigantes*, which included the inhabitants of all the
northern part of England.   In like manner they comprized part of the
Saxon kingdom of *Northumberland*.   The diftrict was named by the
Saxons *Lonkaflerfcyre*.   It had its particular lords under the Norman
government, and gave the title of earl to Edmund, younger fon of
Henry III.; a fucceffor of whom was created duke by Edward III.
On his death without iffue male, the fame king created John of Gaunt,
his fourth fon, (who had married the heirefs of the laft poffeffor) duke
of Lancafter, and advanced the county to the dignity of a *palatinate* in
his favour.   The patent for this purpofe grants to the duke his court of
chancery to be held within the county, his juftices for holding the pleas
of the crown and all other pleas relating to common law, and finally,
" all other liberties and royalties relating to a *county palatine*, as freely
and fully as the earl of Chefter is known to enjoy them within the
county of Chefter."   John of Gaunt was fucceeded in his dukedom by
his fon Henry of Bolingbroke, who afterwards afcended the throne under the title of Henry IV.   This king, by authority of parliament,
fecured to his heirs the poffeffion of this inheritance, with all its rights
and liberties, in the fame manner as he received it before he came to
the crown.   Henry V. annexed to this duchy the great eftates which
fell to him in right of his mother, daughter and co-heirefs of Humphrey Bohun, earl of Hereford.   Since that time, the *duchy of Lancafter*, comprehending, befides the county of Lancafter, great eftates

in

in various parts of the kingdom, has fubfifted, as a feparate poffeffion belonging to the kings of England, having its own chancellor, attorney, receivers, and other officers. The law offices for the county palatine are held at Prefton.

With refpect to common judicial adminiftration, Lancafhire is a part of the northern circuit, and the affizes for the county are held twice a year at the county-town, Lancafter.

Lancafhire fends 14 members to parliament, provides 800 men to the national militia, and pays only five parts out of the 513 of the land-tax of England.

The county is divided into fix hundreds, viz. thofe of Salford, Weft Derby, Leyland, Blackburne, Amoundernefs, aand Lonfdale. They are fubdivided into the following townfhips :

SALFORD *Hundred.*

Manchefter,	Barton,	Crompton,
Salford,	Pendleton,	Afhton,
Stretford,	Pendlebury,	Hundersfield,
Withington,	Urmfton,	Caftleton,
Heaton Norris,	Flixton,	Spotland,
Chorlton Row,	Preftwich,	Butterworth,
Reddifh,	Pilkington,	Bolton with hamlets,
Cheetham,	Oldham,	Turton with Longworth,
Worfley,	Royton,	
Clifton,	Chadderton,	Edgworth with hamlets,

* Pays $\frac{14}{100}$ of the county rates ; raifes 293 militia men.

E   Harwood,

Harwood with hamlets,
Blackrod with Afpull,
Rivington, Loftock, and
    Anglezark,
Hulton magna,

Hulton parva,
——— middle,
Weft Haughton,
Farnworth, Rumfworth,
    and Kerfley,

Heaton, Horwich, and
    Halliwell,
Radcliffe,
Bury with hamlets,
Tottington.

WEST DERBY *Hundred.**

Wigan,
Ince and Pemberton,
Holland and Dalton,
Hindley and Abram,
Billinge, Orrell, and
    Winftanley,
Haigh,
Winwick and Hulme,
Newton,
Lowton and Kenyon,
Haydock and Gol-
    bourne,
Afhton in Mackerfield,
Culcheth,
Southworth, Croft, Mid-
    dleton, and Arbury,
Prefcott,
Whifton,
Rainhill,
Ecclefton,
Rainford,
Windle,

Parr,
Sutton,
Widnes and Appleton,
Bold,
Cuerdley and Crouton,
Ditton and Penketh,
Sankey,
Walton and Fazakerley,
Formby,
Derby,
Liverpool,
Kirkdale,
Bootle and Linacre,
Everton,
Ormfkirk,
Burfchough,
Latham,
Scarifbrick,
Bickerfteth and Skelmerf-
    dale,
Warrington,
Burtonwood,

Woolfton and Poolton,
Rixton and Glafsbrook,
Leigh and Pennington,
Atherton,
Weft Leigh,
Bedford,
Aftley,
Tildefley with Shacker-
    ley,
Childwall,
Hale and Halewood,
Great Woolton,
Little Woolton,
Wavertree,
Speak,
Garfton,
Allerton,
Huyton and Robey,
Knowfley,
Tarbock,
Hallfall,
Melling,

* Pays $\frac{24}{100}$ of the county rates; raifes 202 militia men.
I   Down

Down Holland,
Lydiate,
Maghull,
Sephton, Netherton, and
Lunt,

Ince, Blundell, and Little Crosby,
Thornton and Great Grosby,
Litherland, Ayntree, Or-

rett, and Ford,
Aughton,
North Meales, Crosby, and Birkdale,
Altcar.

LEYLAND *Hundred.**

Leyland,
Euxton,
Hoghton, Withnall, Wheelton, and Heapey,
Clayton, Cuerden, and Whittle in the Woods,
Crofton and Rufford,
Tarleton, Much Hoole, and Little Hoole,
Mawdefley, Brifpham,

Hefketh, and Beconfall,
Bretherton and Ulfefwalton,
Standifh with Langtree,
Copull and Worthington,
Heath Charnock, and Anderton,
Charnock Richard,
Skevington, and Walfh Whittle,

Duxbury and Adlington,
Penwortham and Hutton,
Longton,
Farrington and Howick,
Ecclefton and Hefkin,
Wrightington and Parbold,
Bindle,
Chorley.

BLACKBURNE *Hundred.†*

Blackburne,
Mearley,
Altham,
Downham,
Clitheroe,
Chatburne,
Worfton,
Church,

Cliviger,
Haflingden,
Ofbaldcfton,
Balderftone,
Cuerdale,
Simonftone,
Little Harwood,
Great & Little Pendleton,

Hapton,
Burnley,
Padiham,
Samlefbury,
Livefay with Tockholes,
Ofwaldtwifle,
Aighton, Bailey, and Chaidgley,

* Pays $\frac{2}{100}$ of the county rates; raifes 44 militia men.
† Pays $\frac{18}{100}$ of the county rates; raifes 123 militia men.

E 2   Sailfbury,

Sailſbury,
Huntcoat,
Chipping,
Brerecliff with Extwiſle,
Great Harwood,
Billington,
Clayton in le moors,
Nether Darwen,
Thornley with Wheat-
ley,
Riſhton,
Foulrigg,
Pleaſington,
Mellor with Eccleſhill,

Marſden,
Over Darwen,
Whilpſhire with Dink-
ley,
Clayton in le dale,
Wiſwall,
Colne,
Worſthorne,
Dutton,
Mitton, Henthorne and
Colecotes,
Read,
Ribcheſter with Dil-
worth,

Witton,
Twiſton,
Whalley,
Walton in le dale,
Bolland Foreſt,
Pendle Foreſt,
Ightenhill Park,
Heyhouſes,
Trawden,
Roſſendale,
Old Accrington,
New Accrington.

AMOUNDERNESS *Hundred.*[*]

Preſton,
Barton,
Broughton,
Lea,
Aſhton,
Fiſhwick,
Grimſargh with Brock
holes,
Ribbleton,
Haighton,
Elſton,
Alſton with Hotherſall,
Gooſnargh,

Whittingham,
Garſtang,
Catterall,
Bilſborough,
Claughton,
Kirkham,
Weſtby with Plumpton,
Clifton,
Newton with Scales,
Freckleton,
Warton,
Brining with Kellamergh,
Ribby with Wrea,

Weeton with Preeſe,
Medlargh with We-
·ſham,
Newſham,
Trayles,
Great and Little Single-
ton,
Wood Plumpton,
Lythom,
Greenhalgh with Thiſ-
leton,
Elſwick,
Poulton,

[*] Pays $\frac{18}{100}$ of the county rates ; raiſes 64 militia men.

Thornton,

Thornton,
Marton,
Hardhorn with Newton,
Carleton,
Little Eccleston with Larbreck,

Great Eccleston,
Inskip with Sowerby,
Bispham with Norbreck,
Layton with Warbreck,
Hambleton,
Stalmin with Staynall,

Preesall with Hackinsall,
Upper Rawcliffe,
Outer Rawcliffe,
Myerscough Forest,
Bleadale Forest.

LONSDALE *Hundred.* *

Lancaster,
Caton with Claughton,
Middleton,
Tatham with Ireby,
Leek,
Skirton,
Whittington,
Ellell,
Urswick,
Burrow,
Slyne with Hest,
Kirby Ireleth,
Pennington,
Leese,
Poulton, Bare and Torrisholme,
Scotforth,

Ulverstone,
Carnforth and Burnwick,
Aldingham,
Holker,
Nether Kellett,
Buck with Aldcliffe,
Warton,
Causfield,
Tunstall,
Melling with Wreaton,
Wrea,
Wennington,
Arkholme with Cawood,
Hornby,
Heaton with Oxcliffe,
Bolton,

Dalton with Hutton,
Halton,
Overton,
Yealand with Silverdale,
Gressingham,
Ashton,
Thurnham,
Farleton,
Dalton with Furness,
Heysham,
Alithwaite lower,
————— upper,
Broughton,
Cockerham,
Overkellet,
Quarmoor,
Wyersdale,

* Pays $\frac{16}{100}$ of the county rates ; raises 74 militia men.

With

With refpect to ecclefiaftical jurifdiction, Lancafhire is part of the diocefe of Chefter, and is divided in the following manner:

ARCHDEACONRY OF CHESTER.

DEANRY *of* MANCHESTER.

Parifh Churches.	Chapels, &c.	Patrons.
Afhton-under-line, R.	- - -	E. of Stamford,
	Hey or Lees,	Rector of Afhton.
	Mofley,	Ditto.
	Stayley-bridge,	E. of Stamford.
Bury, R.	- -	E. of Derby.
	St. John's Bury,	Rector of Bury.
	Heywood,	Ditto.
	Holcombe,	Ditto.
	Edenfield,	Ditto.
Bolton le moors, V.	- - -	Bifhop of Chefter.
	Little Bolton,	G. Gartfide, Efq.
	Blackroad,	V. of Bolton.
	Bradfhaw,	Ditto.
	Turton,	M. Green, Efq.
	Walmfley,	V. of Bolton.
	Rivington,	Inhabitants.
Dean, V.	- - -	The King.
	Horwich,	V. of Dean.
	Weft Houghton,	Ditto.
Eccles, V.	- - -	The King.
	Ellenbrook,	D. of Bridgewater.
Flixton, Cur.	- - -	Preb. Flixton.
Middleton, R.	- - -	Ld. Suffield.
	Afhworth,	W. Egerton, Efq.

Cockey,

Parish Churches.	Chapels, &c.	Patrons.
	Cockey,	R. of Middleton.
Manchester, Coll. ch.	- - -	Warden, by the king; 4 fellows and 2 chaplains, by the College.
——, St. Anne's, R.	- - -	B. of Chester.
——, St. John's, R.	- - -	Manchester College.
——, St. Mary's, R.	- - -	Ditto.
——, St. Paul's, Cur.	- - -	Ditto.
*	Ardwick,	Ditto.
	Birch,	J. Dickenson, Esq.
	Blakeley,	Manchester College.
	Cholerton or Chorlton,	Ditto.
	Denton,	Ld. Grey de Wilton.
	Didsbury,	W. Broom, Esq.
	Goston or Gorton,	Manchester College.
	Heaton Norris,	Ditto.
	Newton,	Ditto.
	Salford,	J. Gore Booth, Esq.
	Stretford,	Manchester College.
Radcliffe, R.	- - -	Ld. Grey de Wilton.
Prestwich with Oldham, R.	- - -	Rev. James Lyon.
	Oldham St. Mary, P.	R. of Prestwich, Bury, and Middleton.
	Ringley,	Ditto.
	Shaw,	R. of Prestwich.
	Unsworth,	Ditto.
	Royton,	Ditto.
	Hollingwood,	Ditto.
	Oldham chap.	Ditto.
		Rochdale,

* Other churches have been erected or are now erecting in Manchester.

Parish Churches.	Chapels, &c.	Patrons.
Rochdale, V.	- - -	Archb. Canterbury.
	Rochdale,	V. Rochdale.
	Friarmere,	Ditto.
	Hundersfield,	Ditto.
	Littleborough,	Ditto.
	Milnrow,	Ditto.
	Todmerden,	Ditto.
	Whitworth,	Ditto.

DEANRY *of* WARRINGTON.

Parish Churches.	Chapels, &c.	Patrons.
Aughton, R.	- - -	T. Plumbe, Esq.
Childwall, V.	- - -	B. of Chester.
	Hale,	J. Blackburne, Esq.
	Garston,	Heirs of Topham Beauclerk, Esq.
Hallsal, R.	- - -	C. Mordaunt, Esq.
	Maghull,	R. of Halsall.
	Melling,	Ditto.
Huyton, V.	- - -	Ld. Sephton.
Leigh, V.	- - -	Starkey and Gwillim.
	Astley,	Inhabitants.
	Atherton or Chowbent,	—— Gwillim, Esq.
Northmeols, R.	- - -	Rev. J. Baldwin.
Ormskirk, V.	- - -	E. of Derby.
	Latham dom. chap.	R. W. Bootle, Esq.
	Skelmersdale,	V. of Ormskirk.
Prescott, V.	- - -	King's Coll. Camb.
	St. Helen's in Windle,	V. of Prescott.
	Farnworth,	Ditto.
	Rainford,	

Parish Churches.	Chapels, &c.	Patrons.
	Rainford,	V. of Prescott.
	Sankey,	R. V. Atherton Gwillym, Esq.
Sephton, R.	- - -	
	Crosby Magna,	R. of Sephton.
Walton, R.	- - -	
———, V.	- - -	R. of Walton.
	Formby,	Ditto.
	Toxteth Park,	Ditto.
	Kirkby,	Ditto.
	West Derby,	Ditto.
	Richmond,	Corporation of Liverp.
Liverpool two medieties, R. (St. Peter and St. Nicholas.)	- - -	Ditto.
*	St. George's, Liverpool,	Ditto.
	St. Paul's, ditto,	Ditto.
	St. Thomas's, ditto,	Ditto.
	Altcar cur.	E. of Sephton.
Warrington, R.	- - -	R. V. A. Gwillym, Esq.
	Burtonwood,	R. of Warrington.
	Hollinfare,	Ditto.
	Trinity, Warrington,	T. Legh, of Lyme, Esq.
Wigan, R.	- - -	Sir H. Bridgeman.
	Billinge,	R. of Wigan.
	St. George's Wigan,	Ditto.
	Hindley,	Ditto.
	Holland,	Ditto.
Winwick, R.	- - -	E. of Derby.

* Other churches have since been erected in Liverpool.

F   Ashton,

Parish Churches.	Chapels, &c.	Patrons.
	Ashton,	R. of Winwick.
	Newchurch,	R. of Winwick.
	Lowton,	Ditto.
	Newton,	T. Legh, Esq.

DEANRY of BLACKBURNE.

Parish Churches.	Chapels, &c.	Patrons.
Blackburne, V.	- - -	Arch. Canterb.
	Balderston,	V. of Blackburne.
	Darwen,	Ditto.
	Harwood,	Ditto.
	Lango,	Ditto.
	Law or Lowchurch, or Walton in le Dale,	Ditto.
	Samlesbury.	Ditto.
	Tockholes,	Ditto.
Whalley, V.	- - -	Archb. Canterb.
	Accrington,	V. of Whalley,
	Altham,	Asheton Curzon, Esq.
	Burnley,	E. Townley, Esq.
	———— Castle, demolished (the profits given to Whitwell.)	
	Churchkirk,	A. Curzon, Esq.
	Clithero,	Ditto.
	Colne,	V. of Whalley.
	Downham,	A. Curzon, Esq.
	Haslingden,	Ditto.
	Goodshaw (under Haslingden,)	V. of Whalley.
	Holme (under Burnley,)	Ditto.

Marsden

Parish Churches.	Chapels, &c.	Patrons.
	Marſden (under Colne,)	V. of Whalley.
	Newchurch in Pendle,	A. Curzon, Eſq.
	Newchurch in Roſen-dale,	V. of Whalley.
	Padiham,	Legendre Starkie, Eſq.
	Whitwell,	V. of Whalley.

DEANRY of LEYLAND.

Croſton, R. and V.	- - -	Rev. Dr. Maſter.
	Beconſall,	R. of Croſton,
	Chorley,	Ditto.
	Rufforth,	Ditto.
	Tarleton,	T. Legh, Eſq.
Brindle, R.	- - -	D. of Devonſhire.
Eccleſton, R.	- - -	R. Whitehead, Eſq.
	Douglas,	R. of Eccleſton.
Leyland, V.	- - -	Rev. T. Baldwin.
	Euxton,	V. of Leyland.
	Heapy,	Ditto.
Hoole, R.	- - -	Mr. Barton of Ormſkirk.
Penwortham, perp. cur.	- - -	Mr. Barton of Penwor-tham.
	Longton,	Ditto.
Standiſh, R.	- - -	Mr. Standiſh.
	Copull,	S. Crooke, Eſq.

ARCHDEACONRY OF RICHMOND.
DEANRY of AMOUNDERNESS.

Chipping, R. and V.	- - -	B. of Cheſter.
Garſtang, V.	- - -	Truſtees of Mr. Pedder.

Gar-

Parish Churches.	Chapels, &c.	Patrons.
	Garstang,	V. of Garstang.
	Pilling,	G. Hornby, Esq.
Kirkham, V.	- - -	Christ Ch. Coll. Oxon.
	Goosenargh,	V. of Kirkham.
	Hambleton,	Ditto.
	Lund,	Ditto.
	Ribbey with Wray,	Ditto.
	Singleton,	Mr. Shaw.
	Warton,	V. of Kirkham.
	Whitechapel,	Ditto.
Cockerham, V.	- - -	F. Charteris, Esq.
	Ellell,	V. of Cockerham.
	Shirehead,	Ditto.
Bispham, perp. cur.	- - -	B. Hesketh, Esq.
Lancaster, V.	- - -	Dr. Marton.
	Admarsh,	V. of Lancaster.
	Caton (Lonsdale deanry)	Ditto.
	Gressingham (ditto)	Ditto.
	St. John, Lancaster,	Ditto.
	Littledale (under Caton)	Inhabitants.
	Overton,	V. of Lancaster.
	Poulton,	Ditto.
	Stalmin,	Ditto.
	Wyresdale,	Ditto.
Lytham, perp. cur.	- - -	Prior. of Durham.
Poulton, V.	- - -	R. Hesketh, Esq.
Preston, V.	- - -	Sir H. Hoghton.
	Broughton,	Ditto.
	St. Laurence, (domest.)	Mr. Shuttleworth.
	St. George, Preston,	V. of Preston.

Grimsargh,

Parish Churches.	Chapels, &c.	Patrons.
	Grimfargh,	V. of Prefton.
Ribchefter,	- - -	B. of Chefter.
	Longridge.	Sir H. Hoghton.
	Stidd,	V. of Ribchefter.
St.Michael'sonWyre,V.	- - -	Mr. Swainfon.
	Copp,	V. of St. Michael's.
	Wood Plumpton,	Ditto.

DEANRY of FURNESS and CARTMELL.

Aldingham, R.	- -	The King.
	Dendron,	R. of Aldingham.
Dalton, V.	- - -	The King.
	Irelith,	V. of Dalton.
	Ramfide,	Ditto.
	Walney (ifland)	Ditto.
Cartmell, perp. cur.	- - -	B. of Chefter.
	Cartmell Fell,	L. Geo. Cavendifh.
	Flookborough,	Ditto.
	Lindall,	Ditto.
	Staveley,	Ditto.
	Field Broughton,	Cur. of Cartmell.
Coulton, perp. cur.	- - -	Inhabitants and owners paying falary.
	Tinfthwait or Finfth- wait,	Cur. of Coulton.
	Rufland,	Ditto.
Hawkfhead, perp. cur.	- - -	The King.
	Satterthwaite,	Land Owners.
Kirkby Irelith, V.	- - -	Dean and Ch. York.
		Broughton,

Parish Churches.	Chapels, &c.	Patrons.
	Broughton,	Efther Sawrey.
	Seathwaite and Dunner-dale,	W. Penny, Efq.
	Woodland,	Land Owners.
Pennington, perp. cur.	- - -	The King.
Ulverfton, perp. cur.	- - -	W. Bradyll, Efq.
	Blawith,	Ditto.
	Conifton,	Inhabitants.
	Lowick,	W. F. Blencowe, Efq.
	Torver,	Cur. of Ulverfton.
Urfwick, V.	- -	Inhabitants.

DEANRY of KIRKBY LONSDALE.

Claughton, R.	- - -	T. Legh, Efq.
Tatham, R.	- - -	Fr. Charteris, Efq.
	Tatham Fell,	R. of Tatham.
Whittington, R.	- - -	Rev. G. Hornby.
Melling, V.	- - -	The King.
	Archolm,	V. of Melling.
	Hornby,	F. Charteris, Efq.
Tunftall, V.	- - -	Heirs of Mrs. Borret.
	Leck,	V. of Tunftall.

DEANRY of RICHMOND.

Bolton in the Sands, V.	- - -	B. of Chefter.
	Over Kellet,	Mr. Leapor and Inhab.

II. *General*

CHESHIRE.

YORKSHIRE

DERBY SHIRE

STAFFORD SHIRE

SHROP SHIRE

FLINT S.

DENBIGH SHI.

FLINT SHI.

LANCASHIRE

British Statute Miles.

RIVER MERSEY

RIVER DEE

Published October 13, 1794, by J. Stockdale, Piccadilly.

3° Longitude West from 3° London.

II.—*General Account of* CHESHIRE.

*C*HESHIRE is bounded by Lancafhire on the whole northern fide, except a fmall point to the north-eaft where it touches Yorkfhire ; by Derbyfhire and Staffordfhire on the eaft; by Shropfhire and a detached part of Flintfhire on the fouth ; by Denbighfhire and the reft of Flintfhire on the weft, touching alfo upon the Irifh fea at its north-weftern extremity.

The form of this county is diftinguifhed by two horns or projections running eaft and weft from its northern fide ; one of which is made by the hundred of Wirral lying between the eftuaries of the Merfey and Dee, the other by a part of Macclesfield hundred, pufhing out between Derbyfhire and Yorkfhire. A line drawn from the extremities of thefe two projections, meafures 58 miles ; but the extent of the county from eaft to weft acrofs its middle, does not exceed 40 miles. Its greateft extent from north to fouth is about 30 miles. It contains about 1040 fquare miles, or 665,600 acres.

Face of the Country.—Chefhire is for the moft part a flat country, whence it has obtained the name of the *Vale Royal of England*, though this name properly refers to its central part, in which was fituated the Abbey of Vale Royal, founded by Edward I. The principal hilly part is on the eaftern border, where a chain of hills, fome of them of confiderable height, runs along its confines with Derbyfhire and the north of Staffordfhire, and joins the mountainous diftricts of thofe counties. There is likewife a lower and narrower chain of emi-

2

nences,

nences, which beginning at Helfby and Overton, near Frodfham, in
bold promontories above the Merfey, runs fouthward acrofs the foreft of
Delamere, to Tarporley, ftarts up in the infulated rock of Beefton, and
again appearing in the wooded Broxton hills, at length finks in the
vale of the Dee on the borders of Denbighfhire. About a mile to the
fouth of Altringham rifes an elevated tract of ground called Bowden
downs, which extends to a confiderable diftance from eaft to weft. Its
weftern extremity is covered with the wood of Dunham park. Bowden church is fituated on the fummit of this tract, from whence there
is a moft extenfive view of a large part of Chefhire and the fouthern
part of Lancafhire. In various other parts the furface is varied by rifings and depreffions ; but the general character is unanimated flatnefs.
Four-fifths of the county are probably not elevated more than from 100
to 200 feet above the level of the fea.

Many ftreams wind through its levels, moft of which take their
courfe northwards to join the great bordering river, the *Merfey*. This
we fhall firft trace.

R I V E R S.

The *Merfey* takes its origin from a conflux of fmall ftreams near the
junction of Chefhire with Derbyfhire and Yorkfhire, and firft forms
the eaftern limit of the eaftern horn of Chefhire, under the name of the
Etherow river. When arrived at the place where the Goyt meets it
coming from the fouth, they together, taking a middle direction, flow
acrofs the root of the horn (as it may be termed) and reach Stockport.
Here the *Tame*, which may be reckoned the other parent of the Merfey,
and which forms the weftern limit of the eaftern horn, falls in.
From this junction, the Merfey, under its proper name, forms the

4   boundary

boundary between Lancafhire and Chefhire quite to the fea. It takes a very winding courfe, receiving continual acceffions, of which the principal are the river Irwell out of Lancafhire, and the Bollin from Chefhire, both which join it on its way to Warrington. Below this town it foon widens, having a large fhallow channel, full at tide time, but exhibiting little except bare fand at low water. Oppofite Runcorn it is fuddenly contracted by a tongue of land from the Lancafhire fide, forming Runcorn Gap. It then fpreads again, and foon receives the large addition of the Weaver from the heart of Chefhire. With this it fwells into a broad eftuary, and taking a north-weftern courfe, dif-embogues into the Irifh channel below Liverpool.

The *Goyt* rifes near the place where the road from Macclesfield to Buxton croffes the limits of the county, and it forms the boundary be-tween Chefhire and Derbyfhire till it meets the Etherow river near Chad-kirk, as before defcribed. The united ftreams keep the name of Goyt till they reach the Merfey at Stockport.

The *Bollin* rifes in the hilly moors to the fouth of Macclesfield, and paffing that town, takes a north-weft courfe through Preftbury and Wil-moflow, and joins the Merfey below Warburton.

The *Dane* rifes near the junction of Derbyfhire and Staffordfhire with Chefhire, and forming for fome way the limit between the two laft counties, flows wefterly by Congleton and Holms-chapel, to Mid-dlewich, where it receives the Wheelock from the fouth. It then, turning northerly, paffes Davenham in its courfe to Northwich, where it falls into the Weaver.

G   The

The *Wheelock*, rifing near Lawton on the borders of Staffordfhire, flows a little to the fouth of Sandbach in its courfe to join the Dane at Middlewich.

The *Weaver*, the principal river of the middle of Chefhire, rifes on the edge of Shropfhire, and holding a courfe almoft directly north, paffes Namptwich to Northwich, where, receiving the Dane, it turns wefterly, and in a very winding courfe, flows to Frodfham-bridge, below which it mixes with the Merfey.

The *Dee*, coming from Denbighfhire, reaches the border of Chefhire in the fouth-weft, and forming for fome way the limit of the two counties, paffes between Holt and Farndon, and runs directly north to Chefter. From this city it turns weftward; and after flowing fome miles in an artificial channel formed by embankment, at length fpreads into a broad eftuary feparating Flintfhire from the hundred of Wirral, and empties into the Irifh fea.

There are in various parts of Chefhire fmall lakes or meers, of which the principal are *Budworth-meer*, *Rofthern-meer*, *Meer-meer*, and *Tatton-meer*, all in Bucklow hundred, fome meers on Delamere foreft, *Comber-meer* in Namptwich hundred, and *Bar-meer* not far from Malpas. Several of thefe are of confiderable depth, and well furnifhed with fifh.

The proportion of cultivated to wafte land has been ftated as follows:

Arable,

	Acres.
Arable, meadow, pasture, &c. about - - -	615,000
Waste lands, heaths, commons, greens, woods, -	30,000
Peat bogs and mosses, - - - - - -	20,000
Common fields, probably less than - - -	1,000
Sea sands within the estuary of the Dee, - - -	10,000
	676,000

SOIL.

There are a great variety of soils in Cheshire; clay, sand, black moor or peat; marl and gravel, in various intermixed proportions, abound in different parts of the county. The three first, however, form the most predominant parts in the generally prevailing soils, and of these the largest proportion is a strong retentive clay. The substratum is generally rammel or clay, marl, sand, gravel, or red rock; but most commonly one of the two former, viz. clay or marl. The numerous mosses, marshy meadows, and peat bogs, which abound in different parts of the county, seem sufficiently to prove, that either clay, marl, or some other unctuous earth, is very generally at no great depth below the surface.

STATE of PROPERTY and FARMS.

There are in Cheshire many very considerable estates possessed by gentlemen who have residencies within the county; and, indeed, it has been observed, that no county in England has preserved more of the race of its ancient gentry. The number of proprietors of land, possessing from 500 to 1000l. per annum rent, are also many. But the race of yeomanry is supposed to be much diminished; another species

of

of freeholder, however, has increafed in thofe parts bordering on Lancafhire and Yorkfhire, where a number of fmall farms have been purchafed by the manufacturers of cotton, &c. The tenure is almoft univerfally freehold. There are fome few copyholds, or what may be
called cuftomary freeholds, paying fines and rents certain, in Macclesfield, Halton, and one or two other manors. The land is occupied in
farms of various extent; fome may contain 500 acres and upwards;
there are few, however, of more than 300 acres; though the practice
(but too frequently a pernicious one) of laying farms together, feems
to be increafing. On the whole, it is probable that there is at leaft one
farmer to every eighty ftatute acres.

AGRICULTURE and PRODUCTS.

About three-fourths of the county is paftured or mown; the other
fourth is ploughed. The land is generally ploughed in rotation. The
ufual courfe for ftiff clayey land is to plough four years; firft, oats;
fecond, fallow for wheat; third, wheat; fourth, oats; and then laid
down with clover or grafs feeds, or both, and paftured five or fix years
before it is again broken into tillage. Sandy land is ploughed only three
years, and frequently bears a crop every year.

The *Manures* are, marl, lime, farm-yard dung, and various kinds
of compoft. On the eaftern part of the country, lime is chiefly ufed;
and on the weft and fouth, marl is the moft general manure, of which
there are various forts, viz. the clay marl, the blue flate marl, the red
flate marl, ftone marls, &c. The clay marl is fuppofed to prevail
moft. The quantity of marl ufed, varies according to its quality, and
the quality and nature of the foil on which it is laid. The quantity is
from one to two roods, each rood being feventy-two folid yards and

I   upwards,

upwards, on an acre; the expence of it filled into the cart is about two-pence a yard. Marl is generally laid upon the turf, and after the froft has had its effect upon it, it is fometimes harrowed before the field is broken up. When lime is ufed, it is commonly mixed with gutter clods, fcourings of ditches, or foil; and laid on the land for barley. Farm-yard dung is frequently mixed with the foil off the fides of lanes, with furrows drawn from between the butts of paf-ture land, with gutter clods, ditchings, &c. and to thefe, marl or lime are fometimes added. Sand is frequently ufed as manure on ftiff lands with great fuccefs.

Foul or dirtied falt is a moft excellent manure, either for pafture land or fallows, when properly incorporated with foil, or other fubftances; and it is much to be regretted, that fo large a quantity as 7 or 800 tons annually, in Chefhire alone, fhould be loft to the community. The heavy duty laid upon refufe, or dirtied falt, almoft totally prevents its ufe for manure.

The markets for the overplus grain grown in Chefhire are chiefly Manchefter, Stockport, and Macclesfield. The oats are generally firft ground into meal, which is made into bread or cakes, and confumed in the N. E. of Chefhire and fouth of Lancafhire.

Green crops, as winter food for cattle, are very little cultivated : there are, however, very confiderable quantities of potatoes and carrots grown on the north fide of the county, which are chiefly intended for the fupply of the Lancafhire markets.

Potatoes

Potatoes are cultivated in the parifh of Frodfham, with as much fuccefs, and probably to as great an extent, as in any other parifh in the kingdom. It is eftimated, that not lefs than 100,000 bufhels of 90lb. weight, have annually, for fome years paft, been grown in this parifh; and a ready fale has generally been found for them, owing to the great demand for this root in Lancafhire, and to an eafy and cheap communication with Liverpool, by means of the river Merfey, and with Manchefter, by the duke of Bridgewater's canal. In years of plenty, when the market is overftocked with potatoes, and the price is fo low as one fhilling per bufhel, confiderable quantities have been given to different kinds of ftock, viz. to feeding cattle, milch cows, horfes and hogs.

Dairies and cattle.—The moft noted part for the production of cheefe is faid to lie in the neighbourhood of the Wiches, efpecially Namptwich, where the foil is more clayey than in other parts; but there is more or lefs made in every part of the county. The beft Chefhire cheefes run from 60 to 140 pounds weight. Their excellence depends partly on the fize, and partly on various nice and minute circumftances in the making, only to be learned by experience, and which conftitute the art of the very able and careful dairy-women of this county. The cheefe is generally made with two meals milk, and that in dairies where two cheefes are made in a day. In the beginning and end of the feafon, three, four, and even five or fix meals are kept for the fame cheefe. The proportion of cream withheld from the milk before it is put together, varies; but the general cuftom in the beft dairies is to take out about a pint of cream when two meal cheefes are made, from the night's milk of twenty cows. The principal late improvement in

3   cheefe-

cheefe-making has been the mode of preparing the *fteep* or *rennet*, by infufing all the maw-fkins at once, and faturating the ftrained liquor with falt. The colouring of cheefe is Spanifh arnotta. On the dairy farms one woman fervant is generally kept to every ten cows, who is employed in winter in fpinning and other houfehold bufinefs, but in milking is affifted by all the other fervants of the farm. The cheefe is chiefly fold in London, being exported from Chefter, Frodfham-bridge, and Warrington. The Liverpool merchants buy fome. A good deal is difpofed of to country dealers in Yorkfhire and Lancafhire, and fome goes into Scotland. The cattle in Chefhire are probably kept to a greater age than in moft other counties; for as the chief object with the farmers is their milk, when they meet with a good milker, they generally keep it till very old. The proper feafon for calving is reckoned to be from the beginning of March to the beginning of May; and during thefe months more veal is probably fed in Chefhire than in any other county, though generally killed young in order to fpare the milk. As cows are kept chiefly for milking, and very few are fed, the farmers are lefs attentive to the beauty of their cattle than in many other counties, though they begin to be more curious in their breeds than formerly.

Horfes, fheep, fwine.—The horfes employed in hufbandry are generally of the ftrong black kind, the beft of which are purchafed in Derbyfhire. The breed of the county is nothing remarkable, but has been improved by mixtures with the Leicefterfhire kinds. Few fheep are kept on the farms; what are kept, the farmers chiefly purchafe in the neighbouring counties. Each common or wafte maintains a few; but on Delamere foreft great numbers are kept, which are fmall, and of a fine-wooled kind. This breed has been lately improved by croffes

with

with the Herefordfhire. The breed of hogs ufually kept is a mixture between the long and fhort-eared.

Woods and Timber.—Chefhire is in general a very woody county. It is probably owing to this circumftance, and to the large fupply of hides from the manufacturing towns of Lancafhire, that great numbers of tanners are fettled in it, particularly in the middle and north parts. Befides the hides of cattle flaughtered at home, they have a large fupply from Ireland. The oak bark, in order to prepare it for ufe, was formerly univerfally, and is now by many tanners, ground down by a heavy ftone wheel turned by a horfe. Inftead of this, feveral now ufe caft-iron cylinders, between which the bark is paffed, and is thus more completely ground with lefs labour. Some experiments were lately made by an ingenious tanner in Afhley with the twigs and ends of the boughs of oak as a fubftitute for the bark. His fuccefs has been fuch as to convince him that leather may be tanned with them almoft equally well as with the bark. The leather prepared in Chefhire is principally confumed in the circumjacent parts, and very little of it is exported. Befides the common ufe of it in fhoes, boots, faddlery, &c. a very confiderable quantity is employed in the machinery of the cotton manufactory, for ftraps, coverings for the rollers, &c.

Some of the largeft oaks in the kingdom grow in Lord Stamford's park at Dunham. There are fingle trees elfewhere larger than any here, but no where fo many large trees together. At Morley near Wilmflow a remarkable oak was felled in fpring 1793. The principal trunk rofe above fix yards from the ground, and there gave off four large branches at nearly equal diftances, each itfelf being a large tree. All together contained about 470 feet of timber. The trunk immediately

ately above the ground was 41 feet in circumference; at four yards height, 32 feet. It was hollow, and its cavity would eafily admit fix or eight people.

MINERALS.

The mineral product for which Chefhire is moft remarkable is its falt, with which it is ftored in inexhauftible quantities. The particulars refpecting this article will hereafter be mentioned more minutely. It is enough here to obferve, that it is found in the two ftates of folid rock, and brine fprings. The firft is obtained only at Northwich, where large quantities are raifed, part of which is refined on the fpot, and part exported in its rough ftate. Brine fprings are met with in feveral places in the county, and the falt is procured from them by boiling. The average quantity of falt made annually in Chefhire is upwards of 74,000 tons, of which, as well as of the unrefined rock falt, a great proportion is exported abroad, forming a very beneficial article of commerce. That confumed at home pays a large fum to the public revenue.

Coals are procured in confiderable quantity in the north-eaftern part of the county near Poynton. They are fmall and of a foldering quality. Some are alfo got in the hundred of Wirrall.

Quarries of ftone of various kinds are wrought in different parts. Slate and flags are got at Kerridge on the hills near Macclesfield. Stone for building is procured from the eaftern hills, alfo at Millington near Bucklow-hill, at Hill-cliff near Warrington, at Hefswell near Parkgate, and in many other places. It has been remarked, that almoft every village on the north fide of Chefhire is fituated upon a bed of

H red

red rock, which in many parts lies bare. Mill-ftones are got on Mole-cop, which are fent to various parts of the country.

At Newbold Aftbury, about three miles from Conglèton, at the edge of Mole-cop, laige quantities of lime-ftone are dug. It is burned upon the fpot, the coal for the purpofe being procured from Stafford-fhire, at the diftance of about three miles. This lime-ftone is heavier than that of Buxton, and when burnt has more of a grey afh colour. It has lately come into very general ufe as a manure, and many farmers upon comparifon prefer it to the Buxton lime. It is longer in break-ing down, but fwells more, and is thought to be more durable in effect. Its price is about 5½d. per bufhel.

About five miles to the north-weft of Macclesfield is an elevated tract of ground called Alderley-edge. Some ftone ufed for building and other purpofes is got here; and both copper and lead ore have been found, the former in pretty confiderable quantity. The ore lies near to the furface, but is of too poor a quality to pay the expence of get-ting and fmelting. It was attempted to be worked many years ago, and the attempt was not long fince renewed, but without fuccefs.

CIVIL AND ECCLESIASTICAL STATE.

This county is one of thofe which in the time of the Romans was inhabited by the people named *Cornavii*. By the Saxons it was termed *Ceftrefcyre*; and its modern appellation is the *County Palatine* of Chef-ter. The reafon of the title *Palatine* was, that the earls of Chefter enjoyed palatine jurifdiction; that is, the inhabitants were tenants in chief to them alone, and they to the king. The courts of law were held in their name; and they had a fort of miniature parliament at

which

which their great tenants or barons, and their vaffals, attended. The fucceffion of earls becoming extinct in the reign of Henry III. the king made his eldeft fon earl of Chefter, which title has ever fince been attached to the eldeft fons of the crown.

The jurifdiction of the county palatine extends as well over the county of the city of Chefter, as over the county of Chefter. The Chief Juftice of Chefter has the fame jurifdiction over the courts of the city, as the Chief Juftice of the King's Bench has over the different courts of the kingdom at large; and iffues writs of latitat and certiorari into the city, the latter of which writs removes indictments and plaints into the county-palatine court before the Chief Juftice. His determinations have the fame weight and effect as thofe of the Chief Juftice of the King's Bench, and are impeachable only in the fame way. The exchequer court of the county-palatine is a court of equity; and the decrees of the chamberlain or his vice-chamberlain are only fubject to revifion and appeal in the Houfe of Lords. In this court is alfo a Baron, anfwering to the Remembrancer in the Court of Exchequer above; alfo a Seal-keeper, Filazer, Examiner, Cryer, &c. Its fittings, which were till lately held twice a year, are now only held once.

Chefhire is divided into feven hundreds, exclufive of the city of Chefter, which is a county of itfelf. It contains one city and 11 market towns; fends four members to parliament; pays feven parts out of 513 of the Englifh land-tax, and furnifhes 560 men to the national militia. Each hundred has two fubdivifions, for each of which there are two high conftables. The following is a lift of townfhips, vills, and places contained in each hundred.

MACCLESFIELD. *Hundred.*

Bredbury,
Brinnington,
Bromhall,
Cheadle,
Duckinfield,
Difley and Standley,
Etchels,
Godley,
Hyde,
Hatterfley,
Hollinworth,
Marple,
Matley,
Mottram, in Longden-
    dale,
Norbury,
Northenden,
Newton,
Offerton,
Romiley,
Stayley,

Stockport,
Tintwiftle,
Taxall,
Torkington,
Werneth,
Yeardley cum Whaley,
Adlington,
Alderley Superior,
Alderley Inferior,
Birtles,
Bollin Fee,
Bollington,
Bofley,
Butley cum Newton,
Capefthorne,
Chelford cum Old Wi-
    thington,
Chorley,
Eaton,
Falibroome,
Gawfworth,

Hurdsfield,
Henbury cum Pexall,
Kettlefhulme,
Marton,
Macclesfield,
Mottram Andrew,
Poynton,
Pownall Fee,
Preftbury,
Pott Shrigley,
Rainow,
Rode, *vulgo* North Rode,
Snelfon,
Sutton Downes cum
    Wincle,
Siddington,
Somerford Booth,
Tytherington,
Upton,
Warford Magna,
Withington Inferior.

BUCKLOW *Hundred.*

Agden,
Altrincham,
Afhley,
Afhton fuper Merfey,
Baguley,

Bexton,
Bollington,
Bowden,
Carrington,
Cogfhul,

Dunham Maffey,
Hale,
Knutsford Inferior,
Knutsford Superior,
Legh, *vulgo* High Legh,
             Marfton,

Marston,
Marthall, cum Little Warford,
Mere,
Millington,
Mobberly,
Ollerton,
Partington,
Peover Superior,
Peover Inferior,
Pickmeir,
Plumbley,
Rosthern,
Sale,
Tabley Superior,
Tabley Inferior,
Tatton,
Timperley,
Toft,
Warburton,

Wincham,
Acton Grange,
Aston juxta Sutton,
Aston Grange,
Aston juxta Budworth,
Anderton,
Barnton,
Batherton,
Budworth, *vulgo* Great Budworth,
Clifton, *alias* Rock Savage,
Cumberbach,
Daresbury,
Dutton,
Groppenhall,
Halton,
Hatton,
Hull and Appleton,
Kekewick,

Lymme,
Little Leigh,
Latchford,
Marbury,
Middleton Grange,
Moore,
Newton prope Daresbury,
Norton,
Preston,
Runcorn,
Stockham,
Stretton,
Sutton,
Thelwall,
Walton Inferior,
Walton Superior,
Weston,
Whitley Inferior,
Whitley Superior.

NORTHWICH *Hundred*.

Artclid,
Buglawton,
Bradwell,
Brereton cum Smethwick,
Congleton,
Cotton,
Davenport,

Elton,
Gooftrey cum Barnshaw,
Hulme and Walfield,
Church Hulme,
Church Lawton,
Kermincham,
Moreton cum Alcomlow,
Mosebarrow cum Parme,

Moston,
Newbold Astbury,
Odd Rode,
Smallwood,
Summerford cum Radnor,
Sandbach,
Sprofton,
Swettenham,

Swettenham,
Twemlow,
Tetton,
Warminsham,
Weelock,
Allowstock,
Byley cum Yatehouse,
Birches,
Bostock,
Clive,
Cranage,
Croxton,
Davenham,
Eyton prope Davenham,

Hulse,
Lach Dennis,
Lees,
Leftwich,
Lostock Gralam,
Kinderton cum Hulme,
Middlewich,
Minshull Vernon,
Moulton,
Newhall,
Newton,
Northwich,
Occleston,

Nether Peover,
Ravenscroft,
Rudheath Lordship,
Shipbrooke,
Shurlach cum Bradford,
Stanthorne,
Stubs and Lach,
Sutton,
Wharton,
Whatcroft,
Witton cum Twambroke,
Wimboldsley.

Eddisbury *Hundred.*

Alpraham,
Beeston,
Bunbury,
Budworth,
Calveley,
Eaton cum Rushton,
Heighton,
Idenshall,
Merton,
Over cum Darnhall,
Oulton Lowe,
Peckforton,
Ridley,
Spurstow,

Tarporley,
Tiverton,
Tilston Fernal,
Utkinton,
Wardle,
Weever,
Wettenhall,
Alvanley,
Ashton,
Acton,
Burton,
Bridge Trafford,
Barrow Magna,
Barrow Parva,

Bruen Stapleford,
Cuddington,
Crowton,
Clotton Hoofield,
Castle Northwich,
Dunham,
Duddon,
Elton,
Frodsham,
Hapsford,
Helsby,
Horton cum Peele,
Hockenhull,
Hartford,

2

Kelsall,

Kelfall,
Ince,
Kingfley,
Manley,
Mouldfworth,
Newton,

Norley,
Oulton, *alias* Oufton,
Tarvin,
Thornton,
Wallerfcoat,

Waverham cum Milton,
Walaton, *alias* Willington,
Wimbolds Trafford,
Winnington.

NAMPTWICH *Hundred.*

Afton,
Alfager,
Alvanderfton,
Afton juxta Mondrum,
Aufterton,
Baddington,
Barthomley,
Betchton,
Brindley,
Burland,
Cholmondefton,
Church Coppenhall,
Monks Coppenhall,
Crewe,
Edlafton,
Faddiley,
Haflington,
Haffall,
Henhull,
Hurlefton,
Leighton,

Minfhull,
Namptwich,
Poole,
Stoake,
Willafton,
Wiftafton,
Worlefton,
Wolftanwood,
Audlem,
Baddiley,
Bridgemere,
Basford,
Batherton,
Blackenhall,
Bromhall,
Buerton,
Checkley cum Wrinehill,
Chorley,
Chorlton,
Coole Pilate,
Dodcot cum Wilkefley,

Dodington,
Hankilow,
Hatherton,
Hough,
Hunfterfton,
Lea,
Marbury cum Quoifley,
Newhall,
Norbury,
Rope,
Shavington cum Grefty,
Sound,
Stapeley,
Titley,
Walgherton,
Wefton,
Wybunbury,
Wirefwall,
Wrenbury,
Woodcott.

BROXTON

BROXTON *Hundred.*

Aldford,
Aldersey,
Agden,
Barton,
Bulkeley,
Burwardsley,
Broxton,
Bickley,
Bickerton,
Bradley,
Chowley,
Coddington,
Chidlow,
Cuddington,
Chorlton,
Church Shocklach,
Caldecot,
Cholmondeley,
Crewe,
Carden,
Clutton,
Edge,
Edgerley,
Egerton,
Farndon,
Grafton,
Handley,
Hampton,

Horton,
Harthill,
Duckington,
Larckton,
Macefen,
Malpas,
Newton juxta Malpas,
Old Castle,
Overton,
Stockton,
Shocklach Oviat,
Stretton,
Tushingham cum Grind-
    ley,
Tilston,
Wigland,
Wighalgh,
Boughton,
Buerton,
Bach,
Coghull,
Christleton Parva,
Church Christleton,
Row Christleton,
Claverton,
Cotton,
Cotton Edmunds,
Churton Heath,

Dodleston,
Eccleston,
Eaton,
Golborn David,
Golborn Bellow,
Hoole,
Huxley,
Hatton,
Kinnerton,
Lea and Newbold,
Lach,
Moston,
Marlston,
Newton juxta Suxton,
Newton juxta Tatten-
    hall,
Pickton,
Poulton,
Pulford,
Sutton,
Stapleford,
Saighton,
Trafford,
Tattenhall,
Upton,
Wervin,
Waverton.

WIRRAL

WIRRALL *Hundred.*

Backford,
Bromborow,
Burton,
Blacon cum Crabhall,
Copenhurſt,
Childer Thornton,
Croughton,
Chorlton,
Eaſtham cum Plimyard,
Hooton cum Ranacre,
Lea,
Ledſham,
Leighton,
Mollington Baniſter,
Mollington Torrett,
Neſſe,
Neſton Magna,
Neſton Parva cum Har-
    greave,
Poole Superior,
Poole Inferior,
Puddington,
Raby,
Rough Shotwick,

Saughall Magna cum
    Woodbank,
Saughall Parva,
Shotwick,
Stanney Magna,
Stanney Parva,
Stoake,
Sutton Magna,
Sutton Parva,
Thornton Mayes,
Whitby,
Willaſton,
Arrow,
Brimſtage,
Bebbington Superior,
Bebbington Inferior,
Barnſton,
Bidſton cum Liſcard,
Caldey Magna, or
    Grange,
Caldey Parva,
Claughton cum Grange,
Frankby,
Greaſby,

Gayton,
Heſwall cum Oldfield,
Irby,
Knoctorum,
Kirkby cum Wallaſey,
Liſcard,
Landican,
Moreton,
Meols Magna,
Meols Parva,
Newton cum Larton,
Oxton,
Poulton cum Seacombe,
Poulton cum Spittle,
Prenton,
Penneſby,
Saughall Maſſie,
Storeton,
Thurſtaſton,
Thingwall,
Tranmore,
Upton,
Weſtkirby.
Woodchurch.

In the aſſeſſments for county rates, when the whole ſum to be raiſed
is £.1000 the following proportions are levied on each hundred :

	£.	s.	d.
Macclesfield Hundred, - - - - - -	166	9	2
Bucklow ditto, - - - - - -	141	15	5
Northwich ditto, - - - - - -	128	18	4
Eddisbury ditto, - - - - - -	108	9	2
Namptwich ditto, - - - - - -	168	14	7
Broxton ditto, - - - - - - -	150	0	5
Wirrall ditto, - - - - - - -	135	12	11

ECCLESIASTICAL DIVISION.

The county of Chester is contained within the diocese of the same name, which was erected into a bishopric by Henry VIII. in the year 1541, and belongs to the province of York. It contains two archdeaconries, those of Chester and Richmond. Cheshire is entirely within the former. It is subdivided into the following deanries and parishes:

DEANRY of CHESTER.

Parish Churches.	Chapels, &c.	Patrons.
St. Mary on the Hill, Chester, R.	- - -	M. Wilbraham.
St. Oswald, Chester, V.	- - -	D. and Ch. of Chester.
	Bruera, or Church on the Heath,	
St. Peter, Chester, perp. cur.	- - -	B. of Chester.
Trinity Chester, R.	- - -	E. of Derby.
	St. Bridget's Chester, R.	B. of Chester.
	St. John Baptist, Chester, V.	T. Adams, Esq.

Little

Parish Churches.	Chapels, &c.	Patrons.
	Little St. John's, Chester, cur.	Corp. of Chester.
	St. Martin, Chester, R.	B. of Chester.
	St. Michael, Chester, cur. p.	Ditto.
	St. Olave, Chester, cur.	Ditto.
Barrow, R.	- - -	E. Cholmondeley.
Christleton, R.	- - -	Sir R. Mostyn.
Dodleston, R.	- - -	D. and Ch. Chester.
Eccleston, R.	- - -	Ld. Grosvenor.
Pleniston, perp. cur.	- - -	Sir H. Bridgman.
Pulford, R.	- - -	Sir P. Warburton.
Tarvin, V.	- - -	Preb. of Tarvin in Litchf. Cath.
	Hargrave,	Trustees.
Thornton, R.	- - -	T. Hill, Esq.
Tarporley, R.	- - -	J. Arden, Esq.
Waverton, R.	- - -	Bishop of Chester.
	Farndon, P.	Ld. Grosvenor.
	Gilden Sutton, cur. p.	Sir J. Stanley.
	Ince, p.	R. Hill Waring, Esq.

DEANRY *of* FRODSHAM.

Ashton upon Mersey, R.	- - -	Rev. W. Johnson.
Bowden, V.	- - -	B. of Chester.
	Carrington,	E. of Stamford.
	Ringey,	J. Crewe, Esq.
Budworth, V.	- - -	Christ Ch. Oxon.
	Little Leigh,	V. of Budworth.

Parish Churches.	Chapels, &c.	Patrons.
	Nether Peover,	Sir J. Fl. Leycester.
	Nether Whitley, dom.	Sir J. Chetwode.
	Whitton P. Northwich,	Sir J. F. Leycester.
Frodsham, V.	- - -	Christ Ch. Oxon.
	Alvandley,	J. Arden, Esq.
Grappenhall, R.	- - -	Rev. P. Halstead.
	Latchford,	R. of Grappenhall.
Lymme, R. (two medieties)	- - -	Sir P. Warburton.
	- - -	Egerton Leigh.
	Warburton, supplied by the Rector of one mediety,	
Runcorn, V.	- - -	Christ Ch. Oxom
	Aston,	H. Harvey Aston, Esq.
	Daresbury, P.	
	Halton,	J. Cheshyre, Esq.
	Thelwall, P	E. Pickering, Esq.
Rosthern, V.	- - -	Ld. Vernon.
	High Leigh, (domest.)	
	Knutsford, V.	Lords of four adjacent manors.
	Over Peover,	Sir H. Mainwaring.
Waverham, V.	- - -	B. of Chester.
Whitegate, R.	- - -	Mr. Cholmondeley.

DEANRY of MACCLESFIELD.

Alderley, R.	- - -	G. Hartley, Esq.
Cheadle, R.	- - -	S. Buck, Esq.
Gawsworth, R.	- - -	Mrs. Parrott.

Mob-

Parish Churches.	Chapels, &c.	Patrons.
Mobberley, R.	- - -	T. Mallory.
Mottram, R.	- - -	B. of Chester.
	Woodhead,	Ditto.
Northenden, R.	- - -	D. and Ch. Chester.
Prestbury, V.	- - -	C. Legh, Esq.
	Adlington, dom.	Mrs. Legh.
	Bosley, P.	V. of Prestbury.
	Capesthorn, C.	D. Davenport, Esq.
	Chelford, P.	Mr. Parker.
	Forest Chap.	E. of Derby.
	Macclesfield, P.	Mayor of Macclesfield.
	Chrift Church, Macclesfield,	W. Roe, Esq.
	Marton,	D. Davenport, Esq.
	Pott Chap.	P. Downes, Esq.
	Poynton,	Sir G. Warren.
	Rainow,	V. of Prestbury.
	Wincle,	Ditto.
	Saltersford,	Ditto.
	Siddington.	D. Davenport, Esq.
Stockport, R.	- -	Mary Prescott.
	Chadkirk,	R. of Stockport.
	Disley,	T. Legh, Esq.
	Norbury,	Ditto.
	Marple,	R. of Stockport.
	St. Peter, Stockport,	Rev. H. O. Wright.
Taxall, R.	- - -	Rev. J. Swain.
Wilmslow, R.	- - -	Gilb. Berresford, Esq.

DEANRY

DEANRY *of* MALBAN WICH, *alias* NAMPTWICH.

Parifh Churches.	Chapels, &c.	Patrons.
Acton, V.	- - -	Wilbrah. Tollemache, Efq.
	Burleydam,	Sir R. S. Cotton.
	Wrenbury,	V. of Acton.
Audlem, R.	- - -	Rev. W. Wickfted.
Baddiley, R.	- - -	Sir H. Mainwaring.
Barthumley, R.	- - -	E. Mainwaring, Efq.
	Haflington,	Sir T. Broughton.
Coppenhall, R.	- -	B. of Litchf. and Cov.
	Church Minfhull, P.	T. Brooke, Efq.
Namptwich, R.	- - -	J. Crewe, Efq.
Wibunbury, V.	- - -	B. of Litchf. and Cov.
Wiftafton, R.	- - -	P. Walthall, Efq.
	Bunbury, cur.	Comp. of Haberdafhers, London.
	Burwardfley, chap. to Bunbury,	
	Marbury, fupplied by the R. of Whitchurch,	

DEANRY *of* MALPAS.

Aldford, R.	- - -	Ld. Grofvenor.
Malpas, (two portions)	- - -	W. Drake, Efq.
Tattenhall, R.	- - -	B. of Chefter.
Tylfton, R.	.. - -	Ld. Cholmondeley.

DEANRY *of* BANGOR.

Parish Churches.	Chapels, &c.	Patrons.
Coddington, R.	- - -	D. and Ch. Chester.
Handley, R.	- - -	Ditto.
	Harthill, cur. p.	W. Drake, Esq.
	Shocklach, p.	T. Puleston, Esq.

DEANRY *of* MIDDLEWICH.

Astbury, R.		P. Brooke, Esq.
	Congleton,	Corp. of Congleton.
	Little Budworth, cur. p.	B. of Chester.
Brereton, R.	- - -	Sir Lister Holt.
Davenham, R.	- - -	T. Brock, Esq.
Sandbach, V.	- - -	Mary Haddon.
	Goostrey, ch. p.	V. of Sandbach.
	Holms-chapel,	
Swetenham, R.	- - -	Ab. Painter.
Warmingham, R.	- - -	Ph. Egerton, Esq.
Lawton, R.	- - -	J. Lawton, Esq.
Middlewich, V.	- - -	If. Wood, Esq.
Over, V.	- - -	B. of Chester.
	Wetenhall, p.	V. of Over.
Whitegate, *alias* New-church, V.	- - - - - -	Mr. Cholmondeley.

DEANRY *of* WIRRALL.

Eebington, R	- - -	Rev. S. Jackson.
Backford, V.	- - -	B. of Chester.
Eastham, V.	- - -	D. and Ch. Chester.

Heswall,

Parifh Churches.	Chapels, &c.	Patrons.
Hefwall, R.	- - -	R. Davenport, Efq.
Weft Kirkby, R.	- - -	D. and Ch. Chefter.
Nefton, V.	- - -	Ditto.
Woodchurch, R.	- - -	—— Crookhall.
Thurftafton, R.	- - -	D. and Ch. Chefter.
Wallifey, R. Med.	- - -	B. of Chefter.
	Biditon cum Ford,	Ditto.
	Birkenhead, Ch. to Bid-fton,	R. P. Price, Efq.
	Bromborow,	D. and Ch. Chefter.
	Burton, cur.	Maft. of Hofp. of St. John Bapt. Litchf.
	Over Church in Upton, cur.	Rev. S. Jackfon.
	Shotwick, cur.	D. and Ch. Chefter.
	Stoke, cur.	Sir T. C. Bunbury.

III. DERBY.

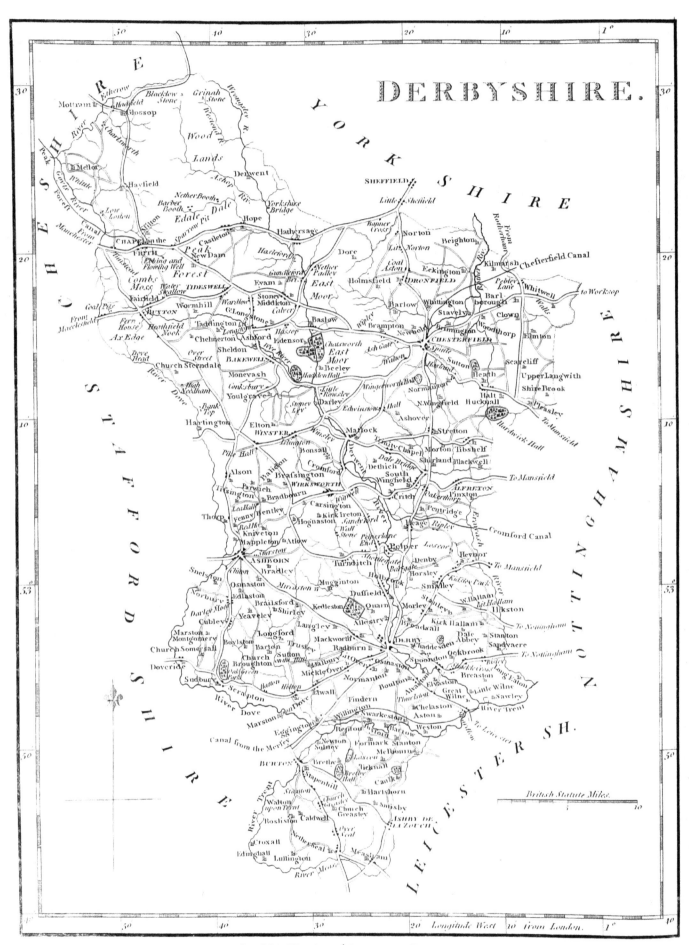

DERBYSHIRE.

British Statute Miles.

Published November 1.1794. by I.Stockdale, Piccadilly.

III.—DERBYSHIRE *in General.*[*]

*D*ERBYSHIRE is bounded to the north by Yorkſhire and part of Cheſhire, the river Etherow being its ſeparation from the latter; to the weſt, by Cheſhire and Staffordſhire, its limits almoſt all the way being the Goyt, and the Dove and Trent; to the ſouth and ſouth-eaſt by Leiceſterſhire; and to the eaſt by Nottinghamſhire. It is ſituated nearly in the middle of the iſland, at an equal diſtance from the eaſt and weſt ſeas. Its principal extent is almoſt directly from north to ſouth, in which direction it meaſures about 55 miles. Its greateſt breadth is at the northern extremity, where it meaſures about 33 miles, from which it contracts, though irregularly, on advancing towards the ſouthern, where it is very narrow. A portion of this extremity is inſulated by Leiceſterſhire. The county is eſtimated to contain 720,640 acres.

Face of the Country.—A conſiderable part of the county is diſtinguiſhed from the reſt by being a mountainous tract, and one of the moſt celebrated of the kind in England. From nearly the middle of Derbyſhire, that chain of hills ariſes, which ſtretching northwards, is continued in a greater or leſs breadth quite to the borders of Scotland, and forms a natural boundary between the eaſt and weſt ſides of the northern part of the kingdom. Its courſe in this county is inclining a little to the weſt. It ſpreads as it advances northerly, and at length fills up the whole of the north-weſt angle, alſo overflowing a little, as it were, towards the eaſtern parts. The hills are at firſt of ſmall eleva-

---

[*] For the general and particular accounts of Derbyſhire we are much indebted to the Rev. Mr. Pilkington's accurate and valuable hiſtory of that county.

K

tion;

tion; but being in their progrefs piled upon one another, they form very elevated ground in the tract called the *High Peak*, though without any eminences which can rank among the loftieft mountains even of this ifland. The two moft diftinguifhed heights in the Peak are Ax-edge on the limits of the county near Buxton, and Kinder-fcout, in the centre of the north-weft angle. The former was calculated by Mr. Whitehurft to be about 2100 feet higher than the town of Derby, and 1000 feet above the valley in which Buxton-hall ftands. Kinder-fcout has not been meafured; but as it overlooks all the furrounding eminences, it is fuppofed to have a ftill greater elevation. The fuperior height of thefe two points is further confirmed by the obfervation that clouds reft on them when they pafs over the intermediate high grounds.

The High Peak is a region of bleak barren heights and long-extended moors, interfperfed with deep narrow vallies, through which the fmall ftreams take their courfe. Some of thefe offer agreeable profpects of fertility; but on the whole, the tract is one of the leaft pleafing, being deftitute of moft of the romantic beauties of other mountainous countries. It contains feveral natural curiofities, fuch as deep caverns and apertures in the ground, which have had their full fhare of admiration under the name of the *Wonders of the Peak*: they will hereafter be more particularly mentioned. The tract called the *Low Peak*, lying near the centre of the county, likewife contains hills of various height and extent, affording large profpects into the neighbouring counties. The eaft fide of the county has alfo a high ridge extending from Hardwick in a northern direction to the Yorkfhire border. The fouthern part of Derbyfhire is for the moft part a pleafant and fertile country, not diftinguifhed in its appearance from the other midland counties.

The

The banks of the Trent are a range of low meadows, fubject to inundations.

RIVERS.

The principal river of this county is the *Derwent*. It rifes from the junction of various rills out of the High Peak, which appear in one ftream near Hatherfage. Taking a fouthern courfe a little inclining to the eaft, it paffes through Chatfworth park, below which it receives the *Wye* coming down from Buxton and Bakewell. It flows through the romantic dale of Matlock, and at length reaches Derby, having fo far divided the county into an eaftern and weftern part nearly equal in dimenfions. From Derby it fuddenly turns more to the eaft, and mixes with the Trent on the Leicefterfhire border near Wilne. It is made navigable from Derby to the Trent. The current of the Derwent is rapid, and the temperature of its waters has been obferved to be warmer than that of rivers in general, which may be afcribed to the mixture of warm fprings. It frequently in the fummer raifes the thermometer to 66 degrees.

The *Dove*, rifing a little to the fouth of Buxton, on the Staffordfhire limit, holds a courfe nearly parallel to the Derwent, ferving for the boundary of the two counties all the way to its junction with the Trent a little below Burton. In its tract it paffes through the very romantic Dove dale. It is augmented by many little ftreams on the fouthweftern fide of Derbyfhire.

The *Trent* itfelf holds but a fhort part of its courfe through this county. Coming out of Staffordfhire, it reaches the border of Derbyfhire at its fouth-weftern point. After making the boundary for fome

K 2   miles,

miles, at its junction with the Dove it enters the county, and paffing from weft to eaft acrofs its narroweft part, it reaches the Leicefterfhire border. It there becomes again the boundary, till it enters Nottinghamfhire. It is navigable during all this courfe.

The *Errewafh*, rifing about the middle of the eaftern border, runs fouthward, forming the boundary between Derbyfhire and Nottinghamfhire till its junction with the Trent.

The *Rother*, taking its rife to the fouth of Chefterfield, paffes that town, and holds a north-eaftern courfe till it enters Yorkfhire.

CLIMATE.

The mountainous part of Derbyfhire is diftinguifhed from the reft by the greater quantity of rain which falls in it. At Chatfworth, which is by no means the higheft part, about 33 inches of rain have been found to fall annually at a medium. The High Peak is peculiarly liable to very violent ftorms, in which the rain defcends in torrents, fo as frequently to occafion great ravages in the lands: it is alfo fubject to very high winds. Thefe caufes, together with the elevation of the country, render it cold; fo that vegetation is backward and unkindly. Some kinds of grain will not grow at all in the Peak, and others feldom ripen till very late in the year. The atmofphere is, however, pure and healthful, and the higher fituations are generally free from epidemic difeafes, though agues and fevers fometimes prevail in the vallies. One difeafe is, however, endemic in thefe parts, and even as far fouth as Derby, which is the bronchocele or Derby-neck: it is an enlargement of the glands of the throat, and is a degree of the fame difeafe that is known in the Alps, and in fome other mountainous tracts.

SOIL.

SOIL.

The moſt common ſoil in Derbyſhire is a reddiſh clay or marl. The ſouthern part of this county is in general compoſed of it, with little or no ſtone beneath the ſurface. This ſoil alſo appears on the north-weſt ſide of the county. Its quality is very various in different ſituations, in ſome containing much calcareous earth, in others not at all effervefcing with acids. Its colouring principle is iron. That large tract of country which produces coal, is covered with a clay of various colours, black, grey, brown, and yellow; eſpecially the laſt. It is in ſome places mixed with a large proportion of ſand. This kind of ſoil is alſo found in ſome parts where grit-ſtone is met with; but there it is frequently of a black colour and bituminous quality. On the eaſt moor, and in the northern extremity of the county, are large tracts of land conſiſting of this ſoil. That in the lime-ſtone country on the north-eaſt ſide is of a brown colour and looſer texture. Small tracts of gravel or ſand are interſperſed through the marl diſtrict. In the north part of the county are peat bogs, ſome upon the higheſt mountains, in which trees have been found nearly perfect. The ſoil in the vallies near the banks of the larger rivers is very different from that of the adjacent parts, and has been evidently altered by the depoſitions from inundations.

PRODUCE.

The ſouthern parts of this country are nearly equally divided between paſture and tillage. The banks of the Dove are chiefly occupied by dairy farms. On the eaſtern ſide of the county, tillage chiefly prevails. The midland tracts have a mixture of paſture and arable according to the ſoil and ſituation, and large improvements are carrying on upon the

moors

moors of this diſtrict. In the High Peak the ground is chiefly devoted to the raiſing and feeding of cattle, very little corn beſides black
oats being grown. On the whole, Derbyſhire is more of a grazing
and dairying than a corn country. The grain principally cultivated is
barley, of which much is grown for the ſupply of the breweries at
Burton. Of the whole produce, calculated at 5000 quarters annually,
about half is ſuppoſed to be exported to the neighbouring counties,
ſome in the ſtate of malt. The produce of wheat is ſcarcely equal to
the conſumption ; that of beans and oats about anſwers the home demand. Of cheeſe, nearly 2000 tons are thought to be annually exported to London and ſeveral ſea-ports on the eaſt coaſt. Its quality is
mild, and its taſte reſembles the Glouceſterſhire.

An uncommon ſpecies of culture, in which about 200 acres of this
county are employed, is that of *camomile*. A loamy ſoil is choſen for
the purpoſe, in which, after proper preparation, ſlips from the roots of
an old plantation are ſet about the end of March. The collection of
the flowers begins in September, and continues in ſucceſſion till
ſtopt by the froſts. The plants uſually ſtand three years, of which the
firſt affords the ſmalleſt, the ſecond the beſt and largeſt produce. A
dry year is moſt favourable to them. When the flowers are gathered,
they are carefully dried in a kiln or on a heated floor, packed in bags,
and ſold to perſons in the neighbourhood, who ſend moſt of them to
the druggiſts in London. The produce and price are ſubject to great
variation ; but on an average the former may be reckoned at four cwt.
an acre, the latter at four pounds per cwt.

The horſes of Derbyſhire are of very different breeds in the ſouthern
and northern parts. In the former they are of the ſtrong and heavy
kind ;

kind; but in the latter, light and flender. They are much employed in the Peak for carrying lime-ftone on their backs, and fhow great agility in afcending and defcending the fteep mountains.

The neat cattle are almoft univerfally horned, and rather large and handfome. The cows are diftinguifhed for their beautiful fhapes, and have the property of becoming fat in a fhort time. Their yield of milk is but moderate. Notwithftanding the numbers bred here, many are brought every year from Yorkfhire and Lancafhire, and fold to the Derbyfhire graziers.

The fheep on the Leicefterfhire border refemble thofe of that county in weight and fize. They diminifh on proceeding northwards; and in the High Peak weigh from 14 to 17 pounds per quarter, thofe on grit-ftone land being three pounds lighter than thofe on lime-ftone. But the difference in their fleeces is more remarkable, thofe of the grit-ftone fheep being much lighter and thinner than of the others. There are now few or no goats kept in Derbyfhire, though once they were common Other animals, tame and wild, offer nothing remarkable.

SUBTERRANEOUS GEOGRAPHY.

This may in general be confidered as dividing the county into the three diftinctions of lime-ftone, coal, and grit-ftone land.

Lime-ftone.—The moft extenfive tract of this land is fituated on the north-weft fide of the county. Its northern extremity is at Caftleton: its weftern line runs along the weft fide of Peak Foreft to Buxton, thence, keeping along the eaft fide of Ax-edge, it proceeds to the head of the Dove, and follows the boundary of the counties about 12 miles,

and

and croffing the river, extends a few miles into Staffordfhire. The moft fouthern point in which it appears in Derbyfhire is about two miles north of Afhborne. Hence, its limit runs eaftward in a line by Wirkfworth as far as Matlock : its courfe then points northward, extending on the eaft fide of Winfter, Bakewell, Stony-Middleton, and Bradwell, to its termination in the valley of Edale. Befides this large tract of lime-ftone, there is a fmaller one on the eaft fide of the county, forming the ridge already mentioned from near Hardwick, through Bol-fover and Barlborough to the border of the county. This lime-ftone tract fpreads eaftwards into Nottinghamfhire, and northwards, quite through Yorkfhire, with little interruption, as far as Tinmouth-caftle in Northumberland. There are likewife feveral detached beds of lime-ftone in other parts of Derbyfhire, but none exceeding two miles in length or breadth.

Coal.—The principal coal country begins a little north-eaft of Derby, at Stanton, Dale, and Morley. It runs on the weft fide of Morley and Belper, and appears again at Lea, Afhover parifh, Dronfield parifh, and fo to the Yorkfhire border. This tract of coal is faid to extend, under the name of the *great northern rake*, quite to the border of Scotland, being only interrupted by a lime-ftone bed of three miles in breadth near Ferrybridge in Yorkfhire. Coal has alfo been found at Chinley hills near Chapel-le-frith, in the neighbourhood of Buxton, and at various places in the fouthern extremity of the county.

Grit-ftone.—This occupies a much greater extent than the two former divifions, particularly the north and north-weft extremity of the county, and the tract lying between the principal beds of coal and lime-ftone, of which diftrict the eaft moor forms the moft confiderable part.

This

This laſt extends, with various breadth, almoſt as far ſouth as Derby. Small beds of grit-ſtone appear alſo in a few other parts.

Gypſum or *Plaſter-ſtone.*—This ſubſtance, which is found in nearly a ſtrait line acroſs the kingdom, appears in Derbyſhire at ſeveral places, particularly at Chellaſton, Aſton, and Elvaſton, three contiguous pa-riſhes, about five miles ſouth-eaſt of Derby. It lies about eight yards beneath the ſurface, and is found, not in regular layers, but in large lumps or blocks indented together, but which may be eaſily ſeparated. The thickneſs of the beds is from two to four yards.

It has been already obſerved, that a conſiderable tract in the ſouthern part contains no beds of ſtone of whatever kind near the ſurface. If a line be drawn from Aſhborne through Derby to the Nottinghamſhire border, it will have ſuch a tract to the ſouth, with the exception of a few places mentioned above.

CAVERNS and SUBTERRANEOUS PASSAGES.

The ſtrata of different kinds of ſtone, or *meaſures* as they are here termed, differ in reſpect to arrangement, thickneſs, and inclination, in the ſeveral parts of the mountainous tracts of Derbyſhire. It often happens that theſe meaſures are broken, in conſequence of which clefts and chaſms are formed in the earth. Theſe are extremely various in figure and ſize, and are more frequent in ſome parts than in others. The moſt remarkable which has been diſcovered in the clefts of the lime-ſtone, is ſituated at Caſtleton, and known by the name of

Peak's-hole.—It is ſituated in a deep and narrow receſs of the valley in which the town ſtands. On each ſide and near the end of this re-

L

cefs, two large faces of rock are feen rifing to a great height. At the
foot of the rock the mouth of the cavern opens: it is about 14 yards
high and 40 wide; the arch at the entrance is regularly formed, and extends nearly 300 feet in a direct line: this part is tolerably light, and is
inhabited by a number of poor people who manufacture pack-thread.
They have built fmall dwellings in this fpacious vault, where they are
fheltered from the extremes both of heat and cold. Beyond the firft
turning the ground gently declines, and the path is made wet by droppings from the roof. At the diftance of 130 yards from the entrance,
all further progrefs was formerly ftopped by a projection of the rock,
but a paffage is now opened through it. The cavern, which has been
gradually contracting, appears about 20 yards from hence to be entirely clofed; but on a near approach, a low paffage under the rock, almoft full of water, is difcovered. The opening juft admits a fmall
boat, but the paffenger muft lie almoft flat while it is pufhed under the
rock. On landing, he finds himfelf in a cavern more fpacious than the
former, faid to be 70 yards wide, and 40 high, but totally dark. A
path on its right fide leads up a fteep afcent to the top of a rock; another declines and leads to a much lower and narrower part. The whole
length of the fubterranean paffage is faid to be 750 yards, and attempts
have been made by blafting the rock to extend it further in order to
communicate with another cavern, but without fuccefs. A ftream of
water runs through the whole length, which muft be croffed feveral
times, and after heavy rains is fo much fwelled as to cut off accefs to
the further parts.

Poole's-hole is a cavern formed in the lime-ftone, and fituated a
fhort diftance from Buxton. Its entrance is low and narrow, requiring a perfon to ftoop confiderably. After proceeding 20 or 30 yards

in

in this pofture, you open into a fpacious and lofty cavern, the roof and fides of which are covered with ftalactitical incruftations, called here *water-icle*. Large piles and maffes of the fame fubftance appear on the floor, which are continually receiving increafe from the droppings of water loaded with calcareous matter, and put on various fingular figures. The cavern, after contracting at a large water-icle called the flitch of bacon, enlarges again, and continues of the fame dimenfions till you come to Mary queen of Scots' pillar, which is a large column of ftalactite. It is not eafy to go farther. The path has hitherto lain along the fide and fome height from the bottom of the cavern. On defcending to examine the interior extremity, the bottom is at firft tolerably even, but after 20 yards it rifes with a perpendicular afcent to the height of 80 yards. On returning by the bottom, you pafs under the queen of Scots' pillar, and view various other incruftations, fome of extraordinary fize and form. The whole length of the cavity is faid to be 560 yards.

Elden-hole, fituated in Peak-foreft, is alfo a cleft in a lime-ftone meafure. Its entrance is perpendicular. It is a deep chafm extending lengthwife in the direction of north-weft and fouth-eaft. Near the furface it is about 10 yards wide and 30 long; bu it gradually contracts, and at the depth of 90 feet is very much confined. At this place is a projection of the rock, and behind it a fmall cave admitting the light. Miners and other perfons have defcended much below this, and found various other chinks and caverns lined with ftalactite. At a vaft depth water has been found, and there is fome reafon to believe that this is part of a fubterraneous river which appears in the mouth of the cavern at Caftleton. All the ground between Perry-foot and Caftleton abounds in clefts and caverns, a feries of which reaches from the neighbourhood

of

of Peak's-hole nearly to Elden-hole. Thefe have been difcovered by miners in finking their fhafts, and purfued under ground to a great extent.

There are other fubterraneous caverns and paffages near Eyam, particularly Charlefworth and Bamforth-hole. The latter is a feries of ftalactitical caverns of confiderable extent.

MINES AND MINERALS.

Lead.—Lead mines in Derbyfhire are of great antiquity, undoubted proof exifting that they were worked in the time of the Romans. They may be traced from the Saxon and Norman eras down through fucceffive periods to the prefent time. The extent to which the bufinefs has been carried on at different periods cannot with certainty be determined, but the produce of the mines during the laft century has undoubtedly been very confiderable. At prefent, lead ore is found in various parts of the country. Indeed, it has been difcovered in different quantity throughout all the tract of lime-ftone land; but it is met with in the greateft abundance about ten miles to the north and fouth of the river Wye.

Veins of lead ore, on account of their pofition in the earth, are diftinguifhed by the different names of *pipe*, *rake*, and *flat* works. A pipe-work lies between two meafures of lime-ftone regularly extending above and below. It confifts of feveral lines or branches running nearly parallel to each other, which have a general communication by means of flender threads, or leadings, as they are called by the miners. The rock is fometimes pierced through by thefe leadings, which it is thought right to follow, as they often conduct to a frefh range. Should no ore be

found

found on such a pursuit, the breadth of the work is ascertained: its length is indeterminate, depending much upon the dipping of the measures. If this be great, it begins to decline, or cannot be pursued further on account of water. The rake-vein is found in the chasms or clefts of the lime-stone, and consequently breaks through the measures and sinks into the earth. It sometimes penetrates 150 or 200 yards, generally in a slanting direction; and it has been followed to the distance of four miles from the place where it was first discovered. The flat-work resembles the pipe, but has no leader or stem like that. It spreads wider, and seldom extends above 100 yards. It is also found near the surface and in the solid rock, and is very weak and poor, being seldom thicker than a man's finger.

The veins of lead ore are generally enclosed in a yellow, red, or black soil, and are firmly connected with cauk, spar, or some other mineral. Their direction is not uniform. The pipes, never penetrating the measures, follow the dip of the country in which they are found. The rakes run still more variously; in the High Peak, generally pointing east and west; in the wapentake of Wirksworth, north and south. Sometimes two veins cut each other at right angles: sometimes the pipe and rake unite and run together a short way, becoming stronger and richer. It is difficult to determine which of these two veins is most common, or most productive; the pipe, however, seem most generally valuable.

Veins are discovered various ways; sometimes by attention to the nature of the ground, which leads the experienced miner to make a search by boring; often by accidents laying open some branch which rises to-day. The more the branches which accompany a vein, the

richer

richer it is, and when they begin to diminifh, it becomes poorer. Alfo, for the moft part, a vein is impoverifhed when it runs in fuch a direction as to receive over it a greater number of meafures. In working mines, a principal point is to free them from water ; the moft common and effectual method of doing which is to drive a fough or level from the bottom of fome neighbouring valley, as far as the works ; where this cannot be done, pumps muft be employed, which are either worked by a water wheel, or by a fire engine. Mines are freed from bad air by the introduction of a pipe down the fhaft to the work, whence it is extended along the roof of the gallery. The circulation this occafions proves an effectual remedy.

There are numerous and various regulations refpecting the rights of miners, and the dues payable for the ore, in different parts of the mining country. The principal tract containing lead is called the *King's-field*. Under this denomination nearly the whole wapentake of Wirkf-worth is comprized, as well as part of the High Peak. The mineral duties of the King's-field have been from time immemorial let on leafe. The prefent farmer of thofe in the High Peak is the duke of Devon-fhire ; and of thofe in the wapentake of Wirkfworth is Mrs. Rolles. They have each a fteward and bar-mafters in the diftricts they hold of the crown. The fteward prefides as judge in the Barmote courts, and with twenty-four jurymen determines all difputes refpecting the working of mines. The courts are held twice a year ; thofe of the High Peak at Money-afh, and thofe of the wapentake at Wirkfworth. The principal office of the bar-mafter is putting miners in poffeffion of the veins they have difcovered, and collecting the proportion of ore due to the leffee. When a miner has found a new vein of ore in the King's-field, provided it be not in an orchard, garden, or high-road, he may obtain

an

an exclufive title to it on application to the bar-mafter. The method of giving poffeffion is, in the prefence of two jurymen, marking out in a pipe or rake work two *meares* of ground, each containing 29 yards; and in a flat work 14 yards fquare. But if a miner neglect to avail himfelf of his difcovery beyond a limited time, he may be deprived of the vein of which he has received poffeffion, and the bar-mafter may difpofe of it to another adventurer. As to the other part of the bar-mafter's office, that of fuperintending the meafurement of the ore, and taking the dues of the leffee or lord of the manor, it is attended with fome difficulty from the variety of the claims, which differ greatly in different places. In general, a thirteenth of the ore is the due in the King's-field, but a twenty-fifth only is taken. Befides this, there is a due for tithe. In mines that are private property, fuch tolls are paid as the parties agree upon.

The miner having fatisfied the feveral claims, proceeds to difpofe of his ore to the merchant or fmelter. There are four denominations of ore; the largeft and beft fort is called *Bing*; the next in fize and almoft equal in quality is named *Pefey*; the third is *Smitham*, which paffes through the fieve in wafhing; the fourth, which is caught by a very flow ftream of water, and is as fine as flour, is ftiled *Belland*: it is inferior to all the reft on account of the admixture of foreign particles. All the ore as it comes from the mine is beaten into pieces and wafhed before it is fold. This bufinefs is performed by women, who can earn about 6d. per day.

Smelting furnaces are of two kinds, the hearth and cupola. The hearth confifts of large rough ftones placed fo as to form an oblong cavity about two feet wide and deep, and 14 long, into which fuel and

ore

ore are put in alternate layers; the heat is raifed by means of a large pair of bellows worked by a water wheel. The fuel is wood and coal. The lead procured this way is very foft, pure, and ductile, but a confiderable quantity of metal remains in the flags. Thefe are, therefore, fmelted over again with a more intenfe fire of coke; but the metal produced is inferior in quality to the former. At prefent, a fmall proportion of ore is fmelted this way, only two hearth furnaces remaining in Derbyfhire. The cupola, introduced about fifty years fince, is of an oblong form, refembling a long, but not very deep, cheft, the top and bottom of which are a little concave. The fire being placed at one end, and a chimney at the other, the flame is drawn over the ore placed at the bottom, and by its reverberation fmelts it without any contact of the fuel.

The lead when fmelted is poured into moulds of various fizes, according to the different markets for which it is intended, Hull, Bawtry, or London. Two of the blocks make a pig. Some of it, however, is firft rolled into fheets at works erected for the purpofe near the furnaces. A confiderable quantity is alfo converted into red-lead. This procefs is performed in a kind of oven, the floor of which is divided into three parts. The middle of thefe contains the metal, and the two others, the fire. The flame being reverberated on the metal, converts it to a calx or powder; which, on being a fecond time expofed to the action of the fire, acquires a red colour.

Attempts were made fome years ago to extract filver from the lead; but no fuch work now exifts in Derbyfhire. The fulphur driven off from the ore in fmelting is collected at two furnaces.

The

The annual produce of lead from the Derbyshire mines is not exactly ascertained, but may be estimated at an average of between 5 and 6000 tons. It is generally thought to be on the decline, some of the richest mines being either exhausted, or become more difficult to work; but on the other hand, from the improvements in the art of smelting, and the more effectual methods employed to clear the mines of water by new levels and improved fire engines, advantages have been gained that may, perhaps, supply the deficiency.

Iron.—The ore of this metal occurs throughout all that tract in which coal has been discovered, Chinley-hills excepted. The depth at which it lies from the surface is extremely various. Frequently from the great dipping of the measures, it bassits out to-day. In this case, a hole is made like the shaft of a coal-pit. This is gradually enlarged on going deeper, so as to assume the form of a bell. It is seldom sunk lower than 18 yards; after which fresh ground is broken and a new pit sunk: by this means the lower beds are mixed with the soil near the surface, so as to injure the land greatly; whence it is not thought worth while to dig for iron ore unless the beds are very valuable. Their thickness varies from two to 12 inches. The most valuable beds which have yet been discovered are in Morley-park near Heage, at Wingerworth, Chesterfield, and Stavely. At all these places furnaces are built; these are of a circular or conical form, having the fire with a blast at the bottom. When the furnace is prepared and duly seasoned, the process of smelting begins. Fuel, ore, and flux, in alternate layers, are continually put in day and night, and the fire is not suffered to go out till the furnace wants repair, which is frequently a period of some years. The fuel is generally coke, though charcoal has been used. Lime-stone is the universal flux. The ore undergoes the previous preparation of

M   being

being burned in the open air in beds, firft with coke, then with coal flack; it is then broken into fmall pieces and fcreened. The procefs of fmelting takes different times according to the fize of the furnace and other circumftances. Different forts of iron are produced by varying the proportions of ore, flux, and fuel. The metal firft obtained is brittle and void of due malleability. To give it this property it is carried to the forge, and wrought into bars. The quantity of iron produced in this county amounts to about 5600 tons.

Calamine.—The value of this mineral, which is an ore of zinc, has but lately been attended to in this county. The chief places in which it is difcovered, are Caftleton, Cromford, Bonfall, and Wirkfworth. It occurs at various depths, but is generally found near a vein of lead ore. The two minerals are fometimes mixed, or run a confiderable way by the fide of each other; but more commonly, one ceafes where the other begins, and a good vein of both is never found in the fame place. Calamine generally lies in a bed of yellow or reddifh brown clay. The beds refemble pipe works, and confift of lumps of various fizes and fhapes: their direction is the fame with the dip of the mea-fures.

The calamine is firft wafhed in a current, and then again in fieves in a veffel of water, and all the foreign matters, as fpar, cauk, and lead ore are picked out from it. It is next calcined in a reverberatory fur-nace, after which it is again picked, ground to a fine powder, and wafhed. The quantity of calamine at prefent annually produced in Derbyfhire is about 500 tons. Its value in its crude ftate is from 35 to 40 fhillings per ton; in its prepared ftate, five or fix guineas. It is in-ferior in value to the calamine of Mendip in Somerfetfhire. Blend or

black

black jack, alfo got in Derbyfhire, is another ore of zinc, lefs valuable than calamine.

Copper.—This metal has hitherto been found only in fmall quantity in Derbyfhire. Confiderable pieces detached from any vein are frequently met with at Matlock and Bonfall. A flender vein of ore was difcovered fome years fince at Creat Roch Dale, between Tidefwell and Buxton; and another lately near Chapel-le-frith; but neither is worked.

Coal Mines.—The tract of country producing coal has already been mentioned. It is got in great abundance in Derbyfhire. Coal is met with at various depths, and in fome places feveral beds are paffed by one fhaft, but the upper ones are thin and foft, and feldom worked. Befides the home confumption of coal, which is very great, a confiderable quantity is conveyed by the Errewafh canal into Leicefterfhire, and by the Chefterfield, into Nottinghamfhire and Lincolnfhire. Large quantities alfo go to Sheffield from Dronfield parifh.

Plafter-ftone.—The moft valuable kind of this fubftance was got at Elvafton, but the pits are now clofed. That of Chellafton, though neither of a fine colour nor texture, is equally ufeful for common purpofes. About 800 tons are got annually from thefe pits, of which 500 are fent by the canal into Staffordfhire to the potteries, where it is ufed for the formation of moulds. A confiderable quantity is alfo ufed for laying floors in buildings. For both thefe purpofes a previous calcination is neceffary, after which the addition of water makes it fet firm and folid. In its native ftate, this fubftance is called gypfum and alabafter, and when wrought, takes a high polifh, and is ufed for ornamental works. The calcined gypfum is ufed for all the purpofes of

M 2

plafter

plafter of Paris, and is fometimes mixed with lime in making the finer kinds of mortar.

Lime-ftone.—The extent of country which yields this ftone has been already mentioned. Its qualities are various. At Buxton, Peak-foreft, and Stony-Middleton, it is of a light grey, and when burned is much ufed in agriculture. For this purpofe much is difpofed of in the northern part of the county, and alfo in Chefhire and Lancafhire. At Crich are feveral kilns, which burn a lime remarkably white, and much valued for ceilings and other ornamental purpofes. This lime-ftone is free from metallic particles, and forms a manure for cold lands, which is reckoned to bring the crops a fortnight forwarder than that which is darker-coloured. At Ticknal and Kniveton the lime-ftone is very dark, and fets very ftrongly. That of the latter place is thought nearly equally to the lime of Barrow in Leicefterfhire. At Hopton is a kind of a light colour, hard, and abounding with fmall fragments of entrochi. It is much ufed for hearths, chimney-pieces, floors, and ftaircafes. On Braffington moor a fpecies of a fimilar nature, but fuperior quality, has been difcovered.

Marble is found in various parts of the High and Low Peak : it is either black or mottled grey. The black abounds chiefly at Afhford ; it may be had in large blocks, and is in general very black, clofe, folid, and capable of a high polifh. The mottled grey is found in many places. but particularly near Money-afh. It has a great diverfity of fhades, but may be diftinguifhed into two kinds ; that with a lightifh grey ground, and that with a light blueifh ground. The latter is rendered very beautiful by the purple veins that fpread over its furface. But the chief ornament of the grey marble is the vaft quantity of entrochi

trochi that it contains, the tranfverfe and longitudinal fections producing an incredible variety of forms. In general, the more fuperficial the beds of marble, the lighter its colour, and the more abundant the entrochi.

Water-icle or *Stalactite* is very common in the Peak, and of a great variety of colours. They are polifhed and ufed for making ornaments of various figures ; as are likewife the *tranfparent calcareous fpars*, of the rhombic kind.

Porcelain Clay, of a delicate white and very fine texture, has been got from a lead mine near Braffington. What is now dug, is fent to the Staffordfhire potteries. *Pipe-clay* is got at Bolfover, where pipes are made with it, and both it and potter's clay are found in various other parts. *Rotten-ftone* is met with near Bakewell, and is much ufed by the lapidaries of Derby.

Slate of a grey colour is got in Chinley-hills, and at Hayfield, and is much ufed for covering houfes in that neighbourhood.

Chert is found in ftrata, and may be feen running through the rocks in the Peak. A large quantity of it is carried from the neighbourhood of Bakewell into Staffordfhire and Yorkfhire, where it is ufed in the manufacture of earthen ware. Some kinds of it are made into mill-ftones.

Moor-ftone is found in the north-weft part of the county, and the eaft moor. Mill-ftones are made of it on Kinder-fcout, and in the parifh

of

of Eyam. *Free-ftone* is found in various places, and fome of the fineft houfes in Derbyfhire have been built with it.

A fpecies of *pyrites* got near Dronfield is ufed for the production of copperas, but in no great quantity.

Black wad.—This earth, which on analyfis is found to be chiefly compofed of iron and manganefe, is met with principally at Elton near Winfter. After calcination it is ufed as an oil colour in houfe and fhip painting. It is chiefly employed for the latter purpofe, and there is a confiderable demand for it in the royal navy.

Medicinal Waters.—Derbyfhire abounds beyond moft counties with mineral and medicinal waters; they are of various kinds, warm, cold, faline, calcareous, fulphureous, and chalybeate. Some of the moft noted, which come within the limits of this work, will be particularized hereafter.

CIVIL AND ECCLESIASTICAL DIVISION.

In the Roman times, Derbyfhire formed part of the country of the Coritani; in the Saxon, part of the kingdom of Mercia. It is divided into fix hundreds; the names of which are,

> *High Peak hundred,* in the north-weft.
> *Scarfdale hundred,* in the north-eaft.
> *Wirkfworth wapentake,* in the weft
> *Appletree hundred,* in the weft.
> *Morlefton hundred,* in the eaft.
> *Repington hundred,* in the fouth.

Thefe are faid to contain 11 market towns, and about 440 hamlets.

The

The number of inhabitants in the year 1788, from the moſt accurate inquiry that could be made, was 124,465; of houſes, 25,642. An eſtimate made in the late reign reckons the inhabitants at 126,900, but there are good grounds for ſufpecting its accuracy, as population ſeems in moſt parts to have been increaſing. Derbyſhire pays ſix parts of the land-tax, and provides 560 men to the national militia.

Some remains of the ancient civil policy of the county ſtill appear, the court of the duchy of Lancaſter, and the Peverel court, being of this kind. The honor of Tutbury and the hundred of Appletree belong to the former; and courts are regularly held, called three weeks courts, for the honor, at Tutbury, and for the hundred, at Sudbury The Peverel courts are held at Basford near Nottingham. A conſiderable number of townſhips belong to each of theſe. The courts of High Peak and the wapentake of Wirkſworth have already been mentioned, as regulating the mineral concerns of thoſe parts. With reſpect to its common judicature, Derbyſhire is included in the midland circuit.

Derby, the capital, is the only parliamentary borough in the county. It ſends two members to parliament, and the county two more.

In its eccleſiaſtical concerns, it forms a part of the dioceſe of Litchfield and Coventry, and is divided into one archdeaconry, and five deanries, which are the following:

ARCHDEACONRY OF DERBY.

Deanry of Aſhborne.
——— *of Caſtillar*
——— *of Cheſterfield.*

Deanry

Deanry of Derby.
———— *of Repington.*

Its-parochial churches, from the beſt inquiry, amount to 116; its chapels, of which two are extra-parochial, to 71.   There are 39 meeting-houſes of different denominations of Diſſenters.

IV.—*General*

WEST RIDING
of
YORKSHIRE.

British Statute Miles.

Published December 1. 1794. by J. Stockdale Piccadilly.

IV.—*General Account of the* WEST-RIDING OF YORKSHIRE.

THE great county of York is divided into three diftricts called *Ridings*, the Eaft, Weft, and North, of which the two latter have each the magnitude of a large county. A confiderable part of the Weft-Riding coming within the limits of the prefent undertaking, it has been thought proper to prefix to the account of the particular places, a general defcription of the diftrict itfelf.

The *Weft-Riding of Yorkfhire* is bounded to the north by the North-Riding, the river Ure making part of the divifion ; to the eaft, by the Ainfty Liberty, and by the Eaft-Riding, the rivers Wharf and Oufe being the limits, and alfo by the counties of Lincoln and Nottingham ; to the fouth, by Derbyfhire and Chefhire ; to the weft, by Lancafhire and Weftmoreland. Its length, if meafured from north-weft to fouth-eaft, exceeds 90 miles, upon an average breadth of about 40. It is computed to contain 2450 fquare miles, or 1,568,000 ftatute acres.

RIVERS.

A number of rivers take their courfe through it, the principal of which terminate in the Oufe.

N   The

The *Nidd*, rising in Nidderdale or Netherdale forest, passes Paitley-bridge, Ripley, and Knaresborough, and joins the Ouse a few miles above York.

The *Wharf* takes its rise in Langsterdale Chace, and passing by Otley, Harewood, Wetherby, and Tadcaster, empties into the Ouse near Cawood.

The *Aire* deriving its sources from about Malham moor, flows near Skipton and Keighley; thence to Leeds, below which it is joined by the *Calder*, and they pass on together by Ferry-bridge and Snaith, to the Ouse near Howden.

The *Calder* rises in the hills on the Lancashire border, west of Halifax, and after receiving the *Coln* from Huddersfield, flows by Wakefield to its junction with the *Aire*.

The *Don* or *Dun* rises near the Cheshire border west of Penifton, which place it passes, and being augmented by many small streams from the Derbyshire border, flows to Sheffield, where it receives the *Sheaf*. These together run by Rotherham and Doncaster to meet the Ouse a little above its opening into the Humber.

The *Ribble* coming down by Settle, and joined by the *Hodder* from Bolland forest, takes its course westward into Lancashire.

These numerous rivers bestow beauty and fertility on the vales through which they flow, and afford, along with the navigable canals,

the

the advantage of water carriage to the bufy manufacturing towns on their banks.

FACE OF THE COUNTRY.

The face of the country is in many parts ftrongly irregular. In the weftern and northern divifions a confiderable portion is hilly and mountainous, but interfected with numerous vales rich in the fineft grafs.

The hills of *Ingleborough*, *Whernfide*, and *Penigent*, to the north and north-weft of Settle, rank among the higheft mountains of South-Britain. In their neighbourhood are various caverns and other natural curiofities belonging to a mountainous country. One of the moft noted of thefe is *Malham-cove*, a kind of amphitheatre of fmooth perpendicular lime-ftone, 288 feet high in the centre from its fummit to its bafe. On the top of the moor on which the cove is fituated is an elevated lake called *Malham-tarn*, of clear and very cold water, abounding in trout. It difcharges itfelf by a fubterraneous paffage into the river Aire, of which it forms the head. *Gordal-fcar* in its neighbourhood forms a deep and romantic bed for the river, through which it rolls in a grand cafcade, over-hung by rugged rocks above 100 feet high, projecting above their bafes till they almoft meet at top. Near *Chapel-in-the-dale*, on the north fide of Ingleborough, are other remarkable pits or caverns, containing within them pools of water and cafcades, giving birth to fubterraneous ftreams which at length burft out to day. The river Ribble near its origin in thefe parts tumbles into a deep cavern, and is loft in the bowels of the mountains for three miles, when it emerges and makes its way to Settle. Many other romantic fcenes are met with in this part of the diftrict, which is a favourite fpot for botanifts on account of the number of rare and curious plants it contains.

N 2

The

The greater part of the Riding, however, is a flat country, with no other elevations than such as serve to vary the profpect. Towards the border of Lincolnfhire, and the lower part of the Oufe, are large tracts of marfh, which have been drained by canals and dykes, firft made in the reign of Charles I. Hatfield moor or chace, and Thorne wafte, contain the principal part of thefe lands.

The whole cultivated part of the Riding is almoft completely enclofed with ftone dikes and hedges, kept in excellent order; and there are few open fields, except where the land is common or wafte.

SOIL.

The nature of the foil in this extenfive tract differs greatly. There are all kinds, from deep ftrong clay, and rich fertile loam, to the pooreft peat earth, and it is not afcertained which fort prevails moft. Much ground, originally barren, has been rendered productive by vicinity to great towns, and fuperior culture. In general, it may be faid that a large proportion is of a quality favourable to the purpofes of hufbandry. By a calculation made, it, however, appears, that the wafte lands in this Riding amount to 405,272 acres, of which it is computed that 265,000 are capable of cultivation, or of being turned into pafture, while the reft are incapable of improvement, except by planting.

CLIMATE.

The climate is, in general, moderate. The mountainous parts in weft are colder and more fubject to rain than the others. The moft eaftern parts are fomewhat damp and fubject to fogs from their low fituation near the great rivers, and they are lefs healthy.

The

AGRICULTURE.

The hufbandry of the Weft-Riding is very different in different parts; in general, it may be diftributed into the following fyftems.   1ft. The pafture lands, where grafs is the chief object, and cultivation by the plough is only a fecondary concern.   The parts of the Riding in which this fyftem prevails are, at leaft, one-third of the whole.   From Ripley to the weftern extremity almoft all the good land is in grafs, and corn is raifed only upon the inferior foils, and in fo fmall a quantity, that a ftack of corn is a rare object.   Upon the higher grounds in thefe parts are immenfe tracts of wafte, which are generally common among the adjacent poffeffors, and are paftured by them with cattle and fheep. Some of them are ftinted paftures, but the greater part are under no li- mitation, and in confequence, the ground is exhaufted and the ftock poor.

2dly. The lands adjoining the manufacturing towns. The greateft part of thefe are occupied by perfons who do not follow farming as a bufinefs, but regard it only as a matter of convenience. The manufacturer has his enclofures, in which he keeps milch cows for the fupport of his family, and horfes for the conveyance of his goods. Much ground under thefe circumftances is not kept under the plough, yet more corn comparatively is raifed than in the divifion before de- fcribed.

3dly. The parts in which tillage is principally attended to, and grafs is confidered only in connexion with the beft corn-hufbandry. If a line be run from Ripley fouthward by Leeds, Wakefield, and Barnf- ley, to Rotherham, the greateft part eaftwards of it, to the banks of

the

the Oufe, is employed in raifing corn. About Boroughbridge, Wetherby, and Selby, one half of the fields is under the plough; further
fouth, about Pontefract, Barnfley, and Rotherham, two-thirds; and
to the eaftward of Doncafter, to Thorn and Snaith, three-fourths.
There is not much wafte in this divifion, and what there is appears capable of great improvement.

4thly. The common fields. Thefe are fcattered over the whole of
the laft divifion, but are moft numerous in the country to the eaftward
of the great north road, from Doncafter to Boroughbridge. In all
thefe there is room for much fubftantial improvement by better modes
of culture.

5thly. The moors. Thefe, befides the large tracts in the firft divifion, moftly lie in the fouth-weft parts of the Riding, above Penifton
and Sheffield. Upon them fheep are chiefly bred, which are fold to
the graziers in the lower parts. A great part of them is common.

STATE OF PROPERTY.

A confiderable part of the landed property of the Weft-Riding is in
the hands of fmall freeholders and copyholders; but there are likewife
a great number of extenfive proprietors. Few of the latter refide upon
their eftates, at leaft for a confiderable part of the year, and the management of them is chiefly committed to ftewards and factors. The
greater part of the farms are comparatively fmall; many on the arable
lands under 50 acres, and none above 300; and they are ftill fmaller in
the grafs divifion. Moft of the land is fet without leafe, or the occupiers are removeable at fix months warning—a practice very difcouraging

ging to improvements in agriculture. Some of the proprietors who are fenfible of this, grant leafes from three to twenty-one years.

MANURES.

Befides thofe in common ufe in other parts, the farmers employ ground bones, horn fhavings, and rape duft.

PRODUCTS.

The corn raifed is of all kinds according to the foil; but the whole quantity grown in the Weft-Riding is much fhort of the confumption. Towards the banks of the Oufe a good deal of flax is grown. The turnip hufbandry prevails over a great part of the Riding, but the mode of cultivation would admit of improvement. The artificial graffes are laid down with red and white clover, fain-foin, and hay feeds. Winter tares are fown in many parts. Pontefract has long been famous for the culture of liquorice. A great deal of oak and afh wood is grown in the Riding, which meets with a ready fale at the towns.

Not many horfes are bred except in the eaftern parts. Thofe in the weftern are generally fmall, but hardy, and capable of undergoing great fatigue. Of neat cattle there are four different breeds. 1. The fhort-horned kind, which principally prevail on the eaft fide of the Riding, and are diftinguifhed by the name of the Durham, Holdernefs, or Dutch breed. 2. The long-horned or Craven breed, either bred and fed in the weftern parts, or brought from the neighbouring part of Lancafhire. Thefe are a hardy kind, and fit to endure the viciffitudes of a wet climate. 3. A crofs between the two former breeds, which makes the beft kind of all. A great number of milch cows of this

I

kind

kind are kept about Nidderdale, and are both uſeful and handſome. 4. Scotch cattle, which are brought in great numbers into the county to be fed, and produce the beſt beef in the markets. The graziers in Craven are very large dealers in this branch of buſineſs.

Of ſheep there are a great many kinds both bred and fed; but that which appears to have been the native breed is met with upon the moors in the weſtern part of the Riding, and is uſually called the Peniſton breed, from the name of the market town where they are ſold. They are horned, light in the fore-quarter, and well adapted for ſeeking their living in a hilly country. When fat, they weigh from 14lb. to 15lb. per quarter. They are a hardy kind of ſheep, and when brought down to the lower paſtures fatten kindly, and prove excellent mutton. Wool of all ſorts meets with a ready ſale in conſequence of the manu-factures of the county.

MINERALS.

Coals are cheap and plentiful throughout moſt parts of the Riding, an advantage ineſtimable to a manufacturing diſtrict. Stone for build-ing and various other purpoſes is every where at hand in the hilly parts.

There are ſeveral *mineral waters* in this Riding, of which the moſt noted is the ſulphureous water of Harrowgate, much reſorted to in cu-taneous and cachectical complaints, and uſed both for drinking and bathing. There is alſo a chalybeate ſpring at the ſame place, and ano-ther at Thorpe Arch in conſiderable repute. At Knareſborough is a noted petrifying ſpring called the dropping well; and near Settle is one of the moſt remarkable ebbing and flowing wells in the kingdom.

CIVIL

CIVIL AND ECCLESIASTICAL DIVISION.

The Weft-Riding of Yorkfhire is for the moft part divided into Wapentakes, but alfo contains fome detached diftricts. The names of the divifions are as follows:

Agbrigg Wapentake,	Skyrack Wapentake,	Liberty of Cawood,
Barkfton Afh ditto,	Staincliffe ditto,	Wiftow, and Ottley,
Claro ditto,	Staincrofs ditto,	Liberty of Rippon,
Ewcrofs ditto,	Strafforth and Tickhill	Doncafter Soke,
Morley ditto,	ditto,	Leeds Borough.
Ofgoldnefs ditto,		

Within thefe limits are contained twenty-nine market-towns, and five parliamentary boroughs.

Ecclefiaftically, this Riding is within the province and diocefe of York, and forms an archdeaconry, called the

ARCHDEACONRY OF YORK, or WEST-RIDING,
divided into the following deanries:

Craven,
Doncafter,
Pontefract,
City of York and Ainfty, (not in this Riding.)

Rippon, within the Archdeaconry of Cleveland, is a peculiar jurifdiction.

O   V.—*General*

V.—*General Account of the* NORTHERN PART OF STAFFORDSHIRE.

THE northern portion of the county of Stafford forms a broad angle, of which the eastern side joins to Derbyshire, and the western to Cheshire. The greater part of it consists of a tract called the *Moorlands*, a region in general hilly, steril, and open, composing the southern extremity of the mountainous ridge which divides the north of England. Its height is shown by the number of streams which take their rise in it, most of which flow southwards.

RIVERS.

The *Trent*, generally accounted the third river in England for length of course and quantity of water, rises near Biddulph towards the Cheshire border, out of New-pool, and two springs flowing from Molecop, many more little springs soon contributing to form it into a rivulet. It passes not far from Newcastle, and visits Trentham, where it distinguishes itself by its proper name. Its further course passes out of our circuit, through a great part of Staffordshire, the southern end of Derbyshire, almost the whole of Nottinghamshire, and terminates in the Humber.

The *Churnet*, formed by a conflux of two principal branches near Leek, themselves composed of many moorland streams, takes a south-eastern course to join the Dove a little to the north of Utoxeter.

Further

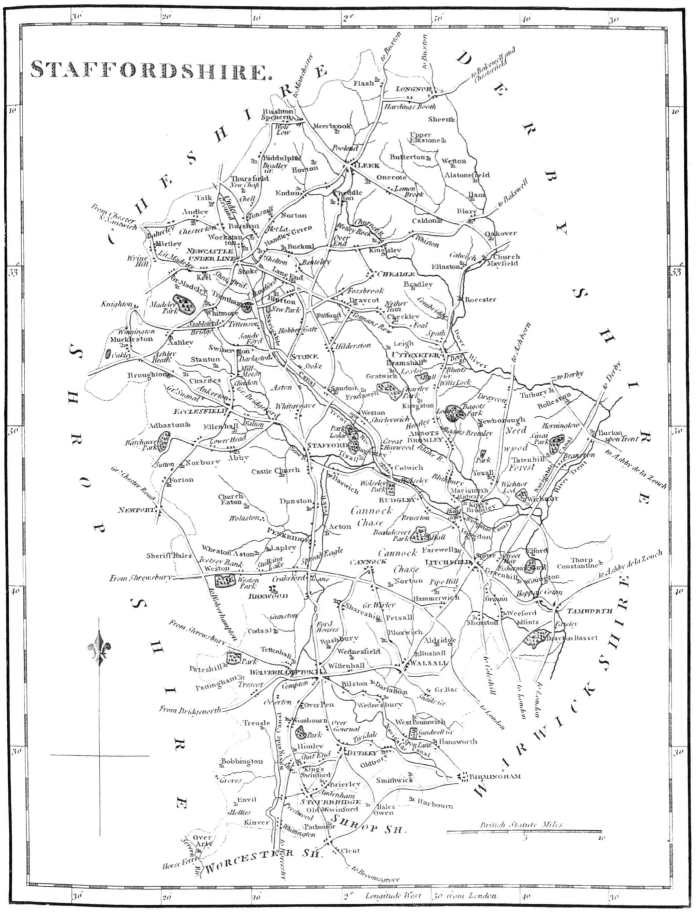

STAFFORDSHIRE.

British Statute Miles

Published November 12.1794.by I.Stockdale Piccadilly.

Further to the north-eaft, the two mountain rivulets, *Hamps* and *Manifold*, come down to the neighbourhood of Wetton, where, on an extenfive and romantic common, they both fink into the earth, and rife again conjoined, three miles below, in Ilam gardens, and foon empty themfelves into the Dove. This fubterraneous tranfit is defcribed by that celebrated poet Dr. Darwin, in a paffage glowing with images of nature and fancy, from which we fhall copy only the *natural* part:

Where *Hamps* and *Manifold*, their cliffs among,
Each in his flinty channel winds along;
With lucid lines the dufky moor divides,
Hurrying to intermix their fifter tides.
* * * * * * * * *
* * * * * * * * *
Three thoufand fteps in fparry clefts they ftray,
Or feek thro fullen mines their gloomy way;
On beds of Lava fleep in coral cells,
Or figh o'er jafper fifh and agate fhells.
Till where fam'd *Ilam* leads his boiling floods
Thro' flowery meadows and impending woods,
Pleas'd, with light fpring they leave the dreary night,
And 'mid circumfluent furges rife to light;
Shake their bright locks, the widening vale purfue,
Their fea-green mantles fring'd with pearly dew;
In playful groups by towering *Thorp* they move,
Bound o'er the foaming wears, and rufh into the *Dove*.

Botan. Gard. Part II.

The *Dove* rifes near the northernmoft point of the county, in the very bordering line of Derbyfhire, and flowing fouth-eaftwards, makes the limit of the two counties as far as its junction with the Trent below Burton. The channel of the Dove has a great declivity, and in many places tumbles over the rocks in cafcades. Its water has a greyifh caft.

O 2

owing

owing to the particles of limeftone it brings down with it, whereby, in its flood, it imparts great fertility to the meadows on its banks, fo as to have given rife to the old proverb,

> In April, Dove's flood
> Is worth a king's good.

After it has received the Churnet, this colour is almoft wafhed away, and the meadows below are lefs diftinguifhed for fertility.

All the above-mentioned rivers fpring out of the Moorlands; but one which has its fource within our circuit, rifes weft of the Trent, near the Chefhire border : this is the *Sow*, the head of which is near Great Madeley, between Betley and Newcaftle. It runs acrofs the county by Stafford, and mixes with the Trent above Burton.

FACE OF COUNTRY and SOIL.

The northern part of Staffordfhire exhibits a variety of country, but it is chiefly characterized as a hilly tract, with interjacent vales, and bleak extenfive moors. Its general elevation above the fouthern parts of the county may be eftimated at from 100 to 200 yards; but it has fome diftinguifhed eminences of much more confiderable height. The hill called *Bunfter*, near Ilam, is calculated to rife 1200 feet above the level of the Trent; and the *Wever* hills, and fome of the other moorland peaks, 1500 feet. A pretty extenfive part of the moorlands is upon a lime-ftone bottom. This portion reaches in length from the Wever hills to Longnor, and in breadth from the Dove to the parallel of Morredge. In this, the quantity of lime-ftone is inexhauftible, lying in many places in ftrata of immenfe thicknefs. The

Wever

Wever hills are vaſt heaps of this ſtone, and are covered with a rich calcareous, loamy earth, which bears a fine turf. They are encloſed in large tracts by ſtone walls, which are almoſt the only boundaries in this part of the county. The fall even from the foot of theſe hills to the Dove and Churnet is very great, and thoſe rivers are very rapid. The hill of *Bunſter* is alſo a calcareous rock, and vaſt precipices from it overhang the Dove. The ridge of this mountain terminates in ſome places in conical ſugar-loaf peaks of bare lime-ſtone. *Mill-dale*, near Alſtonfield on the Dove, is a long narrow glen of great depth, the ſides of which conſiſt of perpendicular lime-ſtone precipices, which nearly equal in height the breadth of the dale. The vale in which the Manifold runs is extremely romantic, and contains a curious excavation in the ſide of a precipice called *Thyrſis's Cavern*

The country weſt of the lime ſtone is generally ſandy or gravelly clay, or grit-ſtone rock, and is the worſt part of the moorlands. Its ſurface is uneven, and large tracts of waſte land, though on elevated ſituations, are mere peat bogs or moſſes. Large quantities of peat are cut upon *Morredge* and *Axedge*, which is ſpongy and retentive of moiſture. The *Cloud Heath*, *High Foreſt*, *Leek Frith*, and *Mole Cop*, are ſimilar pieces of ground. But the ſummits of ſome of the hills are rocky cliffs, particularly thoſe called *Leek rocks* or *roches*, and *Ipſtone cliffs* which are compoſed of huge piles of rugged rocks, heaped upon each other in a tremendous manner. Leek rocks conſiſt of a coarſe ſandy grit; thoſe of Ipſtones are gravel or ſand, and ſmall pebbles cemented together. Many of the cliffs overhang ſteep precipices; and large maſſes detached from them are ſcattered on the moors around. To the ſouth of theſe, between Oak-moor and Cheadle, are Commons or waſtes, conſiſting of an immenſe number of rude heaps of

3

gravel

gravel upon an under-ſtratum of ſoft ſandy rock, thrown confuſedly together into all ſorts of fantaſtical forms.

Between Mole-cop and Newcaſtle the country does not merit the name of Moorlands, but is various in appearance, divided by quickſet hedges and trees, and reſembling other cultivated tracts. The ſoil is generally cold and ſtiff. Towards Betley the ſoil is a mixed gravelly loam, with an underſtratum of ſand, gravel, marl, or grit. It produces fine timber trees, and is equally fit for paſture and arable. Between Betley and Newcaſtle is a good deal of light land. To the ſouth of the road towards Eccleſhall, is a ſtronger ſoil of friable clayey or marly loam, intermixed with peat and poor land on the eminences.

CLIMATE.

The *climate* of the north of Staffordſhire is cold and wet, like that of the adjacent parts of Derbyſhire and Cheſhire ; ſnow lies long in the Moorlands, and the weſt wind ſeldom fails to bring rain.

AGRICULTURE and PRODUCTS.

The *Agriculture* of this diſtrict is not entitled to particular obſervation. The Moorlands are chiefly devoted to the feeding of ſheep and cattle ; the arable being a ſmall proportion, and the grain produced, almoſt ſolely oats and barley. The principal manure uſed is lime. The ſheep are of two kinds : thoſe on the eaſt Moorlands are white-faced and polled, with long or combing wool ; upon the lime-ſtone bottom they are ſtrong and heavy, and are thought to be the moſt valuable breed on waſte land in the county. Thoſe upon the waſtes in the weſt part of the Moorlands, and on the grit and gravel bottom, are a much inferior ſort, and ſeem to have originated from the ancient

Moorland

Moorland breed, continued without attention. They have fome white, fome grey or dark faces, with legs generally of the fame colour; fome are with, and fome without horns; and their fleeces are too coarfe for clothing, and too fhort for combing wool. The cattle of the long-horned kind are of a good fize and form, and thrive better on the fhort grafs of the lime-ftone hills than might be fuppofed. They are fuperior to the breeds in the fouthern part of the county. Thofe fed on the Dove and the other rivers are in high efteem. On the weftern fide a mixture of arable and pafture prevails, and the products are the ufual ones of that part of the kingdom.

MINERALS.

The *mineral* productions of this tract are various and important. The hill of Mole-cop, of which part is in Chefhire, and part in this county, has been already noticed as yielding ftone of feveral kinds, particularly excellent mill-ftones. Lime-ftone is common in the Moorlands, and alfo on the weftern fide, near Madeley. Great quantities of lime are burned upon Caldon Low, and in the neighbourhood of the Wever hills. Clays of various fpecies and colours, fome tenacious, fome friable, are found in great quantity near Newcaftle, and have given rife to the potteries of that diftrict, which are of ancient ftanding. Coals abound in moft parts of which a fingular kind, called *peacock coal,* from the prifmatic colours appearing on its furface, is dug at Handley-green. This diftrict poffeffes the ores of iron, copper, and lead. Iron-ftone is met with plentifully to the weft of Newcaftle: it is fmelted at the Madeley furnaces, and yields a cold-fhort metal. Lead-ore is got not far from thence, which is ufed at the potteries. A copper mine is wrought at Mixon, near Leek; but the principal in thefe parts is that at Ecton-hill, in the parifh of Wetton, belonging to

the

the Duke of Devonſhire. The hill in which the mine is ſituated is conical, and riſes 700 feet above the river Dove which flows at its foot. Its diameter is about half a mile. The mine was worked in the laſt century, but after ſome years was neglected as unprofitable. About thirty-five years ago it was re-opened by a Corniſh miner, and ſome adventurers at Aſhborne took a leaſe of it, and expended 13,000*l.* in ſearching for ore without ſucceſs. At length, after making a ſhaft 200 yards deep, they came to vaſt beds of the ore, which repaid their coſt. The leaſe has ſince fallen to the Duke, and it is ſaid to have cleared annually from 8000 to 10,000*l.*; but to be now leſs productive than formerly. More than 300 perſons, men, women, and children, are employed in the works; the men in digging, the women and children in breaking and picking the ore. On the oppoſite ſide of the hill a lead mine has been diſcovered, which promiſes to be valuable.

Staffordſhire was part of the country inhabited by the Roman *Cornavii*. Under the heptarchy it belonged to the *Mercian* kingdom. It is now, as to its civil juriſdiction, compriſed within the Oxford circuit; and with reſpect to its eccleſiaſtical, within the dioceſe of *Litchfield* and *Coventry*. It is divided into five hundreds, of which about half of that of *Totmanſlow* in the north-eaſt, and a ſmaller portion of that of *Pyrehill* in the north-weſt, are included within the limits of this work.

VI.—*Account*

VI.—*Account of* RIVER *and* CANAL NAVIGATIONS.

THE great advantages accruing to trade from water-carriage have at all times been well known to commercial nations; and in proportion as this ifland has advanced in manufactures and commerce, plans for connecting the internal parts of the country with the fea-ports by means of navigations have been encouraged and multiplied. It was natural, that extending and improving the navigation of rivers fhould be the firft expedient thought of for this purpofe; and many projects of this kind were brought to effect in this kingdom, before the more expenfive and artificial conftruction of canals was ventured upon. As our fea-ports are for the moft part fituated at, and indeed formed by, the mouths of rivers, which nature has made capable of admitting veffels to a certain diftance up their channels; the extenfion of this natural navigation by deepening their beds and removing obftacles has generally been attempted.

The port of Liverpool, at the mouth of the river Merfey, obvioufly depends for its confequence upon the facility of communication that can be eftablifhed with the interior country; and, on the other hand, the cheap conveyance of the yarn, cotton, and other raw materials to Manchefter and its neighbourhood, and of the wrought goods to a port for exportation, is of evident importance to the interefts of the manufacturers. By the affiftance of the tide, which flows with rapidity up the channel of the Merfey, veffels were enabled, without any artificial help, to navigate as far as the neighbourhood of Warrington.

P   To

To render the higher parts of the river, through its communicating branch the Irwell, acceffible to veffels as far as Manchefter, was an improvement, which could not fail of fuggefting itfelf to the enlightened inhabitants both of Manchefter and Liverpool

IRWELL and MERSEY NAVIGATION.

In the year 1720 an Act of Parliament was obtained, empowering certain perfons in each town (but moft of them refident in Manchefter) to make navigable the rivers Irwell and Merfey from Liverpool to Manchefter—fo the words of the act run; but as it is mentioned in the act, that the Merfey is already navigable from Liverpool to Bank-key near Warrington, and as all the ftipulated demand for tonnage is confined to the navigation between that place and Manchefter, it appears that the undertakers meant only to employ themfelves in the improvemnt of the upper part of the river. This has been effected by the ufual contrivances of wears, locks, &c. and the very winding courfe of the river has in feveral places been corrected by cuts acrofs the necks of the principal bends. The want of water in droughts, and its too great abundance in floods, are circumftances under which this, as well as moft other river-navigations, has laboured. It has been an expenfive concern, and has, at times, been more burthenfome to its proprietors than ufeful to the public. At prefent it is managed in a fpirited and intelligent manner, and proves an ufeful addition in water-carriage to the rival canal-navigation.

WEAVER NAVIGATION.

In the fame year, 1720, an important acceffion was obtained to the internal communications of the port of Liverpool, by an act for making

navigable

navigable the river Weaver, from Frodſham bridge, which is near its conflux with the Merſey, up to Winsford-bridge beyond Northwich.

This act appointed certain perſons to be undertakers and truſtees of the propoſed navigation, with power to borrow a ſum of money to be advanced by other perſons named, at five per cent. intereſt, and one per cent. for the riſk, payable out of the firſt rates and duties accruing from the tonnage. If this ſum ſhould prove inſufficient, the under-takers were empowered to borrow more, ſecured in the like manner. After all the borrowed money, and all coſts and charges ſhould be fully repaid, the clear produce of the rates and duties was directed to be applied towards amending and repairing the public bridges in the county of Cheſter, and ſuch other public charges as the juſtices in quar-ter ſeſſions ſhould appoint; as alſo to the repair of highways leading from the ſalt-works to the river, and of other highways in the county. The ſum at firſt thought ſufficient to complete this work was 9000*l.*; but in an act to explain and amend the former, paſſed in 1759, it ap-pears that a debt of 20,000*l.* had been contracted, the greateſt part at five per cent. and the reſt at four and half, ſecured by mortgages on the rates and duties of the navigation. This debt has now for ſome years been paid off, and a large annual balance is produced in favour of the undertaking. The annual income of the navigation is about 8000*l.* In the year ending April 1794, the amount of caſual profits and whar-fage was 286*l.* 5*s.* 7*d.*; of tonnage, 8736*l.* 9*s.* 8½*d.*; and notwith-ſtanding a large ſum expended in new improvements, beſides the uſual repairs, there was paid to the County Treaſurer for public purpoſes 3000*l.* The length of this navigation is twenty miles. It has a fall of 45 feet 10 inches, divided between ten locks. The rate of tonnage limited by the act is not more than one ſhilling per ton for all goods

what-

whatfoever, and this is the charge now made for moft goods. There are about 120 veffels conftantly employed on the navigation, from 50 to 100 tons burthen. The kind of goods carried are principally white and rock falt downwards; and coals and fome merchants goods (but the latter to no confiderable amount) upwards. The rock falt comes from the pits at Northwich; and its cheap conveyance to Liverpool has proved of material benefit to that port, by furnifhing a profitable article for loading or ballaft to outward-bound fhips. The coal is brought from Lancafhire, and fupplies a large tract of the internal parts of Chefhire.

The principle upon which this work was undertaken, (almoft the only one of the kind which can be called a *public work,*) and the fuccefs with which it has been attended, feem to entitle it to particular notice.

DOUGLAS NAVIGATION.

While the Merfey and its communicating rivers were thus objects of commercial fpeculation, another ftream had its fhare of attention. The neighbourhood of Wigan is particularly rich in coal, and the little river Douglas flows from that town to the eftuary of the Ribble. A year before the above-mentioned acts were obtained, viz. in 1719, an act paffed for making the river Douglas, alias Afland, navigable from the river Ribble to Wigan. By means of this undertaking (which was not effected till 1727) the northern parts of Lancafhire, and even Weftmoreland, which produce no coal of their own, were fupplied coaft-wife with this neceffary article; and the lime-ftone and flate of thofe parts were brought back in return.

The Douglas navigation has fince been purchafed by the proprietors of the Leeds and Liverpool canal, who have in part fubftituted an artificial cut to the natural channel of the river.

AIRE, CALDER, AND DUN NAVIGATIONS.

Confiderably before this period, the clothing country of Yorkfhire had applied its rivers to the purpofes of water-carriage. An act for making navigable the rivers Aire and Calder to Leeds and Wakefield, paffed in the year 1699, and various extenfions and improvements in this navigation have been fucceffively made: and in 1725, another river in the Weft-Riding, the Dun, was made navigable from Doncafter to the diftance of two miles from Sheffield.

Various other projects of river navigations were fet on foot during the firft half of this century in Lancafhire and Chefhire, fome of which, however, were never carried into execution. One of thefe abortive fchemes was that of making navigable Worfley brook, to its junction with the Irwell, for which an act was obtained in 1737. It is worth mentioning only as the parent in defign of the duke of Bridgewater's firft canal.

SANKEY CANAL.

But an undertaking particularly deferving of notice took place in the year 1755, which, under the general powers of an act for making navigable a river, in reality gave rife to the firft canal-navigation made in England. In that year an act paffed, by which certain undertakers were authorized to make Sankey brook or river navigable from the Merfey, which it joins about two miles below Warrington, up its three branches;

viz.

viz. to Boardman's ftone bridge near St. Helen's, on the fouth branch;
to Gerrard's bridge on the middle branch; and to Penny bridge on the
north branch. From Sankey bridges to the ftone bridge next above the
mouth of Holme-mill-brook, was to be a new canal not communicating with Sankey brook. The owners of Sankey quays upon the old
natural navigation of the brook from the Merfey were not to be preju-
diced by the erection of quays or warehoufes interfering with them.
The new navigation was to be entirely free and open upon the payment
of ten-pence per ton tonnage to the undertakers. They were empowered to extend the navigation 800 yards from the three bridges before-
mentioned, as they found it convenient.

In a fubfequent act granted in the year 1761, it is fpecified in the
preamble, that the navigation is completed from the loweft lock on Sankey brook to Gerrard's bridge and Penny's bridge; but that in neap
tides the navigation is rendered impracticable for want of water in the
brook. The undertakers are therefore empowered to make a canal to
be begun within 250 yards from the loweft lock, and carried to the
Merfey at a place called Fiddler's ferry. This new part is about one
mile and three quarters in length; and in confideration of it the undertakers are empowered to levy two-pence per ton more tonnage. The
diftance above the three bridges to which they are allowed to extend
the navigation, is enlarged to 2000 yards.

The prefent ftate of the canal is as follows :—It runs entirely feparate from Sankey brook, except croffing and mixing with it in one
place about two miles from Sankey bridges. Its length from Fiddler's
ferry to the place where it feparates into three branches is 9¼ miles.
From thence it is carried to Penny bridge and Gerrard's bridge without

going

going further; but from Boardman's bride it runs nearly to the limits of 2000 yards, making the whole diftance from the Merfey 11¾ miles. There are eight fingle and two double locks upon the canal, and the fall of water is about 60 feet. The chief article carried upon it is coal, of which, in the year 1771, by an account given in to Parliament, there were taken to Liverpool 45,568 tons, and to Warrington, Northwich, and other places, 44,152 tons. There are, befides, flate brought down, and corn, deal balk, paving and lime-ftone carried up.

This navigation is never obftructed by floods, and feldom for any length of time by froft; upon an average perhaps about a week every winter. The higheft fpring tides rife within a foot of the level of the canal at the loweft lock. Loaded veffels are generally neaped about three days, but unloaded, can pafs to or from the river at every tide.

The old lock by which it at firft communicated with Sankey brook ftill remains, but is feldom ufed, unlefs when a number of veffels are about entering from the Merfey at once, in which cafe fome of the hindmoft fometimes fail for Sankey brook in order to get before the others.

This canal has proved very beneficial both to the public and the undertakers. Some of the firft collieries upon its banks are worked out, but others have been opened. Its bufinefs has been increafed by the large copper-works belonging to the Anglefea company, erected on one of its branches, and by the plate-glafs manufactory and other works founded near it, in the neighbourhood of the populous town of St. Helen's. Its original furveyor was Mr. John Eyes.

DUKE

DUKE OF BRIDGEWATER's CANALS.

Thofe magnificent plans which have rendered the name of the *Duke of Bridgewater* fo celebrated in the hiftory of canal-navigation, commenced in the years 1758 and 1759, when acts were paffed enabling him, firft, to carry a canal from Worfley to Salford, and alfo to Hollinferry on the Irwell; and fecondly, to deviate from that courfe, and carry his canal from Worfley acrofs the river Irwell to Manchefter, through the townfhip of Stretford. Poffeffing an extenfive property at and near Worfley, rich in coals, which could not by land carriage be conveyed to Manchefter fo advantageoufly as thofe from the pits on the other fide of that town, the Duke was naturally led to confider of a better mode of conveyance. The formerly projected, but unexecuted, fcheme of making navigable Worfley brook to the Irwell, evidently fuggefted the defign; but the original and commanding abilities of his engineer, that wonderful felf-inftructed genius *James Brindley*, pointed out a much more eligible mode of effecting his purpofe, than by means of the waters of a winding brook, fubject to the extremes of overflow and drought.

This firft undertaking was marked with the features of greatnefs. At its upper extremity in Worfley it buries itfelf in a hill, which it enters by an arched paffage, partly bricked, and partly formed by the folid rock, wide enough for the admiffion of long flat-bottomed boats, which are towed by means of hand-rails on each fide. This paffage penetrates near three quarters of a mile before it reaches the firft coalworks. It there divides into two channels, one of which goes 500 yards to the right, and the other as far to the left, and may be continued

nued

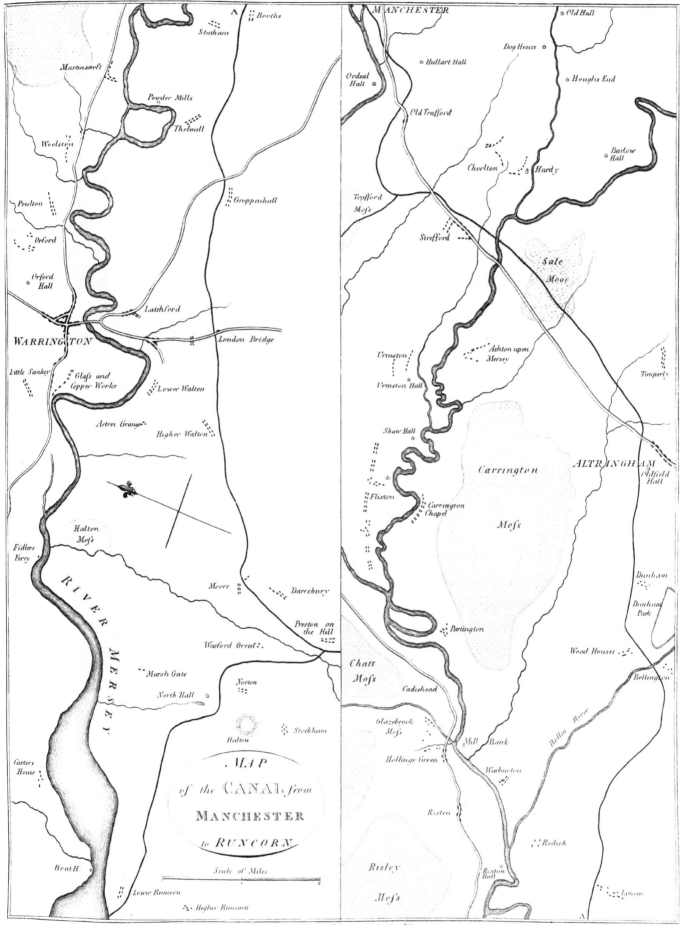

MANCHESTER

Old Hall

Booths

Statham

Martinscroft

Dog House

Hullart Hall

Houghs End

Powder Mills

Ordsal Hall

Thelwall

Old Trafford

Barlow Hall

Woolston

Chorlton

Hardy

Greppenhall

Poulton

Trafford Mofs

Orford

Strefford

Sale Moor

Orford Hall

Latchford

WARRINGTON

Urmston

Ashton upon Mersey

Timperly

London Bridge

Little Sankey

Glafs and Copper Works

Urmston Hall

Lower Walton

Acton Grange

Shaw Hall

ALTRINGHAM

Higher Walton

Carrington Mofs

Oldfield Hall

Halton Mofs

Flixton

Fidlers Ferry

Carrington Chapel

Dunham

RIVER MERSEY

Dunham Park

Moore

Daresbury

Partington

Wood Houses

Preston on the Hill

Warford Green

Marsh Gate

Bollington

Norton

North Hall

Chatt Mofs

Bollin River

Cadishead

Halton

Stockham

Glazebrook Mofs

Mill Bank

MAP

of the CANAL, from

Hollings Green

Warburton

Carter's House

MANCHESTER

to RUNCORN

Rixton

Redish

Scale of Miles

Boat H.

Risley

Rixton Hall

Lower Runcorn

Mofs

Lymm

Higher Runcorn

Published May 20. 1795 by I. Stockdale, Piccadilly.   I. Muden Sc.

I. Swertner del.t

Pollard sculp.t

Publish'd July 11 1794 by I Stockdale, Piccadilly

VIEW OF BARTON BRIDGE.

nued at pleafure. In the paffage at certain diftances air funnels are cut through the rock, iffuing perpendicularly at the top of the hill. The arch at the entrance is about fix feet wide and about five in height from the furface of the water. It widens within, fo that in fome places the boats may pafs each other. To this fubterraneous canal the coals are brought from the pits within the bowels of the hill in low waggons holding about a ton each, which, as the work is on the defcent, are eafily pufhed or pulled by a man along a railed way to a ftage over the canal, whence they are fhot into one of the boats. Thefe boats hold feven or eight tons, and feveral of them being linked together, are eafily drawn out by the help of the rail to the mouth of the fubterraneous paf-fage, where a large bafon is made, ferving as a dock. From hence they are fent along the canal to Manchefter, in ftrings drawn by a horfe or two mules.

It was the principle of this, as it has been that of all Mr. Brindley's canals, to keep on the level as much as poffible; whence it has been neceffary to carry them over the roads or ftreams upon arches after the manner of an aqueduct, and to fill up vallies by artificial mounds for their conveyance, as well as to cut down or bore through hills. The moft ftriking of all the aqueduct works is in this firft canal, where it paffes over the navigable river Irwell at Barton bridge. The aqueduct begins upwards of 200 yards from the river, which runs in a valley. Over the river itfelf it is conveyed by a ftone bridge of great ftrength and thicknefs, confifting of three arches, the centre one fixty-three feet wide and thirty-eight feet above the furface of the water, admitting the largeft barges navigating the Irwell, to go through it with mafts and fails ftanding. The fpectator was, therefore, here gratified with the extraordinary fight, never before beheld in this country, of one vef-

Q

fel failing over the top of another; and thofe who had at firft ridiculed the attempt, as equivalent to building a caftle in the air, were obliged to join in admiration of the wonderful abilities of the engineer, from whofe creative genius there was fcarcely any thing within the reach of poffibility which might not be expected. This work is not the proper place for details of thofe admirable contrivances, in which every department in the making of his canals have abounded. They have introduced numerous improvements into the practice of fimilar works, and have received many additions from other ingenious perfons, among whom the duke of Bridgewater's fteward, Mr. Gilbert, merits a diftinguifhed place.

This canal, after paffing Barton bridge, was conveyed on the level, with great labour and expenfe, in a circuitous tract of nine miles, to Caftlefield adjacent to Manchefter. The moft remarkable part of its courfe is that where it croffes the low grounds near Stretford upon a vaft mound of earth, of great length, the conftruction of which exercifed all the inventive powers of the conductor. At its termination it is fed by the river Medlock, and in order to keep up the water to a proper height, and prevent a fuperabundance of it in time of floods, a large circular wear is conftructed, having in its centre an aperture, or fwallow, which conveys the fuperfluous water by a fubterranean paffage into the brook below. Another wear of a fimilar kind is formed at Cornbrook, three miles further. By the act for making this canal, the Duke was limited to a rate of tonnage not exceeding two and fix-pence per ton, and was bound to fell his coals at Manchefter and Salford for no more than four-pence per hundred. On the execution of the undertaking, the poor of thofe towns were benefited by a reduction in the price of coals of one half of what they before paid, and vaft quantities were taken away by them from the wharf in Caftlefield, in wheel-bar-rows, at three-pence halfpenny per hundred.

But before this firft defign was completed, a much greater and more important plan had opened itfelf to the Duke: which was an extenfion of his canal by a branch which, running through Chefhire parallel to the river Merfey, fhould at length terminate in that river below the limits of its artificial navigation, and thus afford a new and rival water-carriage from Manchefter and its vicinity to Liverpool. The execution of this bold idea was authorifed by an act of parliament obtained in 1761, which enabled the duke of Bridgewater to make a canal from Longford-bridge in the townfhip of Stretford, to the river Merfey, at a place called the Hempftones in the townfhip of Halton. It was oppofed, but ineffectually, by the proprietors of the old river-navigation, on which its operation could not but be highly injurious, however benefi-cial it might be to the public. This canal, which is more than twenty-nine miles in length to its termination at Runcorn-gap, (which place was preferred to the Hempftones on account of the fuperior advantage it offered in entering the mouth of the canal at neap tides) was finifhed in five years. It is carried acrofs the Merfey by an aqueduct-bridge fimilar to that over the Irwell at Barton, but lower, as the Merfey is not navigable in that part. Further on, it alfo croffes the fmall river Bollin, which, running in a tract of low meadows, has made a mound in that part neceffary for the conveyance of the canal, of a height, breadth, and length, that forms a fpectacle truly ftupendous. The principle of keeping the level has been rigoroufly purfued, in defiance of expenfe and difficulty, for the whole length of the canal, till it is brought in full view of the Merfey at Runcorn. There it is precipi-tately lowered ninety-five feet in a chain of locks, of admirable con-

Q 2　　　　　　　　ftruction,

struction, furnished at different heights with capacious reservoirs of water, in order to supply the waste incurred by the passage of vessels.

When the duke of Bridgewater undertook this great design, the price of carriage on the river-navigation was twelve shillings the ton from Manchester to Liverpool, while that of land-carriage was forty shillings the ton.   The Duke's charge on his canal was limited to six shillings, and together with this vast superiority in cheapness, it had all the speed and regularity of land-carriage.   The articles conveyed by it were likewise much more numerous than those by the river-navigation: besides manufactured goods and their raw materials, coals from the Duke's own pits were deposited in yards at various parts of the canal, for the supply of Cheshire; lime, manure, and building materials were carried from place to place; and the markets of Manchester obtained a supply of provisions from districts too remote for the ordinary land conveyances.   A branch of useful and profitable carriage hitherto scarcely known in England, was also undertaken, which was that of passengers.   Boats on the model of the Dutch treckschuyts, but more agreeable and capacious, were set up, which at very reasonable rates and with great convenience carried numbers of persons daily between Manchester and the principal extent of the canal.   All these objects of traffic on the new canal became more and more considerable with the increasing trade of Lancashire; but other circumstances also greatly operated in its favour.

TRENT and MERSEY COMMUNICATION.

There is a period in which the mind of man, rouzed to attend to any particular subject, whether of art, science, or regulation, is irre-

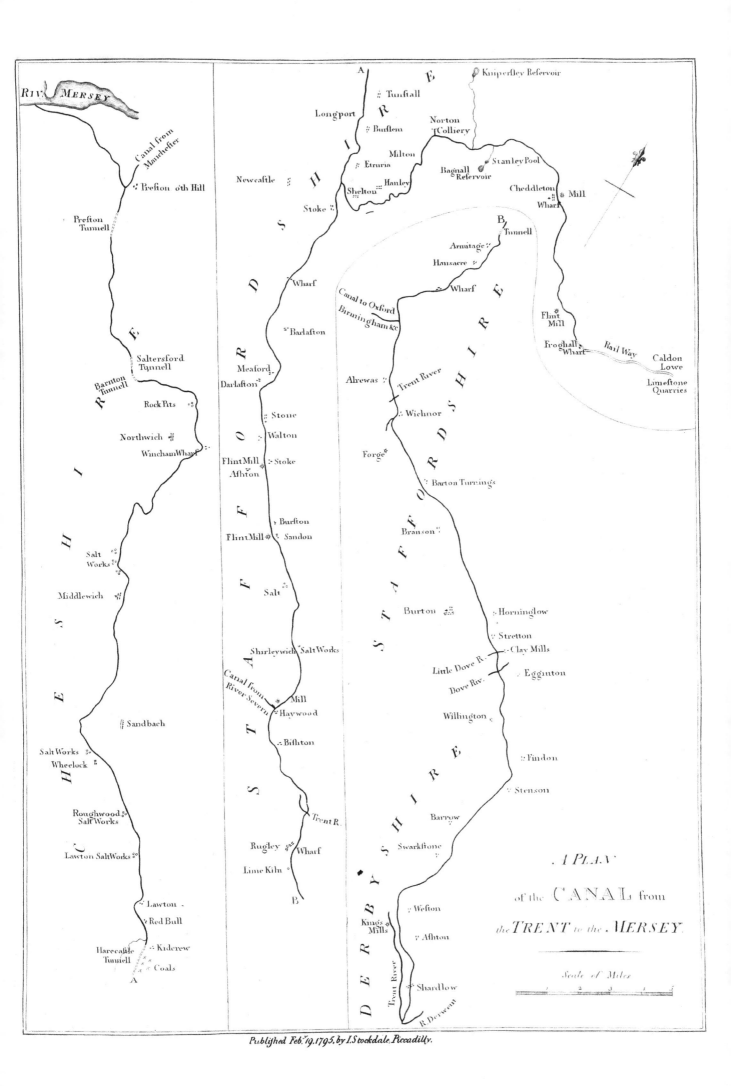

A PLAN of the CANAL from the TRENT to the MERSEY.

Published Feb.r 19.1795. by I. Stockdale, Piccadilly.

fiftibly impelled to proceed in its career; and this crifis was now arrived with refpect to the internal communication between the different parts of this kingdom by means of navigable canals.

As early as the year 1755, the corporation of Liverpool, (which, perhaps, has diftinguifhed itfelf beyond any other fimilar body in the kingdom for a liberal and fpirited attention to commercial improvement) employed two perfons, Mr. Taylor of Manchefter, and Mr. Eyes of Liverpool, to take furveys with a view of determining the practicability of joining the river Trent with the Weaver or Merfey, and thus opening an inland communication between the great fea-ports of Liverpool and Hull. It was propofed that this navigation fhould go through the counties of Nottingham, Derby, Stafford, and Chefter; and on an accurate furvey the defign was reported to be practicable. The late Mr. Hardman, an intelligent merchant of Liverpool, and one of its reprefentatives in parliament, was the chief promoter of this furvey. Another furvey, under the patronage of the prefent marquis of Stafford, and the late lord Anfon, was made in 1758 by Mr. Brindley, and afterwards revifed by him and Mr. Smeaton jointly; and their opinions were equally in favour of the projected undertaking. An union with the river Severn and port of Briftol alfo became part of the defign, which thus embraced the vaft idea of connecting almoft all the midland counties of England with each other, and with the different feas, by a chain of water communication. In the two plans offered to the public for effecting this purpofe, one of the principal differences confifted in the manner of communicating with the Merfey. One propofed doing this by terminating the canal in the navigable river Weaver at Winsford-bridge: the other, by terminating it in the duke of Bridgewater's canal at Prefton-brook. The latter, which was Mr.

4

Brindley's

Brindley's plan, was preferred, apparently on reasonable grounds, as it afforded a direct communication with Manchester, without the intervention of a single lock. In December 1765, a numerous meeting of land-owners and persons concerned in trade held at Wolseley-bridge in Staffordshire, agreed upon an application to parliament for leave to bring in a bill for making a navigable canal from the river Trent near Wilden-ferry in Derbyshire, to the river Mersey near Runcorn-gap; and the bill was accordingly brought in and passed in 1766.

GRAND TRUNK CANAL.

This canal which, by its planner, was ingeniously termed the *grand trunk*, (in allusion to the main artery of the body from whence branches are sent off for the nourishment of the distant parts) and which is commonly known by the name of the *Staffordshire* canal, takes its course from north-west to south-east, across the county of Chester, and thence across Staffordshire beyond its middle, when, turning short in a north-eastern direction parallel to the Trent, it accompanies that river into Derbyshire, and enters it near the place where the high road from Derby to Leicester crosses the Trent over a bridge, substituted to the former Wilden-ferry. In length it is ninety-three miles. Its fall of water from its greatest elevation at Harecastle-hill, is 326 feet on the northern side, and 316 on the southern; the former effected by thirty-five locks, the latter by forty. Six of the most southern locks are fourteen feet wide, adapted to the navigation of large barges, and one of the northern is of the same width. The common dimensions of the canal are twenty-nine feet breadth at the top, sixteen at the bottom, and the depth four feet and a half; but in the part from Wilden to Burton, and from Middlewich to Preston-on-the-hill, it is thirty-one feet broad at the top,

eighteen

eighteen at the bottom, and five and half deep. The canal is carried over the Dove in an aqueduct of twenty-three arches, the ground being raifed to a confiderable height for the fpace of a mile and two furlongs. Over the Trent it is carried by an aqueduct of fix arches of twenty-one feet fpan each; and over the Dane, on three arches of 20 feet fpan. There are befides near 160 leffer aqueducts and culverts for the conveyance of brooks and fmall ftreams. The cart bridges erected over it are 109; the foot bridges eleven.

For the fake of preferving a level as much as poffible, the hills and elevated grounds in the courfe of the canal have been pierced by five tunnels. Of thefe, that through the mountain at *Harecaftle* is the principal, and has proved a work of vaft labour and expenfe, in confequence of unforefeen difficulties. Its length is 2880 yards, with a width of nine feet, and a height of twelve, lined and arched with brick; and it runs more than feventy yards below the furface of the earth. The other tunnels are at *Hermitage*, 130 yards; at *Barnton*, in Great Budworth parifh, 560 yards; at *Saltenford* in the fame parifh, 350 yards; and at *Prefton-on-the-hill*, 1241 yards. Each of thefe is feventeen feet four inches high, and thirteen feet fix inches wide. The boats employed upon the canal carry about twenty-five tons, and are drawn by one horfe. The tonnage paid to the proprietors for the liberty of navigating is three-halfpence per mile. This great work was begun on July 17th, 1766. It was carried on with great fpirit by Mr. Brindley while he lived, and was finifhed by his brother-in law, Mr. Henfhall, who put the laft hand to it in May 1777.

Soon after this canal was undertaken, Mr. Brindley planned and executed a canal from the Grand Trunk at Haywood, to the river Severn

near

near Bewdley; thus completing the communication between the three principal ports of the kingdom, (after London) thofe of Briftol, Liverpool, and Hull, and all the inland country lying between them.

As the Staffordfhire canal, or Grand Trunk, has a peculiar connection with the country which is comprized within the circuit of this work, it will be proper to ftate the chief fources of employment which it was expected to open, and the greater part of which have in effect accrued to it. They may be diftributed into three heads : 1ft. Natural products of the adjacent tracts of country.—2dly. Products of cultivation and manufacture.—3dly. Imported raw materials and objects of general commerce.

From Northwich to Lawton in Chefhire lies a vaft bed of rock falt, eftimated at forty yards in thicknefs, which, befide being purified for home and foreign confumption, might, were liberty obtained for fuch ufe, be employed to great advantage in agriculture and feveral of the arts depending on chymiftry. At prefent, indeed, the Weaver navigation conveys to Liverpool all the rock falt wanted at that port; but the poffeffion of fuch a ftore on the banks of this canal may reafonably be accounted an advantage for futurity.

The hill called Mole or Mow-cop near Lawton, contains feveral ufeful kinds of ftone enumerated in the general account of Chefhire. Thefe are already carried to great diftances by land-carriage, and of courfe muft be conveyed by the much cheaper medium of canal-navigation to the various parts near its courfe. Several other valuable fpecies of ftone are met with near the canal; as a fine free-ftone near Wolfeley-bridge, and near Burton upon Trent; a whole mountain of lime-ftone near the

termination

mination of the canal, on which the village of Breden in Leicefterfhire is built; lime-ftone quarries of note at Tickenhall in Derbyfhire, and at Barrow in Leicefterfhire; gypfum or alabafter at Clay-hill. At Rudgeley is found the curious kind of coal called cannel, as well as other fpecies of coal; and it is fuppofed that a fubterraneous canal, like that of the duke of Bridgewater at Worfley, might be carried to the under-ftrata of the mines, at the fame time laying them dry, and affording a conveyance for their contents. Marl in large quantities would be thrown out in digging the canal, and might eafily be procured clofe to its banks; whence this, as well as other manures, will be cheaply conveyed along the courfe of the navigation to the lands which want it.

That kind of iron ore which is called iron ftone, proper for making cold-fhort iron, is contained abundantly in many parts of the country through which the canal runs. This has been found of great ufe for mixing with the red iron ore of Cumberland, in manufacturing the beft tough iron, and has been conveyed by land-carriage to the Weaver in large quantities, in order to be fhipped for the north for that purpofe. It is to be prefumed that greater quantities of it will be fent by the cheaper conveyance of the canal. Various other mineral products from diftricts more remote may probably find their way to this navigation, which will carry them to works where they may be ufefully employed.

With refpect to the products of culture, corn deferves the firft confideration. The mutual advantage of conveying the products of the agricultural counties to the markets of the manufacturing towns, which can only be fed by means of diftant fupplies, and are enabled to pay the beft prices, is obvious; and a cheap conveyance of the fuperfluity of plentiful years to the fea-ports for exportation is alfo a matter of

R

great

great confequence to the farmer. The Staffordfhire and duke of Bridge-water's canal have derived a large fhare of their employment from the tranfport of articles of provifion, fome of which have been carried in quantities beyond all previous calculation. Timber growing in the in-terior country, efpecially oak for fhip-building, cord-wood for char--coal, oak-bark for tanning, madder and woad for dying, muft alfo from certain diftances be brought to the canal for conveyance to the places of demand. The cheefe of Chefhire deftined for the fupply of Lancafhire, as well as part of that intended for London, will naturally go by this road; as well as the manufactured falt of that county for the ufe of the inland diftricts.

Of manufactures properly fo called, the pottery wares, bricks, tiles, &c. of Burflem and the other villages in Staffordfhire employed in that trade, being commodities of great weight in proportion to their value, will moft certainly take the benefit of a canal running through the midft of them, and communicating with fuch an extenfive tract of country as well as with the fea-ports. The fame may be faid in fome degree of the heavy metallic manufactures carried on to fuch prodigious extent in Birmingham, Walfall, Wolverhampton, Dudley, &c. from whence the grand trunk receives communicating branches. The manufactures of Manchefter rather concern the duke of Bridgewater's and the other Lancafhire navigations; but thofe of Derby, Nottingham, and Lei-cefter will find their cheapeft conveyance to Liverpool along the grand trunk. The ale of Burton, fo much valued for exportation, may alfo be fent to Liverpool by its means, as it has been to Hull by the Trent.

As to raw materials for the fupply of manufactures, the flint ftones and pipe-clay brought from vaft diftances coaft-wife to the ports for the

ufe

CANAL

from

LIVERPOOL to LEEDS.

Scale of Miles

YORKSHIRE

LANCASHIRE

LEEDS

SKIPTON

COLNE

BURNLEY

KEIGHLEY

CHORLEY

WIGAN

ORMSKIRK

LIVERPOOL

MERSEY RIVER

Air River

NAVIGATION

Douglas

A. G. Harwood
Whalley
Reed Hall
Clayton Hall
Huncote
Roft Greve
Higham
Marfden
Barnolswick
Church Marton
Thornton
Salterforth
Gargrave
Thorlby
Broughton
Carlton
Woodfide
Eaftburn
Bradley
Kildwick

Bingley
Cottingley
Shipley
Helwick
Baildon
Parkgate
Nether Yeaden
Horfforth

Fatherley
Woodhall
Maddling Water
Grenshaw Park
BLACKBURN
Withnell
Moorgate Fold
Wheelton
Heapy
Brindle

Martin Lane
Halsall
Down Holland
Aughton
Rufford
Burfcough
Latham Hall
Newburgh
Dalton
Up Hollande
Dyhsbury Hall
Adlington
Standifh
Blackrod
Hugh Hall
Hirdes Hall
Horwich
Rivington

Hefkayne
Lidiale
Maghull
Sephton
Warbreck Moor
Ainfree
G. Crofby
Lunaere
Walton

L.Haulon, A.Jones St.

Publifhed Dec:r 21.1794. by I.Stockdale. Piccadilly.

ufe of the Staffordfhire potteries, and to which, from their fmall value, the price of carriage is of peculiar confequence, cannot but afford an abundant fource of employment to the canal, to the mutual benefit of the carriers and manufacturers. Birmingham and its neighbourhood will alfo receive part of their fupply of metals by the fame conveyance. Of other imported goods, fir timber for building, mahogany for cabinet work, wine, fpirits, and heavy groceries, will be fent from the fea-ports to the interior country along this and its communicating canals.

To this view of the expected and experienced benefits arifing to the undertakers of this great fcheme of inland navigation, and to the public, it is proper to add, that the fyftem of communication has fince been rendered more complete by the junction of a branch paffing from the great trunk to Coventry, with another proceeding from Oxford directly northwards through Oxfordfhire and Warwickfhire. Thus the firft of our rivers, the Thames, and the firft of our ports, that of the metropolis, have been added to the comprehenfive chain of canal-navigation; and it cannot be doubted that fuch an acceffion muft be felt through every part of it. We fhall now return to the limits of our own circle, to mark all the undertakings of this kind within its boundaries which fucceeded thofe of the duke of Bridgewater and of the Staffordfhire company.

LEEDS AND LIVERPOOL CANAL.

A navigation between the eaftern and weftern feas by means of the rivers Aire and Ribble, had for many years been thought of as a practicable and ufeful work, and fome endeavours had been ufed to draw the public attention to it, but ineffectually. At length, the fuccefs of

the

the duke of Bridgewater's canals excited Mr. Longbotham in 1767 to conceive the defign of making a communication between Leeds and the port of Liverpool by fimilar means; and having made a furvey of the interjacent country, with plans and eftimates of the propofed work, he produced them before various public meetings in Yorkfhire and Lancafhire, at which they were approved. Mr. Brindley was called in to determine on the fcheme; and after furveying all the tract pointed out by Mr. Longbotham, he made his report in its favour at two numerous meetings held at Bradford and at Liverpool in December 1768. The plan was there adopted, and an act for carrying it into execution was obtained in the beginning of 1770, and the work was begun in the latter end of the fame year.

This defign was the greateft and moft adventurous that had then, or has fince, been undertaken. The great direct diftance between the two extremities, much augmented by the very winding courfe which the nature of the country demanded; together with the high elevation of the tract on the borders of the two counties, which the moft circuitous courfe could only in part avoid; rendered the work fo difficult and expenfive, that nothing but the extraordinary zeal with which fchemes of this kind now began to be purfued, could have ftimulated the perfons concerned to put it into execution. The whole length of the courfe from Leeds to Liverpool is 107 miles and three quarters: the fall from the central level is on the Lancafhire fide 525 feet; on the Yorkfhire, 446 feet. Its courfe is feen on the map. It may in general be remarked, that on the Liverpool fide after making a large circuit round Ormfkirk, it croffes the river Douglas, and proceeding north-eafterly, runs for fome miles parallel and near to the Ribble then follows the courfe of the Lancafh re Calder, which it croffes and re-croffes, till it arrives at its head in

2   the

the great bafon of Fouridge, near Pendle-hill and the town of Colne. Thence, declining on the Leeds fide, it runs north-eaftward to the banks of the Aire near Gargrave, which river it croffes, and afterwards clofely accompanies in its whole courfe to Leeds, paffing the towns of Skipton and Bingley. Of the two fide-branches, that to Wigan is upwards of feven miles and a half, with a fall of thirty-fix feet; that to Bradford is a little more than three miles, with a fall of eighty-feven feet fix inches.

On a curfory furvey of the tract of country through which this canal paffes, it will probably appear not extremely inviting to fuch an undertaking upon the whole; it is but lightly peopled; and though the great towns at the oppofite extremities abound in objects of commercial importance, yet their connection with each other is not very intimate, nor does it feem likely to be much promoted by fuch a circuitous communication. Coal and lime-ftone are the chief natural products of the intermediate country; and as the diftricts abounding in the one often want the other, a confiderable tranfport of thefe articles on the canal may be expected, as well as of other ufeful kinds of ftone found in quarries near its courfe. That confiderable benefits will accrue to the the country, from the canal, cannot be doubted; in particular, agricultural improvements of its wafte and barren tracts by means of the eafier conveyance of lime and other manures may certainly be expected.

That part of the canal which goes from Liverpool to the Douglas, and thence, by a collateral branch (fubftituted to the old Douglas navigation) to Wigan, was finifhed with great celerity, and has proved of great advantage to the proprietors, and to the town of Liverpool, by the new and plentiful fupply of coals it has brought, which have caufed

a cona confiderable exportation of that commodity from thence. The part adjacent to Leedswas likewife foon finifhed to the extent of feveral miles. By another act paffed in 1783, liberty was obtained by the proprietors to purchafe the Douglas river-navigation ; and by a third in 1790, a power was given to raife an additional fum of money, and alfo to make a variation in the courfe of the canal.

A further and much more confiderable variation in the courfe of the canal, projected in confequence of the interference of the new Lancafter canal, was permitted by an act paffed in May 1794. By this a deviation begins from Barrowford in the townfhip of Whalley, and taking a more fouthern line than the former, paffes through Burnley, Accrington, Blackburn, Chorley, Adlington, Blackrod, Weft Houghton, Ince, and fo to Wigan. This line will form a longer and more circuitous courfe, but will go through the centre of a country full of manufactures, and abounding in coal.

CHESTERFIELD CANAL.

In 1769 Mr. Brindley furveyed the courfe of an intended canal from the town of Chefterfield to the river Trent ; and in 1770 an act was obtained for putting his plan into execution. The tract of the canal is by Stavely forge and coal-works, to Harthill, which it penetrates by a tunnel, thence to Workfop, to Retford, where it croffes the Idle, and at length to the Trent, which it enters at Stockwith, a little below Gainfborough Its whole length is forty-fix miles: its rife from Chefterfield to Norwood is forty-five feet, and its fall from thence to the Trent 335 feet, for which it has fixty-five locks. The tunnel at Norwood through Harthill is 2850 yards ; and that at Drake-hole 153 vards. The canal was completed fo as to be navigated in 1776 ; but

the

the expenfe of the work, amounting to 60,000*l.* was fo much beyond the eftimate, that fhares fell to a very depreciated value; and though they have lately recovered themfelves confiderably, they are ftill below par. The principal trade on the canal is the conveyance of coal, got near Chefterfield, and fent to Workfop and Retford, and by the Trent to Gainfborough and Lincoln. Lead is the next valuable article, of which a large quantity, the produce of the Derbyfhire mines, is exported by its means. Wrought iron, pottery, and a few manufactured goods are alfo carried downwards upon it. The carriage upwards confifts in large quantities of corn; lime, timber, groceries, &c.

CHESTER CANAL.

The ancient port of Chefter had long feen her younger rival, Liverpool, opening new fources to her extenfive traffic, without any exertion to obtain a fhare in fimilar benefits. But in the years 1767, 1769, and 1770, the courfe of a canal from thence to the midland parts of the county was furveyed by different engineers, and after an unfuccefsful attempt in 1769, an act was obtained in 1772 for making a navigable canal from Chefter to the towns of Namptwich and Middlewich, but with the reftriction, that it fhould not at the latter town join the Grand Trunk canal, which flows by it. Such a reftriction, the fruit of a monopolizing fpirit, though a manifeft difadvantage to the fcheme, did not prevent the execution of a great part of it. The canal to Namptwich was completed at the unforefeen expenfe of 80,000*l.* Its length is eighteen miles; its rife from Chefter 170 feet ten inches. For want of money the branch to Middlewich was never cut; and thus the principal objects of the undertaking, the carriage of falt from that place to Chefter, and the communication (though not by abfolute junction)

tion) with the Grand Trunk, being never effected, the scheme has proved more totally abortive than any other in the kingdom. Its employment, at present, is not sufficient to keep it in repair, and shares have been sold at one per cent. of the original cost. There is now, however, some prospect of connecting it with the eastern line of the newly undertaken Shrewsbury canal, which may give an extension to its business.

HUDDERSFIELD CANAL TO THE CALDER.

The manufacturing town of Huddersfield has obtained the advantage of a communication by canal with the river Calder. In 1774 an act passed enabling Sir John Ramsden, Bart. (proprietor of the town of Huddersfield) to make a canal from the Calder at Cooper's-bridge, where the river Colne falls into it, to King's-mill, near the town of Huddersfield. This has been executed, and is eight miles in length, with a fall of fifty-six feet ten inches divided into nine locks. It opens a communication with Hull and all its associated rivers and canals, and its benefits are manifest.

LANGLEY-BRIDGE, OR ERREWASH CANAL.

Another Derbyshire canal, which it is proper to mention for the sake of connection, though out of the limits of our work, is that called Langley-bridge or Errewash canal. In 1777, the owners of the extensive coal-mines lying in the south-eastern part of the county, obtained an act for making a navigable canal from Langley-bridge to the Trent opposite to the entrance of the Soar near Sawley-ferry. It begins in the parish of Heanor, and runs very near and parallel to the

little

little boundary river Errewafh in the greateft part of its courfe, paffing through the above-mentioned callieries. Its length is eleven miles
and a quarter; its fall, 108 feet eight inches, by means of fourteen
locks. It furnifhes an additional fupply of coals to the diftricts bordering the Trent.

MANCHESTER, BOLTON, AND BURY CANAL.

The vaft extenfion of the Manchefter manufactures after the peace
of 1783, gave rife to various new fchemes of water communication
between the centre of that traffic and its principal ftations in the furrounding country. The firft of thefe was a canal from Manchefter to
Bolton with a branch to Bury, for which an act was obtained in 1791.
It begins on the weftern fide of Manchefter from the river Irwell, to
which it runs nearly parallel in a northerly courfe, croffing it at Clifton,
and again near Little Lever, where its two branches, to Bolton and to
Bury, feparate. Its total length is fifteen miles one furlong, with a
rife of 187 feet. The country with which this canal opens a communication, abounds in coals, together with other mineral products, which
will by its means obtain a cheap and eafy conveyance to the town and
neighbourhood of Manchefter. Mercantile goods, raw and manufactured, may alfo be expected to afford much carriage in this populous
tract of country.

MANCHESTER, ASHTON-UNDER-LYNE, AND OLDHAM.

In 1792 an act was granted for making a canal from Manchefter to
Afhton-under-Lyne, and to the neighbourhood of Oldham. This
commences from the eaft fide of Manchefter, croffes the Medlock, paffes
Fairfield, and terminates at Afhton-under-Lyne. At Fairfield a branch

S   goes

goes off to the New Mill near Oldham ; from this there is a cut to Park Colliery. The whole length of the canal is eleven miles, and its rife is 152 feet. Coal, lime, lime-ftone, and other minerals, and manure, are its principal objects of carriage. The two above-mentioned under-takings are nearly completed. A branch is intended to go from this canal to Stockport, a town which has hitherto been fomewhat unac-countably fruftrated of the benefits of water communication, though an extenfion to it was included in the powers firft granted to the duke of Bridgewater.

A connection between Manchefter and Rochdale by canals has been a matter of much difcuffion, and different plans have been propofed, and met with their abettors and opponents. One of thefe was an ex-tenfion of the Bury canal, the diftance from which town to Rochdale is not confiderable : but this plan was given up for a defign of much greater magnitude, which, in effect, is another junction of the eaft and weft feas.

ROCHDALE CANAL.

An act paffed in April 1794 authorizes the opening of a navigation from the duke of Bridgewater's canal at Manchefter, to the Calder na-vigation at Sowerby-bridge near Halifax. Beginning from the fouth-weft fide of Manchefter, it leaves that town at the north-eaft corner, and takes its courfe nearly parallel to the Oldham road as far as Failf-worth. Here it turns directly north, and proceeds through the tract of coal country about Fox Denton, Chaderton, Middleton, and Hop-wood, to a fmall diftance to the eaft of Rochdale, whence it fends off a fhort branch to that town. Having paffed Littleborough it gains its head level about Dean-head. It was originally intended to enter the hill at this

place

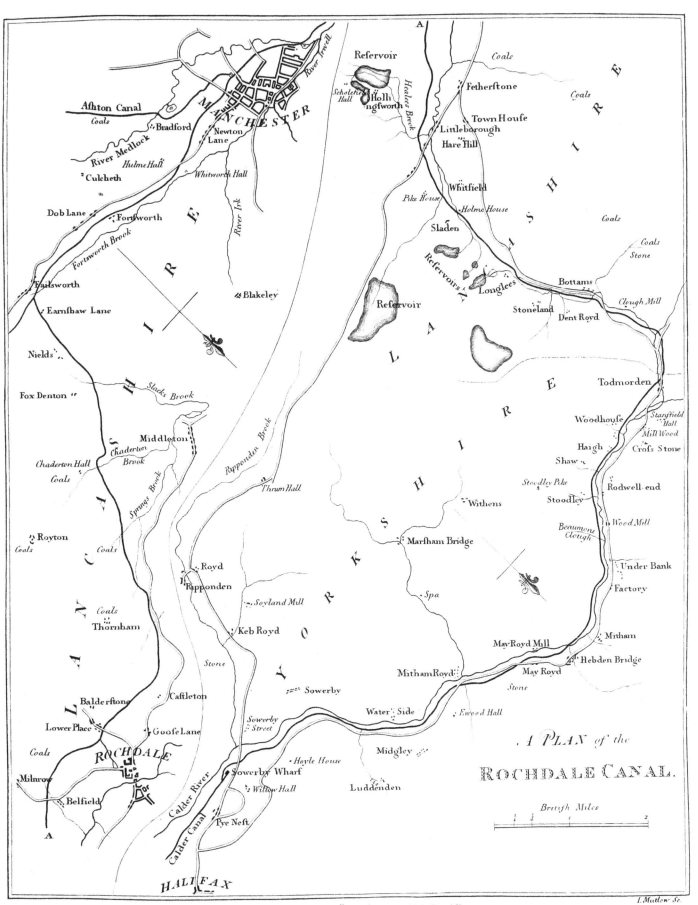

A

Coals

Reservoir

Coals

Ashton Canal
Coals
Bradford
Newton Lane
MANCHESTER
River Irwell
Scholefield Hall
Hollingsworth
Healens Brook
Fetherstone
Coals
Town House
Littleborough
Hare Hill

River Medlock
Hulme Hall
Whitworth Hall
Culcheth

Dob Lane
Fortworth
Fortworth Brook
River Irk
Whitfield
Pike House
Holme House
Coals

Failsworth
Earnshaw Lane
Blakeley
Sladen
Reservoirs
Longlees
Bottams
Coals Stone
Clough Mill

Nields
Reservoir
Stoneland
Dent Royd

Fox Denton
Slacks Brook
Todmorden

Middleton
Chaderton Brook
Rupponden Brook
Woodhouse
Stanfield Hall
Mill Wood

Chaderton Hall
Coals
Springs Brook
Thrum Hall
Haigh
Shaw
Crofs Stone

Royton
Coals
Coals
Withens
Stoodley Pike
Stoodley
Rodwell-end
Wood Mill

Coals
Thornham
Royd
Rupponden
Marsham Bridge
Spa
Beaumont Clough
Under Bank
Factory

Soyland Mill
Keb Royd
May Royd Mill
Mitham
Hebden Bridge

Stone
Mitham Royd
May Royd
Stone

Balderstone
Castleton
Goose Lane
Sowerby
Water Side
Ewood Hall

Lower Place
Sowerby Street
Midgley

Coals
ROCHDALE
Hoyle House
Luddenden

Milnrow
Calder River
Sowerby Wharf
Willow Hall
Luddenden

Belfield
Pye Nest

A

Calder Canal

HALIFAX

A PLAN of the
ROCHDALE CANAL.

British Miles

Published Jan^r 11. 1795, by I Stockdale, Piccadilly.

L. Mutlow Sc.

A PLAN of the CANAL from HUDDERSFIELD to ASHTON under LYNE.

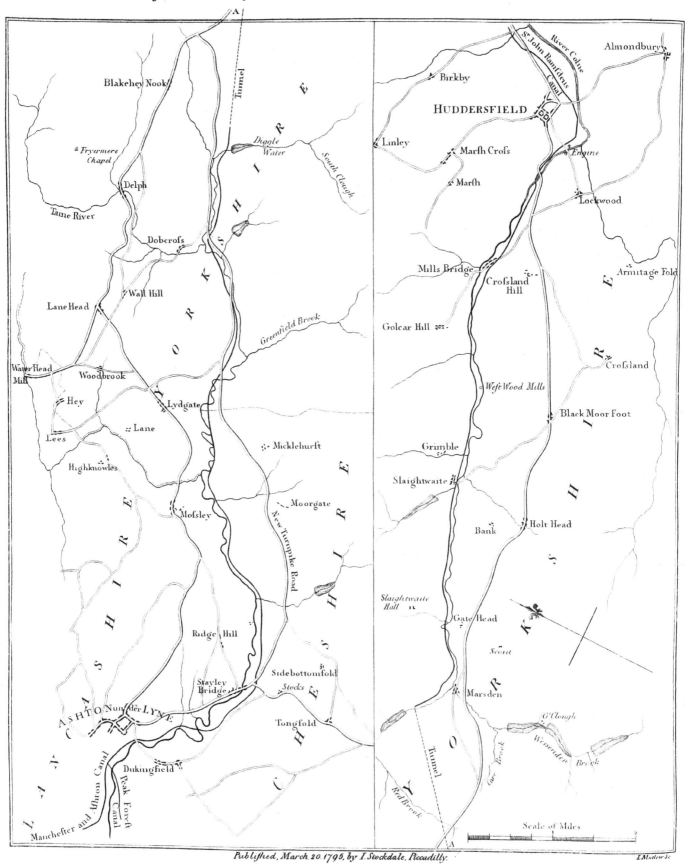

Published, March 20. 1795, by I. Stockdale, Piccadilly.

T. Mutlow Sc.

place by a tunnel, but this is now avoided. Hence it proceeds to Todmorden, where it turns north-eaft to Hebden-bridge, and then bends somewhat to the fouth-eaft, till it reaches the Calder navigation at Sowerbybridge, having during the latter part of its courfe clofely accompanied the river Calder. Its whole length from one extremity to the other is thirty-one miles and a half; that of two fhort collateral branches, about a mile and quarter. From its head level it falls 275 feet on the Halifax fide: 438 feet feven inches, on the Manchefter fide. In order fully to obviate an objection which was the caufe of a ftrong oppofition to it—the danger of cutting off thofe ftreams which feed the river Irk, by which the fchool-mills at Manchefter are worked, as well as thofe which feed the mills on the Roach and Calder—great refervoirs have been made in the hilly country near different parts of its courfe, abundantly fufficient to fupply all the wafte of locks or leakage, without borrowing from any of the above-mentioned ftreams. The advantages ftated to be expected from this defign, are thofe of a complete canal-navigation from fea to fea, a communication of import and export between the ports of Liverpool, Briftol, and Hull, and the populous and manufacturing towns of Rochdale, Halifax, Oldham, and their vicinities, and a general mutual communication between thefe diftricts and all the other great manufacturing places vifited by the canals with which this is mediately or immediately connected. The work is at this time carrying on with celerity and fuccefs.

HUDDERSFIELD CANAL to ASHTON.

So active was now become the fpirit of adventure, that another communication between the two feas, paffing through a line of country fomewhat to the fouth of the former, was undertaken. This is the Huddersfield canal, the act for which paffed in April 1794. Its two

extremi

extremities are the Afhton-under Lyne canal on the weftern fide, and Sir John Ramfden's canal to the Calder on the eaftern. Its general direction is north-eaft. From Afhton it takes its courfe parallel to the Tame, often crofling its windings, by Stayley-bridge, and enters York-fhire in the manufacturing townfhip of Saddleworth. Arriving at its head level, it penetrates the high grounds by a tunnel of three miles in length, pafling beneath Pule Mofs, and coming out near Marfden: thence it proceeds by Slaighthwaite to Huddersfield, clofely accompa-nying, and often crofling, the Coln. Its extreme length is nineteen miles and near three quarters; its fall from the head level is 436 feet on the Huddersfield fide, and 334 feet eight inches on the Afhton fide. Several of the little brooks in the hills are widened into refervoirs for its fupply of water. This navigation claims fimilar advantages with the Rochdale canal with refpect to general communication; and as it pafles through one of the moft populous tracts of the clothing country, it may expect a proportionate fhare of employment in the export and import of raw materials, manufactured goods, and other articles. The fup-ply of lime to the lands in its courfe is alfo likely to be very beneficial in promoting agricultural improvements.

PEAK-FOREST CANAL.

Another newly projected canal, called the Peak-foreft, the act for which pafled in March 1794, will augment the communications of the preceding navigation, as well as of the general fyftem. It proceeds from Milton near Chapel-le-Frith in the Peak of Derbyfhire, and en-tering Chefhire near Whalley-bridge (to which a branch is carried) crofles its eaftern horn by Difley, Marple, Mellor, and Chadkirk, and joins the Afhton-under-Lyne canal near Dukinfield-bridge. The great object of this undertaking is to convey at a cheap rate the lime with

which

LANCASTER CANAL.

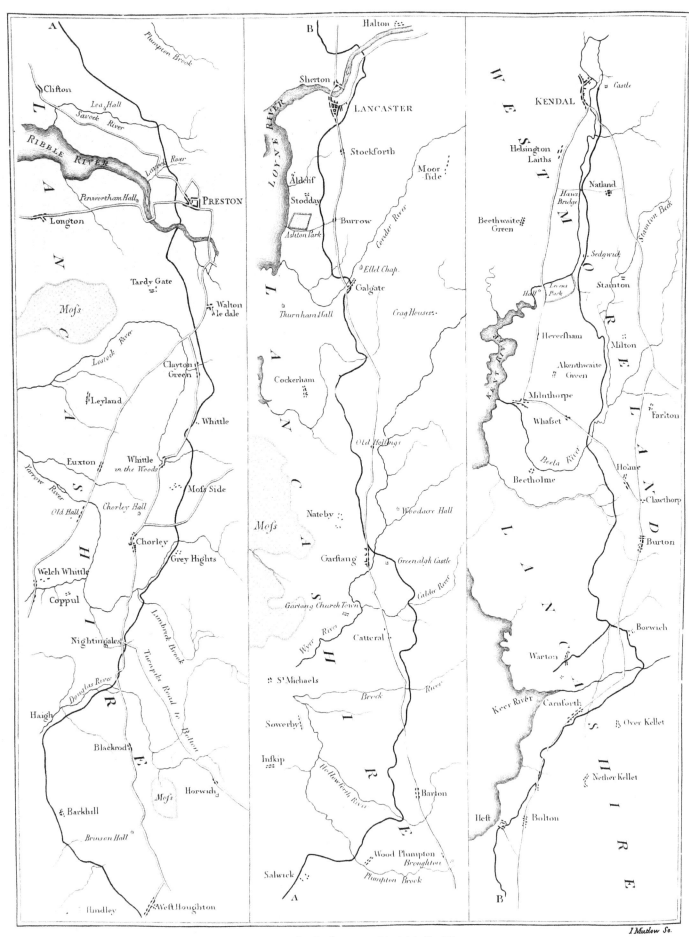

Published Jan.ʳ 2. 1795, by I. Stockdale, Piccadilly.

I Mutlow Sc.

which that part of the peak is ftored, to all the country of Chefhire, Yorkfhire, and Lancafhire, with which the canal communicates.

CROMFORD CANAL.

A new canal, which commences within the limits of our circle in Derbyfhire, begins at Cromford, and running fome way parallel to the Derwent, paffes Critch Frithley, Todmoor, Heage, and Heynor, and joins the Errewafh canal at Langley-bridge. Its total length is about fourteen miles, of which the firft eleven are level; the latter three have a fall of about eighty feet. There is a collateral cut to fome coal-works upon the level, about three miles in length. Befides feveral fmall tunnels, there is one on this canal of about 3000 yards. By this navigation a water-communication is eftablifhed between the centre of Derbyfhire and the Trent; and the reciprocal conveyance of coal and other mineral productions, as well as merchant-goods, to the feveral connected parts, cannot fail of being highly beneficial to the whole tract. Some of the moft important articles to be expected, are raw materials to, and manufactured goods from the very extenfive cotton works of Mr. Arkwright at Cromford, near Matlock, and Holme, near Bakewell; Mr. Strutt's large cotton factory at Belper; and another at Wirkfworth; the carriage of pigs of lead from different works; and the bufinefs of the iron-forge at Critch-chafe on the Derwent.

While thefe additional communications between the eaft and weft feas, and different parts of the interjacent country, were projecting, a new and fingular defign was fet on foot of carrying a canal from Weftmoreland to the centre of Lancafhire in a line parallel to the fea-coaft.

LANCASTER CANAL.

The Lancafter canal, for which an act was obtained in 1792, commences at Kendal, having a feeder from a rivulet about a mile beyond

the

the town. It proceeds directly fouthwards, and enters Lancafhire near Burton, having paffed under ground for about half a mile, near midway. At Borwick, a little fouth of Burton, it finks to its mid-level, which it preferves for more than forty-two miles, making for this purpofe a very winding courfe, in fome places approaching almoft clofe to the fea-beach. It croffes the Loyne a little above Lancafter in a magnificent aqueduct, and paffes by the eaft and fouth of that town. At Garftang it croffes the Wyre, and having made a bend weftward, by which it is brought within two miles of Kirkham, it next paffes the weftern fide of Prefton, and croffes the Ribble. Afcending then through a feries of locks, it croffes the Leeds and Liverpool canal, and reaches its higheft level, on which it proceeds a little to the eaftward of Chorley, acrofs the Douglas, through Haigh, (noted for its cannel pits) and bending to the eaft of Wigan, arrives at its termination at Weft Houghton. The whole of this courfe is feventy-five miles and upwards of five furlongs. The fall from Kendal to the mid-level is fixty-five feet; and the rife from thence on the fouthern fide, 222 feet. A collateral cut in the neighbourhood of Chorley is near three miles in length; and another near Borwick is near two miles and a half.

The principal objects of this canal are to make an interchange of product between the coal and lime-ftone countries, and to form a communication between the port of Lancafter and the interior parts to the north and fouth. All the country north of Chorley is deftitute of coal, with which it has hitherto been fupplied either by a burthenfome land-carriage, or by a coaft-wife navigation by means of the Douglas canal to the mouth of the Ribble. The prefent canal, in its tract from Chorley to Weft-Houghton, paffes through a country replete with inexhauftible ftores of coal of various fpecies. On the other hand, the

country

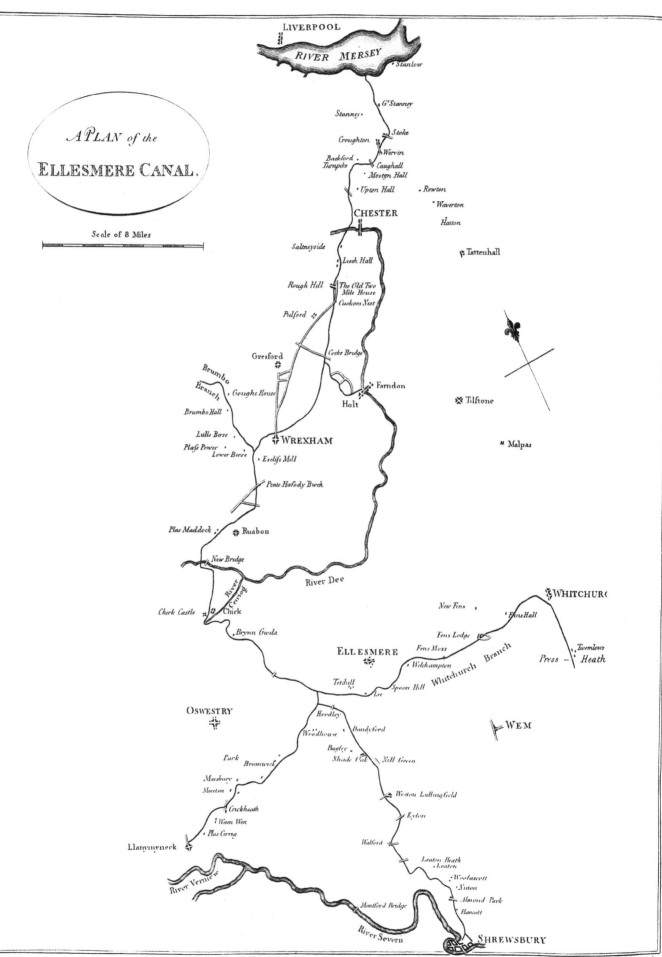

A PLAN of the
ELLESMERE CANAL.

Scale of 8 Miles

LIVERPOOL

RIVER MERSEY

Stanlow

G.r Stanney

Stanney

Stoke

Croughton

Wervin

Backford
Turnpike

Caughall

Mostyn Hall

Rowton

Upton Hall

Waverton

CHESTER

Hatton

Saltneyside

Tattenhall

Leech Hall

Rough Hill

The Old Two
Mile House

Cuckoos Nest

Pulford

Gresford

Cocks Bridge

Brumbo
Branch

Goughs House

Farndon

Holt

Brumbo Hall

Tilstone

Lulle Berse

WREXHAM

Plafs Power

Lower Berse

Ecclifs Mill

Malpas

Pente Hafody Bwch

Plas Maddock

Ruabon

New Bridge

River Dee

WHITCHURCH

River Ceriog

New Fens

Fens Hall

Chirk Castle

Chirk

Fens Lodge

Brynn Gwda

Fens Moss

Twemlows
Heath

Press

ELLESMERE

Welchampton

Tetchill

Lee

Spoon Hill

Whitchurch Branch

OSWESTRY

Herdley

Dandyford

WEM

Woodhouse

Bagley

Shade Oak

Nill Green

Park

Bromwich

Maesbury

Weston Lullingfield

Moreton

Eyton

Crickheath

Waen Wen

Walford

Plas Cerrig

Leaton Heath
Leaton

Llanymyneck

Woolascott
Yaton

River Verniew

Almond Park

Montford Bridge

Hancott

River Severn

SHREWSBURY

Published May. 16. 1795. by I. Stockdale, Piccadilly

I. Mutlow Sc.

country for fixteen miles to the fouth of Kendal is full of lime-ftone, of which all the northern part of Lancafhire is deftitute. The port of Lancafter, having a large importation of cotton as well as other foreign merchandize, will be enabled to convey its commodities on eafy terms to various populous and manufacturing places in the courfe of this canal. A confiderable part of this defign is completed.

ELLESMERE CANAL.

We have only one other navigation to mention, the termination of which is within our boundaries. It forms a direct junction between the Severn, and the Dee and Merfey, and is commonly called the Ellefmere canal. The act for it paffed in April 1793. Taking its rife at Shrewfbury, it firft bends to the north-weft, paffing near Ellefmere and Chirk, to the river Dee, which it croffes; and then turning north-eaft, it goes by Ruabon and Wrexham, to the city of Chefter, which it paffes on the weft fide, communicating with the navigable channel of the Dee. Hence it takes its courfe acrofs the neck of the peninfula of Wirral, to the eftuary of the Merfey. The whole length of this intended canal is fifty-five miles and a half; viz. from the Severn to the Dee at Chefter, forty-feven miles; from the Dee to the Merfey, about eight miles and a half. Several collateral branches are projected, viz. to Llanymynech, ten miles; to Whitchurch, fixteen miles fix furlongs; to Brumbo collieries, three miles; to Holt, three miles and a quarter. It will communicate with many extenfive collieries, lime-ftone, blue flate, and other quarries, iron-works, and lead-mines. It will connect three confiderable rivers; the town of Shrewfbury with the ports of Chefter and Liverpool, and thefe with each other; and will provide a large tract of intermediate country, with all the ufual advantages of an inland navigation, of which it is at prefent deftitute.

Of

Of the vaſt and multifarious deſigns above deſcribed, which a few late years have ſpread over this tract of country, all may be ſaid to be in a ſtate either of completion or of progreſs, though in different degrees. Of ſome, the immediate benefits are ſo apparent, that they have ſtimulated the undertakers to the moſt vigorous exertions. Others, which have great difficulties to encounter, and the objects and advantages of which have, perhaps, not been ſo deciſively conſidered, will probably require many years for their complete execution; nor is it unlikely that various deviations from the original plans may be made during the progreſs of the works. Competitions and interferences have ariſen between the different undertakings, in proportion as the number of them has increaſed, by which the proſpects of advantage which at firſt offered themſelves to the projectors have materially altered. In particular, the moſt extenſive of all the deſigns, the Leeds and Liverpool canal, ſince its commencement, has felt the rivalry of two nearer communications between the eaſt and weſt ſeas, and of a readier conveyance of coal from the middle to the northern parts of Lancaſhire; on which account a conſiderable variation of its courſe has been propoſed, as already mentioned.

Meantime, the prodigious additions made within a few years to the ſyſtem of inland navigation, now extended to almoſt every corner of the kingdom, cannot but impreſs the mind with magnificent ideas of the opulence, the ſpirit, and the enlarged views which characterize the commercial intereſt of this country. Nothing ſeems too bold for it to undertake, too difficult for it to atchieve; and ſhould no external changes produce a durable check to the national proſperity, its future progreſs is beyond the reach of calculation. Yet experience may teach us, that the ſpirit of project and ſpeculation is not always the ſource

of

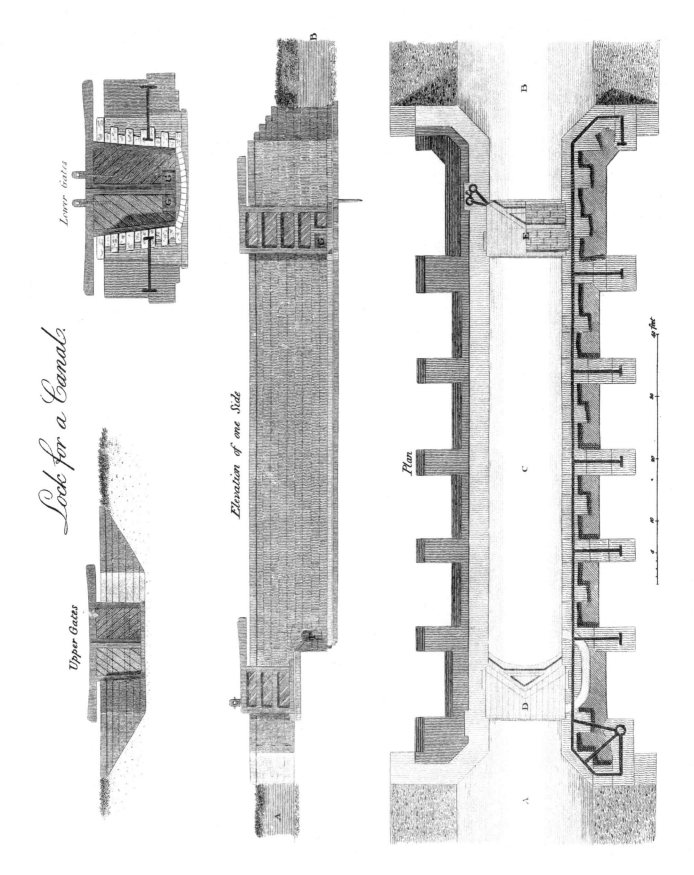

Lock for a Canal.

Upper Gates

Lower Gates

Elevation of one Side

Plan

40 Feet

Plate 2

Aqueduct for a Canal.

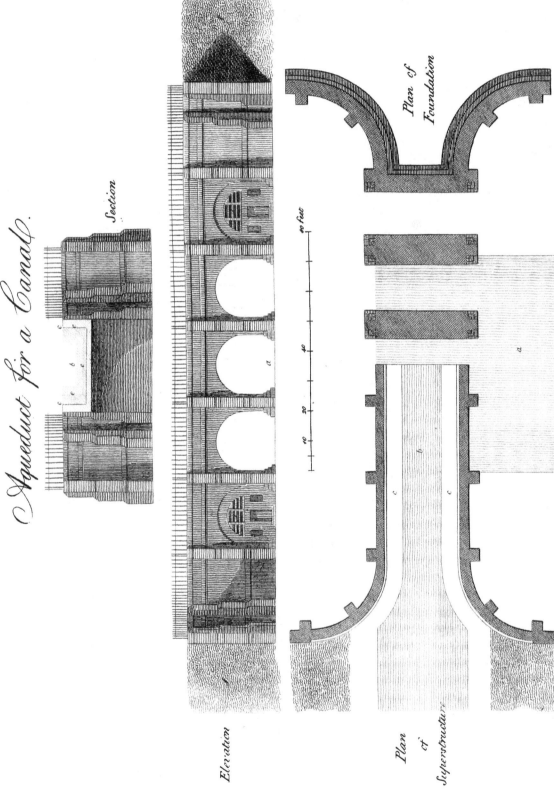

Section

Elevation

Plan of Foundation

Plan of Superstructure

Publish'd Dec.ʳ 22. 1794. by I. Stockdale. Piccadilly.

of folid advantage, and poffibly the unbounded extenfion of canal navigation may in part have its fource in the paffion for bold and precarious adventure, which fcorns to be limited by reafonable calculations of profit. Nothing but highly flourifhing manufactures can repay the vaft expenfe of thefe defigns. The town of Manchefter, when the plans now under execution are finifhed, will probably enjoy more various water-communications than the moft commercial town of the Low Countries has ever done. And inftead of cutting them through level tracts, fo as only to make a wider ditch, its canals are carried over mountainous diftricts, where the fole method of avoiding the difficulties of fteep afcent and defcent, has been to bore through the very heart of hills, and navigate for miles within the bowels of the earth. At the beginning of this century it was thought a moft arduous tafk to make a *high road* practicable for carriages over the hills and moors which feparate Yorkfhire from Lancafhire; and now they are pierced through by *three navigable canals!* Long may it remain the centre of a trade capable of maintaining thefe mighty works!

It has been thought proper to add to this chapter fome plates illuftrative of canal navigation, with their explanations, from *Mr. Phillips's Hiftory of Inland Navigation.*

DESCRIPTION *of Plate I. which fhews the* PLAN, *&c. of a* LOCK *for a* CANAL.

A. The upper water of the canal.
B. Lower ditto.
C. Chamber of the lock.
D. The platforms on which the upper gates are hung.

T   E. The

E.   The lower ditto, fhewing the manner of conftruction.

F.   Sluices through which the water paffes into the chamber, to raife it equal with the upper level.

G.   Paddles in the gates, to reduce the water to the lower level. There is a *chain-bar*, run with lead in a courfe of ftone, fet at water level.

Plate II. fhews a defign for an aqueduct which croffes a river the width of the three centre arches; and, to occupy the remaining fpace ufefully, the extreme arches are converted into warehoufes.

a. The river. b. The canal. c. Towing-path. d. Warehoufes. e. A bed (technically a *punn*) of clay, to prevent the water weeping through the arches. f. The canal continued by embankment.

Plate III.   *Elevation, &c. of a bridge.*

a. The canal. b. Plan of the foundation. c. Towing-path under the bridge. d. Plan of the fuperftructure.

Alfo, a canal in its courfe often divides lands with which fome communication is neceffary for the purpofes of hufbandry. The eafieft method is fhewn on plate IV. This is called *an accommodation bridge*. It hangs by large hooks and eyes, or hinges, and is worked up and down with eafe, by means of the balance poles. This view alfo fhews a towing-path gate, which is ufed for dividing grounds, and is hung fo as always to fall to.

A bio-

Plate 3

Bridge for a Canal.

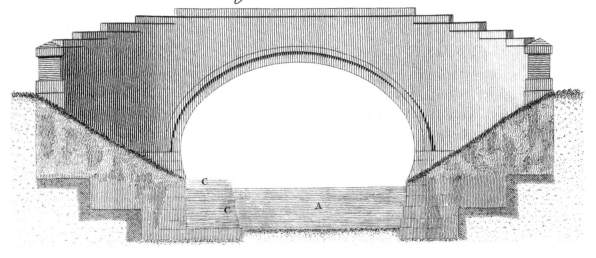

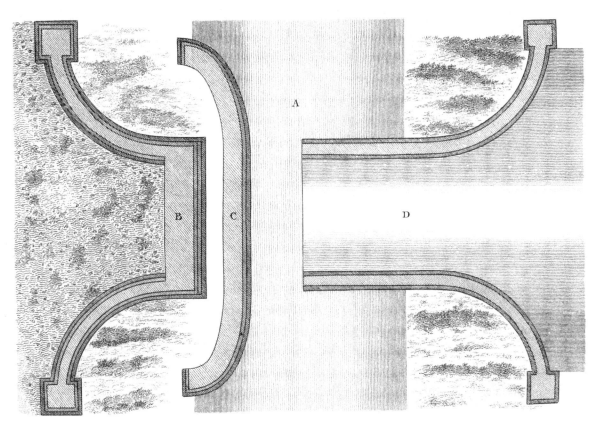

Publifh'd Dec.ᵣ 22, 1794, by I. Stockdale, Piccadilly.

Accommodation Bridge for a Canal.

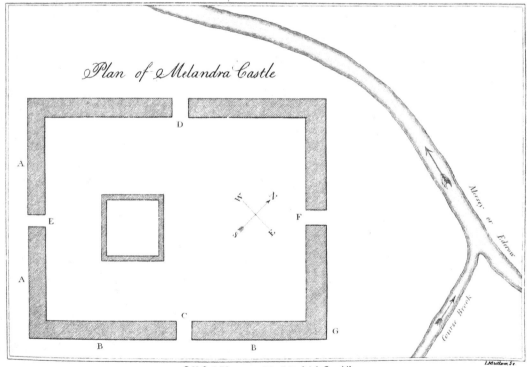

Plan of Melandra Castle

Published May 27. 1795. by I. Stockdale. Piccadilly

I. Mutlow. Sc.

A biographical account of the late celebrated *Brindley* properly belongs to this work, as he was born within the limits of its inquiries; but from the intimate connection between his life and the fystem of canal navigation, it is imagined that fuch an account will be read with more intereft and advantage in this place, than where it would have come in according to the order of the work.

ACCOUNT of Mr. BRINDLEY.

JAMES BRINDLEY was born at Tunfted in the parifh of Wormhill, Derbyfhire, in 1716. His father was a fmall freeholder, who diffipated his property in company and field-amufements, and neglected his family. In confequence, young Brindley was left deftitute of even the common rudiments of education, and till the age of feventeen was cafually employed in ruftic labours. At that period he bound himfelf apprentice to one Bennet, a mill-wright, at Macclesfield, in Chefhire, where his mechanical genius prefently developed itfelf. The mafter being frequently abfent, the apprentice was often left for weeks together to finifh pieces of work concerning which he had received no inftruction; and Bennet on his return was often greatly aftonifhed to fee improvements in various parts of mechanifm of which he had no previous conception. It was not long before the millers difcovered Brindley's merits, and preferred him in the execution of their orders to the mafter or any other workman. At the expiration of his fervitude, Bennet being grown into years, he took the management of the bufinefs upon

T 2   himfelf;

himfelf ; and by his fkill and induftry contributed to fupport his old mafter and his family in a comfortable manner.

In procefs of time, Brindley fet up as a mill-wright on his own account, and by a number of new and ingenious contrivances greatly improved that branch of mechanics, and acquired a high reputation in the neighbourhood. His fame extending to a wider circle, he was employed in 1752 to erect a water-engine at Clifton, in Lancafhire, for the purpofe of draining fome coal-mines. Here he gave an effay of his abilities in a kind of work for which he was afterwards fo much diftinguifhed, driving a tunnel under ground through a rock nearly 600 yards in length, by which water was brought out of the Irwell for the purpofe of turning a wheel fixed thirty feet below the furface of the earth. In 1755 he was employed to execute the larger wheels for a filk mill at Congleton; and another perfon, who was engaged to make other parts of the machinery, and to fuperintend the whole, proving incapable of completing the work, the bufinefs was entirely committed to Brindley ; who not only executed the original plan in a mafterly manner, but made the addition of many curious and valuable improvements, as well in the conftruction of the engine itfelf, as in the method of making the wheels and pinions belonging to it. About this time, too, the mills for grinding flints in the Staffordfhire potteries received various ufeful improvements from his ingenuity.

In the year 1756 he undertook to erect a fteam-engine upon a new plan at Newcaftle-under-Line ; and he was for a time very intent upon a variety of contrivances for improving this ufeful piece of mechanifm. But from thefe defigns he was, happily for the public, called away to take the lead in what the event has proved to be a national con-

I   cern

cern of capital importance—the projecting the fyſtem of *canal naviga-tion*.—The duke of Bridgewater, who had formed his defign of carry-ing a canal from his coal-works at Worſley to Mancheſter, was in-duced by the reputation of Mr. Brindley to conſult him on the execu-tion of it; and having the fagacity to perceive, and ſtrength of mind to confide in, the original and commanding abilities of this ſelf-taught genius, he committed to him the management of the arduous undertaking. The nature and progreſs of this enterpriſe have already been deſcribed; it is enough here to mention, that Mr. Brindley, from the very firſt, adopted thoſe leading principles in the projecting of theſe works, which he ever afterwards adhered to, and in which he has been imitated by all ſucceeding artiſts. To preſerve as much as poſſible the level of his canals, and to avoid the mixture and interference of all natural ſtreams, were objects at which he conſtantly aimed. To accompliſh theſe, no labour and expenfe was ſpared; and his genius feemed to delight in overcoming all obſtacles to them by the difcovery of new and extra-ordinary contrivances.

The moſt experienced engineers upon former fyſtems were amazed and confounded at his projects of aqueduct bridges over navigable rivers, mounds acroſs deep vallies, and ſubterraneous tunnels; nor could they believe in the practicability of fome of theſe fchemes till they faw them effected. In the execution, the ideas he followed were all his own; and the minuteſt, as well as the greateſt, of the expedi-ents he employed, bore the ſtamp of originality. Every man of ge-nius is an enthuſiaſt. Mr. Brindley was an enthuſiaſt in favour of the fuperiority of canal navigations above thoſe of rivers; and this triumph of art over nature led him to view with a fort of contempt the winding ſtream, in which the lover of rural beauty fo much delights. This

fenti-

fentiment he is faid to have expreffed in a ftriking manner at an examination before a committee of the Houfe of Commons, when on being
afked, after he had made fome contemptuous remarks relative to rivers,
what he conceived they were created for :—he anfwered, " To feed
" navigable canals."—A direct rivalry with the navigation of the Irwell and Merfey, was the bold enterprize of his firft great canal ; and
fince the fuccefs of that defign, it has become common all over the
kingdom to fee canals accompanying with infulting parallel the courfe
of navigable rivers.

After the fuccefsful execution of the duke of Bridgewater's canal to
the Merfey, Mr. Brindley was employed in the revived defign of carrying a canal from that river to the Trent, through the counties of
Chefter and Stafford. This undertaking commenced in the year 1766 ;
and from the great ideas it opened to the mind of its conductor, of a
fcheme of inland navigation which fhould connect all the internal parts
of England with each other, and with the principal fea-ports, by means
of *branches* from this main ftem, he gave it the emphatical name of
the *Grand Trunk*. In executing this, he was called upon to employ
all the refources of his invention, on account of the inequality and various nature of the ground to be cut through : in particular, the hill of
Harecaftle, which was only to be paffed by a tunnel of great length,
bored through ftrata of different confiftency, and fome of them mere
quickfand, proved to be a moft difficult as well as expenfive obftacle,
which, however, he completely furmounted. While this was carrying
on, a branch from the Grand Trunk to join the Severn near Bewdley
was committed to his management, and was finifhed in 1772. He
alfo executed a canal from Droitwich to the Severn ; and he planned
the Coventry canal, and for fome time fuperintended its execution, but

on account of fome difference in opinion, he refigned that office. The Chefterfield canal was the laft undertaking of the kind which he conducted, but he only lived to finifh fome miles of it. There was, however, fcarcely any defign of canal-navigation fet on foot in the kingdom during the latter years of his life in which he was not confulted, and the plan of which he did not either entirely form, or revife and improve. All thefe it is needlefs to enumerate; but as an inftance of the vaftnefs of his ideas, it may be mentioned, that on planning a canal from Liverpool to join that of the duke of Bridgewater at Runcorn, it was part of his intention to carry it by an aqueduct bridge acrofs the Merfey, at Runcorn-gap, a place where a tide fometimes rifing fourteen feet rufhes with great rapidity through a fudden contraction of the channel. As a mechanic and engineer he was likewife confulted on other occafions; as with refpect to the draining of the low lands in different parts of Lincolnfhire and the ifle of Ely, and to the cleanfing of the docks of Liverpool from mud. He pointed out a method which has been fuccefsfully practifed, of building fea-walls without mortar; and he was the author of a very ingenious improvement of the machine for drawing water out of mines by the contrivance of a lofing and a gaining bucket.

The intenfity of application which all his various and complicated employments required, probably fhortened his days; as the number of his undertakings, in fome degree, impaired his ufefulnefs. He fell into a kind of chronic fever, which, after continuing fome years with little intermiffion, at length wore out his frame, and put a period to his life on September 27th, 1772, in the 56th year of his age. He died at Turnhurft, in Staffordfhire, and was buried at New Chapel in the fame county.

In

In appearance and manners, as well as in acquirements, Mr. Brindley was a mere peafant. Unlettered and rude of fpeech, it was eafier for him to devife means for executing a defign, than to communicate his ideas concerning it to others. Formed by nature for the profeffion he affumed, it was there alone that he was in his proper element; and fo occupied was his mind with his bufinefs, that he was incapable of relaxing in any of the common amufements of life. As he had not the ideas of other men to affift him, whenever a point of difficulty in contrivance occurred, it was his cuftom to retire to his bed, where in perfect folitude he would lie for one, two, or three days, pondering the matter in his mind, till the requifite expedient had prefented itfelf. This is that true *infpiration*, which poets have almoft exclufively arrogated to themfelves, but which men of original genius in every walk are actuated by, when from the operation of the mind acting upon itfelf, without the intrufion of foreign notions, they create and invent. A remarkably retentive memory was one of the effential qualities which Mr. Brindley brought to his mental operations. This enabled him to execute all the parts of the moft complex machine in due order, without any help of models or drawings, provided he had once accurately fettled the whole plan in his mind. In his calculations of the powers of machines, he followed a plan peculiar to himfelf; but, indeed, the only one he could follow without inftruction in the rules of art. He would work the queftion fome time in his head, and then fet down the refult in figures. Then taking it up in this ftage, he would again proceed by a mental operation to another refult; and thus he would go on by ftages till the whole was finifhed, only making ufe of figures to mark the feveral refults of his operations. But though, by the wonderful powers of native genius, he was thus enabled to get over his want of artificial method to a certain degree, yet there is no doubt,

that

that when his concerns became extremely complicated, with accounts of various kinds to keep, and calculations of all forts to form, he could not avoid that perplexity and embarraffment which a readinefs in the proceffes carried on by pen and paper can alone obviate. His eftimates of expenfe have generally proved wide of reality ; and he feems to have been better qualified to be the contriver, than the manager, of a great defign. His moral qualities were, however, highly refpectable. He was far above envy and jealoufy, and freely communicated his improvements to perfons capable of receiving and executing them ; taking a liberal fatisfaction in forming a new generation of engineers able to proceed with the great plans in the fuccefs of which he was fo deeply interefted. His integrity and regard to the advantage of his employers were unimpeachable. In fine, the name of *Brindley* will ever keep a place among that fmall number of mankind, who form *eras* in the art or fcience to which they devote themfelves, by a large and durable extenfion of their limits.

U   PART

PART II.

ACCOUNTS OF PARTICULAR PLACES.

I.—*LANCASHIRE.*

SALFORD HUNDRED.

MANCHESTER.

THIS diftinguifhed town, one of the firft with refpect to commercial confequence in England, and the centre of our prefent undertaking, has been dignified by a very learned and ingenious hiftorian of
its earlieft ftages, the *Rev. Mr. Whitaker.* The elaborate work of that
writer rather deferves, however, to be confidered as an account of the
ftate of this ifland in general, during its early periods, than as the hiftory of a fingle town, then of little comparative confequence, and the
principal events of which are rather to be deduced from inference, than
to be laid down from authentic monuments or records. What alone
appears certain is, that the Roman invaders of this country fixed a ftation for a body of troops in a place fince called *Caftlefield*, to which
they gave the appellation of *Mancunium*, probably borrowed from a

U 2

name

name given it by the Britifh inhabitants of the vicinity ;—that a town was raifed in the neighbourhood of the ftation, probably on the fite of the prefent *Aldporton*, where a caftle was built, which had the name of *Mancaftle*; and that the erection of a parifh church in the Saxon times drew round it a new town on the banks of the Irwell, the commencement of the prefent *Manchefter*, and caufed the old one to be deferted. Mr. Whitaker fixes the date of this new town to be A. D. 627.

In the Danifh invafion and conqueft of the kingdom of Northumberland, towards the latter end of the ninth century, Manchefter, in common with many other towns, was totally or in great part deftroyed. At this time it was a borough or city; and about 920 it appears, that Edward king of the Mercians gave orders for the fortifying of the city of Manchefter, and placing a garrifon in it. Doomfday book mentions a church of St. Mary, and a church of St. Michael, as being in *Mamceftre*, which it calls a manor or hundred. In 1301, Thomas Grelle granted to the burgeffes of Manchefter a charter conftituting it a free borough with certain privileges. This perfon was likewife patron of the church. In 1313 John de la Warr, knight, was lord of the manor and patron. The manor-houfe ftood in or near the place where the college now ftands, and was called Baron's court, or Baron's yard.

Thomas lord de la Warr, the laft male heir of that family, who was firft rector of Manchefter, and then fucceeded to the peerage, procured a licenfe in the ninth year of Henry V. 1422, for founding a collegiate church at Manchefter. The college confifted of a warden and eight fellows, of whom two were parifh priefts, two canons, and four deacons, two clerks and fix chorifters. The building of the houfe coft at that time 300*l*. and to the value of twelve lordfhips were beftowed by

the

S. Daye del.

Recard sculp.

VIEW OF CHRIST'S CHURCH.

Published July 10 1791, by I. Stockdale, Piccadilly.

the founder on the college and to other pious ufes. At that period the following lift of prices of commodities is given, continuing to the year 1524.

	£.	s.	d.		£	s.	d.
A horfe, - - -	2	4	0	A calf, - - - -	0	4	1
An ox, - - - -	1	15	8	A cock, - - - -	0	0	3
A cow, - - - -	0	15	6	A hen, - - - -	0	0	2
A colt, - - - -	0	7	8	Wheat per quarter, -	0	11	3
A fheep, - - - -	0	5	0	Ale per gallon, - -	0	0	2
A hog, - - - -	0	5	0	Day labourer's wages,	0	0	3

About the time of the foundation of the college the prefent fabric of Chrift's Church, ufually called the Old Church, appears to have been erected. Who contributed moft to the building is not certainly known; but the names and arms of the Stanleys, Wefts, Radclyffes, Byroms, and others, witnefs their affiftance. The church is a fine gothic ftructure, much ornamented with fculpture on the outfide, and enriched with curious tabernacle-work over the ftalls in the choir; with feveral chapels within, belonging to confiderable families in the neighbourhood.

Manchefter was now become a place of note. Cambden, fpeaking of the town in his time, mentions its having been famous in the laft age for its manufacture of ftuffs, called *Manchefter cottons*, which were a fpecies of *woollen* cloths. It is alfo recorded, that about 1520 there were three famous clothiers living in the north country, viz. Cuthbert of *Kendal*, Hodgefkins of *Halifax*, and Martin Brian (fome fay Byrom) of *Manchefter*. Each of thefe kept a great number of fervants at work, fpinners, carders, weavers, fullers, dyers, fhearmen, &c. This Martin is alfo related to have given much money towards the

building

building of a free-school at Manchester; which institution, however, did not take place till some time after.

Leland, who travelled through the kingdom in the reign of Henry VIII. mentions *Mancestre* as " the fairest, best-builded, quickest, and " most populous town of Lancashire." He says, " It has but one " parish church, but that collegiate, and almost throughout double- " isled with very hard squared stone. There are several stone bridges " in the town, but the best, of three arches, is over the Irwell, di- " viding Manchester from Salford, which is a large suburb to Man- " chester. On this bridge is a pretty little chapel. The next is the ' bridge over Hirke (Irk) river, on which the very fair-builded college " stands. On this river are divers fair mills that serve the town. In " the town are two market-places.

Hugh Oldham, bishop of Exeter, a native of Oldham in Lanca- shire, who died in the year 1519, founded a free grammar-school in Manchester, and endowed it with certain lands, and a long lease which he had purchased of the corn mills of Manchester: and in 1524, Hugh Bexwick, clerk, and Joanna Bexwick, widow, made a full convey- ance of the property of the said mills, lands, and tenements, to trustees for accomplishing the same purpose. In the ordinances concerning the school, it is directed, that no scholar or male infant of whatever coun- try or shire be refused admission. The choice of the head-master and usher is vested in the President of Corpus Christi Coll. in Oxford for the time being, and on his default, in the warden of Manchester college.

Manchester having been originally a place of sanctuary, was one of the eight places to whom this privilege was confirmed by stat. 32 Hen. VIII.

5   A. D,

A. D. 1540; but the next year, the privilege having been found prejudicial to the " wealth, credit, great occupyings, and good order" of Manchefter, was transferred to Chefter, which (fays the ftatute) had no fuch trade and merchandize, and had a ftrong goal, and a mayor, bailiffs, &c.

By an act of parliament in the firft of Edward VI. the college of Manchefter was diffolved, and the land and revenues belonging to it were taken into the king's hand, and by him demifed to Edward earl of Derby, who, however, took care to provide three or four minifters to officiate in the church. Queen Mary refounded the college, and re-ftored almoft all the lands, the earl of Derby ftill keeping the colle-giate houfe and fome fmall things.

A document concerning the trade of Manchefter occurs in an act paffed fifth and fixth of Edward VI. 1552, entitled, for the true ma-king of woollen cloth; in which it is ordered, " That all the cottons " called *Manchefter, Lancafhire,* and *Chefhire* cottons, full wrought " to the fale, fhall be in length twenty-two yards, and contain in " breadth three quarters of a yard in the water, and fhall weigh thirty " pound in the piece at the leaft. Alfo, that all other clothes called *Man-* " *chefter rugs,* otherwife named *Manchefter frizes,* fully wrought for " fale, fhall contain in length thirty-fix yards, and in breadth three " quarters of a yard coming out of the water, and fhall not be ftretched " on the tenter or otherwife above a nail of a yard in breadth, and " being fo fully wrought and well dried, fhall weigh every piece forty- " eight pound at the leaft."—From this it is clear that the Manchefter cottons at that period were made of wool. An act paffed in 1557 to

amend

amend the above act, recites in the same terms the Manchester, Lancashire, and Cheshire manufactures.

In the eighth of Q. Elizabeth 1565, an act was passed respecting the fees of the queen's *Aulneger* (the officer appointed to examine and set the seal to manufactured cloth) for the county of Lancaster. In the preamble to this act it is recited, " That it has been a practice with " divers clothiers inhabiting the said county, to send clandestinely " out of it cottons, frizes, and rugs, without being previously sealed " by the queen's Aulneger, and sometimes counterfeiting and setting " to their clothes seals of their own." For the prevention of this, the towns of *Manchester, Rochdale, Bolton, Blackburn*, and *Bury*, are appointed, wherein the Aulneger is to have his deputies. His fees are regulated by the act, and the requisite length, breadth, and weight of the cottons, rugs, and frizes are determined.

In the twentieth year of Queen Elizabeth, A. D. 1578, a new foundation was given to the college by her Majesty, in which it is incorporated by the name of *Christ's Coll. in Manchester*, and made to consist of one warden priest, by degrees batchelor of divinity; four fellows, priests, batchelors of arts; two chaplains or vicars; four singing men, and four children; the warden to be appointed by the crown, the fellows and others to be elected by the warden and fellows. In the preamble to this foundation, the number of parishioners residing in the town of Manchester is asserted to be ten thousand.

In the year 1605, the town was visited by a pestilence, of which upwards of 1000 persons are said to have died.

In

The college having fuffered great loffes from mifmanagement and ufurpation of its revenues, was re-founded by king Charles I. in the year 1635. The chief alterations made by this foundation were to abridge the power of the wardens and augment that of the fellows, and to confine the power of granting leafes to tenants to twenty-one years, inftead of three lives as formerly. The fines which accrued for fome time, were applied to the repairing and beautifying the church, which had become greatly dilapidated.

At the breaking out of the civil war in 1642, poffeffion was taken of Manchefter in behalf of the Parliament by the militia of the country, who were joined by many of the inhabitants and people of the vicinity; and fortifications were thrown up at the end of the ftreets. At this time the town chiefly confifted of Market-ftreet-lane, Dean's-gate, Miln-gate, and a few ftreets about the market-place. In September 1642, the earl of Derby marched from Warrington with a force of about 4000 foot and 300 horfe, with feven pieces of ordnance, in order to feize upon Manchefter for the King. On being refufed admiffion, he commenced an affault upon the defenders from Salford and the end of Dean's-gate, which proving unfuccefsful, he retired after a few days. This petty attempt, in which the town is faid to have loft only four men killed and as many wounded, cannot but give a contemptible idea of the ftate of military fkill in this ifland at the commencement of thofe troubles. In the next year the town was fortified and ftrongly garrifoned, and it continued in the hands of the Parliament during the remainder of the war.

By an ordinance of Parliament dated 9th December, 1645, it appears that Manchefter had for a long time been fuffering under a peftilence,

X   fo

fo that for many months none had been permitted to come in or to go out. In confequence of this, (the ordinance fays) " moft of the inha-" bitants living upon trade are not only ruined in their eftates, but " many families are like to perifh for want, who cannot be fufficiently " relieved by that miferable, wafted country." On this account the Parliament orders that a collection be made for the poor of the faid town in all the churches and chapels of London and Weftminfter; the money to be tranfmitted to Mr. John Hartley, of Manchefter.

A Defcription of the towns of Manchefter and Salford annexed to a plan of the towns taken about 1650, affords the following circumftances of information. It is to be obferved, however, that the defcription is written in a very turgid ftyle, abounding in terms of exaggeration.

The people in and about the town are faid to be in general the moft induftrious in their callings of any in the northern parts of this kingdom. The town is a mile in length, the ftreets open and clean kept, and the buildings good. There are four market-places; two market days weekly, and three fairs yearly. The trade is not inferior to that of many cities in the kingdom, chiefly confifting in *woollen frizes, fuftians, fack-cloths, mingled ftuffs, caps, inkles, tapes, points,* &c. whereby not only the better fort of men are employed, but alfo the very children by their own labour can maintain themfelves. There are befides, all kinds of foreign merchandize brought and returned by the merchants of the town, amounting to the fum of many thoufands of pounds weekly. There are in the town forty-eight fubfidy-men, befides a great number of burgeffes; and four quarter-feffions are held in it. The town is governed by a fteward, a head-borough, aad two confta-bles, with a deputy-conftable, and feveral inferior officers; and great

commen-

commendation is given to the regular and orderly manner in which things are conducted. The parish is said to be at least twenty-two miles in compass, within which are eight chapels; and to contain above twenty-seven thousand communicants. This last number appears to be totally incredible.

The town was dismantled of its fortifications in 1652.

Humphrey Cheetham, Esq. of Clayton, by his will dated Dec. 16, 1651, founded and endowed an hospital and library in Manchester. The purpose of the hospital was to maintain and educate forty poor boys to the age of fourteen, when they were to be bound apprentice or otherwise provided for. They were to be elected out of various town-ships named in the will; and it is recommended to the trustees to purchase the old college for a place of residence for the children, and for the use of the library. For commencing the library, a thousand pounds are bequeathed to be expended in books; and the residue of his personal estate is given for the augmentation of the library. The college was accordingly purchased; and by a charter granted by Charles II. in 1665, the trustees of this noble charity were incorporated into a body politic.

What the increase of the town was during the latter part of the last century does not appear from any authentic documents; but probably it was not very considerable. From the register of the collegiate church, the average number of burials appears to have been,

From 1580 to 1587 inclusive, 184.
From 1680 to 1687   286.
From 1720 to 1727   359.

It

It was not till 1708 that an act paffed for the erection of another church or chapel, St. Ann's. An account of the inhabitants taken in 1717 ftates them at 8000. From that period the increafe has been rapid. An act for a third church, St. Mary's, was obtained in 1753. In 1757, on account of an application to Parliament in order to exonerate the town from the obligation of grinding its corn at the mills belonging to the free-fchool, which were now unable to fupply its wants in a proper manner, two enumerations were made by the oppofite parties, which came within 1000 of each other. The number moft to be confided in, for Manchefter and Salford conjointly, appears to have been 19,839.

In 1773 a furvey of Manchefter was executed with accuracy, which gave the following refults:

	Manchefter.	Salford.	Total.
Houfes (inhabited	3402	866	4268
Families,	5317	1099	6416
Male inhabitants,	10,548	2248	12,796
Female ditto,	11,933	2517	14,450
Both fexes,	22,481	4765	27,246

Perfons to a houfe, 6⅓   To a family, 4¼.

At the fame period, the townfhip of Manchefter (detached from the town) contained 311 houfes, 361 families, 947 males, 958 females; total, 1905.

And the whole parifh of Manchefter, comprizing thirty-one townfhips in a compafs of fixty fquare miles, contained 2371 houfes, 2525 families, 6942 males, 6844 females; total, 13,786 inhabitants.

The

The whole number, then, of inhabitants in the town, townſhip, and pariſh of Mancheſter, and in Salford, amounted to 42,927.

At Chriſtmas 1788, the numbers by enumeration were, in the townſhip of Mancheſter, 5916 houſes, 8570 families, 42,821 perſons ; in the townſhip of Salford, about 1260 houſes. The whole number of people in both towns might then be reckoned at more than 50,000.

During the year 1791, the chriſtenings in theſe towns amounted to 2960 ; the burials to 2286. Theſe numbers, by the uſual mode of calculating, will give from ſixty-five to ſeventy-four thouſand inhabitants—an increaſe almoſt unparalleled!

Having thus traced to the preſent period the progreſs of population in Mancheſter, we ſhall give a ſummary account of that of the trade and manufactures, by which the population is ſupported.

It has been ſeen that the original trade of this place was in thoſe coarſe woollen fabrics which were eſtabliſhed in various parts of the north of England ; but that, as long ago as the middle of laſt century, it was alſo noted for the making of fuſtians, mixed ſtuffs, and ſmall wares. An original branch of the trade of Mancheſter was leather laces for women's boddice, ſhoe ties, and points for other uſes, which were tagged like laces, and ſold under the general denomination of *Congleton points*. Theſe were ſlips of leather dyed various colours. Upon the introduction of Dutch looms, woven laces were ſubſtituted to theſe, and tagged in like manner. Inkle, tapes, and filleting, which had before been made in frames or ſingle looms, were now like-

2   wiſe

wife wrought in thefe new engines; and coarfe felts were made for country wear, but none of finer quality. Bolfters, bed-ticks, linen-girth-web, and boot-ftraps were manufactured here as early as 1700; but the weft of England has long out-rivalled Manchefter in ticks and webs, though it keeps its fuperiority in woollen webs. Sixty years fince, upon the decline of ticks, the manufacturers in that branch took more to the making of coarfe checks, ftriped hollands, and hooping, and fome yellow canvas was then made. At the fame time the filk branch was attempted in cherry-derrys and thread fatins. Fuftians were manufactured about Bolton, Leigh, and the places adjacent; but Bolton was the principal market for them, where they were bought in the grey by the Manchefter chapmen, who finifhed and fold them in the country. The fuftians were made as early as the middle of laft century, when Mr. Cheetham, who founded the blue-coat hofpital, was the principal buyer at Bolton. When he had made his markets, the remainder was purchafed by a Mr. Cooke, a much lefs honourable dealer, who took the advantage of calling the pieces what length he pleafed, and giving his own price. The Manchefter traders went regularly on market days to buy pieces of fuftian of the weaver; each weaver then procuring yarn or cotton as he could, which fubjected the trade to great inconvenience. To remedy this, fome of the chapmen furnifhed warps and wool to the weavers, and employed perfons on commiffion to put out warps to the weavers. They alfo encouraged weavers to fetch them from Man-chefter, and by prompt payment and good ufage endeavoured to fecure good workmanfhip.

The kinds of fuftian then made were herring-bones, pillows for pockets and outfide wear, ftrong cotton ribs and barragon, broad-raced lin·thickfets and tufts, dyed, with whited diapers, ftriped dimities,

and

and lining jeans   Cotton thickfets were made fometimes, but as frequently dropped for want of proper finifhing. Tufts were much in demand at that time, and reached their full perfection, in refpect to the price.   The Irifh were particularly fond of them, till fome of the leading people there found means to get them out of ufe.   When tufts ceafed to be in demand, more figured goods were made for whiting, and a greater variety of patterns attempted, by weavers, who had looms ready mounted for the former purpofes. But as figures made with treadles are confined to a fcanty range, beyond which they grow too complicated, the workmen had recourfe to the ufe of draw-boys, which gave name to a new and important branch of trade.   Some yard-wides being made upon this plan were bought up with avidity, and great encouragement was given to the moft ingenious weavers, and looms were mounted for them by their employers at a great expenfe.   In the fubfequent courfe of trade, great ftocks of thefe draw-boys have come to lie on hand, and the article has met with great checks; yet the variety of figures it is capable of exhibiting, the diftinctnefs of quality in the forts, the many ufes to which it is adapted, and its cheapnefs upon the whole, have rendered it a ftanding branch of trade; although quilting with draw-boys upon an improved plan invented above forty years fince, counterpanes, and the various kinds of corded dimities lately introduced, have rivalled it.

About the time when draw-boys were firft made, cotton velvets were attempted, and brought to fome perfection in the manufacturing part; and cotton thickfets were well manufactured; but thefe wanted the prefent methods of dreffing, bleaching, dying, and finifhing, to give them the general perfection they have now obtained.

The

The manufacturers of check had by this time made great advances, and introduced new articles; for as the coarse and narrow goods were chiefly made for sea use, or sent to the plantations abroad, upon the conclusion of a peace, or a glut of the foreign markets, the demands fell off; whence the manufacturers made broader checks, besides the yard-wides of a finer and better quality, for home consumption. Gowns striped acrofs with cotton in a variety of patterns and colours were introduced sixty years ago, and had a confiderable run; and silk was at last shot with the cotton, which gave them superior richness, and contributed to greater variety in the patterns. To these succeeded washing hollands, all cotton in the warp, which were a valued article, till yarn was mixed with the warp, and ruined their character. But the methods of hardening and stiffening single cotton, and the facility with which it had been wrought in these hollands, induced some capital houses about fifty years since, to undertake the manufacture of slight cotton goods for the African trade, upon a failure of imports from the East Indies. In this they succeeded, and had large demands, though they were afraid of a stock, since the East India Company could command the article, and sometimes gave them a check. But the Company seem to have given up the object; and this branch of trade continued till the unhappy contest with America interrupted the intercourse with Africa.

An application of the lighter open striped checks to bed-hangings and window-curtains forty years since introduced the making of furniture checks, which have almost set aside the use of stuffs in upholstery. The use of soft coloured silk in striped gowns was followed by the introduction of it in warps for the several species of ginghams, damasks, morees, &c. The tying and dying of silk handkerchiefs is brought to great perfection, so as to imitate those imported from India; and the

variety

variety of printed handkerchiefs here, both cotton and linen, is scarcely to be enumerated.

The perfecting of silk handkerchiefs was owing to Mr. Richard Meadowcroft, who, in 1770, observing a poor family, that had usually been employed in the tying, destitute of work, found that the reason was, the want of dying them properly. Having a turn to chymistry, he made experiments till he produced fast colours in different shades of chocolate, and a colour approaching to scarlet, which he long kept to himself, and established the article to his own deserved emolument. The tying is now extended to fine callico, and silk with cotton hand-kerchiefs.

About the time that silk handkerchiefs began to be tyed for dying, velverets began to be stamped with gold spots and figures by the inge-nuity of Mr. Mather, who had before that time contrived to get thick-sets dyed of one colour uncut, and after cutting, of another, which gave a novel appearance to the article. An attempt was made to stamp the pile of velverets in figures by heated rollers, as linseys and harra-teens had formerly been done for bed-furniture; but without success. The striping of callicoes by rollers, and printing them with copper-plates in the rolling-press has, however, succeeded.

The manufacture of hats has been as much improved at Manchester as any original branch of its trade. At first the felt-makers only wrought the coarse sheep's wool, and it was not till about sixty years since that they used the fine Spanish, or the goat's wool from Germany, or that from the Levant, which is a species of goat's wool, though commonly called camel's hair, or any of the furs called stuff. The

Y   process

procefs of felting coarfe wool is quite different from that of working thefe finer matters ; being, firft to put the wool flightly together in a conical form, and then to boil it with common aftringents of native growth ; whence it is now carried on in the country where fuch materials are at hand, by undertakers who have the wool from Manchefter, and bring back the felts to be finifhed : but the manufactory of fine hats at Manchefter is now inferior to none ; as the workmen early began to handle the fine wools, ftuffs, and beaver, and are now perfect in the procefs of working them with beer grounds, fpirits, &c. and are equally expert in dying and finifhing blacks, while they have a decided fuperiority in fancy hats, in which they rather lead than follow the fafhion. The linings have been glazed and cut here as long as forty years fince, and now ferve other manufactories befides thofe of Manchefter. The looping is made in the fwivel engines here, and other trimmings in the neighbourhood.

To the manufactory of laces, inkles, tapes, and filleting, was early added that of the divers kinds of bindings and worfted fmall wares ; but fuch has been the demand for Englifh worfted of the beft quality by the manufacturers of furniture checks and Turkey ftripes, that the fmall-ware-makers were conftrained to ufe Irifh worfted, which, being cheaper, made them drop the prices : and the competition fince has rather been in the cheapnefs than the goodnefs of the article. Thefe furniture checks have grown into difrepute from the cockling of the worfted upon wafhing ; and the upholfterers now choofe cotton ftripes made on purpofe, or prints with furniture patterns. White cotton binding, lace and fringe for curtains is now an article of extenfive demand. As it was found that the Dutch enjoyed the manufacture of fine holland tapes unrivalled, plans were procured, and ingenious mechanics invited

vited over to conftruct fwivel engines at a great expenfe, which have been employed in moft branches of fmall wares with fuccefs. This manufacture alone, however, has not been fufficient to employ large capitals without the aid of fome other branch, and the fuftian trade has been added to it, firft as an auxilary, then as a principal.

The former deficiency as to finifhing the cotton velvets and thickfets put the manufacturers upon feveral methods to remedy that defect; all which, however, were imperfect, till the prefent mode of dreffing was invented and brought to perfection, which not only contributed to the eftablifhment of thofe articles to which it was applied, but foon raifed velverets, which were made as a middle fpecies between velvets and thickfets, to a rivalfhip with the former; and gives to many other articles, both dyed and white, their higheft degree of perfection. The fuftian trade has alfo been improved by the addition of velveteens, fifteen years fince, approaching nearer to real velvets than the velverets; likewife ftrong and fancy cords.

The practice of dreffing caufed a revolution in the whole fyftem of bleaching and dying. Before this time, the lighter drabs and fancy colours might be faid rather to hang on the furface, than to be fixed in the fubftance of cotton goods. But the neceffity of paffing through the ordeal of dreffing over glowing hot iron, caufed them to employ more fixed drugs and aftringents, with more powerful menftruums, in order to difcharge the ruftinefs contracted by the fire; in all which attempts they kept improving till dreffing in the grey took place, and goods were brought to confiderable perfection by alternate dreffings and bleachings before they were dyed. Notwithftanding this improvement, the dyers found fufficient fcope for their invention in the variety of pat-

terns

terns they were encouraged to produce for pattern-cards, which now began to be circulated, not only through thefe kingdoms, but all over Europe; and the printing of many articles in the fuftian branch gave a greater variety to thefe pattern-cards, while it afforded full employment for invention in dying grounds preparatory to them, and following the prints with other fhades. Thus the art of printing here came to rival that of London, and that branch has in great meafure been tranf-ferred from thence to the town and neighbourhood of Manchefter.

A perfon to whom thefe improvements have been particularly owing, is Mr. John Wilfon of Ainfworth. He was originally a manufac-turer in the fuftian branch in Manchefter, and early engaged in the ma-king of cotton velvets, which by unwearied efforts he brought to their utmoft degree of perfection. By attending carefully to the inftruction and fuperintendance of weavers, he foon brought that part of the ma-nufacture to fuch perfection, that nothing could be added but an altera-tion of tabbies to Genoa backs, chained or otherwife. The dying and dreffing, however, were ftill imperfect. Mr. Wilfon ufed various means of rubbing and brufhing the piles, clearing off the loofe hairs with razors, and then burning them off with fpirits of wine, in which operations many others began to engage equally with him. But he firft began to dye them himfelf; at firft in an experimental way at home, when firing off the pile with hot irons took place. Thefe were firft ufed upon blacks only, and were much like the weaver's drying irons, only of a rounder form, and were heated by ftoves; and the perfon who firft employed them was Mr. Whitlow, governor of the houfe of correction. This method faved the expenfe of fpirits, and fucceeded equally well.

Mr.

Mr. Wilſon having a turn for chymical inquiries, inveſtigated the different known proceſſes for dying, and found that thoſe employed by the thread dyers were better adapted to fix black upon cotton, than thoſe uſed by the fuſtian dyers. He found frequent waſhing and rincing of great uſe in opening the pile to favour the new method of dreſſing. Reſolving to give full ſcope to his improvements, he took a houſe and grounds at Ainſworth near Cockey-moor, and commenced a capital dreſſer, bleacher, and dyer, firſt and principally of his own goods, which he brought to ſuch high perfection, as to acquire the higheſt character both at London and in foreign markets. Before he could bring his plans to full execution, he had perſons articled to him for ſeven years, and carefully taught all the various operations in the different departments; for none of the workmen previouſly employed in dreſſing, bleaching, or dying, would ſuit his purpoſe, on account of their attachment to the old methods. He continued the method of dreſſing by hand irons ſome time after the preſent one obtained of drawing them over red-hot cylinders, as there was leſs danger of firing or tearing the pieces; but he effectually opened and ſoftened the pile by repeated operations of various kinds; finiſhing it quite upright, with a peculiar gloſs and brightneſs, inſomuch that pattern-card makers could at firſt ſight diſtinguiſh ſlips of his working from all others.

Having ſucceeded to his ſatisfaction in dying the other rich colours, he procured from the Greek dyers of Smyrna the ſecret of dying Turkey red, which has been deſcribed at large in two eſſays read before the *Philoſophical and Literary Society of Mancheſter*, which he printed and diſtributed among his friends after he had retired from buſineſs. This red he found required too tedious and expenſive a procefs, leſs ſuited to manufactured goods, than to cotton in the ſkain; nor even ſuited to

that.

that fpun upon the fingle fpindles then in ufe, though it might be applicable enough to that fpun on machines. The character Mr. Wilfon's finifhing had acquired was a great recommendation of velverets
when they firft came up, and induced the manufacturers to get moft of
the rich colours dyed by him. He was prevailed upon by much en-
treaty to dye fome drabs, which he performed in fuch perfection, that
the dyers of fancy drabs could only fucceed in proportion as they followed
his proceffes. The china blues that he dyed upon velvets and velverets
were likewife of his own invention.

Several circumftances have occurred to fix the printing bufinefs here.
A principal one was, that cotton greys and callicoes are manufactured
in thefe parts; whence, by printing here, the former expenfe of land-
carriage to London is faved. Further, the rent for bleaching grounds
is here lower, and workmen can live cheaper. A fucceffion of capital
artifts were thus induced to come down, who not only inftructed others,
but added to their former experience by printing upon grounds which
the dyers followed with other fhades. Hence there was a communication of methods and chymical fecrets between printers and dyers, to
the advantage of both parties. Thefe improvements left the London
printers no fuperiority but in light airy patterns, upon which thofe in
Lancafhire are making a confiderable progrefs, while the large capitals
employed in the bufinefs fecure all the improvements that are made.

Muflins have been made to a great extent of late, and many printed
ones; hence from a great demand both articles have been too flightly
made, and have received a check.

The

The acquifition of thefe laft branches, with the great increafe of the export trade, have given fuch employment to large capitals here, that the interior bufinefs of the country is in great meafure given up to the middle clafs of manufacturers and petty chapmen; but no exertions of the mafters or workmen could have anfwered the demands of trade without the introduction of *fpinning machines.*

Thefe were firft ufed by the country people on a confined fcale, twelve fpindles being thought a great matter; while the awkward pofture required to fpin on them was difcouraging to grown up people, who faw with furprize children from nine to twelve years of age manage them with dexterity, whereby plenty was brought into families formerly overburthened with children, and the poor weavers were delivered from the bondage in which they had lain from the infolence of fpinners. The following ftate of the cafe will explain this matter. From the time that the original fyftem in the fuftian branch, of buying pieces in the grey from the weaver, was changed, by delivering them out work, the cuftom of giving them out weft in the cops, which obtained for a while, grew into difufe, as there was no detecting the knavery of fpinners till a piece came in woven; fo that the practice was altered, and wool given with warps, the weaver anfwering for the fpinning. And the weavers in a fcarcity of fpinning have fometimes been paid lefs for the weft than they gave the fpinner, but durft not complain, much lefs abate the fpinner, left their looms fhould be unemployed. But when fpinning-jennies were introduced, and children could work upon them, the cafe was reverfed.

The plenty of weft produced by this means gave uneafinefs to the country people, and the weavers were afraid left the manufacturers

3   fhould

should demand finer weft woven at the former prices, which occasioned some risings, and the demolition of jennies in some places by the uninformed populace.   At length Dorning Rasbotham, Esq. a worthy magistrate near Bolton, wrote and printed a sensible address to the weavers, in order to convince them of their own interest in encouraging these engines, which happily produced a general acquiescence in their use to a certain number of spindles.   These were soon multiplied to three or four times the number; nor did the invention of mechanics rest here, for the demand for twist for warps was greater as weft grew more plentiful, whence engines were soon constructed for this purpose.

The improvements kept increasing, till the capital engines for twist were perfected, by which thousands of spindles are put in motion by a water wheel, and managed mostly by children, without confusion and with less waste of cotton than by the former methods.   But the carding and slubbing preparatory to twisting required a greater range of invention.   The first attempts were in carding engines, which are very curious, and now brought to a great degree of perfection; and an engine has been contrived for converting the carded wool to slubbing, by drawing it to about the thickness of candlewick preparatory to throwing it into twist.   When these larger machines that moved by water were first set to work, they produced such excellent twist for warps, that they soon out-rivalled the warps made on the larger jennies, which had yielded good profits to the owners.   In consequence of this, according to the usual short-sighted policy of narrow-minded and interested men, the country was excited against the water-machines, and some of them were demolished before protection could be obtained. Yet a little reflection would have shown the country people, that if more warps were made, there would be a greater demand for weft from

their

their jennies, and a better price for it. This has fince been fully experienced in the introduction of muflins; for no contrivance in the other
machines can make the thread hold when it is fo flack thrown as to fuit
for weft; nor can it be fuppofed that the attempt would be made, as
the demand for twift for warps will fully employ them. For when
cotton bears a reafonable price, the warps made of this twift will be as
cheap as thofe made with yarn, and keep the money at home which
ufed to be fent abroad for that article; there being no comparifon between yarn and cotton warps in goodnefs. In fact, cotton warps have
lately been introduced to a great extent, where yarn had before been
ufed. As thefe machines are now to be feen by the curious, and fpeci-
fications of their conftruction may be had at the Patent office, no delicacy is neceffary in laying defcriptions of them fully before the public.
We fhall, therefore, attempt to give fuch an idea of them as can be
communicated by words, beginning with the machine for carding
cotton.

The fpinners had begun to pick the hufks of cotton feeds from their
wool, and pafs it through a lather of foap, preparatory to carding, before carding engines were invented; and upon their introduction, the
firft operation was to pick and foap the wool, wring it out well from
the lather, dry it, then fpread a given quantity upon the feeder of a
carding engine. This feeder was a coarfe cloth, fewed together at the
ends, and ftrained upon fmall rollers; upon the cotton ferved by this
feeder, a roller faced with tin punched through like a common grater,
made a flow revolution, pinching up the cotton; and the feeder, anfwering its motion, kept delivering more, while the vacant part of the
cloth coming up was ferved with more cotton. Thus the cotton was
delivered to fets of cylinders with cards nailed upon them; as many

Z. of

of thefe as had a revolution onward from the feeder, were governed by one ftrap, from the firft mover, fixed on feveral pullies or whorles upon the fpindles paffing through the centres of thofe cylinders. Other cylinders had a contrary motion, to ftrip the cotton from thofe of the firft defcription, delivering it to the next, in the direct motion onward to the largeft cylinder of all, which received the cotton thoroughly carded by the inverfe and direct revolutions of thefe intermediate cylinders.

An invention was neceffary at the end of the motion, to take off the cardings, which was firft attempted by a fluted roller put in motion by a ftrap from the inverfe fyftem of cylinders, which preffing upon the card teeth of the large cylinders, rubbed off the cardings, which fell into a receptacle below; but thefe cardings were rubbed too clofe in the operation, and hence not fo open for the purpofe of fpinning as could be wifhed. A moft curious contrivance produced the remedy defired; this was effected by cafting a worm-like or fpiral fluxion at the centre of the great wheel, which was fixed upon the cylinder to be divefted of the cardings; this fpiral worm worked a fmall wheel upon a fpindle which governed a tumbler by a crank, and threw a crofs plate of metal garnifhed with fmall teeth againft the cards at intervals, and took off the carding as open as could be wifhed.

This contrivance Mr. Arkwright claimed as his own invention till a verdict in the King's-Bench fet afide his claim. This gentleman, knighted in the prefent reign for his ingenuity, is worthy of being celebrated for his induftry in the early obfervations which he made of new inventions in carding and fpinning, and his capacity in forming them into a perfect fyftem in the twift machine, for which he obtained

a patent.   But finding feveral improvements not in his firft fpecifica-
tion, he got it extended, and fpecified in particular the above invention
to take off the cardings.   Before this time he had fued feveral cotton
fpinners for an invafion of his patent.   They joined iffue with him,
and in the event he was non-fuited.   On the extenfion of his patent,
care being taken to fpecify the additional improvements, he inftituted
another fuit for invafion of his patent, and obtained a verdict in the
court of Common Pleas.   This occafioned a great alarm among many
who had at a great expenfe erected machines for cotton fpinning, of
whom an acknowledgement of fo much a fpindle was demanded under
the threat of immediate fuit.   The perfons concerned got the matter
removed into the court of King's-bench, where, upon trial, it was
proved that the apparatus above defcribed for taking off the cardings
was a prior invention of an ingenious mechanic, Mr. Heys by name,
in confequence of which a verdict was given againft Mr. Arkwright.
In fact, the roller upon which Mr. Heys's fpindle-ftrings ran was immediately adopted after his public exhibition of it; his contrivance alfo
of flipping his handle from a fquare to a round, which checked the
operation of fpinning and pufhing on to an interior contrivance to wind
up the fpin thread, is adopted in the machines for fpinning of twift,
which procefs we fhall now defcribe.

The cotton for this purpofe is of the firft ftaple, but not too long
grained; being beaten out to open the grain, it is picked very carefully,
and the ufual procefs purfued to the carding, with this difference, that
inftead of feveral cylinders, there is one only to take cotton wool from
the pincher, and deliver it to a very large one, whence it is received by
another, and ftript by the tumbler, and carried to the ferver of others
in rotation, till it rifes from the laft in a fine well-corded fheet.   This

is

is kept from returning to the cylinder by the attendants; and being gently clofed together, is conducted over a pulley high enough to make it fall by its own weight, as it is continually detached from the cards. A deep tin-can is fet under, into which the carded wool coils itfelf, much refembling the wool drawn from Jerfey combs : many of thefe tin-cans are in readinefs to replace the filled ones, which are removed to ferve a machine for roving, as the firft operation of fpinning is called; where the cardings of three cans put together are paffed through rollers moved by clock-work, which alfo puts in motion fmall circular brufhes to clear the loofe flying hairs of cotton from the rollers ; thofe deliver every three fleeces of carded cotton fo connected, that when a can is emptied and another is fupplied, care is taken that two whole fleeces preferve the continuity of the preparation for twifting, which paffes from the rollers to fpindles furnifhed with a curious apparatus to give it a very flight throw and wind it on bobbins in rovings. Thefe undergo feveral courfes of drawing by rollers and throwing, till it is wound upon bobbins in an open and even ftate, for the final operation of fpinning by the machines for making twift.

Thefe machines exhibit in their conftruction an aggregate of clockmaker's work and machinery moft wonderful to behold. The cotton to be fpun is introduced through three fets of rollers, fo governed by the clock-work, that the fet which firft receives the cotton makes fo many more revolutions than the next in order, and thefe more than the laft which feed the fpindles, that it is drawn out confiderably in paffing through the rollers; being laftly received by fpindles, which have every one on the bobbin a fly like that of a flax wheel; both the flyers and the bobbin in like manner are loofe on the fpindle, which are whirled with amazing rapidity; but every bobbin refting upon a board, is

checked

checked in its courfe, and only can wind up what twift is fpun; and to avoid the inconvenience of winding it in ridges, as in flax-fpinning, the board upon which they reft has an alternate motion, which raifes and depreffes the bobbins, fo that the twift winds to and fro, the whole length of each bobbin. A confiderable number of fpindles may be wrought in one twifting frame, but they are connected in fyftems of four to each fyftem, fo that when a thread breaks, thofe four of the fyftem to which it belongs may be ftopped, while the others are twift-ing. This advantage is obtained by lifting that fyftem from the fquare part of a fpindle, which by a whorl from the machinery governed the four, to a round part above, which moves without giving motion to the fyftem, till the thread is again connected with the prepared cotton, by pinching off what was unfpun, and clapping it to the laft roller, where it lays hold of the untwifted cotton, when that fet on four is dropped again upon the fquare of the fpindles, and the twifting goes on. Children are foon very dexterous at connecting broken ends with prepared cotton at the rollers, their fmall fingers being more active and endued with a quicker fenfibility of feeling than thofe of grown perfons; and it is wonderful to fee with what difpatch they can raife a fyftem, connect threads, and drop it again into work almoft inftantaneoufly.

Upon thefe machines twift is made of any finenefs proper for warps; but as it is drawn length way of the ftaple, it was not fo proper for weft; wherefore on the introduction of fine callicoes and muflins, mules were invented, having a name expreffive of their fpecies, being a mixed machinery between jennies and the machines for twifting, and adapted to fpin weft as fine as could be defired, by adding to the jen-nies fuch rollers, governed by clock-maker's work, as were defcribed above, only with this difference, that when the threads are drawn out,

the

the motion of the rollers is fufpended by an ingenious contrivance, till
the weft is hardened and wound up ; in which operation the fpindles
are alternately drawn from and returned to the feeding rollers, being
fixed on a moveable frame like thofe of the billies to make cardings
into what are called rovings for the common jennies.

Thefe mules-carry often to a hundred and fifty fpindles, and can be
fet to draw weft to an exact finenefs up to 150 hanks in the pound,
of which muflin has been made, which for a while had a prompt fale ;
but the flimfinefs of its fabric has brought the finer forts into difcredit,
and a ftagnation of trade damped the fale of the reft.

The worfted and woollen manufactories are alike benefited by improvements in carding and fpinning, taken from the cotton machines,
and adapted to their particular branches, which improvements make
the work people uneafy till they experience that an increafed fale of
goods in proportion to improvements finds them employment, and that
children, who had nothing to do before, earn wages by employment at
the machines, whether employed in fpinning woollen yarn, Jerfey or
cotton.   Flax is now attempted by the fame machinery, but the length
of its ftaple in fine dreffed flax may render it difficult to draw ; yet
the fhort hards dreffed out of it may be fpun this way evener and more
compact than by the flax wheel, and what was too fhort for making
yarn before, may now be wrought up, which will be good economy
and leffen the imports.

The new-invented fteam engines by a fingle cylinder clofed above,
pufhing over water to an overfhot-wheel, which returns to the refervoir, fuppofe a common pump-fpring, were a great improvement,
                                                                    and

and employed to advantage as the application of machinery to several branches of bufinefs was extended. For by this means, there is lefs occafion for horfes, and any power may be applied by enlarging the diameter of the cylinders, as one of twenty-four inches will force over more than fixty gallons at a ftroke. This improvement, which is as fimple as ingenious, was the invention of a common pump-maker, Wrigley by name, of this town, who never applied for a patent, but imparted freely what he invented to thofe who thought proper to employ him.*

Some attempts have been made to work a number of looms together by machinery. The firft was upon the introduction of fwivel-looms, above thirty years fince, by Mr. Gartfide, with a capital water-wheel at his factory near Garret-hall, now a very large one for cotton fpinning by water. Mr. Whitehead, the chief projector, and a partner, has there fixed a fteam engine to return the water occafionally, and another fixed in a cafe of brick on the principle of thofe to quench fire; upon the leaft alarm of fire he can fcrew on his pipe, fet the engine to work by the great wheel, and no deficiency of water can occur, the engine forcing up water from the mill-race, fo that a fingle perfon can fend a continued ftream of water to any part of the factory or over it; a contrivance worthy to be adopted in all cotton fpinning factories, where there is a powerful wheel and plenty of water, which is the cafe here: for Mr. Gartfide fpared no coft in his fcheme of working fwivel-looms

* Raifing water by fteam engines, and throwing it back into the mill-dam or refervoir was firft practifed about thirty-feven years fince by the late Mr. Wilkinfon, at Berfham-furnace, near Wrexham, by an engine of great magnitude which brought up the contents of the river as it were at one ftroke. This engine fhook the buildings and ground for a confiderable diftance, and required ten times more fuel than thofe at prefent conftructed.

by

by water, and continued to employ them for a confiderable time to very little advantage; for one weaver was neceffary to take care of a loom, and if the divifion where the fhuttle ranges in any piece was clogged with knots in the warp or broken ends, the whole of a piece or a great part of it was liable to be cut down before a loom could be thrown out of gear; but weavers who work a fwivel-loom by the hand themfelves, have a facility acquired by habit of checking the motion in fuch cafes, returning back the fhuttles from a half-fhoot to prevent any misfortune.

Mr. Grimfhaw of Gorton attempted the conftruction of machinery to weave piece goods, in a capital factory at Knott-mill, which was burnt down before any judgement could be formed how it would have fucceeded.

The prodigious extenfion of the feveral branches of the Manchefter manufactures has likewife greatly increafed the bufinefs of feveral trades and manufactures connected with or dependent upon them. The making of paper at mills in the vicinity has been brought to great perfection, and now includes all kinds, from the ftrongeft parcelling paper to the fineft writing forts, and that on which banker's bills are printed. To the ironmongers fhops, which are greatly increafed of late, are generally annexed fmithies, where many articles are made, even to nails. A confiderable iron foundry is eftablifhed in Salford, in which are caft moft of the articles wanted in Manchefter and its neighbourhood, confifting chiefly of large caft wheels for the cotton machines; cylinders, boilers, and pipes for fteam engines; caft ovens, and grates of all fizes. This work belongs to Batemen and Sharrard, genmen every way qualified for fo great an undertaking. Mr. Sharrard is a very ingenious and able engineer, who has improved upon and brought

the

the fteam engine to great perfection. Moft of thofe that are ufed and fet up in and about Manchefter are of their make and fitting up. They are in general of a fmall fize, very compact, ftand in a fmall fpace, work fmooth and eafy, and are fcarcely heard in the building where erected. They are now ufed in cotton mills, and for every purpofe of the water wheel, where a ftream is not to be got, and for winding up coals from a great depth in the coal pits, which is performed with a quicknefs and eafe not to be conceived.

Some few are alfo erected in this neighbourhood by Meffrs. Bolton and Watts of Birmingham, who have far excelled all others in their improvement of the fteam engine, for which they have obtained a patent, that has been the fource of great and deferved emolument. The boilers are generally of plate iron or copper; but fome few for the fmaller engines are of caft iron.

There are five other iron foundries in Manchefter, which do a great deal of bufinefs. In one of them Mr. Alexander Brodie of Carey Street, London, is concerned, who is well known for his very extenfive manufactory of grates and ftoves, as well for kitchens and dining rooms, as fhips.*

The quantity of pig iron ufed at the different foundries in Manchefter within thefe few years, has been very great, and is moftly brought (by

* The firms of the iron foundries are,
Bateman and Sharratt; Salford.
Brodie, M'Niven, and Ormrod; Manchefter.
Smiths and Co. ditto.
Baffett and Smith, ditto.
Mrs. Phœbe Fletcher, ditto.
John Smith, ditto.

A a

canal

canal carriage) from Boatfield and Co.'s iron furnace, Old Park, near Coalbrook Dale; and Mr. Brodie's furnace, near the Iron Bridge, both in Shropfhire.

The tin-plate workers have found additional employment in furnifhing many articles for fpinning machines; as have alfo the braziers in cafting wheels for the motion-work of the rollers ufed in them; and the clock-makers in cutting them. Harnefs-makers have been much employed in making bands for carding engines, and large wheels for the firft operation of drawing out the cardings, whereby the confumption of ftrong curried leather has been much increafed.

We fhall conclude this account of the trade of Manchefter with fome facts to fhow the rapid increafe and prodigious amount of the cotton manufactures of this ifland, extracted from a pamphlet publifhed in 1788, entitled, " An Important Crifis in the Callico and Muflin Ma- " nufactory in Great Britain, explained;" the purpofe of which was to warn the nation of the bad confequences which would refult from the rivalry of the Eaft India cotton goods which then began to be poured into the markets in increafed quantities, and at diminifhed prices.

The author afferts, that not above twenty years before the time of his writing, the whole cotton trade of Great Britain did not return £.200,000 to the country for the raw materials, combined with the labour of the people; and at that period, before the introduction of the water machinery and hand engines, the power of the fingle wheel could not exceed 50,000 fpindles employed in fpinning the cotton wool into yarn: but at the prefent moment, the power of fpindles thus employed

amounts

amounts to two millions; and the grofs return for the raw materials and labour exceeds feven millions fterling. It was about the year 1784 that the expiration of Sir Richard Arkwright's patent caufed the erection of water machines for the fpinning of warps in all parts of the country, with which the hand engines for the fpinning of weft kept proportion. At the time he wrote he eftimates the number of

Water mills or machines, at - - - - - 143
Mule jennies or machines, confifting of 90 fpindles each, - - - - - - - - - 350
Hand jennies of 80 fpindles each, - - - - 20,070

Of the water mills, 123 are in England, and nineteen in Scotland. Of thofe in England,

Lancafhire has - -	41	Chefhire, - - -	8
Derbyfhire, - - -	22	Staffordfhire, - -	7
Nottinghamfhire, -	17	Weftmorland - -	5
Yorkfhire, - - -	11	Flintfhire, - - -	3

Thefe eftablifhments, when in full work, are eftimated to give employment to about 26,000 men, 31,000 women, and 53,000 children, in fpinning alone; and in all the fubfequent ftages of the manufacture, the number of perfons employed is eftimated at 133,000 men, 59,000 women, and 48,000 children; making an aggregate of 159,000 men, 90,000 women, and 101,000 children, in all, 350,000 perfons, employed in the cotton manufacture.

The increafe of raw material ufed, and goods made, is fhown in the following lifts:

Cotton

Cotton wool remaining in the country after exportation, in

					℔.
1783	-	-	-	-	9,546,179
1784	-	-	-	-	11,280,238
1785	-	-	-	-	17,992,888
1786	-	-	-	-	19,151,867
1787	-	-	-	-	22,600,000

Grofs value of cotton goods made, in

					£.
1783	-	-	-	-	3,200,000
1784	-	-	-	-	3,950,000
1785	-	-	-	-	6,000,000
1786	-	-	-	-	6,500,000
1787	-	-	-	-	7,500,000

The cotton imported for the manufactures in 1787 was of the follow-growths:

				℔.
Britifh iflands eftimated at	-	-	-	6,600,000
French and Spanifh fettlements	-	-	-	6,000,000
Dutch fettlements -	-	-	-	1,700,000
Portuguefe ditto -	-	-	-	2,500,000
Eaft Indies, procured from Oftend	-	-		100,000
Smyrna or Turkey	-	-	-	5,700,000
				──────────
				22,600,000

The

The application of this cotton to the different branches of manufacture was supposed by intelligent persons to have been as follows :

		℔.
To the candlewick branch	- - -	1,500,000
To the hosiery ditto	- - - -	1,500,000
To silk and linen mixtures	- - -	2,000,000
To the fustian branch	- - - -	6,000,000
To callicoes and muslins	- - -	11,600,000
		22,600,000

The increase of value acquired by the raw material in the labour expended upon it in manufacturing, is generally from 1000 to 5000 per cent. By the dexterity of the spinners, specimens of yarn have been produced from East India cotton in which 205 hanks, weighing one pound, have been drawn out from two pounds of the raw cotton ; each of these hanks measures 840 yards, and the whole would reach near 100 miles.

To this sketch of the progress of the *trade* of Manchester, it will be proper to subjoin some information respecting the condition and manners of its *tradesmen*, the gradual advances to opulence and luxury, and other circumstances of the domestic history of the place, which are in reality some of the most curious and useful subjects of speculation on human life. The following facts and observations have been communicated by an accurate and well-informed inquirer.

The trade of Manchester may be divided into four periods. The first is that, when the manufacturers worked hard merely for a livelihood,

hood, without having accumulated any capital. The fecond is that, when they had begun to acquire little fortunes, but worked as hard, and lived in as plain a manner as before, increafing their fortunes as well by economy as by moderate gains. The third is that, when luxury began to appear, and trade was pufhed by fending out riders for orders to every market town in the kingdom. The fourth is the period in which ex- penfe and luxury had made a great progrefs, and was fupported by a trade extended by means of riders and factors through every part of Europe.

It is not eafy to afcertain when the fecond of thefe periods com- menced; but it is probable that few or no capitals of 3000*l*. or 4000*l*. acquired by trade, exifted here before 1690. However, towards the lat- ter end of the laft century and the beginning of the prefent, the traders had certainly got money beforehand, and began to build modern brick houfes, in place of thofe of wood and plafter. For the firft thirty years of the prefent century, the old eftablifhed houfes confined their trade to the wholefale dealers in London, Briftol, Norwich, Newcaf- tle, and thofe who frequented Chefter fair. The profits were thus di- vided between the manufacturer, the wholefale, and the retail, dealer; and thofe of the manufacturer were probably (though this is contrary to the received opinion) lefs per cent. upon the bufinefs they did, than in the prefent times. The improvement of their fortunes was chiefly owing to their economy in living, the expenfe of which was much below the intereft of the capital employed. Apprentices at that time were now and then taken from families which could pay a mode- rate fee. By an indenture dated 1695 the fee paid appears to have been fixty pounds, the young man ferving feven years. But all apprentices were obliged to undergo a vaft deal of laborious work, fuch as turning

warping

warping mills, carrying goods on their shoulders through the streets, and the like. An eminent manufacturer in that age used to be in his warehouse before six in the morning, accompanied by his children and apprentices. At seven they all came in to breakfast, which consisted of one large dish of water-pottage, made of oat-meal, water, and a little salt, boiled thick, and poured into a dish. At the side was a pan or bason of milk, and the master and apprentices, each with a wooden spoon in his hand, without loss of time, dipped into the same dish, and thence into the milk pan; and as soon as it was finished they all returned to their work. In George the First's reign many country gentlemen began to send their sons apprentices to the Manchester manufacturers; but though the little country gentry did not then live in the luxurious manner they have done since, the young men found it so different from home, that they could not brook this treatment, and either got away before their time, or, if they staid till the expiration of their indentures, they then, for the most part, entered into the army or went to sea. The little attention paid to rendering the evenings of apprentices agreeable at home, where they were considered rather as servants than pupils, drove many of them to taverns, where they acquired habits of drinking that frequently proved injurious in after life. To this, in part, is to be attributed the bad custom of gilling, or drinking white wine as a whet before dinner, to which at one period a number of young men fell a sacrifice.

When the Manchester trade began to extend, the chapmen used to keep gangs of pack-horses, and accompany them to the principal towns with goods in packs, which they opened and sold to shop-keepers, lodging what was unsold in small stores at the inns. The pack-horses brought back sheep's wool, which was bought on the journey, and

fold

fold to the makers of worsted yarn at Manchester, or to the clothiers of Rochdale, Saddleworth, and the West-Riding of Yorkshire. On the improvement of turnpike roads waggons were set up, and the pack-horses discontinued; and the chapmen only rode out for orders, carrying with them patterns in their bags. It was during the forty years from 1730 to 1770 that trade was greatly pushed by the practice of sending these riders all over the kingdom, to those towns which before had been supplied from the wholesale dealers in the capital places before mentioned. As this was attended not only with more trouble, but with much more risk, some of the old traders withdrew from business, or confined themselves to as much as they could do on the old footing, which, by the competition of young adventurers, diminished yearly. In this period strangers flocked in from various quarters, which introduced a greater proportion of *young* men of some fortune into the town, with a consequent increase of luxury and gaiety. The fees of apprentices becoming an object of profit, a different manner of treating them began to prevail. Somewhat before 1760, a considerable manufacturer allotted a back-parlour with a fire for the use of his apprentices, and gave them tea twice a day. His fees in consequence rose higher than had before been known, from 250*l.* to 300*l.*; and he had three or four apprentices at a time. The highest fee known as late as 1769, was 500*l.* Within the last twenty or thirty years the vast increase of foreign trade has caused many of the Manchester manufacturers to travel abroad, and agents or partners to be fixed for a considerable time on the Continent, as well as foreigners to reside at Manchester. And the town has now in every respect assumed the style and manners of one of the commercial capitals of Europe.

Some

Some other anecdotes refpecting the manners of the place in the laft age may prove amufing from comparifon, however trivial in their own nature.

About the year 1690 there was a great quarrel between the mafter and fcholars of the grammar-fchool. The boys locked themfelves in the fchool, and were fupplied by the town's people with victuals and beds, which were put in at the windows. They even got fire arms and ammunition, which they employed in firing at the legs of perfons who attempted to get in. This petty rebellion continued a fortnight, fomewhat to the difgrace of thofe who ought to have exerted a better difcipline.

In 1693, a manufacturer, being in London, learned that one of his cuftomers, a mercer in Manchefter, was bound in a large fum for a Londoner who was expected to break : he thereupon prudently wrote to his wife to go and dun the mercer, adding, " if thou canft not get " money, take goods—thou mayft buy thyfelf a filk manteau and pet- " ticoat." For a fenfible and frugal man, who fet out with very little capital, to fend fuch an order to his wife, proves that thofe articles of finery were not at that time very uncommon.

In a manufacturer's private expenfe-book, under the date 1700, are different fums paid for two of his daughters who were at London in the houfe of a perfon who managed a warehoufe for him. Among the reft is paid for a fpinet 5*l*. 3*s*. 0*d*. In the fame book, in 1701, is paid 26*l*. 18*s*. 9*d*. for a journey to Scarborough, and hire of a coach 13*l*. 6*s*. 2*d*. This was the fea-bathing place of the time, for the journey was on account of a child five years old who died there ; and

B b   at at her funeral, though fo young, there was paid for gloves 2*l*. 5*s*. o*d*. When this reputable perfon went to London, his conftant annual luxuries wcre Brunfwick mum, beer, and tobacco. In the expenfes for 1702 there is a charge, for the firft time, of ten fhillings for coffee and tea. His houfe rent was forty pounds per annum, perhaps including his warehoufe. For feveral years, ten fhillings a quarter is put down for *chapel wages*, or his fubfcription to the diffenting meeting-houfe. In 1704 is five pounds for an afs; an enormous price for the time, from which it is probable that few were then bred near Manchefter. For the fame year is 2*l*. 10*s*. o*d*. for a perriwig, but this was preparatory to a wedding, and double the price of thofe charged before. This was an expenfive piece of finery for fuch frugal times.

A proof of the early hours then kept appears in the following faĉt: In 1705 a manufaĉturer married a phyfician's daughter who had been genteelly educated and kept a good deal of company. The hour of afternoon vifiting was then *two o'clock*, fo that for fome years after her marriage, fhe had always finifhed her vifit foon enough to go to the Old Church prayers at four. They then dined at twelve; and there being no fuch thing as a hair-dreffer, it was eafy to be ready for vifiting at two.

In 1708 the aĉt paffed for building St. Ann's church, which in a few years was followed by the fquare and ftreets adjoining, where was difplayed a new ftyle of light and convenient rooms, very different from thofe in the reft of the town. The front parlours however were referved for company only; and the family ufually lived in the back parlours. This fafhion continued to our own times, and in fmall houfes, fubfifts in fome degree at prefent. The great fums of money brought into circulation by the wars and taxes in queen Ann's reign, and by the fubfequent commercial fpeculations, muft have rapidly forwarded the progrefs of luxury in Manchefter. Lady Bland of Hulme, who was herfelf a great heirefs, and had married a gentleman of large fortune, was then the chief promoter of whatever could embellifh the town, or polifh the tafte of its inhabitants. She had fubfcribed liberally to the building of St. Ann's church, and the initials of her name were put upon the cover of the communion table. A few years afterwards fhe was the principal patronefs of a dancing affembly; and a handfome room for the purpofe was erected upon pillars, leaving a fpace beneath to walk in. This was in the middle of the new fafhionable ftreet called King-ftreet, and opened a convenient paffage to the new church-yard. The affembly was held once a week at the low price of half a crown a quarter; and the ladies had their maids to come with lanthorns and pattens to conduct them home; nor was it unufual for their partners alfo to attend them. Lady Bland was of a cheerful difpofition, and fo fond of young company, that fhe had frequent balls in her hall at Hulme, and often, when an old woman, danced in the fame fet with her grandfon.

About 1720 there were not above three or four carriages kept in the town. One of thefe belonged to a Madam D—— in Salford. This refpectable old lady was of a fociable difpofition, but could not bring herfelf to conform to the new-fafhioned beverage of tea and coffee; whenever, therefore, fhe made her afternoon's vifit, her friends prefented her with a tankard of ale and pipe of tobacco. A little before this period a country gentleman had married the daughter of a citizen of London: fhe had been ufed to tea, and in compliment to her it was introduced by fome of her neighbours; but the ufual afternoon's

entertain-

entertainment at gentlemens' houfes at that time was wet and dry fweet-meats, different forts of cake and gingerbread, apples, or other fruits of the feafon, and a variety of home-made wines. The manufacture of thefe wines was a great point with all good houfe-wives both in the country and the town. They made an effential part of all feafts, and were brought forth when the London or Briftol dealers came down to fettle their accounts and give orders. A young manufacturer about this time having a valuable cuftomer to fup with him, fent to the tavern for a pint of foreign wine, which next morning furnifhed a fubject for the farcaftic remarks of all his neighbours. In order to perfect young ladies in what was then thought a neceffary part of their education, a paftry-fchool was fet up in Manchefter, which was frequented, not only by the daughters of the town's-people, but thofe of the neighbouring gentlemen. At this time there was a girl's boarding-fchool; and alfo a dancing-mafter, who, on particular occafions, ufed to make the boys and girls parade two by two through fome of the ftreets; a difplay which was not very pleafing to fome of the bafhful youths of that day.

About this period there was an evening club of the moft opulent manufacturers, at which the expenfes of each perfon were fixed at fourpence halfpenny, viz. four-pence for ale, and a halfpenny for tobacco. At a much later period, however, a fix-pennyworth of punch, and a pipe or two, were efteemed fully fufficient for the evening's tavern amufement of the principal inhabitants.*

Annual

* As a proof that even at the *prefent day* ftrong features of ancient manners exift here, we fhall copy the following anecdote lately communicated:

There now refides in the market place of Manchefter, a man of the name of John Shawe, who keeps a common public houfe, in which a large company of the refpectable

Manchefter

Annual horfe-races at Kerfal-moor were eftablifhed about 1730. A ferious diffuafive againft them was publifhed in a pamphlet printed at Manchefter in 1733, the writer of which was probably the celebrated Mr. Byrom. Several circumftances relative to the town and neighbour-hood are mentioned in it; particularly, that even the dancing affembly, though from the teftimony of this writer conducted with the utmoft decorum, was then confidered as an improper place for a clergyman to appear at; bifhop Peploe, warden of Manchefter college, having thought fit to inhibit his clergy from attending it as derogatory from the gravity becoming their characters. The races were however conti-nued till about the year 1745, when they were laid afide for feveral years; but afterwards revived, and are annually held in Whitfun-week to the prefent day, probably not without much injury to fuch a popu-lous and manufacturing country. By the thoughtleffnefs of the young people frequenting this diverfion, who make a practice of riding races

Manchefter tradefmen meet every day after dinner, and the rule is to call for fixpenny-worth of punch. Here the news of the town is generally known. The high change at Shawe's is about fix; and at eight o'clock every perfon muft quit the houfe, as no liquor is ever ferved out after that hour; and fhould any one be prefumptuous enough to ftop, Mr. Shawe brings out a whip with a long lafh, and proclaiming aloud, " Paft eight o'clock, " Gentlemen !" foon clears his houfe.

For this excellent regulation Mr. Shawe has frequently received the thanks of the ladies of Manchefter, and is often toafted; nor is any one a greater favourite with the townf-men than this refpectable old man. He is now very far advanced in life, we fuppofe not much fhort of 80, and ftill a ftrong, ftout, hearty man. He has kept ftrictly to this rule for upwards of fifty years, accompanied by an old woman fervant for nearly the fame length of time.

It is not unworthy of remark, and to a ftranger is very extraordinary, that merchants of the firft fortunes quit the elegant drawing room, to fit in a fmall dark dungeon, for this houfe cannot with propriety be called by a better name—but fuch is the force of long-eftablifhed cuftom !

to

to their refpective homes, many melancholy accidents annually happen, and many lives are loft.

In 1710, a manufacturer taking his family up to London hired a coach for the whole way, which, in that ftate of the roads, muft probably have made it a journey of eight or ten days. And in 1742, the fyftem of travelling had fo little improved, that a lady wanting to come with her niece from Worcefter to Manchefter, wrote to a friend in the latter place to fend for her a hired coach, becaufe the man *knew the road*, having brought from thence a family fome time before, and alfo becaufe he travelled on cheaper terms than the Worcefter hired coaches.

We are not inclined to enter into the party-hiftory of Manchefter, unfortunately too copious a topic. But it feems proper to mention, that in 1730-1 a violent parliamentary conteft was carried on between the whigs and tories refpecting a workhoufe, the general plan of which feems to have been judicioufly laid, and to have met with univerfal concurrence, but the *management* would by the propofed bill have been thrown almoft entirely into the hands of the whigs. Thefe, though fupported by the miniftry at that time, met with a defeat, and the fcheme fell through. Neither can the effects of the laft rebellion be totally paffed over, which infufed fuch a fpirit of party-rancour, that the pleafures of fociety were greatly interrupted by it. From fome quarrels that arofe in the affembly between the people of the town and the officers quartered there, the whigs made a feceffion, and two dancing affemblies were for fome years kept up with fpirit; till the patriotic adminiftration of the great William Pitt having made an union of parties, the whigs returned to their old room.

In

In the year 1750, there was a ſtand of hackney-coaches in St. Ann's ſquare; but theſe vehicles being found leſs convenient for ſome pur-poſes than ſedan chairs, the latter took place of them, and few country towns have been better ſupplied with them. Some perſons who had quitted trade began to indulge in the luxury of a chaiſe of their own to take an airing; but it was not till 1758 that any perſon actually in buſineſs ſet up a carriage.

Mancheſter has long been famous for a pack of remarkably large hounds, which the learned Mr. Whitaker conceives to be the true breed of old Britiſh hounds, once general to the kingdom, though lat-terly confined to a ſmall tract of the north-weſtern part of it. A pack of a ſmaller breed has alſo for many years been kept there; and the pleaſures of the chace have been ardently purſued by many of the in-habitants.

We ſhall conclude this article with ſome further particulars of the *preſent ſtate* of Mancheſter.

With reſpect to *government*, it remains an open town, deſtitute (pro-bably to its advantage) of a corporation, and unrepreſented in parlia-ment. Its municipal officers are a borough-reeve and two conſtables, elected annually in October at the court leet. The borough-reeve is an officer almoſt peculiar to this place, and who ſeems formerly to have been the chief magiſtrate; but at preſent his proper office is the diſtri-bution of certain charities, though in point of rank he is conſidered as the firſt man at all public meetings, and takes the chair. The con-ſtables are the real executive officers.

Mancheſter

Manchester and Salford, in several streets and the market place, bear great marks of antiquity, as there are still standing nearly whole streets of houses built of wood, clay, and plaister.

The new streets built within these few years have nearly doubled the size of the town. Most of them are wide and spacious, with excellent and large houses, principally of brick made on the spot; but they have a flight of steps projecting nearly the breadth of the pavement, which makes it very inconvenient to foot passengers. When two people meet one must either go into the horse road, or over the flight of steps, which in the night time is particularly dangerous, as the lamps are not always lighted. In the first year after obtaining the act for lighting and paving the town, a considerable debt was incurred. On this account, Manchester was, as before the act, in total darkness; but by receiving the money and using no oil, the fund has recovered itself and the town is now well lighted. But very few of the streets are yet flagged, which makes the walking in them, to strangers, very disagreeable. There is little doubt but this will in a short time be remedied, and the great ugly projecting flight of steps to the houses taken down. As Manchester may bear comparison with the metropolis itself in the rapidity with which whole new streets have been raised, and in its extension on every side towards the surrounding country; so it unfortunately vies with, or exceeds, the metropolis, in the closeness with which the poor are crowded in offensive, dark, damp, and incommodious habitations, a too fertile source of disease! The mischievous effects proceeding from this cause are so clearly stated, and the remedies so ably suggested, in a paper addressed by Dr. Ferriar to the Committee for the regulation of the police in Manchester, that we are persuaded

we

we fhall do an ufeful fervice in making it more extenfively known by reprinting the moft material parts of it.*

The new churches are noble buildings, and moft of them conftructed at great expenfe, chiefly of free-ftone brought by the duke of Bridge-water's canal. Some of the diffenting meeting houfes alfo are well built and very large.

The number of churches and chapels of the eftablifhment in Man-chefter and Salford, actually built and building, amount to twelve; and

* 1. In fome parts of the town, cellars are fo damp as to be unfit for habitations; fuch places fhould be reported to the Commiffioners, by whom proper reprefentations may be made to the owners, that the cellars may be appropriated to other purpofes. I have known feveral induftrious families loft to the community, by a fhort refidence in damp cellars.

2. The poor often fuffer much from the fhattered ftate of cellar windows. This is a trifling circumftance in appearance, but the cofequences to the inhabitants are of the moft ferious kind. Fevers are among the moft ufual effects; and I have often known confumptions which could be traced to this caufe. Inveterate rheumatic complaints, which difable the fufferer from every kind of employment, are often produced in the fame manner. This fource of difeafe may be expected to admit of eafy removal, for it cannot be the intereft of the proprietor of a cellar to have his tenants conftantly fick.

3. I am perfuaded, that mifchief frequently arifes, from a practice common in many narrow back ftreets, of leaving the vaults of the privies open. I have often obferved, that fevers prevail moft in houfes expofed to the effluvia of dunghills in fuch fituations.

In a houfe in Bootle Street, moft of the inhabitants are paralytic, in confequence of their fituation in a blind alley, which excludes them from light and air. Confumptions, diftortion, and idiocy, are common in fuch receffes.

4. In Blakeley Street, under No. 4, is a range of cellars let out to lodgers, which threaten to become a nurfery of difeafes. They confift of four rooms, communicating with each other, of which the two centre rooms are completely dark; the fourth is very

C c

ill

and there are about as many places of worſhip for different ſects of diſſenters. By improvements in the revenues of Cheetham's hoſpital, the number of boys now educated in it is eighty. The public library, which was a part of this foundation, has now a very valuable collection of books in all ſciences and languages, amounting to the number of 10,000. By the laſt ſtatement of the rents

and

ill lighted, and chiefly ventilated through the others. They contain from four to five beds in each, and are already extremely dirty.

5. The lodging houſes, near the extremities of the town, produce many fevers, not only by want of cleanlineſs and air, but by receiving the moſt offenſive objects into beds, which never ſeem to undergo any attempt towards cleaning them, from their firſt purchaſe till they rot under their tenants. The moſt fatal conſequences have reſulted from a neſt of lodging houſes in Brook's entry, near the bottom of Long-mill-gate, a place which I beg leave to recommend to the ſerious attention of the Committee. In thoſe houſes, a very dangerous fever conſtantly ſubſiſts, and has ſubſiſted for a conſiderable number of years. I have known nine patients confined in fevers at the ſame time; in one of thoſe houſes, and crammed into three ſmall, dirty rooms, without the regular attendance of any friend, or of a nurſe. Four of theſe poor creatures died, abſolutely from want of the common offices of humanity, and neglect in the adminiſtration of their medicines. In ſome other houſes in the ſame neſt, I have known a whole ſwarm of lodgers expoſed to infection by the introduction of a fever patient, yet ſo far infatuated, as to refuſe to quit the houſe till all of them have been ſeized with the diſorder. It muſt be obſerved, that perſons newly arrived from the country are moſt liable to ſuffer from theſe cauſes, and as they are often taken ill within a few days after entering an infected houſe, there ariſes a double injury to the town, from the loſs of their labour, and the expenſe of ſupporting them in their illneſs. A great number of the home-patients of the Infirmary are of this deſcription. The horror of thoſe houſes cannot eaſily be deſcribed; a lodger freſh from the country often lies down in a bed, filled with infection by its laſt tenant, or from which the corpſe of a victim to fever has only been removed a few hours before.

6. The beſt method, perhaps, of giving an effectual check to theſe evils, would be to oblige all perſons letting lodgings to take a licenſe, and to limit them in the number of their lodgers. By the terms of the licenſe, they might alſo be obliged to white-waſh their houſes twice a year, which is a powerful method of preventing infection. When a fever

5   appears

and other income of the Free-fchool, (including improvements to take place in 1794) the total amount was 2448*l*. from which all expenfes and deductions of every kind, amounting to 1079*l*. being taken, the capital fum of 1369*l*. is left for future advantages in the literary education of the natives of this town. At the time of the ftatement, there were one upper, and one under mafter, two af-

fiftants,

appears in a houfe full of lodgers, all who are uninfected fhould be immediately removed to a clean houfe, and their clothes fhould be wafhed and fcoured. When the fever has ceafed, the bed-clothes and curtains of the infected room ought to be fcoured, or other-wife cleaned, and a frefh application of white-wafhing fhould be made. With proper care, indeed, the worft kind of fever may be confined to the patient's room, without dan-ger to the reft of the family ; but no dependance can be placed on the conduct of the perfons to whom I allude.

When the fick are deftitute of beds, they fhould be fupplied by the town. It is obvi-ous, that fevers, flight in their commencement, muft be greatly aggravated, and muft often become dangerous, when the patient lies on a few rags, in a cold garret, or damp cellar.

7. This plan would require the appointment of Infpectors of lodging-houfes, whofe bufinefs it would be to vifit houfes which fhould be reported to them as infected, either by the neighbours, or by any medical gentleman, under whofe obfervation fuch places fhould fall. They fhould be empowered to take proper fteps for checking infection where-ever it appears, and occafional inquiries might be made, refpecting the compliance of perfons letting lodgings with the condition of their licenfes. This would anfwer a very defirable purpofe refpecting the police, independent of the advantages propofed regarding health. The keepers of the lodging houfes might be required to give an account of the name and occupation of every lodger whom they receive, and to become refponfible, to a certain degree, for the truth of thefe reports. By this means, a conftant check might be maintained on houfes, which at prefent are the refuge of the moft profligate and dan-gerous part of fociety.

8. There is a practice, very common in fmall new buildings, which ought to be dif-couraged; that of putting up fixed windows without cafements. Some part, if not the whole of the window fhould always be moveable ; efpecially where there is but a fingle window in the room. From the want of fuch a regulation, I have been often obliged to order feveral panes to be taken out of the window of a fever-room, to obtain a tolerable degree of ventilation.

fiftants, an Englifh mafter, and eight exhibitioners at the univerfity. Such of the fcholars as are entered of Brazen-nofe Coll. Oxon. have alfo a chance of obtaining fome valuable exhibitions arifing from lands in Manchefter bequeathed by Mr. Hulme.

In 1786 an Academy was eftablifhed in Manchefter, chiefly by fub-fcriptions among the diffenters, for the education of youth in the higher branches of literature, which has continued to flourifh under able and attentive tutors.

No town in England has been more exemplary in the number and variety of its charitable inftitutions, and the zeal by which they have been fupported—a zeal in which all ranks and parties have united.

9. It is fometimes difficult to prevent the mafter of a lodging-houfe from turning a patient out of doors, in the height of a fever, when he apprehends that his other lodgers will defert him. Some interpofition of authority fhould take place, in fuch cafes, both for the fake of humanity, and to prevent the unfortunate patient from fpreading the difeafe into a frefh houfe.

10. When a houfe is infected in every room, a nurfe fhould be provided, on whom dependance can be placed, to prevent unneceffary vifits from neighbours and acquaintances. About two years ago, a fever of the worft kind was carried from a lodging-houfe in Salford, where it had attacked all the inhabitants, to another in Milk Street, near the Infirmary, where it feized feveral perfons, in confequence of a thoughtlefs vifit made by an acquaintance lodging in Milk Street. In this way, fevers are fometimes introduced among the fervants in opulent families.

11. The prevalence of fevers among perfons employed in cotton mills, might be leffened by an attention on the part of the overfeers to the following circumftances, befides a due regard to ventilation. Perfonal cleanlinefs fhould be ftrongly recommended and encouraged ; and the parents of children fo employed, fhould be enjoined to wafh them every morning and evening, to keep their fhoes and ftockings in good condition, and above all, never to fend them to work early in the morning without giving them food.

It is greatly to be wifhed, that the cuftom of working all night could be avoided. The continuance of fuch a practice cannot be confiftent with health, and I am glad to find that it does not prevail univerfally.

1   The

The charities annually diftributed by the Borough-reeve are the following, according to the ftatement printed by Mr. Thomas Walker,
when he ferved that office in 1792.

CHARITIES, commonly called THE BOROUGH-REEVE's CHARITIES.

The late Mr. MARSHALL's Charity.

For the relief of " *the poor, aged, needy, and impotent Inhabitants*
" *of the Town of Manchefter*," was bequeathed in the year 1624, and
confifted of buildings and lands fituated in Manchefter, which in the
year 1750, produced only twelve pounds per annum. This property
was fold in 1781 to the Commiffioners under an Act of Parliament for
Improving certain Streets in the Town of Manchefter; with the money arifing from which fale, 2250*l.* ftock in the three per cent. Confolidated Annuities was purchafed, which yields annually 67*l.* 10*s.*

The late Mr. CLARKE's Charity.

For the relief of " *the poor, aged, needy, and impotent Inhabitants*
" *of the Town of Manchefter*," was given by deed dated the 13th of
December, 1636, when the whole income was 100*l.* per annum—
the neat proceeds the laft year were 320*l.* 0*s.* 6*d.* arifing principally
from lands in Crumpfall, and buildings in Manchefter.

The late Mr. SHUTTLEWORTH's Charity.

The intereft of fifty pounds to be given about Chriftmas, in linen
cloth, " *to poor Perfons inhabiting Deanfgate.*" The principal is
now

now in the hands of Mr. Edward Place, and produces annually 2l. 10s.—This bequeſt was made in the year 1696.

The late Mrs. BENT's Charity.

The intereſt of fifty pounds to be given " *to poor Houſekeepers in* " *Mancheſter, who are not chargeable to the Town,*" was bequeathed the 31ſt of December, 1773.—The principal is now in the hands of the executors of the late Rev. Humphrey Owen, and produces annually 2l. 10s.

At the ſame time, Mrs. Bent left the intereſt of fifty pounds, which is likewiſe in the hands of the executors of the late Rev. Humphrey Owen, " *to be given to poor Houſekeepers in the Townſhip of Chetham,* " *who are not chargeable thereto.*"—The annual produce is 2l. 10s.

The following account will ſhew the number of poor perſons who have been relieved by the different charities, and the manner in which ſuch relief has been diſtributed :

By the late Mr. SHUTTLEWORTH's Charity.

Two yards one-half of linen cloth, to   -   20 poor perſons.

By the late Mrs. BENT's Charity.

Money, to   -   -   -   -   -   -   47 ditto.

By the late Mr. MARSHALL's, and the late
Mr. CLARKE's Charities.

Five yards of linen cloth, to   -   -   -   958 ditto.
One gown, ſeven yards one quarter, to   -   228 ditto.
One coat, four yards, to -   -   -   -   26 ditto.
                                    Carried over   1279

One

Brought over   1279

One blanket, to   -   -   -   -   -   217 ditto.

Money, to   -   -   -   -   -   -   112 ditto.

Total number of perfons relieved by the above ——

charities,   -   -   -   -   -   -   1608

In 1752 an Infirmary was opened, which has gone on gradually increafing its funds and the extent of its benefits. It accommodates about feventy patients in the houfe. In addition to the original plan of out and in-patients, has been added the clafs of home-patients, or thofe who are attended at their own houfes by the medical gentlemen of the Infirmary, and thus a Difpenfary has been joined to the firft inftitution. The total number of patients admitted in thefe feveral claffes for the laft year was 6704; the amount of the laft year's fubfcription was 2449*l.* Annexed to this building, but a feparate foundation, is a Lunatic Hofpital, eftablifhed near thirty years fince, and fucceffively enlarged. It accommodates above feventy patients at a time. To the edifices of the Infirmary and Lunatic Hofpital have been added a range of very commodious baths; cold, warm, and vapour, which are not only ufed by the patients, but admit, at fixed rates, all others who require them.* In 1789 a Lying-in-Hofpital

* *A Table of the Rates of Subfcription to the Public Baths at Manchefter, from and after the firft Day of Auguft, 1790.*

SUBSCRIBERS OF

	Non Subfcribers, each time.	Half a Guinea, to be charged each time.		One Guinea, each time.		One Guinea and Half, each time.		Two Guineas, each time.	
		Individuals.	Families.	Individuals.	Families.	Individuals.	Families.	Individuals.	Families.
	s. d.	s. d.	s. d.	s. d.	s. d.	s. d.	s. d.	s. d.	s. d.
Cold Bath - - - -	0 9	0 5	0 6	0 4	0 5	0 3	0 4	0 2	0 3
Matlock Ditto - - -	1 8	0 10	1 0	0 8	0 10	0 6	0 8	0 5	0 6
Buxton Ditto - -	1 8	0 10	1 0	0 8	0 10	0 6	0 8	0 5	0 6
Hot Ditto - - - -	4 0	3 0	3 6	2 6	3 0	2 0	2 6	1 6	2 0
Vapour Ditto - - -	6 0	4 3	5 0	3 3	4 0	2 6	3 0	2 0	2 6
Vapour and Hot when ufed together -	7 6	5 3	6 0	4 3	5 0	3 6	4 0	2 6	3 0

in-Hofpital and Charity for delivering poor women at their own houfes, was eftablifhed ; and in the fame year, a Humane Society for the recovery of perfons apparently dead by drowning, &c. was inftituted. A truly philanthropical fociety under the name of the Stranger's Friend, for the purpofe of relieving thofe poor who are not entitled to parochial affiftance, was formed in 1791. The favourite plan of Sunday-fchools has been extended to about 5000 children annually in this town.

Manchefter has long been the feat of an Agricultural Society, which takes in a circuit of thirty miles round the town, and by its annual premiums has done much to diffufe a fpirit of improvement in that effential branch of political economy through the neighbourhood.

In 1781 this town had alfo the merit of fetting an example to the provincial towns of this kingdom by the inftitution of a *Literary and Philofophical Society*. The purpofe of uniting the purfuits of fcience and literature with commercial opulence was highly laudable ; and the fuccefs with which the plan has been attended, has been manifefted to the public by the appearance of four volumes in octavo of its Me-

---

It is propofed, that individuals or families, fubfcribing according to the foregoing rates, fhall have liberty to ufe any of the baths, during the fpace of twelve months, from the time of paying their refpective fubfcriptions : but that at the termination of this period, if the amount of the bathings fhall exceed that of the fums advanced, the fubfcribers fhall pay the difference, according to the rates fpecified in the feveral divifions of the table. Under the denomination of a *family*, all perfons conftantly refident within the houfe of the fubfcriber, excepting lodgers, boarders, and fervants, are meant to be included. Higher prices are propofed for fingle bathings, as an additional inducement to fubfcribe ; and this can be deemed no burdenfome impofition on the fick, becaufe, whenever the baths are wanted for medicinal purpofes, a continued ufe of them is required.

Wrapping gowns and towels are to be provided without any expenfe to the bathers ; and the fervants are not allowed to receive gratuities.

moirs,

moirs, which have met with a very favourable reception both at home and abroad.

Of other public plans and edifices in this town, we fhall firft mention the new prifon or penitentiary houfe called the *New Bayley*, in honour of that very refpectable man and active magiftrate, Thomas B. Bayley, Efq. of Hope, to whom the police of this diftrict has for many years been moft highly indebted. In this are adopted all the improvements relative to that part of the police, propofed in the works of that celebrated philanthropift, Mr. Howard, with whofe name it is infcribed.* There are cells for feparate confinement, different wards and yards for different claffes of prifoners, and work-rooms for various occupations; as likewife a large feffions-houfe and rooms for magiftrates, council, and jurors. It is fituated in Salford near the river.

Manchefter poffeffes a neat theatre, an elegant and capacious concert room, and large and commodious affembly rooms. It has two commodious market-places near the centre of the town. Another market at the New Crofs, top of Oldham Street, has in fome meafure formed

---

* *Copy of the Infcription on the Firft Stone of the New Goal in Salford.*

On the 22d of May, 1787, and in the 27th year of the reign of George III. King of Great Britain, France, and Ireland, this GAOL and PENITENTIARY-HOUSE, (at the expenfe of the Hundred of Salford, in the County Palatine of Lancafter) was begun to be erected; and the firft Stone laid by THOMAS BUTTERWORTH BAYLEY: and that there may remain to pofterity a MONUMENT of the affection and gratitude of this county, to that moft excellent perfon, who hath fo fully proved the wifdom and humanity of feparate and folitary confinement of offenders, this prifon is infcribed with the name of JOHN HOWARD.

D d itfelf,

itfelf, and is very convenient for this new and populous part of the town. The Crofs ftands in a wide ftreet, four great thoroughfares meeting at this point. Over the Irwell are three bridges uniting Manchefter and Salford; the old ftone bridge, a wooden bridge flagged over for foot paffengers, and the new or lower ftone bridge, which was built by private fubfcription.

In the year 1776, an act paffed for widening feveral ftreets near the centre of the town, for which purpofe a confiderable fum of money was raifed by fubfcription. The effects produced by it were very advantageous as far as they went; but ftill, as in almoft all other old towns, the central parts are too clofe; and it is only in the more modern ftreets that elegance and convenience are to be found united..

Salford, which is to Manchefter what Southwark is to London, is a royalty belonging to the crown, and gives name to the hundred. It has two fairs, one at Whitfuntide, the other in November, for cattle, and alfo for peddling merchandize, hardware, woollen cloths, blanketing, &c. A market would have been opened in Salford, had it not been prevented by a ftatute requiring a certain diftance of new markets from thofe of eftablifhed manors. The main part of Salford confifts of a wide and long ftreet leading from the old ftone bridge to the entrance of the town from Warrington and Bolton. Trinity Chapel in this ftreet was founded in the reign of Charles I. but has fince been repaired with an entire new cafe of ftone. A new church called St. Stephen's was confecrated in 1794,* and the increafe of the town has kept pace with that of Manchefter. The erection of the new ftone bridge has afforded

* The ground on which this church is built was given by Mr. John Bury, a very opulent and refpectable timber merchant in Salford.

3   a much

a much fhorter road for carriages to moft parts of Manchefter than the former one through the whole length of Salford; and fome capital breweries have been erected in its vicinity, which will have the advantage of being near the courfe of the Bolton canal. In a ftreet running perpendicularly from the end of Salford next to the foot of the old bridge, and which appears to be the oldeft part of the town, are the ancient crofs and court-houfe for the hundred.

The fupply of provifion to this populous town and neighbourhood is a circumftance well deferving of notice. Formerly, oatmeal, which was the ftaple article of diet of the labouring clafs in Lancafhire, was brought from Stockport; and the prices of meal and corn in the Friday's market there, ruled thofe of Manchefter. In the town, however, corn ground at the fchool mills was chiefly ufed by families, who fearced it themfelves, and feparated it into fine and bread flour, and bran, for domeftic ufe. About eighty years ago the firft London baker fettled in Manchefter, Mr. Thomas Hadfield, known by his ftyptic. His apprentices took the mills in the vicinity, and in time reduced the inhabitants to the neceffity of buying flour of them, and afterwards at the flour fhops. Monopolies at length took place in confequence of thefe changes, which at different times produced riots, one of which, occafioned by a large party of country people coming to Manchefter in order to deftroy the mills, ended in the lofs of feveral lives at a fray known by the name of *Shude-hill fight*, in the year 1758. Since that time, the demand for corn and flour has been increafing to a vaft amount, and new fources of fupply have been opened from diftant parts by the navigations, fo that monopoly or fcarcity cannot be apprehended, though the price of thefe articles muft always be high in a diftrict which produces fo little and confumes fo much.

D d 2

Early

Early cabbages, and cucumbers for pickling, are furnished by gardeners about Warrington; early potatoes, carrots, peas, and beans, from the sandy land on and about Bowden downs. Potatoes, now a most important auxiliary to bread in the diet of all classes, are brought from various parts, especially from about Runcorn and Frodsham, by the duke of Bridgewater's canal. Apples, which form a considerable and valuable article of the diet even of the poor in Manchester, used in pies or puddings, are imported from the distance of the cyder counties by means of the communicating canals, and in such quantities, that upwards of 3000*l.* in a year has been paid for their freight alone. The articles of milk and butter, which used to be supplied by the dairy-farmers in the vicinity, at moderate rates, are now, from the increase of population, become as dear as in the metropolis, and are furnished in a similar manner; viz. the milk, by means of milk houses in the town, which contract for it by the great, and retail it out; and the butter from considerable distances, as well as salt butter from Ireland and other places. Of butcher's meat, veal and pork are mostly brought by country butchers and farmers; mutton and beef are slaughtered by the town butchers, the animals being generally driven from a distance, except the milch cows of the neighbourhood, which are fattened when old. The supply of meat and poultry is sufficiently plentiful on market days; but on other days it is scarcely possible to procure beef from the butchers; nor is poultry to be had at any price, there being no such trade as a poulterer in the whole town. Wild fowl of various kinds are brought to market in the season.

With fish, Manchester is better provided than might be expected from its inland situation. The greatest quantity of sea-fish comes from the Yorkshire coast, consisting of large cod, lobsters, and tur-

bots,

bots, of which laft, many are fent even to Liverpool, on an overflow of the market. Soles, chiefly of a fmall fize, come from the Lancafhire coaft. Salmon are brought in plenty from the rivers Merfey and Ribble, principally the latter. The rivers in the neighbourhood abound in trout, and in what is called *brood*, which are young falmon from one to two years old, and not eafily diftinguifhed from trout, which they clofely refemble in fhape, but are more delicate to the tafte. Salmon trout is alfo plentiful, and likewife fine eels. The Irwell at Manchefter and for fome diftance below is, however, deftitute of fifh, the water being poifoned by liquor flowing in from the dye-houfes. Many ponds and old marl-pits in the neighbourhood are well ftored with carp and tench, and pike and other frefh water fifh are often brought to market. The poor have a welcome addition to their ufual fare, in the herrings from the Ifle of Man, which in the feafon are brought in large quantities, and are fold at a cheap rate.

The fupply of coals to Manchefter is chiefly derived from the pits about Oldham, Afhton, Dukinfield, Hyde, Newton, Denton, &c. at prefent by land carriage; but the canals now cutting will pafs through that tract of country, and greatly facilitate the conveyance. The fupply from the duke of Bridgewater's pits at Worfley is lefs confiderable, though a very ufeful addition for the poor.

At each extremity of Manchefter are many excellent houfes, very elegantly fitted up, chiefly occupied by the merchants of the town, which may in fome meafure be confidered as their country refidences, being from one to two miles from their refpective warehoufes. Ardwick-green, to the fouth of the town, on the London road, is particularly diftinguifhed by the neatnefs and elegance of its buildings.

Some

Some years ago it was regarded as a rural fituation ; but the buildings of Manchefter have extended in that direction fo far as completely to connect it with the town ; and this quarter is principally inhabited by the more opulent claffes, fo as to refemble, though on a fmall fcale, the weft end of the city of London. There is a chapel at Ardwick, and a fhort time ago, Nathan Hyde, Efq. who poffeffes a fpacious houfe fituated in the midft of pleafure grounds at this place, made a liberal offer of a piece of land for a new church and burial ground, which will probably be accepted, fhould the times become again favourable for improvements.

To conclude our defcription of Manchefter—we may without hefitation pronounce it to be that of the modern trading towns of this kingdom, which has obtained the greateft acceffion of wealth and population. The fortunes which have been raifed by the fpirit and ingenuity of its inhabitants from fmall capitals, have probably exceeded thofe acquired in any other manufacturing place ; and it is but juftice to fay, that in no town has opulence been more honourably and refpectably enjoyed. Upon all occafions, public or private, the purfes of Manchefter have been open to the calls of charity and patriotifm ; and whatever differences may have prevailed as to the *mode* of promoting the good of the community, the ardent *defire* of doing it has pervaded all parties. We are concerned to obferve the check its profperity is now undergoing, which is rendered too manifeft by a variety of circumftances.* May its caufes prove only temporary, and be fucceeded by renewed and augmented fuccefs !

* The regifter of the Collegiate Church from Chriftmas 1793 to 1794 ftates a decreafe of 168 marriages; 538 chriftenings; and 250 burials.

In

In the neighbourhood of Manchester are several old mansions, which are deserving of some notice.

Strangeways-hall is an ancient seat of the *Hartleys*, who once owned considerable property in and near the town. The last descendant left his estate, it is said, to his housekeeper, who conveyed it to Mr. Reynolds, father of lord Ducie, the present possessor. Many portraits of the family of Hartley are still remaining there.

An old house in Pool-fold, now converted into two public houses, was the seat of a *Ratcliff* in the reign of Charles I. at which time it was surrounded by a moat, with a draw-bridge. The posts and chains were taken away, and probably the moat filled up, about 1672.

Broughton-hall, about or a little before the time of queen Ann, was the property of a *Mr. Stanley*, a descendant of one of the earls of Derby, who bestowed it upon his ancestor about the time of queen Elizabeth. It is now the seat of Samuel Clowes, Esq.

Smedley-hall was once the seat and property of the last of the family of *Cheethams* of *Cheetham*. It is now owned by James Hilton, Esq.

Collyhurst-hall, about the reign of Charles II. was the seat of *Nicholas Moseley, Esq.* of the Ancoats family. The late Sir Ashton Lever possessed it, and it has since been in several hands.

Hough-hall, commonly called *Hough's-end*, was the seat of *Sir Edward Moseley, Bart.* whose daughter married Sir John Bland of Kippax Park, Yorkshire.

Hulme

Hulme-hall, an old half-timbered houfe, was the feat of the *Preſt-wiches*, Baronets, and of the ancient family of *Preſtwich* of *Preſt-wich* in the time of the Conqueror. This family, by embarking in the royal caufe in the civil wars of Charles I. loft much of their pro-perty ; fo that in the reign of king William, *Hulme-hall* and eftate was fold and purchafed by Sir Edward Mofeley, who left it, together with his other eftates, to his daughter Ann, wife of Sir John Bland, Baronet, who made it her chief refidence. At the death of their fon, Sir John Bland, it was fold to G. Lloyd, Efq. and it now belongs to the duke of Bridgewater.

Garrat-hall, in the time of Henry VII. belonged to *George Trafford*, Efq. and his wife Margaret, for whom the boys of the free-grammar fchool in Manchefter were bound to pray daily along with other bene-factors.

Trafford-hall is enjoyed by a family of the fame name, which traces its defcent from anceftors as far back as the conqueft.

Ordfall-hall was once owned by a family of *Ratcliffs*, a branch of the Ratcliffs of Ratcliff, which race has fpread into many once flou-rifhing branches, as the Ratcliffs of Ordfall, Foxdenton, Smethels, Wimerley, Chaderton, Manchefter, Todmorden, and Mellor, and the earls of Fitzwalter and Derwentwater. This moated manfion is now occupied by Mr. Richard Alfop, who holds it under William Eger-ton, of Tatton, Efq.

Clayton-hall, furrounded by a moat, in the time of Charles I. was owned by the *Byron* family, now lords Byron, barons of Rochdale. It was afterwards fold to the Cheetham family, and at the death of the laft Mr. Cheetham, was inherited by Mordecai Green, Efq. His fon has fince parted with it to feveral proprietors.

Kerfall-hall is in part owned by the refpectable family of Byroms, and in part by Samuel Clowes, Efq. of Broughton. On this fite once ftood a fmall religious houfe founded by the lord who owned the place, and who ended his days here in folitude. Coffins and bones have been found in the gardens and orchard of late years.

Edgcroft-hall is poffeffed and occupied by the Rev. *John Dauntefey,* whofe anceftor married one of the co-heirs of Sir Robert Langley of Edgcroft in the time of queen Elizabeth.

Clifton-hall was once the feat of a family of the name of *Holland,* a branch of the ancient family of Holland near Wigan, from whence fprung the Hollands, earl of Exeter, duke of Suffolk, &c. in the time of the civil wars between the houfes of York and Lancafter. A family of this name refided at *Denton-hall* in this parifh: funeral monuments and coats of arms to their memory are now remaining in Denton Chapel. This family likewife owned *Heaton-hall* and eftate, till the laft heir female became the wife of Sir John Egerton, Bart. of Rine-hill, Staffordfhire, great grandfather of the prefent lord Grey de Wilton, who refides at Heaton.

Birch-hall, about the reign of king John was granted by Matthew de Haverfege, to Matthew de Birch, with fome land in Widdinton (perhaps Withington) by a latin deed without date. Of this family was William Birch, firſt warden of the collegiate church after the re-formation; alſo colonel Birch of Birch, a commander in the Parliament army, and one of thoſe who defended Mancheſter when beſieged by James earl of Derby. In a large old houſe at Ardwick near Ancoats-hall, reſided during the latter part of his days Major Birch, an officer in the Parliament army; from whom is deſcended the preſent major-general Samuel Birch, who owns the lime works* and other lands in Ardwick.

Barlow-hall was the reſidence of a family of the ſame name as far back as the reign of Henry VI. but deſcending from a family of the ſame name ſeated at Barlow or Barley, in the county of Derby, as early as the conqueſt. The laſt of the Lancaſhire family who poſſeſſed Bar-low, was Thomas Barlow, Eſq. who died about thirty years ago. One Ambroſe Barlow, an Engliſh Benedictine monk, who ſuffered death at Lancaſter on a political account in 1641, is ſuppoſed to have been of this family.

Chorlton-hall within theſe few years was owned and inhabited by the *Minſhull* family, ſprung from the Mynſales, lords of Mynſale in Che-ſhire, in the reign of Henry I. It was demiſed in 1590 by Edmond Trafford, Eſq. to Ralph Sorocold for 320*l.*; and in 1644, by Ellis Hey, of Monk's-hall, in Eccles, to Thomas Minſhull, apothecary,

---

* This lime is of a very valuable ſort, as it anſwers all the purpoſes of plaiſter of Paris, and is uſed in all the aqueducts and works on the canals. In water it becomes as hard and ſolid as ſtone, and is exported to moſt parts of this kingdom. It is uſed for water ciſterns, and feels in the hand ſmooth and ſleek like ſoap. It is wound up from pits of a conſiderable depth by a horſe-gin.

been

VIEW OF HARTSHEAD PIKE.

E. Dayes delt.   Fearer sculpt.

Published June 1. 1796. by J. Stockdale, Piccadilly.

E. Dayes delt.   S. Rothwell sculp.

VIEW OF ANCOATS

in Manchester, for 300*l.* If these sums are compared to the many thousand pounds (some say sixty or seventy) for which it has lately been sold, an idea will be given of the amazing increase in the value of property near Manchester.

Ancoats-hall, a very ancient building of wood and plaister, but in some parts re-built with brick and stone, is the seat of Sir John Moseley, Bart. lord of the manor, but is now occupied by William Rawlinson, Esq. an eminent merchant in Manchester.—The annexed view, though on a small scale, is a just representation of the front of the house. It is the back part that is chiefly rebuilt.

The parish of Manchester is extensive, being computed to contain a compass of somewhat less than sixty square miles, within which are thirty-one townships exclusive of those of Manchester and Salford. It is bounded on the north, by the parishes of Prestwich, Middleton, and Oldham; to the east, by that of Ashton-under-line; to the west, by those of Eccles and Flixton; to the south, it reaches the borders of Cheshire. The population of the townships, exclusive of those of Manchester and Salford, was found, at the enumeration in 1773 and 4, to be somewhat less than half the amount of that in those towns; and as they are filled with the various branches of the Manchester manufactory, it may be supposed that their increase of population has gone on proportionally to that of the population of Manchester. Many parts of the parish appear like a continued village bordering the high roads for miles. The land is chiefly employed in pasture and meadow, as well as in bleaching and printing grounds, and other purposes connected with manufactures. The parish contains ten chapelries.

E e 2

The

The annexed view of Manchefter is taken from Kerfall-moor, at the diftance of about three miles. The fituation affords a pleafing landfcape, for the fore-ground, enlivened by the beautiful windings of the Irwell.

Manchefter has not yet afforded much matter for biographical anec-dote. The printed accounts of its college have generally contained a brief biography of the wardens; moft of whom, however, were ftrangers, and none (except the mathematician and myftic, Dr. Dee) became fufficiently eminent in literature to be entitled to particular commemoration. One perfon, who may properly be called a Manchefter man, has obtained by literary merit the diftinction of a place in the *Biographia Britannica*, and certainly deferves notice here. The following account of him is drawn chiefly from that work, though with fome additions and remarks from other fources.

ACCOUNT OF JOHN BYROM, *M. A.*

JOHN BYROM, the younger fon of Mr. Edward Byrom, linen-draper, a branch of a genteel family in Lancafhire, was born at Kerfall, near Manchefter, in the year 1691. Having received the rudiments of education in his native place, he was removed to Merchant Taylor's fchool in London, where he went through the ufual claffical ftudies with reputation. At the age of fixteen he was fent to the Univerfity of Cambridge; and on July 6th, 1708, was admitted a penfioner of Trinity College, under the tuition of Mr. (afterwards Dr. and Vice-mafter) Baker. Here he purfued the graver ftudies of the place far enough to take both his degrees in arts; but the bent of his mind declared itfelf for poetry, and the pleafanter parts of literature. The *Spectator* was at that period the popular work of the time; and it was not uncommon for

men

E. Dayes del.r

VIEW OF MANCHESTER.

Publish'd Feb: 27. 1795. by I. Stockdale. Piccadilly.

W.m Wilson sculp.t

men of ingenuity to eſſay their powers of entertaining the public, in ſome of the papers of that pleaſing and inſtructive miſcellany. Mr. Byrom is ſaid to have contributed the two letters concerning dreams in the 586th and 593d numbers. They are not diſtinguiſhed by any great depth of thought, or vigour of ſtyle, but may deſerve the praiſe of lively conception and elegant morality. But a poem, more certainly of his compoſition, in the 603d number, has obtained a very general and laſting approbation. It is the well-known paſtoral ſong of *Colin and Phœbe*, which has had a place in moſt poſterior collections of poetry of that kind ; and by the familiar ſimplicity of its language, and its natural ſentiment and imagery, ſeldom fails to give pleaſure, eſpecially to young readers. Some of the thoughts, neverthelefs, are not free from the quaintneſs of the Italian ſchool ; and the diction ſometimes goes to the extreme verge of the *ſimple*.

In 1714 Mr. Byrom was choſen fellow of his college ; and the ſuavity of his manners and pleaſantry of his humour endeared him to his companions, and gained him the favour of his maſter, the celebrated Dr. Bentley. In 1716, however, he was obliged to quit his fellowſhip, not chuſing to comply with the condition required by the ſtatutes of the college, that of taking holy orders. Probably, in common with many other conſcientious men of that period, he was prevented by political ſcruples. Not long after, his health being impaired, he went to Montpellier. During his reſidence in France, he received a ſtrong impreſſion from reading Father Malebranche's *Search after Truth*, and ſome of the devotional pieces of Antoinette Bourignon. The effect of this ſeems to have continued through life ; and he remained warmly attached to the viſionary philoſophy of the former, and not a little addicted to the myſtical enthuſiaſm of the latter. In more advanced life it appears from his works that he adopted the congenial

notions

notions of the Behmenifts. If apology were at all neceffary for a man's fpeculative opinions, it would be eafy to adduce examples of a fimilar turn of mind in perfons highly eftimable for the qualities both of head and heart.

On his return, he was for fome time wavering in the choice of a pro-feffion, and that of phyfic fuggefted itfelf to him, but he did not carry his purpofe into effect. Either, however, from this intention, or from his character of a literary graduate, he obtained from his ac-quaintance the title of Doctor, by which he was afterwards univerfally known and addreffed at Manchefter. *Some* profeffion was very defira-ble to him, on account of an attachment which at this time took place between him and his coufin, Mifs Elizabeth Byrom; which, after much preffing folicitation on his part, and much oppofition on that of the young lady's parents, who were rich, terminated at length in mar-riage. As he received no fupport from his father, his little fortune was foon exhaufted in this new condition; on which account he was obliged to leave his wife with her relations in Manchefter, and refort to London in order to make the beft of his abilities. When at Cam-bridge, he had invented a new kind of fhort hand, which for beauty and legibility has obtained great praife from the beft judges in the prin-ciples of that ufeful art. This he began to teach profeffionally at Man-chefter, and he purfued the fame employment on the greater theatre of London. Among his pupils were feveral perfons of rank and quality, one of whom was lord Stanhope, afterwards the celebrated earl of Chef-terfield. It was his cuftom occafionally to deliver to his fcholars a lec-ture on the utility and importance of fhort-hand writing, (in which he was an enthufiaft) and this, being interfperfed with his natural ftrokes of humour and vivacity, proved very entertaining. His pupils were

much

much attached to him, and uſed to treat him with the jocular title of Grand Maſter. Either from his proficiency in this art, or from his general character as a literary man, he was created a fellow of the Royal Society in March 1724.

The death of his elder brother without iſſue, at length relieved him from this ſtraightened condition. He ſucceeded to the family eſtate at Kerſall, and was at liberty to enjoy that domeſtic felicity which the ſociety of a truly faithful and affectionate wife, and a riſing family of children, aſſured to a man of his amiable diſpoſition. Of the after events of his life, none are recorded of ſufficient importance to give to the public, except that in this work it may be proper to mention the part he took in the oppoſition to the propoſed Mancheſter Workhouſe-bill, at the beginning of the year 1731. In conjunction with Thomas Pigott, Eſq. barriſter at law, he conducted the buſineſs in London; and a ſeries of MSS. letters from them to the committee of the party at Mancheſter, is in the poſſeſſion of the writer of this account. Mr. Byrom's letters, written to an intimate friend and old companion, are an agreeable mixture of buſineſs and pleaſantry, and contain many particulars of the public news of the day, as well as the progreſs of their particular affair. To ſhew the ſpirit with which he entered into the matter, we ſhall tranſcribe a paſſage from his firſt letter after reaching London. " We hope in a little time to be able to communicate our " own endeavours to obviate unfair play, amongſt ſome lords and gen- " tlemen, whoſe intereſt we have begun to lay wait for at ſecond hand, " and hope to do it in perſon; to which if any one ſhall object, as " a piece of medding and impertinence in us, we ſhall anſwer, that " we are not of the man's humour, who being on board a ſhip at ſea, " and a ſtorm ariſing, and being deſired to work a little, for that the

" ſhip

" fhip was in danger of being funk, replied, ' What have I to do
" with the fhip? I am but a paffenger.' We look upon ourfelves em-
" barked in the *good fhip Manchefter*, and whenever we apprehend her
" in the leaft danger, are ready to work as hard as if we were never fo
" confiderable fharers in her cargo. We profefs a love and fervice to
" the fellow inhabitants of our country, although we fhould not have
" a foot of land in it, not meafuring our affection for our brethren by
" our's or their acres, but by juftice, kindnefs, and liberty."

The latter part of Mr. Byrom's life paffed in the calm round of domeftic and focial employments, and in the amufement of writing, particularly pieces of verfe on a variety of topics. Verfification of the
eafy unfhackled kind he practifed, was fo familiar to him, that no
fubject, however abftrufe or uncommon, came amifs; and he poffeffed the facility, if not the graces, of Ovid, in this refpect. Even
religious controverfies and literary differtations were carried on by him
in verfe; but it may readily be imagined, lefs to the delight of the
reader, than to his own gratification. Nothing was fo well fuited to
his ftyle of writing and thinking as familiar humorous ftory-telling;
and if any of his works deferve to furvive their author, they are a few
pieces of this kind. His relation of the combat between Figg and
Sutton, two prize-fighters, and of his purchafe of the head of his
favourite Malebranche at an auction, are perhaps the beft fpecimens of
thefe light effufions. The latter is unaccountably left out of the collection of his works printed at Manchefter after his death in two vols.
12mo. in 1773. One of the moft ferious of his critical differtations in
verfe was an attempt to prove, that the true patron faint of this kingdom was not the dubious St. George of Cappadocia, but pope Gregory the Great, under whofe aufpices the Saxons of England were con-

verted

verted to Chriftianity. But this fingular hypothefis was fully confuted in profe, by that accurate antiquary, the Rev. Mr. Pcgge.

Mr. Byrom was much beloved and refpected at Manchefter and its vicinity, and though particularly connected with one party, yet gained the efteem of all, by an inoffenfive cheerfulnefs of manner, and benignity of difpofition. He died on the 28th of September, 1763, in the 72d year of his age.

ECCLES PARISH.

THE parifh of Eccles in its greateft extent from eaft to weft is about nine miles long. Its greateft breadth from north to fouth extends four miles. It is a vicarage in the gift of the crown. The church, which ftands in the village of Eccles, diftant from Manchefter four miles and a half, is ancient and large. It formerly (with the parifh of Dean) belonged to Whalley Abbey in this county; but at the diffolution of the monafteries it was made parochial; the great tythes were taken from it, and after paffing through many lay impropriators, they are now nearly all fold to the owners of the feveral eftates in the parifh. From thefe a fmall referved payment, and the glebe, with the dues, form the vicar's ftipend.

There is nothing peculiar in the climate or foil of this parifh, except its containing Chat mofs, and Trafford mofs, and other fmaller portions of moraffy ground, which there is now a reafonable profpect of re-

F f   claiming,

claiming, by the spirited and judicious exertions of Mr. Wakefield of Liverpool.

The agriculture of the parish is chiefly confined to grazing, and would be more materially benefited by *draining*; but the tax upon brick, a most essential article in this process, has been a very great hindrance to it. The use of lime (imported from Wales, and brought by the inland navigations to the neighbourhood of our collieries) has become very general in the improvement of the meadow and pasture lands; experience proves its great efficacy in improving the quality of the grass on all kinds of soil, where it is laid on in sufficient quantities; and on lands properly drained, it nearly has superseded the use of marle. The roads in this, as in all other counties, are become an object of very general and serious concern. To make and preserve these in as perfect a manner as possible, is indispensable for the interests of agriculture and commerce. Much labour, and a very great expense of money, have been expended on the roads of this parish; but they still remain in a very indifferent state, and from one plain and obvious cause, the immoderate weights drawn in waggons and carts. To prevent this, vain and useless are all the regulations of *weighing machines*; and the encouragement of broad and rolling wheels still increases the evil, which must soon destroy all the best roads of *Great Britain*, and by their irresistible crush exhaust all the ballast or gravel, materials required to repair the mischiefs they occasion.

It is the duty of the legislature not only to authorize and require good roads to be *made* throughout the kingdom, but also to enact such regulations as may *preserve* them when made; and it is now proved that this can only be done by " such a construction of carriages as will

" *oblige*

" *oblige* them to carry *light* loads, and *not* enable them to carry *heavy*
" ones." In short, by encouraging or enforcing the use of *short* teams,
or *one horse carts*. Almost all the reports of counties to the Board of
Agriculture agree in this *important* fact.

The bills of mortality will shew the extent and increase of the population of the parish of Eccles, which is the effect of the great demand for hands in our manufactures.

The invention and improvements of machines to shorten labour, has
had a surprising influence to extend our trade, and also to call in hands
from all parts, especially children for the *cotton mills*. It is the wise
plan of Providence, that in this life there shall be no good without its
attendant inconvenience. There are many which are too obvious in
these cotton mills, and similar factories, which counteract that increase
of population usually consequent on the improved facility of labour.
In these, children of very tender age are employed; many of them
collected from the *workhouses* in *London* and *Westminster*, and trans-
ported in crowds, as apprentices to masters resident many hundred
miles distant, where they serve unknown, unprotected, and forgotten
by those to whose care nature or the laws had consigned them. These
children are usually too long confined to work in close rooms, often
during the whole night : the air they breathe from the oil, &c. employed in the machinery, and other circumstances, is injurious ; little
regard is paid to their cleanliness, and frequent changes from a warm
and dense to a cold and thin atmosphere, are predisposing causes to
sickness and disability, and particularly to the epidemic fever which
so generally is to be met with in these factories. It is also much to be
questioned, if society does not receive detriment from the manner in

which

which children are thus employed during their early years. They are not generally ſtrong to labour, or capable of purſuing any other branch of buſineſs, when the term of their apprenticeſhip expires. The females are wholly uninſtructed in ſewing, knitting, and other domeſtic affairs, requiſite to make them notable and frugal wives and mothers. This is a very great misfortune to them and the public, as is ſadly proved by a compariſon of the families of labourers in huſbandry, and thoſe of manufacturers in general. In the former we meet with neatneſs, cleanlineſs, and comfort; in the latter with filth, rags, and poverty; although their wages may be nearly double to thoſe of the huſbandman. It muſt be added, that the want of early religious inſtruction and example, and the numerous and indiſcriminate aſſociation in theſe buildings, are very unfavourable to their future conduct in life. To mention theſe grievances, is to point out their remedies; and in *many* factories they have been adopted with true benevolence and much ſucceſs. But in all caſes " The public have a right to ſee that its mem- " bers are not wantonly injured, or careleſſly loſt."

The advance of population in the pariſh of Eccles has been attended with a due care reſpecting public worſhip, and the religious education of children. Two new chapels of eaſe have been built ſince the year 1775 at Pendleton and Swinton, with competent ſalaries for the clergymen from ſeat rents. In *this mode* of providing the miniſters ſtipend in new-erected churches and chapels, there does not appear a ſufficient recollection of the decreaſing value of money, or a requiſite proviſion to obviate its effects, by a clauſe in the conſecration deeds, to authoriſe a proper advance of the ſtipend as the circumſtance may require, by the direction of the biſhop, or otherwiſe.

The

The excellent inftitutions of Sunday fchools were early patronized in
Eccles parifh, and continue to receive the fteady and liberal fupport of
the parifhioners. There are now, it is calculated, near one thoufand
children regularly taught in thefe fchools, and with very confiderable
improvement.

In the laft twenty-five years only two have been added to the number of alehoufes in this parifh.

Accurate bills of mortality for Eccles parifh have been yearly printed
ever fince 1776, from which the following extracts are made.——It is
to be obferved, that the diffenters of all forts are included in the general
enumeration of families and perfons, though not generally in the lifts of
births and burials.

Year.	Chrifts.	Burials.	Marr.	Year.	Chrifts.	Burials.	Marr.
1776	303	331	95	1785	423	310	110
1777	347	248	76	1786	429	363	111
1778	347	207	86	1787	440	327	131
1779	340	337	86	1788	485	384	108
1780	364	289	74	1789	474	392	102
1781	362	248	87	1790	479	455	117
1782	386	237	74	1791	526	415	128
1783	329	358	72	1792	586	480	183
1784	418	268	122	1793	542	560	121

From the parifh regifter before the bills were kept in the new form
the following lifts are made, in which the average numbers during periods of ten years each, are ftated.

5

Years.

Years.	Chrifts.	Bur.	Years.	Chrifts.	Bur.
1700—1710	118	89	1740—1750	194	138
1710—1720	120	106	1750—1760	178	151
1720—1730	152	197	1760—1770	229	177
1730—1740	168	134	1770—1776	321	223

An uncommon and very valuable article in the new bills, is an annual ftatement of the population of the whole parifh, from which we fhall copy a few periods to fhow the gradual increafe.

		Families.		Inhab.
1776	In Worfley	522	- -	2725
	Barton	735	- -	3742
	Pendleton, Pendle-bury, and Clifton	391	- -	2256
		1648	- -	8723

		Families.		Inhab.
1780	In Worfley	560	- -	3020
	Barton	740	- -	3958
	Pendleton, Pendle-bury, and Clifton	390	- -	2170
		1690		9148

		Families.		Inhab.
1785	In Worfley	609	- -	3464
	Barton	785	- -	4341
	Pendleton, Pendle-bury, and Clifton	437	- -	2717
		1831	- -	10,522

In

		Families.			Inhab.
	In Worfley - -	742	-	-	4227
1790	Barton - -	922	-	-	5085
	Pendleton, Pendle-bury, and Clifton	542	-	-	3118
		2206	-	-	12,430

		Families.			Inhab.
	In Worfley - -	817	-	-	4693
1793	Barton - -	1004	-	-	5646
	Pendleton, Pendle-bury, and Clifton	634	-	-	3926
		2455	-	-	14,265

ASHTON-UNDER-LYNE PARISH.

THIS parifh is fituated in the fouth-eaftern corner of the county. Afhton itfelf is a fmall but populous town, which has received a great increafe of late years, and now confifts of feveral ftreets of well-built, commodious houfes. It ftands on a rifing fituation on the north fide of the Tame. There was formerly a market held here every Wed-nefday, at a place where an ancient crofs is ftill ftanding; but it has been difcontinued above thirty years, though fuch a convenience is now particularly wanted from the augmented population.

The earl of Stamford, to whom the town and a principal part of the parifh belongs, holds a court leet here yearly, where his agent prefides

as judge, and all difputes, breaches of truft, rights of tenants, together with actions of debt under forty fhillings, are cognizable. It appears from a very ancient manufcript now in the poffeffion of Jofeph
Pickford, Efq. of Royton, containing the rent-roll and feveral very
curious particulars concerning the eftate, drawn at a remote period, to
have been a borough; but why the charter was withdrawn, or by what
means the privilege was loft, there is no account: yet the cuftom of
yearly nomination, and the infignia of office, are ftill kept up by the
inhabitants.

There is nothing that excites the curiofity of a ftranger fo much at
this place as the annual cuftom of *Riding the Black Lad*, which is always celebrated on Eafter Monday. There are different traditions concerning the origin of this extraordinary circumftance, and the idea is
generally prevalent, that it is kept up to perpetuate the difgraceful actions of Sir Ralph Afhton, who in the year 1483, under the authority
of vice conftable * of the kingdom, exercifed great feverity in this part
of the country. The following are the particulars of the ceremony.
An effigy in the human form, which is made of ftraw, inclofed in a
coarfe wrapper, and feated on a horfe, is firft led through the town,
after which it is hung up at a crofs in the market-place, and there fhot
away in the prefence of a large concourfe of the neighbouring people,
who always attend to be fpectators of the exhibition. Yet from a fum
iffued out of the court to defray the expenfe of the effigy, and from a
fuit of armour which till of late it ufually rode in, together with other
particulars handed down by tradition, a very different account of the
origin of this cuftom is preferved, of which the following is the fubftance:

* The commiffion is ftill to be feen in *Rymer's Fœdera.*

In

In the reign of Edward the Third, furnamed of Windfor, lived Thomas Afhton, of Afhton-under-lyne, of whom nothing but the following particulars are known : In the year 1346, when the king was in France, David king of Scotland brought an army into the middle of this kingdom; and at Nevil's Crofs near Durham, Edward's queen, with the earl of Northumberland as general, gained a complete victory over the Scots, about the fame time that her hufband obtained a great victory in France. In this battle, Thomas Afhton, one of her foldiers, but in what ftation is unknown, rode through the ranks of the enemy, and bore away the royal ftandard from the king's tent, who himfelf was afterwards taken prifoner. For this act of Afhton's heroifm, when Edward returned from France, he gave him the honour of knighthood, and the title of Sir Thomas Afhton, of Afhton-under-lyne : and to commemorate this fingular difplay of his valour, he inftituted the cuftom above defcribed, and left the fum of ten fhillings yearly to fupport it, (within thefe few years reduced to five) with his own fuit of black velvet, and a coat of mail, the helmet of which is yet remaining.

Afhton has a large and ancient church, furnifhed with a fine ring of ten bells, and a large organ erected by the fubfcription of the inhabitants. Under the feats of fome of the pews are rude carvings on wood, relating to different families in the neighbourhood, of a very old date. Several of thefe are preferved, though the church has been newly pewed. A popular tale is current concerning a fuppofed ace of fpades cut upon the fouth fide of the fteeple. This has been found by Mr. Barritt to be an old triangular fhield charged with a mullet, the arms of Afhton, impaling the arms of Stealey, of Stealey, in that neighbourhood, which feems to denote that a lady of that family married to an Afhto n was a liberal contributor towards the building. The living is a valuable rectory in the gift of the earl of Stamford, now in the poffeffion of the Rev. Sir George Booth, Bart. Near the church is a building of great

G g   antiquity,

antiquity, called the Old Hall, which is fuppofed to have been built about the year 1483, at prefent occupied by Mr. Brooke. Adjoining to it is an edifice which has the appearance of a prifon, and till of late years has been ufed as fuch; it was formerly regarded by the inhabitants as a fort of Baftille to the place. It is a ftrong rather fmall building, with two round towers overgrown with ivy, called the dungeons, but which appear to have been only conveniences for the prifoners, as they have door places, a flag for the feet, and a rail to prevent them from falling backwards, with drains from the bottom; and they are not large enough for a perfon to live in. The prifon is now occupied by different poor families. It has two court-yards, an inner and an outer, with ftrong walls. Over the outer gate was a fquare room afcended to from the infide by a flight of ftone fteps, and very ancient. It has always gone by the name of the Gaoler's Chapel, as it was fuppofed that prayers were occafionally read in it to the prifoners. The annexed view will give a good idea of its ftate in 1793, juft before it was taken down. The houfe to the inner court is ftill ftanding, and in tolerable repair. It is inhabited by a venerable and very aged man, who remembers the gate being open through the houfe about fixty years ago. The other view annexed is of the two fuppofed dungeons and back part of the prifon, taken at the fame time. On the other fide is a view of the back front of the Old Hall adjoining the prifon, overlooking the gardens and river Tame, with a beautiful profpect. On this fide of the building are ftrong parts of immenfe thicknefs with numbers of loop holes. This view was taken from Spring Pafture. At a fhort diftance is a meadow well known by the name of Gallows-field, doubtlefs the place of execution when the lord of Afhton had power of life and death.

Afhton is joined by two very confiderable hamlets of houfes, built in the beginning of the American war, and called *Bofton* and *Charleftown*, after the places of that name in New-England. It alfo extends in every
direction

E. Dayes delin.ᵗ   R. Newman sculp.ᵗ

VIEW OF JAILERS CHAPEL.

C. Dayes del.ᵗ   Sansom sculp.ᵗ

THE DUNGEONS.

Pub.ᵈ June 4. 1795. by J. Stockdale, Piccadilly.

VIEW OF OLD HALL.

Publish'd May 4, 1793, by I. Stockdale, Piccadilly.

VIEW OF ASHTON UNDER LINE.

Publish'd July 21, 1794, by I. Stockdale, Piccadilly.

direction towards the neighbouring towns. It is well fupplied with water, except about two months in the fummer, when the inhabitants, are obliged to fetch their foft water in carts from the Tame. This river abounds with trout. It is alfo of the higheft utility to the machinery of the woollen and cotton factories of the neighbourhood ; it being reckoned that within the fpace of ten miles from Afhton there are near 100 mills upon this ftream and its tributary branches. The annexed view of the town was taken from the terrace in the front of Dukinfield-lodge, an eminence looking down to the Tame and Dukinfield-bridge, about half a mile from the church. On the right is the prifon ; on the left, the town, ftretching towards Manchefter.

Coals are got at the very edge of the town in abundance, whence they will be conveyed to Manchefter by the canal which is now nearly finifhed. Its advantages to the town and neighbourhood will be ineftimable, particularly in the improvement of the foil by lime and other manures. At a fhort diftance from Afhton, on the Manchefter road, is an extenfive mofs, from the edges of which the furrounding poor cut turf, which fupplies them with fuel. The turf is cut away till the diggers come, at about ten feet depth, to a tolerable foil of loam, which on proper improvement becomes good meadow land. The mofs itfelf is a fhaking bog, which neverthelefs can be croffed in any feafon, and probably might be made folid ground by means of judicious draining. Red fir trees are frequently found in it, which, being frefh and full of turpentine, ferve, when fplit, the purpofe of candles to the poor ; alfo numbers of large oak trees perfectly found and as black as ebony.

Afhton and its townfhips have rapidly increafed in population, with the increafe of manufactures. From an enumeration made in 1775, it appears that there were,

G g 2

In

In the town,   553 houfes, 599 families, 2859 inhabitants.
In the parifh,   941 ditto.   971 ditto.   5097 ditto.

The parifh regifter of births and burials is as under :

Years.	Chriften.	Bur.	Years.	Chriften.	Bur.
1765	235	159	1784	422	187
1770	281	167	1785	427	201
1775	323	239	1786	409	175
1776	230	131	1787	428	351
1777	324	180	1788	438	244
1778	350	174	1789	412	232
1779	342	199	1790	469	259
1780	348	180	1791	461	185
1781	364	200	1792	572	308
1782	373	186	1793	545	348
1783	353	237	1794	399	399

The following Epitaph may be feen on a tomb in Afhton church-yard in pretty good repair :

" Here refteth the body of JOHN LEECH, of Hurft, buried the
" 16th day of October 1689, aged 92 years, who by ANNE his
" wife had iffue 12 children, and in his life-time was father to 12,
" grandfather to 75, great grandfather to 92, great great grandfather
" to 2, in all 181 perfons."

Upon the tomb there has been fomething or other like a coat of arms, upon the top of which is entwined a Serpent, which tradition fays he kept tame in his houfe.——Motto, " *Virtus eft venerabilis.*"

The following lift of houfes in the feveral diftricts, paying the window taxes, was taken in 1793.

3   Afhton

Afhton town - - - 279	Mofley - - - 65
Bofton - - - - 28	Smallfhaw - - 22
Charleftown - - - 23	Hurft - - - 108
Audenfhaw, including Hoo-	Luzly and Towracre - 40
ley-hill - - - 238	Ridghill-lane, or Sta-
Knott-lanes - - - 202	ley-bridge - 112
Hartfhead - - - 37	
	Total 1154

It is certain, however, that this is very fhort of the real number, as evidently appears by comparifon with the return of houfes in the town in 1775, fince which period it has manifeftly received a great increafe.

The town of Afhton, including Bofton, Charleftown, Botany-Bay, Hurft, and the adjoining buildings on the Manchefter, Mofley, and Staley-bridge roads, with the new ftreet, &c. near the church, cannot be much fhort of 1,600 houfes. In this town five inhabitants may fafely be reckoned to a houfe, making in all 8000 fouls. Staley-bridge, Oldham, Dukinfield, Hooley-hill, Audenfhaw, Openfhaw, with the other towns and villages in this neighbourhood, have increafed nearly in the fame proportion as Afhton.

With refpect to the fchool, the appointment of a mafter is jointly betwixt the earl of Stamford and the Rev. Sir George Booth, Rector. The infcription is as follows :—" Given by the Right Hon. George " earl of Warrington, and rebuilt by the parifh anno Domini, 1721." The falary is three pounds per annum with a fmall houfe over the fchool ; the three pounds paid from Crime eftate.

Staley-bridge, near two miles above Afhton-under-lyne, has an excellent ftone bridge acrofs the Tame. A little below it another was

lately

lately built by the late John Aftley of Dukinfield, Efq. for the convenience of his own eftate.   The place is now a very large and extenfive
village, the houfes well built, fome of ftone, but the greateft part of
brick.   On an eminence ftands an octagon chapel of the church of
England, in which is an organ.   Part of the village is on the Chefhire
fide of the Tame, but by far the greateft in Lancafhire, in a continued
ftreet of half a mile, well paved.   The greateft part of this village, as
well as the chapel, has been built in the laft eighteen years.

This place has been famous, for a great length of time, for woollen
cloth, dyers and preffers, as well as weavers.   Thefe branches ftill continue to flourifh.   Here and in this neighbourhood commences the woollen manufactory, which extends in various directions as we proceed to
Saddleworth.   Here is an old hall, long in the poffeffion of a family of
the Kenworthy's, who are principally concerned in the clothing bufinefs,
but the great fupport of the place has for fome time paft been the cotton trade.   The annexed view was taken from below the bridge.

On a high ground on the Chefhire fide of the Tame, about two miles
above Staley-bridge, is fituated Staley-hall, the old family feat of the
Staleys.   It is a roomy, fpacious houfe with extenfive barns and ftables
of modern date, ftrong and well built with ftone.   The annexed view
was taken at the bottom of the yard.

In the back ground is a diftant view of Bucton Caftle.   The ftabling,
&c. forms a wing on the left, but being of great extent could not be
brought into fo fmall a compafs.   It is now a farm-houfe in the occupation of a Mr. Morfe, with very extenfive poffeffions belonging to it,
bordering on the Yorkfhire moors.   A new turnpike road from Staley-

5   bridge

C. Dayes delin.   Murray sculp.

VIEW OF STALEY HALL.

C. Dayes delin.   Eastgate sculp.

VIEW OF STALEY BRIDGE.

Publish'd June 7. 1794 by J. Stockdale Piccadilly.

E. Dayes delin.t

Eastgate sculp.t

VIEW OF SCOUT MILL.

bridge paffing this hall into Yorkfhire, is nearly finifhed, and the canal from Afhton, running up this valley at the fide of the Tame, is carrying on with fpeed.

A little above Staley-hall, on the Lancafhire fide of the Tame, ftands *Scout Mill*, a place well known to the furrounding neighbourhood, partly from its very rural and romantic fituation, and partly for its melancholy and unfortunate inhabitants. For many years it has been in the occupation of Mr. Wilfon, a refpectable man, now very far advanced in life, who has long had the care of infane perfons, but has now in a great meafure declined it. A few are ftill under the care of his fon. The mill is now ufed in the cotton branch. It is defcended to from the turnpike road near Mofley by a long fteep hill, with a lofty broken ground, nearly perpendicular to the river, overhung by a fine wood. The annexed view was taken from a rock in the middle of the river, in order to comprehend the beautiful fall of water at the Wear. In the back ground is a view of the high hill on which ftood Bucton Caftle.

Mofley is a confiderable village, with upwards of 100 houfes, many of them large and well built, chiefly of ftone. It is about three miles from Afhton, in the high road to Huddersfield, with a large chapel in the gift of or under the rector of Afhton.

Near this ftands Hart's-head Pike,* a favourite and well-known object for the furrounding country, which is feen at a confiderable diftance, and in general has been fuppofed to be a fea mark. It is fituated

* For a view of this Pike fee page 211.

on

on very high ground betwixt Oldham and Mofley, from whence the traveller has a moft delightful view of the furrounding country. We have afcertained, from good authority, that it was formerly ufed as a beacon, and there are others in the neighbourhood to anfwer it. It was rebuilt of folid ftone in 1758, and is of confiderable height and circumference. It is now fplit from top to bottom near half a yard in width. A few pounds laid out in repairs, if done in time, might preferve this pile for a century to come. On the top are the fmall remains of a weather-cock, probably a hart's-head.

Fairfield is a new fettlement belonging to the Moravians, near four miles from Manchefter and within two fields of the Afhton turnpike road. Though eftablifhed within thefe twenty years it has the appearance of a little town. There is a large and commodious chapel, with an excellent organ. The ground plot is laid out with great tafte and judgement. It forms a large fquare. The chapel and fome large dwelling houfes well built of brick form the front. On each fide of the chapel are two deep rows of dwelling houfes; on the back front behind the chapel is a row of elegant large houfes. Thefe, with the chapel, form a large fquare mafs of buildings, round which is a broad paved ftreet, and the whole is flagged round. On the outer fide of the ftreet is another row of excellent buildings, which furrounds the whole, except the front; at a fhort diftance from which is a fine row of kitchen gardens, and oppofite to the chapel a large burying ground; the whole divided and furrounded with quickfet hedges. One of the houfes is a convenient inn with ftabling, &c. for the accommodation of thofe who frequent the place.

The

VIEW OF FAIRFIELD

J.Farrington del.

Mutlow Sculpt.

Publish'd July 25 1794, by J.Stockdale, Piccadilly

The neatnefs of the whole has a very pleafing appearance, and the place is frequented by numbers from Manchefter. The annexed view is taken from the right of the turnpike road leading from Manchefter.

The cotton manufactory forms a principal part of the employment of the inhabitants, including fpinning, weaving, &c. Tambour and fine needle-work is carried to a great pitch of perfection, and is chiefly fent to London. There are alfo in this fettlement taylors, fhoemakers, bakers, and a fale fhop for moft articles, as well for the convenience of the fettlement, as for the neighbourhood.

The Manchefter, Afhton, and Oldham canal comes clofe to this place, which will be of infinite advantage to it, as well for the carrying of goods to and from Manchefter and Afhton, as for procuring a fupply of coals nearly as cheap as at the pit.

At a fhort diftance is *Shepley-hall,* pleafantly fituated on the banks of the Tame, and now in the occupation of Thomas Phillips, Efq. adjoining to it are the very large cotton factories and extenfive bleaching grounds of Meffrs. Phillips and Lowe.

The people of Afhton and the neighbourhood about fixty years ago were almoft wholly employed in fpinning cotton wefts for check-makers or twift to make fuftian warps. They likewife furnifhed fingle cotton harder thrown to make warps for flight goods. Of late they have fallen more into the practice of making twift and warps for velverets, cotton thickfets, &c. The inhabitants of feveral of the townfhips near Hooley-hill are employed in a hat manufactory lately fet up at a new village called Quebec, on the road from Afhton to Stockport.   H h   PREST.

PRESTWICH PARISH.

PRESTWICH-CUM-OLDHAM conftitutes one rectory, though the parifhes are, in fome refpect, feparate. The proper parifh of Preftwich contains the following townfhips, to which the number of families, taken at three different periods, is annexed :

	In 1714	1789	1792
Preftwich - - -	94 - - -	282 - - -	291
Two Heatons - -	40 - - -	141 - - -	148
Whitefield - - -	148 - - -	149 - - -	556
Unfworth - -	(not returned) -	115 - - -	151
Outwood - - -	63 - - -	156 - - -	183
Alkrington and Tong -	25 - - -	129 - - -	152
Families	370 - -	1314 - -	1481

The progrefs of population is further fhown by the following extracts from the parifh regifter of Preftwich :

Year.	Bapt.	Bur.	Marr.	Year.	Bapt.	Bur.	Marr.
1700 -	51	58	23	1760 -	78	61	78
1710 -	50	41	27	1770 -	126	139	126
1720 -	48	53	28	1780 -	155	126	199
1730 -	49	89	46	1790 -	201	209	244
1740 -	101	73	48	1791 -	210	185	259
1750 -	83	64	40	1792 -	174	192	257

It is to be remarked, that the building of new chapels of eafe (of which there are now feven in the united parifhes) caufes great fluctuations in the articles of chriftenings and burials at the parifh church.

Preft-

Preftwich parifh is about fifteen miles in length and three in breadth. Its foil is very indifferent, though it has been much improved of late years by manuring and draining. Lime is the principal manure made ufe of. The great demand for milk and butter at Manchefter has diminifhed the quantity of tillage, fo that there is probably little more than half the land in that fpecies of cultivation that there was about fifteen years fince. The grain and ftraw produced are generally for the farmer's own confumption, and the land is only now and then broken up to keep it in good condition, and turn up the lime, which naturally keeps finking. The tithes are for the moft part paid by a moderate compofition: 20s. per Chefhire acre for wheat; 15s. for barley, (of which very little is grown;) and 10s. for oats. The living is of the clear yearly value of about £.700. The principal feats in the Preftwich part of the parifh are thofe of lord Grey de Wilton at Great Heaton; the late Sir Afhton Lever at Alkrington; Peter Drinkwater, Efq. at Irwell-houfe; and Thomas Phillips, Efq. at Sedgeley.

The air of Preftwich is pure and falubrious, as the following note will teftify:———In the year 1747, May the 1ft, the ages of the then rector, curate, churchwarden, clerk and his wife, fexton and his wife, were as under:

	Years.
Doctor Goodwin - - - - -	70
Mr. Scholes, curate - - - - -	78
Ralph Gueft, churchwarden - - - -	85
Robert Diggle, parifh clerk - - - -	85
Ann Diggle his wife - - - - -	78
Edmund Berry, fexton - - - - -	76
Mary Berry - - - - - -	86
	558

Heaton-houfe, the feat of lord Grey de Wilton, about four miles from Manchefter, is beautifully fituated on an eminence in a rich park, highly manured and well wooded.

This truly elegant feat is built from a defign of Wyat. The centre is a circular projection with a dome at the top, that gives the whole a fine effect. It is not compofed of either of the five orders, but approaches neareft to the Ionic. The apartments are truly noble, and fitted up in the firft ftyle of elegance. One room in particular is ornamented in the compartments by the inimitable pencil of Rebecca. From the temple in the park is a moft delightful view over an extenfive and well-wooded country.

The annexed view will give a better idea of the fimplicity and elegance of the building than any defcription.

OLDHAM PARISH.

OLDHAM is a parochial chapelry, connected with Preftwich, confifting of four townfhips, *Oldham*, *Royton*, *Chaderton*, and *Crompton*.

OLDHAM contains one church and a chapel of the eftablifhment, and a methodift and a diffenter's meeting-houfe. The town is pleafantly fituated on a high eminence commanding an extenfive and delightful profpect, and is inhabited by a number of refpectable families. The chief feat in the townfhip is that of the Greggs of Chamber-hall;

now

E. Dayes del.^t

Bovis sculp.^t

VIEW OF HEATON HOUSE.

now Hopwood of Hopwood. The hat manufactory and that of strong fustians are carried on to a considerable extent in this town, chiefly for the Manchester market. Coals are found in great plenty in the several townships, which, besides supplying the neighbourhood, are sent in large quantities to Manchester. The price of those of the best quality is 5*d*. per cwt. at the pit. Branches of the rivers Irk and Irwell extend through these townships, by which a considerable number of machines are worked in the cotton and woollen manufactories. The soil is chiefly black loam and clay. Marl is met with in most parts. The produce of corn, potatoes, and other articles of provisions, is very inadequate to the supply of the inhabitants, who are chiefly fed out of the neighbouring counties. The enclosed land is estimated at about 3590 statute acres, and the waste land at 435. The trees are a little oak, ash, plane, and fir, chiefly in the hedge-rows. Lime for manure and other purposes is brought from the Peak in Derbyshire and from Ardwick, and comes high. A good deal of hay is brought every year from Yorkshire and Cheshire. The poor's rate for 1793 was about 3*s*. per pound of the full value of land. The farms are small. The value of land varies from 7*s*. to 7*l*. per acre, seven yards to the perch. The tithe of grain is taken in kind. The small tithes are compounded for by a small modus. A turnpike road from Manchester to Huddersfield runs through Oldham, and another from Mumps near Oldham through Lees and Saddleworth joins the former at Stand-edge.

ROYTON, ten miles east of Manchester, contains 576 statute acres of enclosed land, and has (Octob. 1793) 424 inhabited and 26 new houses, total 450; and 2511 inhabitants. Of the houses, only 118 are assessed to the window tax, though almost all the omitted ones are

rated

rated to the church and poor.   There are in this townſhip five mills
moved by water, four horſe mills for carding cotton, one fulling mill
for the Rochdale baizes manufactured in the neighbourhood, and one
large malt kiln.   From this variety of employ population has more
than doubled ſince 1772, in which year the inhabitants were 1105.

The ſoil is for the moſt part dry and ſandy, a few acres only wanting draining.   There is no waſte land.   The proportion of arable is
ſmall to that of meadow and paſture.   The manures are marl, got in
the townſhip ; lime, brought from Ardwick near Mancheſter or Buxton ; and black muck.   The products are oats, potatoes, and a few
turnips ; ſeldom any wheat, the vicinity of the hills making it ſubject
to mildew from damps.   Theſe are conſumed on the ſpot, but are not
ſufficient for the wants of the people, who are ſupplied from the Mancheſter market.   The timber is in hedge-rows and ſome ſmall plantations.   There are no woods.   The farms are ſmall, from 10 to 30 and
40l. per annum.   The rent per acre very various, the meadows higheſt.
Tithes are compounded for at 7s. 8¼d. per acre, Lancaſhire meaſure,
for oats, and double that for wheat.   The greater part of the vicarial
tithes are compounded for by a modus, and paid with the Eaſter dues.
The living is a chapelry under Preſtwich, value about eighty pounds ;
preſent curate, Rev. Richard Berry.   The chapel was erected by ſub-
ſcription in 1754.   There is a quaker's meeting-houſe in the townſhip.

Three branches of the *Irk* take their riſe in this townſhip, as alſo
one of the *Bail*, a ſtream which joins the Roch.   Theſe ſtreams are
ſubject to frequent floods from the quantity of rain which falls here,
but on account of the height of the ground they ſoon ſubſide.

3   The

J. Swinton del.   Wilson sculp.t

VIEW OF ROYTON HALL.

The manufactures of the place are the different branches of the cotton trade, efpecially the heavy fuftians. The raw materials come from Manchefter by land carriage, and the made goods are fent thither to the Tuefday's markets. A number of hands are alfo employed by the *putters-out* on account of the merchants in Manchefter. The manufactures employ all the people, except fome colliers, fhop-keepers, and hufbandmen. The gains are from 2*d.* per day by young children, to 3*s.* 6*d.* and 4*s.* by grown people. Women will fometimes earn 16 and 17*s.* per week by fpinning with a jenny.

Coals are a confiderable product in this townfhip, more than half of it containing valuable beds of this mineral. They have been worked here about 100 years back. The prefent price at the pit is 10*d.* the horfe load, weighing 280lb. and meafuring two bafkets, each thirty inches by twenty, and ten inches deep. The quantity worked is, by the neareft computation, about 315 tons 17½ cwt. per week. They lie from 20 yards to 100 and upwards from the furface, in different beds, dipping to the S. S. W. one yard in five and a half. Some of the beds are fix feet thick. The coals are fent to Manchefter and other parts in the neighbourhood in carts. Some free-ftone is got in the townfhip, and fold at 4*d.* per foot.

There is a good chalybeat fpring in the townfhip.

Royton-hall, the feat of Jofeph Pickford, Efq. formerly belonged, together with vaft poffeffions in thefe parts, to the lords Biron. It is pleafantly feated in a deep valley, furrounded by high grounds. It is a firm, well-built ftone edifice of ancient date, remarkable for an uncommonly ftrong and heavy round ftaircafe, like that of a church, but

more

more maſſy.   In the front of the houſe runs a ſmall ſtream, dividing the
gardens from rich meadows.   The annexed view gives a juſt repreſen-
tation of the houſe, and part of the town of Royton, with a ſummer-
houſe in the adjoining walled park, built upon a hill called the Sun
Low, whence is a very extenſive proſpect of the circumjacent country,
as far as the Welch mountains.

A very providential eſcape from danger which happened in the houſe
of Mr. Pickford, is worth recording.   On April 10th, 1790, in the
morning, a tremendous guſt of wind blew down two very large chim-
nies in the front of the houſe, each raiſed to the height of eighteen feet,
in order to prevent ſmoaking.   They fell acroſs the weſt gable roof covered with thick and ponderous ſlates, broke the beams, and brought
the whole down together through three heights of chambers, into the
cellars.   Two of Mr. Pickford's daughters were in bed in the upper-
moſt chamber, and one in that beneath.   Their beds with all the furniture were ſhivered to pieces.   Two of the young ladies were precipitated
into the cellar; one of whom was ſoon diſcovered ſcrambling up the
rubbiſh, without any material hurt, having only received ſome ſlight
bruizes on the head and arms.   The other, who was buried in the rubbiſh, was found in about twenty minutes, after the exertions of a number of neighbours, lying in the midſt of a feather-bed, not at all injured except by the fright.   The third was caught in the ſecond floor,
acroſs a beam, and fixed down by a heavy piece of wood.   She was
much bruiſed and hurt, but had no bones broken except one or two of
her ribs and recovered after a month's confinement in bed. Their maid,
who was juſt retiring from the door after calling them up, when the accident happened, was confined in the narrow ſpace of the door-way,
and obliged to remain in that ſituation till the carpenter relieved her

2   from

E. Dayes del.

Newman sculp.

VIEW OF CHADDERTON HALL.

Published July 22. 1794. by L. Stockdale. Piccadilly.

from it by cutting the door from the hinges; for had it been pushed open, she would have fallen headlong down the breach.

CHADERTON contains a chapel of the establishment. In this township is situated *Chaderton-hall*, the residence of the ancient family of the Hortons, much improved by the present owner, Sir Watts Horton. It is rather a modern house, built of brick, and nearly surrounded by shrubberies and pleasure-grounds, laid out with great taste. In the front of the house is a beautiful park, from several eminences in which are delightful prospects. The park contains several clumps of trees, and much fine timber. A commodious shooting-ground is laid out within view of the house, for the amusement of the archers in the neighbourhood, who frequently resort to this hospitable retreat. Sir Watts possesses some valuable paintings. The annexed view is taken from the park, at a small distance from the fir-trees which appear in the fore-ground. On the right, near the house, is an elevation which was formerly a tumulus, a considerable part of which has been lately taken away. Several relics of antiquity were dug up on the occasion.

Chaderton also contains a seat of Robert Ratcliffe, Esq. of Fox-Denton.

CROMPTON has a chapel of the establishment.

The increase of population in the parish of Oldham will appear from the following comparison of three periods:

I i

Oldham

Years	1714.			1789.			1792
Oldham (families)	433	-	-	2003	-	-	2370
Chaderton do.	190	-	-	601	-	-	628
Royton do. -	65	-	-	396	-	-	432
Crompton do. -	218	-	-	479	-	-	514

MIDDLETON PARISH.

THE parifh of Middleton is of large extent, and comprifes feven or eight hamlets, confifting altogether of between 7 or 8000 ftatute acres. The parifh church and town of Middleton are pleafantly fituated, with the great road leading from York to Manchefter paffing by that, and through the town. It is fifty-nine miles from York, five and a half from Rochdale, and fix and half from Manchefter. The townfhip of Middleton and much the greater part of the parifh have long been in the poffeffion of the family of the Afhetons, even previoufly to the 1ft of Richard III. anno 1483, at which time an extraordinary grant paffed to Sir Randolph Afheton, as lord of the manor of Middleton. This property was increafed, and remained in the poffeffion of the Afhetons until 1766, when the late Sir Raphe Afheton, Bart. whofe anceftors had been created fo in 1620, dying without male iffue, the eftates devolved to his two daughters as co-heireffes, the eldeft of whom, before the death of Sir Raphe Afheton, was married to the prefent lord Suffield of Gunton in Norfolk; and in three or four years afterwards the youngeft was married to the prefent lord Grey de Wilton, of Heaton, in Lancafhire. The ancient family feat at Middleton,

5   the

the manor and prefentation to the rectory of Middleton, together with that townfhip, and other adjoining property, are now in the poffeffion of lord Suffield, and the village of Middleton is rapidly increafing. Many buildings have been erected, and a grant from the crown was obtained in 1791 for holding a weekly market on a Friday, and three fairs annually, viz. on the firft Thurfday after the 10th of March, the firft Thurfday after the 15th of April, and the fecond Thurfday after the 29th of September, for the fale of all kinds of cattle, goods, and merchandize, &c.; and for the accommodation of thofe who refort thither, lord Suffield has, at a very confiderable expenfe, erected ware-houfes, and an elegant market houfe, as well as fhambles adjoining. The market, though in its infancy, is well fupplied with butcher's meat and other provifions.

The neighbourhood is populous, and nothing will more forcibly point out the increafing population of this place, than the annexed ex-tract from the parifh regifter. Yet we muft further ftate, that though little more than twenty years fince there were fcarcely more than twenty houfes in the village, there are now between 4 and 500, which contain more than 2000 inhabitants. Buildings are increafing daily, and we here view with pleafure the outlines of what one day promifes to be a great flourifhing town.

The police of the town is managed by two conftables chofen annu-ally at the court leet held in and for the manor. The church, a rec-tory, is dedicated to St. Leonard, and moft delightfully fituated on a fmall hill. It is a venerable old ftructure, has a peal of fix fweet bells, and, together with the plantation adjoining, forms an agreeable object, and heightens much the fcenery of the adjacent country. The body

or

of the church was lately very neatly pewed, and two galleries erected on the north and south, at the expense of the parish. In this church are deposited the remains of the ancient family of the Ashetons, who for many centuries resided in this parish. The Rev. Richard Asheton, D. D. and warden of Chrift's college in Manchester, is the present rector, who resides in a neat parsonage house not far distant from the church. The hall, a mansion house, formerly the place of residence of the Asheton family, is part ancient and part modern. It is at present unoccupied by any person except the steward; what was once the park lies a short distance from the house, but is now in a great measure inclosed. The free grammar school is pleasantly situated in a valley just below the church, upon the banks of the river Irk. It was founded by Dr. Alexander Nowel, then dean of St. Paul's, and principal of Brazen-nose-college in Oxford, in the year 1572, and endowed with a small stipend for two masters, wherein for some years past have been educated seldom fewer than 150 children. The present head master is the Rev. James Archer. The river Irk rises a few miles from, and passes close by, the town. The soil of the country round this place is in general sand and a strong clay: the proportion of arable land to pasture is about four acres to twenty. The crop grown principally is oats and potatoes. The size of the farms in general is from twenty to thirty acres, which are occupied mostly by weavers, who alternately engage themselves in the pursuits of husbandry, and the more lucrative one of the shuttle. The rent of land is various, being from 40s. an acre (customary measure) to 10l. The inhabitants are well supplied with coals at a moderate price and easy distance. The cotton trade is carried on in this place in all its different processes. A large twist manufactory is established here, and very considerable printing and bleaching works.

The

The weaving of filk was originally more general than at prefent, but now gives way to the more profitable branches of muflin and nankeen.

We know of no particular difeafe which the inhabitants are fubject to, and from its good air and water we confider it as a peculiarly healthy fituation.

The following extracts from the regifter will fhow the progreffive increafe of population in this parifh.

From Nov. 1582 to ditto 1590.

Marriages 46. Baptifms. { Males 117 Females 94 } Burials 134

211

From April 1680 to ditto 1699.

Marriages 108. Baptifms { Males 191 Females 190 } Burials { Males 212 Females 126 }

381   338

From 1780 to 1784 inclufive, five years.

Baptifms { Males 465 Females 456 } Burials { Males 246 Females 280 }

921   526

From 1785 to 1789 inclufive, five years.

Baptifms { Males 589 Females 544 } Burials { Males 324 Females 371 }

1131   695

Marriages for the above ten years, 490.

Marriages for ten years, from Jan. 1784 to Dec. 1793, 588.

ROCH-

ROCHDALE PARISH.

THE parifh of Rochdale is of great extent, meafuring from eaft to weft, nine miles; and from north to fouth, eleven; and, except on the wild moors, is full of inhabitants, the number of which is eftimated at 50,000 fouls, of which about 10,000 are refident in the town.

The townfhips in the parifh are four: *Hundersfield, Spotland, Butterworth*, and *Cafleton*. The inclofed land (except in the laft-named townfhip, which is chiefly of a fandy foil) is moftly of clay and black earth, which under the care of good farmers yields great crops, efpecially in the meadows. The corn grown is chiefly oats; but the whole quantity of grain raifed is fo much fhort of the confumption of the inhabitants, that perhaps nineteen parts in twenty of what is ufed are brought out of the counties of York, Nottingham, Lincoln, &c. or coaft-wife from Wales and the fouth of England, to the ports of Liverpool and Hull. The rent of good land in this parifh is as high as in moft parts of England. Meadow land may be averaged at 3*l*. 10*s*. per acre, Lancafhire meafure, (forty-nine yards to the pole;) but near the town, little or none is let under 7*l*. and fome as high as 9*l*. The farms, being generally occupied by manufacturers, are fmall, feldom exceeding 70*l*. per annum. William lord Byron is lord of the manor, and takes his feat as an Englifh peer under the title of baron Byron of Rochdale. At his court leet, the officers and conftables for the civil government of the parifh are annually appointed.

The vicarage of Rochdale is fuperior in value to every other living of that defcription in the kingdom. In the valuation of livings made in

The

the reign of Henry VIII. it is rated as low as 11*l*. 4*s*. 9½*d*. a fum that little, if at all, exceeds a hundredth part of its prefent produce. Probably no other in England has increafed in an equal proportion. The emoluments arife from lands and houfes. It is in the gift of the archbifhop of Canterbury, to whom the tithes belong, which are let for a term of years. Nine chapels of eafe belong to the church of Rochdale, viz. St. Mary's in the town, Littleborough, Milnrow, Todmorden, Whitworth, Friermeer, Lydyate, Saddleworth, and Dobcrofs; moft of them in the patronage of the vicar, Dr. Thomas Drake.

The town of Rochdale is fituated in a vale, through the middle of which runs the river Roch, which joins the Irwell below Bury. Befides the places of worfhip of the eftablifhment, it has a meeting-houfe of the prefbyterians, another of the baptifts, and a very large building lately erected for the methodifts. There are two charity-fchools, viz. a free-grammar fchool founded by archbifhop Parker, and an Englifh free-fchool endowed by Mrs. Hardman, deceafed. Sixteen Sunday fchools have been eftablifhed fince 1784. The rapid increafe of inhabitants will appear from the following extract from the regifter of the parifh church alone:

Years.	Chrift.	Bur.	Mar.	Years.	Chrift.	Bur.	Mar.
1700	268	177	91	1760	355	255	160
1710	210	212	66	1770	457	403	144
1720	231	206	57	1780	517	392	185
1730	307	247	99	1790	618	644	238
1740	275	228	66	1791	673	504	279
1750	308	261	110	1792	746	646	339

A melancholy reduction appears in the yearly bill for 1794, the articles being, *Chrift.* 373; *Bur.* 671; *Mar.* 199.

The

The markets, on Mondays and Saturdays, are fupplied chiefly from Manchefter with meal, fruit, vegetables, and roots of all kinds. The unfold flefh meat at Manchefter Saturday's market is fometimes carried to Rochdale, but the fubftantial butchers there get their chief fupply of fheep and cattle from the fortnight fairs at Skipton and Wakefield. The bread in common ufe at Rochdale is oat-cakes, of which they make brewis by pouring on them broth and the fkimming of the pot. This is eaten with black puddings, for the making of which this place is noted. The ufe of oat-cake extends from this town over moft of the Weft-Riding of Yorkfhire, infomuch that a regiment firft raifed in thefe diftricts is called the Haver-cake regiment, and recruiting parties for it commonly beat up with an oat-cake mounted on a fword's point.

Three fairs are held annually in Rochdale, on May 14th, Whitfun-Tuefday, and November 7th, for cattle, horfes, toys, &c.

There is no prifon in the town, offenders being fent to the houfe of correction for the hundred in Manchefter.

A fmall, but very neat playhoufe has lately been erected under the management of Mr. Stanton.

The parifh of Rochdale, though not able to boaft of its fertile corn-fields, is yet rich in the mineral products of flate, ftone, and coal. It is alfo, and has long been, diftinguifhed for its trade. A branch of the woollen manufacture is its ftaple, of which the principal articles are bays, flannels, kerfeys, coatings, and cloths, the greateft part of which are fent abroad to Holland, Portugal, Spain, Italy, Ruffia, and Germany. Part of thefe are exported or fent to London by the York-

fhire

fhire merchants; but confiderable quantities are fent directly abroad by the merchants of Rochdale itfelf. The manufactures extend eight or ten miles to the north of the town. The cotton trade has likewife fpread greatly in the neighbourhood; and a very confiderable hat manufacture is in an increafing ftate.

Rochdale hitherto has not had the advantage of a navigation; but a canal is now cutting which will connect it with the navigable river Calder on the one fide, and with the duke of Bridgewater's canal at Manchefter on the other; and thus afford a communication with the ports of Liverpool and Hull, and with the whole fyftem of internal canal navigation. Upwards of 290,000*l.* has been fubfcribed to carry this fcheme into execution, which muft be of the greateft benefit to the town, as well in refpect to its manufactures, as its fupply of provifions and merchandize.

The ancient families of note in the parifh are Chadwick of Healey, Entwiftle of Foxholes, Buckley of Buckley, Townley of Belfield, Hamer of Hamer, Halliwell of Pike-houfe, Bamford of Shore. There are likewife other gentlemen of confiderable landed property in the parifh, who are alfo engaged in its commercial concerns.

In the chapelry of Whitworth refide Meffrs. John and George Taylor, better known by the name of the *Whitworth Doctors*. The fame of thefe ruftic artifts is almoft equal to that of the celebrated Swifs doctor, mentioned by Mr. Coxe, and has fpread not only over their more immediate neighbourhood, but to remote parts of the kingdom, and even the metropolis itfelf. They are chiefly noted for fetting broken and diflocated bones, and for the cure of cancerous and other

K k

tumours

tumours by cauftics, properly termed by themfelves *Keen*. Not lefs than 100 perfons annually take lodgings in Whitworth to be under their care, befides the great refort of occafional vifitants. With very rea-fonable charges they have realized handfome fortunes, which they en-joy with the general efteem of their neighbours.

Rochdale and its vicinity may be confidered as the centre of the genuine *Lancafhire dialect*; a variety of the Englifh tongue, which, though uncouth to the ear, and widely differing in words and grammar from cultivated language, is yet poffeffed of much force and expreffion. Its peculiar aptnefs for humorous narrative has been difplayed in the noted dialogue containing the adventures of a Lancafhire clown, of which this diftrict is the fcene, written by Mr. Collier, under the name of *Tim Bobbin*. The following memoirs of this perfon, obligingly communicated to us by Richard Townley, Efq. will, we doubt not, agreeably entertain our readers.

ACCOUNT OF TIM BOBBIN,

Mr. JOHN COLLIER, alias Tim Bobbin, was born near War-rington in Lancafhire.* His father, a clergyman of the eftablifhed church, had a fmall curacy, and for feveral years taught a fchool. With the joint income of thofe, he managed fo as to maintain a wife and feveral children decently, and alfo to give them a tolerable fhare of

---

* Mr. Wardleworth, mafter of the free fchool at Mottram, affures us that he was born at Harrifon's Fold, near this village. He was intimately connected with him from his youth.

ufeful

useful learning, until a dreadful calamity befell him, about his 40th year, the *total* loss of sight. His former intentions of bringing up his son John, of whose abilities he had conceived a favourable opinion, to the church, were then over, and he placed him out an apprentice to a Dutch loom-weaver, at which business he worked more than a year; but such a sedentary employment not at all according with his volatile spirits and eccentric genius, he prevailed upon his master to release him from the remainder of his servitude. Though then very young, he soon commenced itinerant school-master; going about the county from one small town to another, to teach reading, writing, and accounts; and generally having a night school (as well as a day one) for the sake of those whose necessary employments would not allow their attendance at the usual school hours. In one of his adjournments to the small, but populous town of Oldham, he had intimation that Mr. Pearson, curate and schoolmaster at Milnrow, near Rochdale, wanted an assistant in the school; to that gentleman he applied, and, after a short examination, was taken in by him to the school, and he divided his salary, twenty pounds a year, with him. This Tim considered as a material advance in the world, as he still could have a night school, which answered very well in that very populous neighbourhood, and was considered by him too as a state of independency, a favourite idea *ever afterwards* with his high spirit. Mr. Pearson, not very long afterwards, falling a martyr to the gout, my honoured father gave Mr. Collier the school, which not only made him happy in the thought of being *more* independent, but made him consider himself as a *rich* man. Having now more leisure hours by dropping his night-school there, though he continued to teach at Oldham and some other places during the vacations of Whitsuntide and Christmas, he began to instruct himself in music and drawing, and soon was such a proficient in both as to be able to instruct

K k 2   others

others very well in thofe amufing arts. The hautboy and *common* flute were his chief inftruments, and upon the former he very much excelled, the fine modulations that have fince been acquired or introduced upon that noble inftrument, being then unknown to all in England. He drew landfcapes in good tafte, underftanding the rules of perfpective, and attempted fome heads in profile, with very decent fuccefs; but it did not hit his humour, for I have heard him fay, when urged to go on in that line, that drawing heads and faces was as dry and infipid as leading a life without frolic and fun, unlefs he was allowed to *fteal in* fome lears of comic humour, or give it a good dafh of the caricature. Very early in life he difcovered fome poetic talents, or rather an eafy habit for humorous rhyme, by feveral anonymous fquibs he fent about in ridicule of fome notorioufly abfurd, or very eccentric characters; thefe were fathered upon him very juftly, which created him fome enemies but more friends. I had once in my poffeffion fome humorous relations, in tolerable rhyme, of his own frolic and fun with perfons he met with, of the like defcription, in his hours of feftive humour, which was fure to take place when releafed for any time from fchool duty, and not too much engaged in his lucrative employ of painting. The firft regular poetic compofition which he publifhed was ftyled the *Blackbird*, containing fome fpirited ridicule upon a Lancafhire juftice, more renowned for political zeal and ill-timed loyalty, than good fenfe or difcretion. In point of eafy, regular verfification, perhaps this was his beft fpecimen, and it alfo exhibited fome ftrokes of *true* humour. About this period of his life he fell *ferioufly* in love with a handfome young woman, a daughter of Mr. Clay of Flocton, near Huddersfield, and foon afterwards took her unto him for wife, or as he ufed to ftyle her, his crooked rib, who in proper time increafed his family, and proved to be a virtuous, difcreet, fenfible, prudent woman; a good wife, and

an

an excellent mother. His family continuing to increafe nearly every year, the hautboy, flute, and *amufing* pencil were pretty much difcarded, and the brufh and pallet taken up *ferioufly*. He was chiefly engaged for fome time in painting altar pieces for chapels, and figns for publicans, which pretty well rewarded the labours of his vacant hours from fchool attendance; but after fome time family expenfes increafing more with his growing family, he devifed, and luckily hit upon, a more lucrative employment for his leifure time—this was copying Dame Nature in fome of her humorous deformities and grotefque fportings with the human race (efpecially where the vifage had the greateft fhare in thofe fportings) into which his pencil contrived to throw fome pointed features of grotefque humour; fuch as were beft adapted to excite rifibility, as long as fuch ftrange objects had the advantage of novelty to recommend them. Thefe pieces he worked off with uncommon celerity; a fingle portrait in the leifure hours of two days at leaft, and groups of three or four, in a week: as foon as finifhed, he was wont to carry or fend them to the firft-rate inns at Rochdale and Littleborough in the great road to Yorkfhire, with the loweft prices fixed upon them, the inn-keepers willingly becoming Tim's agents. The droll humour, as well as fingularity of ftyle of thofe pieces, procured him a moft ready fale from riders-out, and travellers of other defcriptions, who had heard of Tim's character. Thefe whimfical productions foon began to be in fuch general repute, that he had large orders for them, efpecially from merchants in Liverpool, who fent them upon fpeculation into the Weft Indies and America. He ufed at that time to fay, that if Providence had ever meant him to be a *rich* man, that would have been the proper time, efpecially if fhe had kindly beftowed upon him two pair of hands inftead of one; but whenever cafh came in readily it was fure to go merrily: a cheerful glafs with a joyous com-

panion

3

panion was fo much in unifon with his own difpofition, that a temptation of that kind could never be refifted by *poor Tim;* fo the feafon
to grow rich never arrived, but Tim remained *poor* Tim to the end of
the chapter.

Collier had been for many years collecting, not only from the ruftics
in his own neighbourhood, but alfo wherever he made excurfions,
all the aukward, vulgar, obfolete words and *local* expreffions which
ever occurred to him in converfation amongft the lower claffes. A
very retentive memory brought them fafe back for infertion into his
vocabulary or gloffary, and from thence he formed and executed the
plan of his *Lancaſhire dialect;* which he exhibited to public cogni-
zance, in the adventurers of a Lancafhire Clown, formed from fome
ruftic fports and gambols, and alfo fome whimfical modes of circulating fun, at the expenfe of filly, credulous boobies, amongft the *then*
cheery gentlemen of that *peculiar* neighbourhood. This publication, from
its novelty, together with fome *real* ftrokes of comic humour interlarded
into it, took very much with the middle and lower claffes of the people
in the northern counties, (and I believe every where in the fouthern too,
where it had the chance of being noticed) fo that a new edition was
foon neceffary. This was a matter of exultation to Tim, but not of
very long duration; for the rapid fale of that fecond edition foon brought
forth two or three *pirated* editions, which made the honeft, unfufpect-
ing owner exclaim with great vehemence, " That he did not believe
" there was *one* honeft printer in Lancafhire;" and afterwards to lafh
fome of the moft culpable of thofe infidious offenders with his keen,
farcaftic pen, when engaged in drawing up a preface to a future publication.

The

The above-named performances, with his pencil, his brush, and his pen, made Tim's name and repute for whimsical archness pretty generally known, not only within his native county, but also through the adjoining districts in Yorkshire and Cheshire; and his repute for a peculiar species of pleasantry in his hours of frolic, often induced persons of much higher rank to send for him to an inn (when in the neighbourhood of his residence) to have a *personal* specimen of his uncommon drollery. Tim was seldom backwards in obeying a summons to good cheer, and seldom, I believe, disappointed the expectations of his generous hosts; for he had a wonderful flow of spirits, with an inexhaustible fund of humour, and that too of a very peculiar cast. Blessed with a clear, masculine understanding, and a keen discernment into the humours and foibles of others, he knew how to make the best advantage of those occasional interviews, in order to promote *trade*, as he was wont to call it; though his natural temper was very far from being of a mercenary cast; it was often rather too free and generous, more so than prudence, with respect to his family, would advise, for he would sooner have had a *lenten* day or two at home, than done a shabby or mean thing abroad.

Amongst other persons of good fortune who often called upon him at Milnrow, or sent for him to spend a few hours with him at Rochdale, was a Mr. Richard Hill of Kibroid and Halifax in Yorkshire, then one of the greatest cloth merchants, and also one of the most considerable manufacturers of baizes and shalloons, in the north of England. This gentleman was not only fond of his humorous conversation, but also had taken up an opinion that he would be highly useful to him as his head clerk in business, from his being very ready at accounts, and writing a most beautiful *small* hand in any kind of type, but especially in imitation

tion of *printed** characters. After several fruitless attempts, he at last, by offers of an extravagant salary, prevailed upon Mr. Collier to enter into articles of service for three years certain, and to take his family to Kibroid. After signing and sealing, he called upon me to give me notice that he must resign the school, and to thank me for my long continued friendship to him. At taking leave, he, like the honest Moor,

> Albeit unused to the melting mood,
> Dropp'd tears as fast as the *Arabian* trees
> Their medicinal gum,

and in faltering accents entreated me not to be hasty in filling up the vacancy in that school, where he had lived so many years contented and happy; for he had *already* some forebodings that he should never relish his new situation and new occupation. I granted his request, but hoped he would soon reconcile himself to his new situation, as it promised to be so advantageous both to himself and to his family. He replied, it was for the sake of his wife and children that he was at last induced to accept Mr. Hill's *very tempting* offers; no other consideration whatever could have made him give up Milnrow school and independency.

About two month's afterwards, some business of his master's bringing him to Rochdale market, he took that opportunity of returning by Belfield. I instantly perceived a wonderful change in his looks; that countenance that used ever to be gay, serene, or smiling, was then covered and disguised with a pensive, settled gloom. On asking him

---

* The Lord's Prayer in the size of a split pea of the *garden* kind; the Apostle's Creed in the size of a sixpence, both most distinct.

how

how he liked his new fituation at Kibroid, he replied, Not at all; then enumerating feveral caufes for difcontent, concluded with an obferva-tion, that he never could abide the ways of that country, for they nei-ther keep *red letter* days themfelves, nor allow their fervants to keep any.—Before he left me, he paffionately entreated that I would not give away the fchool, for he fhould never be happy again till he was feated in the crazy old elbow chair, within his *old* fchool. I granted his re-queft, being lefs anxious to fill up the vacancy, as there were two other free fchools for the fame ufes, within the fame townfhips, which have decent falaries annexed to them.

Some weeks afterwards I received a letter from Tim, that he had fome hopes of getting releafed from his vaffalage; for that the father* having found out what very high wages his fon had agreed to give him, was exceeding angry with him for being fo extravagant in his allowance to a clerk; that a violent quarrel betwixt them had been the confequence, and from that circumftance he meant, at leaft hoped, to derive fome advantage in the way of regaining his liberty, which he lingered after and panted for as much as any galley-flave upon earth.

Another letter announced, that his mafter perceiving that he was de-jected, and had loft his wonted fpirits and cheerfulnefs, had hinted to him, that if he difliked his prefent fituation, he fhould be releafed from his articles at the end of the year; concluding his letter with a *moft earneft imploring*, that I would not difpofe of the fchool before that time. By the interpofition of the old gentleman and fome others, he got the agreement cancelled a confiderable time before the year expired; and

* The father and fon were not in partnerfhip, but carried on diftinct branches of the woollen trade.

L l   the

the evening of the day, when that liberation took place, he hired a large Yorkfhire cart to bring away bag and baggage by fix the next morning to his own houfe* at Milnrow. When he arrived upon the weft fide of Blackfton-edge, he thought himfelf once more a *free man*, and his heart was as light as a feather. The next morning he came up to Belfield to know if he might take poffeffion of his fchool again, which being readily confented to, tears of gratitude inftantly ftreamed down his cheeks, and fuch a fuffufion of joy illumined his counte- nance as plainly befpoke the heart being in unifon with his looks. He then declared his *unalterable* refolution never more to quit the hum- ble village of Milnrow: that it was not in the power of emperors, kings, or their prime minifters, to make him any offers, if fo difpofed, that would allure him from his tottering elbow chair, from humble fare with liberty and contentment. A hint was thrown out that he muft work hard with his pencil, his brufh, and his pen, to make up the deficiency in income to his family—that he promifed to do, and was as good as his promife, for he ufed double diligence, fo that the inns at Rochdale and Littleborough were foon ornamented, more than ever, with ugly grinning old fellows, and mumbling old women on broom- fticks, &c. &c.

Tim's laft literary productions, as I recollect, were remarks upon the Rev. Mr. Whitaker's Hiftory of Manchefter in two parts. The remarks will fpeak for themfelves. There appeared rather too much feafoning and falt in fome of them, mixed with a degree of acerbity, for which he was rather blamed.

* His father-in-law built a very decent houfe for him and his daughter, upon a fmall plot of ground near the fchool on a 999 year leafe, at the fmall chief of a fhilling per ann.

Mr. Collier died in poffeffion of his mental powers but little impaired, at near eighty years of age, and his eyes not fo much injured as might have been expected from fuch a fevere ufe of them during fo long a fpace of time. His wife died a few years before him, but he left three fons and two daughters behind him. The fons were all attached to the pallet and brufh, but in different branches of the mimetic art.

RATCLIFFE PARISH.

THE parifh of Ratcliffe confifts only of the townfhip of that name, and takes in a circuit of between fix and feven meafured miles. The number of houfes contained in it is 399; of families, 409; and of inhabitants, 2032. The houfes for the moft part are of an inferior fort, and the inhabitants are chiefly weavers, crofters, or employed in the coal works which abound in this country. Thofe who live by farming in this parifh are very few, and the lands are much divided. Nearly the whole is the property of the lord Grey de Wilton, who is likewife the patron of the rectory.

Year.	Bapts.	Burials.	Marr.	Year.	Bapts.	Burials.	Marr.
1700	12	23	4	1770	83	73	18
1710	32	22	9	1780	60	37	10
1720	36	14	9	1790	92	72	15
1730	25	44	5	1791	118	82	14
1740	28	38	10	1792	123	95	17
1750	61	53	15	1793	120	57	15
1760	75	24	16				

BOLTON.

BOLTON.

BOLTON-LE-MOORS, fo called to diftinguifh it from a town of the fame name in the Weft-Riding of Yorkfhire, has been known as the feat of a manufacture belonging to the fyftem of the Manchefter trade, as far back as that trade itfelf can be traced. Leland, in his Itinerary, notices the cottons (then a fpecies of woollen manufacture) and coarfe yarn which its markets afforded, and fays that many villages in the moors around were employed in making thofe cotrons. At that period, too, the coal pits in its neighbourhood were wrought, which, with cannel and turf, afforded the fuel of the diftrict. The early manufacture of fuftians at Bolton has been mentioned in our account of the trade of Manchefter, and it has continued to be celebrated for thefe and a variety of kindred articles to the prefent day. The barrennefs of its fituation has probably aided its progrefs in wealth and population by operating as a ftimulus to the induftry and ingenuity of the people. It is faid that the manufactures originated from proteftant refugees from Flanders; but this could not have been the cafe with thofe eftablifhed before Leland's time, who lived in the reign of Henry VIII. Poffibly, foreigners might have been the introducers of the *real cotton* branches, which fuccceded to the coarfe woollens fo called.

In the civil wars of Charles the Firft's time, Bolton underwent a ftorm in 1644 from prince Rupert, in which many perfons were killed: and in 1652, James earl of Derby, who had been taken in the battle of Worcefter, was beheaded at Bolton, in retaliation, it was faid, for the feverities inflicted there under his command.

Bolton

Bolton has no other magiſtrates than conſtables. It has a free-ſchool, of which Ainſworth, author of the Latin Dictionary, was once a maſter. There are two principal fairs in the year, one in winter and the other in ſummer. The market is on Monday. It is ſupplied with oat-meal from both Preſton and Mancheſter, beſides from oats grown in the neighbourhood. Jannock or oat bread was formerly the only kind uſed at Bolton, and was proverbially as noted as Cheſhire cheeſe. The cattle killed by the butchers are brought chiefly from Yorkſhire, and moſtly conſiſt of Scotch cows, called cuſhes, fattened in Craven. So greatly is the conſumption of fleſh meat increaſed, that, whereas in the memory of ſome perſons now living, not more than one cow uſed to be killed weekly in Bolton, or if two, the unſold beef uſed to be ſent to Bury market,—before the beginning of the preſent war, a tanner in Anderton bought weekly thirty-five cow hides of the Bolton butchers, and yet was ſuppoſed not to take half the whole produce. The fruit and vegetables ſold here come principally from the Mancheſter markets, or from the vicinity of Warrington, its own neighbourhood not being favourable to theſe productions.

In 1773 an enumeration was made of the inhabitants of the manor of Bolton, which gave the following reſults :

	houſes,		inhabitants,	
In the town of Bolton, - - -	946		4568.	
In Little Bolton and the manor - ditto -	232	ditto - -	771	
Total	1178		5339	

So rapid was the increaſe after this period, that in 1789 an enumeration of the inhabitants of the townſhip of Bolton gave the amount

of

of 11,739 perfons; and the augmentation vifibly went forwards till the beginning of the prefent war. Even at this time, notwithftanding the great numbers who have enlifted, houfes for the working clafs are not procured without difficulty; and laft fummer many houfes were built in the fkirts of the town, which are now occupied. Upwards of a thoufand children attend the Sunday fchools of the methodifts, and are inftructed in their chapel by teachers without pay.

This original feat of the cotton trade is ftill the centre of the manu-facture of ornamental or fancy goods. It is only by emigrants from this place that any branches of this trade have been tranfplanted elfe-where; but the moft ingenious part of the workmanfhip ftill remains rooted as it were to the foil, and flourifhes even amidft prefent difcou-ragements fo far, that the poor fuffer lefs here than in any of the fur-rounding diftricts. The muflin trade is that which feems to anfwer beft at prefent. Since the oppofition of the populace to the ufe of ma-chines for fhortening labour has been quelled by convincing them of their utility, fpinning factories have been erected throughout all the furrounding country, efpecially where water is plentiful. The ftreams near Bolton are too near their fources to furnifh the water that large works require; there are few, therefore, in its neighbourhood of the larger kind, though feveral of the fmaller. Much water is alfo occu-pied by the bleachers, who have extenfive crofts here. The new and more expeditious mode of bleaching by the dephlogifticated marine acid is now generally known, but it is not often ufed unlefs when there is a very brifk demand for a particular fort of goods; for if great care be not taken, it is often injurious to the pieces, and takes out the marks. The want of water in this diftrict is made up by the ingenious inven-tion of the machines called mules, or *hall-in-the-wood* wheels, from

an

an old hall in the neighbourhood feated in a moft romantic fituation, in a part of which the inventor refided. This machine admits of a great number of fpindles; the greateft yet known is 304. Had the inventor fought a patent, he might probably have acquired a large fortune; but fome gentlemen in Manchefter purchafed the invention for 100l. and made it public.

The Bolton manufacturers almoft univerfally repair to Manchefter to fell their goods on the Tuefday, fome few on the Thurfday, and a great number on the Saturday, of every week. Manchefter on thofe days is crowded with traders and makers of cotton goods from the country round, on the Tuefdays particularly. The goods are not expofed in a public hall as the Yorkfhire cloths are; their vaft quantity and variety would not admit of fuch a mode. The expenfes of importing the raw materials, and the extent of the trade, have enabled men of fome property to ftep in between the weaver and merchant, and to obtain a profit upon the materials and goods in every ftage of their progrefs.

The fuftian tax impofed about ten years ago was, of courfe, a matter of very near concern to the manufacturers of this place; and upon its repeal, obtained by the determined oppofition of the people, and the able and active exertions of the gentlemen delegated from Manchefter for the purpofe, a filver cup was prefented from Bolton to Mr. Thomas Walker and Mr. Richardfon, with the following infcription, drawn up by Dorning Rafbotham, Efq.:—" To ————, this cup is moft " refpectfully prefented by the inhabitants of the town and neighbour- " hood of Bolton in the Moors, the original feat of the fuftian manu- " facture in this kingdom, as a token of their gratitude for his lauda- " ble and unwearied exertions, in conjunction with his affociates, in " foliciting,

" foliciting, and in the year 1785, in procuring a repeal of an odious
" and oppreffive tax upon ftuffs made of cotton and linen mixed, or
" wholly of cotton wool."

Bolton, as we have already noticed, is upon the eve of obtaining the
benefit of a canal connecting it with Manchefter, and with all the circuit of inland water communication. It will run along the edge of
the hills on the banks of the Irwell and its tributary ftreams, through a
moft beautiful and romantic country. Thrice it is carried over thefe
ftreams by aqueducts much grander than that at Barton-bridge. One
is at Clifton; another at Preftolee; and a third, at leaft twenty yards
high, and confifting of three arches, within two miles of Bolton.
Coals, which alone can repay the expenfe of fuch an undertaking, are
met with all round the town. Steam engines are much ufed, not only
for draining the mines, but on a fmaller fcale, for drawing up the coals.
But few of them are on the plan of Meffrs. Bolton and Watt.

The neighbourhood of Bolton has been diftinguifhed for producing
men of great talents in mechanical invention, who have generally been
wholly uneducated, and indebted only to native powers and the habit
of obfervation. The moft celebrated of thefe was Sir Richard Arkwright, of whom falfe pride and prejudice alone can think it derogatory to fay, that he paffed a great part of his life in the humble ftation
of a barber in the town of Bolton. His mind was fo ardently engaged
in the improvements of the mechanifm ufed in the manufactures, that
he could fcarcely keep himfelf above want by the exercife of his proper
profeffion; but his perfeverance and ingenuity were at length rewarded
with a meafure of opulence which nothing but the full tide of profperity

rity in a commercial nation could beftow. His fhare of merit in invention has already been ftated in the account of the trade of Manchefter.

At *Smithels* an old hall to the north of Bolton, anciently belonging to the Fauconberg family, is ftill remaining a large wainfcotted room, the pannels of which are adorned with upwards of fifty heads cut in the wood, which are fuppofed to reprefent different perfons of the family. The hall has been much vifited, on a fuperftitious account, by zealous proteftants, in order to view the fuppofed impreffion of a foot made in the ftone floor by one Marfh, a martyr, in the reign of queen Mary.

Rivington, in the parifh of Bolton, is diftinguifhed by a lofty hill crowned by a building called *Rivington Pike*, a confpicuous object to the country round. In this townfhip fome promifing veins of lead and calamine were difcovered many years fince in the eftate of Sir F. Standifh, which were worked, and lead enough got to pay the expence. They have fince been purfued by miners out of Derbyfhire, but not much more has been done than to clear the old works of water. The veins follow the dip of a great rock into the eftate of James Hammerton, Efq.

B U R Y.

BURY is pleafantly fituated about nine miles north of Manchefter, with the Irwell running clofe on its weft fide, and the Roch about a mile's diftance on the eaft, both which rivers unite about two miles below. In Leland's tour Bury is mentioned as a poor market, having a ruin of a caftle by the parifh church, which, with the town, belonged formerly to the Pilkingtons, but then to the earl of Derby. Yarn was made about the town. At the prefent day, Bury may be confidered

M m

as a confiderable appendage to the cotton and woollen trades. It is a market town of tolerable fize, the market day on Thurfday. The buildings are moftly of brick, and generally good. The church, which has been lately rebuilt, is very handfome. There are likewife a chapel of the eftablifhment, and places of worfhip for the prefbyterians, independents, and methodifts. There is a very handfome free-fchool well endowed, with two mafters, who have each a good houfe befides their falaries; and alfo a charity fchool for boys and girls. One half of the town is leafehold under the earl of Derby; the other half glebe, belonging to the rectory. The living, in the gift of the earl of Derby, is a very valuable one, and has of late years been much improved, owing to an act of parliament paffed in 1764, empowering the rector for the time being to grant building leafes for 99 years, renewable at any period in the interim as the rector and tenant can agree. By an account taken in 1773, the number of houfes in Bury was 463; of families, 464; and of inhabitants, 2090. Thefe numbers are fuppofed fince that time to have doubled, from the natural increafe, and the influx of new people. The following extract of the regifter of the parifh church will fhow the progrefs of population during the laft ten years.

	Marr.	Chrift.	Bur.
From July 1784 to ditto 1785	167	411	257
———— 1785 to ditto 1786	166	425	291
———— 1786 to ditto 1787	135	450	222
———— 1787 to ditto 1788	137	457	373
———— 1788 to ditto 1789	159	468	266
———— 1789 to ditto 1790	160	456	357
———— 1790 to ditto 1791	185	481	257
———— 1791 to ditto 1792	182	477	239
———— 1792 to ditto 1793	156	530	255
———— 1793 to ditto 1794	196	481	272

The

The parifh is large, and divided into the following townfhips : Tottington Higher and Lower End, Bury, Walmerfley, Heap, and Elton. The four laft are commonly called the lordfhip of Bury, and are moftly leafehold, under the earl of Derby. The Tottingtons compofe what is called the royal manor of Tottington. There are three chapels of eafe in the parifh, Holcombe, Edenfield, and Heywood.

The cotton manufacture, originally brought from Bolton, is here carried on very extenfively in moft of its branches. A great number of factories are erected upon the rivers and upon many brooks within the parifh, for carding and fpinning both cotton and fheep's wool, alfo for fulling woollen cloth. The inventions and improvements here in different branches are aftonifhing. One of the moft remarkable is a machine made by Mr. Robert Kay, fon to the late Mr. John Kay, inventor of the wheel or flying fhuttle, for making feveral cards at once to card cotton or wool. The engine ftraightens wire out of the ring, cuts it in lengths, ftaples it, crooks it into teeth, pricks the holes in the leather, puts the teeth in, row after row, till the cards are finifhed ; all which it does at one operation of the machine, in an eafy and expeditious manner, by a perfon turning a fhaft, and touching neither the wire nor leather.

Formerly there lived in this town Mr. Thomas Whitehead, who was at the fame time clerk and apparitor, and alfo an ingenious artift. He was noted for being the firft maker of a very ferviceable metal button, much efteemed by country people, and ftill fold by the name of Clerk-of-Bury buttons.

M m 2

The

The town and neighbourhood of Bury have been highly benefited by the eſtabliſhment of the very capital manufacturing and printing works belonging to the Company, of which that very reſpectable gentleman, Robert Peel, Eſq. member of parliament for Tamworth, is the head. The principal of theſe works are ſituated on the ſide of the Irwell, from which they have large reſervoirs of water. There is likewiſe a ſeparate reſervoir ſupplied by a ſpring of fine clear water, which is uſed for the waſhing of goods when the river is muddied by floods. The articles here made and printed are chiefly the fineſt kinds of the cotton manufactory, and they are in high requeſt both at Mancheſter and London. The printing is performed in the moſt improved methods, both by wooden blocks and copper rollers, and the execution and colours are ſome of the very beſt of the Lancaſhire fabric. The premiſes occupy a large portion of ground, and cottages have been built for the accommodation of the workmen, which form ſtreets, and give the appearance of a village. Ingenious artiſts are employed in drawing patterns, and cutting and engraving them on wood and copper, and many women and children in mixing and pencilling the colours, &c. The Company has ſeveral other extenſive works in the neighbourhood, as well on the Irwell as on the Roch. Some of theſe are confined to the carding, ſlubbing, and ſpinning of cotton; others to waſhing the cottons with water wheels, which go round with great velocity, but can be ſtopped in an inſtant for taking out and putting in the goods. Boiling and bleaching the goods are performed at other works. In ſhort, the extenſiveneſs of the whole concern is ſuch as to find conſtant employ for moſt of the inhabitants of Bury and its neighbourhood, of both ſexes and all ages, and notwithſtanding their great number, they have never wanted work in the moſt unfavourable times. The peculiar healthineſs of the people employed may be imputed partly to the judicious and humane regulations

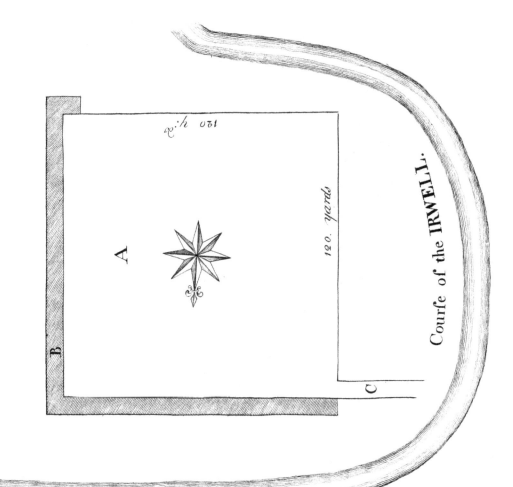

CASTLE STEADS in Walmesley.

120 y.ds

120. yards

A

B

C

Course of the IRWELL.

Pub.d 14. Nov. 1792 by I. Stockdale Piccadilly.

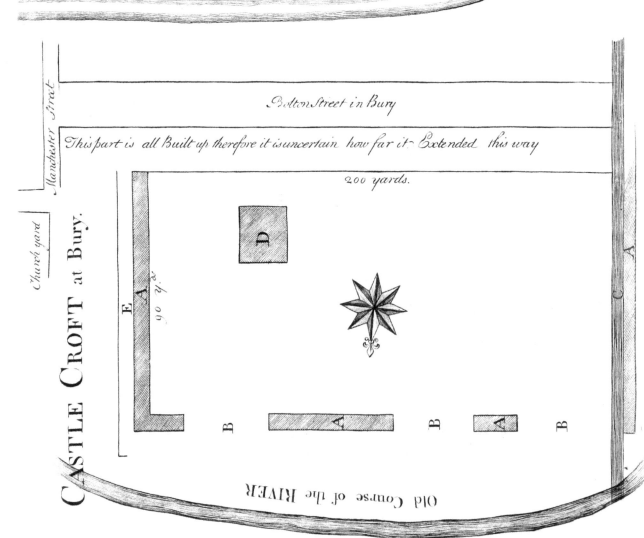

CASTLE CROFT at Bury.

Manchester Street

Church yard

Bolton Street in Bury

This part is all Built up therefore it is uncertain how far it Extended this way

200 yards.

D

E

90 y.ds

A

B

A

B

A

B

A

C

A

Old Course of the RIVER

tions put in practice by Mr. Peel, and partly to the falubrity of the air and climate. At a fhort diftance from Bury and the works is a large well-built houfe, called Chamber-hall, in which Mr. Peel himfelf refides, and in an adjoining meadow is a cottage or nurfery for his young family. The whole is fitted up in a ftyle of neatnefs and elegance, and furrounded with ornamental grounds and rifing plantations.

The canal from Bury to Manchefter, which will come within the breadth of the Irwell from Mr. Peel's works, will greatly facilitate the conveyance of goods and raw materials.

Tradition preferves the memory of two caftles in and near Bury. One is at a field called *Caftle Croft* clofe by the town of Bury, on its weft fide, about 80 yards from the crofs. There are no remains of ancient buildings here, but in the adjacent gardens have often been dug up parts of the foundation walls. It was a good fite for a fortrefs; and the old courfe of the river feems to have winded in the valley which fkirts it below, where the printing and bleaching grounds of Meffrs. Peel and Co are fituated. The other, viz. *Caftle Steads* in Walmefley, placed in a bend of the Irwell, is faid to have been only an entrenchment of the Parliament's army, when Bury was befieged, and its caftle battered by cannon planted at the head of a wood in Walmefley. Nothing remains of thefe works but the name of the clofe, the tenant occupying it having levelled the trenches. Not far from thence, at a place called *Caftle-hill*, there feems to have been in the feudal times a lordfhip of the royalty tenure, with power of imprifonment and execution of criminals. A hill juft by is ftill called *Gallows-hill*.

The turnpike road from Bury northwards to Haflingden is an excellent one, being made with a coarfe ftone between flag and free ftone,

of

of which material the houses and many of the fences of the country are constructed   The face of the country is greatly diversified with hills and vallies, in which many rivulets wind, of great service in working the numerous machines used in the thriving manufactures of these parts.

———————————

BLACKBURN HUNDRED.

BLACKBURN PARISH.

THE parish of Blackburn is one of the two parishes which comprehend almost the whole hundred of that name. This entire territory was bestowed by the Conqueror on Ilbert de Laci, one of his potent followers. He and his descendants parcelled it out again to their dependents, and most of the estates in the hundred derive their titles from these grants.

The *town of Blackburn* is seated in a bottom surrounded with hills. It has long been known as a manufacturing place, but within the memory of man the population was very inconsiderable to what it has lately been. It was formerly the centre of the fabrics sent to London for printing, called *Blackburn greys,* which were plains of linen warp shot with cotton. Since so much of the printing has been done near Manchester, the Blackburn manufacturers have gone more into the making of calicoes. The fields around the town are whitened with the materials lying to bleach. The town itself consists of several streets, irregularly laid out, but intermixed with good houses, the consequences of commercial wealth. Besides the parish church, there is a newly-

erected

erected chapel of the eftablifhment, and five places of worfhip for different perfuafions of diffenters. There is a free-fchool in the town founded by queen Elizabeth, and a very good poor-houfe, with land appropriated to the ufe of the poor, where cattle may be paftured.

Blackburn has a market on Mondays, but its chief fupply of provifions is from Prefton, particularly the articles of butcher's meat and fhelled groats. The latter are bought by the town's people about Michaelmas, ground to meal, and ftowed in arks, where they are trodden down hard while new and warm, to ferve for the year's bread, which is chiefly oat cakes. It has an annual fair on May-day, and a fortnight fair for cattle, chiefly milch kine.

The church of Blackburn before the reformation belonged to the Abbey of Whalley. The archbifhop of Canterbury is now rector, and the living is ferved by a vicar, who has feven chapelries in his gift, but which are independent of him in point of revenue. Half of the fite of the town belongs to the rector, who lets it on leafes for twentyone years. The tythes of the rectory are let to farmers, who compound by a modus, and rarely take in kind. A mortuary is due throughout the parifh (which comprifes twenty-four townfhips) for every houfekeeper dying worth £.40 perfonalty free of debts. The value of land and price of provifions are increafed here within the laft fifty years in as great proportion as in moft parts of the kingdom.

To the eaft of Blackburn is Fore-gate, where are fome good new buildings. The new road to Haflingden, Bury, and Manchefter, paffes this way. A little to the fouth is a capital brewery, clofe by which the new canal from Leeds to Liverpool takes its courfe. A mile on

the

the Preston road is a large printing ground, and a factory for spinning cotton twist. On the south of the town lies Hoadley-hall, which, with its land, belongs to the rectory.

Extract from the parish register of Blackburn.

	Chrift.	Bur.	Marr.
From Dec. 21, 1779 to ditto 1780	418	255	159
———————— 1780 to ditto 1781	431	484	180
———————— 1781 to ditto 1782	450	298	163
———————— 1782 to ditto 1783	353	232	168
———————— 1783 to ditto 1784	432	296	197
———————— 1784 to ditto 1785	502	432	210
———————— 1785 to ditto 1786	475	315	232
———————— 1786 to ditto 1787	541	287	186
———————— 1787 to ditto 1788	506	327	140
———————— 1788 to ditto 1789	431	388	176
———————— 1789 to ditto 1790	582	341	218
———————— 1790 to ditto 1791	539	361	240
———————— 1791 to ditto 1792	513	400	222
———————— 1792 to ditto 1793	495	400	225
———————— 1793 to ditto 1794	389	393	185

The land about Blackburn is in general barren, and much of it sandy. Coal is found in plenty in the southern end of the parish, and in several parts much stone slate is got, which is used for covering the houses. In one of the hills there is a mine of alum stone, which Fuller says was worked in his time, but had long been neglected on account of the increasing expense of removing the super-incumbent strata. When Sir G. Colebrook's project of monopolizing alum took place, he purchased

and

and worked thefe mines; but fince its failure they have again fallen into neglect.

At *Darwen*, four miles fouth of Blackburn, there are plenty of coals. This was formerly a fmall village, but is now a populous diftrict, manufacturing a large quantity of cotton goods. It contains two printing works, and there are a proportional number of mechanics and fhop-keepers. Twenty years fince, a return was made to Dr. Percival of a diffenting congregation here, confifting of 1850 individuals, among whom the annual proportion of births was more than double that of deaths. Darwen is in a bleak and elevated fituation, furrounded with moors, and little cultivated.

WHALLEY PARISH.

THIS large parifh, comprifing a great portion of Blackburn hundred, contains fifteen chapelries. *Whalley* itfelf is only a village. The parifh church is a vicarage in the gift of the archbifhop of Canterbury. In the church-yard are three remarkable croffes. Two are carved in a form fimilar to that of Maen y Cwynfan, in Flintfhire; the other is of an extremely eccentric fhape. Dugdale fuppofes thefe to be fome of thofe erections in the time of Auguftine the monk, which were called croffes of the bleffed Auguftine. There is a fmall fchool at Whalley founded by Edward VI. This fchool and thofe of Middleton and Burnley have thirteen fcholarfhips in Brazen-nofe College in Oxford.

Whalley-abbey, a place formerly of great note and confequence in thefe parts, is feated on the bank of the river Calder, beneath the fhade of a lofty brow clothed with trees impending over the oppofite fide. The boundaries of this religious houfe were very large. Two fquare towers yet remain with pointed gateways. Beneath are the ancient entrances to the place. One is finely vaulted, and the arch fecured with ftone ribs curioufly interfecting each other. There are ftill left part of the conventual church, and fome of the old dwelling part of the abbey. On a bow window are cut in ftone feveral coats of arms of founders and benefactors, as the Lacies, the Stanlies, &c. There are the ruins of a vaft length of room, perhaps the refectory, with windows on each fide, fome rounded, others pointed. Above this had been the lodging rooms. A great court lies to the weft of thefe, and on one fide is a great pile with two rows of rounded windows with Gothic ftone work within.

The name of this place in the Saxon language was *Valeleg*. Auguftine, the firft miffionary of Chriftianity to this ifland, founded a church in thefe parts, which was long parochial to the wide tract of Blackburnfhire and all Bolland. As converts increafed, more places of worfhip were erected. Thefe had no particular patrons, but the lords of the foil in which they lay, appointed their relations or friends to the cure, who were called rectors, and were married men and perfons of property. The country was at that time very thinly peopled; the bifhops, therefore, left the government of thefe churches to the owners with the powers of deans, which ftyle they bore among the people, and the office was hereditary. In the reign of Will. Rufus, the laft dean being prohibited marriage by a council, conveyed the prefentation of Whalley and its chapels to his relation John, conftable of Chefter, and

lord

lord of Blackburn.   Henry Lacy, earl of Lincoln, a fucceffor of his, beftowed this church on the white monks of Stanlaw in Wirral, with the provifo, that if the number of monks fhould be augmented from forty to fixty, they fhould remove to Whalley.   This was effected in 1296, when the new convent was built by the munificence of the earl, who tranflated to it the bones of his anceftors interred at Stanlaw. This abbey flourifhed till the year 1536; when, encouraged by Afke's rebellion, or the pilgrimage of grace, the abbots and monks of feveral convents who before had either furrendered their houfes, or been driven out, repoffeffed themfelves, and refumed their functions.   Among them were the religious of this houfe, as well as others in the north. The earl of Shrewfbury, however, who commanded againft the rebels, had them taken out, and martial law executed upon them.   John Paf- lew, the 25th abbot, and one of his monks, were hanged at Lancafter. At the diffolution, the place was granted by Edward VI. to Richard Afhton of Darcy-Lever, a branch of the family of Middleton, toge- ther with great part of the demefne; the reft to John Braddyl, which his defcendants ftill poffefs.   Afhton made the abbey his refidence. Confiderable buildings were added, which ftill fubfift, though in a ruin- ous ftate, a good fpecimen of ancient fplendour.   The gallery is a wainfcotted room 150 feet long, and coarfely painted.   The houfe and manor continued the property of the Afhtons till the prefent century, when it was transferred by marriage to the Curzons, to a branch of which family it now belongs.

HASLINGDEN.

THIS is a fmall market town upon the turnpike road leading from Bury to Blackburn. The church ftands upon the brow of a hill, which was alfo the fituation of the old part of the town; but the buildings have now extended into the valley beneath.. The river Swinnel fkirts the weftern part of the town, and winds away through a populous country. Haflingden has been greatly improved within the laft twenty years, chiefly from the increafe of the woollen manufacture; though much of the cotton trade has likewife been introduced within a few years, particularly the branch of making twift for warps, for which purpofe alone feveral factories have been erected in its neighbourhood.

The church is under the vicar of Whalley, who appoints a curate. It has been rebuilt about twenty years fince, but the old fteeple is left ftanding. The town is governed by a conftable and fix churchwardens, who have under their care fix divifions, or pofts, as they are here termed. Two of thefe divifions, however, have a chapel of eafe of their own, fubordinate to Haflingden, called *Goodfhaw chapel*, fituated about two miles on the Burnley road, and near it is a quaker's meetinghoufe, at a place called Crawfhaw Booth.

The town and hamlets of Haflingden are reckoned now to contain about 3000 inhabitants, which is triple the number they contained forty years fince. The people were at that time chiefly employed by monied men at Rochdale; but now the trade is fupported by capitals acquired

on

on the fpot by the induftry and enterprifing fpirit of the manufacturers, who have erected inns for the entertainment of travellers, fhops, and handfome houfes for their own refidence. A fquare is lately planned here, and fome capital houfes are already built in it. A turnpike road from Halifax to Blackburn runs through Haflingden, which is kept in excellent condition, from the goodnefs of the materials every where at hand. Some bulky goods, as oil for the woollen manufactory, treacle, &c. are brought from London by the Selby navigation into Yorkfhire, and thence hither by land carriage; but the newly-projected canals will afford the benefit of water carriage directly to this neighbourhood. The following is an extract from the church regifter for the laft twenty years.

Year.	Chrift.	Bur.	Marr.	Year.	Chrift.	Bur.	Marr.
1775	157	77	52	1785	210	124	72
1776	178	129	48	1786	206	113	72
1777	204	96	52	1787	237	119	68
1778	196	83	56	1788	201	133	56
1779	173	100	48	1789	200	151	64
1780	194	111	52	1790	228	146	68
1781	184	145	52	1791	213	125	52
1782	196	106	52	1792	251	147	56
1783	176	97	58	1793	210	169	72
1784	191	102	72	1794	165	171	52

A number of mills for carding cotton and fheep's-wool, and fpinning them into cotton-twift and woollen yarn for the flannels made here, are erected upon the Swinnel. There is alfo a corn-mill on the river, formerly belonging to the Holden family, now extinct, whofe hall, an

ancient

ancient manſion, ſtands about a mile from Haſlingden. Near it is Cold-hutch-bank, under a hill from which the fineſt flags and ſlate are quarried out. On the other ſide ſtands Todd-hall, an old manſion. Hud-hey on the Blackburn road is another ancient reſidence, near which ſtands Carter-place, belonging to Mr. Taylor, a handſome houſe built of the excellent ſtone abounding in this country. In the Grane poſt or diſtrict are many good houſes, ſome of them ancient.

About five miles from Haſlingden on the Whalley road is the ancient manſion of *Dungnow*, belonging to lord Petre, where a prieſt of the Roman Catholic religion is ſtill kept. It is ſituated in a noble park, and ſome antiquities worth notice yet exiſt in it. At this houſe was formerly entertained an ideot, called *Nick of Dungnow*, of whoſe ſimplicity, united with a natural ſhrewdneſs, many tales are ſtill current in popular tradition.

At *Church-bank* near *Church-kirk*, Mr. Jonathan Peel has erected very extenſive buildings, where he carries on the printing buſineſs in great perfection. There are other large printing works at a place called Oakenſhaw, in which a number of hands are employed. In its neighbourhood is an excellent coal-pit.

BURNLEY.

BURNLEY has a market on Mondays, chiefly for corn. Its trade was formerly only in woollen or worſted goods, but the cotton ma-

2   nufactures

COLNE. 279

nufactures are now introduced in it. Some fulling mills for woollens are still kept up, and there are many cotton machines and printing works about the town. The church of Burnley is under Whalley, and though only a curacy, is reckoned one of the best livings in these parts. The intended course of the Leeds and Liverpool canal will nearly surround the town. Several good families reside in the country round, and stone and slate are plentiful, and some lead mines have been discovered. Roman coins have been found at this town.

C O L N E.

COLNE has a church under Whalley, and a baptist and methodist meeting, with a free-school. It is a small market-town, the market on Wednesdays. The trade formerly consisted in woollen and worsted goods, particularly shalloons, calamancoes, and tammies; but the cotton trade is of late introduced, the articles consisting chiefly of calicoes and dimities. There is an elegant cloth-hall, or piece-hall, as it is here called, where goods are sold during the ringing of a bell, fines being levied on sales after the stated time. Much money is turned in this town, in proportion to its size, it being situated on the edge of the district of Craven, where cattle for slaughter are procured for a large surrounding country. Colne stands only a mile from the course of the Leeds canal, at a part where a subterraneous tunnel is to be carried at vast expense through a quicksand. The country about Colne is hilly, and the town is seated upon coal, with stone beneath, and slate for building. Lime is plentiful four miles on the Skipton road. Roman

coins

coins have been found at Colne, but there are no other marks of its being a Roman station.

CLITHEROE.

THIS is a small borough town, seated on an infulated eminence,
with a high limestone rock at one end, crowned by its little castle,
whose remains are a square tower surrounded at a distance by a strong
wall.   This castle was possessed by the royalists in the latter end of the
civil wars, and was ordered to be dismantled by the Parliament in 1649.
The town had been entirely moated round except on the inacceffible
parts.   The castle is of great antiquity, being mentioned in a grant
of William Rufus.   The lordship or honour of Clitheroe, anciently
belonging to the Lacy family, having been part of the duchy of Lancaster, became the property of the crown, till on the Restoration it was
bestowed on Monk, duke of Albemarle, from whom it came to its
present possessors, the dukes of Montague.   The church is a chapelry
belonging to the parish of Whalley.

Clitheroe had an ample charter from the first Henry de Lacy, who
granted its townsmen the fame privileges with the citizens of Chester.
This was confirmed by another of Edward I.   The town is governed
by two bailiffs, who jointly have the power of one justice of the peace.
They are the returning officers of the borough, which fends two members to parliament.   It is not incorporated, but the right of voting
is in the resident owners of the houses, or, according to the resolution

of

of the Houfe of Commons in 1661, in fuch freeholders only who have eftates for life or in fee. It did not fend members till the firft of Elizabeth. The prefent number of voters is 42. Thomas Lifter, Efq. and Lord Curzon, are joint proprietors of the borough, and by compromife now fend one member each.

RIBCHESTER.

THIS is a poor village, containing a parifh church; the living a rectory, in the gift of the bifhop of Chefter. Ribchefter is celebrated as having been a Roman ftation of confiderable note. The place is bounded on its north-eaft fide by a little brook, on its fouth-eaft by the river Ribble, both which ftreams annually make great encroachments on it, efpecially the latter, which has croffed over from the other fide of the vale, and threatens ruin by undermining the banks on which the village ftands. A row of houfes and fome gardens have already been fwept away. Except a rampart and fofs near the church, there are no veftiges of the exiftence of the ancient town. The evidences which remain, are the multitude of coins and other Roman antiquities which, even to the prefent time, continue to be found there. Moft of thefe are difperfed into different places; a few remain on the fpot. Various infcriptions found here are copied by our antiquarian writers; one of them proves that a part of the Sarmatian cavalry was quartered here. As to the Roman name of the place, it is a difputed point. Camden fuppofes it to have been the *Coccium* of Antonine, and the *Rigodunum* of Ptolemy. Horfeley inclines to the firft name, and makes Warrington

O o   the

the ancient Rigodunum. From the difcovery of anchors here, and rings of fhips, and even a whole veffel, it is evident that it was formerly ufed as the haven of the upper end of the *Setantiorum portus*, or eftuary of the Ribble. The view of the tract evidently fhews that the water muft formerly have flowed over the whole plain quite up to Ribchefter. The flat is bounded on both fides by high banks. The intervening level on examination exhibits a different kind of foil from the furrounding country, being deep and muddy, and evidently of recent formation. The gradual retreat of the tide is fupported by very good evidence. Leland was an eye-witnefs to its flowing more than half way between Prefton and Ribchefter, at the time he made his furvey, which was between the years 1536 and 1542. At prefent, the tides never reach higher than Brocket-hall, two miles above Prefton, and eight from this ftation; fo that from Leland's time they have retreated three miles in this river. Probably no large veffels ever came up hither. The true Portus Setantiorum, or haven of Lancafhire, lay within the *Neb of the Nefs*, a point jutting into the eftuary of the Ribble ten miles below Prefton, on which *neb* a Roman fort is faid to have been built, now wafhed away by the fury of the tides. Veftiges of a Roman road from this place pointing to Ribchefter are to be traced. A quarter of a mile from Ribchefter is a new and elegant bridge of three arches over the Ribble. Two or three former ones have been fwept away by floods. Oppofite Ribchefter ftand feveral ancient feats, and on each fide the river, defcending to Prefton, are many refpectable houfes, now deferted, once the habitations of old families in this diftrict. They all ftand on the edge of the bank, embofomed once in thick woods of oak, which flourifhed greatly on the fteep flope. Their fite is another proof of a former eftuary or wafh, as they are placed beyond the reach of the tide, but yet near enough to enjoy the benefit of navigation. The

ride

ride along the meanders of this river, from Ribchester to Cuerdale, and thence to Preston, is extremely pleasing.

AMOUNDERNESS HUNDRED.

PRESTON.

AMONG the Lancashire towns, *Preston* is that which has always taken the lead in point of gentility. Its agreeable and central situation, the number of good families resident in its neighbourhood, the gentlemen of the law belonging to its courts, and its freedom from the bustle of traffic and manufacture, are what have given it this prerogative.

Preston is situated on a rising ground ascending from the river Ribble, over which, at about a mile's distance, is a bridge at the village of Walton. The walks on the edge of this elevation command a beautiful view of tracts of meadow bounded by gentle wooded risings, and the river meandering till it terminates in its broad estuary. The town is of ancient origin, having, according to Camden, risen out of the ruins of Ribchester, and acquiring its name from its religious foundations, *Preston* being derived from *Priest's-town*. Edmund earl of Lancaster, son of Henry III. founded here the Grey Friars; and there was an hospital at a remote period.

Preston

Preſton is a market town and a borough. The town was firſt incorporated by Henry II. The corporation conſiſts of a mayor, recorder, eight aldermen, four under-aldermen, ſeventeen common-
councilmen, and a town-clerk. It has the peculiar privilege of holding
a guild every twenty years, which is reſorted to as a kind of jubilee by
the people of faſhion and leiſure from all the country round. It is held
in Auguſt, and laſts a month. The corporation walks in ſolemn pro-
ceſſion, followed by the trading companies under their proper banners,
and decorated with the inſignia of their profeſſions. Plays, concerts,
and other public amuſements, have made part of the entertainment in
modern times.

Preſton enjoys the advantage of being the ſeat of ſeveral law courts.
The duchy of Lancaſter holds a court of chancery here, appointed to
hear and determine all cauſes according to ſome peculiar cuſtoms held
among themſelves. The chancellor of the duchy is chief judge of this
court, and has proper officers under him, viz. a vice-chancellor, an at-
torney-general, chief clerk, regiſter and examiner, five attorneys and
clerks, a prothonotary and his deputy, and clerks of the crown and
peace. There is alſo a county court, which ſits every Tueſday in the
year, and iſſues writs which compel appearance without bail for any
ſum above forty ſhillings, and on failure of appearance execution follows. Another court is called the county arreſt, whence proceſs iſſues
for ſums under forty ſhillings, alſo without bail. Another is that of
the wapentake, in proceſs like the laſt mentioned, but only for the
hundred of Amounderneſs. Writs holding to bail are iſſued from the
prothonotary's office, upon which the ſheriff grants a warrant for apprehenſion. Other writs are iſſued from this office, not holding to bail,
but on ſerving a copy a proceſs takes place in the common pleas. The

1   borough

borough court iſſues proceſſes for debts up to ten pounds, which compel appearance, or, on failure of it, attach goods in execution to be
ſold within a limited number of days. This court can likewiſe ſend
criminals to the new priſon, as it takes place of the former houſe of
correction. The quarter ſeſſions are held at Preſton by adjournment
from Lancaſter, on the Thurſday in the week after Epiphany.

The new priſon, or penitentiary houſe, as it is called, is ſituated
near the entrance to Preſton from Chorley. No criminals are confined
in it but thoſe from Lonſdale, Amoundernefs, Blackburn, and Weſt
Derby hundreds. It was erected at the charge of thoſe hundreds upon
Mr. Howard's plan, much reſembling the New Bayley priſon at Mancheſter. The purpoſe is only for ſalutary confinement and reformation.
The priſoners have a daily allowance of one pound and half of bread
with a lump of butter, and the value of a halfpenny in potatoes. If
they cannot conſume this allowance, they may exchange it for tea and
ſugar; but no liquors of any kind are ſuffered to enter the priſon.

Preſton is a parliamentary borough, and ſends two repreſentatives.
Few towns have been the ſeat of more violent party conteſts, in ſome
of which it has nearly ſuffered the fate of a town beſieged by an
enemy. A queſtion has been at iſſue for near a century and a half,
whether the right of election was in the in-burgeſſes of the laſt guild
and thoſe admitted ſince by copy of court-roll, or in the inhabitants at
large, or pot-wallers. Two deciſions by the Houſe of Commons before
the paſſing of Mr. Grenville's act, and two ſince, have all agreed in
determining the caſe in favour of the inhabitants at large, whence it will
probably be no more conteſted. The earl of Derby has great influence

ence in this borough. The mayor and two bailiffs are returning officers.

The weekly markets are held on Wednefday, Friday, and Saturday, the latter the principal, and are extremely well regulated to prevent foreftalling and regrating. None but the town's-people are permitted to buy during the firft hour, which is from eight to nine in the morning: at nine others may purchafe; but nothing unfold muft be with-drawn from the market till one o'clock, fifh excepted, which, after the town is ferved, may be taken off in panniers to other places, left it fhould be fpoiled, and the fupply of this article is moft abundant for the town. This market is remarkable for great quantities of meal and fhelled groats from the Filde diftrict, upon which the poorer inhabitants in great meafure fubfift, making their oaten bread called jannock. The flaughter houfes are contiguous to the fhambles, which is a nuifance to that quarter; but it contributes to make flefh-meat reafonable. There are three fairs in the year, in March, (which lafts three days) September, and January. Prefton is fupplied with coals by means of the Douglas navigation, which enters the Ribble fomewhat lower than Walton-bridge, and it will have another fource of fupply from the new Lancafter canal, which is to pafs clofe on the weftern fide of Prefton, in its way fouthwards to the great coal country about Chorley.

Prefton is a handfome well-built town, with broad regular ftreets, and many good houfes. The earl of Derby has a large modern man-fion in it. The place is rendered gay by affemblies and other places of amufement, fuited to the genteel ftyle of the inhabitants. Though it is not characterized by trade, yet it is not deftitute of mercantile houfes of reputation. Formerly it was a fort of mart for the Lancafhire

linens,

linens, and sheetings are still sold here; but of late the cotton branches have obtained possession, and the house of Watson and Co. manufacture all the articles of dimities, muslins, and calicoes, from the raw cotton to the printing, and have a warehouse for their sale at Manchester. Preston has a parish church, and a chapel for the establishment, and places of worship for different sects of separatists. It has likewise several alms-houses and charity schools. The parish register has afforded the following extracts:

Year.	Christ.	Burials.	Marr.	Year.	Christ.	Burials.	Marr.
1781	142	184	51	1788	220	189	73
1782	149	250	78	1789	202	209	73
1783	170	159	80	1790	197	179	72
1784	139	266	81	1791	209	279	84
1785	168	180	96	1792	224	282	77
1786	206	214	97	1793	243	218	72
1787	204	277	83	1794	223		91

From its situation, Preston has been an important post in the civil commotions of this kingdom, and the scene of various military actions. The most considerable of these was in 1648, when the duke of Hamilton and Sir Marmaduke Langdale with a combined army of English and Scotch of the royal party were defeated with great slaughter by a much inferior number under Cromwell and Lambert. The battle was fought on Ribbleton moor, to the eastward of the town, and also at the pass of the bridge. The Scotch were pursued by Lambert quite to Wigan. In the year 1715, Preston was taken possession of by the rebel general Forster, with a mixed body of Scotch and English, and defended for some time against the king's troops by means of barricades, but he was at length obliged to surrender at discretion.

KIRKHAM.

K I R K H A M.

THIS is a market town, fituated eight miles weftward of Prefton, in the Filde or Field country. The church is a vicarage, in the gift of Chrift Church college, Oxford, and has under it feven chapels. There is a well-endowed free-fchool, with three mafters. The market-day is Tuefday; the annual fairs in June and October. The chief trade of Kirkham is coarfe linens, and efpecially fail cloth, of which it makes a confiderable quantity for the ufe of the navy. Though fituated near the mouth of the Ribble it has no river or port; but the Lancafter and Kendal canal will come very near the town.

Leyland Hundred.

AT *Walton-le-Dale*, a pleafant and populous village on the Ribble, a mile from Prefton, is the feat of Sir Henry Hoghton, reprefentative in parliament for that borough. The ancient feat of this family is *Hoghton-tower*, placed upon an eminence about half way between this place and Blackburn, and alfo in Leyland hundred. This laft is a great pile confifting of two courts with three fquare towers in the front, beneath the middlemoft of which is the gateway. The firft court contains the offices; the fecond, the dwelling apartments, numerous, but very ruinous. The draw-well is eighty yards deep. This place was garrifoned during the civil wars, and part of it blown up accidentally, but afterwards repaired. In the reign of Henry II. it was

called

called *Hocton*, and gave name to the firſt of the family mentioned in hiſtory, Adam de Hocton.

CHORLEY.

THE road from Preſton to Chorley is a good turnpike, made with gravel out of the beds of the Ribble and Douglas. Further ſouthwards the only materials are pebble ſtones bruiſed with hammers, with nothing proper to fill up interſtices.

Chorley is a ſmall, neat market town, taking its name from a rivulet called the Chor, which iſſues from ſeveral ſprings to the eaſt of the town, and after flowing through the pleaſant valley beneath, joins the Yarrow. In its courſe it turns ſeveral mills, engines, and machines for carding and ſpinning of cotton. The Yarrow is a larger ſtream of limpid water, which encircles the extremities of Chorley towards the ſouth. On its banks are many bleaching and printing grounds, with cotton factories intermixed. The ſituation of Chorley is on the great north road, and nearly central to the main part of the county. Its markets are on Tueſdays and Saturdays; the former plentifully ſupplied with every neceſſary. Fiſh of various kinds are brought from Preſton and Lancaſter. Its fairs are held in March, May, Auguſt, and September; the ſpring and ſummer fairs for cattle, the autumn for toys, ſmall wares, and Yorkſhire cloth. Chorley has an ancient chapel, lately made parochial; the ſtructure is ſuppoſed to be Saxon, dedicated to St. Laurence. The walls are ornamented with ancient coats of arms and Saxon characters, and there are hieroglyphic paintings in the windows. The living is in the gift of the rector of Croſton,

P p which

which is the mother church to Chorley.   In the church-yard is a
grammar fchool, endowed with feveral legacies, but not free to fcholars.
A dungeon or prifon for the confinement of malefactors has fome time
fince been erected.   Plenty of coals and cannel are procured about
Chorley, and the country alfo poffeffes quarries of afhler, flag, and
mill-ftone, and mines of lead and alum.   Thefe, and other mineral
treafures, will obtain a ready conveyance from the intended canals
which are to pafs through them.   The population and trade of this
town and neighbourhood have been greatly increafed of late years.

Extracted from the church regifter from 1779 to 1795.

Years.	Chrift.	Bur.	Marr.	Years.	Chrift.	Bur.	Marr.
1779	101	39	11	1787	99	60	29
1780	96	62	17	1788	139	118	28
1781	108	41	22	1789	122	56	21
1782	103	50	18	1790	148	66	25
1783	90	73	27	1791	143	72	36
1784	118	53	34	1792	156	83	35
1785	120	80	27	1793	163	91	26
1786	104	65	22	1794	168	122	23

LEYLAND PARISH.

LEYLAND, from whence the hundred takes its name, is a pleafant and dry village.   The church is a noble room of fixty-five feet
by thirty-three, a fine arch without a fingle pillar.   The living is a
vicarage : the impropriate rectory belonged to the abbey of Penwortham.   In the church are feveral monuments of the Faringtons.   The

feat

feat of this family is *Shaw-hall*, at a fmall diftance from Leyland. This is a large but irregular houfe, containing fome fine apartments, among which is a mufeum for natural hiftory. There is a collection of pictures, fome of them very valuable; particularly fome frefco paintings taken from the walls of Herculaneum. The views from the houfe are pleafing; the grounds are laid out in a modern ftyle, and there is a very excellent kitchen garden with fruit ftoves, &c. The late owner, Sir William Farington, fpent the greater part of his life at this place, and amufed himfelf with improvements of all kinds. The family are lords of this manor, and alfo of the fee or honour of Penwortham, and of feveral other adjoining manors; but the manor of Farington, the ancient feat of the family, was long ago in the poffeffion of the church, and at the diffolution was fold to the Fleetwoods.

STANDISH PARISH.

THE village of *Standifh* has a very handfome church with a fpire fteeple. The pillars within fhew an attempt at the Tufcan order. It was rebuilt in 1584, chiefly by the affiftance of Richard Moodie, the rector, who maintained the workmen with provifion at his own coft during the time. He was the firft proteftant paftor, conformed, and procured the living by the ceffion of the tythes of Standifh. He lies in effigy on his tomb in the church dreffed in his Francifcan habit, with an infcription declarative of his munificence. There is likewife a handfome tomb of Sir Edward Wrightington, knight, king's council, who died in 1658, and lies recumbent in alabafter, in his gown. The rectory is at prefent worth £.700 per annum. There is only one chapel of eafe in the parifh, which is Coppull.

The

The principal grain produced in the parifh is oats; fome barley and a little wheat are fown. The farms are generally fmall, fcarcely any exceeding, and few reaching, £.100 per annum. Land lets from 35s. to 50s. per acre of eight yards to the rood, and a little, particularly rich, at £.3. Manual labour is from 1s. 8d. to 2s. a day. Coals are met with plentifully in the parifh, and a tunnel is about to be carried from the mines in the Standifh eftate to convey them to the Liverpool canal. The cotton manufacture is the ftaple trade of the parifh; but fome coarfe linens are alfo woven. Poor's rates are high.

The gentlemens' feats are,

Standifh-hall; an old houfe of the Standifh family. It contains a few relics of the Arundel collection.

Duxbury; Sir Frank Standifh.

Adlington; Sir Richard Clayton. This is a new houfe, with a few good pictures, efpecially one of a dead head of Charles I. extremely well painted. The Clayton family were originally fettled at Clayton near Leyland, which was granted to Robert de Clayton by William the Conqueror. They removed to Adlington about a century ago.

In Coppull is *Chifnal-hall*, formerly the feat of the family of Chifnals, to one of whom, a colonel in the civil wars, there is a memorial in the church. The laft reprefentative of this family having built for his refidence *Tompfon-houfe* in Langtree near Standifh, fuffered the old hall to be occupied by tenants. The family eftate is now poffeffed by James Hammerton, Efq. of Hellifield Peel, near Craven, whofe

grand-

grandfather married one of the co-heireffes. Coal abounds in this eftate.

Wrightington-hall, near Standifh, the feat of William Diccoufon, Efq. is faid to have been the firft fafh-window houfe in Lancafhire, and the firft to the north of the Trent in the kingdom.

The Kendal and Lancafter canal will pafs through this parifh.

WEST DERBY HUNDRED.

WIGAN.

THIS borough is fituated near the fmall river Douglas, on the north road. It is a confiderable town, which, as far back as the time of Leland, is called a " paved town as big as Warrington, but better builded, " and inhabited by fome merchants, artificers, and farmers." It was firft incorporated by Henry I. and poffeffes a charter from queen Elizabeth, and a later one from Charles II. The corporation confifts of a mayor, recorder, twelve aldermen, two bailiffs, and an indefinite number of freemen admitted by a jury in the mayor's court. The rector of the parifh, as fuch, is lord of the manor, and has a rectory-houfe and glebe land annexed to it. The living is valuable. Wigan fends two members to parliament, the right of election fuppofed to belong to the free burgeffes, in number about 200. The power vefted in the corporation of admitting out-ftanding or honorary burgeffes is a powerful engine in elections, and has been greatly abufed. Many very expenfive contefts have happened in this borough. The prefent

patrons

patrons are the duke of Portland and lord Bradford. It has a town hall, erected in 1720 at the joint expence of the then reprefentatives, lord Barrymore and Sir Roger Bradfhaigh.

The parifh church is antient beyond any traditionary account, and has four chapels under it. One of thefe is St. George's chapel in the town of Wigan. The church has a ring of bells remarkably deep-toned and tuneable, the tenor weighing 29½ cwt. There is a free-grammar fchool, and one for blue-coat boys, fome alms-houfes founded by lady Bradfhaigh, and a good workhoufe for the poor of the townfhip. The main ftreets of the town are broad, but irregularly built, with a mixture of old and modern houfes.

Wigan has long been noted for the making of checks and braziery work. The Wigan checks were in much eftimation, nor have they yet loft their fuperiority over thofe of Manchefter; but the cotton manufactory, as in all other places, intrudes upon the old ftaple of the place. The braziery is now on the decline. Some fail-cloth is made here in time of war. An ingenious perfon works cannel coal into vafes, fnuff boxes, beads, and other toys. The market days of Wigan are Mondays and Fridays; the fairs are in July and October. The ftate and progrefs of population will appear in the following extract from the regifter:

Years.	Marr.	Chrifts.	Bur.	Years.	Marr.	Chrifts.	Bur.
1780	92	425	240	1785	115	458	240
1781	86	414	252	1786	129	492	222
1782	101	440	207	1787	104	467	349
1783	95	415	191	1788	110	482	341
1784	91	462	327	1789	122	496	316

Years.

Years.	Marr.	Chrift.	Bur.	Years.	Marr.	Chrift.	Bur.
1790	117	507	200	1793	123	595	330
1791	136	518	411	1794	104	565	373
1792	147	630	338				

We have already mentioned, that the river Douglas many years fince was made navigable to the Ribble, by which means a large vent for the coals with which this diftrict abounds was obtained, and the town received other advantages. Thefe have been augmented by a canal cut within a few years to Liverpool, (part of that between Leeds and Liverpool) whereby a direct communication has been opened with that port. There is a mineral water at Wigan, of a fimilar nature with that of Harrowgate, and ufed for cutaneous and fcorbutic diforders. The town derives a plentiful fupply of fpring water from refervoirs at Whittle.

Near the north end of the town is a monument erected to the memory of Sir Thomas Tildefley, who was flain on this fpot in an action, in which the earl of Derby, having rifen in favour of the young king Charles II. in 1651, was defeated by Lilburne.

The parifh of Wigan contains twelve townfhips. One of thefe is *Haigh*, noted for yielding the fineft cannel coal. It is gotten in large blocks, as black as jet, and bearing a fine polifh. The beds are about three feet in thicknefs; the veins dip one yard in twenty, and are found at great depths, with a black bafs above and below. On an eminence in this townfhip is fituated *Haigh-hall*, the feat of the Bradfhaighs; an ancient houfe, built at different times, the chapel fuppofed to be of the age of Edward II. In front are the Stanley arms, and beneath

I

neath

neath them thofe of the Bradfhaigh family, which in all civil commotions has united with the former. It poffeffes many excellent pictures,
particularly portraits. A fummer-houfe belonging to the hall is entirely
built of cannel coal.

Ince, to the eaft of Wigan, produces cannel equally good with that
of Haigh.

Up-Holland, a village to the weft of Wigan, had formerly a priory of
Benedictines, of which nothing now remains but the church and a few
walls. The pofterity of its founder, Robert de Holland, rofe to the
higheft dignities of the ftate, with the titles of earls of Surry and Kent,
and dukes of Exeter, but underwent many calamities, and at length
came to a miferable end.

Billinge, near the former, is diftinguifhed by a lofty eminence,
crowned by an old beacon, whence is a very extenfive profpect over the
flat part of Lancafhire.

Winftanley in its neighbourhood has a valuable fpecies of coal, excellent for the fmith's ufe, which is fetched for that purpofe from the
country round to a great diftance.

L E I G H.

THIS is a fmall market town, the market-day Saturday. Its church
is ancient; the living a vicarage, which has under it two chapels.
The country around is populous and manufacturing. The trade was

formerly

formerly in fuftians, fuch as pillows, barragons, thick fets and velve-rets; latterly, they have made here fine yard-wide jeans, in imitation of India, with figured and flowered draw-boys. Their fpun cotton for warp and weft is moftly got from Manchefter. At a mile's diftance are good coal pits, which fupply the town at a cheap rate. Lime is got at Bedford near Leigh, of a kind like that of Sutton, harden-ing fpeedily under water, and therefore fit for lining refervoirs, and the like purpofes. It is much ufed in the duke of Bridgewater's canal. The rapid increafe of population, or the improvement in the mode of living (probably both) in this town and neighbourhood, may be judged of from the following fact—in 1758 one beaft was flaughtered at Chrift-mas, and proved too much for the market; in 1792, thirty-five beafts (cows) were flaughtered at Chriftmas, and proved too little. The parifh regifter for the laft twenty years affords the following refults:

Year.	Chrift.	Bur.	Marr.	Year.	Chrift.	Bur.	Marr.
1774	240	173	96	1785	371	159	104
1775	280	126	82	1786	373	230	90
1776	276	130	98	1787	399	164	92
1777	248	176	77	1788	361	211	106
1778	280	107	82	1789	417	215	75
1779	279	160	75	1790	371	153	96
1780	332	174	79	1791	382	194	91
1781	310	143	104	1792	412	165	96
1782	314	262	69	1793	392	177	80
1783	372	113	90	1794	341	170	56
1784	300	140	131				

Q q

Leigh

Leigh parifh is famous for its cheefe, of a mild and rich kind, and peculiarly excellent for toafting. It is produced from the pafture and meadow land on the banks of feveral little ftreams which flow through the parifh, and unite to form the brook which enters the Merfey at Glaze-brook. Leigh, it is hoped, will fhortly have the advantage of a navigation by means of a branch extended from the duke of Bridge-water's canal at Worfley to Pennington.

From Leigh an avenue and pleafure grounds near a mile in length lead to *Atherton-hall*, formerly the feat of the Atherton family, from which it paffed by marriage to the Gwillyms. This is a noble man-fion, erected at great expence, and which took a long time in finifhing. Its plan is in the *Vitruvius Britannicus;* the architect was Gibbs. A vaft cubical hall at the entrance gives it an air of magnificence, but at the expence of utility.

The very populous village of *Chowbent* is contiguous to Atherton. In it are made a great quantity of cotton goods, chiefly of the coarfer kinds, and feveral branches of iron work, particularly nails; but thefe laft have been in great meafure driven out by the cotton trade, and have migrated towards Afhton in the willows. Five and twenty years ago, Chowbent was reckoned to contain 2400 inhabitants, and it is fuppofed to have doubled its inhabitants within that period. A diffenting con-gregation here was returned to Dr. Percival, in 1773, as containing by exact enumeration 1160 perfons. The chapel of the eftablifhment at Atherton or Chowbent formerly belonged to the diffenters, but was taken from them in confequence of an election difpute, and confecrated by the celebrated Dr. Wilfon, bifhop of Sodor and Man, and to this day it remains out of the jurifdiction of the diocefe of Chefter, and in

the

the gift of the Atherton family. In the rebellion in 1717, Mr. Wood, the then diffenting minifter of Chowbent, led a confiderable body of his flock to join the royal army, and to them was committed the cuftody of the pafs over the Ribble at Walton. From this exertion of loyalty Mr. Wood obtained the popular title of General, by which he was ever after known; and many ftories are ftill current of his cheerful fingularities.

We have been favoured with the following particular account of the new village of *Tildfley* in this parifh:

The *Banks of Tildfley*, in the parifh of Leigh, are about one mile and a half in length, and command a moft beautiful profpect into feven counties. The air is pure and healthy; the fprings remarkably foft and clear, and moft excellently adapted to the purpofes of bleaching. The land is rich, but moftly in meadow and paftures, for milk, butter, and the noted Leigh cheefe. This eftate had, in the year 1780, only two farm houfes and eight or nine cottages, but now contains 162 houfes, a neat chapel, and 976 inhabitants, who employ 325 looms in the cotton manufactories of Marfeilles quiltings, dimities, corduroys, velvets, velveteens, thickfets, muflins, muflinets, and new ftripes for furniture. Lately Mr. Johnfon has erected a large factory fix ftories high, and a fteam engine, with dye-houfes and other extenfive buildings for the woollen bufinefs, which confifts of kerfeymeers and various fancy goods in all woollen, and filk and woollen. There are two other factories upon the eftate, intended to be let for the woollen bufinefs, and one very large building newly erected, intended for the fpinning of woollen and worfted. It is Mr. Johnfon's intention to introduce the woollen branches into this part of the country, and it certainly appears

a very

a very eligible fituation, having great plenty of coal, fine water, being in the centre of fome thoufand weavers, and only diftant four miles from the duke of Bridgewater's canals at Worfley ; and the Lancafter canal will run near the eftate. Mr. Johnfon has been at a confiderable expence in fetting up the neweft and moft approved machinery for willowing, fcribbling, carding, roving, and fpinning of fine woollen yarn, which he means to employ, not only for himfelf, but for the accommodation of all others who may be induced to fettle upon the eftate in the woollen bufinefs. There are a number of boys from twelve to fixteen years of age at the factory, who are with great care progreffively inftructed in the manufacture of various fancy woollen articles, with a view of eftablifhing the fine woollen bufinefs in the neighbourhood ; and Manchefter being the firft repofitory of manufactures, is daily frequented by foreigners, and town and country buyers, which has already induced feveral capital woollen houfes to fettle there. Every fort of new machinery feems to be encouraged by the work people in Tildfley, and the great advantages of fcribbling and fhearing by fteam or water, with the ufe of the fly fhuttle, will moft probably be a means of eftablifhing manufactories there.

WARRINGTON.

THIS town, fituated on the Merfey, nearly central to the limit between the two counties of Lancafter and Chefter, is of confiderable antiquity. From the fite of the church it would appear that the whole town was originally confined to its prefent eaftern extremity, which lies oppofite to that old ford of the river which gave name to the village of Latchford. But on the building of the prefent bridge, (which was

erected

erected by the firft earl of Derby, for the purpofe, it is faid, of accommodating Henry VII. on a vifit to him) the buildings collected in its neighbourhood, and the vicinity of the church, was deferted. This was already the cafe in the time of Leland, who defcribes Warrington as " a paved town of pretty bignefs, with an Auguftine friary at the town's end, and the parifh church at the tail of all the town." He fays it has a better market than Manchefter. The friary, which exifted before 1379, ftood near the bridge, its fite being ftill indicated by the name of an adjacent ftreet, though not a veftige of the building remains. The charter for markets and fairs was obtained in the reign of Edward I. by Sir Thomas Boteler, head of an ancient family near this place, of whom, with his lady, there is a magnificent alabafter tomb, ornamented with variety of fculpture, in a chapel of the parifh church. He refided at the houfe of Bewfey near this town, and tradition reports that he and his lady were murdered by affaffins who croffed the moat in leathern boats. An ancient moated manfion is ftill in being at Bewfey.

The principal part of the town confifts of four ftreets croffing at the centre, one of which runs directly from the bridge, and from its narrownefs and mean building, gives but an unfavourable idea of the place to a ftranger. But fome of the other ftreets are much opener, and contain many good houfes interfperfed, the ufual effect of commercial opulence rifing in a place of antiquity. It has the common fault of being moft ftraightened at the centre; a great inconvenience to a town which is one of the principal thoroughfares of the north, being the only entrance from the fouth to all the north-weftern part of England, and the bufy port of Liverpool. There is no bridge over the Merfey between Warrington and the fea, and none for many miles upwards between it and Manchefter. From this circumftance Warrington has

2 always

always been a poft of confequence in the civil commotions of this kingdom, and various actions have taken place on this fpot, of which one of the moft confiderable was the flaughter and capture of a large body of the fugitive Scotch'army under the duke of Hamilton in 1648, after the defeat of the combined royal forces near Prefton. Lambert was the parliamentary general on this occafion, who likewife made a ftand here againft the Scotch army which advanced under the young king in 1651, but was obliged to retreat. In the rebellion of 1745 the bridge at Warrington was broken down, whereby the Pretender's army was induced to vary from their intended route fouthwards, and take the road through Manchefter.

Warrington has long been of fome note as a trading town. In the firft part of this century a great quantity of coarfe linens and checks was made in the town and neighbourhood, and fold at its markets; but in later years, the manufacture of fail-cloth or poldavy, was introduced, and rofe to fuch a height, that half of the heavy fail-cloth ufed in the navy has been computed to be manufactured here. Sail-cloth is for the moft part made of hemp and flax mixed, but fome is made of flax alone. The raw materials are chiefly brought from Ruffia to the port of Liverpool, whence they come to Warrington by water-carriage. This manufacture has brought wealth and population to the place; but a branch of trade fubject to fuch variation in the demand, according to the prevalence of peace or war, has had its inconveniences; and, in fact, Warrington has partaken lefs of the increafed profperity of the county than many other towns. During the interval between the laft and the prefent war, feveral of the manufacturers exerted themfelves to introduce the cotton branches here, and fuccceded to a confiderable de-gree. As the coarfer cotton goods were thofe chiefly attempted, many

.of

of the fail-cloth weavers, for the fake of more employment and better wages, turned their hands to the new manufacture, which caufed a confiderable decline of the old; but fince the commencement of the war the cafe has been reverfed. Various other trades have added to the bufinefs of the town. The making of pins has been, and ftill is, carried on to a pretty large extent; and locks, hinges, and other articles of hardware are fabricated here. Large works for the fmelting of copper were eftablifhed near the town, and ufed for feveral years, but have for fome time been difcontinued. The refinery of fugar, and the making of glafs, have employed many hands; and the latter, particularly, is a flourifhing branch of manufacture. An iron foundry has likewife been fet up, which makes a variety of common articles. Warrington has been long noted for its malt and ale, and deals pretty largely in the corn and flour trade. Befides thefe fources of gain and employment, the great refort of travellers to the town promotes a confiderable circulation of money. Its markets (the principal of which is on Wednefday, the other on Saturday) are frequented by an extenfive and populous circumjacent country; though the Bridgewater canal, which paffes a mile and a half to the fouth of Warrington in its courfe to Manchefter, has drawn off a good deal of the Chefhire bufinefs from this neighbourhood to the latter town. At the latter of the two annual fairs, in November, bufinefs to a confiderable amount is tranfacted, particularly in Irifh linen and Welch flannel from Chefter fair, and in Yorkfhire cloths. Much butcher's meat of an inferior kind killed here is carried to the Liverpool and other markets; and quantities of fruit and vegetables grown round the town are fent away for the fupply of Manchefter, Bolton, and other parts in the manufacturing diftricts.

The

The population of Warrington has received a large increase within the latter half of this century. The parish register affords the following annual averages:

	Marr.	Chrift.	Bur.
From 1750 to 1769 inclusive, - - -	73	237	199
From 1770 to 1772 inclusive, - - -	95	331	258

In 1773 exact bills of mortality were begun to be kept, which comprehended the diffenters of all kinds, as well as the eftablifhment. The following annual refults are taken from them.

Year.	Marr.	Births.	Deaths.	Year.	Marr.	Births.	Death.
1773	93	356	473	1779	105	392	295
1774	69	398	208	1780	93	413	362
1775	50	370	199	1781	93	435	270
1776	101	378	234	1782	84	387	267
1777	78	415	364	1783	87	325	265
1778	96	400	214				

In the year 1781 an enumeration of the houfes and inhabitants of Warrington and its vicinity was made, of which the particulars were as follows:

	Houfes.	Inhab.
Town and townfhip of Warrington, - -	1941	8791
Poulton and Fearnhead, - - - -	73	343
Woolfton, - - - - - -	76	367
Suburb in Chefhire, - - - - -	55	269

In that year, the births, as stated in the preceding bills, ran highest, and after it population seems to have been upon the decline. But the introduction of the cotton trade gave it fresh vigour, and many new houses for the accommodation of working people were built. The result is shewn in the following extracts from the bills:

Year.	Marr.	Births.	Deaths.	Year.	Marr.	Births.	Deaths.
1785 to 1789 } Aver.		430	315	1792	127	478	314
1790	102	418	407	1793	103	514	361
1791	127	444	286	1794	81	423	319

In the last yearly bill are subjoined the births and burials for two country chapelries in the parish, viz.

Hollingfare, - - - 47 births, 22 burials,
Burtonwood, - - - 38 ditto, 11 ditto.

Warrington may, in some measure, be confidered as a port town, the Mersey admitting, by the help of the tide, vessels of seventy or eighty tons burthen, to Bank-quay, a little below the town, where warehouses, cranes, and other conveniences for landing goods are erected. The spring-tides rife at the bridge to the height of nine feet. Upwards, the river communication extends to Manchester. The Mersey naturally is well stored with fish. In the proper seasons large quantities of salmon have been caught in the vicinity of the town, so as formerly to afford a cheap article of food to the inhabitants; but the demands for the luxury of the great towns in its neighbourhood, and of the distant metropolis itself, together with the diminution of the number of fish, owing to too frequent molestation and want of proper

R r

atten-

attention, have latterly made a rarity what was once a plentiful variety. The fame may be faid of the fmelts or fparlings, which annually in fpring come up the river in fhoals, formerly confifting of vaft numbers, and of a fize fuperior to thofe of other parts. But both the fize and numbers have been much diminifhed, as is fuppofed, by the conftant fifhing in the lower parts of the river, whereby the fpawn and young fry are deftroyed.

Warrington is well fupplied with coals, partly by land carriage from the pits of Haydock and its neighbourhood, partly by the Sankey canal, which comes within a mile and a half of the town.

The land around Warrington confifts of rich meadows bordering on the river, and occafionally flooded, and of pafture and garden ground. It is noted for its goofberries, which are fuperior in fize, and of greater variety of kinds, than in moft parts of the kingdom. A very fine kind of damfon is alfo common here. Potatoes are raifed in large quantities, and thirty or forty thoufand bufhels have been fhipped at Bank-quay in a year.

Befides the parifh church, Warrington contains a chapel of eafe, and there is another chapel of the eftablifhment in the fuburb over the bridge, belonging to the parifh of Groppenhall. There are alfo places of worfhip for the Roman catholics, prefbyterians, anabaptifts, metho-difts, and quakers. There is a very well endowed free fchool in the town ; and a charity for educating and maintaining poor children of both fexes.

About thirty-feven years fince, a feminary for educating youth upon a liberal academical plan was inftituted in this town, and fupported by

4

fubsubscriptions, chiefly among the diffenters. It flourished during a considerable period under the care of tutors of eminence, feveral of them well known in the republic of letters, but at length funk, through want of adequate fupport, and the difficulties in maintaining proper difcipline.

Near to Warrington is *Orford*, the feat of the Blackburne family, rendered celebrated by its late venerable poffeffor, for its botanical treafures. A tribute to his memory was inferted in the *Gentleman's Magazine* for March 1787, which we fhall tranfcribe.

" JOHN BLACKBURNE, Efq. of Orford, near Warrington, Lancafhire, was one of the venerable relics of the laft century; for at his death he had attained to, I think, his 96th year. This uncommon age was the reward of a very regular and temperate life, and a mind undifturbed by any violent emotions. His health and tranquillity were alfo not a little promoted by the turn he took early in life to the cultivation of plants. He was, as I have been well informed, the fecond gentleman in England who cultivated that delicious fruit, now fo common, the Pine-Apple; and his garden always continued one of the chief objects of botanical curiofity for its products, both foreign and domeftic, in the north of England. Of this a catalogue was printed by his gardener, Mr. Neal, in the year 1779, which was well received by the lovers of that delightful fcience. Here, as Mr. Pennant, in one of his tours, obferves, the venerable owner, like another Evelyn, fpent the calm evening of his life, under the flourifhing fhades of his own planting. He retained his faculties in very confiderable perfection, till within two or three years before his death; and the writer of this account has frequently enjoyed the pleafure of hearing him converfe

with

with cheerfulnefs, and ready recollection, on the events of former years, and on topics of horticulture and natural hiftory. He was exemplary in the difcharge of religious duties, and in charity to the poor; and his numerous houfehold was governed with that order, decorum, and regular economy, which fo well fuited his ftation and character.

" By his lady, of the family of Afhton, in Lancafhire, he had a numerous progeny, feveral of whom are now living in very refpectable fituations. Mrs. Anna Blackburne, his furviving daughter, who imbibed his tafte for botany, and added to it the other branches of natural hiftory, is well known as the poffeffor of an elegant and valuable mufeum, little inferior to that of her relation, Sir Afhton Lever. This was enriched with many curious fpecimens from North America, by a brother who died in that country feveral years ago. Mr. Blackburne's eldeft fon fettled at Hale, in Lancafhire. The prefent John Blackburne, Efq. knight of the fhire for Lancafhire, is *his* fon and fucceffor."

To this we fhall add, that the laft-mentioned gentleman now inhabits the feat of his grandfather, which he has greatly improved by alterations in the modern tafte, but without infringing upon its *botanical* eftablifhment. Mrs. A. Blackburne is fince dead, but her mufeum is preferved at her late houfe near Warrington.

The Liverpool and Manchefter road on each fide of Warrington is now made with flag or drofs from the copper works, broken with hammers into fmall pieces, and raifed in the middle. This makes an excellent and durable road. That part between Warrington and Prefcott is equal to any in the kingdom.

WINWICK

WINWICK PARISH.

THE village of Winwick, three miles north of Warrington, is re-markable for being the feat of the richeft rectory in England. The parifh is large and fertile, and the whole townfhip of Winwick, one eftate excepted, is glebe land to the church, the rector being lord of the manor. The whole value of the living is fuppofed at prefent to be little fhort of £.3000 per annum. It is in the gift of the earl of Derby. The prefent very refpectable incumbent, the Rev. Geoffry Hornby, has made great additions to the parfonage houfe, and improvements of the grounds about it, fo as to render it an adequate refidence for fuch a be-nefice. There is alfo a good free-fchool in the village. The church is an ancient edifice with a fpire fteeple, a confpicuous object from a great diftance. A Latin infcription in monkifh rhyme, written in old characters, runs round the fouth fide of the church, intimating that the place was once a favourite feat of Ofwald, king of Northumber-land, in the time of the heptarchy. Dr. Sherlock, grandfather of the bifhop of London of that name, died rector of this place in 1689.

Newton, in Winwick parifh, once a fmall market town, and though now but a village; ftill retaining the more important privilege of fending two members to parliament, lies on the north road between Warring-ton and Wigan, forming a broad ftreet diftinguifhed by its numerous public houfes—the true borough badge. The right of election is in the free burgeffes, who are occupiers of certain houfes; their number is about thirty-fix. The fteward of the lord of the manor, and the bai-liff, are returning officers. The property of the borough is in the fa-mily of Legh of Haydock in this parifh, and Lyme in Chefhire.

Newton

Newton has a chapel of the eſtabliſhment.

Aſhton in Makerfield, or *in the Willows,* a village in the ſame pariſh, agreeably ſituated on the north road, is become a thriving place of traffic, having employment both in the cotton trade, and in ſome branches of the hardware manufaƈtory. This laſt is managed by workmen, who perform their work at home, and take it to their employers, as the weaver does his piece. Aſhton has likewiſe a chapel.

Throughout the whole of Winwick pariſh there is much ſpinning of cotton and flax.

PRESCOTT.

THIS is a moderate-ſized market town, ſituated about eight miles to the eaſtward of Liverpool, and on the turnpike road between that port and Warrington. Its ſituation is dry and elevated, ſo that the ſpire ſteeple of its church is an objeƈt from all the low part of this county and Cheſhire to the diſtance of a great many miles. The town may be ſaid almoſt to be built over coal-pits, ſeveral being worked cloſe to its extremities, and its neighbourhood ſupplying large quantities of this article to Liverpool and the circumjacent parts. The town is ſtraggling and of conſiderable length. Its market-day is Tueſday; it has two yearly fairs, in June and November. The church is a vicarage, and of conſiderable value. There is likewiſe a diſſenting meeting, and a free-ſchool, and a number of alms-houſes.

Prescott has several manufactories of coarse earthen ware; but it is particularly distinguished as the centre of the manufacture of watch tools and movements, of which we shall proceed to give an account.

The watch-tools made here have been excellent beyond the memory of the oldest watch-makers; and the manufacture has been much extended by improvements in making new tools of all sorts, and the inventions for first cutting teeth in wheels, and afterwards for finishing them with exactness and expedition. The drawing of pinion wire originated here, which is carried as far as to fifty drawings, and the wire is completely adapted for every size of pinions to drive the wheels of watches, admirable for truth and fitness for the purpose, but left for the workmen to harden. This pinion wire is now very cheap, the price having been lowered by a single workman in that branch, who left the country forty years since and settled at Islington, where he offered it at half price to the tool shops in London.

They make here small files, the best in the world, at a superior price, indeed, but well worth the money, from the goodness of the steel, and exactness of cutting. They do not attempt making the larger files.

They make watch-movements most excellent in kind, which is greatly owing to the superior quality of their files and tools. They likewise excel in what is called motion-work, such as dial wheels, locking springs, hour, minute, and second hands, &c. Main springs, chains for movements, and watch-cases, were not part of the original manufacture, but are now made here.

All

All thefe branches extend from Prefcott to the furrounding villages, and all along the road to Liverpool, in which town the bufinefs feems finally to have centered : the drawing of pinion wire particularly, is now principally carried on at a place called the Park, near Liverpool. Upon the whole, this tool-making bufinefs keeps removing to Liverpool, in the fame manner as the fuftian making, which originated at Bolton, has removed to Manchefter. The tool and watch-movement makers are numeroufly fcattered over the country from Prefcott to Liverpool, occupying fmall farms in conjunction with their manufacturing-bufinefs, in which circumftance they refemble the weavers about Manchefter. All Europe is more or lefs fupplied with the articles above-mentioned made in this neighbourhood.

The parifh of Prefcott is extenfive, and contains various objects deferving of notice.

St. Helens has of late years rifen from a fmall village to be a well-built and populous market town. Its increafe has been owing to the various works eftablifhed in its neighbourhood. In the year 1773, was erected at Ravenhead, near St. Helens, the *Britifh Plate-Glafs Manufactory*, incorporated by act of parliament, occupying near thirty acres of land enclofed by a wall. The buildings have coft near £.40,000. Between 300 and 400 men are conftantly employed in the works. The metal table upon which the glaffes are caft and rolled is fifteen feet long, nine feet wide, and fix inches thick. The manufacture was introduced by workmen from France, and is brought to great perfection. Glaffes have been caft here of the following fizes :

133 inches by 72	135 inches by 62
139 ditto by 69	144 ditto by 54

The

The glafs is chiefly fent to London, and lodged for fale in the Company's warehoufe near Blackfriars bridge. It is as brilliant in colour and perfect in every refpect as the French, though the want of wood fewel was for fome time a difadvantage, which has been overcome by great induftry and care in the choice and ufe of the coals employed. In 1789 a fteam engine was erected to grind and polifh the plates of glafs, which is a very curious piece of mechanifm, and not only faves a great deal of labour, but does the work with more exactnefs and expedition. This invention is faid to perform as much work as would employ 160 men.

Near St. Helen's a few years ago was alfo eftablifhed a manufactory for window glafs, and for blowing fmall plates.

At St. Helen's, about the year 1780, a moft extenfive copper-work was erected by Meffrs. Hughes, Williams, and Co. for the purpofe of fmelting and refining copper-ore from Paris mountain in Anglefey. Of this ore, 20,000 tons per annum are fmelted here and at another work upon the fame navigation, which is the Sankey canal. The Raven-head works manufacture thirty tons weekly of fmall copper bars, not feven ounces troy weight, for the Eaft India Company, which are exported to China, and are fuppofed to pafs for coin. Thefe bars are dropped from the mould into water, when an effervefcence begins in a few minutes to take place at one end, and proceeds quickly to the other, by which the bar is changed from a leaden hue to the colour of red fealing wax. The bar refembles in fhape a ftick of wax.

In the adjoining townfhip of *Sutton*, an excellent clay is found, and made ufe of for making fugar moulds and coarfe earthen-ware; and in the townfhip of *Rainford*, about five miles from St. Helen's, there is

S f good

good clay for making crucibles and fire bricks. In *Sutton* townſhip
and *Parr* iron ſtone has been found in large quantities above the coals,
and in ſome places beds of cokes or cinders have been diſcovered, three
feet thick, ſaid to have been made from the iron works of the Danes,
when in poſſeſſion of this part of the country—and this ſeems probable,
from the manner of their getting the ore, which is proved to have been
by ſinking a ſhaft to the iron ſtone, and excavating the ſame by enlarging the aperture, in the form of a cone, ſo long as they durſt venture
to truſt the roof, and then ſinking a new ſhaft near, and filling up the
old one with the ſoil, &c. ſo produced. The cinders appear to have
reſiſted the efforts of time, and to remain in the ſame ſtate they were in
when buried ; and as diſcovered, they have been made uſe of for the repair of roads.

KNOWSLEY.

ABOUT a mile and a half from Preſcott lies Knowſley, in Huyton
pariſh, the reſidence of the earls of Derby, ſeated in a park, high, and
much expoſed to the weſt winds, the effects of which are viſible in the
ſhorn form of the trees towards that quarter. This was a manor apper-
taining to Lathom. The houſe conſiſts of two parts joining to each
other at right angles. The more ancient is of ſtone, and has two round
towers. This was built by Thomas, firſt earl of Derby, for the reception of his ſon-in-law king Henry VII. The other part, which
is of brick, was built by the two laſt earls. The noble family of
Stanley, the title of which is derived from Weſt Derby in Lancaſhire, not from the county of that name, has for many generations
been ſettled in Lancaſhire, in which it holds large poſſeſſions and the

firſt

firſt intereſt. In this houſe is a long ſeries of portraits of the family, many of whom have been highly diſtinguiſhed by the virtues which ſhould adorn an Engliſh nobleman. It contains likewiſe a capital collection of pictures by ſome of the firſt Italian and Flemiſh maſters, which was purchaſed by James earl of Derby, who ſent abroad for that purpoſe Hamlet Winſtanley, a painter, a native of Warrington. Winſtanley etched twenty plates of the fineſt of theſe paintings in the years 1728 and 1729.

ORMSKIRK PARISH.

ORMSKIRK is a neat market town, with four well-built ſtreets croſſing each other at right angles, leaving a handſome opening at the centre. Its only trade is the ſpinning of cotton for the Mancheſter manufactures, and thread for ſail-cloth. It has long been in poſſeſſion of a fair and market by virtue of a grant from king Edward I. (confirmed by Edward II.) to the canons of Burſcough, to whom the church and manor belonged. The manor and patronage of the church now belong to the earl of Derby. The living is a vicarage. The church is remarkable for its two ſteeples placed contiguous, one, a tower, the other, a ſhort ſpire, concerning the erection of which various ſtories are told. In a chapel within the church is the cemetery of the Derby family, being a vault, the deſcent to which is cloſed by folding doors. me monuments of this family were removed hither from Burſcough priory, at the diſſolution.

From the top of the ſteeple is a fine proſpect of the adjacent country, the Iriſh ſea, the mouth of the Ribble, and the towns of Liverpool

and Preston at indistinct distances, with moors and washes inter
sperfed.

The parish of Ormskirk contains the townships of *Ormskirk*, *Burfcough*, *Lathom*, *Scarisbrick*, and *Bickerstaff* with *Skelmersdale*. In
the sandy loams of these districts carrots are successfully cultivated for
the supply of the Liverpool market. The gardeners about Ormskirk
are likewise famous for their culture of early potatoes.

Burfcough Priory was founded in the reign of Richard I. by Robert Fitzhenry, lord of Lathom. At the time of the dissolution it maintained a prior and five canons of the Augustine order, and forty servants.
Nothing is left of the pile but part of the centre arch of the church.
Instead of its magnificent tombs of the Stanleys before the reformation
a few modern grave-stones peep through the grass, the memorials of
poor catholics, who still prefer this burial place.

Lathom-house, a magnificent edifice built by Sir Thomas Bootle,
knight, chancellor to Frederick, late Prince of Wales, is the present
feat of Richard Wilbraham Bootle, Esq. The house consists of a
ground-floor, principal and attic, and has a rustic basement, with a
double flight of steps to the first story. It is built of stone, after a plan
of Leoni's. The front extends 156 feet by 75, and has nine windows
on each floor. The offices are joined to it by two corridors supported by
Ionic pillars. It contains, among other good apartments, a hall of forty
feet by forty, and thirty-eight high. The back front was begun by
William earl of Derby. The house is situated in the centre of a park
five miles round, commanding an extensive but uninteresting view towards the north.

2   The

The ancient celebrated houfe of Lathom ftood between the north-eaft offices of the prefent edifice, and the kitchen-garden. It originally belonged, with great furrounding property, to the family of Lathoms, from whom it came in 1369 to the Stanleys. The fiege which it underwent from the Parliament forces in 1644 and 1645, and its gallant defence by the famous countefs of Derby, Charlotte de la Tremouille, are events well known in the hiftory of our unfortunate civil wars. It returned into the poffeffion of the Stanley family after the Reftoration, and was inhabited within the prefent century. The houfe and this part of the eftate were transferred in 1714, by marriage, to lord Afhburnham. He fold it to a Mr. Furnefs, who parted with it to Sir Thomas Bootle. His neice and heirefs married the prefent owner, then Richard Wilbraham, Efq. of Rode-hall, Chefhire. Near the houfe is a fmall chapel and fome alms-houfes, founded by one of the Stanleys. A chaplain belongs to them, who bears the name of Almoner of Latham.

Searifbrick-hall is at prefent occupied by Thomas Ecclefton, Efq. a gentleman to whofe fpirited improvements in agriculture and the breeding of ftock, the neighbourhood is greatly indebted. For his exertions in the draining and improvement of *Martin-Meer*, he obtained the gold medal of the *Society for the Encouragement of Arts, Manufactures, and Commerce*. His account of that great work, communicated to the fame fociety in 1786, and publifhed in the feventh volume of their *Tranfactions*, is fo inftructive, that we cannot more ufefully employ a few pages than in reprinting it.

" MARTIN-MEER was formerly a large pool, or lake of frefh water, of an irregular form, furrounded chiefly by moffes or boggy land; containing near one thoufand feven hundred and feventeen acres,

of

of eight yards to the pole, which is the cuftomary meafure of the neighbourhood, (about three thoufand fix hundred and thirty-two ftatute
acres.)   It lies in the different manors of Scarifbrick, Burfcough, North-
Meols, Tarleton, and Rufford.

" About the year 1692, Mr. Fleetwood, of Bank Hall, propofed to
the feveral other proprietors to drain Martin-Meer, on condition that a
leafe (for the whole) of three lives and thirty-one years fhould be granted
him, which they agreed to; and Mr. Fleetwood obtained an act of
parliament the fame year to empower him to effect it.   The following
year he began the work: his plan was, to difcharge the waters immediately into the fea, at the mouth of the river Ribble, which before had
forced themfelves a paffage into the river Douglas, when the Meer waters were raifed above their ufual height by the land floods, as is noted
by Camden in his *Britannia*.

" The intermediate ground between Martin-Meer and the Douglas,
lying confiderably higher than the Meer, occafioned the ftagnation, and
kept it continually full.

" Mr. Fleetwood began the undertaking by making a canal, or fluice,
twenty-four feet wide, of a depth fufficiently lower than the Meer,
which he cut from the Ribble mouth through an embanked falt marfh,
and then through a mofs or bog in North Meols, about a mile and a
half in length; and he continued it through the loweft parts of the
Meer.   To prevent the fea from rufhing up the canal, and overflowing
the Meer, which lies ten feet lower than high-water mark at the fpring
tides, he erected in his canal, near the fea, a pair of flood-gates, which
fhut when the fea waters rofe higher than thofe in the canal, and opened

I   again

again by the fluice ftream when the fea retired. In this place, the mouth of the Ribble is nearly five miles over at the fpring tides; but the bed of the river at low water is no more than a furlong in breadth, and it lies under the Lytham, or oppofite fhore to the flood-gates, about the diftance of four miles from them. This is a very unfavourable circumftance to the draining of the Meer, as it greatly diminifhes the effect of the out-fall by the length of the way the waters have to run over a very flat, loofe, flying, fandy coaft, before they can difembogue into the river. Thefe fands in a few years after the drainage was finifhed, drifting by the winds into the out-fall fluice, foon obftructed the flow of the waters, and in a fhort time choaked up the paffage, which had been made fufficiently deep to carry them off.

" The fpring tides in boifterous weather brought up great quantities of mud to the flood-gates; here it lodged in fediment for want of a powerful current in dry feafons to wafh it away: thus the wifhed-for effect of fo much labour was fruftrated, for the Meer was once more nearly reduced into its primitive ftate. In order to remove this deftructive obftacle of mud and fand, the managers for Mr. Fleetwood, in the year 1714, thought it moft advifeable to raife the fill or threfhold of the flood-gates, which they elevated twenty inches: this, with fome other meafures then adopted, did, for fome time, enable them to keep the flood-gates free from the above-mentioned obftructions.

" But it proved very detrimental; for fo much fall was loft, that the arable and meadow grounds upon the Meer diminifhed greatly in value, by the water remaining upon them all the winter, and very late oftentimes in the fpring feafon.

" By

" By a gradual, continual lofs of out-fall amongft the fands, and by the fluice on the marſh and other parts wrecking up, the Meer lands for many years were only made uſe of as a poor, fenny, watery paſture for the cattle of the neighbourhood, and that for a part of the fummer months only

" Some time after, Mr. Fleetwood's executors continued their fluice farther upon the ſhore, and erected a new pair of flood-gates, winged with ſtone walls, confiderably nearer to the out-fall, and they found great benefit from it, as the gates were much lefs liable to be obftructed by the fand and mud brought up with the tide.

" About the year 1750 Mr Fleetwood's leafe expired; and in 1755 the flood-gates and walls were wafhed down by a very uncommon high tide, but were rebuilt (fourteen feet wide) at the joint expence of the proprietors, in whofe hands it remained in a neglected ſtate for many years; for, as before, from inattention to the cleanfing of the fluice, and from the narrow paffage at the flood-gates, which were ſtill liable to be choaked with mud, &c. and much of the out-fall being loft, the lands upon the Meer became again of little value, being covered with water all the winter, and liable to be flooded by very trivial fummer rains   In this condition the beſt Meer lands let for a few ſhillings the large acre only.

" In the year 1778 I fettled here; and as the moſt extenſive and va- luable wear of the Meer belonged to this eſtate, I had the levels taken from low-water mark; and finding a confiderable fall, I had recourſe to Mr. Gilbert, of Worfeley (who had judicioufly planned, and happily executed the aftonifhing works of his grace the duke of Bridgewater.)

To

To his friendſhip and abilities I am indebted for the ſuccefs of the drainage; for, after the moſt minute inſpection, he gave me every encouragement, and kindly aſſiſted me in directing the undertaking. By his
advice I applied to the other four proprietors of Martin-Meer for a
leaſe for the term of three lives for their ſeveral ſhares, and opened to
them my intention of effectually draining the whole at my own expence. In 1781 I obtained the leaſes from all the proprietors (one only
excepted,) and immediately began the work.

" The plan Mr. Gilbert ſtruck out, which I have executed, was to
have in the main ſluice three different pair of flood-gates. The firſt
are to keep the ſea out, which are called the Sea-gates. The ſecond
pair are erected at about half a mile diſtance nearer to the Meer, to ſtop
the ſea there, in caſe any accident ſhould happen to the firſt: theſe are
termed the Stop-gates. The third pair are built cloſe to, and in the
ſame walls with the Sea-gates, but open and ſhut in a contrary direction to them: theſe are named the Fluſhing-gates. All theſe three
flood-gates are kept open, to give a free paſſage to the waters from the
Meer, when the tide has ſufficiently retired; and when the tide riſes
again above the level of the waters on the Meer, the ſea-gates are ſhut.
In dry ſeaſons, when a ſufficient quantity of water does not come down
from the Meer, to keep the out-fall ſluice open acroſs the looſe flying
ſands on the ſhore, the tide itſelf is permitted to flow up the ſluice to
the ſtop-gates, which are then ſhut; and at high water the fluſhing-
gates are cloſed to keep the ſea water in.

" N. B. All theſe three ſeveral gates have four paddles at the bottom, three feet in length, and two feet in depth, which are drawn up

T t by

by fcrews, to flufh away any obftacle that may chance to impede their working.

" At low water the paddles of the flufhing-gates are drawn up, and the retained fea-water rufhes out with fo much violence, that the fluice to low water is in a very fhort time cleanfed from every obftruction, fand, mud, &c. that may have been brought up by the tide.

" Thus, by the great fkill and fuperior ingenuity of one man (Mr. Gilbert,) the great obftacle to the perfect drainage of Martin-Meer is done away, which had baffled the many vain efforts of the proprietors for almoft a century.

" By an accurate examination of the out-fall, Mr. Gilbert found it would admit of the fill or threfhold of the new gates being laid five inches lower than it formerly had been; and he recommended the fea-gates to be advanced about two hundred yards nearer to the out-fall upon the open marfh. To prevent the fea flowing into the fluice behind thefe gates, large and ftrong banks are thrown up on each fide, which are continued to the ftop-gates; and at the fame time they anfwer another effential purpofe, viz. by containing a larger quantity of fea-water to flufh with.

" The new fea-gates are eighteen feet wide, and nineteen feet and a half high, and the fill five feet lower than the former: this makes the paffage in rainy feafons, when the water would have run four feet upon the old fill, to bear the proportion of one hundred and fixty-two feet in the prefent gates, to fifty-fix in the old ones.

" When

" When we had funk to the proper depth of the foundations of the new gates, we found a quickfand, and built upon it. The walls are twelve bricks in thicknefs at the bottom, and there is no fettlement, nor have they funk in the leaft.—N. B. Large flat ftones were laid under the brick and ftone work, and were the only precaution ufed.

" Whilft the gates were building, I employed all the hands I could procure in deepening and widening the fluice upon a dead level with the fill up to the Meer, fix yards wide at the bottom, allowing a foot and a half flope to every foot in elevation. In fome places the cutting was near twenty feet deep; and at the depth of fixteen feet in fand, I found an entire trunk of a tree, which fquared a foot.

" In April 1783 the level was carried up completely to the Meer, which then (owing to the waters having been dammed up,) was flooded higher than it had been for feveral years. As foon as the dam-head was cut, the fuperior efficacy of the new works appeared, and this un-common flood ran off in five days, which would have required as many weeks to have been difcharged through the old flood-gates.

" After the waters had run off, the fluice was deepened nearly to the fame level through the loweft parts of the Meer. The fluice is nearly five miles in length from the fea-gates.

" The ditches were next attended to; and fince the drainage, above a hundred miles in length have been perfected; but as fmall open drains were neceffary to carry off the rain-water into the ditches, I procured a drain-ing or guttering plough, on Mr. Cuthbert Clark's conftruction, which was drawn by eight, fometimes ten able horfes, and which I can with certainty recommend as a moft ufeful implement in all fenny countries.

" I am greatly indebted to the inventor; for with this, in one day, I cut drains nearly eight miles in length, thirteen inches in depth, twenty inches wide at the top, and five at the bottom, more perfect than could have been done in that land by the hand, and which would have coft, if done by hand, feven pounds five fhillings and ten pence.

" The fummer in 1783 was employed wholly as above, in laying the land dry. In the year 1784 fome few acres were ploughed, and yielded a tolerable crop of fpring corn; fome yielded a very inferior kind of hay : the reft was paftured. Early the laft year I prepared for oats and barley, and ploughed nearly two hundred large acres.

" The effects of the drainage appear from the crops; for I have fold barley for eleven pounds feventeen fhillings and fix-pence the large acre, the produce of the land which before let at no more than four fhillings the acre; and oats at ten pounds feventeen fhillings and fix- pence per acre, off land, which would bring no price before; the pur- chafer to cut, carry off, &c. all at his own expence.

" From the lands which before afforded a very poor pafture in the drieft fummers, I laft year fed feveral head of Scotch cattle, which did better than any that were fattened upon the beft grazing lands in our neighbourhood. The beft meadow lands in the moft favourable fea- fons did not let for more than about nine fhillings per acre.

" Laft

" Laft year I mowed many acres, worth three pounds, and let off feveral of inferior grafs, at two pounds per acre, referving the after-grafs for my own cattle."

A fubfequent account, communicated by Mr. Ecclefton in 1789, begins with informing the Society of various loffes fuftained in confé-quence of the failure of the banks of the river Douglas, and of the Leeds and Liverpool canal, which inundated the drained lands of the Meer, and caufed much damage. In the mean time, the works erected for the drainage itfelf had fully anfwered expectation, and had not failed in a fingle inftance. From thefe accidents, however, Mr. Ec-clefton was induced to adopt the grazing rather than the tillage line. He found grafs-feeds and rape mixed, a very ufeful crop in keeping his lambs; and flax fucceeded well, being fit to pull earlier than any dan-ger can raife from the autumnal floods. Good roads over fome of the fofteft parts of the Meer, for feveral miles, have been made by means of faggots covered a confiderable thicknefs with fand. Of all ftock, horfes have been found to anfwer beft on the natural coarfe grafs and weeds on the fofteft lands; on which account he has greatly increafed his breed of thofe animals, of the coach kind. Lambs while on the ewe improve greatly on the Meer, but the ewes themfelves get out of con-dition, and old fheep are very fubject to the rot. Black cattle have not fucceeded well, great numbers of calves having been taken off by a dif-eafe here called the *hyon*.

L Y D I A T E.

THIS is a townfhip in the parifh of Halfall. It is chiefly remarkable for a ruined edifice, formerly a chapel of eafe to Halfall church. It is

a fmall,

326   SEPHTON PARISH.

a fmall, but moft beautiful building, having a tower fteeple, with pin-
nacles and battlements, venerably overgrown with ivy.   Over the door
are the letters L. I. for Lawrence Ireland, probably the founder, of the
family of Irelands of Lydiate-hall.   The prefent owner is Henry
Blundell, Efq. of Ince.

SEPHTON PARISH.

SEPHTON parifh contains the townfhips of *Sephton*, *Netherton*,
and *Lunt*, *Ince Blundell* and *Little Crofby*, *Thornton* and *Great Crofby*,
Litherland, *Ayntreee*, *Orrell*, and *Ford*.   The farms in this neighbourhood are for the moft part fmall, few rifing to £.100 per annum.   The
country is moftly divided into very fmall tenements or leafeholds granted
for three lives.   As a proof of their fmallnefs, the late Henry Blundell, Efq. of Ince, had in Formby, Aynfdale, and Birkdale, 230 fuch
tenements, confifting of about 1300 Lancafhire acres.   This mode of
letting is difadvantageous to the landlord, whofe rents and fines amount
to a fmall proportion of the real value, but feems to have had a good
effect on the country, by filling it with inhabitants and comfortable
buildings, and caufing feveral branches of manufacture to be fet up.
For thefe leafehold tenants confider themfelves as better than the common fmall farmers, and are above going to fervice or day labour; in
confequence of which the men betake themfelves to fome trade or bufinefs, and the women to fpinning cotton, which caufes their living and
dreffing better, and the confequent greater confumption of articles of
provifion and cloathing.   Few landlords, however, now chufe to renew
the old way of leafing.

The

The fea-fhore all along this coaft is remarkable for its flatnefs and number of large fand banks, highly dangerous to fhipping in ftrong wefterly winds, which are very prevalent here. The fea is fuppofed to abound with fifh, but few are taken, and thofe only with hook and line, the fifhermen either not poffeffing boats to go out to fea, or not chufing to truft themfelves on fuch a boifterous coaft. The kinds taken are chiefly cod, ray or fkaite, and flounders. The fhore is protected by a barrier of fand hills, held together by the *ftar* or fea-reed, the roots of which penetrate deep into the fands, and offer a fixed point round which they may collect. This ftar is ufeful for making mats, befoms, thatch, &c. but the law is very ftrict with regard to cutting it, fince when it is deftroyed, the hills are prefently blown away, and the lands behind overwhelmed by a moving fand. Thefe hills are in fome places half a mile broad, with feveral large openings or flats of land between them; and when in the midft of them, no defarts of Arabia can appear more dreary. There is little or no timber growing on the coaft; and a perfon, from obferving that all the trees to a great diftance up the country are, as it were, fhorn on the weft fide, and bent the oppofite way, would be apt to conclude that none would grow; yet it is certain that the country was once very woody, for in the mofs lands, large quantities of oaks are often found within a foot or two of the furface, lying with their heads all one way, as if blown over by a violent weft wind, or overthrown by a fudden irruption of the fea. A gentleman in this parifh got up near fifty loads out of one field, the wood moftly ordinary, and fit only for fuel. Sometimes trees of value are met with. The wood is ufually dark-coloured and of little durability, though often ufed for pofts and fencing. Many of the mofs lands are fo full of it that they are with difficulty ploughed. Along the fea-fhore, and near the Grange land-mark, are the ftumps of feveral large trees, which, by

2   being

being in a line and at equal diftances, were undoubtedly planted: whence it would feem as if formerly either the climate was not fo rough, or the fea did not advance fo far, fince there would now be no poffibility of raifing trees in the fame fituation. It appears, however, as if the fea had formerly overrun a good deal of this country, from the ftrata of fea-flutch, mofs, fand, and fhells found in various parts; and the fea now again feems retiring.

The village of *Sephton* is placed on a range of fine meadows that reach almoft to the fea, and in great meafure fupply Liverpool with its hay. It is watered by the *Alt*, a fmall trout ftream which empties into the fea near Formby, but for want of fufficient fall to carry off its waters, its banks remain inundated the whole feafon after the firft winter floods. Sephton is a rectory. The church is a large and handfome edifice, confifting of a body and two aifles, battlemented and crenellated. The fteeple is an elegant fpire. The prefent church was built in the time of Henry VIII., as is faid, by Anthony Molyneux, its rector, a celebrated preacher, and diftinguifhed for acts of piety. The chancel is divided by a fcreen from the body, and contains fixteen ftalls of elegant fculpture. The family of Molyneux had their ancient feat in this town, where their Norman anceftor, William de Moulins, fettled on the grant made him by Roger de Poictiers. In the chancel of the church has been for many ages the burying-place of this race, of many of whom monumental memorials are ftill preferved. One of thefe records Sir Richard Molyneux, who diftinguifhed himfelf in the battle of Agincourt, and was knighted by Henry V.; another, Sir William, who was in three actions againft the Scots in Henry VIII.'s time, and in that of Floddon, with his own hand took three banners, for which fervice he was thanked

by

by a letter under Henry's own feal. The Lancashire archers greatly contributed to this victory.

A chapel on the north fide of the chancel contains feveral modern monuments of the Molyneux family. There is in the church another chapel, belonging to the ancient family of Blundells, of Ince-Blundell.

Litherland in the parifh of Sephton is a manor belonging to the Molyneux family, which had an old hall, now demolifhed, but the extent of which may yet be traced by the ruins. The family fe_t is now removed to Croxteth.

WALTON PARISH.

THIS is a large parifh, adjoining on the north to Liverpool, which town it formerly included. The living is a very valuable rectory, containing, befides the parifh church, five chapels of eafe. The church, feated upon a fine eminence, is a fea-mark, and its fituation affords a very extenfive profpect in all directions. The parifh of Walton includes the townfhip of Toxteth-park, Derby, Croxteth-park, Kirkby, Simon's-wood, Walton, Bootle, Everton, Kirkdale, Fazakerly, Formby, Anfdell, Ravers-meals, and Linacre. There was an ancient family of the Waltons of Walton. The laft of the name, who owned all the lands in Walton, left three daughters, co-heireffes. By one of them, a third part paffed to the family of Fazakerly, in which it continued till fold to the late James earl of Derby. Another part went to the Chorleys, of Chorley, but being forfeited in the rebellion of 1715, it was purchafed by Mr. Crompton and others. The other third went to the family of Hoghton, of Hoghton-tower by the defcendants of which, moft of the eftate was fold to Mr. Atherton.

Bootle

Bootle lies near the sea, on a very sandy soil, and contains some good houses. A very copious spring of soft, pure water rises near it, which turns a mill about half a mile below, and soon after falls into the sea at Bootle-bay.

Linacre, a pretty rural village, is a member of the manor of Bootle, and lies adjacent to the sea.

Kirkdale, in the same manor, to the south of Bootle, is a pleasant village, agreeably seated on the declivity of a hill. It was part of the estate of the family of More, or de la More, who established themselves here about the year 1280, and built More-hall near Liverpool. They also built Bank-hall, situate in Kirkdale, near the sea, which was a curious specimen of ancient architecture, with many relics of family antiquities, but all demolished twenty or thirty years since.

West Derby and *Everton* belong to the earl of Derby, under whom they are held by copyholders paying fixed rents and fines. The latter place is now joined to Liverpool by new buildings.

Croxteth-hall, the seat of the earl of Sefton, was rebuilt by William lord Molyneux, grandfather to the present earl.

CHILDWALL PARISH.

THIS lies south-east of Liverpool. It is very extensive, and includes Hale, Speke, Garston, Wavertree, Allerton, and Great and Little Woolton. Its living is a vicarage, containing two chapelries.

In

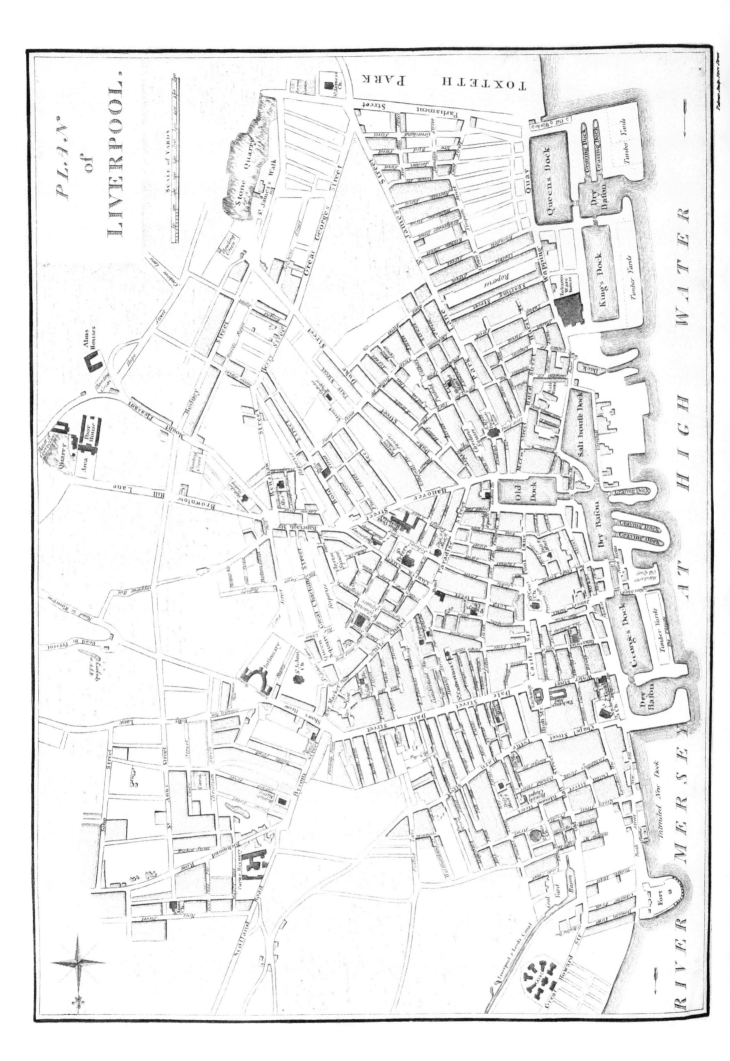

In the manor of *Speke* is a hall, where are feveral remains of antiquity, particularly a curious piece of wainfcot, brought by Sir Edward Norris from the library of the king of Scotland, after the battle of Flodden-field.

In *Garfton* is an ancient houfe, called *Aighburgh-hall*, formerly a feat belonging to the Tarleton family.

Woolton-hall is a noble manfion, purchafed from the Molyneux family by Nicholas Afhton, Efq. who has made large additions to it. It is placed on an eminence, and commands a fine and extenfive profpect.

All the villages in the vicinity of Liverpool are filled with the country feats and places of retirement of the merchants and other inhabitants of Liverpool, which give an air of cheerfulnefs and culture to a tract of country, not of itfelf much favoured by foil or climate.

***

LIVERPOOL.

THE great fea-port of Liverpool, the other eye of Lancafhire, bears fo important a relation to the fyftem of commerce which we have traced from Manchefter through the furrounding country, and is, befides, fo diftinguifhed an object in the maritime hiftory of this kingdom, that we fhould do injuftice to our plan not to beftow on it a large fhare of attention. Our labours are abridged by the elegant and valuable Effay towards its Hiftory, publifhed by Dr. Enfield, partly from

U u 2

papers

papers left by Mr. George Perry, and partly from original materials. As far as this work comes down (which is to the year 1772) we shall not scruple to make use of its authorities, which are drawn from the best sources. For later periods we shall trust to the results of our own inquiries.

The river Mersey, having held nearly a western course till within a few miles of its termination, makes a sudden bend to the north, and at length enters the sea by a channel forming almost a continued line with the coast of Lancashire. On the eastern side of this channel, about three miles within the mouth of the river, at a place where the channel is most contracted, Liverpool is situated. It is proper here to observe, that it appears from Leland, that in his time, the whole broad estuary of the Mersey turning from Runcorn to the sea, was commonly called *Lyrpoole*, (as, indeed, the termination *pool* properly denotes a detached or enclosed piece of water;) whence it would seem, that the town was originally named from its situation, as being, probably, the most remarkable collection of buildings belonging to this *pool* or *haven*.

The quantity of water running down the Mersey being small in proportion to its breadth, its fitness for a haven depends solely upon the tides. At Liverpool, the water, at spring tides, rises to the height of about thirty feet, and in neap tides of about fifteen feet. This great body of water, rushing up the bed of the river, causes, at the narrow parts of the channel, a head similar to that of the *hygre* in the rivers of the Bristol channel. The breadth of the channel of the Mersey opposite Liverpool, at its most contracted part, is 1200 yards at high water, but it soon widens both above and below.

The

The firft exiftence of a town in this fpot is traced by Cambden to the time of William the Conqueror, when Roger of Poictiers, lord of the Honour of Lancafter, built a caftle here. Charters were granted to the town in 1129 by Henry I., in 1203 by John, and in 1227 by Henry III. In the laft of thefe it was conftituted a perpetual corporation and free borough, with a merchant guild and other liberties. About the year 1360, in the reign of Edward III. the caftle of Liverpool was the property of Sir Thomas Latham, of Latham, who prefented it, with feveral other houfes and certain portions of land in Liverpool, to Sir John Stanley, who had married Ifabel his only daughter and the heirefs of Latham. Sir John, upon this, during his government of Ireland, built here a fpacious houfe, and obtained leave of Henry IV. to embattle it. He called the whole ftructure *the tower*, by which name it was known as long as it continued ftanding.

From this time nothing occurs refpecting the hiftory of Liverpool, except the confirmation of its charters and enlargement of its privileges by feveral fucceffive kings, till the time of Leland's tour through the kingdom at the beginning of the fixteenth century. His defcription of it (divefted of ancient language) is as follows: " Lyrpole, alias Lyverpoole, is a paved town, having only a chapel; its parifh church being Walton, four miles diftant, near the fea. The king has a caftelet, and the earl of Derby a ftone-houfe in it. Irifh merchants refort thither as to a good haven, and much Irifh yarn bought by Manchefter men, and other merchandize, is fold there. The cuftoms paid at Liverpool are fmall, which caufes the refort of merchants." Either, however, the town underwent a fubfequent decline, or the trade was carried on little to the advantage of the inhabitants; for it appears, that in 1565 there were in Liverpool only 138 houfeholders and cottagers, and all the fhipping
ping

ping of the place confifted of ten barks (the largeft of forty tons burthen) and two boats, the whole making 223 tons, and navigated by
feventy-five men: and at Wallafey, a creek oppofite, were three barks
and boats, making thirty-fix tons, and navigated by fourteen men.
That it *had* undergone a decay may probably, though not certainly, be
inferred from the language of a petition fent up by the inhabitants to
queen Elizabeth, in 1571, praying to be relieved from a fubfidy, in
which it is ftyled her Majefty's poor *decayed* town of Liverpool.

From this period to that of the civil wars, the increafe of its population and trade could not be very confiderable, fince we find no mention of the place worthy of being recorded; yet it muft have received
fome augmentation, as it was able to undergo a brifk fiege of a month's
continuance from prince Rupert in 1644. It was ftrongly garrifoned
by the Parliament, and fortified with a mud wall and ditch, defended
by batteries on the land fide; and befides its caftle, which was furnifhed with many cannon, and commanded the river and country
round, a fort of eight guns was erected on the river's fide. It was at
length taken, through negligence or treachery, and fome execution was
done by the Prince's troops on entering it. Not long after, however,
it was re-poffeffed by the Parliament's forces, and colonel Birch was
appointed governor. The importance of the town probably depended
chiefly on its being a ready tranfit to Ireland. At this, and at former
periods, the family of More at Bank-hall appear to have been leading
perfons at Liverpool.

It was not till the end of the century, that Liverpool became confiderable enough to be emancipated from its parochial dependence on Walton, and to be made a diftinct parifh. In the year 1699 the act for this

I   purpofe

purpofe paffed, by which alfo, the corporation was empowered to build a new church, in addition to the former parochial chapel, and it was provided, that two rectors fhould be appointed, one for each, who fhould jointly poffefs all rectorial rights within the town of Liverpool. The patronage of the rectory was vefted in the mayor, aldermen, and common council for the time being. The old parochial chapel was the church of St. Nicholas; the new one, that of St. Peter. The regif-ters of marriages, chriftenings, and burials, to the commencement of the prefent century, give the following numbers:

Year.	Marr.	Chrift.	Bur.	Year.	Marr.	Chrift.	Bur.
1624	4	35	21	1680	3	108	51
1662	5	30	30	1690	10	120	151
1670	5	67	48	1700	34	131	125

The fmall proportion of marriages in the earlier periods, and their fudden increafe in the laft, muft be attributed to the difference in the parochial jurifdiction of the town. From thefe lifts it would appear, that even in the firft year of this century, Liverpool did not poffefs a po-pulation of more than about 4240 perfons.*

In 1710, the increafe of trade had fuggefted the neceffity of a dock, and an act paffed for the purpofe of empowering the town to conftruct one. Before this time, the fhips muft have lain in the open channel oppofite the town, as there is no natural creek or inlet from it. About this period, the number of the fhips belonging to the port was eighty-

* It is ftated in the *Hiftory of Liverpool* at 5714; but by following the rule of multi-plication there laid down, and making the proportional allowance for non-regiftered births, the refult is no more than we have given.

four,

four, averaging fomewhat lefs than feventy tons burthen each, and navigated by eleven men at a medium. The port was, however, frequented by above three times that number of fhips belonging to other
places. As the Irifh trade was the original branch of the Liverpool
commerce, fo it continued to be the principal one; and the decline of
the port of Chefter, with the increafed traffic between the two kingdoms, gave great vigour to this intercourfe. Many natives of Ireland
fucceffively fettled in Liverpool for the purpofe of carrying on their
commercial plans, and laid the foundation of fome of the principal
mercantile houfes in it. They likewife contributed much to form the
local character and manners of the town, which have confiderably
differed from thofe of the inland towns of Lancafhire, as well as of
other fea-ports. The relative fituation of the Ifle of Man with refpect
to Liverpool, caufed the greateft part of its trade alfo to center in this
port. The importation of iron, timber, hemp, flax, and naval ftores,
from the northern countries of Europe, muft have been an early branch
of bufinefs at a thriving port, connected with a country rapidly increafing in buildings and manufactures. And as opulence and elegance
of living gained ground, the fupply of wine, fruits, and other articles
from the fouth of Europe, would naturally be fought for by a direct importation from thofe parts, inftead of the circuitous medium of London
or Briftol.

We have not been able to obtain any documents concerning the commencement of the Weft India trade in Liverpool; but as a fmall veffel
is faid to have failed for Africa in the year 1709, it may be prefumed
that fome portion of the direct traffic to the Weft Indies exifted as early
as that period.

The

The fupply of Liverpool with water was now thought a matter of importance; and an act paffed in the fame year with the dock act, for enabling the corporation to make a grant to Sir Oleave Moore, Bart. for liberty to bring frefh water into the town. This ufeful fcheme, however, for want of money, or fome other circumftances, was never put in execution.

It was in 1709 that the fpirit of charity, a general attendant upon commercial profperity, began to make its appearance at Liverpool in the inftitution of the Blue-coat Hofpital, firft called the Charity-fchool. A fmall building, now part of the free-fchool, was erected by benefactions, and forty boys and ten girls were provided with cloaths and inftruction by an annual fubfcription of about £.30, and £.20 out of the facrament money. In 1714, Bryan Blundell, Efq. a liberal contributor to this charity, became its chief manager. He fet on foot a fubfcription for a building in which the children might live together under proper difcipline and provided with all neceffaries, generoufly fetting the example by a large benefaction of his own; the building was begun in 1716, and completed in 1726, at the expence of upwards of £.2000. It then received fixty children, who were taught to work in the fchool, and employed in fpinning cotton.

To proceed with the gradual increafe of the town, we fhall remark, that in 1715 an act was obtained for the building of a third church, upon the fite of the old caftle. It was not, however, completely finifhed and confecrated till 1734. This is St. George's church, a large and handfome building, fitted up with peculiar elegance on the infide. It is the corporation-chapel, at which the mayor, aldermen, and common-council ufually attend.

X x

The

The number of inhabitants in 1720 is computed at 10,446, confiderably above double that in the firft year of the century. In the fame year, an act paffed for making navigable the rivers Merfey and Irwell as far as Manchefter; the firft of thofe fchemes for internal navigation in Lancafhire, which have fince multiplied to fuch a degree, to the benefit of the whole country, and efpecially of Liverpool, the great centre of its export and import trade.

The fame year, 1720, likewife gave rife to a ftill more important defign of water-communication, which was that by means of the river Weaver, with Northwich and Winsford-bridge. The great utility derived to the trade of Liverpool from the inexhauftible quantity of falt brought down from thefe places, has already been noticed, and fome particulars of this branch of commerce will hereafter be given under the head of Northwich. But although the act paffed this year, it was not till a confiderable time afterwards that its purpofes were fully brought into effect.

About the fame time, attention was paid to the improvement of its communications by land, and the roads to Prefcott and other parts were enlarged and repaired by the aid of turnpikes.

In the year 1730 the number of people exceeded 12,000. This is the firft year in which we find an account of fhips failing to Africa, the fingle floop in 1703 excepted. Concerning the flave trade, for which Liverpool has fince become fo peculiarly diftinguifhed, it is difficult to fpeak with the coolnefs of difcuffion that belongs to commercial topics in general. On the one hand, it has been warmly arraigned by the friends of juftice and humanity, and, indeed, by the common feelings of the uninterefted part of mankind; on the other hand, it has been as warmly defended

fended by thofe who are ardent in the purfuit of every extenfion of individual and national wealth. To confider only its *commercial* effects upon
this place, we may fay, that it has coincided with that fpirit of bold adventure which has characterifed the trade of Liverpool, and rapidly carried
it to its prefent ftate of profperity; has occafioned vaft employment for
fhipping and failors, and greatly augmented the demand for the manufactures of the country. Some, however, are of opinion that it has
pufhed this adventurous fpirit beyond all due bounds; has introduced
pernicious maxims and cuftoms of tranfacting bufinefs; has diverted to
itfelf the capital and attention which might have been better employed
on other objects, and has occafioned a great wafte of lives among the
feamen. Meantime, its being ftill an object in which the town regards
its interefts as deeply involved, feems a fufficient proof that its benefits,
in a commercial view, have at this port apparently exceeded its mifchiefs.

An act had paffed in 1717 for enlarging the time granted by the firft
dock act, which contained powers for making an additional dock and
building a pier in the open harbour, and for enlightening the faid dock;
and in 1738 another act paffed for enlarging the time of the laft act;
whence it may be concluded, that its purpofes as to the making of the
fecond dock were not yet completed. It was probably for the
want of thefe conveniences, that the tonnage of fhips entering inwards
was no greater in the year 1737 than it had been in 1716; but after
this period, the increafe became rapid. The augmentation of inhabitants was proportional; for in 1740, they were by computation more
than 18,000.

About the year 1745, a fubfcription was opened at Liverpool for the
eftablifhment of one of thofe excellent charities, an infirmary. The
work was begun the fame year; but owing to the national difturbances

at that period, its completion was retarded, so that the house did not open for the reception of patients till 1749. This, however, was earlier than the date of the greater part of those institutions of the like kind, with which so many of our provincial towns are now honoured.

At the same period (that of the last rebellion) the town of Liverpool displayed its consequence, and its attachment to the present royal family, in a very spirited manner. A regiment of foot, called the Liverpool Blues, was raised in the town, consisting of eight companies of seventy men each, with proper officers, &c. They continued in pay about fifteen weeks, during eight of which they were under marching orders, and were at the taking of Carlisle, where they were reviewed by the duke of Cumberland. The whole expence of this armament amounted to £.4859, of which the corporation contributed £.2000, and the town raised the rest. Besides this regiment, five companies of volunteers, consisting of sixty men each, exclusive of officers, were raised in the town, and instructed in the military exercise: one of which kept guard nightly while the disturbances of the kingdom lasted. Though Liverpool was then only in its early youth, few towns in England were probably capable of a similar exertion.

In 1749 an act passed for building another church in Liverpool, and for lighting and cleansing the streets. The church was St. Thomas's, consecrated the next year, and distinguished by the simple beauty of a lofty and elegant spire.

An institution of peculiar use, the design of which was formed in 1747, was carried into execution in 1752. This was an hospital for decayed seamen, their widows and children, supported by a monthly

contri-

contribution of fixpence, which every feaman from this port is obliged to pay out of his wages. The building forms the wings of the infirmary; it coft £.1500 The bufinefs of the inftitution is conducted by a committee chofen annually.

An act for the more fpeedy recovery of fmall debts in the town and its liberties, fimilar to what has been found neceffary in all populous and trading towns, paffed in 1753.

The internal water-communications of Liverpool were increafed by the Sankey canal, the act for which paffed in 1755, and which for many years after continued to improve in the facility and extent of its navigation. It afforded from the firft a new fupply of coals to Liverpool, and by the works fince eftablifhed upon it, has in various ways added to the bufinefs of this port.

By the year 1760, the population of Liverpool had reached, by computation, 25,787 fouls, and the tonnage of the fhipping belonging to its port was above four times that of the year 1709. It was provided with a convenient cuftom-houfe, a large and handfome exchange, a neat playhoufe, and all the other ufeful and ornamental ftructures belonging to a wealthy commercial town. In 1762, fuch was the prefent ftate and future profpects of the town, that an act was obtained for building two new churches at once, and alfo for making an additional dock and pier, and erecting lighthoufes in or near the port. The tafte for fhow and expence, however, caufed more than all the money deftined for the two churches to be confumed in building one, which was St. Paul's, confecrated in 1769. This is a magnificent ftructure, upon a plan in fome meafure imitative of that of the firft religious edifice in England.

England, which bears the same name. Like that, it has a grand portico at the weft end, two inferior projections in the north and fouth fronts, and a dome. This laft, though favourable to its architectural effect, has been found greatly to injure its utility as a place for fpeaking in. It is to be obferved, that the erection of places of worfhip for the various claffes of feparatifts had been keeping pace during thefe periods, in number and elegance, with that of the churches of the eftablifhment.

The new dock, more fpacious than either of the former, was a vaft addition to the accommodation of the port, and its piers and quays greatly improved its beauty and grandeur. It was not finifhed till about 1771.

The duke of Bridgewater's canals had by this time begun to operate in adding to the bufinefs of Liverpool. The Grand Trunk communication between the Trent and the Merfey, fo important to the trade of both rivers, was carrying on with vigour. The vaft defign of a communication between Liverpool and Leeds, croffing one large county, and penetrating into another, was begun to be executed in 1770, and it was not long before that part of it which extends from Liverpool to Wigan was completed, affording fuch plentiful fupplies of coal as greatly to add to the exportation of that commodity from this port.

The increafing number of poor in Liverpool had caufed feveral fucceffive changes in the management of them. At length it was determined to erect a large and commodious poor-houfe in an airy fituation adjoining to this town, and money for this purpofe was borrowed under the corporation feal. The building was begun in March 1770, and finifhed for the reception of the poor in Auguft 1771, at an expence of

near £.8000. It was calculated to contain 600 inhabitants, and few in‑
stitutions of the kind have been better managed.

A new and spacious theatre, by royal patent, built by subscription at
the expence of £.6000, was opened in June 1772. It is probably the
largest in England out of London, and is elegantly finished both on the
outside and within. Its passages and communications are particularly
well managed, and were much superior to those of the London theatres
at the time of its erection. The inhabitants of Liverpool have at all
times been liberal encouragers of dramatic entertainments.

In the beginning of the year 1773 a plan was executed which ought
never to be long neglected in a large town—that of an actual enumera‑
ration of its inhabitants. The result was as follows :

Inhabited houses,	-	-	-	5928
Untenanted do.	-	-	-	412
Families,	-	-	-	8002
Inhabitants,	-	-	-	34,407

Persons to a house, $5\frac{1}{4}$; to a family, $4\frac{1}{3}$.

In this statement, the poor-house, infirmary, and other buildings, where
large numbers live together, were included. With respect to the sea‑
faring men employed in the Liverpool ships, they were found to be
about 6000. Of these, about two-thirds were reckoned to be usually
absent from Liverpool, and therefore not to be accounted among the
stated inhabitants. The annual deaths in Liverpool were estimated
upon an average of three years, at 1240, or one in $27\frac{7}{10}$ of the inhabi‑
tants; the annual births on the same average were computed at 1290.
It is imagined by many, that this enumeration was considerably short
of the real number; the poor, it is said, frequently giving in a defective
list, through fear of a tax. This may in some instances have been the
case;

3

cafe; but, on the other hand, we fhould be on our guard againft that fpirit of exaggeration, which, in *every* town, difpofes its inhabitants to aggrandize all its claims to fuperiority. The proportion of people to families and houfes as ftated, agrees very well with the beft authorities in other places. We fhall further remark, that enumerations of this kind fhould not be left, as this was, to the exertions of individuals, but fhould be undertaken by authority, whence all fufpicion of inaccuracy might be obviated.

Having thus carried our hiftorical fketch of the rife and progrefs of Liverpool to a period in which it takes its fair ftation as the *fecond* fea-port, and one of the largeft and moft important towns, of the kingdom, we fhall compofe the reft of the article of papers and documents refpecting its fubfequent events and prefent ftate, with various detached particulars of its commerce and other circumftances belonging to it.

Government and *Police.*—By the lateft charters granted to Liverpool it is ordained, that the body corporate fhould confift of forty-one perfons, compofing the common council; out of whom fhould be annually chofen a mayor, recorder, and two bailiffs. They who have borne the office of mayor, are ftyled aldermen. The mayor, recorder, fenior aldermen, and preceding mayor, were by the charter of William III. directed to act as magiftrates in the town; but their number, upon the great increafe of population, proving infufficient, the charter of George II. further ordained, that the preceding mayor fhould act as juftice of the peace for four years after he is out of office; and that the four aldermen, next to the fenior aldermen, whilft members of the common council, fhould be additional juftices within the town, and the recorder fhould have a power to nominate a deputy.

Previoufly

Previoufly to the reign of Charles II. the freemen at large exercifed the right of chufing their own corporate officers; but fince that period, here, as in many other places, the corporate body affumed the power of filling up all vacancies within themfelves. The free burgeffes have now, however, reclaimed their right. The mayor and bailiffs are chofen annually on October 18th. The general feffion is held four times a year by two juftices of the peace at leaft, and by adjournment every Monday. The mayor attends daily at the town-clerk's office in the Exchange to tranfact public bufinefs. A court of requefts is held alfo at the Exchange every Wednefday. The number of its commiffioners is feventeen, appointed by the common council monthly.

Liverpool has a bridewell and a borough gaol. The former was built in 1776, upon an improved plan. A new gaol is now juft finifhed, a great and coftly ftructure, containing all the improvements fuggefted in Mr. Howard's works, and introduced into the modern architecture of thofe buildings.

This borough fends two members to Parliament, who are chofen by the votes of all the free burgeffes not receiving alms. All perfons who are born free, who have ferved an apprenticefhip under freemen, or who have obtained their freedom by grant or purchafe from the corporation, have the right of voting. Their number is reckoned at 2300. The freemen of Liverpool are alfo free of Briftol, and of Waterford and Wexford in Ireland.

Many ufeful regulations have been made for the government of the port, including the management of the wet, dry, and graving docks, and the laws refpecting pilots and pilotage. From the difficult ap-

Y y

proach.

proach to the harbour, the pilotage is a matter of great importance, and no pilot boats in England are reckoned to be better found, and more fkilfully managed, than thofe belonging to Liverpool. Some of them are conftantly cruizing in order to meet and conduct the homeward bound fhips.

Charities and other Public Inftitutions.—The *Infirmary*, mentioned above as opened in 1749, is fituated on an elevated fpot at the eaftern entrance of the town. It is a neat brick building ornamented with ftone, connected by handfome colonnades with two wings, which form the failors' hofpital. The principal building is three ftories high, and confifts of large wards, with other neceffary apartments. It has been gradually increafing the number of patients accommodated in it, and its receipts and difburfements have advanced proportionably. The average number of in-patients is now about 130. The number of out-patients is comparatively fmall, on account of the inftitution of a difpenfary. The expenditure of the year ending March 1793 amounted to £.2724, which fum that year (owing to particular circumftances) exceeded the receipts by £.376; but it cannot be queftioned that in fuch a town adequate exertions will at all times be made for the fupport of fo ufeful an eftablifhment. A *Lunatic Afylum* has lately been erected at a confiderable expence, connected with this charity. The concerns of the infirmary are managed by a prefident, treafurer, deputy-treafurers, and auditors, with committees of the fubfcribers. The fick are attended by three phyficians, and three furgeons.

The *Difpenfary* is an inftitution liberal in its plan, and highly beneficial in its effects. Its avowed object is to afford medical relief to the poor at their own dwellings; but medical relief is in many cafes only another phrafe for a more cordial or plentiful diet; and hence this charity

4   has

has often been the means of providing a refource for the unfortunate ftranger, when deprived of all other affiftance, and without any legal claim for fupport. It was inftituted in the year 1778, chiefly by the interpofition of fome of the medical gentlemen of Liverpool, on whofe recommendation a competent fubfcription was fpeedily obtained. It is directed by a prefident, two auditors, and a committee of the fub-fcribers. The profeffional duty was originally performed by three phy-ficians and three furgeons, who receive no compenfation for their trou-ble, and an apothecary, who refides on the fpot and receives a falary; but the number of phyficians was in the year 1791 increafed to feven, who vifit the patients according to regulations eftablifhed among them-felves. In the year 1782 a handfome building was erected in Church-ftreet for the more convenient diftribution of medicines, the accommo-dation of the phyficians and furgeons, and the refidence of the apothe-cary. Of the extenfive ufefulnefs of this charity an idea may be formed from the following extract from the printed report for the year 1794.

Patients admitted in 1794, - - - - -	13,760
Remaining on the books from the former year, - -	642
Of thefe were	14,402
Cured, - - - - - - - -	12,880
Relieved, - - - - - - - -	366
Removed to the Infirmary, - - - - -	30
Irregular, - - - - - - - -	65
Dead, - - - - - - - -	397
Remaining on the books, - - - - -	664

The difburfements of the charity for this year amounted to £.777.

During the fevere and fickly months of February and March 1795, upwards of 3000 applications were made to this charity for relief, and when it is confidered that the infirmary, though an excellent and well-conducted eftablifhment, is in its nature principally confined to fuch patients as choofe to relinquifh domeftic fympathy and affiftance for a public ward, and can only admit within its walls a number much inferior to thofe who ftand in need of relief, the abfolute neceffity of a charity of this nature in a populous town muft be ftrikingly evident. The conftant vifits of the phyficians and furgeons at the dwellings of the fick poor are attended with the moft beneficial effects : order and cleanlinefs are introduced—infectious diforders are oppofed . in the firft ftage of their progrefs—and a fentiment of mutual good-will is excited between the different claffes of fociety, of benevolence on the one hand, and of gratitude on the other, which cannot be too induftrioufly cultivated.

The *Afylum for the Indigent Blind* is an eftablifhment of a more peculiar nature, and was begun in the year 1790, under the aufpices of a humane and public-fpirited clergyman,* who has alfo diftinguifhed himfelf by extending the practice of inoculation in the town and neighbourhood of Liverpool, and other parts of the county, giving his attendance and fupplying medicines gratis.—In reflecting on the fituation of thofe perfons who labour under that heavy calamity, the lofs of fight, it muft occur to every one that this misfortune is aggravated by a want of employment for the mind, and by a confcioufnefs of being ufelefs to themfelves, and in many cafes a burthen to others. Frequent experience has, however, fhewn, that blind perfons are capable of becoming expert in various mechanical employments, and in fome cafes, of making a furprizing proficiency in ufeful accomplifhments. The education of perfons in this fituation requires, however, a different procefs

* The Rev. Henry Dannet, Minifter of St. John's.

from

from that which was ufually adopted; and it was therefore fuggefted, that if a fchool of induftry were eftablifhed for the blind, with proper inftructors, the moft beneficial effects might be derived from it. A fubfcription for this purpofe was accordingly opened, and two houfes, fronting the area before the infirmary, were rented, as a temporary accommodation for the pupils. The earneftnefs with which the benefits held forth by this inftitution were grafped at by the unfortunate objects of its kindnefs, is a convincing proof that their inactivity was not voluntary, nor their fituation hopelefs. Several pupils were immediately admitted of different ages, moft of whom applied themfelves diligently to the particular employment to which their talents or their fancy directed them. The principal occupations which, after a trial of fome years, are found moft fuitable for the blind, independent of the ufe of various mufical inftruments, are the making of bafkets and hampers of various kinds, of white and tarred bears, foot-cloths, lobby-cloths, the weaving of fheeting, hagabag, window-fafh and curtain line, and the manufacturing of riding-whips, the latter of which they execute with particular neatnefs. Befides affording the pupils inftruction gratis, the afylum allows them a weekly fum proportioned to the nature of their work, and the proficiency made by them; which, with a fmall addition, in fome inftances, from their friends or parifhes, enables them to provide for their own fupport, thereby relieving them in a great degree from the painful idea of abfolute dependence on the bounty of others; and, which is fcarcely of lefs importance, affording them an active employment for thofe hours which would otherwife be fpent in defpondency and gloom.

The fubfcription for the fupport of this charity in the year 1794, amounted to £.409 from refidents in Liverpool, and £.121 from refi.

3

dents in other places; besides which, a separate subscription has been entered into for the erection of a suitable building, where it may be practicable to vary the occupations of the pupils; particularly by affording them an opportunity of employments in the open air, to some of which, as the making of ropes, &c. there is no doubt but they would be fully competent. This commendable institution was in the year 1793 in danger of being abandoned—not from the want of pecuniary assistance, but of personal attention to its regulation; but some respectable inhabitants of the town, with a generosity far exceeding the most lavish contribution of money, stepped in to its support, and by devoting to its interests a considerable portion of their time, have regulated its finances and established its utility on a permanent foundation.*

The magistrates of Liverpool have paid particular attention to the *recovering of persons apparently drowned*, and saving them when in danger—such accidents being frequent among the people employed about the docks and shipping. The number brought to the house of reception during part of 1787 and 1788 was seventy, of whom not fewer than sixty-seven were saved—a proportion so far beyond that returned from other places, that it must be imputed to the alacrity with which the ample rewards bestowed have prompted the by-standers to take persons out of the water the instant they have fallen in. It is to be observed, that the accidents happening in the docks must usually have a number of witnesses, and that the art of swimming is very common among the people of this town.

Workhouse.—With the increase of the town, the number of poor, has, of course, increased; and additions have been made to the new

* On this occasion the humane exertions of Mr. Pudsey Dawson are entitled to particular commendation.

workhouse

workhouse above-mentioned to enable it to receive the additional number. The following lift will show the gradation of increase of the poor in the house :

Year ending March 25th.

1782	783	1787	966	1791	909
1783	920	1788	1018	1792	1003
1784	963	1789	1098	1793	885
1785	985	1790	1164	1794	1197
1786	946				

The tax for this period has been from 2s. to 3s. in the pound ; the latter for the four laft years. By great reforms in the management, though the number of poor is greater than ever, the rate has been reduced to 2s. 6d. This is eftimated to produce net about £.15,000.

The money paid by the overfeers to the out, cafual, and fick poor, for the year ending 24th of March 1794, was £.3075 9s. 1d. The expence of cloathing the in and out poor was £.1844 15s. 6d. and of provifions in the houfe, £.6063 16s. 7d. ; total, £.10,984 1s. 8d.—In the year 1790 the parifh was indebted on feveral accounts in the fum of £.11,709 2s. 1d., but fuch has been the management under the guardians of the poor, that at the clofe of the prefent year, viz. on the 24th ult. it was expected there would be a furplus of £.4000.

The following paper affords fo curious and inftructive a fpecies of information, that we have copied it entire from the printed report.

STATE and EMPLOYMENT of PEOPLE in the WORKHOUSE, 25th March, 1794.

Governor,	1	Boys, Weavers,	4
Matron and Chamberlain,	2	Ropers and Knotters,	9
House Servants,	3	Coffin-makers, Joiners, and Boys,	6
Hall and Stair cleaners,	5	Boatbuilders,	4
Keeper of Lock and Servants,	4	Two Smiths and Eighteen Boys,	
Two Cooks and Six Servants,	8	making Nails *for Sale* and own	
Two Salters and Ten Washerwomen,	12	Use,	20
Milk-mistress and Porter,	2	Yeomen of the Smithies,	2
Bread Cutter and Doctor's Assistant,	2	Spinners of Wool, Thread, and	
Mistress and Kneaders of Bread,	11	Linen,	59
Nurses and Servants for Infants,	6	Knitters and Seamstresses,	51
Nurses for Lying-in Women, for		Four Sawyers, Seven Taylors,	11
sick, infirm, venereal, fever, and		Cotton Pickers,	266
lunatic Wards,	14	Ditto Spinners, &c.	42
Brewer, Warehouseman, and Assis-		Tambour Workers,	45
tant,	4		
Two Carters, Two Swineherds,	4	Matron's Family,	4
One Coalman, Ten Labourers,	11	Turnkey,	1
Bell-ringer, Clerk, and Messengers,	5	Working People,	663
Gardener and Assistant, Ten Pum-		Lunatics, Idiots, Sick, Lame, In-	
pers,	12	firm, very old, very young	524
Keeper of Lock's Family,	6		
Schoolmasters and Mistresses,	4	In the House,	1197
Book-keepers,	2		
Barber and Painter,	2	Average Number from 31st March,	
Bricklayers, Plaisterers, and Block-		1793, to 21st March, 1794,	1032
maker,	5	Ditto 29th March, 1792, to March,	
Flax-dresser, Leather-cutter, and		1793,	826
Glazier,	3		
Shoe-makers,	9	Average increase,	206
Boys, ditto,	9		
Weavers,	3		

A consi-

A confiderable number of legacies and benefactions have at different times been made by individuals in favour of the poor of Liverpool, particularly of decayed failors and their widows, for whom alms-houfes have been erected in various parts of the town.

The *Blue-coat* charity, formerly mentioned, has continued to flourifh under the management of attentive and generous truftees. The number of children it receives was, above twenty years ago, increafed to 200. The building erected for it is of brick, ornamented with ftone, containing numerous and commodious apartments, and furnifhed with fuitable out-door conveniences.

Few commercial towns have in any confiderable degree united a tafte for literature and the fine arts with the purfuit of wealth; nor have we any public inftitutions of this kind to enumerate under the head of Liverpool. It has, indeed, a *Subfcription Library* founded many years fince, and well fupported. In a room over the library, fome gentlemen, above twenty years ago, opened an *Academy for Drawing and Painting*, in which it was propofed to deliver lectures on Anatomy, Perfpective, Architecture, Painting, &c. with proper fubjects and figures, and annual exhibitions of performances. But this truly liberal defign was dropped after a fhort trial, for want of encouragement; its only durable relic was a very elegant *Ode* on the Inftitution, written by a gentleman of the town, and read before the fociety in Dec. 1773. A few copies were printed at the time, and it was re-printed in 1777, along with the beautiful defcriptive poem by the fame writer, entitled *Mount-Pleafant*. This laft fhould be peculiarly interefting to a native

Z z of

of Liverpool, of which town and its vicinity it affords a ſtriking view
taken from the eminence bearing that name.

Docks.—It has already been obſerved, that the harbour of Liverpool
is entirely artificial, conſiſting of docks formed within the town, and
communicating with the river   No maritime town in Great Britain,
perhaps in Europe, can vie with Liverpool in the number and extent
of theſe works, which afford conveniences in loading and unloading of
ſhips, ſuperior to thoſe enjoyed by any natural harbours.   Of the docks
there are two kinds, the wet and the dry.   The former are ſo conſtructed with flood-gates, that water enough is pounded in them to
keep the ſhips afloat in all times of the tide.   The latter are the entrances to the others, and partake of the ebb and flow of the river.   The
wet docks are uſually occupied by ſuch ſhips as go foreign voyages ;
the dry, by coaſting veſſels : between theſe are ſeveral graving docks,
which admit or exclude the water at pleaſure, and are capable of receiving two or three veſſels at a time, for the purpoſe of repairing
them.

The docks extend along the river nearly the breadth of the town
In the centre is the *Old Dock*, running up a conſiderable way towards
the heart of the town.   To the weſt of it lies the *Salthouſe Dock*,
and the baſon or dry dock, ſerving as the common entrance to both
Theſe were the firſt conſtructed.   To the north of theſe is ſituated
George's Dock, with its dry baſon, the next of theſe works, hollowed
and embanked out of the river beach.   And to the ſouth are the neweſt
docks, called the *King's* and *Queen's*, with one common dry baſon at
the entrance.   The duke of Bridgewater has a ſmall dock of his own

between

between thefe and the Salthoufe dock. The dimenfions of the feveral docks are as follows :

	Yds.		Yd.			Ft.	In.		Ft.	In.	
Old Dock,	- 195	by	85.	Its gates,		33	0	wide,	25	3	deep.
Salthoufe Dock,	213	by	102.	Do.	-	34	0	——	25	0	——
George's Dock,	246	by	100.	Do.	-	38	3	——	26	2	——
King's Dock,	272	by	95.	Do.	-	42	0	——	26	0	——
Queen's Dock,	280	by	120.	Do.	-	42	0	——	27	0	——

The length of quay afforded by all thefe capacious bafons, will appear on calculation to be fo great, as to eclipfe all the moft famous of the river or fhore quays in the different fea-ports ; and though their magnificence of profpect is diminifhed, their utility is increafed, by having them accumulated within a moderate compafs of ground, rather than extended in one long line.

The vaft labour and expence of thefe works will readily be conceived by one who confiders that they muft all have been hollowed by hand from the fhore, in continual oppofition to the tides, which often in an hour deftroy the labour of weeks; and that the piers muft be made of fufficient height and ftrength to bear the daily efforts of a fea beating in, and conftantly endeavouring to recover its ancient boundaries.

On the fides of the docks are warehoufes of uncommon fize and ftrength, far furpaffing in thofe refpects the warehoufes of London. To their different floors, often ten or eleven in number, goods are craned up with great facility. Government in particular has here a very extenfive tobacco warehoufe, occupying a large compafs of ground. The fpace round the docks is fufficient to give room for

loading

loading and unloading, and all the occupations of the failors, without interruption of each other, or of the crowds of paffengers. Strangers may with eafe drive along the quays, and enjoy the view of the bufy fcene without danger or inconvenience; a pleafure no where to be obtained on the river at London, where the clofe wharfs are abfolutely inacceffible except by carts, and by them not to be approached without great obftruction. The entrance to the docks are croffed by drawbridges, excellently conftructed on the Dutch plan.

On the weft fide of the North Dock, by the river fide, is a pier forming a fine parade, 320 yards in length, and of confiderable breadth, which is a favourite walk of the inhabitants and ftrangers. It commands a noble view of the harbour from the rock point or commencement of the fea, to the diftance of feveral miles up the river, and a beautiful landfcape on the Chefhire fide. Hence all the fhips are diftinctly feen as they work in and out of the harbour, and enter or quit the docks.*

Baths.——

---

* It will not, we truft, be unacceptable to the public, if we here give a fketch of a plan for wet docks in the port of London, now in agitation, and to be brought before Parliament this feffion. The following outlines of the defign have been communicated to us by a friend. The fituation fixed upon is in Wapping; its neareft part about a quarter of a mile from the Tower. The works will confift of

	Acres.	Rs.	Ps.		Ships.
A Bafon or Outer Dock, comprifing	3	0	35	for	33
London Dock,	25	0	17	—	250
Inner Dock,	10	2	0	—	105
	38	3	12	—	388

A large fpace of about thirty acres is to be left about the docks for quays, warehoufes, &c. Ships are to be at liberty to difcharge either on the quays, or into lighters; and for

the

Baths.—A little northwards of the North Dock, Mr. Wright, an eminent fhip-builder of the town, has erected a fet of elegant and commodious fea-baths, divided into feparate baths and rooms for both fexes, each bath fupplied with water from the centre. On the outfide are fteps for the convenience of fwimmers who chufe to launch into the open water, and who may frequently be feen plunging among the waves of a boifterous tide. It is the inconvenience of thefe baths, that they can only be ufed when the tide is in, there being no contrivance, as at Yarmouth, for a perpetual fupply of water by means of a refervoir. They are, however, much frequented. The corporation intend to build another dock upon this fpot, and to erect another fet of baths, upon a much larger fcale and improved conftruction, at their own expence. Being upon the fubject of bathing, we fhall mention an extraordinary mode of taking this falutary amufement *without baths*, practifed upon the beach below the town for fome weeks in the height of fummer. It is a cuftom with the lower clafs of people, of both fexes, for many miles up the country, and even as far as the manufacturing diftricts to the very extremity of the county, to make an annual vifit to Liverpool, for the purpofe of wafhing away (as they feem to fuppofe) all the collected ftains and impurities of the year. Being unable to afford a long ftay, or to make ufe of artificial conveniences, they employ two or three days in ftrolling along fhore, and dabbling in the falt-water for

the greater convenience of difcharging, a large lighter dock is to be connected with the other docks, for the reception of thirty lighters each tide.—It is further in contemplation to form a cut of 2¾ miles from Blackwall to the docks, admitting two loaded fhips to pafs at a time, in order to avoid the navigation round the Ifle of Dogs and through the Pool.

The only docks of any moment now in the port of London are two private concerns, that of Mr. Wells, at Greenland dock, containing about twelve acres of ground, and of Mr. Perry, at Blackwall, containing about eight acres.

hours

hours at each tide, covering the beach with their promiscuous numbers, and not much embarrassing themselves about appearances. As the practice, however, seems conducive both to health and pleasure, it is not to be wished that rigid notions of delicacy should interfere with this only mode which the poor have of enjoying it.

The Fort.—At different periods, the harbour of Liverpool has been protected from temporary dangers of hostile attacks by the erection of occasional batteries; but in the American war, a fort of considerable size and strength was erected at a large expence on a point of land to the north of all the town, near the baths, and the public walk called the *Ladies' Walk.* It is nearly of a semi-circular form, constructed of the soft yellow stone from the quarries near the town, and well-furnished with light and heavy cannon. It contains buildings for the accommodation of the men and officers, by whom it is constantly occupied, and who keep guard with great regularity. Its situation, just above the level of the water, and commanding an uninterrupted range of the whole harbour, from its entrance to opposite the town, gives it every advantage for security that could be wished. But, in fact, the dangerous shoals at the mouth of the harbour, which shift every tide, and could not be passed without the assistance of pilots, and the direction of buoys and sea-marks, are a more effectual security.

Buildings in general.—The central parts of Liverpool, like those of almost all our towns, were close and narrow, the inconvenience of which was more and more felt as business and population increased. The corporation, (which has ever, beyond most in England, been active and liberal in promoting plans of public advantage) obtained from parliament powers for widening and improving the streets, which they have employed

ployed with great judgment and to a vaſt expenditure. About the Exchange, in particular, a great deal has been done; and Caſtle-ſtreet, which leads from it to St. George's church, is converted into a ſpacious and very well-built ſtreet, furniſhed with ſhops almoſt equal to thoſe of Cheapſide. All the new parts of Liverpool are regularly laid out with ſtraight and wide ſtreets, ſome of them truly handſome. The material is for the moſt part brick. Everton, now entirely joined to Liverpool by buildings, forms, as it were, a new town, and is a favourite reſidence to thoſe whoſe occupations do not oblige them to be near the centre of buſineſs.

The *Exchange*, a building of much coſt and magnificence, which contained the town-hall and other public offices, as well as the aſſembly rooms, and was finiſhed with great elegance and expence, unfortunately took fire by accident in the beginning of this year, and was entirely conſumed, except the outer walls. Such a diſaſter, however, was calculated only to rouſe the ſpirit of this enterpriſing town; and the following paragraph, copied from Gore's Liverpool Advertiſer for March 19th, will ſhow what a phœnix is likely to riſe out of its aſhes.

Gore's Liverpool Advertiſer, March 19th, 1795.

" IT is with the utmoſt ſatisfaction we are enabled to ſtate, that the event of the late dreadful fire at the exchange, much as it has been lamented, is likely to be productive of moſt important good conſequences to the public, and to thoſe in particular whoſe buſineſs require their attendance in any of the offices belonging to it. A plan has been adopted by the common council, and ordered to be carried into execution, for

2. the

the re-building of the Exchange, which, from the general difpofition of the whole, and the particular arrangement of the various rooms
and offices, will afford the moft defirable conveniences for the public
and private bufinefs of the mayor and corporation, and their refpective officers, and very ample accommodation for the merchants and the
public at large.

" No other part of the old building will remain but the exterior
walls, the fronts of which are univerfally admired for their architectural beauty, and have received no material injury from the fire; the
principal entrance from Caftle-ftreet will be into a fpacious hall, leading
to the grand ftair-cafe in the *area*, which will now be placed in the
center of the building, and over which will be erected the elegant dome
defigned by Mr. Wyat, a model of which was lately exhibited in the
Exchange. On the eaft fide will be a commodious committee room,
and range of offices for the town clerk, treafurer, furveyors, &c. opening into High-ftreet; and on the weft fide a noble coffee room, eight
feet by thirty-two, the entrance to which will be on that fide oppofite
to the brokers' offices: at the north end, in the new building, will be
the public office for the daily bufinefs of the magiftrates, which, by
means of a moveable partition, can at any time be enlarged to the fize
of fixty feet by forty, and form a moft capacious *court room* for the
feffions, or *hall* on occafions of public meetings, being a third part
larger than the late town hall; and there will be convenient offices at
each end of the court room, for the magiftrates and juries, and for the
purpofe of town's committees, turnpike meetings, &c. By this arrangement, ample accommodation, and every convenience to be wifhed
for, is provided for the public bufinefs *on the ground floor only*; and the
fuite of rooms above ftairs for the ufe of the mayor and council, and for

4   public

public entertainments, will be rendered as complete as poſſible; they will conſiſt of ſix principal rooms on one floor, the *ball room* being ninety feet by forty-five, two other rooms fifty by thirty, and the reſt in proportion.

" The outline and general diſpoſition of this extenſive plan has received the approbation of a profeſſional gentleman of the firſt abilities, who will furniſh deſigns for finiſhing its different parts."

With reſpect to the proper uſe of an Exchange, that of a place where merchants meet to tranſact buſineſs, Liverpool has loſt nothing by the demolition of its late edifice; ſince the merchants, from immemorial cuſtom, always held their 'Change in the open ſpace at the top of Caſtle-ſtreet, and were not, even by a ſhower, driven to ſhelter elſewhere than in the adjoining ſhops.

The *churches* and *chapels* of the eſtabliſhment at preſent in Liverpool are the following :

St. Nicholas's,	St. Thomas's,	St. John's,
St. Peter's,	St. Paul's,	St. Ann's,
St. George's,	St. Catherine's,	St. Stephens.

To which may be added, on account of their connection with the town by contiguity of building, St. Ann's, Richmond; and St. James's, Toxteth-park.

There are likewiſe ſeveral large and handſome places of worſhip, belonging to the different denominations of Diſſenters, Methodiſts, Quakers, and Roman Catholics.

An extenfive *pleafure walk*, called St. James's, handfomely laid out and planted, was made a good many years fince on the high ground above the fouth end of the town. It commands a fine view of the town, river, and diftant country, but the bleaknefs of its expofure makes it agreeable only in very fine weather, and is unfavourable to vegetation. Behind it, is a moft extenfive *ftone quarry*, which offers a very ftriking fpectacle. Labour has here expofed to view one continued face of ftone, 380 yards long, and in many parts fixteen yards deep, forming a vaft perpendicular wall, without a vein or crack. The entrance to it is by a fubterraneous paffage fupported by arches, and the whole has a pleafing and romantic effect. The ftone is a kind of fand ftone of a yellowifh hue, foft when cut, but afterwards hardening. It is ufed in the public buildings and works of the town. A chalybeat water of moderate ftrength fprings in the quarry.

Supply of Provifions, Coals, &c.—The market days of Liverpool are Wednefday and Saturday. Few towns of the fize are more plentifully and regularly fupplied with provifions of all kinds, brought from a great diftance round. The hundred of Wirral in Chefhire, particularly, furnifhes large quantities of vegetables, fruit, butter, and other articles, which the market people bring over in the ferry boats that are continually paffing and repaffing the channel. Potatoes in great quantities, and excellent in kind, are brought from Ormfkirk and the parifhes in its neighbourhood. The farms in the vicinity of the town are much devoted to the production of milk, the demand for which, in fo populous a place, is almoft unlimited. Of the kinds of fifh, occafionally brought to its markets, a pretty long lift may be formed; but upon the whole it is lefs abundant than might be expected in a fea-port town. The Lancafhire coaft, as already obferved, is not favourable for the

I   eftablifh-

eſtabliſhment of fiſheries. The Iſle of Man furniſhes ſupplies of the cheaper ſorts, eſpecially herring. As an article rather of *luxury* than of *proviſion*, turtle may be noticed, which arrives in conſiderable cargoes with the Weſt India ſhips, and is no where better dreſſed or more hoſpitably beſtowed, accompanied with unſparing draughts of beverage made from the excellent rum and limes derived from the ſame quarter of the world. Good *water* is, however, more of a rarity here than could be wiſhed : and a ſtranger is ſtruck with the water-carts driving through the ſtreets, from which this neceſſary article is ſold at a halfpenny per bucket, a circumſtance by no means conducive to cleanlineſs among the poor, or even thoſe of middling condition. It is hoped that the corporation will either themſelves find ſome better mode of ſupplying the town with water, or give permiſſion for that purpoſe to ſome gentlemen who have propoſed to form a reſervoir on Everton, and thence convey it in pipes to every part of Liverpool.

With reſpect to *coals*, Liverpool is fortunate in having its ſources for that eſſential article increaſed, with the increaſe of demand. The pits at Whiſton, near Preſcott, formerly ſupplied the town entirely, and they ſtill ſend a large quantity, by land carriage, the carts for which purpoſe are no ſmall nuiſance at particular times on that road. The Sankey canal opened a new ſource, which, though diſtant, has the advantage of water carriage all the way ; and the Leeds and Liverpool canal, by means of its branch to Wigan, has made an ample addition, both in quantity and kind, much cannel, as well as common coal, being brought to Liverpool by its conveyance. The head of this canal, near the Ladies' Walk, is widened into a kind of baſon, where boats can load and unload with the greateſt convenience, in a large coal-yard. Between this and the Merſey, a ſquare dock of conſiderable ſize is making, which will hold a great number of the navigation craft.

Trade

Trade and Commerce.—The moſt important circumſtances relative to Liverpool are the progreſs and preſent ſtate of its trade, which we ſhall endeavour, in addition to the information already given, to elucidate by tables and other documents drawn from the beſt authorities.

The dock duties are levied upon ſhips according to a certain rate per ton, which rate is determined by the place whence they come, increaſing in a great ratio with the increaſe of diſtance. The following table exhibits the annual number of ſhips paying them, and the whole amount of the duties; and it will be obſerved, that this amount has gradually been in an increaſing proportion to the number of ſhips.

Dock Duties at Liverpool, from the Year 1752, ending the 24th of June each Year.

Year.	Numb. of Ships.	£.	s.	d.	Year.	Numb. of Ships.	£.	s.	d.
1752		1776	8	2	1774	2258	4580	5	5
1753		2034	16	2	1775	2291	5384	4	9
1754		2095	11	0	1776	2216	5064	10	10
1755		2417	13	11	1777	2361	4610	4	9
1756		2187	16	9	1778	2292	4649	7	7
1757	1371	2336	15	0	1779	2374	4957	17	10
1758	1453	2403	6	3	1780	2261	3528	7	9
1759	1281	2372	12	2	1781	2512	3915	4	11
1760	1245	2330	6	7	1782	2496	4249	6	3
1761	1319	2382	2	2	1783	2816	4840	8	3
1762	1307	2526	19	6	1784	3098	6597	11	1
1763	1752	3141	1	5	1785	3429	8411	5	3
1764	1625	2780	3	4	1786	3228	7508	0	1
1765	1930	3455	8	4	1787	3567	9199	18	8
1766	1908	3653	19	2	1788	3677	9206	13	10
1767	1704	3615	9	2	1789	3619	8901	10	10
1768	1808	3566	14	9	1790	4223	10,037	6	2½
1769	2054	4004	5	0	1791	4045	11,645	6	6
1770	2073	4142	17	2	1792	4483	13,243	17	8¼
1771	2087	4203	19	10	1793	4129	12,480	5	5
1772	2259	4552	5	4	1794	4265	10,678	7	0
1773	2214	4725	1	11					

The

The next table gives the whole number and tonnage of ships, native and foreign, that have annually entered or left the port for a period of forty-three years.

The Number of Ships and their Tonnage that have cleared outwards and entered inwards at the Port of Liverpool, from the Year 1751 to the Year 1793.

Year.	Inwards.				Outwards.			
	British.		Foreign.		British.		Foreign.	
	Ships.	Tons.	Ships.	Tons.	Ships.	Tons.	Ships.	Tons.
1751	523	29,178	20	2535	588	31,185	20	2508
1752	529	29,137	46	5430	561	31,777	48	5884
1753	584	34,221	28	3515	601	34,689	22	3085
1754	577	32,255	44	5710	588	33,435	42	5843
1755	507	33,159	29	3425	519	30,660	27	3315
1756	522	29,793	48	5195	607	35,426	42	4542
1757	554	32,386	68	7300	609	37,881	57	7268
1758	602	36,263	63	7296	641	38,502	56	6277
1759	519	33,006	112	17,789	551	35,079	117	14,498
1760	556	36,884	76	10,535	592	37,157	81	11,663
1761	529	32,899	80	11,043	654	40,268	60	8223
1762	623	45,540	94	12,344	614	39,304	102	13,844
1763	574	39,714	78	11,584	700	44,863	92	13,596
1764	695	46,387	71	10,112	772	50,709	58	8132
1765	738	53,030	65	8134	795	53,807	70	9811
1766	646	51,623	54	7825	708	51,012	69	9370
1767	663	51,690	70	8011	784	57,376	66	9482
1768	727	54,949	57	7225	826	60,379	59	7950
1769	759	58,348	77	10,784	907	62,499	78	11,329
1770	743	46,062	63	7965	942	66,516	79	10,381
1771	764	59,734	55	6924	959	73,432	65	10,366
1772	857	68,812	68	8401	1022	81,689	73	11,284
1773	970	70,392	57	7111	1022	76,588	64	9366
1774	989	79,315	61	8032	973	76,892	64	8744
1775	1016	86,382	56	7294	983	76,686	57	7494
1776	901	74,140	81	12,991	937	68,488	75	11,616
1777	893	70,792	101	11,627	979	71,295	96	11,852
1778	838	76,277	100	13,342	857	63,420	95	11,782
1779	742	57,103	136	17,623	908	64,836	149	19,379
1780	739	58,769	133	17,087	880	61,573	151	19,202
1781	801	58,914	169	22,569	1021	65,477	182	25,899
1782	847	66,290	169	23,107	968	64,481	213	30,295
1783	1165	96,089	206	28,376	1355	105,074	222	32,294
1784	1217	122,263	162	26,091	1333	113,481	160	26,958
1785	1427	127,388	129	21,576	1446	122,195	129	21,990
1786	1381	140,224	150	27,611	1337	128,766	140	28,194
1787	1348	153,625	161	26,903	1474	159,834	180	31,715
1788	1570	140,812	152	25,600	1673	186,355	156	26,973
1789	1603	171,672	89	15,202	1486	170,369	87	14,456
1790	1864	205,440	200	35,677	1779	201,641	196	36,143
1791	1814	220,318	254	46,878	1904	225,641	263	46,839
1792	1832	225,242	215	41,166	1926	231,277	212	41,213
1793	1704	188,286	215	41,177	1739	169,770	240	47,719

The

Ships belonging to Liverpool.—Before the regulations of the Manifeſt Act, the number of ſhips properly belonging to each port could not be aſcertained with any certainty. We do not, therefore, copy any earlier accounts of this kind for Liverpool; but content ourſelves with giving thoſe for the ſeven years ending in 1793, which have been copied from the regiſter of the ſhipping of that port.

Year.	Ships.	Tons.	Year.	Ships.	Tons.
1787	445	72,731	1791	528	83,696
1788	475	76,078	1792	584	92,098
1789	479	76,251	1793	606	96,694
1790	504	80,003			

The next table that we ſhall preſent, gives the particulars of the foreign trade of Liverpool, according to the *places* to and from which it has been carried on, for ſix ſucceſſive years, ending in 1793. Theſe exhibit a gradation of increaſe above all former periods, as far as the year 1792, which was the ſummit of the ſcale. Since that time, temporary cauſes have produced a decline here, as in almoſt all other commercial towns. This table has been moſt obligingly furniſhed us by the Inſpector General of ports at the Cuſtom-houſe in London.

An

An ACCOUNT of the Number of Vessels, with the Amount of their Tonnage, that have entered Inwards and cleared Outwards in the Port of LIVERPOOL. in the following Years, distinguished according to the Places whence and to which they made their Voyages. (N. B. Coasters excluded.)

Place	1788 In. Brit. Shs	1788 In. Brit. Tons	1788 In. For. Shs	1788 In. For. Tons	1788 Out. Brit. Shs	1788 Out. Brit. Tons	1788 Out. For. Shs	1788 Out. For. Tons	1789 In. Brit. Shs	1789 In. Brit. Tons	1789 In. For. Shs	1789 In. For. Tons	1789 Out. Brit. Shs	1789 Out. Brit. Tons	1789 Out. For. Shs	1789 Out. For. Tons	1790 In. Brit. Shs	1790 In. Brit. Tons	1790 In. For. Shs	1790 In. For. Tons	1790 Out. Brit. Shs	1790 Out. Brit. Tons	1790 Out. For. Shs	1790 Out. For. Tons
Africa,	18	3310			73	13,394			12	1432			66	11,564			11	1833			91	17,917		
America, viz. British Colonies,	4	1016			14	2745			3	220			8	1807			1	52			20	3731		
—, United States,	58	11,644			66	14,243			62	12,083			110	20,471			78	14,675			77	16,151		
—, West Indies,	168	34,988	49	7170	112	23,442	51	7245	156	33,492	37	5206	76	16,195	39	5689	155	32,158	60	9679	91	19,622	67	10,276
British Fishery,	19	722							41	1318							31	930	1	150				
South Fishery,					1	320			1	320			18	5605							1	320		
Greenland Fishery,	22	6774			22	6774			13	3915							14	4053			13	4401		
Honduras Bay,	4	575							2	434			1	77			3	564						
Ireland,	970	64,131	18	1684	999	63,764			968	67,784	13	1662	890	57,714	1	82	1112	78,491	15	1991	1037	69,351		
Isle of Man,	99	3686	1	89	112	4522			105	4383			111	4240			87	3810			95	4270		
Guernsey,	1	93			3	196			1	72			6	430			1	218			8	992		
Jersey,									2	166			6	324			1	25			1	25		
Denmark and Norway,	5	963	15	2563	15	5293	21	3553	1	91	5	740	23	6989	19	3067	9	1586	20	3744	31	5852	39	7500
Russia,	68	21,346	3	120	22	8608	1	112	47	14,771			18	6417			81	22,328			55	18,390	2	463
Sweden,	5	593	3	382	2	113	2	240	12	1503	5	616	1	100	5	679	7	604	1	110	5	515	1	150
Germany,	10	1447	9	1086	25	5037	18	2258	10	1508			23	4482			9	980	14	1529	24	3788	23	2883
Holland,	19	1818	7	120	7	847			6	696			11	980			25	2647	7	707	9	1158	3	215
Poland and Prussia,	26	8590	46	13,208	17	6917	47	11,375	37	12,407	21	6010	20	7487	16	4239	83	23,174	65	15,742	30	10,450	38	10,741
Flanders,	3	491	1	200	57	9978	7	1336	5	539	1	156	20	12,604	1	156	1	91	1	435	68	11,270	10	2300
France,	29	2958	5	520	70	8278	8	1278	82	8394	4	517	69	6756	1	159	47	5371	7	920	50	5515	1	172
Portugal,	29	2871	4	367	22	2470	8	947	51	5160	3	295	24	2797	5	385	64	6914	4	394	39	4367	5	514
Spain,	18	2026	2	100	15	1713	3	198	19	2109			19	1915			19	2014	2	201	17	1788	2	246
Italy,	14	1492			12	1563			10	1026			18	2092			21	2619	1	75	15	1859	5	683
Turkey,																	3	303						
Total	1589	171,534	155	35,600	1673	180,217	166	28,542	1646	173,425	89	15,202	1587	170,446	87	14,456	1863	205,440	200	35,677	1779	201,741	196	36,143

Account of the Number of Vessels continued.

	1791 INWARDS British		1791 INWARDS Foreign		1791 OUTWARDS British		1791 OUTWARDS Foreign		1792 INWARDS British		1792 INWARDS Foreign		1792 OUTWARDS British		1792 OUTWARDS Foreign		1793 INWARDS British		1793 INWARDS Foreign		1793 OUTWARDS British		1793 OUTWARDS Foreign	
	Shs.	Tons.	Shs.	Tons.	Shs.	Tons.	Shs.	Tons.	Shs.	Tons.	Shs.	Tons.	Shs.	Tons.	Shs.	Tons.	Shs.	Tons.	Shs.	Tons.	Shs.	Tons.	Shs.	Tons.
Africa, viz. British Colonies,	10	1622			102	19610			11	1643			132	22402			14	2260			52	10544		
America, United States,	8	1550	103	18491	22	4650	105	17945	13	3290	102	18964	26	6318	103	18796	6	1411	117	21061	22	4337	117	21429
———, West Indies,	62	14587			97	21844			52	11834			71	15844			37	9115			17	4807		
British Fishery,	185	38196			98	19945			195	38902			115	24317			127	38911			108	22996		
South Fishery,	31	932							26	776							22	670						
Greenland Fishery,	1	320			1	459			1	459			14	5971			1	419			3	710		
Honduras Bay,	15	4373			15	4373			14	3971			3	591			11	2978			11	2978		
Ireland,	2	255			4	731			4	823							7	1463			1	253		
Isle of Man,	998	74551	18	2149	1064	76353			1039	79965	15	2026	1055	76191			1073	82718	32	5347	1289	95250		
Guernsey,	103	4522			101	4258			100	4159			118	4826			136	5734	3	365	151	6860		
Jersey,	1	70	2	330	4	471			1	102			1	59										
Denmark and Norway,	3	437	18	3075	35	8302	46	8281	1	102	12	1884	1	40	31	5376	4	429	9	1343	28	7964	15	2772
Russia,	122	33129	6	738	62	18365	6	199	142	41535			25	6068	1	380	52	16168			28	9811	1	230
Sweden,	8	1035	20	2601	3	547	25	726	11	1365	4	440	83	27011	4	494	3	235	5	611			5	419
Germany,	12	2525	10	784	30	5669	25	3791	16	2267	15	2413	2	522	13	1917	6	941	3	608	22	4194	16	2570
Holland,	23	2409	72	18083	7	839	57	14868	18	2282	11	1083	31	5648	5	242	12	1273	3	270	30	1416	6	928
Poland and Prussia,	84	20409			32	9926			46	12964	29	13628	16	2026	34	10571	71	15740	34	10456	30	8531	30	10127
Flanders,	1	113			67	10165	12	2670					15	5517	11	1788					25	5715	32	6519
France,	41	4273	2	307	50	5533	3	362	27	2391	1	96	71	13096	3	724	4	467	3	340			11	1768
Portugal,	84	9923	3	313	46	5682	4	486	84	10164	4	304	32	3078	7	594	33	3830	5	494	17	2250	3	194
Spain,	27	3110			33	3940	3	464	26	3108	2	328	55	6921	1	331	21	2166	2	282	7	650	1	194
Italy,	15	1882			30	3656			29	4018			26	2920			15	2029			15	1895	3	469
Turkey,	9	1027			1	323							34	3911										
Total	1845	221250	254	46878	1904	225641	263	49839	1858	226018	215	41166	1926	231177	212	41213	1726	188957	215	41177	1836	191191	240	47719

The progress and fluctuation of the *African trade* in this port is a matter of such important speculation, that we have devoted a table to it alone, in which its annual state from its very first existence is shown.

Ships cleared out to Africa from the Port of Liverpool.

Year.	Ships.	Tons.	Year.	Ships.	Tons.
1709	1	30	1771	105	10,929
1730	15	1111	1772	100	10,150
1737	33	2756	1773	105	11,056
1744	34	2698	1774	92	9859
1751	53	5334	1775	81	9200
1752	58	5437	1776	57	7078
1753	72	7547	1777	31	4060
1754	71	5463	1778	26	3651
1755	41	4052	1779	11	1205
1756	60	5147	1780	32	4275
1757	47	5050	1781	43	5720
1758	51	5229	1782	47	6209
1759	58	5892	1783	85	12,294
1760	74	8178	1784	67	9568
1761	69	7309	1785	79	10,982
1762	61	6752	1786	92	13,971
1763	65	6650	1787	81	14,012
1764	74	7978	1788	73	13,394
1765	83	9382	1789	66	11,564
1766	65	6650	1790	91	17,917
1767	83	8345	1791	102	19,610
1768	81	8302	1792	132	22,402
1769	90	9852	1793	52	10,544
1770	96	9818			

The

The *Account of the Inland Navigation to and from Liverpool*, for the years 1786, 1787, 1788, printed in the Report concerning the African and West India trade, is too curious and valuable to be omitted, though we have not been able to complete it to the present time. It may, however, doubtless be concluded to have kept pace in increase with the other parts of the commercial system of this port and the country connected with it.

An Account of the Inland Navigation to and from Liverpool for the Years 1786, 1787, and 1788.

On the Lancashire end of the Leeds canal there are employed between Liverpool and Wigan eighty-nine boats, of thirty-five to forty tons burthen each; which brought to Liverpool in the years

			1786.	1787.	1788.
viz.	Coals, — — —	Tons.	91,249	98,248	109,202
	Flags, Slates, and Millstones	D°.	3,944	2561	3613
	Merchandize — —	D°.	347	393	405
	Oak Timber — —	Feet.	17,403	17,986	13,589
Took from thence,	Merchandize — —	Tons.	3836	4610	4257
	Limestone and Bricks —	D°.	2245	2064	1429
	Lime and Manure —	D°.	10,213	11,129	12,224
	Fine Timber — —	Feet.	160,766	193,706	153,006
Between Liverpool and the river Douglas 36 boats are employed, which brought	Coals — — —	Tons.	1,6724	22,592	20,706
	And took back Limestone — — —	D°.	4589	6164	5921
The tonnage of the vessels employed on the Sankey canal, the business of which is divided between Liverpool, Northwich, and Warrington, amounted to —		Tons.	74,289	98,356	115,828

Between Liverpool on the river Mersey, and Northwich and Winsford on the Weaver, 110 vessels are employed in carrying timber, salt, coals, and merchandize, to the amount of 164,000 tons annually.

Between Liverpool and Manchester there are employed, on the old navigation, twenty-five boats of fifty-five tons each, which make generally

rally three trips every two spring tides ; or, upon an average, allowing for delays from bad weathers, thirty-six trips each in a year.

There are also on the duke of Bridgewater's canal, which communicates with the Staffordshire canal, forty-two boats employed, of fifty tons each, which make on an average three trips to Liverpool every fourteen days : ten boats will be added to this part of the navigation in the summer.

Privateers.—Liverpool has in different wars distinguished itself by the spirit with which it has fitted out armed ships for the purpose of annoying the trade of the enemy. How far this is a useful spirit to a trading town, and in what degree the prizes made have exceeded or fallen short of the expences of the outfits, we shall not inquire. But it ought not to be omitted, as a memorable instance of the power and enterprize of a single British port, that soon after the commencement of hostilities with France in 1778, there sailed from the port of Liverpool, between the end of August 1778 and that of April 1779, 120 private ships of war, carrying 1986 guns, (mostly six and nine-pounders) and 8754 men, and of the burthen of 30,787 tons—a navy of itself, superior to that of all England in some of its most illustrious reigns ! The largest of these ships was a frigate of thirty nine-pounders ; that with the heaviest metal was one of sixteen eighteen-pounders. Some of the prizes taken by the Liverpool privateers were of very great value ; and their effect in cutting off the resources of the hostile powers was very considerable.

A foreign commerce of the vast magnitude above stated, must necessarily give employment to a number of *domestic trades*, some belonging

to

to shipping in general, and some dependent on the peculiar nature of the traffic of the port. On the whole, however, Liverpool is less of a manufacturing town than Bristol, nor does it supply so many articles for the use of the West India islands. It possesses, however, glass houses, salt works, copperas works, copper works, iron foundries, many houses for the refining of sugar, and a number of public breweries, both for home consumption and exportation. A stranger is struck with the number of windmills in and near the town, of which the greater part are devoted to the grinding of corn, but many to the grinding of colours and rasping dyer's wood. The builders' yards are large and well stocked with timber, and there are many considerable roperies. It has already been mentioned, that the watch movement and tool business has established its head-quarters in or near Liverpool. A stocking manufactory, employing a good number of hands, has likewise been set up in the town.

Population.—The progress of population in Liverpool cannot but have borne proportion to that of its commerce and of its size; though, with respect to the latter, it may be remarked, that the improvements in widening the streets at the center, and building large houses instead of small ones, must, as in London, have rendered that part of the town less populous, and thrown its superfluity upon the extremities. It cannot, however, be doubted that the whole number of houses in Liverpool has very greatly increased since the enumeration in 1773; and though we have not been able to obtain a regular account of the bills of mortality since that period, yet from a few of them, together with a pretty late return of houses, a tolerable idea may be formed of the latter progress and present state of its population.

In

In 1773 it appears that there were regiftered,

Chriften. 1397; Burials, 1109; Marriages, 500.

Now, taking the chriftenings as the fteadieft article, and comparing them with the number of inhabitants found that year by actual enumeration, which, allowing for the increafe of the year and for omiffions, we may ftate at 35,000; it will appear, that the proportion of regiftered chriftenings to that of exifting inhabitants was nearly as one to twenty-five.

In 1780 there were,

Chrift. 1709; Burials, 1594; Marriages, 607.

By the above rule of multiplying the chriftenings, the number of inhabitants in that year will turn out to be about 42,700.

In 1785 there were,

Chrift. 2007; Burials, 1778; Marriages, 767.

By the fame rule the inhabitants were about 50,170.

From March 25, 1787 to ditto 1788, there were,

Chrift. 2267; Burials, 1773; Marriages, 804.

The inhabitants, by the above rule, were then 56,670.

From the tax-gatherers books, examined 29th of February, 1789, it appears that the rated houfes for the preceding year were as follows :

Houfes at £.5 per annum, - -	2053
Ditto at above £.5 and under £.10 -	2561
Ditto at £.10 and upwards, - -	2725
	7339
Ditto untenanted and unfinifhed. -	351
Total -	7690

It

It is extremely difficult to know what allowance fhould be made for non-rated houfes and excufed, the proportion of thefe varying fo greatly in different diftricts. It is, however, prefumable, that in Liverpool the proportion would be much fmaller than in many other towns, fince the number of *manufacturing* poor in it, who are always the greateft defaulters in public payments, is but fmall, and from the rate of houfe rent, very few can be fuppofed to let under £.5. If one fourth be added to the number of inhabited houfes on this account, the proportion of inhabitants to a houfe, as eftablifhed by the enumeration of 1773, (viz. 5⅘) will give at that period a population of 51,190. But this is a merely conjectural calculation, and probably too low. The increafe fince that year cannot but have been confiderable. If it has borne proportion to the increafe of the fhipping, it will have exceeded one-fifth.

The Tenures of Liverpool and its Neighbourhood.—The townfhip and manor of Liverpool formerly belonged to the family of Molyneux, now earls of Sefton, which, though an Irifh title, is derived from the ancient family feat at Sefton, or Sephton, in this neighbourhood.

Till very lately the corporation of Liverpool were only leffees of the manor, under this family, for a long term of years; but about twenty years fince they purchafed the reverfionary eftate, and have thereby confolidated the fee in themfelves.

But the corporation, although poffeffed of the royalty, are not the proprietors of all the lands in the townfhip, the northern part of which adjoining to Kirkdale and Everton, and including about one half of the town as now built, is private property, either held in fee, or leafed by private owners upon building leafes. Of thefe owners the moft confiderable is Thomas Crofs, Efq. of Shaw-Hill in this county, whofe eftate

com-

comprehends a large diftrict on the north fide of the town, which he grants out on building leafes nearly on the fame terms as the corporation.

The leafes granted by the corporation are for three lives, and a term of twenty-one years after the death of the furvivor; under which leafe the inhabitants of the town hefitate not to expend large fums of money in buildings, making little difference in their eftimation between a corporation leafehold, and an eftate in fee. This confidence of the public is founded on an idea that the corporation will, in cafe of the death of any of the lives, renew the leafe by nominating others, although it contain no ftipulation to that effect. They are, however, engaged to comply with this by the ftrongeft of all ties, that of their own intereft; and from the fines paid for fuch renewals a principal part of the large income of the corporation arifes. Their terms are, in general (though not without fuch exceptions as they may think expedient) for the infertion of one new life, one year's rent; of two lives, three years rent; of three lives, feven years rent. On thefe terms, the calculation in point of advantage is fuppofed to be favourable to the corporation; but the practice of renewing leafes is general, and the leffees would deem it a peculiar hardfhip if they were compelled to exhauft their term without the power of renewal.

Liverpool, on the fouth fide, is bounded by the townfhip of Toxteth-park, belonging to the earl of Sefton. From its vicinity to the town, and particularly to the new docks, fuch part of it as lies next to Liverpool has been thought convenient for building, and leafes have been granted by the late earl, on terms fuppofed to be equally advantageous with thofe of the corporation. A new church called St. James's was fome years fince built in Toxteth park, near to the boundary between that townfhip and Liverpool. The propofed ftreets are laid out with a proper attention to regularity and convenience. Several good houfes have been erected, and there is no doubt but that as foon as the re-eftablifhment of peace fhall reftore to the town of Liverpool its commerce, and its profperity, the improvements in Toxteth park, if proper encouragement be given by the owner, will keep pace with thofe in other parts of the vicinity. The new town is intended to be called Harrington, in reference to the family of the prefent countefs dowager of Sefton, the daughter of the earl of Harrington; and the propofed ftreets take their names from the friends and relatives of the family.

The village of Everton is fituated on an agreeable eminence about a mile north-eaft from the town of Liverpool, and commands an extenfive profpect of the mouth of the river, opening into the eftuary of Bootle bay, and of the Irifh channel, as well as of the oppofite coaft of Chefter, and the northern part of Wales. This village has of late years become a very favourite refidence, and feveral excellent houfes are built along the weftern declivity of the hill. About half way on the defcent from Everton to Liverpool, is a diftrict of the town called Richmond, forming a pleafant and refpectable neighbourhood, and uniting in an eminent degree the conveniences of a town refidence, with thofe of a country fituation.—The annexed view of Liverpool was taken in the year 1793, from a ftation between Low-hill and Everton, the beft fpot from which the town can be viewed.

The townfhips or manors adjoining to Liverpool on the eaft, and extending from thence to a confiderable diftance, are principally held by the families of Gafcoigne and Blackburne. Thefe extenfive poffeffions were in the earlier part of the prefent century acquired by the induftry

or

S. Dayes del.

VIEW OF LIVERPOOL.

Publish'd April. 9. 1794. by I. Stockdale. Piccadilly.

Wilson. sculp.

or good fortune of Mr. Isaac Greene, an eminent attorney in this neighbourhood; who, with the opportunity, united the prudence to avail himself of the improving state of the neighbourhood, and on terms which would now be thought scarcely adequate to the purchase of as many farms, acquired the lordships of Everton, West-derbey, Great Woolton, Little Woolton, and Childwall, to which he added that of Hale, in right of his wife, the daughter of Sir Gilbert Ireland. On the death of Mr. Greene, his possessions became the property of his daughters and co-heiresses, Mrs. Blackburne of Hale, and Mrs. Gascoigne of Childwall, by whom the manerial rights are now exercised, and the copyhold courts duly held, with all the formalities attending that extraordinary system of vassalage; the copyholders possessing their estates at the will of the lord or lady, according to the custom of the manor, and performing suit and service in person.

Public Property of the Town of Liverpool.—The corporation of Liverpool is one of the most opulent in the kingdom. In the year 1793, when public credit was so much shaken throughout the kingdom, the merchants of this town, on account of the complicated nature of their concerns, laboured under peculiar difficulties, which occasioned numerous failures, and threatened the most alarming consequences. A scheme was at that time formed by some of the leading members of the corporation, to employ the public credit in aid of that of private persons, by procuring an act of parliament to enable the corporation to issue negotiable bills, for which their estates were to be security. It was consequently necessary to lay before parliament an exact account of the state of their affairs, the summary of which is contained in the following schedule:

C c c

General

General Account and Valuation of the Eſtate and Revenue belonging to the Corporation of Liverpool, taken the 21ſt of March, 1793.

Income for 1792.	£.	s.	d.
Fines received for renewal of leaſes, - - -	2270	14	4
Ground rents received for 1792, - - - -	1027	1	10
Rents for buildings in poſſeſſion, let to tenants at will,	5166	17	6
Rents for land in poſſeſſion, let to ditto, - -	1349	1	0
Amount of town's duties, - - - -	12,180	7	0
Graving docks, - - - - - -	1701	16	5
Anchorage, - - - - - - -	211	15	3
Small tolls called ingates and outgates - - -	321	9	7
Weighing machine, - - - - - -	143	4	0
Rents of ſeats in St. George's church, - -	268	11	0
Arrears of intereſt from the pariſh of Liverpool, -	360	0	0
	25,000	17	11

Intereſt and Annuities paid in 1792.			
Annual intereſt upon the bond debts, principally at 4½ per cent. per annum, - - - -	15,835	14	3
Annuities upon bond, - - - - -	2109	12	10
	17,945	7	1
Balance in favour of the corporation, - -	9055	10	10
Valuation of the above articles, adding that of land not built on, and the ſtrand of the river,	1,044,776	0	0
Valuation of the debt, - - - - -	367,816	12	0
Balance in favour of the corporation, - -	676,959	8	0

Excluſive

	£.	s.	d.
Exclusive of a balance due from the trustees of the docks, and of the reversionary interest of certain lots of ground laid out for building, both together estimated at - - - - -	60,000	0	0
Exclusive also of public buildings, and ground appropriated to public purposes, valued at -	85,000	0	0

State of Agriculture about Liverpool, and Account of the Improvement of Chat and Trafford Mofs.—Of the state of agriculture in the neighbourhood of Liverpool a short account may suffice, the lands being chiefly occupied in small pasture farms, producing butter and milk for the immediate use of the town. Little or no cheese is made in the neighbourhood, a supply of which is readily obtained from the adjacent county of Chester. The farm of Mr. Wakefield, in Smetham-lane, within a mile of Liverpool, is, however, deserving of notice, though only an occasional employment for its owner, who carries on an extensive sugar refinery in Liverpool. His stock generally consists of about 100 cows, in the choice of which he prefers the Holderneffe breed; besides which he fats every year a considerable number of cattle for the market. The food which he raises for his cattle is chiefly turneps and potatoes, the latter of which he boils, and has found them by experience to be in this state a cheap and excellent food for his horses. In boiling his potatoes he uses a large wooden veffel, holding about ten bushels, which being clofed with a lid or cover, and perforated at the bottom, is set over a boiler or iron pot, the steam of which, rising through the potatoes, effectually answers the purpose of boiling by immerfion. For a few years past he has tried the fuccory or wild endive (Cichorium Intybus) which he finds to be very

C c c 2   pro-

productive, throwing up a ftrong vegetation which is confumed by his cattle with great eagernefs, though Dr. Withering afferts that cows and horfes refufe it,* and Mr. Curtis confiders it as a noxious weed † A few years fince Mr. Wakefield difcovered a method of applying fteam to the purpofes of vegetation, particularly to the growing of grapes, pines, melons, and other hot-houfe productions, which is now very generally adopted in the neighbourhood, particularly at Knowfley, the feat of the earl of Derby, where, under the directions of Mr. Butler, a fkilful gardener, it has had great fuccefs. This difcovery is likely foon to be made public with the confent and under the patronage of the inventor, whofe attention is at prefent engaged by an undertaking in the neighbourhood of Manchefter, which, as it is likely to be of public utility, deferves particular notice.

This undertaking is the drainage and improvement of the two large tracts of wafte land lying in the parifh of Eccles, called Chat Mofs and Trafford Mofs, of which fome account has before been given. The former of thefe is very confpicuous from the road between Warrington and Manchefter. Its dark furface rifes above the adjoining lands, and extends along the road five or fix miles, approaching to it at times within the diftance of lefs than 100 yards. Trafford Mofs lies on the fouth fide of the river Irwell, and adjoins to the park of John Trafford, of Trafford, Efq. the proprietor both of that and of much the greater part of Chat Mofs.

The very populous country in the midft of which thefe wafte lands are fituated, their elevation above the bed of the river Irwell, the oppor-

* _Botanical Arrangement_, Vol. II. P. 863, 2d Edit.
† _Flora Londinenfis._

tunity

tunity of improvement by materials either found on the fpot, or at a fmall diftance, and the convenience of carriage by the duke of Bridge-water's canal from Worfeley to Manchefter, which divides Trafford Mofs into two unequal parts, and fhoots a confiderable way into Chat Mofs, feems to render the improvement of thefe lands particularly eligible; and accordingly, in the year 1792, Mr. Wakefield agreed to undertake it upon a leafe for a long term of years. In the feffion of 1793 an act of parliament was obtained, enabling the proprietor to complete fuch agreement.

Mr. Wakefield having affociated in his undertaking Mr. Rofcoe of Liverpool, the drainage of Trafford Mofs was begun by them in the fame year, and the principal part of it is now interfected by drains at fix yards diftance from each other. Thefe drains are cut to the depth of about three feet, and are eighteen inches wide. At the bottom a narrow or fpit drain is formed, about fix inches wide and eighteen inches deep, leaving a fhoulder at the bottom of the wide drain to fupport the fod or turf with which the narrow or fpit drain is covered. No material is ufed but the native fod. Thefe drains, it muft be obferved, ought not to be cut at one operation, as in fuch cafe the fides will give way. They muft be allowed time to harden, and drain off the water at every foot, or oftener, according to the nature and confiftence of the Mofs. This precaution is of the utmoft importance. When the fides of the drain are become fufficiently hard, a fod is placed over the fpit drain, the wide drain is covered up, and the furface levelled for cultivation. Thefe fmall drains open into larger ones, at 100 yards diftance from each other, which alfo form the boundaries or fences of the intended fields, and by which the water is carried off to the extremity of the mofs, where it finds an uninterrupted courfe to the Irwell.

The

The next ſtep to be taken is to improve the ſurface, which is done by introducing ſome extraneous ſubſtance, which being mingled with the moſs, may aſſiſt its decompoſition; (the natural proceſs of which, even when expoſed to the air, is very ſlow) and may render it fit for the purpoſes of huſbandry: calcareous ſubſtances of all kinds, and even ſand, are alſo highly ſerviceable. A fine bed of marl which lies about four feet under the ſurface at one end of Trafford Moſs, affords an excellent article for its improvement. The difficulty attending the conveying the marl over the moſs, which is yet too ſoft and ſpongy to bear a cart and horſes, is obviated by the uſe of moveable caſt iron roads, the direction of which is daily changed as the work proceeds, and over which the marl is conveyed in four-wheeled waggons, containing about ſix hundred weight each. One horſe with great eaſe takes ſix of theſe waggons; by theſe means the weight of the marl, bearing on twenty-four wheels, is diſcharged at ſo many points, that the iron road is much lighter, and conſequently leſs expenſive, and more moveable than it would otherwiſe be. This road is caſt in bars of ſix feet long, which join together, and reſt on wooden ſleepers or blocks; every bar weighs about thirty pounds.

In the year 1794, the undertakers made an experiment by planting with potatoes about ten acres of the native moſs, after they had drained it, but before any marl had been introduced, the land being only manured with the common town ſoil of Mancheſter. Although the ſeaſon was unfavourable, the vegetation was ſtrong, and the crop equal to any in the neighbourhood. It is expected that in the preſent year upwards of 100 acres of Trafford Moſs will be in tillage.

The

VIEW OF LIVERPOOL.

Published May 7, 1795, by I. Stockdale, Piccadilly.

E. Dayes delt

W. Ellis sculp.

The potatoes produced on Mofs lands are faid to be more free from blemifh than any other, and are always preferred for planting again to thofe grown on other foils.

The operations on Chat Mofs are, we underftand, intended to be begun immediately.

———————

Before we entirely quit this town and county, we fhall remark, that the affeffment of men for the fervice of the navy laid by a late act of parliament upon the feveral counties in the kingdom, in proportion to the taxed houfes in each, places Lancafhire higher than any one except Yorkfhire; the numbers being, *Yorkfhire* 1064, *Lancafhire* 589, while that for *Middlefex* and *London* together is only 552, and no other approaches near it.

Alfo, by another act for obliging every fea-port to contribute a certain number of men for the navy, which is affeffed according to the tonnage of fhips regiftered in each port, Liverpool ftands fecond; the numbers for fome of the principal ports in England being as follows :

London,	5725	Hull,	731	Briftol,	666
Liverpool,	1711	Whitehaven,	700	Whitby,	573
Newcaftle,	1240	Sunderland,	669	Yarmouth,	506

The whole number to be raifed by the ports of England is 17,948.

The fecond view of Liverpool here annexed is copied from a picture of Mr. Peters, in the poffeffion of Nicholas Afhton, Efq and was taken from the Chefhire fhore oppofite the town.

I II.—*CHESHIRE.*

II.—*CHESHIRE.*

CHESTER.

ON a rocky eminence above the river Dee, and half encircled by a fweep of that river, ftands the ancient city of Chefter. Whatever be the truth concerning its remoter antiquity, it was certainly made a military ftation by the Romans, for which it was well adapted, as commanding the head of the frith or eftuary of the Dee, which then flowed up in a broad channel to its walls, overfpreading all the low grounds between Wirral and Flintfhire. It was the quarters of the twentieth Roman legion, whence the Britons gave it the names of *Caer Legion*, *Caer Leon Vawr*, *Caer Leon ar Dufyr Dwy*. The Roman geographers named it *Deunana* and *Deva* from the river; and the later hiftorians, *Ceftria*, from *caftrum*, a camp or military ftation. Its Roman origin has farther been proved by the difcovery at various periods of remains of antiquity belonging to that nation, fuch as altars, ftatues, coins, and hypocaufts, of which laft, one is at this day to be feen at the Feathers' inn, confifting of a number of low pillars, fupporting perforated tiles for the paffage of the warm vapour. The Saxons called this place *Legancefter* and *Legecefter*. It is ftyled *Weft Chefter* from its relative fituation, to diftinguifh it from many other towns which have the appellation of *Chefter* with fome addition.

With

A PLAN of CHESTER.

REFERENCES

With refpect to its hiftory, we fhall briefly obferve, that after the final departure of the Romans from this ifland in the fifth century, it fell under the dominion of the Britifh princes, from whom it was wrefted, firft, by Ethelfrid, who gained the battle of Chefter againft the king of Powis in 607, and afterwards was finally annexed to the Saxon crown by Egbert. It was feized and almoft ruined by the Danes in the ninth century, and reftored by Ethelfleda, daughter of the great Alfred. King Edgar made a league here in 973 with fix petty kings. After the Norman conqueft, the earldom of Chefter, with almoft regal powers, was conferred on Hugh Lupus, who kept his court at Chefter, reftored its walls, and built its caftle. Before this time it was a guild mercatory, and was noted as a port of confiderable commerce. In the reign of Edward the Confeffor, there were in it 431 taxable houfes, befides fifty-fix that belonged to the bifhop; but this number was greatly reduced before Hugh Lupus took poffeffion of his earldom. In after reigns it was a place of rendezvous for troops in all expeditions againft Wales, and frequently fuffered in the contefts between the two nations. It was at Chefter that the Welch made their final acknowledgement to Edward of Caernarvon, of the fovereignty of England, in 1300. Several of our kings vifited it at different periods, and conferred favours upon it, which were returned by loyal attachment. Its firft royal charter was given by Henry III.; but that which beftowed its moft valuable privileges was granted by Henry VII. In the civil wars of Charles I. it adhered with great fidelity to the royal caufe, and ftood a long fiege in 1645-6, not furrendering to the Parliament till all hope of relief had long been cut off by the defeat of Sir Marmaduke Langdale at Rowton-heath. In the rebellion of 1745 it was put into a ftate of defence and ftrongly garrifoned; but fince that period its importance as a military ftation has happily ceafed.

D d d   Chefter

Chefter principally confifts of four ftreets running from a centre to-wards the four points of the compafs, and each terminated by a gate; thus preferving the original form of a Roman camp. Thefe have been excavated in the rocky foil, which has been the caufe of a very fingu-lar conftruction of the houfes in them. On the level of the ftreet are low fhops or warehoufes; above them, a gallery, running from houfe to houfe, and ftreet to ftreet, and affording a covered walk for foot-paffengers. Over it are the higher ftories of the houfes. The gallery, called here a *row*, is on a level with the kitchens and yards of the houfes, though elevated a flight of fteps above the ftreet. The appear-ance of the whole is as if the firft ftories to the front of all the houfes in a ftreet were laid open, and made to communicate with each other, pillars only being left for the fupport of the fuperftructure. Thus the foot-paffengers feem to be walking along the fronts of the houfes up one pair of ftairs. In thefe *rows* are many fhops; and they give a fheltered walk in all weathers, though difagreeably clofe and often dirty, with the neceffity of afcending and defcending wherever a lane croffes the ftreet. This mode of ftructure is on many accounts fo in-convenient, that it is only kept up in the old ftreets near the centre of the city. The four ftreets are for the moft part of a good breadth, and ftraight. There are various communicating lanes or narrow ftreets, and large fuburbs. Upon the whole, the building of the city is rather vene-rable and fingular than elegant, though within the laft twenty years a confiderable number of houfes in the modern ftyle have been erected in new fituations.

Of the public edifices, few are diftinguifhed for fplendour or beauty. The cathedral is a large, irregular, and heavy pile, become ragged through the decay of its mouldering ftone. It is on the fite of an Abbey founded by a Mercian king in favour of his daughter Werburgh, to whom, afterwards fainted, the cathedral is dedicated. One of its tranfepts is parted off and ufed as a parifh church. The greater part of the prefent edifice was erected in the reigns of Henry VII. and VIII. The chapter-houfe with its veftibule is a more ancient and a truly beautiful ftructure. St. John's church, which was once collegiate, has been a large and magnificent pile of Saxon architecture, but a great part of it has fuffered demolition. The other churches offer nothing extraordinary. The bifhop's palace is a neat, plain ftructure, forming one fide of the Abbey Court, two others of which confift of handfome, modernbuilt houfes.

The caftle, fituated above the river at the fouth end of the town, ftill affords fome appearance of a fortrefs, though much dilapidated. It confifts of an upper and lower ward, the entrance to each protected by gates and round towers. Within the caftle are the county goal, and the courts of juftice. The latter have lately been taken down, and a new goal, fhire-hall, &c. are building upon a much-approved and extenfive plan. The caftle has a governor, lieutenant-governor, and conftable, and is garrifoned by two companies of invalids.

The walls are one of the moft pleafing fingularities of Chefter, being the only ones in the kingdom, thofe of Carlifle excepted, which are kept up entire. Their circuit is 1¾ mile and 101 yards, and they afford a walk on the top for two perfons abreaft, without the neceffity of defcending at the gates over which the walk is carried. It is indeed folely for the purpofe of pleafure and recreation, and not of defence, that they are now maintained: and the extent and variety of profpect enjoyed from them fully juftify the inhabitants in their attention to pre-

D d d 2

ferve

ferve them in a neat and commodious state. The Welch mountains, the Cheshire hills of Broxton, and the insulated rock of Beeston crowned with its castle, the rich flat interposed, and the perpetually changing views of the river, are striking objects in this favourite tour. Three of the arches which afford entrance to the city through the walls are spacious and elegant modern structures. A small duty paid on Irish linen imported is the principal source of revenue for supporting the walls. A considerable and populous part of the city, particularly on the eastern side, is without their circuit.

With respect to the character and consequence of Chester as a town, it has long maintained nearly the same station it at present occupies. It is principally distinguished as a sort of provincial metropolis, not only to its own county, but to the neighbouring counties of North Wales; many of the gentry of which, as well as other persons disengaged from business, from various parts, chuse it as an agreeable residence, offering the pleasures of cultivated society on easy terms, with the advantage of polite education to their families. Its markets are well supplied with all articles both of necessity and luxury, and at a lower rate than in the trading and manufacturing towns of the neighbourhood. Very good fruit and vegetables of all kinds are grown in the spacious gardens underneath and within the walls. The city is supplied with water chiefly from the river by means of water-works at the bridge which raise the water into a reservoir, whence pipes are laid into the houses.

The commercial character of Chester is rather a secondary consideration, nor have the attempts to make it participate in the benefits which its neighbours have received from the surprising increase of trade and manufactures been attended with much success. It has, however, long been

known

known as the great mart for Irifh linens, which are brought over at its two noted fairs commencing on July 5th and October 10th, and fold to a great amount to purchafers from various parts of the kingdom. The quantity is reckoned at a million of yards each fair. For the better accommodation of the linen merchants, a new hall was built in the year 1778, which is a handfome fquare brick building, containing 111 fhops, and enclofing a fpacious area. At thefe fairs are fold large quantities of other commodities, as Yorkfhire cloths, Welch flannels, cheefe, horfes, cattle, &c. but the refort to them is lefs than formerly, as is the cafe with all other fairs.

The only manufacture of confequence in Chefter is that of gloves, which is carried on to fome extent. There are alfo a fmall manufactory of tobacco pipes, an iron foundry, fnuff mills, fhip builder's yards, and other concerns, which afford fome employment; but the poor in general are occupied only in the common trades and labours belonging to a town inhabited by families of opulence.

Chefter, as has already been noted, is an ancient port; but the great breadth of the eftuary of the Dee, and the comparative fmallnefs of the body of water flowing through it, rendered it liable to be choaked up with fand thrown in by the tide. This gradually took place to fuch a degree in the laft century, that in the year 1674, veffels of twenty tons could fcarcely reach the town, and fhips of burthen were obliged to lie under Newton, ten miles lower down, which was the origin of that affemblage of houfes on the adjacent fhore, called *Park-gate*, ftill the ftation of the Irifh packets. In that year, a plan was formed by Mr. Andrew Yarranton to make a new channel for the river, and at the fame time to recover a large tract of land from the fea by embankment. It

was

was not, however, till the middle of the prefent century, that the project was put into execution. A company was formed for the purpofe and different powers were granted by various acts of parliament; bu the firft operations were fo expenfive, that numbers of fubfcribers were obliged to fell out at above 90 per cent. lofs. At length, the fhares falling into the hands of fewer and wealthier perfons, the plan was brought to a confiderable degree of utility, and a fine canal has been made, protected by vaft banks, in which the river is confined for the fpace of ten miles, with fuch a depth of water as to allow veffels of 350 tons burthen to come up to the quays at fpring tides. This canal opens from the fea a little above Flint. A fmall canal from Sir John Glynne's collieries at Afton, near Harwarden, joins the other about two miles below Chefter. At the fame time, crofs embankments have been made, which have gained much land from the; fea and flourifhing farms are now feen where formerly were nothing but bare fands, covered each tide by the water. Two ferries acrofs the new canal make a communication with the oppofite county of Wales. The medium height of fpring tides at the quays is fifteen feet; the greateft, twenty-one feet. The river juft above the bridge is croffed by a ftone caufe-way, which caufes a fall of thirteen feet, and cuts off conftant communication by veffels between the upper part of the river and the lower. There are, however, fix or eight tides which flow over the caufeway, and fome reach upwards of twenty miles up the country, which allows a navigation for fmall barges as far as Bangor. The caufeway ferves as a dam for the purpofe of turning mills. The fnuff mills are fituated directly upon it, and the town corn mills, which are reckoned extremely complete in their conftruction, clofe to the bridge, one arch of which conveys a ftream for their ufe.

The

The maritime bufinefs of Chefter is of no great extent. It chiefly confifts of the coafting and Irifh trades, with a fmall portion of trade to foreign parts. The commodities imported are, groceries from London; linen cloth, wool, hides, tallow, feathers, butter, provifions, and other articles from Ireland; timber, deals, hemp, flax, iron, and tallow from the Baltic; kid and lamb-fkins from Leghorn; fruit, oil, barilla, and cork, from Spain and Portugal, and a large quantity of wine from the latter, which is the principal article of foreign import. Its exports are coal, lead, lead ore, calamine, copper plates, caft iron, and large quantities of cheefe; and it is a fort of magazine for a variety of goods, raw and manufactured, fent to Ireland. From the large cheefe warehoufe in the river, veffels go at ftated periods with loads for London. The number of fhips belonging to this port, notwithftanding the above enumeration of commercial objects, is very fmall; yet the limits of the port extend on the Chefhire fide of the Dee as far as the end of Wirral, and on the Flintfhire fide to the mouth of the river Clwyd. The bufinefs of fhip-building is carried on here continually, and with advantage, many veffels from 100 to 500 tons being built yearly. Thefe are reckoned to be fuperior in point of ftrength and beauty to thofe built at any other port in the kingdom. The materials are entirely Britifh oak.

The canal from Namptwich, which was expected to add much to the trade of this city, but the miferable failure of which has been already mentioned, (fee page 127) enters the river below the quay, after paffing under the north fide of the walls. The new Ellefmere canal is intended to pafs on the weft fide of the city, and after communicating with the Dee, to proceed to join the Merfey. It is hoped this may open new fources of trade which may prove advantageous to this an-

cient

cient port. That part of it which forms the communication between the Dee and Merfey is already finifhed.

The population of Chefter and its fuburbs was found, on an enume-ration in 1774, to be as follows :—families, 3428 ; male inhabitants, 6697 ; female do. 8016 ; total, 14,713 ; and by calculations drawn from the bills of mortality, its proportional healthinefs appeared to be greater than that of almoft any other large town to which it was com-pared. But this was doubtlefs in part owing to the much lefs propor-tion of the loweft clafs of poor than that in manufacturing towns, among whom the great principles of increafe and decreafe are to be looked for In Chefter the _births_ are equally as difproportionate as the _deaths_ to the exifting number.

The government of this city is vefted in a corporation, confifting of a mayor, recorder, two fheriffs, twenty-four aldermen, and forty com-mon councilmen, two of whom are leave-lookers, whofe office it is to inform of all perfons exercifing trades within the city without being freemen. The two fenior officers are murengers, or receivers of the murage duties for maintaining the walls. Two are treafurers, who are ufually next in fucceffion to the mayor. There are likewife a fword and mace bearer, and the other ufual inferior officers.

The right of election into the corporation was by a charter of king Henry VII. confirmed by queen Elizabeth, declared to be in the citizen-freemen ; but this right being fuppofed to be abrogated by a new char-ter in the reign of Charles II. the corporation affumed the exclufive pri-vilege of electing into their own body. About fifteen years ago, Mr. John Eddowes, a very refpectable citizen, fupported by other citizen-

4   freemen,

freemen, inſtituted a ſuit in the court of King's-bench againſt an alderman and common-councilman thus elected; whoſe cauſe being defended by their brethren, came to a hearing, and was decided in favour of the corporation : but Mr. Eddowes removing the cauſe bv appeal to the Houſe of Lords, after a long and ſolemn hearing, the former
verdict was reverſed, and a decree made, that the old charter of Henry
VII. was the only legal one. Both ſides were adjudged to pay their
coſts, which to Mr. Eddowes and his friends amounted to £.300 ;
and the corporation continued to elect as before.

The law courts of the city are the courts of Crown-mote and Port-
mote, and the Seſſions, all held in the Exchange. In the Port-mote the
mayor, aſſiſted by the recorder, holds pleas to any amount. He alſo
holds the ſeſſions of peace, in which criminals are tried, with the
power of paſſing ſentence of death. There is another court, held at
the *Pentice*, an ancient building at the centre of the city, in which the
ſheriffs are judges; this is for civil cauſes only. The city goal is in
the North-gate. In the Exchange, which is a large, handſome pile
of building ſupported on columns, the body corporate hold their aſſemblies for public buſineſs, and the elections of mayors and other officers.
Here likewiſe the mayors give their entertainments, and the citizens
have their dancing aſſemblies.

The city returns two members to parliament, choſen by the freemen
at large, in number about 1000. The ſheriff is returning officer; the
chief intereſt is in the Groſvenor family.

The limits of the city liberties extend to a circumference of about
eight miles. A fine meadow lying between the walls and the river,

called the *Rood-eye*, is ufed as a common pafture for the citizens, and alfo for a race-ground, for which purpofe it is admirably adapted, lying like an amphitheatre immediately beneath the walls, and alfo commanded by the high banks on the oppofite fide of the river.

Chefter contains, befides the cathedral, the following churches :

St. Ofwald, (in the cathedral,)	St. Michael,
St. John Baptift,	St. Mary,
St. Peter,	St. Olave,
Trinity,	St. Martin.
St. Bridget,	

It has fix places of worfhip for diffenters, viz. one Prefbyterian, two Independent, one Quaker, one Methodift, and one Catholic.

Of the charitable inftitutions of Chefter, the Blue-coat Hofpital, fituated near the North-gate, deferves particular mention. It was founded by bifhop Stratford in 1706; and was devoted to the complete maintenance of thirty-five boys for four years, at the expiration of which they were put out apprentices : but in the year 1781, when the income of the hofpital received an augmentation, it was propofed, inftead of adding to the number of thofe educated in the houfe, to take fixty more as out-fcholars, to be taught reading, writing, and fome arithmetic. This propofal was accomplifhed in 1783, and was attended with fuch good effects, that the number was afterwards doubled. Thefe 120 are taught by two mafters; and the whole annual expence of each boy in teaching, books, and a green cap, amounts to no more than 14s. They are received at nine years of age, and when they are of two years ftanding, fifteen of the beft are annually elected

in-

in-fcholars for two years; and thofe not elected remain out-fcholars two years more. By this plan, the benefits of a good education are extended to one-third of all the boys in Chefter. There is likewife a blue-fchool for a fmaller number of girls, both out and in-fcholars, which is fupported by ladies.

Another ufeful charity is one for thirty decayed freemen of fixty years of age and upwards, who receive £.4 yearly, and a gown every third year. There are likewife various alms-houfes in the city.

The Infirmary, erected in 1761, and fupported by fubfcriptions from the town and county and North Wales, is a very well-conducted inftitution of the kind. Its utility has lately been increafed by allowing the admiffion of fever-patients to a ward fet apart for them, and carefully prevented from communicating infection to the reft of the houfe.

In the year 1778 a charitable inftitution of a kind before unknown in the kingdom was fet on foot in Chefter. Its objects were, to prevent the Natural Small-pox in Chefter, and to promote General Inoculation at ftated periods. A fet of rules were drawn up to be obferved whenever the fmall-pox fhould break out, both by the families where it appeared, and by the neighbours, and rewards were annexed to the obfervance of them. Subfcriptions were liberally raifed for the purpofes of this fociety, and in a courfe of four or five years, it was found by various trials that the rules were fufficient to ftop the contagion of the fmall-pox when faithfully obferved: but the obftinacy and fupinenefs of the people, and their rejection of the offer of free inoculation, caufed the fcheme at length to be given up. The attempt, however,

has

has given birth to two very interefting publications of Dr. Haygarth, which may prove the foundation of more extenfive future plans to extirpate this fatal difeafe. They are entitled, *An Inquiry how to prevent the Small-pox*; and *A Sketch of a Plan to exterminate the Small-pox from Great Britain*, &c.

WREXHAM.

FROM Chefter we fhall make a fmall excurfion out of the county, to a town much connected with it in trade, and at a fhort diftance from the Chefhire border; *Wrexham*, in the county of Denbigh. This is the largeft town in North Wales, and its parifh the moft populous. Its ancient name of *Wrightefham* fhews it to have been of Saxon origin; and its language and appearance have always been more thofe of an Englifh than a Welch town. Mr. Pennant has been able to trace its exiftence no farther back than the time of the laft earl Warren, who had a grant of it. Leland mentions it as a place where there were fome merchants and good buckler-makers.

The church of Wrexham is popularly called one of the wonders of North Wales. It was erected in the reign of Henry VII., and is a magnificent and highly ornamented pile of building. The infide of the church is very fpacious, and confifts of a nave, two aifles, and a chancel. Above the pillars are many grotefque carvings in ridicule of monks and nuns, and over the arches of the nave are many of the arms of the old Britifh and Saxon princes. There are various monuments in

the

the church, of which the most striking is a modern one in memory of Mrs. Mary Middleton, daughter of Sir Richard Middleton of Chirk-castle, representing her as bursting from the tomb at the sound of the last trumpet. There is also an elegant monument by Roubillac, of the Rev. Mr. Thomas Middleton and his wife, representing their faces on a medallion in profile, with a delicate curtain hanging on one side. The outside of the church has a great variety of gross and ludicrous sculpture. The steeple is a fine tower, richly ornamented on three sides with rows of saints placed in gothic niches. Among them is St. Giles, the patron of the church, with the hind, by which, according to the legend, he was miraculously fed in the desert. At each corner of the steeple is a light turret with a winding staircase, twenty-four feet high. The whole height of the steeple is 135 feet. The church is a vicarage; formerly an impropriation belonging to the abbey of Valle Crucis, but since restored to the see of St. Asaph. It has two chapels under it; *Minera*, or *Mwyn glawdd*, (*Mine upon the ditch*, that of Offa running by it) in the mountainous part of the parish; and *Berse* or *Bersham*, a recent foundation. Wrexham has a free-school, endowed with £.10 a year, paid by the mayor of Chester, being the bequest of Valentine. Broughton, alderman of that city.

Wrexham has weekly markets on Monday and Thursday; the last, the principal, which is well supplied with provisions of all kinds, brought in by the neighbouring farmers. About thirty-eight years since the prices were as low, probably, as in any part of the kingdom. A fat stubble goose alive might be bought for 1*s.*; beef at 1½*d.* per pound; mutton in proportion; and fresh butter at 3½*d.* per pound. This last article, however, rose in seven years from that time to double the price, which

which was owing to its being carried to the markets of Chefter and Liverpool, and to the increafed confumption in confequence of the prevalence of tea-drinking. The prices in 1795 are little different from thofe of other country towns; mutton 5*d.* per pound, beef 4*d.*, butter 11*d.* The wages of day-labourers are 6*s.* in winter, and 7*s.* in fummer, having only been increafed 1*s.* during the laft thirty years, notwithftanding the vaft rife of provifions, and a proportional advance in houfe rent and the price of coals.

The people of Wrexham moftly make their own bread, which is compofed of wheat, barley, and a little rye: this mixture, baked in large loaves, makes excellent brown bread. It is fermented by a leaven confifting of a piece of the former dough turned four.

Wrexham enjoys a good deal of the fhop-keeping trade into Wales; but its great importance in a commercial view arifes from its noted annual fair in the month of March, which lafts nine days; the three laft, however, being chiefly employed in packing up the goods. This fair is frequented from almoft all parts of the kingdom, and purchafers flock to it, from North Wales in particular, in fuch crowds, that the town is filled to a degree fcarcely to be conceived by any one who has not feen it. The commodities brought by the Welch are chiefly flannels, linen, linfey-woolfey, and horfes and cattle in great abundance. Traders from other parts bring Irifh linen, Yorkfhire and other woollen cloths, Manchefter goods, Birmingham manufactures of all kinds, and ribands, for which laft there is a great demand among the country people for fairings and rural finery. There are two fquares or areas, the old and the new, for the accommodation of thofe who have goods to fell

in

in their little shops or booths. Here is also a convenient town-hall, where the assizes are held. The centre street, where the market is kept, is of considerable length, and proportionably wide; an uncommon circumstance for an ancient town.

Two miles from Wrexham is *Bersham* iron-furnace, belonging to Messrs. John and William Wilkinson. This concern was carried on about thirty-four years ago by Mr. Wilkinson, sen. in company with one son and some Liverpool gentlemen; but it proved unsuccessful, partly in consequence of the failure of an expensive scheme to convey a blast by bellows from a considerable distance, to the works, by means of tubes under ground. It afterwards fell under the sole management of Mr. John Wilkinson, who, by means of very ingenious mechanism brought it to succeed in a wonderful manner, so that the works may be reckoned among the first of the kind in the kingdom. Besides the smelting furnaces, there are now several air furnaces for re-melting the pig iron, and casting it into various articles; such as cylinders for fire engines, water-pipes, boilers, pots and pans of all sizes, box and flat irons, and cannon and ball of all dimensions. The cannon are now cast solid, and bored like a wooden pipe, according to a very capital modern improvement. The small stream here turns machinery for the boring of cannon, the grinding of flat and box irons, &c. There are also forges for malleable iron, and wire works; and likewise a newly-erected brass foundry. All these works employ a great number of hands in various departments. At a short distance, lead ore is got in considerable quantities, and smelted upon the spot; and Messrs. Wilkinsons have a work for the casting of lead pipes of various sizes, and drawing them out to any lengths. Iron-stone and coal are also plentiful in this neighbourhood.

I A num-

A number of waggons are conftantly employed in carrying goods between Berfham furnace and Chefter, which being fourteen miles land carriage, is attended with a great expence. But this inconvenience will be removed by means of the Ellefmere canal, which is to pafs by thefe works; and a cut from it, called Brumbo-branch, will go to a new and large iron foundry now erecting by Mr. John Wilkinfon, who has alfo great iron works in Shropfhire. This canal will be of the greateft fervice to this part of the country, which yields the fine blue flate, limeftone of the whiteft kind and ftrongeft quality, and excellent coals in large blocks, all at prefent carried in fummer to the diftance of twenty or thirty miles by land-carriage at a great expence.

The farms in the neighbourhood of Wrexham are in general of a moderate fize, though there are fome very large dairy ones, capable of keeping cows fufficient to make a large cheefe every day, of equal goodnefs with the Chefhire, and fold as fuch. Many fmall farmers and cottagers who keep teams for drawing coal-carts or other work, have the practice of collecting the fprouts or foft top branches of young gorfe or furze, which they chop fmall on a block by means of a mallet having a crofs fharp knife on its face; this they give as fodder to their horfes, either alone, or mixed with a fmall quantity of oats. It is found to keep them in good heart, and give them a fleek coat; and the practice deferves to be better known than it is in other parts. Moft of the horfes employed in winding up the coal from the pits are alfo fed in this manner. The greater part of the parifh of Wrexham is either flat, or compofed of gentle rifings, affording many very fertile and pleafant fituations, inhabited by an uncommon number of gentry diftinguifhed for their hofpitable mode of living. The beauties of *Erthig*, the feat of Philip Yorke, Efq at a fmall diftance from Wrexham, are

well

well known to the visitors of this romantic tract of country. The house is situated upon a delightful eminence, commanding a most pleasing view, and the lands are bounded by two little vales, watered by a pretty stream, and bordered by hanging woods.

A great dike or fofs, called *Wat's Dike*, and vulgarly the *Devil's Ditch*, runs through the parish, and by Erthig. It is a deep, wide ditch, enclosed between two high banks made of the earth thrown out, and which are now in many parts covered with trees of the largest growth. This work accompanies at irregular distances the better known entrenchment called *Offa's Dike*.

The road from Wrexham to Chester, $11\frac{1}{2}$ miles, is a very fine one. It passes by the village of *Gresford*, distinguished by a very handsome church, built in the same reign with that of Wrexham, and possessing a fine ring of twelve bells, reckoned one of the wonders of Wales. Beneath the church is a most beautiful little valley, affording a landscape perfect in its kind—a model of rural elegance and retirement. Near this place is the beautiful cottage of Mrs. Warrington, and the house lately built by Mr. James Wyatt, for John Parry, Esq.

The following list of gentlemens' seats at the distance of from one to twelve miles from Wrexham, will give an idea of the beauties of this part of the country.

Lord Dacre,	-	-	-	-	- Plas Tneg.
Lord Kenyon,	-	-	-	-	- Gredington.
Sir W. W. Wynn, Bart.		-	-	-	Wynnstay.
Sir Foster Cunliffe, Bart.		-	-	-	Acton Park.

Philip

Philip Yorke, Efq. - - - -	Erthig.
William Lloyd, Efq. - - -	Plas Power.
Sir Thomas Hanmer, Bart. - - -	Bettisfield Park.
Ll. G. Wardle, - - - -	Hartfheath.
John Humberfton, Efq. - - -	Grewfilt Park.
John Parry, Efq. - - - -	Gresford Lodge.
Peter Whitehall Davies, Efq. - -	Broughton.
Trevor Lloyd, Efq. - - - -	Trevor.
William Owen, Efq. - - - -	Plas Kynafton.
Rev. Thomas Youde, - - - -	Plas Madoc.
Richard Pulefton, Efq. - - -	Emrall.
Philip Lloyd Fletcher, Efq. - -	Gwernhaylid.
———— Price, Efq. (minor) - -	Bryn y pys.
Roger Kenyon, Efq. - - - -	Cefn.
———— Wilfon, Efq. - - -	Trevallyn.
Richard Myddleton, Efq. - - -	Chirk Caftle.
———— Lloyd, Efq. - - -	Penyllan.
———— Meredith, Efq. - - -	Pentre bwchan.
Richard Hill Waring, Efq. - -	Leefwood.
Lady Glynne, - - - - -	Hawarden Caftle.
Rev. Dr. Pulefton, - - - -	Pickhill.
Lord Dungannon, - - - -	Bryn kynalt.
Rev. J. W. Eyton, - - - -	Leefwood.
Thomas Apperley, Efq. - - -	Plas Grwnyo.
David Pennant, Efq. - - - -	Rofe Hill.
Thomas Brown, Efq. - - -	Marchwiel.
———— Jones, Efq. - - -	Llwynon.
Frederick Philips, Efq. - - -	Rhyddyn.
Edward Eyton, Efq. - - - -	Eyton.

BROXTON

BROXTON HUNDRED.

THIS hundred, which was called at the time of the Conqueſt Du-, deſtan hundred, ſtretches on the eaſtern bank of the Dee to the ſouth of Cheſter, as far the ſouth-weſtern corner of the county.

About two miles from Cheſter, on the Frodſham road, is *Hoole-heath,* noted for having been an aſylum eſtabliſhed by Hugh Lupus, and particularly allotted to fugitives from Wales.

About the ſame diſtance from Cheſter, on the London road, is the pleaſing village of *Chriſtleton,* the manor of which was held before the Conqueſt by earl Edwin, and after that period was beſtowed by Hugh Lupus on Robert Fitzhugh, one of his followers.

The village of *Eccleſton* is pleaſantly ſituated on the Dee, commanding a fine view of the towers and ſpires of Cheſter, riſing above the wooded banks. It was held after the Conqueſt by a Venables: it is now the property of the Groſvenors.

At a ſmall diſtance from Cheſter is *Eaton,* a hamlet on the Dee, in which is ſituated the family ſeat of the *Groſvenors.* The houſe is of brick, built about the latter end of the laſt century. The ancient family of Groſvenors came in with the Conqueſt, and took their name from the office of chief huntſman, which they bore in the Norman court. Their firſt ſettlement in this county was at Over Loſtock, be-

ſtowed

ſtowed by Hugh Lupus on his great nephew, Robert le Groſvenour. In 1234, Richard le Groſvenour fixed his ſeat at Hulme; but in the reign of Henry VI. it was transferred to this place by the marriage of Rawlin, or Ralph Groſvenour, with Joan, daughter of John Eaton, of Eaton, Eſq.

Near Eaton is *Aldford* bridge, over the Dee, forming a communication between the two parts of the hundred.

Further ſouth is the little town of *Farn*, or *Farndon*, on the Dee, called in Doomſday-book *Ferenton*. Its church was burnt by the parliament army during the ſiege of Holt caſtle, in 1645, and afterwards rebuilt. In one window, over the pew of the family of Barnſton, is ſome beautiful painted glaſs, repreſenting a commander in his tent, ſurrounded with military inſtruments. Around theſe are ſixteen figures of ſoldiery of different ranks, and over the heads of the officers are coats of arms belonging to ſeveral Cheſhire families of loyaliſts during the civil wars. This town is parted only by an ancient ſtone-bridge from that of *Holt*, in Denbighſhire, famous for its caſtle, which was demoliſhed after the parliament had obtained poſſeſſion of it.

Not far diſtant from hence, along a flat country, having a pleaſing view of the Broxton hills, is *Shocklach*, where was an ancient caſtle, held after the Conqueſt by Robert Fitzhugh. It belonged to the barony of Malpas. Nothing except a foſs marks out its ſite. On the the oppoſite ſide of the road is a great mount, probably of much greater antiquity than the caſtle, and once uſed as an exploratory ſtation.

The

The only market town of this hundred is

M A L P A S,

A fmall town, fituated at the fouth-weftern corner of the county, near the detached part of Flintfhire, which is faid to have derived its name from the bad roads by which it is approached. It was an ancient barony, and had a caftle, of which there are now no remains. From one of its barons, who took the name of Cholmondeley from the lordfhip fo called, is defcended the prefent earl of Cholmondeley, with which title is joined that of vifcount Malpas. The town has a grammar-fchool, and a charitable eftablifhment, both founded by Sir Randle Brereton. Its market is on Monday, and it has an annual fair in December. The church is a fine one, endowed with large revenues, which maintain two rectors and two curates. In the church is a family vault belonging to earl Cholmondeley, in which a long race of his anceftors lie entombed.

Cholmondeley-hall, the ancient feat of this family, with its park, is a little to the north-eaft of Malpas.

NAMPTWICH HUNDRED.

THIS hundred, the moft foutherly in Chefhire, is divided into two nearly equal parts by the river Weaver, and is diftinguifhed by the fertility of its paftures, and the richnefs of its dairies. Its capital is the town whence it takes its name,

NAMPT.

NAMPTWICH.

THIS town is situated near the borders of Staffordshire and Shropshire, in a fertile vale on the banks of the Weaver, near a small stream. It is surrounded by some of the finest dairy land in the county, in which the richest and largest of the Cheshire cheeses are made. The town is ancient, and was erected into a barony by Hugh Lupus, who bestowed it on William de Malbedeng or de Malbang, a Norman chieftain, from whom it obtained the name of *Wich Malbang*. The barony was afterwards split into small parcels, which was probably the cause why the town was never incorporated. At present it confers the title of baron upon the earl of Cholmondeley, who has tolls of cattle, roots and fruit sold in it. Mr. Crewe, of Crewe, the patron of the church, has the tolls of corn and fish.

Namptwich was formerly reckoned the second town in the county, but has been out-stript by some others which have obtained more benefit from the modern increase of manufactures. It contains more than 600 houses, mostly old, disposed in spacious streets. It has a plentiful weekly market on Saturday, and three annual fairs, in March, September, and December. It is governed by constables. The church is a very handsome pile, in form of a cross, with an octagonal tower in the centre. The east and west windows are filled with elegant tracery. The roof of the chancel is of stone, adorned with sculpture. The stalls are neat, and are said to have been brought from the abbey of Vale Royal at the dissolution. The living is a small vicarage. In the street called the Welch Row were anciently two hospitals, now entirely destroyed. A large house near the end of it, called *Town's-end*, was till

lately

lately the refidence of the refpectable family of Wilbraham, one of whom, Thomas Wilbraham, Efq. had the honour of entertaining king James I. when he made a vifit to this town. There are in the town various alms-houfes founded by the Wilbrahams and other charitable inhabitants. There is a free-fchool, founded by John and Thomas Thrufh, natives of this place, who exercifed the trade of wool-packers in London. Another fchool, where forty boys are cloathed and taught Englifh, called the blue-caps, has been fupported chiefly by the family of Wilbraham, aided by the liberality of the Crewe family. In the year 1780 was erected a large and commodious workhoufe within that part of the townfhip called *Beam-heath*, and within the barony thereof, in confequence of a grant from the earl of Cholmondeley.

The chief trade of Namptwich is in fhoes, which are fent to London. It has a fmall manufacture of gloves; but thofe of bone-lace and ftockings, once confiderable, are now loft. The tanning bufinefs was a fource of much wealth to the town in the reigns of Elizabeth and James I.

Namptwich is one of the falt towns, commonly called the *Wiches*; and feems formerly to have been one of the principal of them. In the reign of Elizabeth here were 216 falt works, of fix *leads-walling* each.* At prefent there are only two works of five large pans of wrought iron. The Britons, Romans, and Saxons feem fucceffively to have procured falt from the brine pits here, and various laws and ufages have prevailed from old times refpecting the working of them. It was hoped that the Chefter canal to this place (which terminates in a handfome broad bafon near the Acton road) would have increafed its falt trade to the be-

* Probably, at *all* the falt towns.

ncfit

nefit of both towns; but the other falt towns lie more convenient for commerce, and abound almoft to excefs with that commodity.

Namptwich was the only town in Chefhire which adhered to the parliament from the beginning to the end of the civil wars of Charles I. It ftood a fevere fiege in 1643 from Lord Byron, in which its garrifon defended themfelves with great obftinacy, though the place was poorly fortified, and repelled fome attacks with much lofs to the befiegers. It was at length relieved by the fignal victory obtained over the befieging forces by the army commanded by Sir Thomas Fairfax. This town was the refidence of the widow of Milton during the latter part of her life. She was the daughter of Mr. Minfhull, of Stoke, in this neighbourhood.

Near Namptwich is the village of *Acton*, a confiderable place as far back as the Saxon times. At the Conqueft it was a member of the barony of Namptwich. It came fucceffively to the Lovels, the Arderns, and the Wilbrahams, and at prefent belongs to the Hon. Wilbraham Tollemache. It has a handfome new-built church, containing fome curious and well-preferved monuments of the Mainwaring and Wilbraham families.

Wyburnbury, a village on the London road, is fuppofed to have taken its name from Wibba, fecond king of the Mercians. The manor was anciently in the family of the Praers, from whom it came to the bifhops of Litchfield and Coventry, who are ftill patrons of the living. The church is a very handfome building, embattled and pinnacled. It contains various monuments in memory of the Delves's of Doddington; and likewife a magnificent one of Sir Thomas Smith, of the Hough.

3

At

At the ancient hall of *Doddington* are preferved the ftatues of lord Audley and his four 'fquires, Delves, Dutton, Foulhurft, and Hawke-fton, all Chefhire men, who obtained great renown at the battle of Poitiers.

Crewe-hall, the feat of the family of Crewe, was built by Sir Randle Crewe in the time of Charles I. who was the firft perfon who brought a model of good building into this county. It is now occupied by John Crewe, Efq. member of parliament for Chefhire.

On the other fide of Namptwich is *Baddiley-hall*, the feat of the Mainwarings.

Cumbermere-abbey, which takes its name from the adjacent mere, was formerly the fite of an abbey of Ciftercians, founded by Hugh Mal-banc, lord of Namptwich. It now belongs to Sir Robert Salifbury Cotton, Bart. member for the county, whofe feat was built out of its remains.

EDDISBURY HUNDRED.

THIS diftrict chiefly comprifes the tract lying between Broxton hun-dred, and the weftern bank of the Weaver. A great part of it confifts of the foreft of Delamere, which in the time of Leland was a fair and large foreft abounding with red and fallow deer, but now is a black and dreary wafte, compofed of deep fand or fteril heath, and chiefly inhabited by rabbits, with a few black terns which fkim over the pools and plafhes in fome part of it. A few ftunted trees remain near a place called *Chamber of the Foreft*, once the centre of the wood-

G g g

land

land tract. Tradition reports that a large town once exifted in this hundred, of the name of Eddifbury ; but at prefent it is thinly peopled,
and contains no town of confequence.

On entering it from Namptwich, one of the firft places is *Bunbury*,
a village with a parifh church, which was formerly collegiate, on the
foundation of that celebrated foldier of fortune, Sir Hugh de Calvely.
This Chefhire hero was born at Calvely, a neighbouring hamlet, and
became a principal commander in the mercenary bands which ravaged
Europe in the 14th century. He fought under the Englifh general, lord
Chandos, at the battle of Auray in 1364, in which the great Du Guef-
clin was taken prifoner. He then ferved in Spain, firft againft Peter
the Cruel, and then for him, in the fervice of the Black Prince. He
afterwards became governor of Calais, and of Guernfey and the adjacent ifles, and was living in the reign of Henry IV. He has a magnificent tomb in Bunbury church, in which his effigy in white marble,
armed, and of gigantic proportions, lies recumbent ; and prodigious
feats of ftrength and prowefs are recorded of him in the popular tales of
the time. In this church, which is a handfome embattled one, there
are other ancient monuments. The old feat of Calvely now belongs to
the Davenport family.

Somewhat further is

T A R P O R L E Y,

A fmall market-town fituated ten miles from Chefter on the London
road. Its manor and rectory are divided into fix fhares, of which four
belong to the Ardens ; one to the dean and chapter of Chefter ;
and one to Philip Egerton, Efq. of Oulton. The living is a good

2   one,

one, in the gift of John Arden, Efq. The church is large, and contains feveral marble monuments. This town is chiefly remarkable for being the place where a number of the principal gentlemen of the county meet at an annual hunt, equally confecrated to the pleafures of conviviality and thofe of the chace. The neighbouring open heaths of Delamere foreft afford a favourable ground for the latter paftime.

Clofe within view of Tarporley, though at the diftance of two miles fouthwards, rifes the great infulated rock of *Beefton*, a moft ftriking object from the furrounding country. It is compofed of fandftone, very lofty and precipitous at one end, and floping down to the flat on the other. Its height, from Beefton-bridge to the fummit, is 366 feet. From its top is a very extenfive view on every part, except where interrupted by the near approach of the Peckforton-hills. All the level country of Chefhire, the city of Chefter, and the eftuaries of the Dee and Merfey, are diftinctly feen from it. The creft of the rock is crowned with the ruins of the famed *Beefton-caftle*, proverbial in thefe parts for its almoft impregnable ftrength. This fortrefs was firft erected in 1220 by Randle Blundeville, earl of Chefter. It devolved afterwards to the crown, and going through various viciffitudes, the ftory of which is not well known, it fell into ruins, in which ftate it was found by Leland in the reign of Henry VIII. It was afterwards repaired, and partook of the changeable fate of fo many other fortreffes during the laft civil wars. It was firft garrifoned by the Parliament; then taken by the royalifts under the command of the noted partizan, captain Sandford, who fcaled the fteep fide of the rock, and took it by furprize or treachery. The parliament forces then befieged it for feventeen weeks, but it held out to be relieved by prince Rupert. It was

G g g 2 again

again invested, and forced to surrender by famine after a vigorous defence of eighteen weeks. It was soon after dismantled.

The fortress consisted of an outer and inner area. The outer came
about midway of the slope, and was defended by a great gateway, and
a strong wall, fortified with round towers, which ran across the slope
from one edge of the precipice to the other, but did not surround the
hill as represented in an old print. Some parts of this wall, and about
six or seven rounders, with a square tower of the gateway, still subsist.
The area enclosed is four or five acres. The castle itself is near the
highest part of the rock, defended on the side of the area by a vast
ditch cut out of the live rock, on the other side by a steep precipice.
The entrance is through a noble gateway, guarded on each side by a
great round tower with walls of a prodigious thickness. Within the
yard are the remains of the chapel, a rectangular building. The draw-
well was of surprising depth, being sunk to the level of Beeston-brook
that runs beneath. In the outer area was another well. The perpendicular side of the rock from the castle has a tremendous appearance, and
is haunted by a small kind of hawk which builds in its clefts, and
" wings the midway air."

Over, on the other side of the forest, though now an insignificant
village, retains the evidence of its having once been a considerable town,
in its mayor, aldermen, and other corporate officers, still elected according to charter, with great regularity. A little to the north of it, on the
bank of the Weaver, is *Vale Royal*, once the site of a stately monastery
of Cistercians, founded by Edward I. The house is said to have been
fifty-three years in building, and to have cost £.32,000; an immense
                                                              sum

sum in those days! The name of Vale Royal included all the circumjacent tracts, and has by some been extended to all Cheshire. The
estate of the abbey was granted at the dissolution to Thomas Holcroft,
whose grandson sold it to the Holfords, from whom it came by marriage to the Cholmondeleys.

TARVIN.

A SMALL town on the border of Delamere forest on the Cheshire
side, had the privilege of a market obtained for it in the reign of queen
Elizabeth, by Sir John Savage, to whom it was alienated from the bi-
shoprick of Litchfield. Its church, a rectory, still continues part of
the see of Litchfield, and is a prebend in that cathedral. Here is a monument of Mr. John Thomasine, thirty-six years master of the grammar school, who was distinguished for his exquisite skill in penman-
ship. He particularly excelled in copying the Greek characters; and
many specimens of his writing are preserved in the cabinets of the curious, and public libraries.

FRODSHAM.

THIS is a very small market-town, consisting chiefly of one wide
street, situated beneath the hills which form the northern extremity of
Delamere forest, and not far from the junction of the Weaver with the
Mersey. A level, bounded by a large marsh, extends from the town
to the latter river. Frodsham had formerly a castle, which, together
with the town, was allotted by Edward I. to David, brother of Llew-
ellyn, the last sovereign of Wales. It was latterly used as a mansion
by the Savages, earls Rivers, and was burned down in 1652. A handsome

some modern houfe now occupies its fite, which is at the weft end of the town, juft beneath a high eminence.

The church of Frodfham ftands on a very elevated fituation above the town, in a part called Overton; and near it is a fchool, with a good houfe for the mafter, on which is a cupola for an obfervatory. The profpect from hence and the neighbouring eminences is very extenfive, commanding the eftuary of the Merfey and its bordering marfhes, and the more diftant parts of Lancafhire beyond. The brow of a hill behind the fchool, called Beacon-hill, is cut into a very pleafant and ftriking walk. At its foot are four fhooting-buts for the practice of archery. The church regifter of Frodfham exhibits two remarkable inftances of longevity; on March 13, 1592, was buried Thomas Hough, aged 141; and on the next day, Randle Wall, aged 103.

Frodfham bridge, over the Weaver, is near a mile to the eaft of the town. From a warehoufe near it, much cheefe is fhipped for Liverpool. A work for the refining of rock-falt is at fome diftance on the bank of the river. The channel here is deep and clayey, and a difagreeable object at low water.

In the parifh of Frodfham, potatoes are cultivated to a great extent. It is eftimated, that not lefs than 100,000 bufhels of 90lb. weight each have annually, for fome years paft, been grown in it. They meet with a ready fale in Lancafhire, to which they find an eafy conveyance by the river to Liverpool, and by the duke of Bridgewater's canal to Manchefter.

BUCKLOW

BUCKLOW HUNDRED.

THIS hundred occupies the middle of the northern fide of the county, from the junction of the Weaver and Merfey, to the border of Macclesfield hundred. On entering it from Frodfham, there appears to the right, on a high bank above the Weaver,

Afton-hall, a large and handfome modern houfe, the feat of the ancient family of Afton. To the left of it lies

RUNCORN PARISH.

THIS tract of country, lying to the eaft of the river Weaver near its conflux with the Merfey, and thence for fome miles upwards on the banks of the latter river, is well worthy of notice, from the variety of its ground and profpects, and the objects of curiofity it contains. The firft place that excites attention, after croffing Frodfham bridge, is

Rock-Savage, a noble pile of ruins, embofomed in wood, and feated on a rifing ground above the Weaver, facing towards Frodfham. This feat was built in the reign of queen Elizabeth by Sir John Savage. By the marriage of lady Elizabeth Savage, daughter and heirefs of Richard, earl Rivers, with James, earl of Barrymore, the houfe and eftate paffed into that family; but the poffeffion proved tranfient; for the marriage of his daughter, lady Penelope Barry, with general Cholmondeley, tranf-ferred it to a new race, and it is now poffeffed by the general's grand nephew, the earl of Cholmondeley. After the marriage, the place was neglected, and fell into fuch fpeedy decay, that a gentleman who was born in the houfe lived to draw a pack of fox hounds through it

after

after their game. Part of the ſtately front, conſiſting of a fine gateway with a lofty turret on each ſide, is ſtill ſtanding, as well as part of one of the ſides. The reſt of the pile conſiſts only of foundation walls, broken vaults, and heaps of rubbiſh overgrown with weeds; the whole ſurrounded with encloſures of dilapidated walls. Few places in the kingdom recal more forcibly to the memory the very ſtriking lines of the poet Dyer deſcriptive of a ruined manſion:

> 'Tis now the raven's bleak abode;
> 'Tis now th' apartment of the toad;
> And there the fox ſecurely feeds;
> And there the poiſonous adder breeds,
> Conceal'd in ruins, moſs, and weeds;
> While, ever and anon there falls
> Huge heaps of hoary moulder'd walls.   *Grongar-Hill.*

In the time of the Barrymores, a large range of detached offices and ſtabling, in a more modern ſtyle than the main building, was erected, which is now converted to the uſes of a farm-houſe.

At a ſhort diſtance from hence, juſt oppoſite to the junction of the Weaver and Merſey, is the ſmall retired village of *Weſton.* From the brow overhanging the point of land where the rivers meet, is a very magnificent water-proſpect at full tide, when the broadeſt part of the eſtuary of the Merſey, ſtretching many miles before the eye, till it is completely land-locked by a turn in the channel, exhibits the appearance of an extenſive lake, bordered on the Cheſhire and Lancaſhire ſide by a variety of ground, partly naked, and partly finely wooded. The ſecluded ſituation of this ſpot, out of all courſe of roads, renders its beauties leſs known than they deſerve to be. Farther on, upon the bank of the Merſey, is ſituated

I   *Runcorn,*

Runcorn, a place well known as the termination of the duke of Bridgewater's canal in the Merfey.   Its fituation was judicioufly chofen by the renowned Ethelfleda, queen of the Mercians, for the foundation of a town and caftle, erected in the year 916; for here, by the projection of a tongue of land from the Lancafhire fide, the bed of the Merfey is fuddenly contracted from a confiderable breadth to a narrow channel, eafily commanded from the fhore.   It was juft oppofite to this *gap*, as it is called, that Ethelfleda built the laft of the range of caftles by which fhe protected the borders of her extenfive domain; and though no veftiges of the building remain, its fite is marked by the name of the *Caftle*, given to a triangular piece of land, furrounded with a mound of earth, jutting out into the river, guarded on the water fide by ledges of rocks and broken precipices, and cut off from the land by a ditch at leaft fix yards wide.   This fortrefs in its entire ftate muft have afforded an excellent defence againft the naval inroads of the Danes, who ran up the rivers with their fleets at that period, and committed the moft cruel ravages.   The parochial church of Runcorn ftands above the caftle-rock.   Its foundation was, perhaps, co-eval with that of Ethelfleda's town; it was certainly prior to the Conqueft, fince Nigel, baron of Halton, beftowed it, in the reign of the Conqueror, upon his brother Wolfrith, a prieft.   It became afterwards the property of Norton abbey, and on the diffolution was given to Chrift-church college, Oxford.   An abbey of canons regular, or Auguftins, was founded here by William, the fon of Nigel, in 1133, which was removed by his fon William, conftable of Chefter, to Norton.

The confequence of Runcorn was loft in the later reigns, and it funk into an obfcure village, from which it has emerged only fince the completion of the duke of Bridgewater's navigation.   The vaft works

H h h   formed

formed here, confifting of a grand feries of *all* the locks on his canal, through which it defcends precipitoufly to the river, and which are fupplied with water by vaft bafons or refervoirs, occafioned a great conflux of workmen, and the confequent building of a number of dwelling-houfes, inns, fhops, &c.   This hurry of bufinefs has fince been kept up by the erection of wharfs, a fea-wall, and an immenfe warehoufe, conftructed upon a new and excellent plan.   Vaft quantities of good free-ftone are likewife got out of the quarries in this place, which lie contiguous to the canal, and allow of the raifing of blocks of great fize, which are ufed in the works about the canal, and are alfo conveyed to different places in the courfe of it.   At Manchefter this ftone is fold at eight-pence the fquare foot.

On account of thefe curiofities, Runcorn is much vifited by parties of pleafure from the country round, fome of whom make excurfions by water hence to Liverpool.   It has likewife of late become a place of fome refort for falt-water bathing, for in fpring tides the fmall quantity of frefh water in the Merfey does not much dilute the ftrength of the fea-water flowing up this wide eftuary; and the agreeable fituation and good air of the place and its neighbourhood are ufeful auxiliaries to the effects of the bath.   The fhore here, and all round to Wefton point, is protected by a low ridge of rock rifing almoft perpendicularly from the beach.   The lovers of botany may find a pleafing variety of plants, both maritime and inland, in the vicinity of this place.

A mile or two upwards from Runcorn are feated the ruins of *Halton-caftle*, placed on a fteep elevation, and forming a confpicuous object from all this fide of the country.   Hugh Lupus, earl of Chefter, gave the barony of Halton to Nigel, his relation and one of his officers,

whom

whom he also made constable of Chester, and his marshal; and the castle was probably founded by one of the two. The manor had large privileges conferred upon it; the town of Halton was created a free borough and market town, though now no more than a village. From the posterity of Nigel it came to the house of Lancaster, and was a favourite hunting seat of John of Gaunt. It is now a considerable member of the duchy of Lancaster, having a large jurisdiction round it called Halton-fee, or the Honor of Halton, and possessing a court of record and various privileges. The castle has been in a state of demolition ever since the civil wars of Charles I.; but there is a newer building, used as an inn, containing the court-house, and called a prison, though now never used as such. The earl of Cholmondeley is proprietor under the crown. It is, however, for the prospect this place affords that it deserves visiting, which is without question the most delightful in Cheshire. Northwards, from side to side, the Mersey, winding through a fertile plain, may be distinctly traced from the neighbourhood of Warrington, where it is of the breadth of the Thames at Richmond, to its expansion into a wide channel, contracted at Runcorn-gap, and then again dilating into the estuary which continues to the sea. At low water the river is somewhat deformed by the extensive sandy shoals with which its bed is almost filled; but when the tide is in, and the scene is enlivened by a number of vessels passing and re-passing, few water prospects can be more pleasing. Beyond the Mersey, the county of Lancaster, appearing like a vast forest from the numerous hedgerow trees of its enclosures, extends till lost in the distant hills of Lancashire and Yorkshire. Westward, a large reach into Cheshire, bounded by the Welch mountains, is seen, and immediately under the eye lie the scattered houses and farms of Halton; while to the east, the fine house and grounds of Norton, the seat of Sir Richard Brooke, afford a near

H h h 2

landscape

landfcape of great beauty. Through the pleafure grounds of Norton the duke of Bridgewater's canal is led in an elegantly winding courfe, and proceeding beneath Halton to Runcorn, adds another interefting object to the profpect.

Halton has a chapel, under the church of Runcorn, and a neat but fmall library, left for public ufe, furnifhed chiefly with old books of hiftory and divinity, fome of them valuable.

The houfe at *Norton* is built upon the fite of an ancient monaftery of Auguftines, the lands of which were conferred on the family of Brooke at the diffolution.

On purfuing the courfe of the canal eaftwards, we come to *Prefton-Brook*, near the village of Prefton-on-the-hill, where the duke of Bridgewater's canal, after paffing a tunnel, enters the Staffordfhire navigation. Wharfs are erected here for ftoring goods that go by land to Frodfham, Chefter, and parts adjacent, either brought from Manchefter, or landed from the Staffordfhire canal. The banks of the canal are covered with heaps of flint brought by fea for the ufe of the potteries. The paffage boats from Manchefter come as far as this place.

The next remarkable ftation on the duke of Bridgewater's canal is *Stockton quay*, at London bridge, a mile and a half from Warrington. This is a bufy fcene of traffic from the quantity of goods fhipped and landed at its warehoufes, which lie upon the great London road from the north through Chefhire. A number of carriages are alfo generally in waiting to convey the paffengers who land here from Manchefter in

their

their way to Warrington, and thence by the coaches to Liverpool, &c. The foil hereabouts is a deep fand, which renders the roads very heavy.

Not far from this place rifes the pretty eminence called *Hill-Cliff*, ending precipitoufly towards the north, to which quarter it affords a very pleafing profpect of the canal, the Merfey, the town of Warrington, and all the flat part of Lancafhire as far as the Yorkfhire hills. The fides of the hill are cloathed with plantations, and its fummit is crowned with a fummer-houfe, making a picturefque object from the fubjacent country. A neighbouring hill over which the London road paffes has a large quarry of a red grit-ftone.

The village of *Lymm* is a beautiful object in the courfe of the canal, which is here carried at a great height over a ftream, forming a mill dam, and turning a mill for flitting iron and flattening it into hoops for the cooper's ufe. There are feveral good houfes in the village, and the fituation of the parfonage houfe, above a deep and romantic valley, is much admired. In Lymm is an ancient crofs of Gothic architecture.

KNUTSFORD.

THIS is the principal town of Bucklow hundred. It is divided as it were into two towns, called High and Low Knutsford. By a charter granted in the reign of Edward I. it appears that William de Tableigh was lord of both of them. The lordfhip is now in the duke of Bridgewater. The market-day is Saturday. The upper town has a fair on Tuefday in Whitfun week; and the lower has two, in June and October.

Knutsford

Knutsford is a neat town, containing betwixt two and three thousand inhabitants. It has never been a place of much trade. Its principal manufacture has been that of thread, for which it was long noted. A small portion of the flax used in this manufacture is grown in Yorkshire, but the bulk of it is brought from Ireland, Russia, and Hamburgh. A few years ago it was almost entirely brought in its raw state, and was spun in Knutsford and its neighbourhood; but since the increase of the cotton trade, the flax spinners have been led to engage in this more lucrative employment, and the flax is now principally spun abroad, and is brought to Knutsford in the state of yarn. This manufacture, of course, employs much fewer hands than formerly. The thread is sent to the different parts of England, and some to America.

About twenty-five years since, a large building was erected in the town for doubling and twisting of silk for the use of the London manufacturers. It was used for this purpose for some years, and employed a considerable number of hands; but not being found to answer, the employment was discontinued. The building has since been used for the spinning of cotton, a branch of trade in which, within these few years, this town has partaken, though in no considerable degree; and, indeed, since the late check given to trade, very few hands are employed in it.

Knutsford is particularly noted for the numerous families of gentry residing in its neighbourhood, which contribute much to the support of the town. It has an elegant assembly room, where they have frequent meetings; and the races here are inferior to few in the kingdom for the display of fashionable company.

The

C. Dayes del.^t

Pollard sculp.

VIEW OF TATTON HALL.

Publish'd for...

The church is a handfome brick building, of modern erection, and lately furnifhed with an organ. The old church was about a mile from the town, and fome portion of it is ftill kept ftanding, as an ornamental object from the grounds of a neighbouring gentleman (P. Legh, Efq. of Booths.) It is a vicarage, and is reckoned worth betwixt 200 and £.300 per annum.

A cuftom prevails in this town, which is, we believe, confined to it. On the marriage of any inhabitant of the town or neighbourhood, in addition to the common tokens of joy, as ringing of bells, &c. the friends and acquaintances of the parties ftrew the ftreets with brown fand, and on this, figure with white fand various fanciful and emblematical devices, and over the whole are occafionally ftrewed the flowers of the feafon. This cuftom ferves at leaft this good end, that it keeps the ftreets clean.

At a fmall diftance round Knutsford are the following feats : *Tabley-houfe*, Sir J. F. Leicefter's ; *Tatton-hall*, Mr. Egerton's ; *Mere-hall*, Mr. Brookes's ; *Booth's-hall*, Mr. Legh's ; *Arley-hall*, Sir Peter Warburton's ; *Toft-hall*, Mr. Leicefter's ; *High-Legh-hall*, Mr. Legh's ; *Capefthorne*, Mr. Davenport's ; *Aftle*, Mr. Parker's ; *Withington*, Mr. Glegg's ; and many other old family manfions. Of thefe feats, *Tabley* and *Tatton* are the moft confiderable. *Tatton*, of which a view is annexed, has a very extenfive park of near 25,000 acres of arable and pafture land. The houfe is new, and defigned by Wyatt, in a tafte of elegant fimplicity ; only one fide, which is of ftone, and the offices, are yet built. The ftables, which are alfo new and defigned by the fame architect, are in a fimilar ftyle. The fituation of the houfe is very fine, being on an elevated fpot of ground in the middle of the park, from the front of which a lawn falls gradually to a fine piece of water, called

Tatton-mere, at fomewhat more than half a mile's diftance. The view beyond the mere, after taking in a variety of leffer objects, is terminated by Alderly-edge, and the diftant hills dividing Chefhire from the neighbouring counties, among which the bold termination of *the Cloud*, near Congleton, is particularly ftriking. The gardens are very extenfive, and kept with peculiar neatnefs, and the pinery is remarkably large and well conftructed.

Tabley Houfe, the feat of Sir John Fleming Leicefter, Bart. is an elegant and noble edifice, the chef d'œuvre of the celebrated architect Carr. The portico is executed in the Doric order, and is remarkable for the fize of its pillars, which are the largeft in the kingdom, confifting of fingle ftones. The ftables, which are juft finifhed, may be confidered as a perfect model, both as to magnificence and convenience. They confift of a neat, elegant quadrangle, in the middle of which is a fpacious riding houfe. The offices belonging to the ftables, for fuch they may with great propriety be ftyled, are convenient beyond defcription.

A part of the old manfion remains at a confiderable diftance in the park, and forms a very picturefque and venerable ruin. It was the original habitation of that celebrated antiquarian, Sir Peter Leycefter, Bart. author of the Antiquities of Chefhire, &c. The park is evtenfive, through which runs a beautiful ftream that is formed into a fpacious fheet of water.

Booth's-hall, the feat of Peter Legh, Efq. of which a view is annexed, is a plain houfe, built of brick and ftone, with an extenfive park, containing fome fine pieces of water, particularly the lake over which the houfe is feen in the view. The profpect from the manfion is very beautiful, the eye ranging over a great extent of country well di-

3   verfified,

E. Dayes del.ᵗ

VIEW OF BOOTH'S HALL.

C. Barrow sculp.ᵗ

verfified, in which the lake and canal, making a confpicuous figure, render it a truly charming fituation.

Here is a fine picture of Guerchino, the Death of Dido : it contains fome beautiful paffages, and the air of the heads is inimitably graceful. This feat is one mile from Knutsford.

ALTRINGHAM.

THIS is a fmall, but very neat, town, fituated in the courfe of the duke of Bridgewater's canal, eight miles from Manchefter. It is governed by a mayor, and has a guild mercatory for free traffic, granted to it by charter from Hamon de Maffey, lord of Dunham Maffey, about the year 1290. Its trade, notwithftanding, is inconfiderable. It has a market on Saturday, and a fair on St. James's day, formerly extremely crowded by company from Manchefter, but now little frequented. The number of people in Altringham was accurately taken in 1772, when there appeared to be 248 families, and 1029 inhabitants. About twenty years before the number was very near 1000, fo that the population has not greatly been affected by the neighbourhood of manufactures. The fpinning of combed worfted prevailed formerly throughout this diftrict, the wool being delivered out at Manchefter by thofe who employed Jerfey-combers there, to the people when they came to market, and the worfted yarn being fold to the fmall-ware manufacturers : but the introduction of Irifh worfted ruined the bufinefs. Some ftuffs for home wear are, however, ftill made from the houfewifes' fpinning in thefe diftricts. It is fingular that this town has no church or chapel,

I i i

its

its inhabitants being obliged to go to the parifh church of Bowden, above a mile's diftance, for public worfhip.

Not far from Altringham is *Dunham Maffey*, the feat of the earl of Stamford, a houfe of no great appearance, but fpacious and commodious within. It is chiefly built of brick, of a quadrangular form, with a court in the centre, and contains many family pictures. It is feated in the midft of an extenfive park, full of fine timber, the unmolefted growth of many years, through which avenues or viftas are cut, affording views of the hall. Several of the oaks are of extraordinary magnitude, making a moft venerable appearance; and on their tops is a heronry, in which thofe birds build in fociety like rooks. The ground near the houfe has lately been laid out in an ornamental manner with fhrubberies, flower-beds, &c. This manfion was long the feat of the Booths, firft lords Delamere, then earls of Warrington. By the death of George, the late earl, in 1758, the title became extinct; but the eftate came into the poffeffion of the earl of Stamford, who had married his only daughter, the mother of the prefent earl. This noble family have long afforded to the country an inftructive example of the virtues by which rank and fortune are made truly ufeful and refpectable. The annexed view was taken in 1793.

NORTHWICH HUNDRED.

THIS is fituated to the fouth of the laft-mentioned hundred, and principally comprehends the tracts lying on each fide of the rivers Dane and Wheelock. It is well furnifhed with market-towns, of which the principal is that which gives name to the hundred.

C.Dayes del:

Pollard sculp:

VIEW OF DUNHAM.

NORTHWICH.

THIS is a fmall and ancient market-town fituated at the conflux of the Dane with the Weaver. Its market is on Friday. It has two annual fairs, in Auguft and December, which have lately become much frequented, to the great advantage of the inhabitants. It has a well endowed free-grammar fchool. From its central fituation, furrounded with gentlemen's feats; it is a place of confiderable refort for the tranfaction of public bufinefs, and other purpofes.

Northwich is, however, principally diftinguifhed as the chief of the falt towns, and the only one of them which, in addition to brine fprings, poffeffes mines of rock-falt. The difcovery of this valuable mineral was made about a century ago, in the lands of William Marbury, Efq. of Marbury, near this town. It has fince been found in the adjoining townfhips of Wilton, Marfton, Wincham, and Winnington; but in no other part of the kingdom than this neighbourhood. The inhabitants, however, have a tradition that the rock as well as the brine pits were wrought in the time of the Romans.

Rock-falt is found from twenty-eight to forty-eight yards beneath the furface of the earth. The firft ftratum or mine met with is from fifteen to twenty-one yards in thicknefs, perfectly folid, and fo hard as to be cut with great difficulty with iron picks and wedges. Of late, the workmen have blafted it with gunpowder, by which they loofen and remove many tons together. The appearance of the falt is extremely refembling that of brown fugar-candy. Beneath this ftratum is a bed of hard ftone, confifting of large veins of flag, intermixed with fome

rock

rock falt, the whole from twenty-five to thirty-five yards in thickness. Under this bed is a fecond ftratum, or mine, of falt, from five to fix yards thick, many parts of it perfectly white, and clear as cryftal, others browner, but all purer than the upper ftratum, yet reckoned not fo ftrong. Above the whole mafs of falt lies a bed of whitifh clay, which has been ufed in the Liverpool earthen ware ; and in the fame place is found a good deal of gypfum, or plaifter ftone.

Rock-falt pits are funk at great expence, and are very uncertain in their duration, being frequently deftroyed by the brine fprings burfting into them, and diffolving the pillars, by which the whole work falls in, leaving vaft chafms on the furface of the earth. In forming a pit, a fhaft or eye is funk, fimilar to that of a coal-pit, but more extenfive. After the workmen have got down to the falt-rock, and made a proper cavity, they leave a fufficient fubftance of the rock, about feven yards in thicknefs, to form a folid roof, and as they proceed, they hew pillars out of the rock for the fupport of that roof, and then employ gun-powder to feparate what they mean to raife. When well illuminated, the cryftalline furface of the roof, pillars, and fides of a large pit, make a glittering and magnificent appearance. Frefh air is conveyed from the mouth of the pit by means of a tube, to which is fixed a pair of forge bellows, forming a continual current between the outer air and that in the pit. The pits at the greateft depth are dry, and of a comfortable temperature.

The largeft rock-falt pit now worked, is in the townfhip of Witton, and in the lands of Nicholas Afhton, Efq. It is worked in a circular form, 108 yards in diameter, its roof fupported by twenty-five pillars, each three yards wide at the front, four at the back, and its fides ex-

tending

tending fix yards. The pit is fourteen yards hollow; confequently each pillar contains 294 folid yards of rock falt; and the whole area of the pit contains 9160 fuperficial yards, little lefs than two acres of land.

The average quantity of rock-falt annually delivered from the pits in the neighbourhood of Northwich for the laft feven years is 50,484 tons. Another account ftates the annual average (no period mentioned) at about 65,000 tons. Upon this laft calculation, the mode in which the rock-falt is difpofed of is ftated to be, exported to Dunkirk, Oftend, Riga, Bruges, Nieuport, Pillau, Elfineur, &c. from 45 to 50,000 tons : ditto to Ireland, from 3000 to 4000 tons : refined in England, viz.

At Northwich,	5000 tons,	Liverpool,	3000 tons,
Frodfham, -	3000 do.	Dungeon works,	2500 do.

The rock-falt, as well as the white falt, made at Northwich, is conveyed down the Weaver, and thence by the Merfey to Liverpool in veffels from fifty to eighty tons burthen, and there re-fhipped for foreign countries, or kept for refinement. We have already mentioned the great advantage Liverpool has derived from poffeffing fuch an article for the ballaft-loading of its outward-bound fhips.

Northwich likewife much furpaffes the other falt towns in the falt made from brine fprings ; and being, therefore, the centre of the Chefhire falt trade, we fhall take this occafion of concluding all we have further to fay concerning this product.

The

The average quantity of falt made from the Chefhire brine fprings, which are inexhauftible in quantity, and many of them fully faturated, is fuppofed to be nearly,

At Northwich, - - 45,000 tons,	Lawton, - - 1500 tons,
Winsford, - - - 15,000 do.	Namptwich, - 60 do.
Middlewich, - - 4000 do.	

If to thefe numbers be added, for refined rock-falt, at

Northwich, - 5000 tons,   Frodfham, - 4000 tons.

the whole quantity of falt made in Chefhire will appear; viz. about 74,560 tons.

The ufual depth of the brine fprings is from twenty to forty yards. The mode of cryftallifing falt, is by putting the brine into large iron pans, of twenty or thirty feet fquare, and fourteen inches deep, where it is heated till it boils : a light fcum then rifes to the top, which being taken off, the liquor is reduced to a lower degree of heat; the fteam arifing is made to evaporate as quickly as poffible; and the falt cryftallifing forms a cruft on the furface, which finks to the bottom of the pan, whence it is taken out once or twice in twenty-four hours. The quantity annually cryftallifed is computed at about 35,000 tons. All the fine hard bafket falt is not cryftallifed. Of the white falt, about 15 or 16,000 tons are confumed in England and Wales, exclufive of what is refined from rock-falt. The duty on falt confumed at home is 5s. per bufhel of 56lb., or £.10 per ton, grofs duty, fubject to a difcount of 10 per cent. on refined, and 7½ on white falt; the duty paid weekly. All falt is exported duty free, the exporter giving bond for the amount of the duty, which is cancelled by debenture obtained from the cuftom-houfe when the veffel clears. No falt has been allowed to be ufed as manure, fince the year 1778, when an act paffed to levy an equal duty

I   on on all falt of what quality foever. The obftacle this affords to agricultural improvements has already been noted.

The revenue arifing from falt is thought of fo much confequence, that a particular board is appointed for the collection and management of it, having a department quite independent on the excife and cuftoms. Not a peck of falt can go from the works without a permit, under the rifque of forfeiture and high penalties; and officers are ftationed on the roads to demand a fight of permits, and to re-weigh on fufpicion of fraud.

The number of hands employed in Chefhire in getting rock-falt, and making white and refined falt, is fuppofed to be about 1200.

Winnington-hall, very pleafantly fituated on the Weaver within a mile of Northwich, is the feat of lord Penrhyn.

Acrofs the river, and in the hundred of Bucklow, is *Marbury-hall*, the feat of the Barry family, in the parifh, and clofe to the extenfive meer of Great Budworth.

MIDDLEWICH.

THIS place derives its name from being the middlemoft of the *Wiches*, or falt towns. It is feated at the conflux of the Dane with the Croke. Middlewich is an ancient borough, governed by its burgeffes, and poffeffing the fame privileges with the other falt towns. Its market is on Tuefday, and it has annual fairs on July 25th, and on Holy Thurfday. The church is a vicarage, comprehending a large parifh divided into many townfhips. The falt here is made from brine fprings well faturated; the quantity is not very confiderable, but might be increafed on demand. The Staffordfhire canal paffes by the town. Middlewich is a tolerably well-built place, of moderate fize and pleafantly fituated.

Near

Near Middlewich is *Kinderton*, which gave title to one of the ancient barons who compofed the upper houfe of the parliament of the earls of Chefter.   This was the family of Venables, now reprefented by lord Vernon of Kinderton, the only lineal fucceffor of the eight Chefhire barons, who has defcended to our times.

Not far from hence is *Holm's-chapel*, formerly a great thoroughfare for paffengers from Lancafhire to London by Talk-on-the-Hill, but of late years much lefs frequented, on account of the new roads by Buxton and Derby, and by Congleton and Leek.   Its manor belongs to the family of Needham.

Rudheath, a wild and fpacious diftrict in this neighbourhood, was formerly a place of refuge for criminals, who were protected here from juftice for the fpace of a year and a day.   But this noxious privilege was found to be fuch a nuifance to the country, that it was abolifhed even before the fuppreffion of popery.

SANDBACH.

THIS fmall town is fituated on a high bank upon the little river Wheelock, not far from Middlewich.   It was made a market-town in the laft century by its lord, Sir John Radcliffe of Ordfall, Lancafhire: its market-day is Thurfday, and it has two annual fairs, in Eafter week and September.   In the market-place are two fquare croffes, with images, and the ftory of the Paffion engraved on them.   Formerly, worfted yarn, and fome ftuffs for country wear were made here, but its trade has much declined.   It was likewife famous for its malt liquor.

Brereton.

Brereton-hall, in its neighbourhood, was the feat of the ancient family of that name. Near it is a pool, concerning which it was the tradition of the place, that trunks of trees were feen floating upon it for feveral days together before the death of an heir of the family. A fair is kept yearly on Lammas day on Brereton-green.

CONGLETON.

THIS town is fituated on the upper part of the Dane, near the borders of Staffordfhire. It is a fmall corporation, being governed by a mayor and fix aldermen. The buildings are neat; the market-day is Saturday, and there are four yearly fairs. Congleton has two churches, one in the town, one at the bridge end acrofs the river; both under the mother church of Aftbury, two miles diftant. This place was formerly noted for the making of tagged leather laces, called Congleton points. It has now a manufactory of gloves, with fome ferreting; but the chief employment for the poor is derived from a very capital filk mill, erected on the river, and from the manufactory of ribands on account of the Coventry merchants.

Aftbury is a large parifh, containing many gentlemens' feats. It has a handfome church, with a lofty fpire fteeple. In the church-yard are two ancient ftone monuments, with the infignia of knighthood upon them, but it is not determined to what families they belong.

Lawton, at the fouth weftern extremity of the hundred, on the Staffordfhire border, contains the feat of the family of that name, which has inhabited this place for many generations. There is a confiderable

K k k

falt

falt work in this parifh, which has the advantage of the Staffordfhire canal pafling through it.

―――――

MACCLESFIELD HUNDRED.

THIS is the moft extenfive hundred in Chefhire, comprifing all its north-eaftern fide, and partaking of the wild and hilly character of the adjacent parts of Derbyfhire and Yorkfhire. A great part of it was anciently a foreft, and a confiderable diftrict ftill retains the name of Macclesfield foreft, though at prefent a naked and dreary tract. The head of this diftrict, and alfo of the hundred, is

MACCLESFIELD,

A BOROUGH or corporate town. Its firft charter was granted in 1261 by Edward, fon of Henry III., afterwards king Edward I. It conferred the privileges of a merchants' guild free from toll throughout the county of Chefter, and a common pafture, and contained the ufual obligations on the burgeffes to grind and bake at the king's mill and oven, and to pay a fhilling for each burgage. This charter was confirmed by many of the fucceeding kings, with various additional privileges.

The corporation confifts of twenty-four aldermen, four of whom are in the commiffion of the peace, and one is mayor and juftice of the quorum. Its officers are a town-clerk and coroner, two ferjeants at mace, four javelin men, and a conftable or town crier. The mayor is always lord of the manor, the revenue of which amounts to about £.200 per annum, arifing from tolls, and the money paid for water, which is conveyed by pipes from fprings on the common. He alfo has the right of nominating the preacher or minifter of the parochial church.

Macclef-

Macclesfield ſtands upon the deſcent of a ſteep hill, waſhed by a branch of the Bollin, which runs through the loweſt part of the town, commonly named the Waters. It is well ſupplied with good water from the ſprings on the common above-mentioned. It has two churches of the eſtabliſhment, and five other places of worſhip. The old church or parochial chapel of St. Michael was founded by Edward I. and Eleanor his queen, in the ſeventh year of his reign. It was ſome time afterwards enlarged; and being decayed, was taken down to the chancel, enlarged and rebuilt in 1740, at the expence of £.1000. It is a large Gothic building, and has two chapels annexed to it. One of theſe was built by Thomas Savage, archbiſhop of York, whoſe heart was buried here in 1508; and was made the burial-place of the Savages, afterwards earls Rivers, to whom there are various marble monuments. It now belongs to earl Cholmondeley. The other chapel belongs to the Leghs, of Lyme; one of whom, Perkin a Legh, buried here, is ſaid by an inſcription to have obtained the eſtate and lordſhip of Lyme as a reward for his ſervices in the battle of Creſſy.

The new church, called Chriſt-church, built by the late Charles Roe, Eſq. is a regular, elegant ſtructure, having a ſteeple with ten bells, and a handſome organ. Over the altar is a fine buſt of Mr. Roe, executed by Bacon. This church was begun in March 1775, and opened for divine ſervice on Chriſtmas day in the ſame year, with near 800 communicants.

Macclesfield has a large and elegant free-grammar ſchool, with a ſpacious dwelling-houſe for the head-maſter, and a field for the boys to exerciſe. It has been brought into much reputation by the preſent maſter, who has a number of boarders, and aſſiſtants in various branches

of

of learning. The fchool was founded by Edward VI. : its original endowment was to the amount of £.25 in houfes and lands; but fo great
have been the improvements of the town, that they now produce near
£.800 per annum.

The feffions for the hundred and foreft are held at Macclesfield every
Eafter and Michaelmas to try all caufes lefs than felony. An inferior
court is held by the mayor and juftices every Friday for petty caufes,
and a bench of juftices fits every Monday. The market day is Monday, and there are fairs on St. Barnabas and All Souls' days.

In the town's-box is preferved a copy of a petition fent to king Henry
VII. foon after the battle of Bofworth, fetting forth, that having loft fo
many of the principal inhabitants of the town in the battle, they were
unable to fill up the number of aldermen required by the charter; on
which account they petitioned his majefty that their charter might not be
confidered as broken, their townfmen having loft their lives in his fervice.

Henry Stafford, the great duke of Buckingham, the inftrument of
the ambition of Richard III., lived here in great ftate and hofpitality.
Of his manfion there are ftill fome remains.

With refpect to the trade of Macclesfield, that of wrought buttons in
filk, mohair, and twift, is properly its ftaple. The hiftory of this
button trade affords fome curious particulars. The ufe of them may be
traced 150 years backwards; and they were once curioufly wrought
with the needle, making a great figure in full-trimmed fuits. Macclesfield was always confidered as the centre of this trade, and mills

were

were erected long ago both there and at Stockport for winding filk and making twift for buttons, and trimming fuitable to them.

In the wild country between Buxton, Leek, and Macclesfield, called the *Flafh*, from a chapel of that name, lived a fet of pedeftrian chapmen, who hawked about thefe buttons, together with ribands and ferreting made at Leek, and handkerchiefs, with fmall wares from Manchefter. Thefe pedlars were known on the roads which they travelled by the appellation of *Flafh-men*, and frequented farm-houfes and fairs, ufing a fort of flang or canting dialect. At firft they paid ready money for their goods, till they acquired credit, which they were fure to extend till no more was to be had; when they dropped their connections without paying, and formed new ones. They long went on thus, enclofing the common where they dwelt for a trifling payment, and building cottages, till they began to have farms, which they improved from the gains of their credit, without troubling themfelves about payment, fince no bailiff for a long time attempted to ferve a writ there. At length, a refolute officer, a native of the diftrict, ventured to arreft feveral of them; whence their credit being blown up, they changed the wandering life of pedlars for the fettled care of their farms. But as thefe were held by no leafes, they were left at the mercy of the lords of the foil, the Harpur family, who made them pay for their impofitions on others.

Another fet of pedeftrians from the country where buttons were formerly made, was called the *Broken-crofs Gang*, from a place of that name between Macclesfield and Congleton. Thefe affociated with the Flafh-men at fairs, playing with thimbles and buttons, like jugglers with cups and balls, and enticing people to lofe their money by gambling. They at length took to the kindred trades of robbing and pick-

ing

ing pockets, till at length the gang was broken up by the hands of juftice. We cannot but remark, that Autolycus in Shakefpear feems to
have been a model of this worthy brotherhood.

In order to favour the button trade, an act of parliament paffed
about eighty years ago, inflicting a penalty upon the wearing of
moulds covered with the fame ftuff with the garment; and this, after
having fallen into neglect, was again attempted to be enforced with
rigour in 1778, and hired informers were engaged in London and
the country to put it into execution—an odious and very uncommercial
mode of enforcing a manufacture! the refult of which was rather
to promote the ufe of metal and horn buttons. The trade is ftill,
however, confiderable.

Macclesfield has likewife between twenty and thirty filk mills, and
many cotton factories; for here, as well as in the other Chefhire towns,
the cotton trade is gaining ground upon the older branches of manufacture. It has alfo a very extenfive work for fmelting and working
copper, and making brafs. This is fituated upon a large common to the eaft of the town; and confifts, firft, of a large fquare
building, called the fmelting houfes, where the ore is melted and refined, and the metal caft into fhot. In this building large furnace-bricks
and melting pots are likewife made. There is next a large windmill
for grinding the ore; and near it are the calamy houfes, a range of low
buildings, where the calamine is repeatedly wafhed in running water.
The brafs houfes are a number of lofty buildings where copper is made
into fheets for the fheathing of fhips; and pan bottoms, brafs wire and
brafs nails are manufactured. Before the works are three large refervoirs for the fupply of water, and a row of dwelling houfes for the numerous workmen. A large colliery with four feams of coal, one above
                                                    another,

C. Dayes delin.t

The Barr sculp.c

VIEW OF MACCLESFIELD.

Publish'd June 7 1794 by I. Stockdale Piccadilly.

another, is on the fame common, whence the town and the copper works are fupplied with fuel. A capital brewery in the neighbourhood of the works is furnifhed with water from a hill much higher than its roof. In the front of it runs the river, which turns the corn mill and a number of filk mills.

The houfes in Macclesfield are more than doubled within thefe twenty-five years. The town is now a mile and a quarter in length; and the new buildings on each fide of the London road form a confiderable part of the additions. The annexed view of Macclesfield was taken from Stanley's acre.

Coal abounds in the neighbourhood of Macclesfield, which fupplies the furrounding country, and is ufed for the burning of the lime of Buxton. The townfhip of *Bollington* has a very large fteam engine belonging to a coal pit; and on the river here is a curious water machine for grinding bark, and a large cotton work, with very complete machinery for all the branches of that manufacture. The townfhip of *Rainow* has a fmaller one of the fame kind, and likewife a large colliery.

There are various gentlemens' feats in the neighbourhood of Macclef-field, particularly towards the weft and north, fome of which we fhall enumerate.

Henbury-hall, late the feat of Sir William Meredith, is now occupied by Mr. Jodrell, who has rendered it a very delightful refidence.

Capefthorne, a feat with a fmall park, is the manfion of the Davenport family.

On

On the weſt ſide of that elevated tract of ground called Alderley-edge, is ſituated *Alderley-hall*, the property and late reſidence of Sir J. T. Stanley, Bart. to whom the greater part of that tract belongs. This houſe was in great part deſtroyed by fire a few years ago. It is ſurrounded with a fine moat of running water, well ſtocked with fiſh. Adjoining is the old park, which contains ſome remarkably large beech trees.

Northwards from Macclesfield is *Preſtbury*, reckoned the largeſt pariſh in Cheſhire, and having under it a number of chapels in the circumjacent country. Its living, a vicarage, is in the gift of Mrs. Legh, the heireſs of the eſtates of the Leghs of Adlington, whoſe ſeat, *Adlington-hall*, is at á ſmall diſtance on the road to Stockport. Belonging to it is an extenſive park, ſtocked with a great quantity of fine oak timber of conſiderable growth, and moſt of it fit for cutting. A fine ſtream flows through the midſt of the park. The old cuſtom of driving the deer through a ſheet of water is ſtill continued here.

Mottram St. Andrew-hall, Mr. Wright's; and *Pott Shrigley*, Mr. Downes's, lie to the weſt and eaſt of Adlington.

More to the eaſt, among the hills, is *Lyme-hall*, the ſeat of the principal of the families of the name of Legh, which alſo poſſeſſes Haydock in Lancaſhire; at preſent repreſented by Thomas Legh, Eſq. M. P. for Newton, and colonel of a regiment of light-horſe raiſed by himſelf. The building is on a quadrangular plan, forming a large court, with a piazza round three ſides of it, which gives the whole an air of grandeur. It is irregular, the N. and E. angles being of the date of Elizabeth or James I. and the S. and W. a regular Ionic ſtructure from a deſign of Leoni. The ſituation is bad; the country round barren and mooriſh;

and

E. Dayes del.?

VIEW OF LIME HALL.

Publish'd Feb: 27. 1790. by I. Stockdale, Picadilly.

W. Wilson sculp.?

E. Dayes del.

Pollard sculp.t

VIEW OF POYNTON.

Publish'd Nov. 7. 1794. by I. Stockdale, Piccadilly.

and though the elevation is fuch as to render it much expofed to the wind, there is no view from the houfe. It ftands in the midft of a very extenfive park, well ftocked with deer, which are famous for taking the water when driven by the keeper. The foil appears to fuit thefe animals, as the venifon is of a fuperior flavour. On the top of an eminence in the park is a building called Lyme Cage, a very confpicuous object from the country round.

On the road from Macclesfield to Stockport, at four miles diftance from the latter, is *Poynton*, the feat of Sir George Warren, Bart. K. B. The houfe is an elegant piece of architecture of the Ionic order, and is decorated with beautiful pleafure grounds and a fine piece of water, as fhown in the annexed view, which was taken from the Stockport road. The park is very extenfive and well laid out, and from one part of it is a delightful profpect, taking in Stockport and Manchefter, and ftretching away to the remote parts of Lancafhire. The park has lately been much augmented. It contains confiderable quantities of timber in various parts of it, but its fubterraneous riches, confifting of thick veins of coal of the beft quality, are inexhauftible. The following fingular ftory is related of their difcovery. An old tenant of one of the farms had long laboured under the inconvenience of being obliged to fetch his water at a diftance. He had frequently petitioned his landlord that he might have a well funk, which had often been promifed, but its execution neglected. Wearied out at length, he gave notice that he fhould quit the premifes. Sir George not willing to lofe a refpectable farmer, who had long been his neareft neighbour, affured him that his requeft for a well fhould be complied with, and had the work immediately fet about. The fpring lay a confiderable depth; and before they got to the water, the workmen were agreeably furprized with finding one of

L l l

the

the fineſt veins of coal in that country.   It has continued to be worked
with great ſuccefs ever ſince ; and the lucky diſcovery has greatly en-
hanced the value of the park and eſtate.   The farmer ſtill reſides on the
ſpot.

One mile further is *Bullock Smithy*, a village of conſiderable length.
Here Mr. Legh, of Booths, has built an elegant, ſmall houſe, called
Torkington-lodge, placed upon a riſing ground, and ſurrounded with
pleaſure grounds laid out with taſte.   At Torkington, the road turns
off for Buxton, through Diſley.   It is a good road, though hilly, and
commands delightful proſpects in various parts.

STOCKPORT.

THIS town, ſeated on the Lancaſhire border, was one of the eight
baronies of Cheſhire, and has a charter from its ancient lord, Robert de
Stokeport, who granted an homeſtead and an acre of land to each of his
burgeſſes, on the yearly payment of one ſhilling.   The lordſhip, as well
as the patronage of the rectory, is now in Sir George Warren, of
Poynton.   From its vicinity to Mancheſter, the diſtance being only
ſeven miles, it has participated in a great degree in the flouriſhing ſtate
of the commerce of that town ; ſo that it may now be reckoned the ſecond town in Cheſhire for conſequence, and probably ſuperior to Cheſter itſelf in population.   On this account we ſhall deſcribe it with
ſome minuteneſs.

The

The ground on which it ſtands is very irregular. The market place and pariſh church are ſeated on the ſummit of a hill, affording a level of conſiderable extent. This ground conſiſts of a ſolid rock of ſoft free-ſtone, with an extremely ſteep deſcent on the north, towards the Merſey, but eaſy of acceſs on the other ſides. Part of the northern ſide is perpendicular for a height equal to that of the houſes, of which a row encircles the baſe of the hill, having their backs to it, and concealing it from the view of paſſengers. Some of theſe houſes have apartments hollowed out of the rock, and the appearance of the whole to one who ſurveys it cloſely is very ſingular. On the ſummit of the rock is an upper row of houſes, completely encircling the market-place, which is ſpacious and convenient. From this central part the town ſtretches away in different directions, and by the late great increaſe of buildings has extended on every ſide into the country. Its particular objects we ſhall now deſcribe.

Stockport contains two churches of the eſtabliſhment, four diſſenters', and one quakers' meeting. The old or pariſh church of St. Mary is ſuppoſed to have been built 400 or 500 years ſince. It is a large pile of building, of a ſoft, red free-ſtone, ſimilar to that of the rock on which the town ſtands, which by the force of the weather is ſo waſhed and worn, that it has been neceſſary lately to carry up an additional row of ſtone to ſupport the ſteeple. This church has under it four chapels of eaſe ; and by the improvements of the town and country the value of the living is ſo greatly increaſed, as to be reckoned worth at leaſt £.1200 per annum. The preſent rector is the Rev. Charles Preſcott, an active magiſtrate, and very uſeful member of ſociety. The parſonage houſe at which he reſides is at the top of a hill aſcending from the church, and is a large, handſome building in the midſt of a

L l l 2　　　　　　　　　　garden.

garden. It overlooks the whole town and furrounding country, and enjoys a pleafing view of the windings of the Merfey at the bottom of the hill.

St. Peter's church, confecrated in 1768, was built by Peter Wright, Efq. and endowed by him with £.200 from feveral eftates in Chefhire. It ftands on a hill on the weft fide of the town. The patronage is vefted in Henry O. Wright, Efq. of Mottram St. Andrew. Both the churches are furnifhed with organs; the new church with a very fine one.

There is a grammar-fchool in Stockport, founded in 1487 by the Goldfmith's company in London, and endowed by Edmund Shaw, citizen of London, with £.10 per annum, which is fince, by allowances from the town, advanced to £.36. It is now filled by the Rev. Mr. Hoyle.

There are four bridges in and near the town. The old bridge croffing the Merfey on the Manchefter road, called the Lancafhire bridge, has each end built upon rock, and ftands very high above the water, a neceffary circumftance in a river fubject to fuch fudden and violent fwells as the Merfey is in the upper parts of its courfe. Further to obviate the danger of inundations, it is fuppofed that the rock here has been cut deeper and wider, which is rendered probable by the marks of tools upon it. Directly from this bridge the road to Manchefter rifes up a fteep and difficult afcent; but this inconvenience will be remedied in a new turnpike road now making, which will make a fweep round the hill. About half a mile down the river is Brinkfway-bridge, lately built on the Cheadle road. Up the river, a fhort diftance from Lanca-

fhire.

shire-bridge, is Portwood-bridge, leading to Portwood, a new and thriving village on the Lancashire side of the Mersey; and one mile from Stockport, on the Mottram road, is the New Bridge, built about forty years since, which is a noble structure, making a fine appearance from the river. It consists of a single arch, 210 feet in width, thirty-one feet seven inches high, and sixteen feet thick. Near the old bridge is the very ancient town residence of the Ardens, now the property of John Arden, Esq. It is built of wood and plaister, and being kept in good repair, has a venerable appearance.

Stockport is chiefly supplied with water in the old part of the town by open springs rising in Barn-fields, which are considerably higher than the market-place; these are collected into a reservoir behind St. Peter's church, and from thence carried by pipes to different parts of the town, as well as into the houses on the rocks in the market-place.

We shall now say something of the progress of trade to which this town owes its flourishing condition.

In Stockport were erected the first mills for winding and throwing silk, on a plan procured from Italy; and the persons concerned in the silk factories were reckoned the principal people in the place; but on the decline of this trade, the machinery was applied to cotton spinning; and the different branches of the cotton manufacture are now the chief staple of the town. The people of Stockport first engaged in the spinning of reeled weft, then in weaving checks, and lastly in fustians; and they were so ingenious as to attempt muslins, which were introduced about ten years since upon the invention of the machines called mules, whereby the thread was drawn finer and spun softer than that for weft.

The

'The manufacturers here, with this advantage, produced a fpecies of flowered muflin with borders for aprons and handkerchiefs, by cafting a coarfe fhoot for the figures, and trimming of the float by fciffars neatly before bleaching; fo that the figure was a good imitation of needle work. Weaving fuftians has extended from thence over Cheadle, Gatley, and Northenden, where a few checks or furnitures had been woven before. The cotton trade at Stockport is now fo confiderable, that befides a large number of cotton fpinning fhops, there are twenty-three large cotton factories, four of them worked by fteam engines. The making of hats is likewife a confiderable branch of employment.

The weekly market of Stockport is on Friday. A great quantity of corn and oat-meal are fold at it, and it is accounted the beft market for cheefe in the county. There are four yearly fairs; viz. two in March, one on May-day, and one on the 25th of October.

The police of the town is conducted by one refiding juftice of the peace, two conftables, four churchwardens, and three overfeers of the poor.

The population has of late years been amazingly on the increafe, fo that before the war, houfes could not be built faft enough for the demand. The only documents we have for its prefent ftate are the following. In the year 1794 there were, at the old church, 149 marriages, 415 chriftenings, and 600 burials: the latter number is probably nearly that of all the deaths in the town; and, even upon the fuppofition of the year being an unhealthy one, would imply a population of about 15,000 perfons. In the late affeffment of men for the navy, Stockport raifed twenty men, its *rated* houfes being eftimated at 1358.

3

We

E. Dayes delt.

Storer sculp.

VIEW OF STOCKPORT.

We have before obferved how difficult it is to eftablifh a proportion between the taxed and excufed houfes; but from the manner in which
Stockport is peopled, it is probable that the allowance for non-rated
houfes fhould be as high as in almoft any manufacturing town—perhaps
an equality with the rated houfes. Into this account are not taken the
hamlets of Heaton-Norris, and Portwood, on the Lancafhire fide of
the river, of which the former is reckoned to contain 170 houfes, the
latter about 100. The extenfion of the town is very great, as well on
the Macclesfield and Cheadle fides, as on the Manchefter. The hill to
the weft, on which St. Peter's church is built, is now almoft covered
with buildings.

A branch from the Manchefter and Afhton canal, which is to come
to the top of the high ground on the Lancafhire fide of the river, is
nearly finifhed. Its ufe to fuch a populous and trading place cannot but
be very great.

The annexed view of Stockport was taken in 1793 from Brinkfway
Bank. Brinkfway-bridge is on the left, and behind it part of Lancafhire. In the front is the town. The round tower in the centre is
on a level with the market-place; it is called the Caftle, and is a large
cotton work. To the right of it is the old church, and ftill further
to the right the new church. In the back ground on the right is the
noted hill called Wernerth Low, which is pafture to the top: acrofs it
is the old road to Mottram, and from behind it comes down the Merfey. From the fpot whence the view was taken, we diftinctly fee up
the valley between the two hills. The Woodhead, where the light
breaks in, is fixteen miles diftant.

The

The land in the neighbourhood of Stockport is chiefly pasture, and in general very good, supplying the town plentifully with milk and butter. It lets, however, at a very high rate; and the land sold for building before the war brought such prices as were never known.

Very lately, a spring of mineral water, appearing to come from a coal mine or bed of iron stone, was discovered near the town. It was reported to be a cure for weak eyes, and was for a time frequented by great numbers of people, well and ill, some of whom drank the water. About this time the jaundice became very epidemical in and about Stockport, and this was by some imputed to the use of the mineral water; in consequence of which it came to be entirely neglected.

Between Stockport and the New-bridge, a very extensive cotton factory was lately erected at a large expence by Mr. Doxon. The water is brought to it from the Merfey above the New-bridge by means of a subterraneous tunnel, and in summer it takes every drop of the water, to the great surprize of the traveller, who passes over a vast arch which seems thrown over a channel perfectly dry. The erection of this work has caused a number of dwelling houses for the workmen to be built, which form a street on the road side.

On the left, about two miles further, upon the bank of the Tame, stands *Harden-hall*, the old family residence of the Ardens, and now the property of John Arden, Esq. It is said to have been once occupied by John of Gaunt, but it is now no more than a farm house. It is surrounded by a moat, kept in good condition. The building is of a Gothic design, composed of a centre and two wings, making the figure of an H. The centre part on the ground floor is all one room, very

large,

E. Dayes del.

Wilson sculp.

VIEW OF HARDEN HALL.

large, awkward, and high. The windows are large, but give little light. The walls are wainfcotted to the ceiling. A few old-fafhioned chairs, with worked feats, are left in the room, and it is decorated with feveral old portraits, but none of them good ones. The upper rooms are fmall. The houfe ftands on the brow of a fteep hill. At the back of it is a watch tower, which, with the whole of the building, is in good repair, though the date of its erection is 1500 and odd. The annexed view was taken in 1793.

Denton, a long, ftraggling village on the Lancafhire fide of the Tame, one mile from Harden-hall, has increafed much of late, and is principally occupied by hatters, cotton-fpinners, and colliers.

On the weftern fide of Stockport, at three miles diftance, is *Cheadle*, a neat and pleafant village on the Merfey, having an ancient parifh church. Its manor formerly went in two portions, one to the family of Savages, the other to the Bulkeleys.

About an equal diftance on the eaftern fide of Stockport is *Chadkirk*, where is an ancient chapel, in a moft romantic and fequeftered fituation. At the back is a half round of high bank cloathed with wood, concealing it from view on that fide. Part of the bank is now planted with fruit trees forming an orchard. The land in front, to the river, is rich pafture, divided by beautiful hedges kept in nice order. Only one houfe is to be feen near the chapel, though there are many in the neighbourhood. By the river fide is a large printing ground, one of the oldeft in thefe parts. Somewhat lower down is *Otterfcoe-bridge*, with a number of houfes adjoining.

M m m

Marple-

Marple-hall, an extenſive building, is in this neighbourhood, cele-brated for having been the reſidence of Preſident Bradſhaw, where he lived a conſiderable time in retirement. It is now the property and in the occupation of Mrs. Iſherwood.

Near the commencement of the eaſtern horn of Cheſhire, which runs up into the wild country bordering on Yorkſhire and the Peak of Derbyſhire, is *Hyde Chapel*, or, as it is now called, *Gee Croſs*. The chapel is a diſſenting place of worſhip. About twenty-five years ago there was only one houſe beſides; now the place looks like a little town, and forms a continued ſtreet for nearly a mile. Near it is *Red Pump-ſtreet*, a new village lately built by Mr. Sidebottom.

Hyde-hall, the ſeat of George Hyde Clarke, Eſq. a branch of the Clarendon family, is pleaſantly ſituated oppoſite to Denton, on the Cheſhire ſide of the Tame, upon a riſing ground, having gardens ſloping down to the water's edge. The building is an ancient hall with a new front. Adjoining to it are extenſive ſtables and other offices, conveni-ently planned, and the whole ſupplied with water by a running ſpring iſſuing from a height behind the houſe. In the houſe are ſome good paintings, among which is an original whole length of the great earl of Clarendon. Betwixt the bridge and the houſe is a mill for grinding corn, for the uſe of which, as well as for that of a water engine on the Lancaſhire ſide belonging to ſome valuable coal mines of Mr. Clarke's, is a wear, which throws a broad ſheet of water to a conſiderable depth below, where it has worked a hole many yards deep and wide. The appearance and noiſe of this caſcade have a romantic effect: and the ri-ver for half a mile above is made by it to appear like a lake, forming a fine piece of water well ſtocked with trout and eels. On each ſide of

the

J. Swainson del.t

Sparrow sculp.t

VIEW OF HYDE HALL.

the river downwards from the garden are high banks, well wooded, in which the river is loft for fome fpace, and then feen again at a diftance in a fheet of water, formed by a wear belonging to Mr. John Arden, for the purpofe of another coal-mine engine.

In front of the houfe, and at a pleafing diftance, is a bridge, lately built for the convenience of its owner, and the accommodation of thofe who frequent his coal pits. It is a neat ftructure, with a fine arch, and makes a picturefque object from the houfe. The furrounding land is moftly of a good quality, affording excellent arable, meadow, and pafture. The eftate abounds with coal, and will be greatly benefited by the Peak foreft canal, which paffes at a fmall diftance behind the houfe. As the Tame flows through the middle of Mr. Clarke's eftate, he enjoys a right to the water on both fides. On the whole, the fituation of this feat is a very defirable one, being retired and romantic, without much affiftance from art. The annexed view was taken in 1794. In the back ground appear the diftant hills above Mottram.

DUKINFIELD.—This is a fmall townfhip and barony in the parifh of Stockport. The village is pleafantly fituated upon an eminence commanding an extenfive profpect over a populous, varied, and plentiful country. Its name in the Anglo-Saxon dialect was *Dockenveldt*. The river Tame feparates it from the parifh of Afhton-under-Lyne, in Lancafhire, on the north and weft fides. This river, in the time of the heptarchy, was the boundary of two kingdoms, which will account for the ftrong out-works of the caftle or old hall of Afhton, oppofed by equally ftrong fortifications on this fide. Thefe were fituated fomewhere on the grounds now occupied by the lodge; and the manfion, formerly the feat of the Dukinfield family, thus defended, ftood on a

place

place called the Hall-green. No traces of it remain but the name. The hall now bearing the family name was erected in its stead. This family of Dukinfields have resided here since the time of the Conqueror till of late years, when the estate, by marriage, came into the possession of the late John Astley, Esq. His son, a minor, is now lord of the manor.

Dukinfield-hall is an ancient building of a venerable appearance. A chapel of more modern erection forms one wing of it, in which are buried some of the later branches of the Dukinfield family, under large tomb-stones with inscriptions still perfect; but the place itself is only used as a lumber room. The memory of the family is still much respected by the ancient inhabitants. The annexed view of the hall was taken in 1793 from the lower end of a fish pond in its front.

Dukinfield-lodge, the new seat built by the late Mr. Astley, is delightfully situated on an eminence above the Tame. It contains a fine octagon room with painted windows. Most of the others are small, but elegant, and are decorated with pictures chiefly by the hand of Mr. Astley, who had been a painter by profession. The whole building was never finished. It has a fine hot-house, and a large open bath with a dressing-room. In the front of the house is a terrace, affording a very pleasing view; and the precipitous rock descending from it has been cloathed with evergreens and other trees and shrubs. A fine wood occupies the space between it and the river, through which are cut several retired walks. The seat is now occupied by William Robert Hay, Esq. who married Mr. Astley's widow. Its beauties have given rise to a descriptive piece written by a young poet, Mr. William Hampson,

and

Dayes del.ⁿ   Walker sculp.ᵗ

VIEW OF DUKINFIELD HALL.

E. Dayes del.ⁿ   Sparrow sculp.ᵗ

VIEW OF DUKINFIELD BRIDGE.

Publish'd July 19 1794 by J. Stockdale, Piccadilly.

G. Dayes del.t

W. Ellis sculp.t

VIEW OF DUKINFIELD LODGE.

Publish'd May 1 1795 by I. Stockdale, Picadilly.

and publifhed at the requeft of Mr. Hay and his lady. The annexed view of the Lodge was taken in 1794.

Mr. Aftley, upon coming to the eftate, among many other improvements, put the roads in it in good repair, and built two good ftone bridges acrofs the Tame, one at Staley-bridge, the other leading from the lodge to Afhton; of this laft we have given a view, taken from above. At the end of it are two good houfes, affording one of the moft pleafing fituations in the neighbourhood. At this bridge three canals will meet, viz. the Manchefter and Afhton, the Peak-foreft and the Huddersfield, the latter of which will pafs by a tunnel through a large deep fand bank.

On the fummit above Dukinfield-lodge ftands a very ancient diffenter's chapel, built of ftone, and furrounded with a burying-ground planted with firs. It has a large congregation, noted for fine fingers, and was long under the care of the Rev. Mr. Buckley. Here lie buried fome of the Dukinfield family. The chapel is a fine ftation for an extenfive profpect, and is itfelf a ftriking object from the vicinity. Adjoining to it, Mr. Aftley built a large and commodious inn, which ufed to be much frequented by parties from Manchefter. Near to this place he erected a handfome circus of houfes for the accommodation of induftrious inhabitants, which was filled as foon as finifhed. The buildings are of brick, and the road divides it into two half circles. From a water engine which he built in the Tame for the ufe of the lodge, the water is forced up to a refervoir, whence the circus and moft of the town is fupplied.

Between

Between the lodge and the diffenter's chapel is a neat chapel belonging to the Moravians, furnifhed with an organ; and adjoining it is a very extenfive range of buildings, once inhabited by an orderly and induftrious colony of that fraternity, who carried on a variety of trades and occupations. Thefe buildings were erected at a great expence by the community, under the promife of a renewal of the leafes when they fhould drop, which, in confequence of the eftate's going out of the Dukinfield family, became null. Many negotiations were carried on with Mr. Aftley for the purpofe of accommodating the bufinefs upon equitable terms; but after waiting fome years without effect, the fociety determined on a removal, and accordingly erected their prefent fine building at Fairfield, of which an account has already been given. Their former fettlement at Dukinfield now looks like a deferted village. The chapel is ftill their property, held by the life of one old man; and fervice is performed in it by a refident maintained in the place.

A principal perfon in conducting the treaty with Mr. Aftley was the late Rev. Mr. La Trobe, a perfon highly refpected, not only by his own fraternity, but by the public at large, to whom he was known by many ingenious writings, and by a truly Chriftian character. On his death the following character of him was printed in the London Chronicle:

" On Wednefday evening, Nov. 29, 1786, died, at his houfe in Fetter-lane, moft fincerely lamented, in the 59th year of his age, the Rev. Mr. Benjamin La Trobe. By a large circle of acquaintance, he was known, refpected, and efteemed. The goodnefs of his heart, and the affability of his difpofition, endeared him to all his connections. Diftinguifhed in the practice and profeffion of every Chriftian virtue,

few

Painted by John Astley Esqr.

Engraved by Willm Bromley

THE REV.ᴰ BENJAMIN LA TROBE.

Born April 19ᵗʰ 1728. Died Nov.ʳ 29ᵗʰ 1786. in the 59ᵗʰ Year of his Age

London. Pub.ᵈ June 20 1793 by John Stockdale, Piccadilly.

few men poffeffed a greater liberality of fentiment, or a more general and extenfive knowledge of men and things. His laft moments fhewed that he knew his Redeemer liveth, and that he could meet him with joy: and thus, after a long and painful illnefs of nineteen weeks, which he bore with uncommon patience, he died, as he lived, in perfect refignation to the will of his Maker, an ornament to his profeffion, and a friend to mankind. His death will be a lofs to his afflicted family and friends, of which thofe only who knew his value moft can form the idea. In the early part of life he joined the church of the United Brethren, and till his death proved its zealous friend and protector. The truly Chriftian and benevolent principles of the Brethren were ftrictly conformable to his own fentiments ; and, becoming an indefatigable paftor among them, he proved an ufeful inftrument for many years in promoting the laudable purpofes of the Society, both at home and abroad. In a variety of publications, which he carefully fuperintended for the prefs, he removed every afperfion againft the Brethren, and firmly eftablifhed their reputation. To fum up his character in few words, he was an honeft man, and the fruits of his faithful fervices, as a minifter of the gofpel, will long remain an emblem of his worth and integrity."

The annexed portrait of him was, by the favour of Mrs. Hay, taken from an original and excellent painting at Dukinfield-Lodge, executed by Mr. Aftley himfelf, who had a high regard for Mr. La Trobe.

The townfhip of Dukinfield is very valuable, abounding in mines and quarries that yield a confiderable revenue. The coal-pits are from 60 to 105 yards in depth, according to the bearing of the ftrata. Iron ore is found in great abundance, and the fmelting of iron feems to have

been

been carried on here at a remote period; for in a field called the *Brun Yorth*, (a provincial pronunciation of Burnt Earth) the fcoriæ of iron have been met with in confiderable quantity: alfo the ore in one of the mines has been found wanting, while the other ftrata remained in their regular pofition. Among Mr. Aftley's projects was that of the erection of an iron foundry upon the eftate, which, from the number of hands employed, greatly increafed its population. But after a great deal of money fpent in building works and houfes, he gave up his concern in it, and let it to a company at Manchefter, who likewife, after a fhort trial, abandoned it: the foundry was then pulled down, and a large cotton factory is erected in its place, the wheel of which is turned by the fame ftream. It is the property of Mr. Ollivant of Manchefter. Above the bridge is another work of the fame kind. The cotton trade introduced here, while it affords employment to all ages, has debilitated the conftitutions and retarded the growth of many, and made an alarming increafe in the mortality. This effect is greatly to be attributed to the pernicious cuftom, fo properly reprobated by Dr. Percival and other phyficians, of making the children in the mills work night and day, one fet getting out of bed when another goes into the fame, thus never allowing the rooms to be well ventilated. The length of life muft formerly have been remarkable here, if we may judge by the following complaint of fhortnefs of days, in an epitaph on a perfon aged feventy-one buried in the chapel-yard:

> All ye that do behold this ftone,
> Pray think how *quickly* I was gone;
> Make hafte, repent, no time delay,
> Left Death *as foon* fnatch you away.

The number of families in this town in 1794, was 252.

4

One

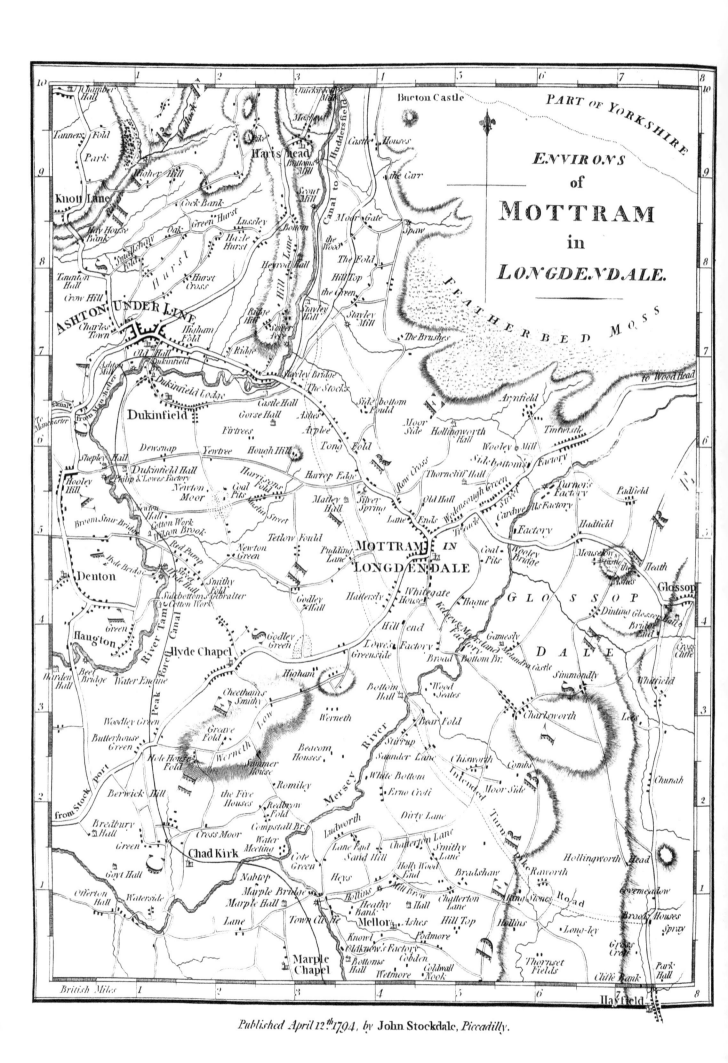

ENVIRONS
of
MOTTRAM
in
LONGDENDALE.

PART OF YORKSHIRE

British Miles

Published April 12th 1794, by John Stockdale, Piccadilly.

One mile from hence is *Newton Moor*, under which coals have been got for ages at different depths. The water is pumped out and the coals raifed by fteam engines, which are now generally taking place of the former horfe-machines. On one fide of the moor is a new-built row of houfes inhabited by weavers, called Muflin-ftreet, erected from the favings of their induftry.

Round many of the old coal pits hereabouts, where nothing elfe would grow, Mr. Aftley planted fir trees, which have thriven well, and now form little woods, which have a pleafing appearance, and in time may be profitable—a practice worthy of imitation!

The greater part of the Dukinfield eftate is good pafture and meadow land, rich as well above as below ground. The manure is principally lime, with marl on the lighter grounds. The Peak-foreft canal paffing through it will be of great advantage. The inhabitants are principally fupplied with provifions from the Afhton market.

MOTTRAM in LONGDENDALE PARISH.

THIS parifh comprehends all the remaining part of the north-eaftern extremity of Macclesfield hundred. It confifts of the parochial town of Mottram, and a number of fmall villages and hamlets, and contains one chapel of eafe, that of Wood-head, befides the parifh church. Mottram, with a confiderable part of the neighbourhood, and the extenfive moors up Longdendale, belong to the Hon. Wilbraham Tollemache, brother to the earl of Dyfart. As lord of the manor he holds a court leet by his fteward, at the court-houfe in Mottram, to which the tenants are fummoned to pay their rents.

N n n   Mottram

Mottram is fituated twelve miles from Manchefter and feven from Stockport, on a high eminence one mile to the weft of the Merfey, from which river the ground begins to rife: half the way being fo fteep as to make it difficult of accefs. It forms a long ftreet well paved both in the town and to fome diftance on the roads. It contains 127 houfes, which are for the moft part built of a thick flag ftone, and covered with a thick, heavy flate, of nearly the fame quality, no other covering being able to endure the ftrong blafts of wind which occafionally occur. Of late, many houfes in the fkirts of the town are built with brick. About fifty years ago, the houfes were few in number, and principally fituated on the top of the hill, adjoining the church-yard, where is an ancient crofs, and at a fmall diftance the parfonage houfe, now gone much to decay, and occupied by working people. It is only of late years that the town has had any confiderable increafe, which has been chiefly at the bottom of the hill, but fome latterly on the top. Many of the houfes are occupied by fhop-keepers of various kinds, for the accommodation of the town and neighbourhood, to which it ferves as a fort of market. There are alfo eight public houfes, which, with twenty-eight more in the vicinity, are certainly many more than can be wanted, and form no fmall nuifance by the encouragement they afford to tippling and idlenefs. The cotton trade is the principal fource of employment to the young people in the town, and the furrounding dif- trict. Within a fmall circuit in this neighbourhood there are twelve large cotton machines worked by water, befides a great number of fmaller ones, turned by horfes, or by fmall ftreams.

The church of Mottram is a large ftately building, of immemorial antiquity, of which the annexed view is an exact reprefentation. It is built of a coarfe, grey ftone, full of fmall pebbles or flints, of a

moft

C. Dayes del.

R. Newman sculp.

VIEW OF MOTTRAM CHURCH,

Publish'd July 5.1794 by I. Stockdale, Piccadilly.

E. Dayes del.t   Sparrow sculp.t

View of a COTTAGE at ROE-CROSS.

T. Barrett del.t

RALPH STEALEY & his WIFE.

Publish'd June 4. 1795. by I. Stockdale, Piccadilly.

moſt durable quality, every ſtone being as perfect as when firſt laid in. The ſtone is ſuppoſed to have come from a rock called Tinſell-Norr, which is of a ſimilar quality. It can be eaſily cut in the quarry, but becomes nearly as hard as flint when expoſed to the air.

In the church is a very ancient and rude monument, called old Roe and his wife. The figures have their hands elevated as at prayer. He is in armour, with a pointed helmet, a collar of S. S. about his neck, and a ſword by his ſide. The dreſs of both is that of the 15th century, and each has an animal at the feet. There is neither date nor inſcription on the monument, and many fabulous ſtories concerning them are handed down by tradition among the inhabitants. But Mr. Thomas Barrett, of Mancheſter, (who made the drawing for the annexed plate in Auguſt 1794) conjectures the effigies to be thoſe of Ralph Stealey and his wife. Tradition ſays, that the perſon interred came the Staley road to Mottram, and ſtopt at a croſs in the way, called Row-croſs, probably Road-croſs; and Mr. Barrett ſuppoſes that all memory relative to the monument being loſt except that of this Row-croſs, the effigy has derived its name from thence.

There is likewiſe a fine monument* of Mr. Serjeant Bretland, having a whole length ſtatue in white marble, on which is the following inſcription:

H. S E.
Quicquid mortale fuit
REGINALDI BRETLAND, A. L. S.
Familia non ignobili orti:
Virtute, Doctrina, Ingenio Præclari.

* William Egerton, Eſq. of Tatton, who purchaſed the Bretland eſtate, pays by way of fine one ſhilling annually for the cleanſing of this monument.

Qui

Confulendo prudens, Eloquendo facundus, Agendo fortis,

Pacis ftudiofus, Rixarum fugax, Clientibus in maximis fidus,

Res aliorum fibi commiffas tam diligenter quam fuas adminiftrabat.

Neque conftituere Litium Actiones, quam controverfias tollere maluit.

Nullus illi per otium dies exît.

Vitæ tandem fatur,

Animam virtutibus onuftam, beneque de repub: meritam,

Placide Deo reddidit, die tertio Aprilis, Anno Dom: 1703,

Ætat. fuæ 62.

Semper Laboremus.

Omnia funt Hominum tenui pendentia filo,

Et fubito cafu quæ valuere ruunt,

Dum loquimur, fugerit invida

Ætas, Carpe diem, quam minimum credula Poftero.

TRANSLATION.

Here lies buried

Whatever was mortal

Of REGINALD BRETLAND, A. L. S.*

Defcended from an honorable family:

Illuftrious in Virtue, in Learning, in Genius.

Who

Prudent in deliberating, eloquent in fpeaking, refolute in acting,

Anxious for peace, avoiding litigation, faithful in the higheft degree to his clients,

Managed the affairs of others committed to his charge as diligently as his own.

Nor ever preferred inftituting a law-fuit to removing the caufe of controverfy.

No day paft by him unemployed.

At laft, fatiated with life,

His foul, replete with virtues, well deferving of his country,

He peacefully furrendered to God, on the third day of April, in the Year of our Lord, 1703,

In the Year of his Age 62.

Let us labour inceffantly.

On a flight thread depend man's tranfient joys,

With fudden lapfe his firmeft hopes decay,

Time, while we fpeak, on envious pinions flies,

Snatch the fleet hour, nor truft a future day.

* A. L. S. probably, Aulæ Lincolnienfis Socius, A Member of the Society of Lincoln's Inn.

The

The church has a gallery on the fouth fide, lately new pewed, at the end of which is the fingers' gallery. It has a fine ring of bells. The afcent from the town is by a flight of about ninety ftone fteps; the hill being fteep and difficult. The living, value about £.100, is in the gift of the bifhop of Chefter; the prefent incumbent is the Rev. James Turner, who this year fucceeded the Rev. Mr. Kinder, deceafed. The church-yard is fpacious, and fo full of tombs, that it muft foon be enlarged. A neat methodift chapel was lately erected, which is well attended. Adjoining the church-yard is an ancient free-fchool, with a fmall houfe for the mafter. This for many years has been of little ufe to the inhabitants, partly owing to the great age of the late mafter, Mr. Warldeworth, who died laft year. It is now in the poffeffion of the rector, Mr. Turner, affifted by the Rev. Mr. Monkhoufe, and it is to be hoped will for the future anfwer the beneficial purpofes of its inftitution. The neglect in the management of this fchool obliged the inhabitants fome years ago to build another on Wednefcough Green at a fmall diftance, which has been well attended fince its commencement by Mr. Heathcote, and has been filled with fcholars, while the free-fchool in Mottram became a finecure.

With regard to the eftablifhment and falary of Mottram fchool, it appears from the deeds, which bear date April 20th, 1632, that one Robert Garfett, citizen and alderman of Norwich, left by his will, bearing date March 4th, 1610, £.100 towards the maintenance of a free-fchool to be erected in Mottram; and that Sir Richard Wilbraham, lord of the manor of Mottram, gave another £.100 to the fame purpofe. In 1618 the £.200 was put into the hands of truftees, who were to employ the intereft of it toward the maintenance of a fchoolmafter till land could be purchafed. In 1632 land was purchafed in Haughton,

2 in

in the parish of Bonebury, near Nantwich, Cheshire. The land is twenty-three Cheshire acres, and letts for £.25 yearly.—There is also a donation of £.5 yearly to the school, which is paid from an estate in Romily, in Chadkirk, in the parish of Stockport. It was left by one Robert Hyde, of Catten-hall, in the county of Chester, grandson of John Hyde, late dean rural of Macclesfield. He married Catherine, only daughter of John Bretland, of Thornecliff-hall, in this parish. He died July 24, 1684, and was buried in this church.

There is also belonging to the school a house in Manchester, which letts for £.14 10s. yearly, subject to leys, taxes, and repairs. It was purchased in 1751 from timber which was sold from the estate in Haughton. The whole salary is £.44 10s. yearly; leys, taxes, and the repairs above-mentioned being deducted. When the school was first built, and by whom, we cannot learn. It was rebuilt in the year 1670 at the expence of the parishioners and neighbouring inhabitants.

Mottram is supplied with water by springs. There is one fine well at the very top of the hill, and two others on different sides of it, from whence pipes might be conveyed to the lower parts of the town at a small expence. Most of the hills in this neighbourhood have springs on the sides, and some on the tops, all of which are of soft water.

Formerly there was not sufficient business in Mottram for one butcher: but few sheep were killed; and seldom more than one cow in a week, except at the wake, which festival is to this time kept up, with all the ceremony of dressing up rush carts, and strewing the church and pews with rushes. At present the town affords a tolerable livelihood for five butchers, and not a week passes without the slaughter of sheep and oxen,

4　　　　　　　　　　　　　　　　　　　which

which are chiefly brought from Huddersfield, Barnsley, and Sheffield. Tea has almoſt expelled the good old diſh of the country, thick porridge, though this is ſtill continued in ſome families, who find it makes a much more ſubſtantial breakfaſt, and, as they ſay, " wears better." Oat cakes, leavened and baked thick, are the principal bread of the place, though wheaten loaves are alſo common.

The gradual increaſe of population in this pariſh may be ſeen in the following extract from the regiſter. It is to be obſerved, that every year ſome chriſtenings and burials from other pariſhes are entered, and ſometimes a conſiderable number. Perhaps theſe may have been balanced by thoſe going out of the pariſh.

Year.	Marr.	Chriſt.	Bur.	Year.	Marr.	Chriſt.	Bur.
1745	22	57	40	1786	48	218	78
1750	26	76	80	1787	55	202	146
1755	23	86	54	1788	45	214	97
1760	19	86	43	1789	32	177	102
1765	30	77	48	1790	54	226	105
1770	31	109	68	1791	37	209	140
1775	40	124	95	1792	46	229	176
1780	40	162	62	1793	41	222	131
1785	46	182	82	1794	24	130	136

From the ſummit of the hill in Mottram is a delightful proſpect up Longdendale to the Wood-head, including the beautiful windings of the Merſey, with the high Derbyſhire hills on the eaſt, gradually riſing from it, among which are ſcattered the villages of Hadfield, Padfield, Whitfield, and Charleſworth; and on the weſt the Cheſhire hills, which as well as the Derbyſhire are, with the villages Tintwiſtle and

and Arnfield, paſtured to their tops. The valley is tolerably well
wooded with trees of various kinds, but rather ſtinted in their
growth. On the other ſide are extenſive proſpects into Lancaſhire,
and as far as the Welch mountains. Notwithſtanding the elevated ſituation of Mottram, it is ſurrounded by eminences much
higher, from which the church and town are viewed far below, and as
if in a deep valley. The principal of theſe hills are Charleſworth-
neck, Mouſelow-caſtle, Werneth Low, Tinſell Norr, Wild-bank, and
Harrop-edge. The latter affords a peculiarly fine proſpect of the ſurrounding country. From the bottom of this hill, at Row-croſs, was
taken, in 1793, the annexed view of Mottram. The ſharp-pointed
hill in the back-ground is Charleſworth-neck, which gradually riſes
about a mile and a half from the Merſey, and extends to the right for
a conſiderable diſtance. At Row-croſs is an ancient favourite cottage
of which a view is given. Near this place is a copperas work.

On the ſummit of Mottram-hill is a neat ſtone houſe called *Whitegate-houſe*, built and occupied by Mr. Solomon Lowe. Near it, his
ſon has built a cotton factory in a deep valley, concealed from the
ſight by an oak wood. From Whitegate-houſe is a ſteep deſcent of
near a mile to *Broad-bottom-bridge*, which croſſes the Merſey, in a
moſt delightful and romantic ſituation. The bridge was built in 1683.
Both its ends reſt on rock. The arch is a fine one, built with ſtone,
and kept in good repair. The annexed view was taken in 1793 from
below the bridge. In the back ground is ſeen a large cotton factory on
the Derbyſhire ſide of the river, lately erected by Meſſrs. Kelſall and
Marſland. This pile of building has much injured the pictureſque
beauty of the view, concealing a fine wood, in which the river loſes
itſelf. The ſpot almoſt equals Matlock in its romantic ſcenery. The
Cat

E. Dayes delt.

VIEW OF MOTTRAM.

Publish'd July 16, 1794, by I. Stockdale, Picadilly.

E. Shent sculp.

E. Dayes del.?

T. Medland sculp.

VIEW OF BROAD-BOTTOM BRIDGE.

Publish'd July 22.1794. by I. Stockdale Piccadilly.

E. Dayes del.

Sparrow sculp.

VIEW OF CAT TOR.

Publish'd April 20.1793.by I. Stockdale Piccadilly.

Cat Torr on the Chefhire fide, and the well-wooded rocks on the Der-byfhire, with the river hurrying between, over its rugged and rocky bot-tom, afford a folemn and ftriking fpectacle.

The *Cat Torr*, of which a view is annexed, is a perpendicular pre-cipice of eighty feet, overhung with vaft rocks at the top, on which, and on the fides, oak trees grow, threatening deftruction to all below. Its face confifts of various ftrata of rock, coal, or flaty matter, and free-ftone at bottom, all laid as regularly as by the hand of the mafon. The height of the fummit of Mottram-hill above that of the Cat Torr is about 450 feet. Below the bridge is Broad-bottom, a houfe belonging to Mr. Boftock, in a very lonely, but pleafing fituation, furrounded by fine meadow ground, which is partly encircled by the Merfey.

Before we quit the town of Mottram, we fhall fay fomething in com-memoration of two of its natives.

Mr. *Lee*, well known as a ftock-broker under the Royal Exchange, was born at Mottram, and owed his fuccefs in life in great meafure to the following circumftance. When a very young boy, he went with a companion into a neighbouring wood in fearch of walking fticks. Co-ming to a plantation of young afh trees, they made free with them by cut-ting as many as they chofe. On returning home they were met by a perfon, who having interrogated them about the manner in which they came by the fticks, pronounced, " that they would both certainly be " hanged or tranfported." This put them into fuch a fright, that lay-ing down their loads, they fled the country, and the end of their ram-ble was London. Lee, being a fhrewd, fenfible young lad, made his way from one ftation to another, till he became partner in a ftock-bro-

king

king houfe, in which he rofe to be head. With great reputation he acquired a handfome fortune, of which he was in his life-time extremely liberal to his countrymen and relations, giving away hundreds at once, and fometimes to thofe who did not make the beft ufe of it. He died fome years ago, leaving the principal part of his fortune to his two fons and relations, with legacies to his friends, and his bufinefs to the late Mr. John Bruckfhaw.

Much more diftinguifhed for the endowments of his mind, though much lefs by the favours of fortune, was *Laurence Earnfhaw*, born at Mottram foon after the commencement of this century, at a cottage on the high road to Wednefcough-green, with fir trees in front, which is looked upon by the neighbourhood with almoft as much veneration as that in which Sir Ifaac Newton was born is by his admirers. From accounts of this extraordinary man in the 57th Vol. Part II. of the *Gentleman's Magazine*, communicated by Mr. Jofiah Beckwith, of Rotherham, and Mr. J. Holt, of Walton, near Liverpool, we fhall copy fome of the moft remarkable particulars.

Lawrence Earnfhaw was put apprentice when a boy to a taylor, and afterwards to a clothier; but neither of thefe employments fuiting his genius, after ferving both for eleven years, he put himfelf for a fhort time to a clock-maker, one Shepley, of Stockport. By the force of native abilities, with the very little inftruction fuch an education could give him, he made himfelf one of the moft univerfal mechanifts and artifts ever heard of. He could have taken wool from the fheeps' backs, manufactured it into cloth, made that cloth into cloaths, and made every inftrument neceffary for the clipping, carding, fpinning, reeling, weaving, fulling, and dreffing, and making it up for wear,

with

with his own hands. He was an engraver, painter, and gilder; he could ſtain glaſs and foil mirrors; was a black-ſmith, white-ſmith, copper-ſmith, gun-ſmith, bell-founder, and coffin-maker; made and erected ſun-dials; mended fiddles; repaired, tuned, played upon, and taught, the harpſichord and virginals; made and mended organs, and optical inſtruments; read and underſtood Euclid; and in ſhort, had a taſte for all ſorts of mechanics, and moſt of the fine arts. Clock-making and repairing was a very favourite employ to him; and he carried ſo far his theory and practice of clock-work, as to be the inventor of a very curious aſtronomical and geographical machine, containing a celeſtial and terreſtrial globe, to which different movements were given, repreſenting the diurnal and annual motions of the earth, the poſition of the moon and ſtars, the ſun's place in the ecliptic, &c. all with the greateſt correctneſs. One of theſe machines curiouſly ornamented was ſold to the earl of Bute for £.150. All the complicated calculations, as well as the execution of this great work, were performed by himſelf. He likewiſe, about 1753, invented a machine to ſpin and reel cotton at one operation, which he ſhowed to his neighbours and then deſtroyed, through the generous, though miſtaken, apprehenſion, that it might take bread from the mouths of the poor. This was previous to all the late inventions of machinery by which the cotton manufactory has been ſo much promoted. He alſo contrived a ſimple and ingenious piece of mechaniſm for raiſing water from a coal-mine. He was acquainted with that equally ſelf-taught genius, the celebrated Brindley, and when they occaſionally met, they did not ſoon part. Earnſhaw was poſſeſſed of an extraordinary degree of ſobriety, never drinking a gill of ale for years after he was grown to manhood. His mien and countenance were far, at the firſt view, from betokening quick parts, but rather announced ſtupidity; but when animated by converſation

O o o 2　　　　　　　　　　they

they at once brightened up.   He had a good flow of words, and clearly explained his fubject in the provincial phrafe and dialect of his country. He had a fick wife and expenfive family, fo that, notwithftanding all his trades and ingenuity, he lived and died poor.   He died about the year 1764.   One of his fons ftill refides in this town.

The neighbourhood of Mottram was formerly famous for the number of halls occupied by their owners, who refided on their own eftates, moft of which are now in the poffeffion of farmers.   A few of them we fhall mention.

Hollingworth-hall, or, as it is now generally called, the Old Hall, is a very ancient, ftrong, ftone building, fituated by the fide of the moors about half a mile from Mottram.   It is furrounded with gardens and excellent meadow land, and enjoys a pleafant profpect.   It ftill belongs to the family of that name; but is now in the occupation of Henry Cardwell, Efq. a very ufeful and active member of fociety.

Somewhat further, on the edge of the fame moors, ftood *Thorncliffe-hall*, belonging to the family of Bretlands.   It was the moft confiderable building in thefe parts; but a few years ago much of it was taken down, and the materials fold.   A confiderable pile is ftill ftanding, converted into a farm-houfe.   The eftates belonging to this family were large; and the extenfive range called Werneth-Low was a part of them.   The whole is now the property of William Egerton, Efq. of Tatton, by purchafe.

Still further, on the very boundary of the moors, is another *Hollingworth-hall*, the property and refidence of John Whittle, Efq.   It is a

large

large ftone building, with fpacious rooms in the antique ftyle, and provided with extenfive and commodious out-houfes.

Half a mile from Mottram, on the road to the Wood-head, are
Wednefcough-green and *Treacle-ftreet*. Thefe two places have of late
increafed very much, owing to the land's being freehold, and fold for
building on. It is chiefly the property of Mr. Egerton, of Tatton.

On the other fide of Mottram, half a mile on the Stockport road, is
Hatterfley, which contains a few ftraggling farm houfes, and a fmall
hamlet called *Brittomley-mill*.

Two miles from Mottram, on the fame road, is the very ancient village of *Tintwiftle*, or *Tinfell*, containing thirty-five houfes and a diffenting chapel. It is entirely built of thick free-ftone flag, got on the fpot.
Tradition reports this to have been a borough in former times.

Half a mile to the left is *Arnfield*, a fmall village of ftraggling
houfes, built like the former, and probably as ancient, there being leafes
in fome of the families dated about 500 years fince, and couched in a
few lines. It is built on the fides of two fteep hills parted by a brook,
and is the laft village adjoining the moors.

Betwixt Tintwiftle and the Wood-head, ftands on the road fide
Wood-head Chapel, furrounded with a fmall burial ground. It has a
fingle bell to call to fervice the furrounding inhabitants, who are thinly
fcattered on the fides of thefe moors. There is not a houfe within a
confiderable diftance. The duty is performed by the Rev. Mr. Broad-
hurft,

hurst, twice a day from the Sunday before Holy Thursday to the middle of October, once a day the rest of the year.

The *Wood-head*, seven miles from Mottram, is a place well known to the weary travellers who have crossed the hills above in their way from Yorkshire. It consists of three public and a few private houses. The Mersey even at this place is a very powerful stream in winter, pouring down with great rapidity, and sometimes overflowing the meadows on its banks. It rises from different springs about one mile from the inn called Salter's-brook-house, within the West-Riding of Yorkshire, and rather more than four miles above the Wood-head, and it is joined in its course to Mottram by several rivulets which take their rise from these barren hills and moors, large tracts of which scarcely yield a blade of grass for the half-starved sheep.

From the Mersey to *Bretland-edge* is a nearly continued ascent of three miles, on the high road to Huddersfield. On the top of the edge is a most extensive view into Yorkshire, all fertile land except the range of moors on which you stand. On the top of this hill where the waters take opposite directions is the boundary between Cheshire and Yorkshire.

The few inhabitants of the Wood-head cultivate small farms with extensive sheep walks. The public houses depend upon travellers, few of whom pass without calling; and, indeed, it would be imprudent for them to neglect feeding their horses here, as they have no other opportunity of doing it for a considerable distance, especially on ascending to Bretland-edge From Wood-head an excellent turnpike road has lately been made across the Mersey to Chapel-le-Frith.

This

BUCTON CASTLE in Micklehurst

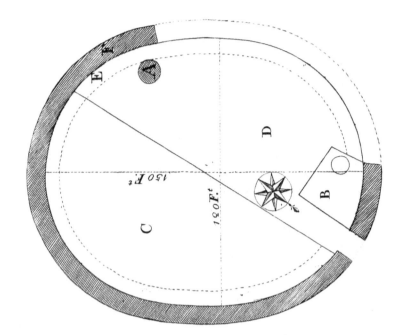

C

150 Ft

120 Ft

D

B

A

E F

Pub.ᵈ 24 Nov.ʳ 1793 by I.Stockdale. Piccadilly.

CASTLE SHAW in Sadleworth

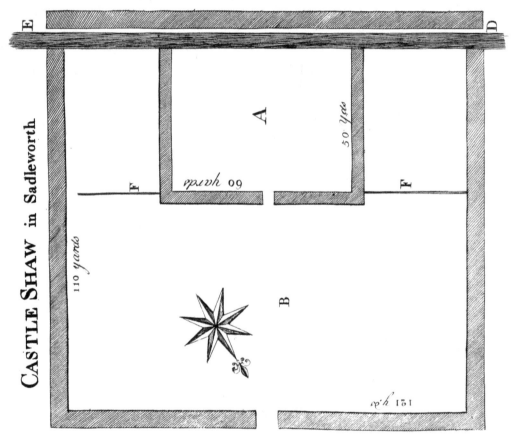

E

D

A

B

C

F

F

60 yards

50 Yards

110 yards

131 y.ᵈˢ

This neighbourhood is not without its antiquities, chains of posts having been anciently established on the heights for the purposes of defence or exploration. Of these are some in Yorkshire and Derbyshire, which will be mentioned in their proper places. A remarkable one in the parish of Mottram and county of Chester, is *Buёton-castle*, in Micklehurst, situated on the north-western edge of the great moss called Featherbed-moss, at about an equal distance between Mottram and Saddleworth. It is of an oval form, consisting of a rampart and ditch, and stands on the summit of a high hill, very steep towards the west and south, commanding a view over the south part of Lancashire and the whole of Cheshire, and easterly to the West Nab in Yorkshire. Its plan is seen in the annexed engraving, taken, with its explanation, from an account drawn up by the late Thomas Percival, Esq. and obligingly communicated by Mr. Pickford, of Royton.

EXPLANATION:

A. The well.

B. Place where the country people dug in 1730, expecting to find treasure.

C. Ruins of buildings, six or seven feet higher than the parade.

D. An inner court or parade.

E. The rampart.

F. The ditch; wanting on the west side, which is the steepest.

The inner slope of the rampart is twenty-seven feet, its perpendicular six feet; outer slope from the top of the rampart to the bottom of the ditch, thirty-five feet; inner slope of the ditch, sixteen feet; depth of the ditch, eight feet; width at bottom, six feet; height of rampart

5   above

above the level of the ground, eight feet; breadth of gateway fixteen feet.

The land in the neighbourhood of Mottram is moftly meadow and pafturage. Some wheat and oats are grown, and potatoes are cultivated. Garden vegetables are fcarce. The foil is generally of a loamy or clayey nature, and marl is found in feveral places. The farms are commonly fmall; from £.10 to £.30 per annum, few exceed £.50. The fmaller ones are let very high; nor could the tenant pay fuch prices but for the induftry of himfelf and family, who are in general weavers, hatters, or cotton fpinners, and fometimes all in the fame houfe. The chief article of the farm is a roomy houfe, and their two or three cows produce milk and butter for family ufe, with a little to fpare for making up the rent. On the commencement of the prefent war and failure of trade, many of the fmall farmers ware ruined, and their little all fold off. The old farm houfes are nearly all built of ftone, with heavy flag-flate roofs.

The climate is cold and inclement, owing to the currents of wind from the hills, and the vaft quantity of rain which falls, keeping the low grounds for a great part of the year a perfect puddle. The roads are feldom dry except in July and Auguft. It almoft daily happens that perfons on the top of a hill are deluged with rain, while thofe in the valley are dry; and, on the other hand, that clouds fail up a valley and drench it, while the furrounding eminences enjoy fair weather.

The manure for land is chiefly lime, of which a confiderable quantity is required; and unlefs the tenant can afford to lay it on, his herbage becomes four and turns to rufhes. The lime is brought from Chapel-le-Frith on the backs of fmall Welch horfes, which

run

run up and down the hills with as fure a foot as goats, and have little other food than what they pick up by the road fide on their return, while the drivers take refreshment. The lime generally cofts at Mottram 1s. 6d. per load, which is only a fmall fack. The Peak-foreft canal, which will come within four miles of Mottram, is expected to reduce the price nearly one half; and there are fome thoughts of having a fmall canal from the above to run up Longdendale, upon Dr. Anderfon's plan, which may be made for lefs than a turnpike road. This would be of the greateft utility to the country, as it would promote the cultivation of the moors to a great extent, and would caufe a demand of its mineral products, of which little is now got, on account of the expence of land carriage.

The vaft rock at Tinfell-Norr confifts of folid blocks of the durable ftone already defcribed as the material of Mottram church. It is well calculated for ufes in which beauty is not the object, as ordinary buildings, kirb ftones, and pofts, &c. Under Bretland-edge is a quarry of flag ftone, lately difcovered by Mr. Boar of the Wood-head, who has obtained a leafe of the fame. The ftone is got fix feet in length, and proportionally broad. Near the top of the hill is a good ftone for building, fofter and of better quality than any in the neighbourhood, and nothing prevents its ufe but the difficulty of conveyance.

Coals of an indifferent quality are occafionally got at Mottram, and on the Derbyfhire fide in different places.

On the top of Tinfell-Norr, Wood-head, and other high hills, are deep and thick peat moffes, in which fuel is got by the poor, and trees are occafionally found in fituations where it would certainly be fcarcely

P p p   poffible

poffible to make them grow at prefent. Thefe peat bogs have fometimes been fet on fire in the fummer, and have long continued to burn
in one grand body of flame..

During the fummer, men, women, and children are conftantly employed in cutting and burning fern on the fides of the moors, the afhes
of which are fold to the foap-boilers..

Cranberries and cloudberries grow on thefe moors, the latter of which
(Rubus Chamæmorus) is a delicate fruit, little known and rare. Whin-
berries grow in great abundance about Tinfell-Norr, and the furrounding rocks, which are in many places covered with ftunted oak trees,
which do not attain a greater height than fix feet. Moor-game or red
groùs frequent thefe moors in great numbers, and the different lords of
the manors are at confiderable expence to preferve them from poachers.

Salmon fwim a great way up the Merfey, and their young, called
brood, and already mentioned under Manchefter, run up the rivulets
among the moors to an incredible height, and are eafily caught in the
fhallow water by perfons fkilled in groping. Trout is alfo plentiful in
thefe ftreams, and is occafionally fold at fixpence per pound. They
are generally caught with a rod and line. Thefe, and a few eels, are the
only fifh in this part of the Merfey.

III.—DERBY-

III.—*DERBYSHIRE.*

HIGH PEAK HUNDRED.

GLOSSOP PARISH.

THIS comprehends a large tract of mountainous country in the north-west angle of the Peak. The living is a vicarage of the clear value of 42*l.* 0*s.* 11½*d.*; the duke of Norfolk is patron. It contains the chapelries of *Mellor*, of *Hayfield*, and of *Charlesworth*; also the liberty of *Chinley*, and several other smaller hamlets. The houses in Glossop and part of the parish have been numbered to 333; the families in the remainder, at 788. The inhabitants of this parish are supported by the manufactures of cotton and wool. In the part bordering on Yorkshire, a considerable quantity of fine woollen cloth is made. In the southern and western parts, the principal employment is spinning and weaving of cotton.

The town of Glossop is three miles east of Mottram, and stands on a rising bank, at the foot of which runs a small stream, that soon joins the Mersey below. It is a small village in which is a very ancient church: the living is now occupied by the Rev. Christopher Howe. The yard has a venerable appearance from the number of railed-in tombs of families of consequence. In the church is a very ancient mo-

num ent

nument fimilar to that of old Roe and his wife at Mottram, and a modern one of the late Jofeph Hague, Efq. of Park-hall. This is a fine marble buft by Bacon, and coft four hundred guineas. The following infcription is under the buft on a tablet of marble :

Sacred to the Memory of JOSEPH HAGUE, Efq.

Whofe Virtues as a Man

Were as diftinguifhed, as his character as a merchant :

Favoured with the bleffings of Providence,

He enjoyed the fruits of his induftry at an early period ;

And by the moft indefatigable purfuits in trade,

Acquired an immenfe fortune,

Which he diftributed with great liberality

Amongft his relations in his own life time.

He was born at Chunal in the Year 1695,

And in 1716 fettled in London, where he married Jane, the only

Daughter of Edmund Blagge, of Macclesfield, in Chefhire,

By whom he had ten fons and two daughters,

Who all died in their minority.

He built and endowed the Charity School at Whitfield, in 1778,

And died at Park Hall in this Parifh, the 12th March, 1786,

Aged 90 Years ;

Leaving the annual Intereft of £.1000 towards the cloathing

12 poor Men, and 12 poor Women, out of the eight Townfhips

Of GLOSSOP DALE for ever ;

Befides other charitable Donations to Gloffop

And the Chapelry of Hayfield.

Mr. Hague was a wonderful inftance of the effects of induftry, joined with integrity and perfeverance. He was the child of poverty, and began while a young boy with a few pence, to buy and fell fmall articles, which he carried in a bafket, that foon became too bulky, and

4   he

he then purchafed an afs. From one ftep to another, the profits of his dealings accumulated in a few years to a large fortune, and he became a very opulent merchant. On the lofs of his children, he adopted a family of the name of Doxon, of about feven children, his nephews and nieces, from Padfield, near Gloffop, and gave them all good educations, and with it handfome fortunes; fome of them are married to the firft bankers in Lombard-ftreet, and others refide in Manchefter. He divided the greateft part of his fortune amongft his relations during his life-time, while in retirement at Park-hall, near Hayfield; an example of good fenfe and true generofity, which it would be happy for mankind if perfons of property were to imitate, inftead of indulging the idle vanity of being recorded as dying worth a vaft fum of money, left to perfons for whom, perhaps, they never fhowed the leaft friendfhip during their lives!

Gloffop lies in one of the deepeft vallies in thefe parts, furrounded on all fides by the higheft hills in the Peak, feveral of which rife a mile and a half from the town. On the top of one of thefe hills, one mile from Gloffop, is a fine round hill called *Moufelow Caftle*, on which there probably was formerly a caftle or ftation, being a fpot well calculated for fuch a purpofe. It ftands very high, and commands a moft extenfive profpect over the furrounding country. About fifteen years fince it was paftured to the top, on which it was plain to be feen that a building had ftood, there being deep holes and a quantity of ftones. The top occupies a large fpace of ground. The whole of the hill, as well as the top, is now planted with firs of about ten years ftanding, and the owner, Mr. Howard, has given it the name of Caftle-hill.

On

On the top of another hill near Gloſſop is a good ſlate quarry of the thick flag ſort, which ſupplies the principal part of the ſurrounding country for a conſiderable diſtance.

There are ſome large cotton factories in this neighbourhood and ſeveral ſmall ones.

The land in this valley is chiefly paſture and meadow, and ſome of it very good.

At a ſmall diſtance from the town ſtands an ancient building, formerly called *Royl-hall*, but now changed by the proprietor, Mr. Howard, to *Gloſſop-hall*. It ſerves as a retreat during the ſhooting ſeaſon of moorgame, of which there is great plenty. Round it are planted large firs, and in front a very extenſive hill is covered with firs, of many years growth, through which are pleaſant roads. The following lines have long remained on one of the panes of glaſs at this hall :

> Here hills, with naked heads, the tempeſts meet,
> Rocks at their ſides, and torrents at their feet.

This hall and neighbourhood, as well as very extenſive moors, are the property of Barnard Howard, Eſq. who has reſolved to continue planting a conſiderable part of theſe moors yearly with firs, which in this diſtrict ſeem to thrive well. As wood in this country is a ſcarce article, the grown firs are now very valuable, the off branches being valuable for fuel, as there are no coals in this neighbourhood of any conſequence.

In

In this parish are the remains of a very ancient building, called *Melandra Castle*, of which the late Rev. Mr. Watson, of Stockport, has given a description in the 3d volume of the *Archæologia*, part of which we shall transcribe. For a plan of this castle, see p. 138.

" On the south side of the river Mersey, (or, as some call it, the Edrow) near Wooley-bridge, in the township of Gamesley, and parish of Glossop, in Derbyshire, is a Roman station which no writer has mentioned, nor did any one know, as far as can be informed, that it had been constructed by that people, till July 1771, when I made this discovery. The country people give it the name of *Melandra Castle*; the area of it is called the Castle-yard, and eleven fields adjoining to it are named in old deeds the Castle Carrs.

" It is situated, like many Roman stations, on moderately elevated ground, within the confluence of two rivers, and was well supplied with good water. Very fortunately the plough has not defaced it, so that the form of it cannot be mistaken. The ramparts, which have considerable quantities of hewn stones in them, seem to be about three yards broad. On two of the sides were ditches, of which part remains, the rest is filled up; on the other sides there are such declivities, that there was no occasion for this kind of defence. On the north-east side, between the station and the water, great numbers of worked stones lie promiscuously, both above and under ground; there is also a subterraneous stream of water here, and a large bank of earth, which runs from the station to the river. It seems very plain that on this, and on the north-west sides, have been many buildings; and these are the only places where they could safely stand, because of the declivity between them and the two rivers.

5   " The

" The extent of this station is about 122 yards by 112. The four gates, or openings into it, are exceedingly visible, as is also the foundation of a building within the area, about twenty-five yards square, which in all probability was the prætorium.

" Very near the east angle, the present tenant of the ground under the duke of Norfolk, found several years ago, as he was searching for stones to build him a house, a stone about sixteen inches long, and twelve broad, which is now walled up in the front of his house, and contains an inscription which I read thus; *Cohortis primae Frisianorum Centurio Valerius Vitalis.*"

From these circumstances, Dr. Watson concludes this to have been a sister fort to that of Manchester, which was garrisoned by another part of the Frisian cohort; and he endeavours to trace the course of the Roman roads leading through it, one of which, from the Roman station at Brough, in Derbyshire, is still used for a good part of the way, being set with large stones in the middle, and having proper drains cut on each side where it runs over mossy grounds. It has the name of the *Doctor's Gate.*

At Melandra was lately found a large sword, and what is more extraordinary, a cannon ball. Tradition reports that there was once under the castle a city or town called Wooley, on the banks of the Mersey, near the bridge of that name. Hearths and ashes have been ploughed up in this place.

A few years ago an act was obtained for the making a new turnpike road, from Buxton to Chapel-in-le-Frith through Hayfield, by Glossop to the Wood-head. From Chapel-en-le-Frith to the Wood-head it is completed. The road fkims along the fide of the Derbyfhire hills half way betwixt their tops and the Merfey. This road is principally intended for the advantage of thofe paffing to and from Buxton into Yorkfhire, inftead of the wide circuit through Manchefter. It is already much travelled, and will be ftill more fo on its being known. The extenfion of this road from Buxton to Chapel-en-le-Frith is not yet finifhed. A new turnpike road paffes from Gloffop to Mottram, through Hadfield, which by the effects of the cotton trade is much improved of late.

Charlefworth, three miles from Gloffop, is a long, ftraggling village of confiderable extent, much increafed within thefe few years, principally by the cotton bufinefs. The buildings reach nearly to the top of Charlefworth Neck, one of the higheft range of hills in this part, extending fouth-eaft to a confiderable diftance. It is a continued range of rocks of free-ftone,* at leaft as far as feen in the back ground of the view of Mottram. The clouds in front hide the face of the rocks, or, as it is called, the coombs. Near this is *Chifworth*, another fmall village ; and not far from hence are collieries, which fupply many of the villages on the Derbyfhire fide, though the coal is but indifferent.

Marple Bridge, is a fmall village equally divided by the Goyt, part being on the Chefhire, and part on the Derbyfhire fide of the river, containing about fixty houfes. The principal employ of the inhabitants is in the cotton manufacture.

---

* Should a canal-branch from the Peak foreft up the fide of the Merfey to Broadbottom-bridge take place, this ftone will find a ready market in the neighbourhood of Stockport, Manchefter, &c.

On

On the Derbyfhire fide, about a mile from the bridge, Mr. Oldknow has erected the largeft cotton mill in this part of the country on the Goyt, turned by a cut from that river ; which of courfe employs the principal part of the young people in this neighbourhood. Mr. Old-know has alfo built, at his own expence, a very fine bridge over the river Goyt, with free-ftone got in the quarry at Charlefworth Neck, and faced and finifhed with a finer fort from the quarries near Buxton.

Near this place, on the Derbyfhire fide, is a diffenting meeting-houfe of modern date, to which belongs a numerous congregation. Here is alfo a very ancient building called *Lower Marple*, and on the Derby-fhire fide, an ancient family feat of the Shuttleworths, pleafantly fituated on a rifing ground, now the property of Mifs Shaw.

Mellor has a chapel of the church of England, round which are only ftraggling houfes.

Hayfield is a long, ftraggling, and confiderable village, betwixt Gloffop and Chapel-en-le-Frith, on the turnpike road. It has a hand-fome church with a new fteeple juft built. The inhabitants are princi-pally clothiers, though the cotton branch of late has gained a fmall footing. A fine ftream of water runs through the village. Near this is *Park-hall*, the feat of the late Jofeph Hague, Efq. A magnificent range of ftabling has lately been added to it.

CHAPEL-EN-LE-FRITH PARISH.

THE living is a donative curacy, of the clear value of 16*l.* 16*s.* 8*d.* It has a handfome church, with a fine organ. The number of families in the parifh is 420, chiefly fupported by the manufacture of cotton, which has caufed a great increafe of population. Chapel-le-Frith is a fmall market-town. About a mile from it is Bank-hall, the feat of Samuel Frith, Efq. At the diftance of two miles from the town are fome works of a military appearance on a mountain called Comb's-mofs, confifting of entrenchments on the edge of the hill and carried down the declivity; but no circumftance has been difcovered by which the people who formed them could be conjectured. A canal is now cutting from this place to join the canal from Manchefter to Afhton-under-Lyne. See p. 132.

The ebbing and flowing well, commonly called *Tidefwell*, and reckoned one of the wonders of the Peak, is two miles from Chapel-le-Frith, clofe to a turnpike road lately made to Sparrow-pit. It is about a yard deep and broad, and rifes and falls about three quarters of a yard. The water gufhes from feveral cavities at once for the fpace of about five minutes, and then fubfides again; and this takes place at uncertain intervals, often feveral times in a day, or even in an hour, in wet weather, but much more rarely in dry weather.

TIDESWELL PARISH.

THIS is a vicarage of the clear value of £.32, the dean and chapter of Litchfield patrons. The church is very ancient and large, and much admired by the curious. Tidefwell is a fmall market-town, containing 254 houfes, and about 1000 inhabitants. A few hands in it are employed in fpinning cotton, but the chief dependence is on the mining bufinefs. The hamlet of *Litton* contains about feventy-

Qq q 2   four

four houſes, and 348 inhabitants. In the village are about fifty-two ſtocking frames, and ten jerſey combers. *Worm-hill* is another hamlet in this pariſh, with a chapel. This place had the honour of giving birth to that extraordinary genius, the late Mr. Mr. Brindley, ſo celebrated for planning navigable canals. Worm-hill contains about twenty-nine houſes. At *Millhouſe Dale* are ten houſes, and a cotton mill which employs many hands from the neighbouring villages. The reſt of the pariſh of Tideſwell contains forty-nine houſes.

Monſal-dale through which the river Wye runs in its courſe between Tideſwell and Bakewell, is one of the moſt pleaſing in Derbyſhire. It is extremely ſteep on one ſide, that on which the road runs, gently aſcending on the other, and ſoftened by a rich covering of wood and herbage. Its prevailing character is tranquil beauty. Towards its head two other beautiful dales open into it; and by following the courſe of the Wye up to Buxton various romantic ſcenes offer themſelves to the eye.

EYAM PARISH.

A RECTORY; lady Burlington, duke of Chandos, and Mr. Bathurſt, patrons. The liberty of Eyam contains about 108 houſes, and 918 inhabitants, who are maintained by agriculture and working the lead mines. In *Foxlow* and *Grindlow* are about ninety-four houſes; in the *Woodlands*, forty; at *Grindleford*, twenty-four. In the two former places the inhabitants depend upon agriculture, cotton ſpinning, and working the lead mines; but population is in a very declining ſtate from a failure in the two laſt branches. When the plague raged in London in 1665, the infection was conveyed in a parcel of

2   clothes

clothes to Eyam, where it broke out in September 1665, and in November 1666, 260 of the inhabitants had died of it. The worthy rector, Mr. Montpesson, would not quit his flock. He used every argument to persuade his wife to leave the spot, but in vain. She would not forsake her husband, and is supposed to have fallen a victim. They sent away their children. Mr. Montpesson continued to employ himself in his pastoral office, and preached in a field under a sort of alcove formed by nature in a rock, which place still retains the appellation of *the church*. He survived the visitation, and the entries of deaths from the plague in the parish register are in his hand-writing. In the fields surrounding the town are many remains denoting where tents were pitched; and tombs still exist of large families swept away by the pestilence.* It ought not to be omitted, that Mr. Robert Standley, the deprived minister of the place, also remained in the village during the whole of this visitation, and performed every good office in his power to the poor sufferers.

EDENSOR PARISH.

A VICARAGE; the duke of Devonshire, patron. In its liberty are about eighty-five houses; and in the hamlet of *Pilsey* about thirty. Several of the inhabitants meet with employment and support at Chatsworth.

* Howard on Lazarettos, p. 24.

BAKEWELL PARISH.

THIS is reckoned the moſt populous and extenſive pariſh in Der-byſhire. It contains nine chapelries, beſides ſeveral large hamlets. The whole number of houſes is 1040. Bakewell is a vicarage; the dean and chapter of Litchfield patrons. The church is built in the manner of cathedrals, and has a croſs aiſle and a handſome ſpire. It contains ſeveral ancient monuments, the moſt remarkable of which are dedicated to the families of Vernon and Manners. In the church-yard is an antique ſtone croſs, with ſeveral figures of rude ſculpture.

Bakewell is a place of great antiquity, and was made a borough by Edward the elder. It is now a ſmall market town, containing about 192 houſes and 930 inhabitants. A few years ago a machine for cot-ton ſpinning was erected here by Sir R. Arkwright, which affords em-ployment to about 300 hands. A few are employed in the lead mines, and in collecting the foſſil productions of the Peak. The curious in natural hiſtory will here be much gratified with the complete collection of the foſſils of Derbyſhire, arranged by the ingenious Mr. White Watſon of this town, who by a tablet of his invention has exhibited a view of the ſtrata of the Peak, with the relative poſition and proportion of the minerals with which it abounds.

Haddon-hall ſtands on a gentle eminence amid thick woods overhang-ing the Wye, two miles below Bakewell. It is an ancient manſion be-longing to the duke of Rutland. It conſiſts of two quadrangular courts, round which the apartments and offices are built; and it is em-battled and caſtellated on every ſide, ſo as to afford a perfect ſpecimen of the reſidence of an Engliſh baron in the 15th century. It is now

entirely

entirely disfurnished, though several of the rooms are still hung with old tapestry. This place was long the seat of the Vernons, a family of distinction during several reigns. After the death of Sir George Vernon, in the reign of Elizabeth, who left two daughters, it came, along with several Derbyshire manors, by marriage into the family of Manners, which continued to reside there during more than a century, but finally quitted it for Belvoir castle. It was formerly surrounded by a park, which is now thrown into enclosures of pasture ground.

Ashford, a chapelry in the parish of Bakewell, has a village of the name situated on the Wye. The whole liberty contains about 119 houses and 540 inhabitants. A few persons here are employed in cotton spinning, and about twenty hands in the manufacture of stockings. About fifty years ago a machine was constructed here by a Mr. Watson, for sawing and polishing the marble which is found in great abundance at this village and in the neighbouring country. The scheme did not at first answer to its author; but the present proprietors have made a beneficial concern of it, and carry on business to a considerable extent. The marble manufactured here is not only much in request in this kingdom, but is exported to distant parts.

The chapelry of *Baslow* contains several hamlets. The houses in all are about 202. A large cotton mill in the centre of them gives employment to a number of people of the vicinity.

In *Great Longstone* the manufacture of muslins has been introduced. *Little Longstone*, *Sheldon*, and *Taddington* are other villages in this district, situated in a part of the Peak little cultivated or inclosed. The inhabitants chiefly depend for their support on working in the lead mines.

mines.   The fame may be faid of *Moneyafh*.   The houfes in all thefe places are about 247.

Chelmorton chapelry.—This village ftands at the foot of a high eminence, and contains about forty houfes.   Its inhabitants are partly employed in the lead mines, partly in a manufacture of ribands lately introduced.   A barrow or low in the neighbourhood was opened fome years ago containing fome human fkeletons entire.

Buxton chapelry.—The part of this town within Bakewell parifh contains about feventy-feven houfes, and 238 ftated inhabitants, the number being much increafed in the bathing feafon.

This place, fituated in a hollow, among naked and dreary hills, has been favoured by nature with the poffeffion of one of the moft valuable mineral waters in this kingdom, which has rendered it the refort of multitudes of invalids of all ranks, and has decorated it with fplendid and commodious buildings.   The following account of its waters and baths has been drawn from the beft authorities.

Buxton waters and baths.—There is little doubt that the warm baths of Buxton were known to the Romans, various remains of Roman workmanfhip having been difcovered about them.   Their celebrity in the later ages is little known, our writers making little mention of them till the 16th century.   Buxton was much frequented in the reign of Elizabeth, and fince that period, the number of perfons reforting to it, and the buildings erected for their accommodation, have been continually increafing.   On a chemical analyfis, the waters have been found to be lightly impregnated with mineral matter, particularly calcareous earth,

fea-falt,

fea-falt, felenite, and acidulous gas, with perhaps fome other perma-
nently elaftic vapour. The baths are three in number, and their degree
of heat from eighty-one to eighty-two. The water is clear, fparkling,
and grateful to the palate. When drank in confiderable quantity, it
proves, for the moft part, heating and binding. The temperature of
the baths is extremely agreeable to the feeling. A flight fhock is felt at
the firft immerfion, which is fucceeded by a pleafant warmth. The cafe
in which bathing is attended with the moft diftinguifhed good effects,
is chronic rheumatifm, many perfons every year abfolutely crippled by
this diforder being reftored to the ufe of their limbs. The water is
found beneficial in gouty, nephritic, and bilious diforders, and in moft
debilities of the ftomach and bowels. In thefe, as ufual in the adminiftration of mineral waters, much of the benefit muft be imputed
to the air, exercife, and change of living.

Buxton water iffues to the day through the fiffures of a rock of
blackifh marble. Some of thefe openings are large, and fome apparent
only from the circumftance of the water running through them,
attended with large air bubbles. The fprings are many, and the water
pouring from them fo copious, that they have enabled the proprietor to
make a number of ufeful and fubftantial improvements.

The place where the water is ufually drunk, and which is yet called
St. Anne's well, is a very elegant building, in the Grecian ftile, and is
certainly a great improvement, both with refpect to its conveyance from
the original fpring, and from the mode of delivering it to the company.
Before the late alterations, the water rofe into a ftone bafon, which,
as has been before obferved, was inclofed in a wall of brick. This
wall remained to the time of Sir Thomas Delves, who built the late

R r r

hand-

handfome arch over the wall, which was about twelve feet fquare, and fet round with ftone benches. The bafon was about twenty-five yards north of the outermoft bath. This was fuppofed always to have been the original fpring; but there is not a fhadow of doubt that the water was conducted into the bafon in a rude and flovenly manner, and from a very confiderable diftance. It muft, indeed, be allowed, that the water is now conveyed from a fomewhat greater diftance into the prefent bafon, which is of white marble. But as it runs through a narrow, neat channel of grit-ftone, by which it is covered to the very edge of the bafon, it is equally beneficial, and at the fame time free from many impurities arifing from foughs and drains to which the other was frequently and unavoidably expofed. The temperature of this water, which does not in any degree depend on rain, or other accidental circumftance, is always eighty-one by Fahrenheit's thermometer.

There is another fountain, called from its fituation the Hall well. This is inclofed in a neat room opening into the corridore, which leads from the hall to the crefcent, and is particularly convenient in bad weather. But, as it lies at a ftill greater diftance from the fpring, its temperature is one degree below the former. In other refpects its qualities are the fame.

An exhalation, or fteam, often hovers over St. Ann's well early in the morning, and late at night; and fometimes, when the atmofphere is very moift and cold, it continues for the whole day. This laft appearance is efteemed almoft a certain fign of rain. There is no fediment of any kind whatfoever in the well.

Dr

VIEW OF BUXTON.

A. Doyen del.ᵗ

Fores sculp.ᵗ

Published Feb. 1 1816 by I.T. Hinton Hilary.

Dr. Denman, from whofe " Obfervations on Buxton Water," lately publifhed, the preceding account of the fprings is copied, has given many judicious directions for their internal and external ufe, formed upon long practice on the fpot. He in general confiders Buxton water as a more active remedy than is ufually fuppofed, and not only diffuades from its ufe in all inflammatory and feverifh complaints, but limits the quantity to be taken, in cafes where it is proper, to a moderate portion. " In common," he fays, " two glaffes, each of " the fize of a third part of a pint, are as much as ought to be drank " before breakfaft, at the diftance of forty minutes between each ; and " one or two of the fame glaffes between breakfaft and dinner will be " quite fufficient " With refpect to bathing, he recommends, for invalids, the time between breakfaft and dinner as the moft proper, and directs that the prefcribed or ufual exercife fhould be taken before the bath. The water fhould never be drunk immediately before bathing.

There is likewife a chalybeate fpring at Buxton, in which the water is pretty ftrongly impregnated with iron held in folution by acidulous gas ; and alfo an artificial bath of the Buxton waters, in which they are warmed by a ftove.

The buildings for the accommodation of company at Buxton were, till of late years, only the *Old-hall*, a fpacious houfe at the bottom of the hill, and a few inns and fmall lodging-houfes in the towns. From the increafing conflux of people, however, new buildings were added yearly ; and at length the duke of Devonfhire erected the large and beautiful edifice called the *Crefcent*, of which a view is here given, which will convey a better idea of it than can be communicated by words. It is built of ftone got on the fpot, and faced with a fine free-

ftone

ftone, from a quarry a mile and a half from Buxton on the Difley road, and confifts of numerous private apartments, fupplied with every convenience, with a grand ball-room on the right, and a coffee-room under it. In the centre of the building is the duke's arms cut in ftone, and furnifhed with a capital pair of *real* ftag's horns, which were once brought down by order of the architect for the purpofe of filencing a ftranger, who, after feverely criticifing the feveral parts of the edifice, finifhed with obferving that the horns were peculiarly ill executed. At the back of the Crefcent are feen the ftables, compofing a grand fquare, and equal in magnificence and contrivance to any thing in the kingdom. A large range of fheds for carriages is annexed to them. To the front of the Crefcent is a fine rifing ground, laid down with grafs, and planted with trees, round which are led agreeable walks. The whole defign of thefe buildings is faid to have coft the duke upwards of £.120,000. They are leafed to a perfon who undertakes the management of them; and the refort of company has been fuch, as to fill them to overflowing. In the front of the Crefcent, to the left, is a building where the waters may be drunk gratis. More to the left are the baths adjoining the Old hall. See the view.

The roads about Buxton are excellent, being made with lime-ftone, which forms a fmooth, even furface. A new road round one of the hills at Buxton was cut in 1794.

One mile from Buxton on the road to Tidefwell is *Fairfield*, a fmall, ftraggling village, with a tolerable church. From this place to Chapel-le-Frith, a new turnpike road will foon run in nearly a ftraight line, to join that from the latter town to the Wood-head. This will be three miles nearer, and alfo more on the level; and will be of great advan-

tage

tage to thofe who have occafion to go to Huddersfield or Leeds without paffing through Sheffield to the eaft, or Manchefter to the weft.

The country round Buxton is celebrated for lime of a very ftrong quality, the kilns for burning which form a principal object in the fcenery of the furrounding hills. It is fent chiefly on the backs of fmall horfes to confiderable diftances in the adjacent counties.

Beeley chapelry. The village ftands in a valley near the Derwent. It has about fifty-four houfes, and its inhabitants are chiefly fupported by agriculture.

In the fmall hamlet of *Haffop* is the handfome feat of Francis Eyre, Efq. whofe family is very ancient and refpectable in this county. The prefent poffeffor has a very large collection of exotic plants in his greenhoufes; and has continued the extenfive plantations begun by his father.

There are various other hamlets in the parifh not worth particular notice. One of the moft diftinguifhed places in it is

Chatfworth-houfe, the feat of the duke of Devonfhire. This is a magnificent building, fituated in a wide and deep valley, near the foot of a high hill, finely cloathed with wood. The gardens are diftinguifhed by their water works, which, from the advantage of their fituation, are rendered fuperior in their kind to any others in the kingdom, and were the objects of much admiration when thofe contrivances of art were in efteem. This houfe has been about two centuries the manfion of the anceftors of the Cavendifh family. The prefent edifice

was

was erected by the laft earl of Devonfhire, a few years before the revolution.   The moft remarkable thing in the infide is an elegant chapel
with a good deal of the exquifite carving of Gibbon.   Some modern
improvements have been made in the grounds, and a noble range of
ftabling was built about 1760.   The annexed view of Chatfworth was
taken in 1793 from the weft fide of the Derwent, in the park.

Y O U L G R A V E   P A R I S H.

ITS living is a rectory; the duke of Devonfhire patron.   The town
of Youlgrave contains 136 houfes, and 614 inhabitants.   Agriculture
and mining are the principal employments of the place.

Winfter is a market town containing 218 houfes.   The inhabitants
chiefly depend upon the lead mines for fupport.   Thefe having been
for fome time in a declining ftate, the poor have employed themfelves
in picking and cleaning cotton for Sir R. Arkwright's works.

Elton, *Birchover*, and *Stanton*, are hamlets in this parifh, containing
together about 216 houfes.   In the neighbourhood of Birchover is a
rocking-ftone of large dimenfions.   There are various works of rude
antiquity in thefe parts.

In a part of this parifh within the wapentake of Wirkfworth is the
village of *Middleton*, near which is one of the moft ftriking monuments
of antiquity in Derbyfhire, known by the name of Arbelows, or Arbor-
low.   It confifts of an area, encompaffed by a broad ditch of a circular
or rather of an elliptical form, leaving entrances to the north and fouth,

and

VIEW OF CHATSWORTH.

Published Nov. 1 1794, by I. Stockdale, Piccadilly.

Holland sculp.

and bounded externally by a mound. The area within is forty-six yards from eaft to weft, and fifty-two from north to fouth. Round its border are thirty oblong ftones intermixed with fourteen fmaller ones, pointing to the centre, where are three others. This was probably a Druidical temple or place of worfhip.

DARLEY PARISH.

THE living is a rectory; patron, the dean of Lincoln. The whole parifh contains 381 houfes, contained in feveral villages. In all of them, agriculture and the mining bufinefs are the chief fupports of the inhabitants.

Darley church lies on the eaft fide of the river Derwent, clofe to it, in the dale leading from Matlock to Bakewell, which is one of the moft beautiful rides in the kingdom. The church is ancient, and in the church-yard is one of the oldeft and largeft yew trees in the kingdom. No traveller can pafs without noticing its appearance, which gives folemnity to the lonely church-yard; there is no building but the parfonage houfe near it, which probably is as ancient as the church. Adjoining it are pleafant grounds and gardens, much improved and beautified by the prefent refpectable incumbent, the Rev. Mr. Wray, who has had the pleafure to fee trees planted with his own hands towering as high as the fteeple of the church, and fhading a confiderable fpace of ground. He remembers in his early youth the branches of the yew tree extending to a length and covering a fpace of ground that would appear almoft incredible. Some of its noble branches have been broken off of late years.

Snit-

Snitterton-hall in this parifh is a good manor-houfe, built about the reign of James I. It fuccefsively belonged to the Sacheverels and Mil-wards, and was, about the year 1680, conveyed to Henry Ferne, Efq. receiver-general of the cuftoms, whofe daughter and co-heir Elizabeth carried it to Edmund Turnor, Efq. of Lincolnfhire.

HATHERSAGE PARISH.

A VICARAGE, value £.35; patron, the duke of Devonfhire. The number of houfes in this liberty is about ninety; in the outfets twenty-feven, and in Bamforth twenty-five. At Hatherfage is a fmall manu-facture of metal buttons. At Bamforth a cotton mill has been worked feveral years back.

Stoney Middleton contains about 104 houfes, and 468 inhabitants. Several perfons in it are employed in the burning of lime-ftone; but working in the lead mines is the chief bufinefs of the place. The dale which takes its name from this hamlet is one of the curiofities of the county. It is a narrow, deep, and winding ravine, not fo much diftin-guifhed for grandeur or beauty, as for the peculiarity of the fhape of its rocks. On the north fide they bear a ftrong refemblance to the round towers and buttreffes of an old caftle; and in fome parts there is fuch a diftinct appearance of mouldings, that one can fcarcely help thinking the chiffel has been employed on them. The rocks, efpecially on this fide, are perpendicular, and rife to the height of 3 or 400 feet, but they are every where naked, except at a point near the entrance of Eyam dale. Here Mr. Longfdon has raifed a beautiful plantation, with a grotto in the midft of it, furnifhed with the moft elegant foffils of the country. The

4   road

road through the dale is fo narrow, and its turns fo acute, that you continually think your way ftopped up by the rocky projections.

At Stoney Middleton is a bath, called *St. Martin's*, enclofed with walls, but open at top; the water of which, in its chemical properties, refembles that of Matlock. Its heat is fixty-three degrees of Fahrenheit. It is little ufed except by the poor of the neighbourhood. There are alfo three warm petrifying fprings on the weft fide of the churchyard, and a chalybeate fpring.

Peak-foreft is a chapelry containing about ninety-five houfes. Its inhabitants are employed in the cotton manufacture, in the burning of lime, and in the mines.

HOPE PARISH.

A VICARAGE; the Dean and Chapter of Litchfield patrons. The village is fmall; a few hands in it are employed in fpinning hemp and weaving facking.

Bradwell, a large village in the parifh, but declining in population, is chiefly fupported by the mining bufinefs; a few perfons are employed in the linen and cotton manufactures. There are various little hamlets in this parifh, the inhabitants of which are chiefly employed in the mining bufinefs. The chapelry of *Fairfield* alfo belongs to it, though fituated near Buxton. The whole number of houfes in Hope parifh is about 611, but fome are uninhabited. *Brough* near Hope affords various proofs of having been a Roman ftation.

S f s   CAS.

CASTLETON PARISH.

A VICARAGE; the Bifhop of Chefter impropriator and patron. The town of Caftleton probably derived its name from the caftle, which is ftill extant in a ruined ftate. It ftands on a high point of ground, one fide being on the edge of a perpendicular precipice above the cavern named Peak's-hole. It is thought to be one of the moft ancient for-treffes in the kingdom, and part of it, at leaft, to have exifted in the Saxon heptarchy. The town of Caftleton was alfo once fortified, and the veftiges of a foffe and rampart are ftill to be feen. The number of houfes in its liberty is about 182. The inhabitants are chiefly fup-ported by the lead mines. The cotton-fpinning in this, as in other places, has declined fince the erection of Sir R. Arkwright's mills, and with it their population has diminifhed. On the noted mountain *Mam Tor* near Caftleton are evident marks of an encampment, fuppofed by fome to have been been a Roman work. The vulgar ftory, that this moun-tain is perpetually crumbling without being diminifhed, is evidently falfe, its diminution being very vifible. Of *Peak's-hole*, or *Caftleton Cavern*, we have given a particular defcription at p. 73. The annexed view, taken in 1793, exhibits the entrance to the cavern, and the ruins of the caftle above.

The valley in which Caftleton is fituated is perhaps the moft ftriking in the high Peak. It is at leaft 800 feet deep, and in many parts nearly two miles wide, and extends eaftward to the diftance of five or fix miles. A number of leffer dales at various diftances are feen opening into it. The fteep fides of the valley are beautified by well-cultivated enclofures rifing above one another to its very edge. To the north the country boldly fwells into hills, terminating in two high points. Weft-

3

ward

C. Donne delt.

VIEW OF CASTLETON.

Publish'd Sep.r 25 1794 by I. Stockdale Piccadilly.

Newman sculp.

ward it does not extend beyond the town of Caſtleton, but it there forms a noble ampitheatre : the back of which riſes in many parts to the height of 1000 feet, and the front meaſures nearly two miles over. The town of Caſtleton, its ruined caſtle frowning over the precipice, and Mam Tor raiſing i s head beyond, are grand and ſtriking objects. This valley communicates with that through which the Derwent holds its courſe to Derby, a tract well worth purſuing from the romantic variety and beauty of the ſcenes it ſucceſſively preſents.

Edale chapelry contains about ſixty-ſix houſes. There are ſome remains of antiquity near this village, imagined to be Druidical.

WIRKSWORTH WAPENTAKE.

HARTINGTON PARISH.

A VICARAGE; patron, the Duke of Devonſhire. This pariſh extends along the weſtern boundary of the county about twelve miles, comprehending all the tract of land between the manors of Buxton and Thorpe. It is divided into the Hartington town quarter, and the lower, middle, and upper quarters. The town quarter contains ſixty-three houſes, and 363 inhabitants. In the village of Hartington about ſixty hands are employed in the cotton, thread, linen, and check manufactures. There are traditions of battles fought near it, and a large barrow is to be ſeen on a high eminence not far from it, called Wolfs-cote hill. The lower quarter contains fifty-ſix houſes and 281 inhabitants; the middle quarter, ſeventy houſes and 338 inhabitants; and the upper quarter, 130 houſes, ſome of them adjoining to the town of Buxton. In the north part of this diviſion a great

S ſ s 2

quantity

quantity of lime is burnt every fummer. There are eight kilns, each
of which employs five hands, and burns about 120 horfe loads daily.
Upon Hartington common, which extends ten miles in the direction of
north and fouth, are many barrows, generally fituated upon the higheft
points of ground.

BRADBOURN PARISH.

A VICARAGE; patron, the Duke of Devonfhire. The village
contains thirty-two houfes. *Braffington*, a large chapelry in the parifh,
contains 130 houfes, and 482 inhabitants. Near it is a remarkable low
or barrow, having a number of vaults carried round its circumference,
feveral of them now expofed to fight. Other hamlets in this parifh
contain about fifty-fix houfes; the inhabitants are employed in mining.

ASHBOURN PARISH.

A VICARAGE; patron, the dean of Lincoln. Afhbourn is a market
town, fituated on the great north road. The view of this town from
the top of the hill on approaching it from London, is particularly delightful. It lies in a deep rich valley, with beautiful high grounds at
the back, as well as on the front. The defcent to it by the turnpike road
is one of the fineft walks in England, being fenced on the inner fteep fide
with a handfome railing, and having a thorn hedge on the outer fide.
The church of Afhbourn is a noble ancient building, with a fine fpire.
There is a good free-fchool in the town, founded by citizens of London, natives of the place and its vicinity. The markets of Afhbourn,

which

which are on Saturday, fupply an extenfive neighbourhood. It has alfo a confiderable fupport from its cattle fairs, which are held frequently, efpecially in fpring and autumn. The trout caught in its river, the Dove, afford a delicious treat, of which moft travellers chufe to partake. In the liberty of Afhbourn are about 480 houfes. The manor of Afhbourn, long in the family of Cockayne, whofe principal feat for many generations was at this place, paffed from them into the Boothby family. Sir Brooke Boothby, the prefent lord, refides at Afhbourn-hall, a delightful fituation. The parifh of Afhbourn extends partly in this wapentake, and partly in the hundred of Appletree. In the latter are the hamlets of *Clifton, Offcote, Underwood, Yelderfley*, and *Hulland*, together containing 103 houfes. In the wapentake are *Mappleton*, a rectory containing thirty-two houfes; *Alfop*, a chapelry, and *Parwich*, a chapelry, both at a confiderable diftance northwards, containing 102 houfes; the inhabitants employed in farming. Near the latter village are veftiges of a Roman ftation, at which a number of coins have been difcovered.

About three miles from Afhbourn is *Dove-dale*, one of the moft fingular and romantic fcenes in Derbyfhire. The river Dove here runs in a deep narrow valley, which leaves only a foot path on its banks. Its fides are almoft in every part fteep and craggy. After having entered it, which is done by a tolerably good defcent near Thorpe, you find yourfelf enclofed between craggy rocks piled above one another to a vaft height on the right, and a fteep afcent cloathed with wood and herbage on the left. On proceeding, the rocks affume the moft extraordinary fhape: in fome places they rife to the height of thirty or forty yards in the form of fpires and pyramids, entirely detached from the fide of the vale; in others, they lean over the river, and feem to menace deftruction to the paffenger. About a mile up the dale a fine natural arch is

feen,

seen, about forty feet high and eighteen wide, in a chain of rocks which extends along the edge of a high precipice, but so detached from it as to have the appearance of a maffy wall built by human hands. The rocks on the oppofite fide are covered with hanging woods, from the midft of which rifes a folitary pointed rock, fublime in its appearance, and ufually called by way of eminence, Dove-dale-church. In the opinion of the ingenious Mr. Gilpin, Dove-dale is one of the moft pleafing pieces of fcenery of the kind any where to be met with. Its perpendicular detached rocks ftamp it with a character entirely its own. It may be added, that it is a favourite fpot to the botanifts, a great variety of plants, fome of them rare, being found in its rocks and woods.

From Afhbourn are two diftinct roads to Manchefter: one through Leek and Macclesfield, the other through Buxton. The firft is the neareft and much lefs hilly, and in general a good road. The latter through Buxton, to Difley and Bullock-Smithy, where the roads join, is nearly a perpetual afcent and defcent of hills, frequently of confiderable length, as much as a mile each way. This road is equally good, if not better than the Leek and Macclesfield road, being principally made with lime-ftone. Until this year (1795) the ftage for poft-horfes from Afhbourn to Buxton was twenty-one miles, perhaps the heavieft in the kingdom, and extremely deftructive to horfes. The duke of Devonfhire's humanity has induced him, as well for the accommodation of the public, as the eafe of the animals, to eftablifh at Newhaven a capital inn with poft-horfes, to divide this unreafonable ftage. It was formerly a fmall public houfe where the horfes were baited for a few minutes.

The

C. Dayes del.ᵗ

Sparrow sculp.ᵗ

VIEW OF ASHBORNE.

The annexed view of Afhbourn was taken from the bend of the hill leading from London to Afhbourn, near to the town. On the right is the feat of Sir Brooke Boothby, Bart.; in the centre, the town, with the Derbyfhire hills behind; on the left, the church, with the Staffordfhire hills in the back ground.

FENNY-BENTLY PARISH.

A RECTORY; dean of Lincoln patron. It contains twenty-fix houfes, and 130 inhabitants. The family of Beresford was feated here towards the end of the fifteenth century, and there are feveral monuments of them in the church.

THORP PARISH.

A RECTORY; dean of Lincoln patron. It contains twenty-eight houfes. Its inhabitants are fupported by the farming bufinefs.

TISSINGTON PARISH.

A CURACY; Sir W. Fitzherbert patron. Its liberty contains forty-four houfes and 192 inhabitants. At this place is the feat of the Fitzherberts (now Lords St, Helen), who have refided here fince the reign of Henry V.

HOG-

HOGNASTON PARISH.

A RECTORY; the King patron. It contains about fifty-two houses, the inhabitants supported by agriculture.

KIRK-IRETON PARISH.

A RECTORY; the dean of Lincoln patron. It contains 120 houses.

CARSINGTON PARISH.

A RECTORY; the dean of Lincoln patron. It contains forty-six houses; the people supported by agriculture and mining.

WIRKSWORTH PARISH.

DEAN and chapter of Lincoln patrons of the living. The town lies in a bottom, eternally enveloped in smoke from the neighbouring lead and calamine works. It has a handsome church, a free-school, and an alms-house. There is a town hall for holding the manor-court; and in this town are held the Barmote courts for the wapentake. Wirksworth has scarcely any supply of common water, but has a strong medicinal water of the sulphureous kind. The number of houses in Wirksworth is 486; in the whole township 648. This place has been supported by the lead mines from before the Norman conquest. At present, several hands are also employed in the spinning of jersey

and

and cotton. A cotton mill erected by Sir R. Arkwright employs nearly 200 perfons.

Alderwafhley is a chapelry in this parifh. It contains fifty-feven houfes; its inhabitants are principally employed in farming. Near it is the feat of Francis Hurt, Efq. formerly belonging to the family of Pole.

Cromford is a hamlet containing about 120 houfes. Population has of late years rapidly increafed here, on account of the great cotton machines erected by Sir R. Arkwright, which employ about 800 hands. This was the firft place in Derbyfhire in which that moft ingenious mechanic eftablifhed his works, the various contrivances of which have contributed to the improvement and extenfion of the cotton manufactures. All operations are performed here upon the cotton, from the raw ftate in which it is imported, to fpinning it to the fineft thread; and thefe in a manner much fuperior to that by former methods, as well as at a much cheaper rate.* Sir Richard's refidence was at Cromford.

His

---

* Dr. Darwin's poetical defcription of thefe works will, we doubt not, gratify many of our readers.

> So now, where Derwent guides his dufky floods
> Through vaulted mountains and a night of woods,
> The nymph, Goffypia, treads the velvet fod,
> And warms with rofy fmiles the wat'ry god;
> His ponderous oars to flender fpindles turns,
> And pours o'er maffy wheels his foaming urns;
> With playful charms her hoary lover wins,
> And wheels his trident,—while the Monarch fpins.
> —Firft with nice eye emerging Naïads cull
> From leathery pods the vegetable wool;
> With wiry teeth *revolving cards* releafe
> The tangl'd knots, and fmooth the ravell'd fleece;

Next

His fon has built a very elegant feat on a rifing ground eaft of the Derwent, commanding a view of his works. and the neighbouring country. This place has lately received great benefit, in a canal carried from it to join the Errewafh navigation at Langley-bridge. See p. 133.

There are other hamlets in this parifh, and among them, *Hopton*, the feat of Philip Gell, Efq. whofe family have refided there fince the time of queen Elizabeth.

BONSALL PARISH.

A RECTORY; dean of Lincoln patron. It contains about 240 houfes. Its inhabitants are employed in the mines, and at the works at Cromford. Here is a free-fchool, built and endowed by Robert Ferne of this place, anceftor of the Fernes, of Snitterton.

MATLOCK PARISH.

A RECTORY; dean of Lincoln patron. The parifh contains 373 houfes. The inhabitants are confiderably employed in the lead

> Next moves the *iron-hand* with fingers fine,
> Combs the wide card, and forms th' eternal line;
> Slow, with foft lips, the *whirling can* acquires
> The tender fkeins, and wraps in rifing fpires;
> With quicken'd pace *fucceffive rollers* move,
> And thefe retain, and thefe extend the *rove*.
> Then fly the fpoles, the rapid axles glow;—
> While flowly circumvolves the labouring wheel below.
>
> *Botan. Gard.* V. ii. p. 56.

5   mines,

mines, and lately feveral hands have been occupied in manufacturing ftockings and in cotton works. There are twenty ftocking frames in the parifh. Two cotton mills have been erected; one in Matlock-dale, a large building belonging to the late Sir R. Arkwright.

The romantic beauties for which Matlock is fo much diftinguifhed, confift in a dale through which the Derwent flows, between vaft ledges of rocks, fome bare, and forming a perpendicular wall of two or three hundred feet in height, others adorned with a variety of trees and fhrubs, thus yielding a combination of the rudely magnificent, with the foft and beautiful features of fuch fcenery. The river itfelf is a great addition to the charms of the place, now flowing with a rapid and broken current, now gliding with a deep and gentle ftream, the fmooth furface of which reflects the rocks and over-hanging boughs on its margin. The moft fublime object here is called the High Tor, which is a ftupendous rock rifing almoft perpendicularly from the river to the height of 300 feet, and projecting its broad front into the valley.

Matlock water and bath.—The warm fprings of Matlock were firft noticed about the year 1698. They have gradually rifen to the reputation they now enjoy, part of which has certainly been owing to the romantic beauties of the place, and the increafed tafte for travelling. Matlock water is grateful to the palate, but without any fenfible appearance of a mineral fpirit or impregnation. Its contents on analyfis afford nothing remarkable, being chiefly calcareous earth. Its temperature is fixty-fix degrees at the fpring, and fixty-eight in the bath; as a bath, therefore, it is rather to be reckoned among the cold than hot. The effects of the water taken internally are fuppofed to be fimilar to thofe of

T t t 2

Briftol;

Briftol; they are accordingly ufed in hectic cafes, fpitting of blood, diabetes, and other difeafes with a quickened circulation. The climate, however, is far from being as fuitable as that of Briftol to confumptive patients. There are two baths at Matlock, the old and the new, and houfes for the entertainment of company at each; of which the old is the largeft and moft frequented; the new the moft pleafantly fituated.

There are two chalybeate fprings near the bridge at Matlock.

The annexed view of Matlock was taken from Mafon's Inn (the Miner's Arms.) On the right are the rocks peeping through the tops of the woods; and on the left, the Zig-Zag walk.

SCARSDALE HUNDRED (Part.)

ASHOVER PARISH.

A RECTORY; John Simpfon, Efq. patron. In the church is a very ancient font, fuppofed by fome to be Saxon. It ftands upon a ftone pedeftal; and around are twenty figures in attitudes of devotion, caft in lead. There are feveral monuments in the church, chiefly of the Babington family. The number of houfes in the liberty is 321. The inhabitants are fupported by the mining bufinefs, and the manufacture of ftockings. *Dethick* in this parifh was long the feat of the Babingtons. Anthony, the principal in a confpiracy againft queen Elizabeth,

3   refided

E. Dayes del.t

VIEW OF MATLOCK.

Heron sculp.t

Publish'd Nov.r 7.1794. by J. Stockdale Piccadilly.

CHESTERFIELD PARISH. 509

resided here. At *Lea*, another hamlet, is the seat of Peter Nightingale, Esq. A cotton mill has been erected here, and there is a small manufacture of muslins.

Overton-hall in this parish is a good mansion house, belonging to Sir Joseph Bankes, Bart. whose family became possessed of it by marriage with the heiress of Hodgkinson.

WINGERWORTH. A curacy; the dean of Lincoln patron. The houses in the liberty are about sixty-one. A furnace for smelting iron ore furnishes employment to a number of persons. *Wingerworth-hall*, the seat of Sir H. Hunloke, is a large ancient house, on an elevated situation, commanding extensive prospects. The family of Hunloke has been settled here from the time of Henry VIII.

CHESTERFIELD PARISH.

A VICARAGE; dean of Lincoln patron. Chesterfield became a borough town in the reign of king John. The corporation consists of a mayor, six aldermen, and twenty-four common-council men. The duke of Portland is lord of the manor. Its church is very ancient. The spire, which rises to the height of 230 feet, appears to lean to each side on which it is approached. The Presbyterians, Independents, and Quakers have each a place of worship in Chesterfield. There are also a free-grammar school, a town-hall, a jail for debtors, five hospitals, six alms-houses for widows, a workhouse, and house of correction. From an enumeration made in December 1788, the town was found to contain 801 houses, and 3626 inhabitants. The following

extract

extract from its annual bills of mortality will give a view of its progreffive increafe.

Year.	Marr.	Chrift.	Bur.	Year.	Marr.	Chrift.	Bur.
1700	43	79	85	1760	37	129	153
1710	19	83	78	1770	40	119	117
1720	35	91	83	1780	43	165	103
1730	51	104	107	1790	46	181	172
1740	31	93	70	1791	46	202	102
1750	41	88	91	1792	71	208	177

Chefterfield flourifhes in various branches of trade. The iron-works fituated in the town and neighbourhood afford confiderable employment. At *Walton* there are a furnace and foundry, which employ about 100 hands. At thefe works are manufactured cannon and ball, engine cylinders, ftoves, grates, ovens, and a variety of other goods. At *Newbold* is a furnace chiefly ufed for fmelting, which employs about forty-feven hands. In the town is a fmaller foundry, at which utenfils of various forts are caft. The manufacture of ftockings is another branch of its bufinefs. The frames in the town and neighbourhood are about 260. A manufacture of carpets employs eighty-four hands. A confiderable number of fhoes are made here for the London market. Three potteries near the town make a large quantity of coarfe earthen ware. A cotton mill and hat manufactory have been lately eftablifhed at Brampton moor.

The canal from Chefterfield to the Trent is a great advantage to its commerce, and is likely at laft to become a profitable concern to the undertakers. We have already given a particular account of it in p. 116.

Several

Several chapelries and hamlets in this parifh contain together about 460 houfes. *Walton* was during many generations the feat of the ancient family of Foljambe.

BRAMPTON PARISH.

A CURACY; dean of Lincoln patron. The church contains feveral ancient monuments, chiefly relating to the family of Clarke of Somerfall. The parifh is very extenfive, and contains 325 houfes. In that part of it which lies near Chefterfield there has been a confiderable increafe in population owing to the iron works. This part of the county is faid to be remarkably healthy, and the grave-ftones in the church-yard afford many inftances of great longevity.

DRONFIELD PARISH.

A VICARAGE; the king patron. It is a fmall market town. In 1783 the houfes in Dronfield were numbered, and amounted to 171, which, with the remainder contained in feveral hamlets, make up 447 in the whole parifh. The inhabitants are principally fupported by agriculture. There is here an excellent free-fchool, with a noble endowment by Henry Fanfhawe, Efq. in the time of Henry VIII. From the Fanfhawes, of Fanfhawe-gate, in this parifh, were defcended lord vifcount Fanfhawe of the kingdom of Ireland, and Sir Richard Fanfhawe, Bart. ambaffador to Spain in the reign of Charles II. There are ftill fome veftiges of a manfion at Fanfhawe-gate, which now belongs to Mrs. Fanfhawe.

At

At *Cawley*, near Dronfield, is a fulphureous fpring and bath, the water of which is gently purgative.

NORTON PARISH.

A VICARAGE; Mr. Lifter patron. The parifh confifts of feveral hamlets, containing 278 houfes. The manufacture of fcythes is carried on here to a great extent. The number of perfons employed in it is 136 makers and twenty-five grinders; and befides this, fome of the principal manufacturers furnifh work for other parifhes. *Norton-hall*, in the village of *Great Norton*, is the feat of Samuel Shore, Efq.: *Norton-houfe*, in the fame village, of Robert Newton, Efq. At a fmall diftance is the large and ancient manfion of John Bagfhaw, Efq.

IV.—*STAFFORDSHIRE.*

———————

THE principal object for which we have included part of this country in our defign having been its potteries, we fhall almoft folely confine our account of particulars to thofe parts connected with them. The town which may be confidered as their capital is

NEWCASTLE.

On the decay of the town or caftle of Chefterton-under-Lyme, which was a place of note before the conqueft, the earl of Lancafter, in the reign of Henry III. built another in the vicinity, in the midft of a great pool, which he called the New-Caftle, and which gave origin to the prefent town of that name. By Camden it is called *Newcaftle-under-Lyme*; but Leland names it *Newcaftle-under-Line*, and fays it is fo called of a brook running thereby, or of a hill, or a wood, fo named. The remains of the caftle have long fince been obliterated, but the town has become a confiderable place of trade.

Newcaftle is fituated on the fide of a hill, defcending rapidly into the vale. It is a corporate town; its corporation confifting of a mayor and twenty-one aldermen, of whom two are juftices of the peace, a recorder, town-clerk, and two ferjeants. It has a court for holding

U u u

pleas,

pleas for any fum under £.40, and the feffions are quarterly. It is likewife a parliamentary borough, fending two reprefentatives, chofen by the refident freemen, whofe number is computed at 664. The mayor is returning officer. The chief intereft is in the marquis of Stafford, which has, however, been lately checked by the fpirited and perfevering oppofition of Thomas Fletcher, Efq. a refident in the place.

The church of Newcaftle is large, but wants repair. There are feveral places of worfhip for diffenters of various denominations. There are twenty alms-houfes, endowed by the Trentham family, for the fupport of as many women, who are allowed each 2s. 11d. per week, and a new gown yearly.

Newcaftle, including the late additions, is nearly a mile in length and breadth. Several of the ftreets are fpacious, the market-place particularly fo, in which ftands the town-hall; but the buildings have a black appearance in confequence of the quantity of coals burnt in the manufactures. The inhabitants are chiefly in trade, and many of them opulent. There are two principal fairs, at Eafter and Whitfunfide. The market-day is Monday, and every fortnight there is a cattle fair. A handfome little theatre was built in 1788 by the fubfcription of twenty gentlemen of the town and neighbourhood. A fingularity which deferves mention, is a boarding-fchool for young ladies built by fubfcription, the houfe of which is elegant, and ftands on the border of an extenfive and delightful public ground, called the Brampton.

The manufacture for which this town has been long noted, is that of hats, which formerly were almoft folely of the coarfe kind, but of

late

late years the manufacturers have been fuccefsful in their attempts to make thofe of the fineft quality. A confiderable quantity of the hats made here are bought for the ufe of the furrounding country, which is very populous; but by far the greater fhare is fent by orders to all parts of the kingdom. There are alfo large quantities of fhoes made here for the London and other markets, as well as for exportation. A pottery has lately been eftablifhed in this town; and this branch of bufinefs is likely to fucceed here to a confiderable degree, provided an act be obtained, now in agitation, for cutting a canal from hence to communicate with the Grand Trunk at Stoke upon Trent.

The fupply of coals to Newcaftle is from the Apedale mines belonging to Sir Nigel Bowyer Grefley, Bart. conveyed from the pits to a wharf adjoining the town by a canal, the exclufive property of that gentleman, and fold at a low price ftipulated in the act of parliament empowering him to cut the canal.

The markets of Newcaftle have declined, fince feveral have been eftablifhed in the potteries; yet they are ftill confiderable, and well furnifhed with corn, butcher's meat, and other articles, generally at moderate prices. The town is alfo well fupplied with water.

The land about the town is in general very good and fertile; the profpects various and beautiful. The principal feats in the neighbourhood are,

Trentham-hall, a noble manfion of the Marquis of Stafford. The houfe has two grand, modern fronts, above a lawn floping to the Trent, and

Uuu 2

is

is furrounded with grounds in which are blended all the beauties of art and nature.

Keel-hall, belonging to colonel Sneyd; a very refpectable, ancient manfion.

Field-houfe, a pleafing, rural villa of Thomas Yoxall, Efq.; and the feats of H. Hatrel, Efq.; James Bent, Efq.; and at Woolftanton, that of Ralph Moreton, Efq.

The POTTERIES.

We fhall begin with a particular account of the places in which this manufacture is feated, communicated by a very intelligent gentleman refident on the fpot.

ABOUT a mile from the borders of Chefhire, the Staffordfhire potteries commence at a village called Golden-hill, from whence to the other extremity of the pottery at Lane End, is fomething more than feven miles; a confiderable part of which, by joining together, ftrikes the traveller as but one town, although under different names. The manufacturing of pottery wares is the general and nearly fole bufinefs of this extenfive and very populous quarter; and from the great increafe of inhabitants and houfes in the laft twenty years, (it being fuppofed that for every inhabitant or houfe then, there are at leaft three now) in all probability, the various towns and villages of Golden-Hill, New-Field, Smith-Field, Tunftall, Long-Port, Burflem, Cobridge, Etruria, Hanley, Shelton, Stoke, Lower Lane, Lane Delf, and Lane End,

E. Dayes del.ⁿ

W.C. Wilson sculp.ⁿ

VIEW OF SMITH-FIELD

will ere long be fo intermixed with buildings, as to form only one town and one name. At a little diftance they are all of them already ranked under the general name of *The Pottery*.

The Village of GOLDEN-HILL.—One fhould fuppofe this from its name to be a confiderable and even fplendid place; but on comparifon it is found to be the leaft fo of any in the pottery; however, its valuable mines of coal make ample amends for its other deficiencies, and from thofe mines the name was given it. At the upper end of this village is Green Lane, which commands a moft unbounded and beautiful profpect. On one fide the greateft part of Chefhire at once fhews itfelf, clofed by the Welch hills; and on the other, a complete and the beft general view of the pottery and country beyond it.

NEW-FIELD—is well fituated for manufacturing purpofes, having plenty of coals in its neighbourhood; but as the place belongs wholly to one individual, Smith Child, Efq. who has a handfome feat here, it is probable that he will not fuffer himfelf to be incommoded by a confequence inevitable where there are a number of manufactories of earthen ware together, the nuifance of the fmoke and fulphur arifing from them. It is therefore fuppofed that the manufactories will not be fpeedily increafed here.

SMITH-FIELD.—The fituation of this place, in point of convenience for manufacturing earthen wares, is not exceeded in the pottery. It has feveral ftrata of coal and coarfe clay, which the potters ufe much of, clofe to its manufactories; but belonging folely to Theophilus Smith, Efq, (a view of whofe feat is here given) this circumftance will

doubt-

doubtlefs prevent the erection of more works. The profpects it commands are very beautiful and extenfive.

TUNSTALL, including its environs, is the pleafanteft village in the pottery. It ftands on high ground, and commands pleafing profpects. The manufacturers in it are refpectable, and do confiderable bufinefs. There formerly was a church here, and various human bones have been dug up; but fuch is the effect of time, that not the leaft trace of either the one or the other remains now. A neat chapel has been lately built here. There are a confiderable number of brick and tile works here, the clay being of a fuperior kind for fuch articles, fo that with good management the tiles made from it are as blue, and look as well on the roof of a houfe, as moderate flate. This place is four miles from Newcaftle, and nine from Congleton, ftanding on the turnpike road from Lawton to Newcaftle; another turnpike road alfo commences here, and ends at Bofley in Chefhire.

LONG PORT, fituated between Burflem and Newcaftle, in a valley; has fome good buildings in it, and feveral confiderable manufactories; but its fituation thereby is rendered at times difagreeable, if not unwholefome, by the fmoke hanging upon it longer than if it was on higher ground. The Staffordfhire canal paffes Long Port, and has a public wharf upon it. This place was formerly called Long Bridge, from a kind of bridge which ran about a hundred yards parallel with the water; on the removal of which, and completion of the canal, added to its rapid increafe in buildings and bufinefs, the inhabitants about twenty years ago changed its name to that of Long Port.

BURSLEM.

BURSLEM.—This is the ancient feat of the pottery, where doubtlefs earthen wares of one kind or other have been made many centuries. Doctor Plot, in his hiftory of Staffordfhire, written in 1686, makes particular mention of the potteries of this place, and points them out as the greateft of their kind. He alfo gives an admirable detail, defcribing moft minutely the procefs and manner of making earthen ware in thofe days. But as the wares of the prefent time are of a different kind, and very different alfo in the compofition and manufacture, from that defcribed by Dr. Plot, we fhall, before we quit this neighbourhood, defcribe the prefent mode of manufacturing earthen ware, from the clay to its completion.—This place has two markets in the week, Monday and Saturday; but the meeting on Monday is the moft confiderable. In the laft four or five years they have eftablifhed regular fairs for cattle, which have been well attended. Burflem is a parifh, and has a good church, lately enlarged and thoroughly repaired, with a good organ. The late Mr. Weftley gained confiderable ground here. The methodifts have a chapel, and are very numerous; they have alfo regular built chapels in feveral towns and villages of the pottery: it is, however, fuppofed that the members of this fociety are not fo numerous now as they were in the life-time of Mr. Weftley. There are alfo great variety of other fects in the pottery: few places have fo great a diverfity of opinion on the fcore of religion as this; but the effufions of loyalty here upon moft occafions may be fairly ftated to be general, warm, and fincere.

COBRIDGE is a large village, has manufacturers of the ftaple article of the country earthen ware in it, and lies part in Burflem, and part in Stoke parifh.

ETRURIA

ETRURIA belongs folely to Jofiah Wedgwood, Efq. who has a very extenfive earthen ware manufactory here, a confiderable village, a handfome feat, and complete grounds. In his pottery purfuits he has moft defervedly acquired a great fortune with an equal fhare of reputation. The name of this place was given to it by Mr. Wedgwood, after an ancient ftate in Italy, celebrated for the exquifite tafte of its pottery, the remaining fpecimens of which have ferved grea.'y to improve the beauty of the modern articles. The Staffordfhire canal goes through Etruria grounds, which of courfe renders it a good manufacturing fituation ; but the whole belonging to one individual will moft likely operate againft an increafe of manufactories.

HANLEY.—No part of the pottery can boaft of more refpectable manufacturers than this place and its vicinity. In point of fize it is the next to Burflem, but built fo irregularly, that to a perfon in the midft of it, it has fcarcely the appearance of any thing beyond a moderate village; yet if the houfes had been properly joined together, it not only would make a capital town, but a well built one. It has a good market every Monday. All the produce of the country about is brought here, except corn, the public fale of which is not allowed, it being fo near the corn market at Newcaftle. All the other markets in the pottery labour under the fame inability, and from the fame caufe; but it is expected that attempts will be made ere long to get over fuch an inconvenience, as the inhabitants in general here, and many in other places, feem determined to deal as little as poffible with Newcaftle, on account of fome inftances of an unaccommodating difpofition which have been fhown by the latter. On the other hand, Newcaftle, which was formerly the general market of the potteries, having of courfe felt fome decline, in confequence of the rapid rife of their markets, has ex-

hibited

hibited fymptoms of diffatisfaction, which have contributed to augment the mutual jealoufy and difcontent between them.

Hanley has a very handfome, new-built and well-finifhed church; there are alfo chapels and meeting-houfes for diffenters. It is an improving and fpirited place.

SHELTON is an extenfive place, and has many confiderable manufactories in it, amongft the reft, one which deferves particular notice; the porcelain or china manufactory, carried on under the refpectable firm of Hollins, Warburton, and Co. The china made here is very little, if at all, inferiour, efpecially in the colours, to that of the Eaft Indies. This kingdom produces all the various ftone and clay which are ufed in this manufactory; and from the number of years it has already been eftablifhed, added to a regular increafe of encouragement and demand for their porcelain, there is no doubt but the worthy proprietors will reap the fruits of their fpirited adventure in fame and emolument. The ingenious Mr. Champion* of Briftol, who difcovered the art of making this porcelain, expended an ample fortune in the various trials. He had the good fortune, however, of bringing it to perfection, and obtained a patent for the exclufive privilege of making it, which he fold to the above gentlemen for fuch a fum of money as enabled him to retire to America, but he has fince returned to England. The navigation paffes this place, upon which there is a public wharf, the confequence of a water conveyance to and from the pottery, in fuch bulky and heavy articles as the raw materials ufed in this country, and the goods when manufactured, muft be obvious to every one.

* Author of " Confiderations on American Commerce."

X x x   STOKE

STOKE UPON TRENT is the parish town; has an ancient, large church, well endowed; is a rectory, and has under it several chapels and churches. It has, like most other parts of the pottery, improved much since the Staffordshire canal was cut. It contains some handsome buildings, and from its contiguity to a wharf upon the canal, is conveniently situated for trade. It has many earthen ware manufactories, some of which are upon an extensive scale. At this place, a gentleman of the name of Spode established a few years ago the first steam engine to grind burned flint for potters' use; which, it is said, answers the expectation. The river Trent passes here, and at times with rapidity; nevertheless the brick arches which carry the navigation above the river do not seem to have sustained much injury. J. Whieldon, Esq. has a pleasant rural seat here. A new road has lately been cut from this place to join the London road between Newcastle and Trentham. Heretofore the road lay through Newcastle, which was considerably round. From this place to Newcastle on the right, the prospects are extremely beautiful; and nearly at the midway, a view so populous, and at the same time so picturesque, is seldom met with.

LOWER LANE, LANE DELF, *and* LANE END, conclude the pottery beyond Stoke. The latter place is by far the most considerable. It has a new-built chapel under Stoke, a methodist chapel, and meeting-houses for other dissenters. These places, particularly the latter, manufacture large quantities of earthen wares; but it is said to be with less attention than in the other parts of the pottery, consequently something inferior in quality; at the same time, there are a few houses whose wares are inferior to none. On the right hand, at Lower Lane, is *Fenton*, the seat of Charles Smith, Esq. To the left, at Lane End, is *Longton-hall*, the seat of Sir John Edenson Heathcote, and to the

4   left

left of it *Park-hall*, the feat of —— Parker, Efq. a defcendant of lord chief juftice Parker. Some earthen ware is alfo manufactured at New Chapel, Wolftanton, Red-ftreet, Newcaftle, Norton, and fome other places; but not in fo extenfive a degree as in moft of the places already mentioned.

With refpect to the manufactures themfelves, we are happy in being able to prefent to our readers a very accurate account of their rife, pro-grefs, and prefent ftate, drawn up by a perfon of great chymical know-ledge, and thoroughly acquainted with the fubject.

Account of the Pottery Manufacture in Staffordfhire.

This part of the county, from the clays and the coal mines which it abounds with, appears better adapted for a manufactory of earthen wares than, perhaps, for any other. The *meafures* or ftrata, by which the beds of coal are divided, confift moft commonly of clays of diffe-rent kinds, fome of which make both excellent fire bricks for building the potters' kilns and faggars,* or cafes in which the ware is burnt. Finer clays, of various colour and textures, are likewife plentiful in many places, moft of them near the furface of the earth; and of thefe, the bodies of the wares themfelves were formerly manufactured. The coals being then alfo got near the furface, were plentiful and cheap: Plot ftates them, fo late as his time, at twopence the horfe load, which, at eight horfe loads to a ton, (the common eftimation) amounts only to fixteen pence per ton. The land, having chiefly a clay bottom, was unfavourable to the productions of hufbandry; and its remotenefs from the feats of commerce contributed further to render labour cheap. All

* This is a corruption of the German word *fchragers*, which fignifies cafes or fup-porters.

X x x 2   thefe

thefe circumftances confidered together, with fome others which will
be mentioned hereafter, may poffibly afford the beft anfwer to a
queftion which has often been afked, why the pottery was eftablifhed
in Staffordfhire preferably to any other place, and why it ftill continues
to flourifh there more than in any other part of the kingdom, or perhaps
of the world ?

How long this kind of manufactory has fubfifted here is utterly unknown.   It can be traced with certainty for at leaft two centuries back ;
and no document or tradition remains of its firft introduction.   Its
principal feat feems to have been formerly the town of Burflem, and
it was then called a *butter* pottery, that is, a manufactory of pots in
which butter was kept ; and we have feen it fo denominated in a very
old map.   As a proof of the antiquity of the manufacture in this neighbourhood, it may be proper to mention, that about feventy years ago,
below the foundation of a building then taken down and fuppofed to
have been not lefs than a hundred years old, the bottom of a potter's
kiln was difcovered, with fome of the faggars upon it, and pieces of
the ware in them ; and that about the fame time a road, which had
long before been made acrofs a field, being worn down into a hollow
way, the hearth of a potter's kiln was found to be cut through by this
hollow part of the road ; and it was not among the then exifting, or
then remembered potteries, that thefe old works were difcovered, but
at a confiderable diftance, in places where no tradition remained among
the oldeft inhabitants of the neighbouring villages that any pot-works
had ever been.   It may be added, that pieces of ware, of the rudeft
workmanfhip and without any glaze or varnifh, are frequently met
with in digging for the foundations of new erections.

2   Though

Though the old remains are undoubtedly the productions of diftant periods, they give little or no light into the fucceffive improvements made in the art; nor indeed could any good purpofe be anfwered by an inquiry of that kind; for though the manufacture has, within our memory, advanced with amazing rapidity to its prefent magnitude, it feems to have continued for a long feries of years almoft uniformly rude and uninterefting. Even fo late as the year 1686, when Dr. Plot publifhed his hiftory of the county, the quantity of goods manufactured was fo inconfiderable, that " the principal fale of them," the doctor fays, " was to the poor crate-men, who carried them *at their backs* all over " the country !" All the ware was then of the coarfe yellow, red, black, and mottled kind, made from the clays found in the neighbourhood, as already mentioned; the body of the ware being formed of the inferior kinds of clay, and afterwards painted or mottled with the finer coloured ones mixed with water, feparately or blended together, much in the fame manner that paper is marbled. The common glaze was produced by lead ore, finely powdered, and fprinkled on the pieces of ware before firing; fometimes with the addition of a little manganefe, for the fake of the brown colour it communicates; and, when the potter wifhed " to fhew the utmoft of his fkill" (to ufe Dr. Plot's expreffion) in giving the ware a higher glofs than ordinary, he employed, inftead of lead ore, calcined lead itfelf, but ftill fprinkled it on the pieces in the fame rude manner.

The æra of improvement commenced a few years after the publication of Plot's work, by the introduction of a new fpecies of glaze, produced by throwing into the kiln, when brought to its greateft heat, a quantity of common falt, the fumes of which occafioned a fuperficial vitrification of the clay. How long this practice might have fubfifted

in

in other countries, is unknown; but it was firſt brought hither about the year 1690, by two ingenious foreigners of the name of Elers,* who eſtabliſhed a ſmall pot-work at Bradwall near Burſlem; and it was in the memory of ſome old perſons, with whom a friend of ours was well acquainted, that the inhabitants of Burſlem flocked with aſtoniſhment to ſee the immenſe volumes of ſmoke which roſe " from the Dutchmen's " ovens," on caſting in the ſalt; a circumſtance which ſufficiently ſhews the novelty of this practice in the Staffordſhire potteries. The ſame perſons introduced likewiſe another ſpecies of ware, in imitation of the unglazed red China from the Eaſt; and the clays in this country being ſuitable for the purpoſe, they ſucceeded wonderfully for a firſt attempt, inſomuch that ſome of their tea-pots are ſaid to have been ſold ſo high as a guinea a-piece; and ſome of the ſpecimens which ſtill remain in the country are very perfect in their kind, as well with reſpect to the texture and quality of the ware itſelf, as to the form and workman-ſhip. The foreigners, however, did not long continue in this ſitua-tion; finding the manufacturers about them very inquiſitive, and not chooſing to have their procedures ſo narrowly inſpected, they quitted Staffordſhire, and ſet up a manufacture near London.

The eſtabliſhment of the new glaze with ſalt was ſucceeded, in a ſhort time, by a capital improvement in the body of the ware itſelf, which the tradition of the country attributes to the following incident: One of the potters (Mr. Aſtbury) in a journey to London, happened to have powdered flint recommended to him, by the oſtler of his inn at Dunſtable, for curing ſome diſorder in one of his horſe's eyes; and for

* A deſcendant of one of theſe ingenious foreigners was lately a reſpectable magiſtrate in the county of Oxford.

that

that purpofe a flint ftone was thrown into the fire to render it more eafily pulverable. The potter, obferving the flint to be changed by the
fire to a pure white, was immediately ftruck with the idea that his
ware might be improved by an addition of this material to the whiteft
clays he could procure. Accordingly he fent home a quantity of the
flint ftones, which are plentiful among the chalk in that part of the
country, and on trial of them with tobacco-pipe clay, the event proved
fully anfwerable to his expectation. Thus originated the *white* ftone
ware, which foon fupplanted the coloured ones, and continued for many
years the ftaple branch of pottery.

Thofe who became firft acquainted with the great improvement produced by the addition of flint, endeavouring, as is ufual in fuch cafes,
to keep the fecret to themfelves, had the flints pounded in mortars by
manual labour, in cellars or in private rooms; but the operation proved
pernicious to many of the workmen, the fine duft getting into the
lungs, and producing dreadful coughs and confumptions, and thefe
alarming complaints of the men may be prefumed to have haftened the
difcovery of the fource from which they had arifen. The fecret becoming generally known, the confequent increafe of demand for the flint
powder occafioned trials to be made of mills, of various conftructions,
for ftamping and for grinding it; and the ill effects of the duft, which
could not be entirely guarded againft when the ftones were either
pounded or ground dry, pointed out an addition of water in the grinding. This method, being found effectual as well as fafe, is ftill continued: the ground flint comes from the mill in a liquid ftate about the
confiftence of cream; and the tobacco-pipe clay being mixed up with
water to the fame confiftence, the two liquids are proportioned to one
another by meafure inftead of weight.

A little

A little after the ufe of flint had been introduced, an improvement was made by an ingenious mechanic in the neighbourhood, Mr. Alfager, in the potter's wheel, by which its motion was greatly accelerated. This enabled the potters to form their ware not only with greater expedition and facility, but likewife with more neatnefs and precifion than they had done before.

By thefe means the manufacture was fo far improved, in the beginning of the prefent century, as to furnifh various articles for tea and coffee equipages, and foon after for the dinner table alfo. Before the middle of the century thefe articles were manufactured in quantity, as well for exportation as home confumption. The falt glaze, however, the only one then in ufe for thefe purpofes, is in its own nature fo imperfect, and the potters, from an injudicious competition among themfelves for cheapnefs rather than for excellence, had been fo inattentive to elegance of forms and neatnefs of workmanfhip, that this ware began to be rejected from genteel tables, and fupplanted by a white ware of finer forms and more beautiful glaze, which, about the year 1760, was imported in confiderable quantities from France.

This inundation of a foreign manufacture, fo much fuperior to our own, muft have had very bad effects upon the potteries of this kingdom, if a new one, ftill more to the public tafte, had not happily been foon after produced here. In 1763, Mr. Jofiah Wedgwood, who had already introduced feveral improvements into this art, as well with refpect to the forms and colours of the wares, as the compofition of which they were made, invented a fpecies of earthen ware for the table, of a firm and durable body, and covered with a rich and brilliant glaze, and bearing fudden viciffitudes of cold and heat without injury : it was

accom-

accompanied alfo with the advantage of being manufactured with eafe and expedition, was fold cheap, and as it poffeffed, with the novelty of its appearance, every requifite quality for the purpofe intended, it came quickly into general eftimation and ufe. To this manufacture the Queen was pleafed to give her name and patronage, commanding it to be called *Queen's Ware*, and honouring the inventor by appointing him her majefty's potter.

This ware is compofed of the whiteft clays from Devonfhire, Dorfetfhire, and other places, mixed with a due proportion of ground flint. The pieces are fired twice, and the glaze applied after the firft firing, in the fame manner as on porcelain. The glaze is a vitreous compofition, of flint and other white earthy bodies, with an addition of white lead for the flux, analogous to common flint glafs ; fo that, when prepared in perfection, the ware may be confidered as coated over with real flint glafs. This compound being mixed with water to a proper confiftence, the pieces, after the firft firing, are feparately dipt in it : being fomewhat bibulous, they drink in a quantity of the mere water, and the glaze which was united with that portion of the water remains adherent, uniformly, all over their furface, fo as to become, by the fecond firing, a coat of perfect glafs.

To the continued experimental refearches of the fame perfon we owe the invention of feveral other fpecies of earthen ware and porcelain, adapted to various purpofes of ornament and ufe. The principal are the fix following :

1. A *terra cotta*; refembling porphyry, granite, Egyptian pebble, and other beautiful ftones of the filiceous or cryftalline order.

Y y y

2. *Bafaltes*

2. *Bafaltes* or black ware; a black porcelain bifcuit of nearly the fame properties with the natural ftone; ftriking fire with fteel, receiving a high polifh, ferving as a touchftone for metals, refifting all the acids, and bearing, without injury, a ftrong fire, ftronger indeed than the bafaltes itfelf.

3. *White porcelain bifcuit*, of a fmooth wax-like furface, of the fame properties with the preceding, except in what depends upon colour.

4. *Jafper*; a white porcelain bifcuit of exquifite beauty and delicacy, poffeffing the general properties of the bafaltes, together with the fingular one of receiving through its whole fubftance, from the admixture of metallic calces with the other materials, the fame colours which thofe calces communicate to glafs or enamels in fufion; a property which no other porcelain or earthen ware body, of ancient or modern compofition, has been found to poffefs. This renders it peculiarly fit for making cameos, portraits, and all fubjects in bas relief, as the ground may be of any particular colour, while the raifed figures are of a pure white.

5. *Bamboo*, or cane-coloured bifcuit porcelain; of the fame nature as No. 3.

6. *A porcelain bifcuit*, remarkable for great *hardnefs*, little inferior to that of agate: this property, together with its refiftance to the ftrongeft acids and corrofives, and its impenetrability by every known liquid, adapts it for mortars and many different kinds of chemical veffels.

Thefe

Thefe fix diftinct fpecies, with the queen's ware already mentioned, expanded, by the induftry and ingenuity of the different manufacturers, into an infinity of forms for ornament and ufe, varioufly painted and embellifhed, conftitute nearly the whole of the prefent fine Englifh earthen wares and porcelain, which are now become the fource of a very extenfive trade, and which, confidered as an object of national art, induftry, and commerce, may be ranked amongft the moft important manufactures of the kingdom.

The evidence given by Mr. Wedgwood to the committee of Privy Council, and at the bars of the two Houfes of Parliament, when a commercial arrangement with Ireland was in agitation, in 1785, will give fome idea of the prefent extent of this manufacture, and of its value to our maritime and landed, as well as our commercial, interefts.

Though the manufacturing part alone, in the potteries and their vicinity, gives bread to fifteen or twenty thoufand people, including the wives and children of thofe who are employed in it; he looks upon this as a fmall object when compared with the many others which depend on it, namely, 1. The immenfe quantity of *inland carriage* it creates throughout the kingdom, both for its raw materials and finifhed goods:—2. The great number of people employed in the extenfive collieries for its ufe:—3. The ftill greater number employed in *raifing* and *preparing* its raw materials, in feveral diftant parts of England, from near the Land's-end in Cornwall—one way along different parts of the coaft, to Falmouth, Teignmouth, Exeter, Pool, Gravefend, and the Norfolk coaft—the other way, to Biddeford, Wales, and the Irifh coaft:—4. The *coafting veffels*, which, after having been employed at the proper feafon in the Newfoundland fifhery, carry thefe materials coaft-wife to

Y y y 2   Liverpool

Liverpool and Hull, to the amount of more than 20,000 tons yearly, at times when they would otherwise be laid up idle in harbour:—5. The further conveyance of them from those ports, by *river and canal navigation*, to the potteries situated in one of the most inland parts of this kingdom:—and 6. The *re-conveyance* of the finished goods to the different ports of this island, where they are shipped for every foreign market that is open to the earthen wares of England.

He observes further, that this manufacture is attended with some advantageous circumstances almost peculiar to itself, viz. that the value of the manufactured goods consists almost wholly in labour; that one ton of raw materials produces several tons of finished goods for shipping, the freight being then charged, not by the weight, but by the bulk;— that scarce a vessel leaves any of our ports without more or less of these cheap, bulky, and therefore valuable articles to this maritime country; and, above all, that not less than five parts in six, of the whole produce of the potteries, are exported to foreign markets.

Important as the pottery may now appear, and rapid as its progression has been within the last thirty years, Mr. Wedgwood, in his evidence to the House of Commons, declares himself strongly impressed with the idea, that the art is still but in its infancy, compared with what it may arrive at *if not interrupted in its growth*. In a history of commerce lately published,* the editor, after quoting Mr. Wedgwood's evidence, supposes that by this last expression he alludes to the introduction of *excise laws* in the pottery, of which, it seems, there was some talk at that time; but adds, very justly, that it would have been too im-

* Appendix to the second edition of Anderson's History of Commerce, vol. iv. p. 700.

politie

politic a ftep to check fo growing a manufacture by excife laws, more efpecially when five-fixths of the duty collected muft have been paid back again upon exportation of the goods, and an opening thereby made for fraud, which, if we may judge from what has been practifed in fome other articles, would have made the drawback amount to more than the original payment.

To the preceding general account of the manufacture, we fhall add a more particular defcription of the procefs ufed in manufacturing the earthen ware, which has been communicated to us by a perfon on the fpot.

A piece of the prepared mixture of clay and ground flint, dried and tempered to a proper confiftence, is taken to be formed into any required fhape and fafhion, by a man who fits over a machine called a wheel, on the going round of which he continues forming the ware. This branch is called *throwing*, and as water is required to prevent the clay fticking to the hand, it is neceffary to place it for a fhort time in a warm fituation. It then undergoes the operation of being turned, and made much fmoother than it was before, by a perfon called a turner; when it is ready for the handle and fpout to be joined to, by the branch called *handling*.—Difhes, plates, tureens, and many other articles are made from moulds of ground plaifter, and when finifhed, the whole are placed carefully (being then in a much more brittle ftate than when fired) in faggars, which in fhape and form pretty much refemble a lady's band-box without its cover, but much thicker, and are made from the marl or clay of this neighbourhood. The larger ovens or kilns are placed full of faggars fo filled with ware; and after a fire which confumes from twelve to fifteen tons of coal, when the oven is

become

become cool again, the faggars are taken out, and their contents removed, often exceeding in number 30,000 various pieces; but this depends upon the general fizes of the ware. In this ftate the ware is called *bif-cuit*, and the body of it has much the appearance of a new tobacco pipe, not having the leaft glofs upon it. It then is immerfed or dipped into a fluid generally confifting of fixty pounds of white lead, ten pounds of ground flint, and twenty pounds of a ftone from Cornwall burned and ground, all mixed together, and as much water put to it as reduces it to the thicknefs of cream, which it refembles. Each piece of ware being feparately immerfed or dipped into this fluid, fo much of it adheres all over the piece, that when put into other faggars, and ex-pofed to another operation of fire, performed in the gloffing kiln or oven, the ware becomes finifhed by acquiring its gloffy covering, which is given it by the vitrification of the above ingredients. Enamelled ware undergoes a third fire after its being painted, in order to bind the colour on.

A fingle piece of ware, fuch as a common enamelled tea-pot, a mug, jug, &c. paffes through at leaft fourteen different hands before it is finifhed, viz.

The flipmaker, who makes the clay;
The temperer, or beater of the clay;
The thrower, who forms the ware;
The ballmaker and carrier;
The attender upon the drying of it;
The turner who does away its roughnefs;
The fpoutmaker;
The handler, who puts to the handle and fpout;

I   The

The firſt, or biſcuit fireman;

The perſon who immerſes or dips it into the lead fluid;

The ſecond, or gloſs fireman;

The dreſſer, or ſorter in the warehouſe;

The enameller, or painter;

The muffle, or enamel fireman.

Several more are required to the completion of ſuch piece of ware, but are in inferior capacities, ſuch as turners of the wheel, turners of the lathe, &c. &c.

We cannot more properly cloſe this account of the Staffordſhire potteries, than with a biographical record of the perſon to whom they have been ſo much indebted, extracted from the *Gentleman's Magazine* for January 1795, the period of his much-lamented death.

" DIED, at Etruria, in Staffordſhire, aged 64, JOSIAH WEDGWOOD, Eſq. F R. and A. SS.; to whoſe indefatigable labours is owing the eſtabliſhment of a manufacture that has opened a new ſcene of extenſive commerce, before unknown to this or any other country. It is unneceſſary to ſay that this alludes to the Pottery of Staffordſhire, which, by the united efforts of Mr. Wedgwood, and his late partner, Mr. Bentley, has been carried to a degree of perfection, both in the line of utility and ornament, that leaves all works, ancient or modern, far behind.

" Mr. Wedgwood was the younger ſon of a potter, but derived little or no property from his father, whoſe poſſeſſions conſiſted chiefly of a ſmall entailed eſtate, which deſcended to the eldeſt ſon. He was the

maker

maker of his own fortune, and his country has been benefited in a proportion not to be calculated. His many difcoveries of new fpecies of
earthen wares and porcelains, his ftudied forms and chafte ftyle of de-
coration, and the correctnefs and judgment with which all his works
were executed under his own eye, and by artifts, for the moft part, of
his own forming, have turned the current in this branch of commerce;
for, before his time, England imported the finer earthen wares; but,
for more than twenty years paft, fhe has exported them to a very great
annual amount, the whole of which is drawn from the earth, and from
the induftry of the inhabitants; while the national tafte has been improved, and its reputation raifed in foreign countries. His inventions
have prodigioufly increafed the number of perfons employed in the
potteries, and in the traffic and tranfport of their materials from diftant parts of the kingdom: and this clafs of manufacturers is alfo
indebted to him for much mechanical contrivance and arrangement in
their operations; his private manufactory having had, for thirty years
and upwards, all the efficacy of a public work of experiment. Neither was he unknown in the walks of philofophy. His communications to the Royal Society fhew a mind enlightened by fcience, and
contributed to procure him the efteem of fcientific men at home and
throughout Europe. His invention of a thermometer for meafuring
the higher degrees of heat employed in the various arts, is of the
higheft importance to their promotion, and will add celebrity to his
name. At an early period of his life, feeing the impoffibility of extending confiderably the manufactory he was engaged in on the fpot
which gave him birth, without the advantages of inland navigation,
he was the propofer of the Grand Trunk Canal, and the chief agent
in obtaining the act of parliament for making it, againft the prejudices
of the landed intereft, which at that time ftood very high, and but juft

3

before

before had been with great difficulty overcome in another quarter by all the powerful influence of a noble Duke, whose canal was at that time but lately finished.—Having acquired a large fortune, his purse was always open to the calls of charity, and to the support of every institution for the public good.   To his relations, friends, and neighbours, he was endeared by his many private virtues; and his loss will be deeply and long deplored by all who had the pleasure of knowing them intimately, and by the numerous objects to whom his benevolence was extended: and he will be regretted by his country as the able and zealous supporter of her commerce, and the steady patron of every valuable interest of society."

We shall add, that the great concerns of the late Mr. Wedgwood are now under the joint management of Messrs. Josiah Wedgwood and Thomas Byerley.

L E E K.

THIS is the principal market-town of the Moorlands.   It is situated on the side of a hill with a steep descent to a small river, which is a branch of the Churnet; and is a middling-sized, clean town, with wide and open streets, and a spacious market-place.   It anciently belonged to the earls of Chester.   The market is on Wednesday, and there are fairs at Candlemas, Easter, Whitsuntide, and other times in the year.   The church is a fine, large edifice, standing on a high ground, which commands a delightful prospect up and down rich vallies to the north and west.   In the church-yard is a tall pyramidal stone, adorned with imagery and fret-work.   The town is well supplied with water, which, together with its situation, contributes to its cleanliness.

Z z z   Leek

Leek long ago participated in the button trade with Macclesfield, of which an account is given under that town. It now poſſeſſes a conſiderable manufacture in the ſilk and mohair branches, the goods made from which materials are ſewing-ſilks, twiſt, buttons, ſilk-ferrets, ſhawls, and ſilk handkerchiefs. In theſe manufactures are employed about two thouſand inhabitants of the town, and one thouſand of the adjacent country. Some good fortunes have been made by the Leek manufacturers, and its trade has been very flouriſhing; but the check on paper credit three years ſince injured it, and the war has leſſened the foreign demand. Still, however, a good deal of buſineſs is done here, and the difficulties with reſpect to credit have in great meaſure been got over.

This town, lying at an equal diſtance between Aſhbourn and Macclesfield, Buxton and Newcaſtle, and being on the London road to Mancheſter, is much frequented by perſons travelling through the country in all directions, from which it derives conſiderable advantage.

The annexed view of Leek was taken from the road leading to Newcaſtle, which is thought to afford the beſt proſpect of the place, though there is no very favourable one.

V.—WEST-

C. Dayes del.t

VIEW OF LEEK.

Sparrow sculp.t

Publish'd May 22.1793 by I.Stockdale, Piccadilly.

V.—*WEST RIDING OF YORKSHIRE.*

THE propofed limits of our work have been fo nearly filled by the details which have crowded upon us from the parts already vifited, that we fhall be obliged to content ourfelves with a concife view of the moft important objects prefented by the large and interefting diftrict to which we have now arrived. Without attending to the topographical divifions of the county, we fhall make a tour through its principal commercial towns; beginning with one in its moft fouthern part, diftinguifhed by a branch of manufacture entirely different in its nature from that which in general characterifes the Weft Riding. This is

SHEFFIELD,

or *Sheaf-field*, a town of ancient note for its trade in cutlery and hardware, and called by Leland the principal market-town in *Hallam-fhire*, a diftrict faid by him to extend fix or feven miles to the weft of Sheffield. The town is fituated near the borders of Derbyfhire, in the deanry of Doncafter, and the united hundreds of Strafforth and Tickhill, upon an eminence at the confluence of the rivers Sheaf and Don, over each of which is a ftone bridge. That over the Don called Lady's-bridge, confifting of three arches, and leading to Barnfley to the north, and Rotherham to the north-eaft, is fuppofed to be fo named from a religious houfe which anciently ftood near it, and was dedicated to the

Z z z 2   Virgin

Virgin Mary, which was afterwards converted into alms-houses for poor widows. But when the bridge was widened, in 1768, these houses were pulled down. It was erected originally in 1485, for 100 marks, the town finding all the materials.—The bridge over the Sheaf was rebuilt by Edward duke of Norfolk in 1769, consisting of one arch; and leads to Sheffield-park, Hansworth-Woodhouse, &c. to the east. The extent of the town from east to west and from north to south is about three quarters of a mile. It is six miles distant from Rotherham, eighteen from Doncaster, thirteen from Barnsley, thirty-six from Leeds, six from Dronfield, eleven from Chesterfield, and 162 from London.

In the north-east part of the town, where the two rivers meet, stood anciently a strong castle, of a triangular form, guarded on two sides by the rivers Don and Sheaf, having a strong breast-work before the gates, which were palisadoed, with a trench twelve feet deep and eighteen feet wide, full of water, and a wall round five yards thick. This castle, with the lordship of Sheffield, was granted (as appears by an ancient record) to Thomas lord Fournyvale, 39 Edward III. to be held by homage and knight's service and the payment to the king and his heirs of two white hares, yearly, on the feast of St. John the Baptist. It was surrendered, upon articles of capitulation, to the parliament forces by commissioners authorized by the governor, major Beaumont, August 10, 1644, and was afterwards demolished; so that there are very few vestiges of it remaining, except that the streets and places thereabouts still retain the names of the Castle-hill, Castle-ditch, Castle-fold, Castle-green, &c.

The

The river Don, which, being joined by the Sheaf, runs hence to Rotherham, is navigable for fmall veffels at about three miles diftance from Sheffield; and thence to and above the town great numbers of works are erected upon it for forging, flitting, and preparing the iron and fteel for the Sheffield manufactures, and for grinding knives, fciffars, fheers, &c.

As a certain portion of ground or tenements in the town belongs to the freeholders at large, fo feven of them (four of the eftablifhed church and three diffenters) are appointed, under the title of *town collectors*, to grant leafes, receive rents, and apply the produce of the eftate to public ufes, fuch as lighting the ftreets, &c.

The corporation here concerns only the manufactory, and is ftiled *The Company of Cutlers of Hallamſhire*. The act for the eftablifh-ment of this corporation was paffed in 1625, and an amendment was made to it in 1791. It is governed by a mafter, two wardens, fix fearchers, and twenty-four affiftants. The mafter is elected annually on the laft Thurfday in Auguft, after having paffed through the inferior offices.

Churches, &c.—There are four places of public worfhip according to the church of England. Trinity church, anciently called St. Peter's, which ftands near the centre of the town, was erected about the year 1100. It is a vicarage, and formerly belonged to the priory of Work-fop, in Nottinghamfhire. The vicar's income chiefly depends upon the fmall tithes, Eafter dues, and fees for marriages, churchings, and bu-rials; the glebe being but fmall, though lately improved. The vicar
has

has three affiftant-minifters, who were firft appointed, and a donation
of land made for their fupport, and other purpofes, by queen Mary, in
1553. They are elected by the twelve capital burgeffes, as they are
ftiled, who are truftees for the donation. The office of thefe affiftant-
minifters or chaplains, according to the grant, was to affift the vicar
in *facramentis et facramentalibus in parochiali ecclefia Sheffieldienfi et
parochianis ibidem.* The church is a Gothic ftructure with a handfome
fpire in the centre. It has eight very tunable bells, and a fet of chimes
made in 1773 by Mr. Whitehurft of Derby. It confifts within of a
nave, two fide aifles, and a large chancel. On the north fide of the
communion-table is the veftry and library, over which is a room where
the twelve burgeffes before mentioned tranfact bufinefs relative to their
truft. On the fouth fide is the Shrewfbury chapel which contains the
monuments of three earls of Shrewfbury, of the family of the Talbots,
viz. George, the fourth earl, and his two wives, Anne the daughter
of William, lord Haftings, and Elizabeth the daughter of Sir Richard
Walden, of Erith, in Kent: he died anno 1538; Francis, the fifth
earl, who died anno 1559; George, the fixth earl, who died in 1599.
On the arrival of Mary queen of Scots in England, fhe was put under
the care of this nobleman, anno 1568, and fo continued till 1584.
Here likewife was interred, Gilbert, the feventh earl of Shrewfbury, fon
of the preceding, who died in 1616. On the fide north of the chancel
is a mural monument to the memory of judge Jeffop and his lady, of
Broom-hall, near this town; and on the fouth fide is another to the
memory of George Bamforth, Efq. of High-houfe, near Sheffield.
The moft ancient epitaph now to be met with in this church is upon a
brafs plate near the north corner of the communion rails, in the following words:

Here lyeth Elizabeth, doughter
of Thomas Erle of Ormond
and Lore his wyf fomtyme
wyf to the Lord Mountjoye,

which Elizabeth deceafed
the xx day of February
the year of our Lord MCCCCCX.
On whofe foul then have mercy men.

Anno 1700, was interred near the chancel door of this church William
Walker, who, from ftrong circumftances, there is reafon to believe was
executioner of king Charles the firft; fee Gent. Mag. vol. xxxvii. 548,
xxxviii. 10, lvii. 759.

St. Paul's church is an elegant modern ftructure in the Grecian ftile.
It was begun to be erected in 1720, but through fome unhappy mifun-
derftandings was not confecrated till 1740. It was founded through
the benefaction of £.1000 from Mr. Robert Downes, a filverfmith in
this town, together with the fubfcriptions of feveral other gentlemen
in the town and neighbourhood. It was finifhed in 1771. This
church has a tower at the weft end, with a bell and clock prefented
by Francis Sitwell, Efq. Within is a good organ erected in 1755 by
Mr. Snitzler, and the galleries are fupported by two rows of Corinthian
pillars. It is a chapel of eafe to Trinity church. St. James's church
is a handfome modern building, erected by fubfcription upon the glebe
land belonging to the vicarage, according to an act of parliament paffed
in 1788, and was confecrated Auguft 5, 1789. The chapel at the duke
of Norfolk's hofpital, rebuilt in 1777 in an octagonal form, was principally defigned for the penfioners, who have daily prayers performed here
by a minifter of the church of England, and two fermons on Sundays.
It is calculated to contain a large congregation, but its conftruction is
unfavourable to the hearers.

Near St. Paul's church to the north-eaft is a diffenting meeting-
houfe built in 1700; another at a little diftance below erected 1710;

near

near to this a methodist meeting-house opened, June 30, 1780. In
Queen-street north of Trinity church a new diffenting meeting-house
was erected in 1784; there is another in Coal-pit-lane, south-west
from St. Paul's; another in Howard-street, east of St. Paul's, opened
April 11, 1790; another in Brick-lane, north-west from Trinity
church; and another in Scotland-street, north-west of the fame church,
where the Liturgy of the establishment is read, but its minister is not
subject to episcopal jurisdiction. A little distance from Trinity church
to the north-east is a quaker's meeting-house; and in Norfolk-row is
a Romish chapel.

Charitable Institutions.—On the east side of the river Sheaf near
the bridge is an hospital, erected in 1670 by Henry, earl of Norwich,
great grandson of Gilbert, earl of Shrewsbury, in pursuance of his
last will and testament, and endowed with divers estates. March 3,
1770, Edward, duke of Norfolk, gave by deed ƒ.1000 for the augmentation of the funds of the said hospital, which sum was applied
by the trustees towards building a new chapel by the side of the old
one. The hospital confists of two quadrangles containing eighteen
dwellings in each. It was intended originally for the benefit of fifteen
men and fifteen women, aged and decayed housekeepers, for each of
whom was provided a house and garden, a pension of 2s. 6d. a week,
three cart loads of coals annually, two new shirts or shifts, and a blue
gown or loose coat every second year, and a purple gown and badge
every seventh year. But, through the improvement of the estate belonging to this charity, three more dwellings have been added to each
quadrangle, and three men and three women penfioners additionally
admitted upon the foundation; and by a still farther improvement of
the estate the trustees were enabled to advance their pensions at Michael-

mas

mas 1763 to 3*s.* 6*d.* and of late to 5*s.* a week. On the north side of the town is another hospital erected in 1703 by Mr. Thomas Hollis, a merchant in London, who, it is said, was a native of this town, for the benefit of sixteen poor cutlers' widows. They have each a separate habitation and 6*l.* 10*s.* a year, which is paid, in some measure, quarterly; two cart loads of coals annually, and a brown gown and petticoat every second year. Upon the same foundation a master is appointed to teach forty boys to read English, and a writing-master to instruct a number of them to write during three or four of the summer months. There is a very good improveable estate belonging to this charity which is under the management of fifteen trustees. At the north-east corner of Trinity church-yard is a charity school for cloathing, feeding, and instructing, in English, writing, and accounts, poor boys from the age of seven to thirteen. They are dressed in a blue uniform with bands and caps, as usual in such places. There are at present fifty-four upon the foundation. This charity was instituted in 1708, and is supported by annual subscriptions, charity-sermon collections, dividends of stock in the funds, some small rents, &c. At the north-west corner of Trinity church-yard is a charity school, erected in 1786, for cloathing, feeding, and instructing poor girls in reading English, sewing, knitting, spinning jersey and line, and in such other particulars as may qualify them to be useful servants. There are at present fifty upon the foundation. They are admitted at the age of seven and continued till they are fourteen or fifteen, at the option of the trustees, when they are engaged out to proper places. This charity is supported by annual subscriptions, charity-sermon collections, &c. West from here is a free grammar school, the patent for which was granted by James the first, though, as appears from a date upon the portal, the building was not completed till 1649. It has a head-master (who must

4 A   be

be a graduate in one of the univerfities) and an ufher. The head-mafter
has a good houfe adjoining to the fchool. A little below the grammar
fchool to the north is a writing fchool, erected in this century, where
fixty poor boys are taught writing and accounts, gratis. About half a mile
weft from the town, September 4, 1793, was laid the firft ftone for an
infirmary upon a large and noble fcale. Towards this inftitution between
£.16,000 and £.17,000 have been fubfcribed; the fubfcription having
been opened by the late Mrs. Fell, of Attercliffe near Sheffield, with a
donation of £.1000. A committee have been appointed to manage every
thing relative to the building, &c.; and there is no doubt that the liberality of the public will be applied with the ftricteft and moft judicious
attention to the important and valuable purpofes which the fubfcribers
have had in view. It is fortunate for the interefts of humanity that the
fubfcription towards this benevolent inftitution was begun, and in
a great meafure completed, before the trade of the town and neighbourhood had experienced any depreffion or interruption from the war.

Public Buildings, &c.—In 1762 were erected in the fouth-eaft part of
the town, in Norfolk-ftreet, an affembly room and a theatre, by the joint
fubfcription of about thirty gentlemen in the town, who, of courfe, remained the proprietors. The theatre has been fince pulled down and rebuilt
upon a larger plan. On the fouth fide of Trinity church-yard is the cutler's
hall, where bufinefs relative to the corporation is tranfacted. A building was
purchafed for that purpofe in 1638; but the prefent ftructure was erected in
1726. At the fouth-eaft corner of Trinity church-yard is the town hall,
built in 1700, where the town's affairs are fettled and the feffions are held.
Auguft 31, 1786, a new market-place was opened, containing extenfive
and commodious fhambles and other conveniences, erected by his grace
the duke of Norfolk, who has a very large and improving eftate in and

almoft

almoſt all round this town. At the ſouth end of the town is a conſiderable work for the purpoſe of making white and red lead, begun about the year 1758. And at the weſt end of the town was erected, about the ſame period, a ſilk-mill, which has ſince been converted into a cotton work, burnt down, February 9, 1792, but ſince rebuilt, and now in full employ. Here are alſo four public breweries. The firſt ſtage-coach from Sheffield was ſet up about 1760, and now there are five. The firſt hackney-coach was ſet up by Nelſon in 1793; of theſe there are not above ſix or eight yet employed.

MANUFACTURES.

It is probable, from the town ſeal and other circumſtances, that Sheffield has been the ſtaple for iron manufactures from the year 1297, eſpecially for falchion-heads, arrow-piles, and an ordinary ſort of knives called whittles. But in proceſs of time, other articles of more importance being invented, the cutlery trade was purſued in the town and neighbourhood, conſiſting of various ſorts of ſheers, knives, ſciſſars, ſcythes, and ſickles. About the year 1600 began to be manufactured an ordinary ſort of iron tobacco-boxes, and " a ſilly muſical inſtrument " called a jew's trump." In 1638, files and razors began to be made. In 1630, claſp or ſpring knives began to be manufactured with iron handles, which, in a ſhort time, were covered with horn, tortoiſe-ſhell, &c. Still, however, it appears that, for near a century ſucceeding, the Sheffield manufactures diſcovered more of induſtry than ingenuity. The workmen dared not exert their abilities in labour for fear of being overſtocked with goods. Their trade was inconſiderable, confined, and precarious. None preſumed to extend their traffic beyond the bounds of this iſland; and moſt were content to wait the coming of a caſual trader rather than to carry their goods, with much labour and expence, to an uncertain market. Old perſons ſtill remember that the

produce

produce of the manufactory was conveyed weekly by pack-horfes to the metropolis. About fifty years ago, Mr. Jofeph Broadbent firft opened an immediate trade with the continent. In 1751 the river Don was made navigable up to within three miles of the town, which greatly facilitated the conveyance of goods abroad. A ftage-waggon was fet up by Mr. Wright, which was foon fucceeded by others. Mafter-manufacturers began to vifit London in fearch of orders with good fuccefs. Several factors now eftablifhed a correfpondence with various parts of the continent and engaged foreigners as clerks in their compting-houfes. The roads began to be greatly improved, and Britain and Ireland were thoroughly explored in fearch of trade. The fairs in different parts of the kingdom annually decreafed in their importance, becaufe fhopkeepers could be eafily fupplied with goods at any time of the year. Buttons of plated metal had been made by Mr. T. Bolfover for a confiderable time. But about 1758, a manufactory of this material was begun by Mr. Jofeph Hancock, an ingenious mechanic, comprehending a great variety of articles, fuch as faucepans, tea-urns, coffee-pots, cups, tankards, candlefticks, &c. &c. Since that time this branch has been purfued by numerous companies to great advantage, and has contributed very confiderably to promote the wealth and population of the town. The Sheffield trade in filver and plated goods was much affifted by the eftablifhment of an affay-office in the town, in confequence of acts of parliament paffed in 1773 and 1784; before which period the manufacturers were obliged to fend their goods to London to be affayed and marked.

POPULATION.

With refpect to the population of Sheffield, it is not eafy to form an accurate account from the parifh regifter, becaufe, though it feems to

I
have

have been kept correctly, yet, as it includes four hamlets or diſtricts, excluſively of the townſhip of Sheffield, the town cannot be conſidered diſtinctly. The ſtate of population and its gradual advance *in the pariſh* may, however, be fully as worthy of attention as that of the town in particular. The regiſter commences in 1561.

	Marr.	Bapt.	Bur.
From 1561 to 1570 incluſive,	234	1085	712
From 1571 to 1580 do.	275	955	721
From 1581 to 1590 do.	340	1245	959
From 1591 to 1600 do.	459	1364	1323
From 1601 to 1610 do.	417	1475	1049
From 1611 to 1620 do.	469	1699	1359
From 1621 to 1630 do.	532	1884	1606
From 1631 to 1640 do.	564	2130	2194
From 1641 to 1650 do.	410	2126	2276
From 1651 to 1660 do.	475	1698	1888
From 1661 to 1670 do.	585	2086	2266
From 1671 to 1680 do.	537	2240	2387
From 1681 to 1690 do.	540	2595	2856
From 1691 to 1700 do.	688	2221	2856
From 1701 to 1710 do.	942	3033	2613
From 1711 to 1720 do.	991	3304	2765
From 1721 to 1730 do.	1212	3874	3828
From 1731 to 1740 do.	1361	4635	3878
From 1741 to 1750 do.	1584	5904	5232
From 1751 to 1760 do.	1833	7036	6270
From 1761 to 1770 do.	2551	8885	7547
From 1771 to 1780 do.	2962	10,697	9898
From 1781 to 1790 do.	3863	13,851	11,849
1791	453	1607	1047
1792	471	1667	1246
1793	444	1732	1482
1794	402	1582	1473

The

The following is a ſtatement of the population of Sheffield at different periods.

Year.	Famil.	Souls.	Year.	Famil.	Souls.
1615	——	2207	1775	4704	——
1736	2152	9695	1785	5256	——
				Houſes.	
1755	2667	12,983	1788	5874	26,538
1768	3842	——	1789	6065	——.

287 empty.

In 1732, according to Mr. Goſling's plan, there were thirty-two ſtreets in Sheffield. In 1771, according to Mr. Fairbank's plan, there appears to have been an addition of twenty-five ſtreets. In 1792, there appears to have been a farther addition of ſeventeen ſtreets. It is not eaſy to give any exact account of the preſent population of either the town or pariſh of Sheffield. In the year 1789 it was found by actual ſurvey of a few ſtreets only, indiſcriminately taken, that the proportion of inhabitants to a houſe was about four three-fourths. This would make the number of perſons in Sheffield leſs than 30,000 at that time. It is generally believed that this number is conſiderably ſhort of the fact, even farther back than that year; but conjecture commonly exceeds the reality. The town is certainly a healthy one; and if it be allowed that in Mancheſter and Liverpool one in twenty-ſeven or twenty-eight (perhaps now a much leſs number) die annually, one death annually among thirty perſons reſident in Sheffield is probably too great for the actual proportion; and comprehending the whole pariſh in the account, ſituated as it is in a hilly country, on a dry ſoil and enjoying excellent air, it is conceived that not more than one in

thirty

thirty-five can be fuppofed to die annually. The average of burials for the laft four years will be found by the above ftatement to amount to 1312. This number multiplied by thirty-five, gives the product of 45,920 for the population of the whole parifh, without making any account of fuch funerals among the quakers and other diffenters as are never entered in the parifh regifter. There is the lefs impropriety in not regarding thefe, becaufe the diffenters here, though numerous, are much in the habit of burying their dead in the church yards.

The foil about Sheffield is generally of a deep clay; and from the quantity of manure beftowed on it, very rich. The duke of Norfolk, earl Fitzwilliam, and the countefs of Bute, are the principal great proprietors; but there are a number of fmall freeholders. In the neighbourhood moft of the farms are fmall, and the land is chiefly devoted to pafture and hay. Labourers obtain large wages, and the price of provifions is high. There is a good deal of wafte land within a few miles of the town, and the country is rather bare of trees. The roads are generally bad, but more attention is now beginning to be paid to them than formerly. The climate is middling; the average of rain, thirty-three inches in a year, which is about a medium between that falling in Lancafhire and on the eaftern coaft.

BARNESLEY,

COMMONLY called *Black Barnefley*, is the principal town of the wapentake of Staincrofs. It is a place of moderate fize, fituated among coal pits and iron-works, and carries on a confiderable trade in wire, with fome other branches of hard ware. It has alfo a manufactory

tory of linen yarn and coarfe linen cloth, which is in a flourifhing ftate. It has a market on Wednefdays, at which much corn and other provifions are fold. Its fairs are in February, May, and October. The farms around it are fmall, and chiefly in tillage.

The church of Barnefley is a chapel under Silkefton; the living in the gift of the archbifhop of York.

HUDDERSFIELD.

WE begin our account of the cloathing country with this town, which is peculiarly the creation of the woollen manufactory, whereby it has been raifed from an inconfiderable place, to a great degree of profperity and population.

The parifh of Huddersfield, fituated in Agbridge hundred, is very extenfive, ftretching from the river Calder on the north and north-eaft, to the borders of Lancafhire on the weft. Its breadth is lefs confiderable. It contains, befides the townfhip of *Huddersfield*, thofe of *Quarmby* with *Lindley*, *Longwood*, *Golcarr*, and part of *Scamanden*, of *Slaughthwaite*, and of *Marfden*. The church is a vicarage, in the gift of Sir John Ramfden; and has under it the chapels of *Dean-head*, and *Slaughthwaite*.

The town of Huddersfield, except two or three houfes, is entirely the property of Sir John Ramfden, who has for fome years paft granted building leafes renewable every twenty years on payment of two years ground rent. He built a very good cloth hall fome years fince, and

made

made a navigation from hence to the Calder, of which an account is given at p. 128. Within the townſhip there are ſeveral freeholders. The higheſt officer is a conſtable, who, with his deputy, is yearly choſen at the court leet held at Michaelmas at Almondſbury, the manor of which alſo belongs to Sir John Ramſden.

The markets of Huddersfield are very well ſupplied with beef, mutton, veal, and pork, which are expoſed for ſale in ſhambles built by the lord of the manor. The market-day is Tueſday, but mutton and veal may be had on other days at the butcher's ſhops. It is alſo tolerably ſupplied for a conſiderable part of the year with ſea-fiſh from the Yorkſhire coaſt. The fat cattle and ſheep are brought out of Lincolnſhire and the neighbouring counties, and generally bought at the fortnight fairs of Wakefield, which ſupply much of the weſtern part of Yorkſhire and the adjacent parts of Lancaſhire. Butter, eggs, and fowls, are not uſually ſold at the market croſs, but may ſometimes be bought in the neighbourhood. A moderate quantity of corn is brought to the market by the farmers round, and a larger quantity is brought by water from the more ſouthern counties, much of which is carried forwards into Lancaſhire.

There are ſmall quarterly fairs, at which ſome horſes and lean cattle are expoſed to ſale; but the principal fair for this purpoſe is on May 4.

The progreſs of population in this town will appear from the following extract from its regiſter:

Year.	Marr.	Chriſt.	Bur.		Year.	Marr.	Chriſt.	Bur.
1710	30	113	112		1730	48	178	149
1720	33	148	133		1740	41	196	100

4 B

Year.

Years.	Marr.	Chrift.	Bur.	Years.	Marr.	Chrift.	Bur.
1750	39	235	120	1790	113	377	267
1760	65	190	99	1791	140	381	270
1770	100	283	132	1792	119	395	274
1780	115	296	135				

The chapelry of *Slaughthwaite* in this parifh, which equally partakes of the increafed population from trade, has afforded the following lift of births and burials for a fpace of five years :

Year.	Chrift.	Bur.
1784	124	53
1785	135	29
1786	140	49
1787	140	90
1788	153	37

From this and the preceding table a very favourable idea may be deduced of the healthinefs of this diftrict, and the advantages it offers for the increafe of the human fpecies. Thefe chiefly proceed from the comparative healthinefs of a manufacture carried on in rural fituations and at the workmen's own houfes ; from the plenty of employ and high price of labour, encouraging to early matrimony ; and from the warm cloathing, good fare, and abundant fuel, enjoyed by the induftrious in this place.

The trade of Huddersfield comprizes a large fhare of the cloathing trade of Yorkfhire, particularly the finer articles of it. Thefe confift of broad and narrow cloths ; fancy cloths, as elaftics, beaverettes, &c. alfo honleys, and kerfeymeres. The qualities run from 10*d.* to 8*s.* per yard, narrows ; and broads as high as the fuperfines in the weft of England. The fineft broads in Yorkfhire are made at Saddleworth,

the

the manufactures of which place are included in this diftrict, being all fold at Huddersfield market. Thefe goods are made from all forts of fhort Englifh wool, from £.6 to £.35 per pack; and from Spanifh wool. The loweft priced Englifh wool is chiefly fhort wool forted from large fleeces of combing wool bought in Lincolnfhire, Leicefterfhire, Nottinghamfhire, and the neighbouring counties. The fineft Englifh wool is from fmall fleeces in Herefordfhire, Shropfhire, and other weftern counties; and alfo from Kent, Suffex, and their neighbourhood.

The markets for thefe goods are almoft wholly Great Britain and Ireland, and America. They are bought up by the merchants of the cloathing towns in a ftate ready for cropping, dreffing, and finifhing, and are then fent to London and the country towns, or exported from Liverpool or Hull. All the branches of trade here may be confidered as in a thriving ftate, making allowance for the temporary check of the war, which, however, has been lefs than might have been fuppofed, as appears from the annual accounts of cloths ftamped and regiftered at Pontefract. It is to be confidered, too, that kerfeymeres and all other goods carried to the market at Huddersfield which are white and quilled, are not regiftered; and thefe forts are on the increafe.

The new canal planned from Huddersfield to join the Manchefter and Afhton canal, which is expected to be of great advantage to its trade, has been mentioned at p. 131.

The principal gentlemens' feats near Huddersfield are, *Whitley-hall*, the feat of Richard Henry Beaumont, Efq. whofe family poffeffed this place in the reign of Henry II.; *Kirklees-hall*, belonging to Sir George Armytage, Bart.; *Fixby-hall* and park, the feat of Thomas Thornhill

hill

hill, Efq.; and *Mills-bridge* to William Radcliffe, Efq. To the weft of Almondfbury is *Caftle-hill*, an old fortrefs, fuppofed by fome to be the Roman *Cambodunum*; but Mr. Watfon conceives it rather to be a Saxon remain, and that *Slack*, to the north of Huddersfield, was Cambodunum.

SADDLEWORTH.

THIS place, though in the county of York, is within the parifh of Rochdale; the caufe of which appears by an old book belonging to Whalley Abbey, to have been an application from Hugo de Stapleton, lord of the manor of Saddleworth, to Hugh, earl of Chefter, for leave to erect a chapel for the ufe of his tenants; to his permiffion for which the earl made it a condition that the chapel fhould be annexed to the abbey of Whalley. On the diffolution of monafteries this was annexed to Rochdale. The minifter of its church or chapel is now put in by the vicar of Rochdale, and the tithes go along with thofe of that parifh.

Saddleworth is a large valley, about feven miles long, and five acrofs in the broadeft part, fituated in an angle of Yorkfhire between Lancafhire and the north-eaftern projection of Chefhire. It is a wild bleak region, of which a very fmall part is under cultivation; but induftry has accumulated in it a large number of inhabitants, who gain a comfortable fubfiftence by the manufactory of woollen cloth, for which the place is peculiarly famous. The diftrict is divided into four quarters, called meres, viz. *Quick-mere*, *Lord's-mere*, *Shaw-mere*, and *Friar-mere*. The latter was once an eftate belonging to the Black Friars, who had a houfe or grange there, near Delph. The manor of Saddleworth was fold by its old lords, the Stapletons, to the Ramfdens; by them,

to

to the Farrers and the Holts of Afhworth. The Holts fold their fhare to the tenants.

Perhaps a more remarkable inftance of rife in the value of an eftate cannot be produced than the following:—On Auguft 9th, 1654, William Farrer, Efq. of Ewood, near Halifax, purchafed a fhare of the lands of Saddleworth from William Ramfden, Efq. of Longley-hall, for £.2950. This, in 1775, brought in a rent of £.1500 per annum to James Farrer, Efq. of Bamborough Grange. In 1780 he fold off to the value of £.10,000, and by advance in the remainder kept up the fame rent as before. At his death in 1791 the rent was about £.2000 much of it in leafes for lives; and the eftate being fold in fmall parcels to the occupiers and others, it produced nearly £.70,000; which, added to the value of that before fold off, makes a product of £.80,000 from lefs than £.3000 in the fpace of 137 years.

There are now about 400 freeholders in Saddleworth; and it is ftated to contain 1822 families, and 10,471 perfons. As this is a much larger proportion to a family than found elfewhere, it is probable fome miftake muft have been made in the ftatement. At the church, and its three chapels, in Dob's-crofs, Lidgate, and Friar-mere, together with a diffenting meeting-houfe at Delph, there were in

1791, 91 marriages, 358 chriftenings, 292 burials,
1792, 73 do. 456 do. - - 267 do.

A remarkable proof of the healthinefs of the place appears in the following fact: A benefit fociety eftablifhed in 1772 confifts of upwards of 300 members, fome of whom were upwards of fifty years old

at

at their entrance. Only twelve members had been buried out of it to the beginning of 1794.

The trade of Saddleworth has increafed in a very rapid degree. In 1740 there were not more than about 8640 cloths manufactured here, and thofe of a very coarfe kind. In 1791 the number was 35,639; and in 1792, 36,637, which at an average were worth £.7 each in an unfinifhed ftate, as fold at Huddersfield market, nearly double the value of cloths made in 1740. For the manufacturing of thefe cloths are ufed 1,480,000 pounds of wool. The number of looms is about 2000; and there are feventy-fix mills, turned by the Tame and the fmall ftreams falling into it. Many of the fuperfine broads made here vie with thofe of the Weft of England.

The land under cultivation in this diftrict lets in fmall farms from 20s. to 40s. per acre. Some meadow land bring five or fix pounds.

Lime is at prefent brought by land carriage from the Peak of Derby-fhire, and fells at about 30s. per ton. Coals are got from the neighbour-hood of Oldham, and are about 15s. per ton. The houfes are all built of ftone, which is in great plenty; but timber comes high, being brought from Hull or Liverpool, and undergoing an expenfive land carriage; hence houfe-rents are dear. This hindrance to improvement it is hoped will be removed in a great meafure by the new Huddersfield and Afhton canal, which will pafs through the midft of Saddleworth.

Caftle Shaw in Saddleworth, a remain of an ancient fortification, of which a plan is given at p. 471, is fuppofed by Mr. Whitaker to have been a fortrefs of the primeval Britons, which he thinks is pretty pla nly

evinced

evinced by the few relics which have been accidentally difcovered at it. Within the area of the caftle, extended as it appears to have been, from the prefent eminence of the ground, and the appellation of the Hufteads and Caftle-hills, and containing feveral ftatute acres in compafs, have been dug up thofe round beads of the Britons, which have equally been difcovered in the Britifh barrows upon Salifbury plain. And within two or three fields from the caftle was lately difcovered a brazen celt Mr. Whitaker alfo fuppofes that a caftrum at Caftle Shaw, feated at the foot of Stanedge, within two furlongs of the Roman road to Slack, was a Roman ftation.

In this neighbourhood are the much frequented and celebrated rocks of *Greenfield*, as well as feveral druidical remains, a rocking ftone, &c. of which, would our limits allow it, a particular defcription fhould be given. Mr. Samuel Bottomley has written a poem defcriptive of this romantic and almoft uninhabited part of the country.

HALIFAX.

Halifax, a town of ancient note for the woollen manufacture, is fituated not far from the river Calder, in the wapentake of Morley, and within a parifh or vicarage of the fame name, which is one of the moft extenfive in the kingdom, confifting of twenty-fix townfhips or hamlets. The parifh is fuppofed to be fully equal in fize to the whole county of Rutland, being about feventeen miles in length, and eleven in breadth; and hence, of courfe, muft originally have been a wafte and barren tract, with a very light population. It is bounded by the parifhes of Whalley and Rochdale in Lancafhire on the weft, by that of Bradford on the north, of Birftall on the eaft, and of Huddersfield on the fouth. The

The era of the introduction of trade into this remote diftrict is not very accurately known; but there is the authority of a MS. paper by Mr. John Waterhoufe, once lord of the manor here, to prove, that at the time of his birth, in 1443, there were no more than thirteen houfes in Halifax; which number in 120 years was increafed to 520 houfe-holders. This probably muft therefore have been the period during which trade was introduced; accordingly, it has already been obferved under the head of Manchefter, that in 1520 one of the three great clothiers of the north of England lived at Halifax. Wright, in his hiftory of Halifax, affirms that the woollen trade was brought hither from Rippon, for the fake of the advantage of coals and water; and there is a tradition that it firft came into Yorkfhire out of Devonfhire, where it had been fettled by fome workmen from Flanders. About 17th Edward IV. two fulling mills were erected in Raftrick within this parifh; but the reign of Henry VII. has by fome been mentioned as the principal period of the introduction of the woollen manufacture in thefe parts.

An act, paffed in the reign of Philip and Mary, in order to prevent the engroffing of wool by perfons of large capitals, gives a lively picture of the ftate of this country. It recites, " that the parifh of Halifax " being planted in the great wafte and moores, where the fertility of " the ground is not apt to bring forth any corne nor good graffe, but " in rare places, and by exceeding and great induftry of the inhabi- " tants; and the fame inhabitants altogether doe live by cloth making; " and the greater part of them neither getteth corne, nor is able to " keepe a horfe to carry wools, nor yet to buy much wool at once, " but hath ever beene ufed only to repaire to the towne of Hali- " fax, &c. and there to buy upon the wool driver, fome a ftone, fome

I " two,

" two, and fome three and foure, according to their ability, and to
" carry the fame to their houfes, fome three, foure, five, and fix miles
" off, upon their heads and backes, and fo to make and convert the
" fame either into yarne or cloth, and to fell the fame, and fo to buy
" more wool of the wool driver, by means of which induftry, the
" barren grounds in thofe parts be now much inhabited, and above
" 500 houfeholds there newly increafed within thefe forty yeares paft,
" &c. &c."

This account exhibits a manufacture in its early ftate, but in a progreffive one: and from lord Clarendon's hiftory we find, that Halifax,
with Leeds and Bradford, were called, in the year 1642, " three very
" populous and rich towns depending wholly on clothiers." As to
the progreffion of population, it is faid in the certificate of the archbifhop of York and others, 2d Edward VI. (1548) " that in the parifh
" of Halifax the number of houflyng people is 8500;" and Camden,
when he travelled in thefe parts about 1580, was informed that the number of inhabitants of this parifh was about 12,000. Archbifhop Grind-
all, in his letter to queen Elizabeth during the northern rebellion, alfo
fays, that the parifh of Halifax was ready to bring into the field for her
fervice 3 or 4000 able men. And thofe who were raifed for the parliament, to whofe caufe Halifax adhered during the civil wars, were
numerous enough to be termed in the town regifter, the *Halifax army.*
We fhall purfue this fubject further hereafter.

The manor of Halifax is parcel of the very extenfive one of Wakefield. Great part of it was anciently called the liberty of the foreft of
Sowerbyfhire, or of Hardwick. Within this liberty a very fingular cuf-
ftom long prevailed, which was that called *Halifax gibbet-law.* It

4 C   confifted

fifted in a fummary mode of trying and capitally punifhing felons (apparently thieves alone) taken within the liberties with the goods found about them, or upon their own confeffion; and the mode of execution was beheading by means of an inftrument called a gibbet, confifting of two upright pieces of timber, joined by a tranfverfe piece, within which was a fquare block of wood fliding in grooves, worked in the uprights, and armed below with an iron axe. This being drawn up, was let fall fuddenly, either by pulling out a pin, or cutting a cord that fupported it; and thus the malefactor's head was at once ftruck off. An engine exactly of the fame kind was for fome time in ufe at Edinburgh under the name of *the maiden*; but which was the original, which the copy, is difputed. It has lately been revived with improvements in France, in the too-famous *guillotine*; which appears, however, to have been an original invention of the perfon whofe name it bears. Indeed, the pile-driving engine would readily fuggeft the idea of it. With refpect to this in Halifax, it feems to have been pretty freely ufed, efpecially after it became a manufacturing town, againft the robbers of tenter grounds. The laft executions by it were in 1650. The practice was then put a ftop to, the bailiff being threatened with a profecution if he fhould repeat it. Forty-nine perfons had fuffered by it from the firft entries in the regifter in the year 1541. A raifed platform of ftone on which the gibbet was placed is ftill remaining in Gibbet-lane.

Halifax is feated in a bottom, on a gentle defcent from eaft to weft, in which direction its greateft length extends. Its ftreets are narrow and irregular; the houfes in general built of ftone, and fome of the more modern ones, large and handfome. The church is a large Gothic ftructure, of good appearance, at the eaft end of the town. It has

4   undergone

undergone various alterations and additions at different times. It has a handfome organ, and a tower fteeple with eight mufical bells. Under the chancel are large rooms upon a level with the lower part of the church-yard, in one of which is a library. Within the church are two chapels, one of them called the Rokefby chapel, in which were buried the heart and bowels of Dr. William Rokefby, vicar of Halifax, and laftly, archbifhop of Dublin. The vicarage is in the gift of the crown. It has under it twelve chapels in different parts of the parifh. There are alfo a number of diffenting places of worfhip within the town, and the parifh. There is a free-fchool in Skircoat, founded by queen Elizabeth; and alms-houfes, and blue-coat hofpital.

Halifax has a fine piece hall, the area of which is 300 feet by 240. Part of it is three ftories high, the remainder two ftories; and it contains 315 different rooms in which the manufactured goods of the town and neighbourhood are expofed to fale. It coft £.12,000; and the value of goods at one time in it is reckoned never lefs than £.50,000. It opens every Saturday at ten o'clock, and fhuts at twelve, a bell ringing at both times. There are other markets on Tuefdays and Thurfdays; but Halifax is not a market-town by charter, but by prefcription.

We fhall now proceed to a more particular account of the trade and population of this place in later times.

The fhalloon trade was introduced here about the beginning of this century; and what are called figured ftuffs and drawboys, within the latter half of it. Formerly much bone-lace was made in Halifax; but this trade fell into a low ftate, till it was again revived, fo as to become no inconfiderable branch. Frame-work knitting was introduced in

4 C 2 1724,

1724, and a good deal of work has been done in it. For some time past, the staple manufactory of the place and neighbourhood has been tammies, shalloons, drawboys, known best under the title of figured lastings and amens, superfine quilled everlastings, double russels, serges de Nisme & du Rome. These are all made from combing wool. They are brought in the unfinished state to the piece hall, where the merchants attend every Saturday to purchase. Formerly the greatest part of these goods were bought by the London merchants for the supply of foreigners; but, for the last fifteen or twenty years, dye-houses and other conveniences have been erected by merchants who finish the goods upon the spot, and are thereby able to undersell the London merchant. Of these goods very few in proportion are sold inland. Large quantities go to all the European continent, of which those sent to Cadiz are chiefly exported to Spanish America. Many shalloons go by land to London for the Turkey trade.

There is, besides, a very considerable manufactory of kerseys, and half-thicks, also of Bockings, and baize, principally in the hands of merchants of property in the neighbourhood of Sowerby, and made in the valley from Sowerby-bridge up to Ripponden, and higher. The whole of the British navy is cloathed from this source. Large quantities are also, in time of peace, sent to Holland, and some to America.

But the most promising branch of manufactory is that of cloth and coatings, which has been introduced within these few years by a few persons of enterprize, who have, at vast expense, erected mills on the Calder, and other smaller streams, the falls of water in this uneven country being very favourable for that purpose. The success of these factories has been such as to excite the jealousy of the Leeds merchants, who are accustomed to buy the same articles from the lower manufacturers at their

cloth

cloth hall; and fo aware were they of the danger of competition, that in 1794 a deputation was fent from thence to petition for an act to prevent any merchant from becoming a manufacturer; but on confideration the idea was dropt. It is evident that merchants concentrating in themfelves the whole procefs of a manufactory, from the raw wool to the finifhed piece, have an advantage over thofe who permit the article to pafs through a variety of hands, each of which takes a profit. This fome perfons in the vicinity of Leeds now fee, and are adopting the fame plan. As machinery is now brought to great perfection, numbers of the fmall manufacturers, who made perhaps a piece in a week, find it more advantageous to work at thofe factories, where their ingenuity is well rewarded. And it appears evident, that the fame number of hands regularly employed, will do more work by one third than when they depend on cafual employ. One day in fix is always loft to the head of a family by attending the mill, and another by attendance at the market.

It may not be amifs to remark an abfurd cuftom prevailing in the manufactory of broad cloths, which is that of the merchants allowing one yard in every twenty as an indemnity for the length of the cloth being ftretched beyond its length from the mill; which has the bad effect of tempting the merchant to ftretch the cloth ftill more in order to gain length, though the quality is injured by it. This practice has thrown the Yorkfhire cloth into difrepute, both at home and abroad, and preference has been given to the Gloucefterfhire fabrics, efpecially by the Eaft India Company. It is, however, notorious, that this great trading body, who are faid to purchafe cloths to the amount of £.200,000 per annum, are groffly impofed upon, as the cloths they buy in the Weft, which meafure forty-eight yards in the white, do not when dyed meafure,

fure, on the average, fo much as forty-five yards. An honeft and intelligent manufacturer would be able to prove this fact to them, *that all cloth manufactured honeftly will be as long when dyed and finifhed, as in the white.*

In the year 1764 an exact account was taken of the number of families in the vicarage of Halifax, of which the following is a tranfcript:

In Halifax	1272 Families	In Eland	242 Families.
Skircoat	251 do.	Greetland	118 do.
Warley	487 do.	Old Lindley	41 do.
Midgeley	217 do.	Stainland	197 do.
Sowerby	587 do.	Barkifland	252 do.
Ovenden	597 do.	Soyland	256 do.
Northowram	630 do.	Rufhworth	130 do.
Shelf	180 do.	Norland	180 do.
Hipperholm	352 do.	Stansfield	464 do.
Southowram	448 do.	Langfield	137 do.
Brighoufe	74 do.	Erringden	177 do.
Raftrick	179 do.	Heptonftall	352 do.
Fixby	55 do.	Wadfworth	388 do.
		Total	8263

On a calculation of 4½ perfons to a family, this will give the number of 35,806 inhabitants. The increafe fince that time muft have been very great, but no new enumeration has taken place. However, we

have

have been favoured with an extract of the lifts of mortality given into the ftamp office for two late years, as follows :

In the whole parifh of Halifax, from October 2, 1791, to October 1, 1792,   -   -   588 marriages; 2246 births; 1273 burials.

In the fame, from October 2, 1792, to October 1, 1793,   524 marriages; 2350 births; 1233 burials.

In this lift, the births of thofe who died unregiftered, and the burials of paupers, are not included. From the beft deduction we can make from thefe facts, a population of between fifty-five and fixty thoufand individuals may be inferred.

Halifax enjoys the benefit of water-carriage to Hull along the Calder, from Sowerby-bridge in its vicinity, the act of parliament for which navigation paffed in 1757. Its communications by water will be much extended by the Rochdale canal, now cutting, which will connect the Calder at Sowerby-bridge with the duke of Bridgewater's canal at Man-chefter, and confequently include the neighbourhood of Halifax in the great fyftem of inland navigation.

The roads about Halifax are generally bad. The farms are moftly fmall, and occupied by manufacturers for the conveniency of keeping a cow or two, and horfes for conveyance of their goods. The land is chiefly in meadow pafture grafs; and the cultivation of the ground is only regarded as a fecondary object with the occupiers. Coals are found in various parts of the parifh.

Halifax has given birth to feveral perfons of eminence, among whom it is fufficient to mention the celebrated *archbifhop Tillotfon*; *Dr. Henry Brigg*, geometrical profeffor at Grefham college, and Savilian profeffor at Oxford; and *Dr. David Hartley*, known among the faculty as the introducer of Mrs. Stephens's medicines for the ftone, but much more known of late years on account of his great work entitled, "Obferva-tions on Man," founded on the doctrine of affociation, the fyftem of which has been adopted with the higheft applaufe by Dr. Prieftley and other ingenious writers.

The hiftory and antiquities of this parifh have been treated of in a large quarto volume by the late learned and Rev. John Watfon, who long refided here, and died rector of Stockport. From his work fe-veral of the materials of the preceding account have been taken.

Near *Horley-green*, a mile and a quarter to the north-eaft of Halifax, a mineral water has been difcovered, on which a pamphlet has been written by Dr. Garnet, of Harrowgate. It appears from his experi-ments to contain a large proportion of vitriolated iron, befides alum, felenite, and ochre; and is reckoned by him the ftrongeft chalybeate water known.

B R A D F O R D.

THIS is a market town fituated in Morley wapentake, about half way between Halifax and Leeds. It belonged originally to John of Gaunt. Its market is on Monday, and it has fairs in March and June. The church is a vicarage, and has under it the chapels of Thornton,

3   Wibfey,

Wibfey, and Haworth. Befides the parifh church, there are places of worfhip for diffenters of all denominations, who are numerous. The methodifts have a large octagon chapel here.

Bradford is a confiderable and populous town, well built of free-ftone got from quarries in its neighbourhood, and is inhabited chiefly by manufacturers, many of whom are opulent. The articles it chiefly deals in are tammies and calamancoes, manufactured in its neighbourhood, and fold in its market, in the fame manner as the Halifax ftuffs, and exported with them. This trade has undergone a temporary diminution from the war; but the return of peace and free exportation would certainly make it revive again. A branch of the Leeds and Liverpool canal was extended to Bradford feveral years fince.

The land about Bradford is poffeffed by fmall proprietors, and occupied by fmall farmers and manufacturers. It is almoft all in grafs, and cows are the principal ftock kept. Where it is in tillage, oats are the moft common crop. The country is all in enclofure.

In the parifh a very capital iron foundry and forge has lately been eftablifhed, which has the advantage of coal and iron ore got on the fpot, and is a very profitable concern. Coals abound in this neighbourhood, and large quantities are fent by means of the canal into Craven, from whence lime ftone is brought in return.

L E E D S.

THOUGH the woollen trade in Yorkſhire has properly no one common centre, yet the town of Leeds has latterly been always reckoned, in opulence and population, the principal place of the Weſt Riding; and it bears a high rank among our manufacturing towns.

Leeds is an ancient place, its name appearing in Doomſday-book, under the reigns of Edward the Confeſſor and William the Conqueror. It had a ſtrong caſtle, probably built by Ilbert de Lacy, which was beſieged by king Stephen in 1139; and here the unfortunate Richard II. was confined about the year 1399. No veſtiges of this fortreſs remain; but its ſite is ſaid to have been on a place now called Mill-hill.

Leeds has long been diſtinguiſhed as one of the cloathing towns of Yorkſhire, though its pre-eminence does not ſeem to have been of very old date. Leland ſays it is " a pretty market town, ſubſiſted chiefly " by cloathing, reaſonably well builded, and as large as Bradford, " but not ſo *quick* as it." Its growth, however, probably ſoon came to be conſiderable, as it was incorporated by Charles I. At the commencement of the troubles of that reign it was held for the king by Sir William Saville; but after a ſharp action, its works were ſtormed by a force which marched out of Bradford under Sir Thomas Fairfax. A ſecond charter was given to it in the 13th of Charles II. under which it is now governed. It is not a parliamentary borough.

The pariſh of Leeds is ſituated on the river Aire, which runs nearly through the middle of it in a direction from weſt to eaſt. It extends,

2   accord-

according to Tuke's furvey, feven miles three furlongs from north to fouth, and feven miles two and half furlongs from eaft to weft, and is thirty miles one furlong in circumference. It is divided into ten town-fhips, exclufive of the townfhip of Leeds, which includes the town properly fo called, and a confiderable village at a mile's diftance. An actual enumeration of the inhabitants of the townfhip was taken in 1775, of which the following is the refult: families, 4099; hufbands, 3121; wives, 3193; widowers, 347; widows, 793; bachelors, 861; fpinfters, 1330; males under twenty-one, 3712; females ditto, 3760; total, 17,117: number to each family, 4⅕. It is to be obferved, that in the loweft rank of people there is often more than one family to a houfe. In that year there were 1140 baptifms, and 781 burials.

The living is a vicarage, in the gift of twenty-feven truftees, who, previous to a prefentation, are required to complete their number by the votes of a majority of the furvivors. The profits of the living arife entirely from fmall tithes and Eafter dues, and are faid to be fhort of £.400 per annum, though they would certainly be much more if the dues were rigoroufly exacted. Befides the parifh church, there are in the town three other churches: two of thefe are fupported by handfome endowments of land, and are in the gift of truftees; the other, lately erected, by the fale and rent of pews, and after two prefentations, is to be in the gift of the vicar. Eight of the ten townfhips have an epifco-pal endowed chapel of eafe, in the gift of the vicar, and are upon an average worth about £.100 per annum each. There are alfo in the town feven diffenting-meeting houfes, viz. two Prefbyterian, two In-dependant, two Baptift, and one Quaker's, exclufive of a large chapel belonging to the Weftley methodifts, and of another where the fervice

of

of the church of England is read by two unordained preachers, educated
at the expence of the late countefs of Huntingdon.

The parifh is governed by a corporation, confifting of a mayor,
twelve aldermen, and twenty-four common council, who fill up the
vacancies in their body, and annually elect the mayor from the aldermen by a majority of votes. As there are no freemen, every inhabitant is eligible to ferve in the corporation, and in return is not liable to
be fummoned to ferve upon any jury out of the parifh.

The market days are Tuefday and Saturday for mixed cloths, that
is, cloths made of dyed wool; and Tuefday only, for white cloths. The
mixed cloths in the laft century were expofed for fale on the battlements
of the bridge over the Aire, and as the manufactory increafed, were removed to the large ftreet called Briggate, fubject to the inconvenience of
bad weather, and of being ftored in adjoining cellars from one market
day to another. The white cloths were fold in a room. Each of them
is now depofited in a feparate covered hall, erected for the purpofe,
where they remain without difturbance till fold.

The mixed cloth hall was erected at the expence of the manufacturers in 1758. It is a quadrangular building, enclofing an open area.
The building is 127½ yards in length, and fixty-fix in breadth; and is
divided into fix covered ftreets, each of which contains two rows of
ftands, the freehold property of feparate manufacturers. Each ftand
is twenty-two inches in front, and the whole number is 1770; but as
about twenty individuals are in poffeffion of two ftands each, the number of mafter manufacturers of mixed cloth, proprietors of the hall,
muft not be eftimated at more than 1750. Thefe have all ferved a regular

gular apprenticeſhip to the making of coloured cloth, which is an indiſpenſable condition of their admiſſion into the hall. Another ſmall hall has lately been erected for the accommodation of irregulars, and near 100 ſtands are already let. Each ſtand originally coſt the proprietor 3*l.* 5*s.* 6*d.*, but they are now worth 5*l.* 10*s.*

The preſent white cloth hall was built in 1775. It is a quadrangle like the other, ninety-nine yards in length, and ſeventy in breadth, and is divided into five ſtreets, each with a double row of ſtands, the number of which is 1210; but there are generally about forty perſons who have two ſtands each. There are ſuppoſed to be about 200 mixed, and more than 100 white cloth manufacturers, of an inferior deſcription, who have ſerved a regular apprenticeſhip, but having no property in the halls, pay a fixed fee for every piece of cloth they expoſe to ſale.

The whole number of maſter broad-cloth manufacturers, in the Weſt-Riding of Yorkſhire is about 3240. The mixed cloth manufacturers reſide partly in the villages belonging to the pariſh of Leeds; but chiefly at Morley, Guilderſome, Adwalton, Driglington, Pudſey, Farſley, Calverley, Eccleſhal, Idle, Baildon, Yeadon, Guiſely, Rawdon, and Horsforth, in or bordering upon the vale of Aire, chiefly weſt of Leeds; and at Batley, Dewſbury, Oſſet, Horbury, and Kirkburton, weſt of Wakefield, in or near the vale of Calder. Not a ſingle manufacturer is to be found more than one mile eaſt, or two north, of Leeds; nor are there many in the town of Leeds, and thoſe only in the outſkirts.

The white cloth is manufactured chiefly at Alverthorpe, Oſſet, Kirkheaton, Dewſbury, Batley, Birſtal, Hopton, Mirfield, Archet, Clackheaton,

heaton, Littletown, Bowling, and Shipley; a tract of country forming an oblique belt acrofs the hills that feparate the vale of Calder from
the vale of Aire, beginning about a mile weft of Wakefield, leaving
Huddersfield and Bradford a little to the left, terminating at Shipley on
the Aire, and not coming within lefs than about fix miles of Leeds on
the right. The diftricts of the white and coloured cloth manufactory
are generally diftinct, but are a little intermixed at the fouth eaft and
north-weft extremities.

The cloths are fold in their refpective halls rough as they come from
the fulling mills. They are finifhed by the merchants, who employ
dreffers, dyers, &c. for that purpofe; thefe, with dryfalters, fhop-
keepers, and the different kind of handicraftfmen common to every
town, compofe the bulk of the inhabitants of Leeds. The difperfed
ftate of the manufacturers in villages and fingle houfes over the whole
face of the country, is highly favourable to their morals and happinefs.
They are generally men of fmall capitals, and often annex a fmall farm
to their other bufinefs; great numbers of the reft have a field or two to
fupport a horfe and a cow, and are for the moft part bleffed with the
comforts, without the fuperfluities, of life.

The markets of Leeds are well fupplied with all kinds of provifion,
partly from the neighbouring agricultural diftrict to the eaft, and partly
from a diftance up the Aire. The whole country from Leeds weftward
into Lancafhire, does not produce grain or feed cattle fufficient to fupply one-fifth of the inhabitants.

The medium price of the beft beef is from fivepence to fixpence
per pound; mutton and veal fourpence halfpenny; pork, fixpence:

upon

upon an average, about a halfpenny a pound dearer than York, and as much cheaper than Manchester.

Leeds has a general infirmary, built by subscription in 1768, and well attended and supported. Also an excellent workhouse, an hospital, alms-houses, charity schools, and other institutions belonging to a great town. It is built of brick, and contains many large and handsome modern houses. From the beginning of the century Leeds has enjoyed the benefit of water-carriage by means of the river Aire, which has been improved by successive acts, the last of which, authorizing a canal from the lower part of the Aire to the Ouse at Selby, passed in 1774.

Its population has kept pace with the general increase of the cloathing trade, as will appear from the following extract from the bills of mortality:

An account of the births and burials in the township of Leeds from 1763 to 1794, including protestant dissenters of all denominations.

Year.	Births.	Bur.	Year.	Births.	Bur.
1764	553	445	1773	699	660
1765	576	459	1774	630	478
1766	584	533	1775	705	574
1767	557	639	1776	712	475
1768	552	560	1777	710	634
1769	637	478	1778	781	656
1770	621	587	1779	709	686
1771	689	533	1780	742	591
1772	650	544	1781	738	673

Year.

Year.	Bir.	Bur.	Year.	Bir.	Bur.
1782	741	600	1788	933	784
1783	725	682	1789	993	671
1784	830	603	1790	1139	969
1785	860	727	1791	1142	688
1786	940	674	1792	1171	929
1787	895	712	1793	1190	1129

Number of houfes in the year 1793, counted from the workhoufe book, where all that are inhabited are inferted, 6691.

The foil of the parifh of Leeds is a coarfe, ftrong clay, fometimes covering a finer ftratum, which is made into pipes, and an inferior kind of pottery, in the neighbourhood. Its northern border is fandy, extending nearly to the ridge which feparates Airedale from Wharfdale, and is a procefs from the great line of hills that form the back bone of the north of England. The higher part of it is incapable of cultivation. That part of the parifh which lies fouth of the Aire abounds in coal; and to the cheapnefs of this indifpenfable mineral, the flourifhing ftate of the manufactory is to be attributed. It is delivered at the coal ftaith in the town, at 13s. per waggon load. The waggon is fuppofed to contain twenty-four corves, and the weight of a corve is near two hundred weight and a half.

There are in the parifh feveral quarries of an argillaceous fchift, which fupply the neighbourhood and the country down the river with flates and flag-ftones for paving. On the north-eaft border begins a bed of imperfect granite, or moor-ftone, of the fame kind as that on the eaft moor in Derbyfhire, which runs to the Chevin near Otley, and forms

I   the

the whole ridge of Romald's-moor as far as Skipton, where the lime-stone commences. On each side, as you approach the level of the rivers Aire and Wharfe, the argillaceous schist occurs, which is evidently a stratum incumbent on the granite. The stone on the south of the Aire is entirely argillaceous schist, as probably is generally the case where coal is found. The land in the greater part of the parish is extremely rich, and on account of the plenty of manure and the populousness of the country, is of course in a high state of cultivation.

Besides the smaller potteries which work up the lower stratum of clay, there is a very considerable one for pottery of a finer kind, the proprietors of which, on account of the cheapness of coal, find it worth their while to bring pot clay and flints from the west and south of England, and export large quantities of goods to Holland, Germany, Russia, &c.

There are also in the town two carpet manufactories; and a large work has lately been erected for spinning flax by machinery.

On the river Aire and the streams that fall into it, there are numerous mills for grinding corn, dyer's-wood, rape seed, &c. and also for fulling cloth, and turning machinery to spin and card wool. Several cotton mills have been lately erected, but these are worked chiefly by the means of steam engines.

The only remarkable antiquity in the parish is *Kirkstall Abbey*, of which an account may be seen in Thoresby's Ducatus Leodiensis. It was a religious house of the Cistercian order, founded in 1157 by Henry

4 E

de

de Lacy, and fituated in a beautiful vale watered by the Aire. There are large remains of the church, a fine gothic building.

At *Fulneck*, near *Pudfey*, between Leeds and Bradford, is a confiderable fettlement of the Moravian brethren, which was begun about 1748, principally by fome Germans, but is now almoft entirely peopled by Englifh, moft of them natives of the place. The chief buildings are the *hall*, containing a chapel, a fchool for girls, and minifter's dwelling : a large fchool-houfe for boys ; a houfe for fingle men ; another for fingle women ; and another for widows ; fituated upon a terrace of confiderable length, and commanding a fine profpect. Thefe, with the houfes for feparate families, form a confiderable village, the number inhabiting which is from four to five hundred Various branches of trade are carried on in it, as fhoemakers, taylors, bakers, &c.; but the chief employment is the woollen manufacture. The fingle women are famous for their fkill in working muflins with the needle and tambour, and their labours fell at a high price. The vocal and inftrumental mufic of the fettlement is reckoned very excellent.

WAKEFIELD.

NEARLY fouth of Leeds, at the diftance of eight miles, ftands the town of Wakefield, on the fide of a hill declining to the Calder. It is an ancient town, and once belonged to the Warrens, earls of Surry. From Leland's defcription, it feems in his time to have been the principal town in thefe parts, having then a fair large church and a chapel of cafe ; with a handfome area for a market place. The buildings were

2   then

then moftly of timber, but fome of ftone; and it is called by him " a
" very quick market town, and meately large, the whole profit of
" which ftandeth by coarfe drapery."

Wakefield is now confidered as one of the handfomeft and moft opulent of the clothing towns, being inhabited by feveral capital merchants,
who have coftly and elegant houfes. It is large and populous, and poffeffes a confiderable fhare of bufinefs. It has a good bridge over the
Calder, on which ftands an ancient chapel with gothic fculptures, commonly faid to have been built by Edward IV in memory of his father,
but exifting in the reign of Edward III. It is now difufed as a place
of worfhip. Its church is large and lofty. The living is a vicarage in
the gift of the king. The lecturefhip is in the gift of the Mercer's
Company, London. There is one chapelry in the parifh, that of
Horbury. In the town are meetings for various fects of diffenters.
There is a charity fchool fupported by fubfcription.

The markets in Wakefield are on Thurfday and Friday. A great
deal of bufinefs is done at them, particularly in the fale of wool, which
is fent from all parts of England to factors in this place, who difpofe
of it among the manufacturers in the different diftricts around. The
goods principally brought to this market are tammies and camlets, and
alfo fome white cloths. But the greater part of the white cloths made
in its neighbourhood, particularly on the weft, are fent to the Leeds
market. The fortnight cattle-fairs of Wakefield have already been
mentioned, as fupplying a great tract of country weftwards with butcher's meat.

4 E 2

The

The Calder was made navigable to this town at the end of laſt century. A canal is now cutting from Wakefield to Barneſley. The banks of the Calder here are a tract of fine meadows.

Near this town was fought the battle between queen Margaret and the duke of York, in which the latter was ſlain, and his ſon, the young earl of Rutland, was put to death in cold blood by the barbarous Clifford. The duke lay before the battle at *Sandall-caſtle*, near Wakefield, an ancient fortreſs built by the earls Warren, of which a few fragments only now remain. It is ſaid to have been demoliſhed in the laſt civil wars.

Acroſs the Calder, about two miles from Wakefield, is the village of *Heath*, reckoned one of the moſt beautiful in England. It is ſituated on an eminence above the Calder, here a conſiderable river, commanding an extenſive and delightful view of the rich and populous country around. The village is built by the ſide of a green, the houſes being all of ſtone found on the ſpot. Of theſe the principal are thoſe of the late Sir G. Dalſton, now Mr. Dillon's, built in the reign of queen Elizabeth; of John Smyth, Eſq. one of the lords of the treaſury; and of Mrs. Smith and Mrs. Hopkinſon. The two firſt of theſe have extenſive pleaſure-grounds ſloping to the water, with walks through the woods on its banks.

The Calder is the eaſtern boundary of the woollen manufacture, which extends hence to the ridge of hills ſeparating Lancaſhire and Yorkſhire. The immenſe importance of this trade, and its late rapid progreſs, will appear from the annexed paper, to which we ſhall premiſe the fact, that in 1769 the quantity of broad cloth ſtamped was only 1,771,667 yards. An

An account of the number of broad and narrow woollen cloths milled at the feveral fulling mills in the Weft-Riding of the county of York from the 25th day of March, 1787, to the 25th day of March, 1793.

| Years. | BROADS. | | NARROWS. | |
	Pieces.	Yards.	Pieces.	Yards.
1788	139,406	4,244,322	132,143	4,208,303
1789	154,134	4,716,460	145,495	4,409,573
1790	172,588	5,151,677	140,407	4,582,122
1791	187,569	5,815,079	154,373	4,797,594
1792	203,623	6,383,589	156,475	5,153,944
1793	214,851	6,760,728	190,468	5,531,698
1794	190,988	6,067,208	130,403	4,634,258

N. B. The above account is made up from 25th of March, 1787, to March, 1788, and fo annually to March, 1794. Kerfeymeres are not included.

ADDI-

ADDITIONS.

THE fubfequent articles came to hand too late to be inferted in their proper places, but were thought too important to be omitted.

CANALS.

Barnſley Canal. In 1793 an act paſſed for a canal to proceed from the Calder below Wakefield, and paſſing Crofton, Felkirk, and Royſton, to arrive at Barnſley, whence it is to make a bend to Barnby-bridge, near Cawthorn, where it is to join another new canal, called the *Dearne and Dove canal,* which goes from Barnſley to the river Dun. The length of the Barnſley canal is about fourteen miles ; its fall from the junction with the Dearne and Dove canal, to the Calder, is 120 feet. There are feveral rail ways for the conveyance of coal to the canal from Barnſley, and others from Barnby-bridge. It is now cutting.

Haſlingden Canal. An act in 1793 authoriſes the cutting of a canal from the Bury and Bolton Canal on the weſt ſide of Bury, through Walmſley, Tottington, Haſlingden, and Accrington, till it joins the Leeds and Liverpool canal at Church, after a courſe of thirteen miles. The undertakers are forbid to make any locks or ſimilar works, and in

their

their stead are to employ the machinery of rollers, racks, or inclined planes; but if it be hereafter found expedient to construct locks, they may do it, on consent obtained from three fourths of the owners of the mills on certain streams.

Lancaster Canal Extension. By an act passed in 1793 the proprietors of the Lancaster canal are enabled to make a cut from the dock at Glasson, at the mouth of the Loyne, to communicate with the Lancaster canal at Galgate, which is about six miles to the south of Lancaster. This cut will be about four miles in length, and will establish an immediate communication between that canal and the sea.

Manchester and Oldham Canal Extension. Under the head of the Oldham and Ashton canal from Manchester, it is mentioned that a design was entertained of cutting a branch to Stockport. Powers for this purpose were given by an act passed in 1793, enabling the proprietors to make a canal from the Manchester and Oldham canal at Clayton demesne, in the parish of Manchester, to Heaton Norris, near Manchester, which distance is about six miles, and parallel to the turnpike road; also, to continue this canal eastward to Denton, a distance of about three miles; likewise to make a cut from the Oldham branch, to Stake-Leach in Hollingwood, a distance of about two miles.

Duke of Bridgewater's canal from Worsley to Leigh. An act passed in 1795, authorises the duke to cut a branch from his canal at Worsley, to the township of Pennington near Leigh. The tonnage of goods of all kinds carried on this canal is not to exceed 2s. 6d. per ton.

M A N.

MANCHESTER,

Bill of Mortality from the earliest Periods,

Year.	Births.	Deaths.	Marr.	Year.	Births.	Deaths.	Marr.
1580	206	158	50	1772	1127	904	427
1590	201	264	25	1773	1168	923	383
1600	210	141	72	1774	1245	958	422
1605	175	1078	61 Pl.	1775	1359	835	473
1610	275	172	63	1776	1241	1220	494
1620	297	284	96	1777	1513	864	577
1630	310	195	71	1778	1449	975	484
1640	303	297	86	1779	1464	1288	448
1645	143	1212	67 Pl.	1780	1566	993	456
1650	144	182	35	1781	1591	1370	495
1660	162	135	37	1782	1678	984	567
1670	188	149	176	1783	1615	1496	682
1680	185	264	66	1784	1958	1175	843
1690	173	183	64	1785	1942	1734	893
1700	231	229	133	1786	2319	1282	872
1710	211	235	128	1787	2256	1761	903
1720	290	273	148	1788	2391	1637	968
1730	305	548	210	1789	2487	1788	920
1740	552	700	194	1790	2756	1940	1120
1750	740	902	279	1791	2960	2286	1302
1760	793	818	380	1792	2660	1605	1657
1770	1050	988	429	1793	2579	1491	1234
1771	1169	993	429	1794	2041	1241	1066

During the years marked (Pl.) the plague was in Manchester. There is a tradition, that for 200 years before this copy commences, the population was upon an average much the same with that stated the first year in this account, neither greatly increasing nor diminishing.

    1   *Copy*

Copy of Thomas Grelle's Grant to the Burgesses of Manchester.

SCIANT prefentes et futuri quod ego Thomas Grelle dedi et conceffi et hac prefenti carta mea confirmavi omnibus burgenfibus meis Manceftrienfis Scill.—quod omnes burgenfes reddent de quolibet burgagio fuo duodecim denarios per annum pro omni fervitio.

Et fi præfectus villæ aliquem burgenfem calumpniaverit de aliquo placito, et calumpniatus non venerit ad diem nec aliquis pro eo infra Laghmot in foris factura eft de duodecim denariis prædicto domino et prædictus dominus habeat placitum fuum fuper eum in Portemanmot.

Item, fi aliquis burgenfis aliquem burgenfem implacitaverit de aliquo debito et ipfe cognoverit debitum præfectus ponat ei diem fcill. octavum, et fi non venerit ad diem reddat duodecim denarios pro foris factura die prædicto domino et reddat debitum et præfecto octo denarios.

Et fi aliquis faciat clamorem de aliqua re et non invenerit vadium et plegios et poftea velit dimittere clamorem fine foris factura erit.

Item, fi aliquis burgenfis in burgo aliquem burgenfem vulneraverit in die dominica vel a nona die Sabatti ufque ad diem lunæ ipfe erit in foris factura viginti folidos. Et fi in die lunæ vel in aliis diebus feptimanæ vulneraverit aliquem ipfe cadet in foris factura duodecim denarios verfus prædictum dominum.

Item, fi aliquis burgenfis cum aliquo certaverit et per iram eum percufferit fine fanguinis effufione et ad domum fuam redire poffit fine calumnia præfecti aut famulorum fuorum liber erit de placito præpofiti;

4 F

et

et fi guerram alius cui commifit fuftinere poterit bene poteft fieri, fin autem per confilium amicorum fuorum cum eo pacem faciat et hoc fine foris factura præfecti.

Item, fi aliquis implacitatus fuerit in burgo de aliquo placito non re-fpondeat nec burgenfi villano nifi in fuo Portemanmot, nec etiam va-fori excepto placito quod ad coronam regis pertinat et de latrocinio.

Item fi aliquis vocat aliquem burgenfem de latrocinio præfectus atta-chiat eum ad refpondendum in curia domini et ftare indicio.

Item fi aliquis implacitatus fuerit de vicino fuo vel de aliquo et tres dies fecutus fuerit fi teftimonium habuerit de præpofito et de vicinis fuis de Portemanmot quod Adverfarius fuus defectus fit ad hos tres dies, nullum poftea det refponfum et de placito illo.

Item burgenfes prædicti fequentur molendinum domini prædicti et ejus furnum reddendo confuetudines prædicti molendini et prædicti furni ut debent et folent.

Item, burgenfes debent et poffunt præpofitum eligere de feipfis quem voluerint et præpofitum removere.

Item, nullus poteft vicinum fuum ducere ad facramentum nifi habeat fectam de aliquo clamore.

Item, nullus poteft aliquid recipere infra villam nifi per vifum præ-pofiti.

2   Item,

Item, líceat cuilibet terram fuam quæ non eſt de hereditate vendere vel dare ſi neceſſitas inciderit cuicunque voluerit niſi hæres eam emere voluerit, ſed hæres debet eſſe propinquior ad eam emendam.

Item, quilibet poteſt vendere de hereditate ſua five majus, ſive minus, five totum per confenfum hæredis ſui. Et ſi forſitan hæres voluerit tamen ſi neceſſitas inciderit licebit ei vendere de hereditate ſua de quacunque ætate hæres fuerit.

Item, præpoſitus debet cui libet tradere burgenfi et cenſario ſendas ſuas in foro et præpoſitus debet inde recipere unum denarium ad opus prædicti domini.

Item, ſi burgenſis vel cenſarius voluerit ſtare in ſenda mercatoris ipſe debet pacare prædicto domino quantumcunque extraneus, et ſi ſtet in propria ſenda tunc nil daturus eſt prædicto domino.

Item, burgenfes poſſunt nutrire porcos ſuos prope nutritos in boſcis domini exceptis foreſtis et parcis domini prædicti uſque ad terminum pannagii et ſi velint ad prædictum terminum diſcedere, liceat eis abſque licentia domini et ſi velint moram facere ad terminum pannagii de pannagio fatisfaciant prædicto domino.

Item, ſi aliquis implacitatus fuerit ante dies Laghmot et tunc venerit oportet eum reſpondere et non debet ſe eſſoniare ſine foris factura et ſi tunc primo implacitatus fuerit tunc habeat primum diem.

Item, burgenfes poſſunt namare homines five milites five facerdotes five clericos, pro debitis ſuis ſi inventi fuerint in burgo.

Item,

Item, fi neceffitas inciderit quod aliquis vendat burgagium fuum ipfe poteft de vicino fuo aliud burgagium recipere et quilibet burgenfis poteft tradere burgagium fuum vicinis fuis per vifum comburgenfium.

Item, liceat prædictis burgenfibus tradere cattalla fua propria cuicunque voluerint in feodo prædicti domini libere et fine licentia prædicti domini.

Item, fi burgenfis homini villano aliquid commodaverit in burgo et terminus inde tranfivit in burgo fumat namium de villano et per namium fuum certificat eum et reddat namium per plegios ufque ad terminum octo dierum et tunc reddat plegii five namium five denarios.

Item, burgenfis de quocunque emerit vel venundaverit in feodo prædicti domini liber erit a tolneto.

Et fi aliquis de alia fhiria venerit qui debeat confuetudinem reddere fi cum tolneto decefferit et retentus a præfecto vel ab alio ejus foris factura erit duodecim folidos ad opus domini et reddat tolnetum fuum.

Et fi aliquis alii aliquid accomodaverit fine teftimonio quicquam non refpondebit ei nifi habuerit teftimonium et fi teftimonium habuerit per facramentum duorum hominum poteft negare.

Item, qui fregit affifam five de pane five de cerevifia ipfe erit in foris factura duodecim denarios ad opus domini.

Item, fi aliquis alium vulneraverit in burgo præpofitus debet attachiare eum fi inventus fuerit extra domum fuam per vadium et plegios.

Item,

Item, quilibet debet et poteſt eſſe ad placitum pro ſponſa ſua et pro familia ſua, et ſponſa cujuſlibet poteſt firmam ſuam reddere præpoſito et placitum ſequi pro ſponſo ſuo ſi ipſe forſitan aliunde fuerit.

Item, ſi aliquis villanus burgenſes calumpniatus fuerit de aliquo, burgenſes non debent reſpondere ei niſi habuerit ſectam de burgenſibus vel aliis legalibus hominibus.

Item, burgenſis ſi non habuerit hæredem ipſe poterit legare burgagium ſuum et cattalla cum moritur ubicunque ſibi placuerit ſalvo tamen domini ſervitio.

Item, ſi aliquis burgenſis moriatur ſponſa ejus debet manere in domo et ibi habeat neceſſaria quamdiu voluerit eſſe ſine marito, et hæres cum illa et ex quo illa voluerit maritari ipſa decedet et hæres ut dominus ibi manebit.

Item, ſi burgenſis moriatur hæres ejus nullum aliud relevium dabit prædicto domino niſi alicujuſmodi arma.

Item, ſi burgenſis vendat burgagium ſuum et velit a villa decedere dabit domino quatuor denarios et liber ibit ubicunque voluerit.

Præterea omnia placita prædita erunt determinata coram ſeneſchallo per rotulationem clerici prædicti domini.

Et omnes libertates prænominatas ego prædictus Thomas et Hæredes mei tenebimus prædictis burgenſibus et hæredibus ſuis in perpetuum
ſalvo

falvo mihi et hæredibus meis rationabili tallagio quando dominus rex fecerit tallagium per liberos burgos fuos per Angliam.

Et ut hæc donatio et conceffio rata fit et ftabilis figilli mei appofi-tione hoc fcriptum roboravi. Hiis teftibus dominis. Johanne Byron ; Ricardo Byron, militibus ; Henrico de Trafford ; Ric: de Hulton ; Ad: de Preftwyche ; Rogero de Pylkington ; Galfro de Chaterton ; Ric: de Mofton ; Johe de Preftwyche, et aliis. Datum apud Manceftr: quarto decimo die Maij, anno domini milleffimo tricenteffimo primo, et anno regni regis Edwardi filii Henricis regis viceffimo nono.

(L. S.)

14th May, 1301.

Thomas Grelle's Grant of the Cuftom of the Mannor pt of Mancheftea

Endorfement upon the Grant.

Between the Right Hon. George Earl of Warrington and others, - - - - Plts. and Sir Ofwald Mofeley, Bart. - - - - Deft.
} In the dutchy of Lancaf. at Weftminfter, at Manchefter.

September 24th, 1733. Shewn on the Execution of a Com-miffion in this Caufe on the Defendant's behalf, and depofed unto by Mr. Richard Davenport,

Before us,

George Haydon,
Thomas Starkie,
William Shaw.

TRANS-

TRANSLATION OF THE ABOVE.*

ALL they that be prefent and to come, know that I, Thomas Grelle, have given, granted, and by this my prefent charter have confirmed to all my burgeffes of Manchefter,

That is to fay,

That all the burgeffes fhall pay of every burgage twelve pence by the year for all fervice.

And if the burgreeve, governor, or ruler of the faid town fummon any burgefs of any plaint, and he fo fummoned come not, nor none for him, at the day within the laghmot, he fhall forfeit to the faid lord twelve pence, and the faid lord fhall have his action upon him in the portmoot.

If any burgefs do fue any burgefs of any debt, and he acknowledge the debt, then fhall the faid governor or ruler affign him a day, (to wit) the eighth, and if he come not at the day, he fhall pay to the lord twelve pence for forfeiture of the day, and he fhall pay the debt, and to the faid governor or ruler eight pence.

And if any man make claim of any thing, and fhall not find fureties or pledges, and afterwards would leave his claim, he fhall be without forfeiture.

Item, if any burgefs in the borough, on the Sunday or from nine o'clock on Sunday until Monday, do hurt any burgefs, he fhall forfeit

* Made by the Rev. Mr. Whitaker, the hiftorian of Manchefter.

twenty.

twenty fhillings. And if upon Monday or any other day of the week he do hurt any perfon, he fhall forfeit to the faid lord twelve pence.

Item, if any burgefs fhall ftrive with any man and with anger ftrike him, without any effufion of blood, and afterwards flee to his own houfe without any attachment of the faid governor, or ruler, or of his fervants, he fhall be free from any plaint of the ruler. And if he can agree with the party of whom he maketh the fray, (well be it) but if he can make his peace with the party by the counfel of his friends, he may do it without forfeiture to the governor or ruler.

And if any man be impleaded in the borough of any plaint, he fhall not anfwer neither to a burgefs nor to a villain, unlefs in the portmoot, except plaint pertaining to the king's crown or to theft.

Item, and if any man do challenge any burgefs of theft, the faid governor or ruler fhall attach him for to anfwer at the lord's court and to ftand to his evidence.

And if any man be impleaded by his neighbour or by any others, and follow the fame three court-days, if he have witnefs of the ruler and his neighbours of the portmoot that his adverfary is in default at thofe three days, the faid defendant fhall make no anfwer unto him of the fame plaint.

Alfo the faid burgeffes fhall follow (or do fuit to) the lord's mill and his common oven, and fhall pay their cuftoms to the faid mill and oven as they ought and were wont to do.

Item,

Item, the burgeffes ought and may chofe a reeve of themfelves whom they will, and to remove the reeve.

Item, no man may bring his neighbour to any oath unlefs he have fuit of fome claim.

Item, no man may receive any thing within the town but by view of the reeve.

Item, it fhall be lawful to every man to fell or give his lands which are not of his inheritance, if need be, to whom he will, except his heir will buy it, but the heir ought to be the next or neareft of kin to buy it.

Item, every man may fell of his inheritance be it more, or lefs, or all, by the confent of his heir. And if peradventure the heir will not, notwithftanding if he fall in neceffity it fhall be lawful for him to fell of his inheritance what age foever the heir be.

Item, the reeve ought to let to every burgefs and ftander his ftall in the market, and the faid reeve ought to receive for every ftanding a penny to the ufe of the faid lord.

Item, if the burgefs or ftander will ftand in the ftalls of the market, he ought to pay unto the faid lord as much as a ftranger; and if he ftand in his own ftall, he ought to pay nothing unto the faid lord.

Item, every burgefs may nourifh his hogs of his own bringing up in the lord's woods, except the forefts and parks of the faid lord, unto

4 G

the

the time of pannage; and if they will at that time go their way, it ſhall be lawful for them without the licenſe of the lord; and if they will tarry the time of that pannage, they ſhall agree or recompenſe the ſaid lord for their pannage.

Item, if any man be impleaded before the day of the laghmot and then cometh, he muſt anſwer, and ought not to be aſſoined without forfeiture, and if it be the firſt time that he be impleaded, he may have the firſt day.

Item, the burgeſſes may arreſt men, whether they be knights, prieſts, or clerks, for their debts, if they be found in the borough.

Item, if neceſſity fall that any ſell his burgage, he may take another of his neighbour, and every burgeſs may let his burgage to his neighbour by view of his fellow burgeſſes.

And it ſhall be lawful to the ſaid burgeſſes to let their own proper chattels within the fee of the ſaid lord to whom they will freely without licenſe of the ſaid lord.

Item, if a burgeſs lend any thing unto any villain in the borough, and the day be expired, he may take a gage of the ſaid villain, and by his gage he ſhall certify and deliver the gage upon ſurety unto the term of eight days, and then the ſureties ſhall anſwer either the gage or the money.

Item, if a burgeſs do either buy or ſell to any man within the fee of the ſaid lord, he ſhall be free of the toll.

And

And if any of any other shire come, the which ought to pay custom, if he go away with the toll and be retained by the governor, or ruler, or any others, he shall forfeit twelve shillings to the use of the lord, and pay his toll.

And if any person do lend any thing to another without witness, he shall answer him nothing, unless he shall have witness, and if he have, the party may deny it upon oaths of two men.

He that breaketh assize either of bread or ale, shall forfeit twelve pence to the use of the lord.

Item, if any man hurt another in the borough, the governor or ruler ought to attach him, if he may be found without his house, by gage or by surety.

Item, every man ought and may answer for his wife, and his household, and the wife of any man may give up his farm to the reeve, and follow any plaint or action for her husband, if he peradventure be absent in another place.

Item, if any villain shall sue burgesses for any thing, the burgess is not bound to answer him, except it be at the suit of burgesses or of other lawful men.

Item, if a burgess have no heir, he may bequeath his burgage and chattels when he dieth to whom he will, saving only service of the lord.

Item,

Item, if any burgefs die his wife ought to remain in the houfe, and there to have neceffaries as long as fhe will be without a hufband, and the heir with her, and when fhe will marry fhe fhall depart, and the heir fhall remain there as mafter.

Item, if any burgefs fhall die, his heir fhall pay no other relief to the lord but fome kind of arms.

Item, if any burgefs fell his burgage, and will depart from the town, he fhall give to the lord four pence, and fhall go free where he will.

Furthermore, all plaints aforefaid fhall be determined before the fteward by the enrollment of the faid lord's clerk.

And all the faid liberties I, the faid Thomas, and my heirs, fhall keep to the faid burgeffes and their heirs for ever, faving to me and my heirs reafonable tallage or taxes when the lord the king maketh tallage, or taxeth his free burgeffes through England.

And that this my gift and grant may be ratified and eftablifhed, to this, my prefent writing, I have caufed my feal to be fet, thefe being witneffes,

Sir John Byron, }	Roger, of Pilkington,
Richard Byron,	Geoffry, of Chadderton,
Henry, of Trafford,	Richard, of Mofton,
Richard, of Hulton,	John, of Preftwich,
Adam, of Preftwich,	and others.

Dated

Dated at Manchefter, the fourteenth day of May, in the year of our Lord one thoufand three hundred and one; and in year of the reign of king Edward, fon of king Henry, the twenty-ninth.

On the bottom fold of the original deed, to which the feal is affixed, are thefe words wrote, viz.

Lett this be inrolled and exemplifyed, per vidimus fexto decimo dio Septembri 1623 viceffimo primo Jacobi regis Angli, &c.

Chr. Baneifter.

LIVERPOOL.

I.—*Its Charters.*

LIVERPOOL is faid to be a borough by prefcription, but its firft charter was granted by king John in the 9th year of his reign. Several fucceeding monarchs have granted either new charters or charters of confirmation. Thofe previous to the reign of Charles I. are, the charters of Henry III. Edward III. Richard II. Henry IV. Confirmation, Henry IV. Charter, Philip and Mary.

The general purport of thefe charters is the eftablifhment of a free borough, and of a guild-merchant in Liverpool. Some of them alfo grant an exclufive privilege of trade, *and that no perfon who fhall not be of that guild, fhall do any merchandize there without the confent of the burgeffes;* but the charters of Richard II. and William and Mary, exprefly except fuch prohibitory claufe.

Under

Under thefe charters the affairs of the corporation were anciently tranfacted by general meetings of the burgeffes at large, affembled in common hall; where they chofe their officers annually, on St. Luke's day, and made bye laws for the good government of the town. Thefe meetings were in all probability not very numerous; but as the population of the town increafed, the inhabitants found it neceffary to intruft the direction of fome part of their public bufinefs to a felect body, who were yearly nominated, and varied in number as circumftances required. In the year 1558 (as appears by a letter from the corporation to queen Elizabeth) there were only thirteen veffels belonging to the port, viz. one of 100, one of fifty, and eleven under thirty tons; and in 1665, the whole number of freemen was 184. In the former-mentioned year, *fixteen perfons were chofen to be a privy council*, and it was afterwards ordered that *twelve burgeffes fhould be every year named, to order all things neceffary for the common hall*: this number was afterwards again changed to fixteen; but notwithftanding thefe delegations, common halls, or public meetings of the inhabitants, ftill continued to be held for the general tranfaction of the bufinefs of the town.

The firft indication of the exiftence of a common council appears in a bye law, or refolution, made in the mayorality of *Edward Halfall*, in 1759; which ftates, *that there had formerly been a cuftom that the town fhould be ordered by a common council, without the reft of the commonality, as in other corporations*, but *that fuch cuftom had been fo defaced by the ufurpations of the commons, that in effect there remaineth no memory thereof at all; faving that twenty-four burgeffes once every year being impanneled, &c. have for fome remembrance of the faid former cuftoms taken upon them to prefcribe rules and orders for the go-*

4   *vernment*

vernment of the town. It is then ordered *that the late ufurped affemblies fhall be abolifhed,* and the *ancient cuftom of common council reftored;* and that in cafe of vacancy, by death or otherwife, the reft of the council fhall choofe another to fupply the place.

This fingular bye law, or order, upon which the common council of the prefent day are faid to found their right to elect the members of their own body, by whatever authority it was ordained, did not prevent the burgeffes from continuing to affemble together and frequently tranfacting their own concerns, till the year 1626; when Charles I. granted the charter, which is yet confidered as the conftitution of the place. By this charter, he gives to the *mayor, bailiffs, and burgeffes,* a power of making bye laws for the government of the town; but no notice whatever is taken of any felect body acting as a common council, nor is any common council there appointed. In the following year the burgeffes, however, met together, and nominated a common council, who, under fuch authority, but not under that of the charter, took upon them the direction of the concerns of the corporation, and frequently filled the vacancies that arofe in their own number. In 1662, feveral of the aldermen and common council-men, together with the town-clerk, were removed from their offices, by commiffioners appointed under the 13th of Charles II. for refufing to take the oath therein prefcribed, from which it may be inferred that they were at this time confidered as eftablifhed officers of the corporation.

The common council, thus purified by the court, feem to have formed a plan for vefting in themfelves and their affociates all the powers of the corporate body, independent of the burgeffes; which they effectually accomplifhed by obtaining a new charter from king Charles II.

in

in 1677, which appointed in exprefs terms a common council, to confift of fixty perfons, who were therein nominated, thirty of whom, together with the mayor and bailiffs, *fhould have power to elect and name the mayor, bailiffs, common council, and freemen of the town*; thereby concentering the whole power of the corporation in the common council themfelves. The burgeffes at large protefted againft this charter, even feveral of the council-men therein named refufed to act under it, and fome tumults took place in the town; but the fpirit of the times ftifled all oppofition, and the common council continued to exercife the whole authority, till the charter of William III. introduced other regulations.

It feems, however, that the corporation were not yet thought fufficiently dependent on the court, for in 1684 chief juftice Jefferies demanded, on the part of the king, a furrender of the charter, which was delivered up to him, and immediately returned to the mayor. This being fuppofed to be a furrender of the privileges of the town, application was made to king James II. for a new charter, which was accordingly obtained, and which directed that the common council *fhould confift of fixty-one, including the mayor and two bailiffs*, and that the council *fhould be elected by fuch perfons as had theretofore been accuftomed to elect them*, or in other words, granting them an exprefs power to elect each other, in perpetuity. But the moft extraordinary part of the charter is a refervation of a power in the king to remove *all the officers of the corporation at pleafure*. This power he did not fail to exercife, by removing fuch as were obnoxious to him; which fo alarmed the council, that on the 12th of September, 1688, they made an order, *That with all due fubmiffion and humble deference to the power of removing any officer in this corporation, James Prefcott, Efq.*

2   *mayor*

mayor for the time being ſhall ſafely keep the wand, mace, and ſword, with all other real and perſonal eſtate of the corporation, and all that concerns the ſame, for the defence of its rights wherewith he is now intruſted, until a ſucceſſor be legally choſen and ſworn, according to our preſent charter and the ancient cuſtom of this corporation.

Soon after the revolution, the common council obtained a new exemplification of the charter of Charles II. and diſavowed that of James, as having been founded on a pretended ſurrender of privileges, which was never recorded. The charter of Charles II. gave them the full command of the corporation, without ſubjecting them to removal at the will of the crown. But great changes had now taken place in public opinions; and applications were made to the king for a charter, which might reſtore to the burgeſſes their ancient rights. The common council were appriſed of theſe attempts, and endeavoured to counteract them, as appears by an order of the 29th of March, 1695, in which they take notice *that endeavours are uſed to take away or make void the charter of Charles II. under which the corporation derives many great privileges and immunities,* and direct *that the mayor and bailiff ſhall, at the charge of the corporation, uſe their utmoſt endeavours to preſerve the ſame;* but theſe endeavours were ineffectual, for on the 26th of September, in the ſame year, king William III. granted the now ſubſiſting charter of the place.

The conteſts that have ariſen as to the conſtruction of this charter, and which have lately been the ſubject of an extenſive litigation in the court of King's Bench, renders the conſideration of it in ſome degree intereſting.

.4 H   After

After *infpecting* or ftating in the fame words the charter of Charles I. and confirming the fame, it proceeds to notice, *that a few of the bur-geffes of the town, by a combination among themfelves, without the affent of the greater part of the burgeffes, and without a furrender of the charter of Charles I. or any judgment of quo warranto, had procured the charter of Charles II. in which fundry material changes were de-figned to be made in the government of the town, which had caufed many differences and doubts concerning the liberties, franchifes, and cuftoms, of the town, and alfo concerning the election and appointment of the mayor, and* DIVERS OTHER OFFICERS *of the fame town.*

The charter then appoints a common council of forty-one burgeffes, one of whom fhall be mayor, and two bailiffs.   And by a fubfequent claufe, it directs that upon the removal or death of any of the mayor, recorder, town-clerk, bailiffs, or common council, another fit perfon fhall be elected *by fuch perfons, and in fuch manner, time, and form, as in that particular was ufed and accuftomed before the making the charter of Charles II.*

It is obfervable, that this claufe which relates to the election of the officers, is in the fame words as the claufe refpecting election in the charter of James II. except that in that of James the election is directed to be *as theretofore accuftomed,* and in that of William it is directed to be made in the fame manner *as before the charter of Charles II.* at which time the common council *did not exift by charter, but by dele-gation from the burgeffes.*   The charter of William III. further directs that the mayor fhall be chofen *by the burgeffes out of the common coun-cil.*

Under

Under this charter it might have been expected, that the burgesses would again have entered upon the exercise of their rights, but the new common council were soon aware of the power they possessed. By the charter of Charles I. now again recognised, as part of the constitution of the place, no common hall, or assembly of the burgesses could be held without the assent and presence of the mayor, and one at least of the bailiffs. By that of William III. the mayor and bailiffs must be chosen from the common council. The council then existing, without adverting to the distinction between the charters of James II. and of William III. respecting the choice of their members, still continued to elect each other; and all that was necessary, therefore, on their parts for securing to themselves the whole government of the town, was to elect *only* such persons into the council as they were satisfied *would not call together the burgesses* for the purposes of making bye laws, or be present at such meeting; and with such precaution have they conducted themselves, that a full century has now elapsed without the burgesses at large having been able to avail themselves of the privileges intended to be granted to them.

This total extinction of their ancient rights has not, however, been submitted to without various struggles. In the year 1735, James, earl of Derby, then mayor of the town, with the concurrence of the bailiffs, called together the burgesses in common hall. The assembly was accordingly held, and sundry bye laws made. But the earl dying in the following year, the common council again assumed the whole authority, and dismissed the two bailiffs from their office of common council-men; declaring in express terms, that in holding the said common hall, they had acted manifestly in breach of the trust reposed in them as common council-men of the borough.

4 H 2   There

There is, however, reason to presume, that notwithstanding the authority exercised by the common council in making bye laws for the government of the town, they could not divest themselves of some doubts as to their power so to do, under the subsisting charter. In order, therefore, to prevent all further opposition, they applied, in the year 1751, to George II. to grant them a new charter, stating in their petition the former charters, and particularly that of William III. which, as they (with some inaccuracy) observe, *ordained that for the future to preserve the peace, tranquillity, and good government, of the town, there shall or may be for ever forty-one good and discreet burgesses, who shall be called the common council, &c.* omitting (as they say) *to give them the least power, in express terms, though it was the manifest if not the sole intent of this charter, to give forty-one the power in the first recited clause of king Charles's charter* (the power of making bye laws) *in order to prevent the populous meetings of the burgesses upon every trifling occasion, as the town was so extremely increased since that time.* They then suggest to the king that it may *thereafter cause disputes, unless the said charter was explained for this purpose, by adding the clause of king Charles's charter, or in such manner as his majesty should think fit.* In plain language, they requested the king would give to the select body of the common council the same power of making bye laws which the body at large possessed under the charter of Charles I. and they conclude with petitioning that the mayor may act as a justice of the peace for four years, and that the recorder may have power to appoint a deputy.

This petition was referred to the then attorney and solicitor general, Sir Dudley Rider, and Mr. (afterwards lord) Mansfield, who recommended to withdraw the whole of their petition, except such as

related

related to the appointment of juftices of the peace, and the nomination of a deputy recorder; to which they prudently affented, and on the report of the attorney and folicitor general a new charter was then obtained which granted their requeft, and confirmed all former privileges; but which left the common council, as to their legiflative authority, in the fame fituation in which they ftood under the charter of William III.

This difappointment made no alteration in the conduct of the common council, who continued to nominate their own members as occafion required, and to make regulations or bye laws for the government of the town; but it is obfervable, that in cafe of refiftance, thefe bye laws were never enforced by legal proceedings. In fact, few of thefe bye laws have at prefent any active exiftence, the town being governed, and the police regulated, chiefly under the authority of various acts of parliament which have been obtained for that purpofe; but the receipts and expenditure of the large income of the corporation refted entirely with the common council, who never audited or publifhed their accompts, or communicated to the burgeffes at large any information as to the real ftate of their concerns. In order to remedy thefe fuppofed abufes, a majority of the refident burgeffes in the year 1791 prefented a petition to John Sparling, Efq. the mayor; Robert Mofs, and Clayton Tarleton, Efqrs. the bailiffs; requefting them to call together a general affembly of the burgeffes in common hall. Thefe officers complied with the requifition, and fuch meeting was accordingly held, and very numeroufly attended, when meafures were taken for bringing to a trial at law, the important queftions which had fo long been the fubject of debate among the burgeffes, viz. in what part of the corpora-

corporation the *making of bye laws and electing the common council* refided.

The caufe refpecting the bye laws came on to be tried at the affizes
at Lancafter in the fame year, before Mr. Baron Thompfon; Mr.
Erfkine being the leading counfel for the felect body, and Mr. Serjeant
Adair for the burgeffes; when the jury being of opinion that the power
of making bye laws was, under the charter of Charles I. recognized by
that of William III. expreffly given to the corporation at large, and
the judge having directed them, that no evidence of a cuftom ought to be
admitted againft the exprefs words of a charter, a verdict was given
for the burgeffes.

A motion was afterwards made in the court of King's Bench for a
new trial, when, after a long argument, the judges of that court were
of opinion that the evidence of the cuftom ought to have been admitted,
and directed a new trial accordingly. The caufe was again tried in
the following year, when the records of the town were produced and
given in evidence; but the fecond jury were alfo of opinion that no
practice could be legal that was in direct oppofition to the claufe in
the charter of Charles I. which gave the power of making bye laws
to the mayor, bailiffs, and burgeffes, on public notice for that purpofe,
and gave a verdict againft the claims of the common council.

A third trial was then moved for, which the court of King's Bench,
on what grounds does not appear, thought proper to grant. But the
expences incurred in thefe proceedings, which were difburfed by individual burgeffes, added to the confideration that the law has prefcribed
no limits to the authority of a court, in remanding a caufe for trial,

4

when-

whenever it is not fatisfied with the verdict, deterred the burgeffes from the further profecution of their claim; and the common council, notwithftanding the opinion of the two juries, ftill continue to exercife the exclufive power of the corporation in the fame manner as before thefe proceedings were commenced.

The queftion refpecting the right of electing the members of the common council was alfo tried, the burgeffes contending, that as the charter of William III. referred to the cuftom before that of Charles II. at which time the common council exifted *not by charter*, but *by the appointment of the burgeffes*, they had a right to elect; and the common council on the contrary contending, that the charter of William meant to refer to *the actual practice* before the charter of Charles II. On this point the jury were of opinion that the cuftom was decifive, and gave a verdict accordingly. The event of this conteft, and of the celebrated Chefter caufe, in which a folemn decifion of the Houfe of Lords was obtained by the exertions, and at the expence, of an individual, without producing the leaft change in the practice of the corporation, will be a ufeful caution to fuch as may be hereafter inclined to engage in fimilar undertakings.

II.—*Project of its Participation in the Eaft India Trade.*

THE active and enterprizing fpirit which has uniformly diftinguifhed the merchants of Liverpool, had led them at different times to turn their attention towards the trade between Great Britain and the Eaft Indies, and it had been repeatedly fuggefted, that there appeared no obvious reafons why the benefits arifing from the being immediately

concerned

concerned in the carrying on this extenfive and growing branch of commerce, fhould be confined wholly to a monopoly by the merchants of
London under an exclufive charter.

On a former occafion there had been an application from the merchants of Liverpool to the Eaft India Company, for a certain number
of their fhips to be fitted out and laden annually from the port of Liverpool; but though this propofition was liftened to with fome attention, yet it failed of being carried into effect.

In the year 1792, the growing wealth and profperity of Liverpool
had led its merchants to believe that they were poffeffed of fufficient capital, and that they were in other refpects competent to the carrying on
of a trade to the Eaft Indies with advantage.   They were the more im-
preffed with this idea, as the merchants of the United States of America had for fome years been engaged in the fame traffic, and were acquiring large fortunes in it.   The approaching expiration of the Eaft
India Company's charter, and the poffibility of a partial or total aboli-
tion of the African Slave Trade, induced the merchants of Liverpool to
hope that this would be a feafon peculiarly favourable for their application.

A public meeting of the merchants and inhabitants was accordingly
held within the Exchange, and the following refolutions were unani-
moufly voted:

" RESOLVED,

" I. THAT the Creator of the Univerfe, by endowing different portions of the earth with different products, has laid the foundation of

com-

commerce; which, having for its object the supply of mutual wants, and the exchange of mutual comforts, may be safely left to the regulations which mutual interest points out, and should, as far as possible, be free from every restraint.

" II. That monopolies are destructive of these principles, because they provide for the interest of the monopolist only, and enable him to fix at his own pleasure, both the rate at which he buys from one country and sells to another, and the charge at which he carries the commodities of each.

" III. That the history of the East India Company affords most striking proofs of the consequence of trusting such powers to the discretion of individuals; and the injuries which their monopoly of the trade between Britain and India has produced to both countries, are of the most serious nature.

" IV. That the principles to which many of these are to be traced, is the temptation which the possession of this monopoly has offered to the East India Company, to exchange the character of merchants for those of warriors and politicians, by which they have assumed the sovereignty of twenty millions of men with whom traffic was their first, and ought to have been their only object.

" V. That to support a dominion by force, which could no otherwise be supported, they have been led to maintain vast and expensive civil and military establishments, the whole charge of which must be defrayed by the people of India or Great Britain, and seems a heavy,

4 I and

and cruel, as well as ufelefs burthen, on the connection between the two countries.

" VI. That peace is the natural, and ought to be the infeparable attendant of commerce ;---that the poffeffion of continental territories is valuable only as it is productive of commercial intercourfe ; and that it is probable the opening of the Eaft India trade will render lefs frequent thofe defolating wars which have fo often deluged the foil of that unhappy country with the blood of its inhabitants, whilft they have been equally fatal to this country by the facrifice of thoufands of Britifh fubjects and the expenditure of millions of Britifh treafure.

" VII. That the Eaft India monopoly prevents the free export of our manufactures to one of the largeft and richeft regions of the world, where there is reafon to believe they might, in the courfe of open trade, be increafed in their vent twenty fold and upwards ;—that under the prefent fyftem the exports are conducted without a proper attention to the change of circumftances and feafons ; and due means are not employed for opening new fources of traffic on the eaftern coaft of Africa, the ifland of Madagafcar, the countries that lie up the ftreights of Babelmandel, and on the fhores of the Perfian Gulph, with many of the vaft profufion of iflands that are fcattered throughout the Indian Ocean, all within the limits of the Company's monopoly, and yielding them little or no advantage, but which the unfettered enterprife and fkill of individuals might foon explore, and render of the utmoft importance.

" VIII. That this monopoly choaks many of the infant manufactures of Britain as they arife, from the power it gives of lowering at pleafure the rival manufactures of India in the home market ; the lofs

fuftained

fuftained being laid on fuch articles as are the produce of the foil of India, which habit has rendered neceffary amongft us, and which are not to be obtained elfewhere; a power that more than once has deftroyed the manufacture of Britifh porcelain, and that was employed to oppofe and bear down the manufacture of cotton, now rifen to fuch national importance.

" IX. That the injuries to commerce and navigation have been proportional, as may be clearly inferred. The practice indeed of employing large veffels on overcharged freights is an open facrifice of the intereft of the Company itfelf to the felfifh views of individuals, and is an undeniable proof of the entire departure from the principles of fair traffic into which this monopoly has diverged :---that all the branches of thofe moft important manufactures employed in the building and equipment of fhipping, are injured under the prefent fyftem, which alfo obftructs the training of mariners, on which our national fafety and profperity fo particularly depend.

" X. That the progrefs of time and experience has now effectually removed the grounds on which the exclufive trade to India was originally fupported, viz. the danger and expence of fo diftant a traffic. The free trade and manufactures of Great Britain have produced fuch an influx of wealth, and accumulation of capital, that there is no adventure too heavy for private merchants, or private companies of merchants, to undertake; the genius, induftry, and talents of our people are fuch, that there is no part of the world to which they cannot make a free trade profitable, and that nearly in proportion to its riches and population; and fuch are the fkill and enterprize of our navigators,

that

ADDITIONS.

that there is no fhore fo dangerous, no region fo remote, as to daunt
their fpirit, or prevent their approach.

" XI. That thefe facts are capable of collateral proof, from the
fuccefs with which the merchants of Portugal carried on a trade to India
without any exclufive charter, for a century and upwards; and ftill more
from the fuccefs of the merchants of North America, who now traverfe
every part of the Indian and Pacific Oceans with veffels of no larger a
fize than thofe ufually employed on the Atlantic, and who with capitals comparatively infignificant, are opening moft advantageous channels
of traffic, from which the Britifh merchant, with prior claims, fuperior
fkill, and irrefiftible capital, is by a falfe policy excluded.

" XII. That as it is the natnre of trade to force its way through lefs
direct channels, when its natural courfe is obftructed, the products of
Great Britain now begin to be fent to the Eaft Indies in American bottoms,
and thofe of China and the Eaft Indies to be fmuggled into Britain and
her colonies, through America and Oftend, to the injury of the Britifh
trader and manufacturer, as well as of the Britifh confumer, all of
whofe interefts are thus palpably facrificed.

" XIII. That thefe facts while they point out the impolicy of the
prefent fyftem of Eaft India monopoly, demonftrate alfo the impoffibility of its being continued without meafures of rigor that the occafion
will not juftify, and more and more violence againft the true principles
of commerce now fo well underftood, and operating with fuch great
and rapid influence on the national profperity.

" XIV.

" XIV. That clear as we are in all thefe views, we are yet aware that difficulties may attend the overthrow of a falfe fyftem that has continued fo long, and connected itfelf fo widely ; and we fhould condemn all attempts for this purpofe that would facrifice the intereft of thofe immediately concerned, in expiation of the miftaken policy of the nation ; but we wifh the public at large to fee the evil of this monopoly in its full extent, and the collected wifdom of the legiflature to be employed in removing it by methods confiftent with true policy and the principles of juftice.

" XV. That a petition be therefore prefented to parliament, praying that the whole of this important fubject may be taken into confideration, and that we may be permitted to be heard by counfel, and, if need be, to adduce evidence in fupport of our allegations againft the renewal of an exclufive charter, by which our interefts in common with the commercial, manufacturing, and by confequence, landed interefts of the kingdom are fo manifeftly injured.

" XVI. That a committee be now appointed to prepare fuch petition for the confideration of a public meeting, to be hereafter called.

" XVII. That the faid committee be requefted to correfpond with fuch other towns and places, as they may think proper, in order to obtain their co-operation with us on this important bufinefs.

" XVIII. That thefe refolutions be publifhed in fuch of the London and country newfpapers, as the faid committee may direct.

3 " XIX.

" XIX. That the following gentlemen be appointed a committee, and that any three of them affembled, on due notice, be competent to act, viz.

The worfhipful the Mayor,

Nicholas Afhton, Efq.	William Earle, Merchant,
John Dawfon, Efq.	Edward Rogers, do.
William Smyth, Merchant.	William Rathbone, do.
Jonas Bold, Banker.	Francis Trench, do.
Thomas Earle, Efq.	Thomas Hodgfon, do.
Willis Earle, Merchant.	Thomas Hodgfon, jun. do.

" XX. That a fubfcription be now opened for defraying the ex-pences that may be incurred in the profecution of this bufinefs, and that Meffrs. Charles Caldwell and Co. bankers in Liverpool, be ap-pointed treafurers.

" XXI. That the thanks of this meeting be given to the Mayor for the attention which he has fhewn to this important bufinefs.

" CLAYTON TARLETON, Chairman."

The preceding refolutions, with circular letters from the chairman of the committee, were addreffed to every member of the Houfe of Com-mons, and to the magiftrate or fome other perfon in almoft every large or trading town in England and Scotland; and they were likewife advertifed in moft of the London and country newfpapers. The fubject excited a confiderable degree of attention; and a correfpondence was entered into

by

by the committee appointed in the preceding refolutions, and committees or other perfons in different trading towns, to the interefts of which the monopoly of the Eaft India trade, under an exclufive charter, was thought injurious. In this number were Manchefter, Birmingham, Exeter, Norwich, Glafgow, Paifley, &c.

In a very fhort time afterwards, however, our fituation with refpect to France became more and more interefting. An uncommon agitation prevailed throughout the kingdom, in confequence of the apprehenfion of difaffection at home, and the profpect of an immediate war. It was feared by many, that any oppofition to the intentions of adminiftration with refpect to the renewal of the Eaft India Company's charter, might be confidered as tending to weaken the hands of government, at a time when it was thought particularly defirable to ftrengthen them. Very foon afterwards the commercial part of the kingdom received a fevere and moft unexampled fhock, in the numerous bankruptcies which took place in every part of the kingdom, and of which Liverpool had its fhare. And from this complication of caufes, the minds of the merchants were fully occupied with the individual diftrefs, either of themfelves or their friends; and no further public exertions were made for the attainment of an object, in which the interefts both of Britain and the Eaft Indies appeared to be deeply concerned.

MACCLESFIELD.

Bill of Mortality.

	Chrift.	Bur.
From March 25, 1712, to ditto 1730,—annual average	148	161
From ditto 1730, to ditto 1740,—annual average	176	133
From ditto 1740, to ditto 1750,—annual average	175	153
From ditto 1750, to ditto 1760,—annual average	203	150
From ditto 1760, to ditto 1770,—annual average	244	166
From ditto 1770, to ditto 1780,—annual average	267	171
1781	292	309
1782	303	213
1783	300	193
1784	288	239
1785	324	246
1786	286	231
1787	313	247
1788	315	256
1789	299	260
1790	316	380
1791	373	252
1792	413	346
1793	418	306
1794	336	263

N. B. Diffenters included.

School

School. The annual value of all its eftates at the firft endowment was £.21 5s. The prefent income is £.300 and upwards; and on the falling in of leafes for lives it will be near £.700. The head mafter is allowed a falary of £.100 per annum, and the fecond mafter of £.60. A new writing fchool has lately been eftablifhed by the governors, for the accommodation of the town and neighbourhood, the mafter of which has a falary of £.25 per annum.

Trade. The manufactures of Macclesfield are mohair buttons; worfted twift, and filk and hair twift, made by twifters alone; alfo filk handkerchiefs and hat-bands, and wafte filk fpun for the making of ftockings; likewife ribbons, ferrets, and galloons, and filk tape for the covering of buttons. There is likewife a confiderable manufactory of fuftians, calicoes, checks, and linen cloth in the town and neighbourhood; and there are feveral capital dyers and hat-makers in the town. There are thirty mills for the throwing of filk for weavers, and making of fewing filk, moft of which are turned by water; alfo twelve mills for the fpinning of cotton, ten of which go by water.

STOCKPORT.
Bill of Mortality.

Years.	Marr.	Bapt.	Bur.	Years.	Marr.	Bapt.	Bur.
1750	47	107	206	1785	249	240	350
1755	50	119	163	1786	191	273	271
1760	73	106	163	1787	190	246	496
1765	82	111	166	1788	201	258	374
1770	93	110	209	1789	215	267	339
1775	108	138	193	1790	224	316	369
1780	108	173	250	1791	276	375	517
1781	146	161	324	1792	278	463	715
1782	157	175	193	1793	232	423	492
1783	159	185	224	1794	157	415	600
1784	207	215	410				

4 K

Expla-

Explanation of the Plate of Melandra Caftle.

On the fides A. and B. were ditches.

C. Road from the Roman ftation at Brough in Derbyfhire, entered at this gate.

From E. it is fuppofed a road went to Buxton.

Not known whether any thing of this fort led from F. into York-fhire.

At G. very near the eaft angle, the prefent tenant under the duke of Norfolk found, feveral years ago, a ftone about fixteen inches long, and twelve inches broad, on which is the infcription already given.

E R R A T A.

Page 378, line 19, for 9055, *read* 7055.

Page 393, line 8, — £.300, *read* £.3000.

Page 521, for Mr. Champion returning to England, *read* died in America, leaving a debt unpaid in England of nearly £.100,000.

Correct the Lift of Patrons of Livings in Chefhire as follows :

St. Mary, Chefter,	—	Mr. Hill.
Pulford,	— —	Reprefentative of Mr. Townfend, rector of Chefter.
Tarporley,	— —	Alfo dean and chapter of Chefter, and Mr. Egerton of Oulton.
Alderley,	— —	Sir J. Stanley.
Preftbury,	— —	Mrs. Legh.
Brereton,	— —	Mr. Bracebridge.
Davenham,	— —	E. Tomkinfon, Efq.
Hefwall,	— —	And —— Mainwaring, Efq.

INDEX.

INDEX.

Buxton

Hul.

Mont-

Small

F I N I S.

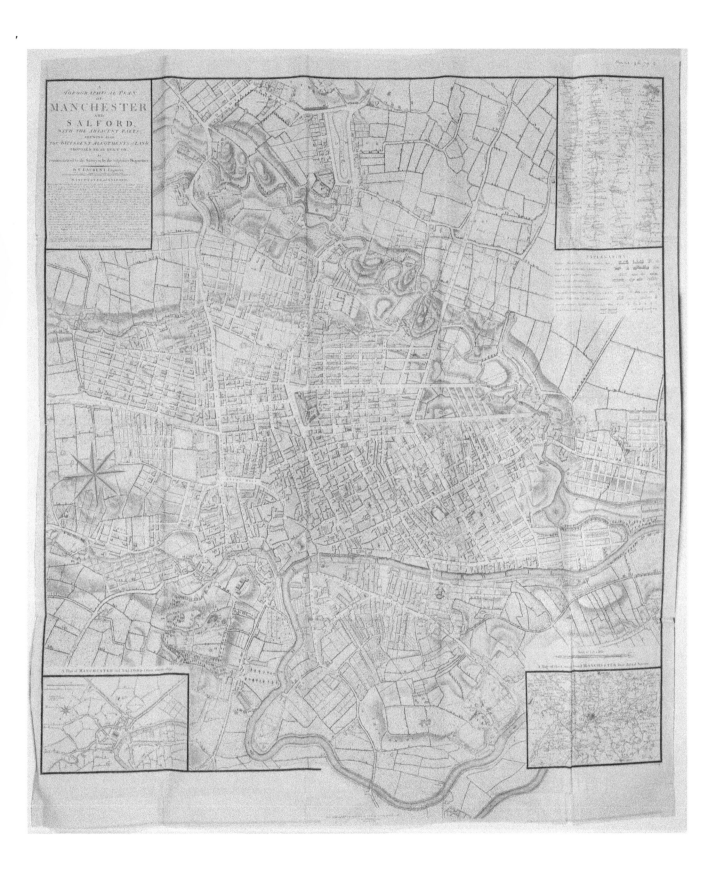

The material originally positioned here is too large for reproduction in this reissue. A PDF can be downloaded from the web address given on page iv of this book, by clicking on 'Resources Available'.

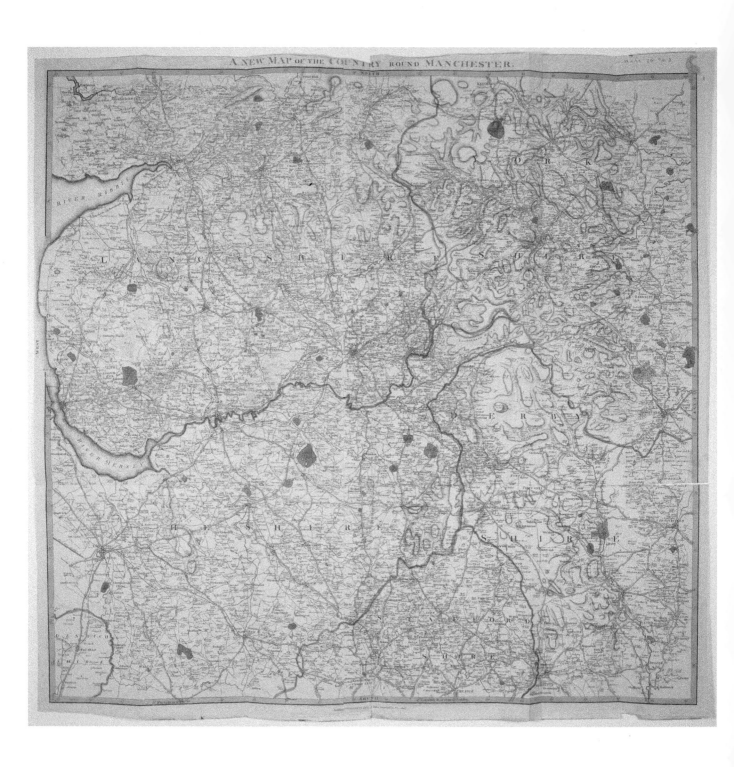

The material originally positioned here is too large for reproduction in this reissue. A PDF can be downloaded from the web address given on page iv of this book, by clicking on 'Resources Available'.

Lightning Source UK Ltd.
Milton Keynes UK
UKHW050711051019
350981UK00018B/371/P

9 781108 075848